The
University of Michigan
Football Scrapbook

Max L. Huey
Hillsdale Mi.

Other titles by Sports Products, Inc.

The Notre Dame Football Scrapbook
The Ohio State Football Scrapbook
The Scrapbook History of Baseball
The Scrapbook History of Pro Football
Pro Football: The Early Years
Pro Football: The Modern Game
The Sports Encyclopedia: Baseball
The Sports Encyclopedia: Pro Basketball
The World Series
The All-Sports World Record Book
The Complete All-Time Baseball Register
The Complete All-Time Pro Football Register
Monday Morning Quarterback
The World Book of Odds

The University of Michigan Football Scrapbook

BY

Richard M. Cohen,
Jordan A. Deutsch,
and David S. Neft

Max Huey —
Hillsdale Mi.

BOBBS-MERRILL
Indianapolis/New York

Library of Congress Cataloging in Publication Data

Cohen, Richard M   1938-
  The University of Michigan football scrapbook.

  1. Michigan. University—Football.
I. Deutsch, Jordan A., joint author.   II. Neft,
David S., joint author.   III. Title.
GV958.M52C63   796.33'263'0977435   78-55640
ISBN 0-672-52494-5

ACKNOWLEDGMENTS

The University of Michigan Football Scrapbook is the third book in a continuing series of major college scrapbooks. The authors are sure you will enjoy this unique and new concept in sports publishing.

The task of assembling all the material and data contained in this book could not have been accomplished by the three authors alone. In order to make this book a reality, the cooperation of many individuals, institutions, libraries, newspapers and news services was needed. The authors, therefore, would like to express their deep appreciation to the following people, who contributed their time and facilities during the preparation of this book:

Nancy McCormack, *Visual and Technical Coordinator and Photo Reproduction Consultant*

University of Michigan Athletic Department:
Don Canham, *Director of Athletics*
Charles Harris, *Assistant Director of Athletics*

University of Michigan Sports Information Department:
Will Perry, *Director*
Jim Vruggink, *Assistant Director*
Phyllis Rogers, *Secretary*
Pat Perry, *Advertising Director*
Don MacLachlan, *Student Assistant*
Kathy Henneghan, *Student Assistant*

University of Michigan Alumni Office:
Dick Emmons, *Editor, The Michigan Alumnus*

University of Michigan Publications:
The Michiganensian
The Michigan Alumnus
The Michigan Daily
University of Michigan Football Guides
University of Michigan Football Game Programs
University of Michigan Sports Archive Collection

Notre Dame International Sports and Games Research Collection:
Herb Juliano, *Curator/Researcher*

The authors would also like to thank the following news services and newspapers for the use of their material:

Associated Press News Service	*The Detroit Free Press*
The Baltimore Sunpapers	*The Detroit News*
The Cleveland Plain Dealer	*The Detroit Times*
The Hartford Courant	*The Ann Arbor News*
The Washington Star News	*The Michigan Daily*

Production:
Sally Lifland

The Authors' Wives:
A special thanks to Nancy Cohen, Thea Deutsch, and Naomi Neft for their continuous faith, understanding, and cooperation throughout all our projects.

All comments and inquiries on this book should be sent to
Sports Products, Inc.
415 Main Street
Ridgefield, CT 06877

Foreword

There will always be heated discussions when former football players talk about school spirit. We all remember our universities for different reasons. Many would undoubtedly have different descriptions of school spirit. Notre Dame, Alabama, Oklahoma, Texas, and Southern California could easily fill the bill. So could my university. Many years have passed since my college days, but I still feel goose bumps when I sit in the stadium and see that great marching band come down the field playing "The Victors." When it comes to tradition, no university in the land stands above the University of Michigan.

Many people today say: "It's too bad that you weren't born twenty-five years later so you could have played today." I disagree. I was most fortunate to have played when I did. My years at Michigan started with two of football's greatest men. My coach was Herbert Orin "Fritz" Crisler, a man I consider to have the finest football mind the game has ever known. And although I played for Crisler, my first touch with college football was in talking with the then Athletic Director, Fielding H. "Hurry-Up" Yost. Being exposed to these men, even being around them, you had to have some of their great knowledge rub off on you. I wouldn't have had that association if I were playing today.

When Michigan men talk of tradition, they talk of Yost and his "point-a-minute" teams. When I think of teams scoring 100 points a game, I get tired. Yost teams accomplished that feat many times. We scored 85 points in a game once. Yet it wasn't in my mind a joyous victory. To me it was sad. In 1939 the University of Chicago was set on deemphasis of their program. A gutty bunch of football players were laboring under Clark Shaughnessy, who was one of the great coaches of the game, but the players and coaches were alone. Their university and student body gave them no support. When I left the dressing room that afternoon, I felt that the ghosts of Stagg, Eckersall, and Berwanger walked uneasily in Stagg field. The game was an 85 to 0 victory for Michigan, but no real competitor enjoys seeing a worthy opponent humiliated.

My first exposure to Michigan tradition happened during my first three weeks on campus at Ann Arbor. In 1937 the Wolverines were not exactly the "Champions of the West." The team had lost its first game when a pep rally was called for Hill Auditorium. The hall was packed, and the spirit was contagious. The team lost their second game the next day, but the following Friday the auditorium was packed again. That type of backing had to be rewarded. And it was. I never questioned Michigan spirit from that day on.

Football memories. I feel they are like precious jewels to be taken from the case and savored. How could anyone on our team in 1940 fail to remember we were the first college team to use air travel for a game? The squad flew from Detroit to San Francisco in three DC 3's. Two for players and coaches and trainers, and one for equipment. The score of that game—Michigan 41, California 0.

Easily the biggest heartache was losing to a great Minnesota team for our only loss of the year, a 7-6 decision in the mud and slop of Minneapolis. Good sportsmanship and all, the Michigan players could never believe they were the "second-best" team in the country that season. We were firm in the belief that the elements had beaten us and even today the pain of that memory overshadows the joy of that year's victories.

How well I remember Nile Kinnick and his "Iron Men" of 1939. And Don Scott and his great teams of Ohio State. Two close friends and great competitors who lost their lives much too young in a war we all shared.

Never could I forget Bruce Smith's twisting run of 83 yards to give Minnesota its touchdown in that heartbreak game of 1940, or the multiple All American talents of Francis X. Reagan of Pennsylvania. Two friends and competitors I admired greatly. Two powerful physical specimens who lost the fight to cancer, a much tougher foe than any of us faced on the field of play.

And finally, no one will ever erase the memory of our last game in Columbus, Ohio, against Michigan's greatest rival, Ohio State. Until you have been there, you cannot visualize what football frenzy is. That cold, wet and snowy November afternoon, 80,000 fans were rocking the stadium at the end of the game as I left the field for the last time, wearing the maize and blue of Michigan. A standing ovation for a Michigan player who had helped beat their beloved Buckeyes 40-0.

No, I will never forget those and many other wonderful memories of my days at Michigan. But although there were moments of great elation, my prize benefit is the friendships that were welded under the sweat and tears and sacrifices of the game.

An understanding and appreciation that only a player can know.

Looking back at my playing days I fully realize how lucky I was to have played at Michigan in those days. What strange fate guided me to Ann Arbor, where I was to share my next four years with Forest Evashevski, Bobby Westfall, Ed Frutig, Al Wistert, Davey Nelson, and all those other talented players who were to form a winning nucleus for Michigan? I wonder how many football fans ever remember that I never played under the coach I went to Michigan to play for. Kipke was the coach in my freshman year. Crisler came in my sophomore year. Who called that play? Without Fritz Crisler as coach, Tom Harmon would have been another name on the long list of unknown football players. It takes players, coaches, and a great share of good luck to be a winner. Four years of college football and never an injury. Yes—I was lucky.

So I hope you will understand why I feel a special twinge in my heart for Michigan. How could a twenty-year-old not feel special thoughts about standing on that field in front of 82,000 screaming fans? No fear, no worry, just the fun of contact in America's greatest game. In my mind everything that has happened in my years since Michigan started there. I have met and known five Presidents of the United States. I have spoken with the Pope and been privileged to know movie stars, sports personalities, and people of history, such as Generals Douglas MacArthur and Claire Chennault. I have lived a very special life. However, my greatest joy is my family, and they too came from football. My lovely wife, Elyse, slammed the phone down in my ear when I called for our first date. Had not her brother remembered her telling him she had met me that day, and had not her brother been a student manager for the University of Pennsylvania the day we met and beat Reagan, I might not ever have met the girl who has given me three beautiful children and so many years of happiness. Yes—I have been blessed.

My football days were not without humor. How many players experienced a fan coming out of the stands to tackle him? It happened to me. During our opening game against California, Bud Brennan (the fan) tried to knock me off my feet in the third quarter. And as strange as that may seem, last year, thirty-seven years after the incident, Bud Brennan and I played together in a golf tournament in San Francisco and almost won it!

How many football players never sold a football ticket during their three years in school? I am probably the only player on record who had his own rooting section of rabid family. There were more than thirty Harmons at every Michigan game, home and away, helping the cheering and box office proportionately. And do you think I will ever forget that same family giving me a football with handles on it for Christmas after I fumbled against Minnesota?

More recently, as I broadcast the games of my son Mark during his playing days at UCLA, I wondered if he felt the same pride and spirit for his university. His mother was probably the only one who realized the war going on in my heart that night in the Los Angeles Coliseum when Michigan played UCLA. The Wolverines won that game, but Mark won the respect of the Michigan players, just as Otto Graham, Nile Kinnick, Don Scott, Bruce Smith, George Frank and Francis Reagan had when we played. Teammate or foe, there is a special bond of football competition. It is on such competition that tradition is built.

Michigan's football tradition is founded in history. The list of their coaches, from Yost and Crisler to Schembechler. Their many All Americans, led by Oosterbaan, Heston, Friedman, Newman and the later crop. These men have lived through the years as a credit to themselves, their families, their university, and their community. One good Michigan player became President of the United States. Gerald Ford's football career was not a fictitious newspaper legend. He was a player. Michigan has had outstanding doctors, dentists, lawyers, businessmen, and just plain good citizens of reputation in this great country. But beyond all, Michigan men have an enviable tradition—they were privileged to wear the maize and blue and be a part of that stirring lyric "Hail to the Victors Valiant."

That's a thrill they'll never forget—and neither will I!

Tom Harmon

THE FIRST MICHIGAN FOOTBALL TEAM. 1879

Top Row—"Jack" A. Green. '80; William W. Hannan. '80; "Dave" DeTar. '80M; Charles A. Mitchell. '80; Frank F. Reed. '80; Albert S. Pettit. '79.

Second Row—Irving K. Pond. '79; "Tom" R. Edwards. '79; John Chase. '79; "Charlie" H. Campbell. '80.

Lower Row—Collins H. Johnston. '81; Gay DePuy. '79; Edmund Barmore. '82.

THE CHRONICLE.

RACINE vs. UNIVERSITY.

May 30, opened exceedingly warm and continued so the whole day. The heat was oppressive, but despite the heat, about 500 students of Racine and citizens of Chicago witnessed what we may call, the finest game of Rugby foot-ball ever played this side of the Alleghanies. The White Stocking grounds were not in the best condition, half of the space being very soft. At about 3:15 a bus took our team from the Clifton House to the grounds, and at 4:15 the game began. A sharp wind was blowing from the south, which was sure to give the advantage to some one, as the goals were in a north and south line. The University team won the choice and let the Racine team have the kick. Johnston made a fair kick which was caught by Campbell and carried forward some distance by good runs and skilled throwing to others of our team. A scrummage then occurred in the middle of the grounds and finally the ball hovered in the direction of their goal. The ball was now brought back by Racine to the middle of the grounds again, and another scrummage, occurred but with no advantage to either party. Soon after this the ball was worked slowly toward their goal. In a short time a touch-down was made by our team and a kick was made by Captain DeTarr for the goal, which, according to the referee's decision, missed; but our umpire and the whole team and the spectators declared the goal was safely made; however, we did not wish to dispute with the referee, yet, we must suggest, he is as liable to be mistaken as anyone else. The ball was brought out and kicked splendidly by Fulforth and caught just as splendidly by Reed, and a place kick was made, but failed. The ball kept going toward the Racine goal, but was now only in the middle of the field. Here Martin made a good run for his team, but was headed off by Edwards. Again Martin made a good run, but carried the ball but a short distance. The ball was now in the middle of the field. The friends of both teams were very enthusiastic and cheered lustily when an inch was made by either team. Here both teams played beautifully. Hard scrummage in the middle of the grounds. A neat kick by Edwards and a good run by Pond brought the ball near their goal. The ball was carried, then, a short distance from the Racine goal by Fulforth, but did very little real good. Wind blowing briskly in our favor. The ball was soon in the middle of the field again. Splendid running and throwing by both teams. Martin here showed himself the player *par excellence* of the Racine team. Torbert shortly had the wind knocked out of him but was soon up again and plucky as ever. Here the ball got out of bounds, near the goal line, and was thrown in by Hannan, but declared by the referee a foul, although the majority of the crowd thought differently. Here DePuy made a run in but it was not counted, on account of the referee's decision. Racine then made a safety touch-down. Edwards made a good kick, and the ball was on the way to the Racine goal. Here time of the first inning was up, and one touchdown scored by the University team. Time, 4:55. Time of inning, 45 minutes.

(continued)

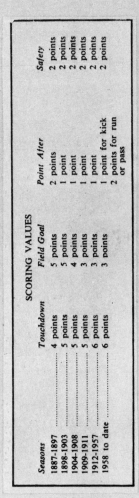

SCORING VALUES			
Seasons	Touchdown	Field Goal	Point After	Safety
1887–1897	4 points	5 points	2 points	2 points
1898–1903	5 points	5 points	1 point	2 points
1904–1908	5 points	4 points	1 point	2 points
1909–1911	5 points	3 points	1 point	2 points
1912–1957	6 points	3 points	1 point for kick	2 points
1958 to date	6 points	3 points	2 points for run or pass	2 points

(Continued)

SECOND INNING.

A rest of ten minutes was given the teams, during which time Mr. Keeler and other graduates amused themselves with a few kicks, but they only succeeded in covering themselves, not with glory, but with dirt. The second inning was opened by a good kick-off by Captain De Tarr, which was prettily caught by Roberts, and succeeded in bringing the ball to the middle of the field. Soon by good playing the ball was carried within about ten feet of the Racine goal, and there it was kept for at least twenty minutes, by drops and pick-ups, by our men. This was the best part of the game, and nothing could have been better. The teams fought like dogs of war. Chase especially distinguished himself, and the shout "Chase is there" was made at least twenty times. De Tarr hung on like a bull-dog, and the other men of our team played exceedingly well, and cheer after cheer went up, "Pond forever." All around we hear, "Racine tackles pretty well, but is not skillful at throwing." The ball is finally got back by Racine, but Edwards brings it up to the Racine goal and another *fight* for it occurs. Again the ball was thrown out, Pond carried it across the grounds, and Hannan got it in touch and threw it to De Puy, and he touched it down behind the goal. A foul was claimed and allowed. The ball thrown in again and the fight renewed. Soon De Tarr put it down in a scrummage and it was kicked by the Racine team and caught by Chase, close behind De Tarr. Only two minutes more and the second inning would have been over. Yet the gods gave the University time to make a goal, which they did in most splendid style,—a place kick by Capt. DeTarr. Here the game closed with a score of one touch-down and one goal for the University team. It is but just to say the Racine team never put the ball back of the University half-back, and Mitchell did not get even a single opportunity to show himself.

Our team was used in a very courteous manner by Racine, and the best of feeling was displayed through the whole game. The University alumni banquet the team this evening at the Palmer House. The boys are feeling splendidly and only regret that more of their University friends are not here. We append the names composing the two teams: Racine Rushers, Parker, Billings, Rogers, Torbert, Cleveland, Roberts; half-backs, Greene, Martin, Ormsby; backs, Johnston, Fulforth. University team Rushers, DeTarr, Chase, Pond, Green, Hannan, Reed, DePuy, Edwards; half-backs, Campbell, Barmore; goal-keeper, Mitchell.

1880 Lettermen
F. G. Allen
E. H. Barmore
R. W. Brown
W. B. Calvert
J. Chase (Capt)
R. G. DePuy
R. M. Dott
W. H. Graham
E. P. Hathaway
W. S. Horton
C. H. Johnston
F. B. Wormwood

MICHIGAN AND PRINCETON PLAYED FIRST INTERSECTIONAL GRID GAME

According to data recently uncovered in the Princeton University files The Tiger can lay joint claim with Michigan to the distinction of having engaged in the first intersectional football contest to be played in the United States. The two schools mixed November 4, 1881, with Princeton emerging from the game on the long end of a 13-4 score.

The account of the game was found in an old scrapbook containing newspaper slippings which had been presented to Princeton by a member of the class of 1882. The account read: "The day was clear, the grounds in good condition, but the weather was exceedingly cold. This combined with the high wind which prevailed during the entire game rendered long-distance kicks or passes unsafe. Except for the absence of Horton of Michigan, both teams were in full force."

The line-ups were:

Michigan—Forwards, Ayers, Captain Woodruff, Olcott, Wilson, Pitney and Depuy; backs, Mahon, H. G. Depuy, Dott, Wormwood, and Gilmore.

Princeton — Forwards, Stone, Benton, Bickham, Rigs, Haxall, and Captain Bryan; backs, Fell, Peace, Baker, Harlan, and Burt.

Records here show that the Wolverines met Princeton, Harvard, and Yale in 1881, losing to Harvard, 4-0, and to Yale, 11-0. The exact dates of these games are unknown, but if the Princeton claim is valid the other games with the remaining schools of the "Big Three" were scheduled sometime after November 4.

Princeton also claims to have been a contestant in the first football game to be played in the United States when they met Rutgers in 1869. The Rutgers eleven emerged victorious from this game 6-4.

This game was the last time that the Tiger and Wolverine have tangled, although Michigan played Yale again in 1883, losing 46-0. The Wolves have met Harvard three times in addition to 1881 in 1883, 1895, and 1914, losing each time, 3-0, 4-0, and 7-0.

1881 Lettermen
F. W. Allmendinger
J. Ayres
H. Bittner
R. G. DePuy
R. M. Dott
T. W. Gilmore
W. S. Horton (Capt)
H. S. Mahon
W. J. Olcott
F. M. Townsend
C. M. Wilson
D. G. deW. Woodruff
F. B. Wormwood

1879 Season   *Won 1, Lost 0, Tied 1*

				Date	Place	Attendance
Michigan	1, Racine College	0		May 30	Chicago	500
Michigan	0, Toronto	0		Nov 1	Detroit	

1880 Season   *Won 1, Lost 0, Tied 0*

				Date	Place	Attendance
Michigan	13, Toronto	6		Nov 5	Toronto	

1881 Season   *Won 0, Lost 3, Tied 0*

				Date	Place	Attendance
Michigan	0, Harvard	4		Oct 31	Cambridge	
Michigan	0, Yale	11		Nov 2	New Haven	
Michigan	4, Princeton	13		Nov 4	Princeton	

1882 Season   *No regular team or outside games*

<table>
<tr><td>

1883

FORWARDS: E. E. Beach. Harry Bitner. H. G. Prettyman, H. J. Killilea, H. P. Borden, R. M. Dott.
QUARTERBACK: T. H. McNeil.
HALFBACKS: R. G. Gemmell, A. I. Moore.
THREEQUARTERBACK: W. J. Olcott.
FULLBACK: T. W. Gilmore.
SUBSTITUTES: R. W. Beach, H. S. Mahon, E. W. Wright.

SCORES

Michigan 0, Yale 46; Harvard 0, 3; Wesleyan 6, 14; Stevens Institute 5, 1.

</td><td>

1884

RUSHERS: E. L. Dorn, E. E. Beach. H. G. Prettyman, H. J. Killilea, H. G. Brock, Dwight Goss, G. C. Schemm.
QUARTERBACK: T. H. McNeil.
HALFBACKS: W. J. Olcott, W. J. Duff.
THREEQUARTERBACK: J. M. Jaycox.
GOALKEEPER: E. F. Duffy.

SCORES

Michigan 0, Albion 18; Chicago Club 48, 10.

</td><td>

1885

FORWARDS: F. G. Higgins, W. M. Morrow, H. G. Prettyman, R. W. Beach, C. N. Banks, J. L. Skinner, F. F. Bumps.
QUARTERBACK: T. H. McNeil.
HALFBACKS: J. M. Jaycox, J. E. Duffy.
GOALKEEPER: J. L. Duffy.
SUBSTITUTES: C. D. A. Wright, L. F. Gottschalk, H. G. Hetzler.

SCORES

Michigan 10, Windsor Club 0; Windsor Club 30, 0; Peninsular Team 42, 0.

</td></tr>
</table>

1883

Harvard—rushers, Simpkins, Kendall, Cabot, Appleton, Bonsal, Crane, Codman; quarterback, Mason; halfbacks, Cowley and Henry; back Peabody.
Michigan—rushers, Bitner, Prettyman, Killilea, Olcott, Beach, Moore, Wright; quarterback, McNeal; halfbacks, Dott and Gemmel; back, Gilmore.
Referee—Mr. Mann of Michigan. Umpires—for Harvard, Mr. Thacher; for Michigan, Mr. Fowler."

THE fourth game of the series was played against Stevens Institute, at Hoboken, N. J. This game was reported as follows: "The Stevens Institute football team had the stalwart eleven of the University of Michigan as opponents in a match on the Institute field yesterday. The visitors won the toss, and took the northerly goal, from which the wind blew fresh, and yet with this advantage to aid them, so well were the Stevens team handled by their able captain (Kletzch), that the best the visitors could do in the first half was to obtain the point of a doubtful safety. In the second half Stevens—this time having the wind with them—went in for a dash, and, by the good rushing of Wurts and Baldwin and some clever passing, their halfback (Wurts) was enabled to score a clean goal from the field, leaving a score of 5 to 1 in favor of Stevens. These figures were not changed, even at the close of the second half, although the contest was full of stirring incidents. The excellent team work of Stevens overcame the heavy weight rushing of the Michigan men. The score was as follows:
Stevens—rushers, Coticert, Williams, Kletzch, Bushorne, Bush, Dilworth and Torrance; quarterback, Baldwin; halfbacks, Wurts and James; back, Campbell. Umpire Mr. Munkwitz.
Michigan University—rushers, Beach, Alcott, E. Beach, Killilea, Wright and Prettyman; quarterback, McNeal; halfbacks, Moore and Gemmel; back, Gilmore. Umpire, H. S. Mahon. Referee, Mr. Hildreth.
Goals scored, by Stevens 1, Michigan 0. Touchdowns, Stevens 0, Michigan 0. Safeties made. by Stevens 1, Michigan 1. Points scored, by Stevens 5; Michigan 1."

Another clipping summarizes the game with: "The game was witnessed by about 200 persons. During the first three-quarters of an hour Michigan showed the greater strength. In the second three-quarters Stevens had the advantage of the wind, and managed, by good running and kicking, to secure a goal from the field. * *."

FOOTBALL, 1884
Couch Rosenthal Beach Jaycox Killilea
Schemn Duff Prettyman John Duffy
Banks McNeil Goss

1886

FORWARDS: H. G. Prettyman, F. F. Bumps.
F. G. Higgins, George Higgins, C. D. A.
Wright, A. C. Kiskadden C. N. Banks.
QUARTERBACK: W. M. Morrow.
HALFBACKS: J. M. Jaycox, J. E. Duffy.
GOALKEEPER: J. L. Duffy.
SUBSTITUTES: W. W. Harless W. R. Trow-
bridge, W. C. Malley.

SCORES

Michigan 50, Albion 0: Albion—24, 0.

1887

RUSHERS: W. W. Harless, E. M. Sprague.
Fred Townsend, J. T. Scott, J. H. Duffie, G.
H. Wood, Lincoln MacMillan, G. W. De
Haven.
QUARTERBACK: R. T. Farrand.
HALFBACKS: J. E. Duffy, E. W. MacPherran.
FULLBACK: J. L. Duffy.
SUBSTITUTES: R. S. Babcock, Mulford Wade.
Leverge Knapp.

SCORES

Michigan 30, Albion 0: Notre Dame 8, 0:
Harvard School: Notre Dame 26, 6.

FOOTBALL, 1887
J. H. Duffie De Haven Townsend Sprague John Duffy Capt.
Harless Wood McMillan
McPherran Farrand Jas. Duffy

Prettyman in 1886

1888 Season				Won 4, Lost 1, Tied 0	
			Date	Place	Attendance
Michigan 26, Notre Dame	6		Apr 20	South Bend	
Michigan 10, Notre Dame	4		Apr 21	Ann Arbor	
Michigan 14, Detroit A.C.	0		Nov 17	Detroit	
Michigan 76, Albion	4		Nov 24	Ann Arbor	
Michigan 4, Chicago U. Club	26		Nov 29	Chicago	

1889 Season				Won 1, Lost 2, Tied 0	
			Date	Place	Attendance
Michigan 33, Albion	4		Nov 9	Ann Arbor	
Michigan 0, Cornell	56		Nov 23	Buffalo	
Michigan 0, Chicago A.A.	20		Nov 28	Chicago	

1888 Lettermen
W. D. Ball
S. S. Bradley
R. W. Beach
E. P. Coman
J. E. Duffy (Capt)
E. P. DePont
A. Hagel
G. M. Hull
L. MacMillan
E. W. MacPherran
W. C. Malley
W. C. Paine
H. G. Prettyman
F. L. Smith
E. M. Sprague
J. Van Ingwagen

FOOTBALL, 1889
Armstrong Mgr. R. Beach Malley McPherran Jas. Duffy Ball
De Pont Bradley Prettyman Payne Hagle
Van Inwagen Smith McMillan

1890 Season — Won 4, Lost 1, Tied 0

		Date	Place	Attendance
Michigan 56, Albion	10	Oct 11	Ann Arbor	
Michigan 18, Detroit A.C.	0	Oct 18	Detroit	
Michigan 16, Albion	0	Oct 25	Ann Arbor	
Michigan 34, Purdue	6	Nov 1	Ann Arbor	
Michigan 5, Cornell	20	Nov 15	Detroit	

1891 Season — Won 4, Lost 5, Tied 0

		Date	Place	Attendance
Michigan 62, Ann Arbor H.S.	0	Oct 10	Ann Arbor	
Michigan 4, Albion	10	Oct 17	Ann Arbor	
Michigan 18, Olivet	6	Oct 19	Olivet	
Michigan 26, Oberlin	6	Oct 24	Ann Arbor	
Michigan 42, Butler	6	Oct 31	Ann Arbor	
Michigan 0, Chicago A.C.	10	Nov 14	Chicago	
Michigan 12, Cornell	58	Nov 21	Detroit	
Michigan 4, Cleveland A.A.	8	Nov 26	Cleveland	5,000
Michigan 0, Cornell	10	Nov 28	Chicago	300

1892 Season — Won 7, Lost 5, Tied 0

		Date	Place	Attendance
Michigan 74, Michigan A.A.	0	Oct 8	Ann Arbor	
Michigan 68, Michigan A.A.	0	Oct 12	Detroit	
Michigan 10, Wisconsin	6	Oct 15	Madison	
Michigan 6, Minnesota	16	Oct 17	Minneapolis	
Michigan 18, DePauw	0	Oct 22	Indianapolis	
Michigan 0, Purdue	24	Oct 24	Lafayette	
Michigan 8, Northwestern	10	Oct 29	Chicago	
Michigan 60, Albion	8	Nov 5	Ann Arbor	
Michigan 0, Cornell	44	Nov 8	Ithaca	
Michigan 18, Chicago	10	Nov 12	Toledo	1,000
Michigan 26, Oberlin	24	Nov 19	Ann Arbor	600
Michigan 10, Cornell	30	Nov 22	Detroit	

1893 Season — Won 7, Lost 3, Tied 0

		Date	Place	Attendance
Michigan 6, Detroit A.C.	0	Oct 7	Ann Arbor	
Michigan 26, Detroit A.C.	0	Oct 14	Detroit	
Michigan 6, Chicago	10	Oct 21	Chicago	
Michigan 20, Minnesota	34	Oct 28	Ann Arbor	
Michigan 18, Wisconsin	34	Nov 4	Ann Arbor	
Michigan 46, Purdue	8	Nov 11	Lafayette	
Michigan 34, DePauw	0	Nov 13	Greencastle	
Michigan 72, Northwestern	6	Nov 18	Ann Arbor	
Michigan 22, Kansas	0	Nov 25	Kansas City	
Michigan 28, Chicago	10	Nov 30	Chicago	

1890 Lettermen
H. T. Abbott
T. L. Chadbourne, Jr.
J. E. Duffy
G. B. Dygert
L. C. Grosh
W. W. Harless
G. S. Holden
G. H. Jewett
T. L. McKeon
W. C. Malley (Capt)
W. W. Pearson
R. Sherman
S. S. Sherman
C. Sutherland
D. Trainer, Jr.

1893 Lettermen
W. I. Aldrich
C. Baird
J. Baird
A. C. Bartel
H. L. Dyer
G. B. Dygert (Capt)
G. H. Ferbert
R. S. Freund
G. F. Greenleaf
C. T. Griffin
W. W. Griffin
L. C. Grosh
F. F. Harding
R. W. Hayes
F. W. Henninger
J. W. Hillister
H. B. Leonard
J. L. D. Morrison
L. P. Paul
W. W. Pearson
H. Powers
E. L. Sanderson
H. M. Senter
R. Sherman
C. H. Smith
G. R. F. Villa

1892 Lettermen
J. P. Bird
F. Decker
E. P. DePont
G. B. Dygert (Capt)
C. T. Griffin
W. W. Griffin
L. C. Grosh
F. F. Harding
R. W. Hayes
G. H. Jewett
H. B. Leonard
L. P. Paul
W. W. Pearson
H. Powers
E. L. Sanderson
C. L. Thomas
V. Tupper
P. Woodworth

Game of 1892

Some past history might be interesting. Just four hundred years after Columbus discovered America the University of Chicago discovered that to advertise the new school it would be best to play athletics for a head liner, and A. Alonzo Stagg was imported from the east to do the trick. He quickly organized a football team out of what material he had, but he did not have eleven men that he could count upon, and so the great Chicago coach of today actually went in and played halfback on his team. In that year Michigan had a date with Lehigh, but this college came out so battered and bruised from a contest with the University of Pennsylvania that they canceled the game and "Stagg's Chicago University team" was taken on as a substitute. The first half stood 12 to 10 in favor of Michigan, and it was anybody's game, but Michigan cinched it in the second half by a touchdown by Jewett, the last colored man to play on a University of Michigan team. Stagg did brilliant work for his team. Chicago made a fumble, but Stagg got the ball and made a touchdown by a long run around an end just as time was called on the first half. For Michigan Henninger, Sanderson, Grosch, Jewett and Dygert starred.

Contest of 1893.

This year Michigan met a Bull Run early in the year, but gained an Appomattox later. On October 21 Chicago trimmed Michigan 10 to 6. It was an off-side play that lost the game for Michigan, but even at that Michigan had the ball within a half yard of Chicago's goal when time was called. It was a hard blow for Michigan, but on Thanksgiving Day revenge was reaped. The old flying wedge was used and Michigan had their opponents 28 to 0 at the end of the first half. A snow storm came up in the second half, and Chicago got two touchdowns, the final score being Michigan 28, Chicago 10. Jack Hollister, former coach of Beloit, made the big run of the day, negotiating a 40-yard run for Michigan. In that year such well known men as Gale, Allen and Flint played for Chicago, while "Dutch" Ferbert, "Mort" Senter, "Fatty" Smith, "Pa" Henninger, "Count" Villa and "Jimmy" Baird were prominent at Michigan.

FOOTBALL, 1891

McCain		Sutherland		Chadbourne		Trainer		Prettyman
	S. Sherman		Grosh	Jennett	Malley Capt.		Codd Mgr.	McMoran
		Dygert		Holden	R. Sherman		James Duffy	

Record of Games.

1.	Oct. 6, at Ann Arbor, M. M. A.,	12,	U. of M.	12
2.	Oct. 13, at Ann Arbor, Albion,	10,	U. of M.	28
3.	Oct. 17, at Ann Arbor, Olivet,	0,	U. of M.	48
4.	Oct. 20, at Ann Arbor, M. M. A.,	6,	U. of M.	40
5.	Oct. 23, at Ann Arbor, Adrian.,	0,	U. of M.	48
6.	Oct. 28, at Cleveland, O., Case Scientific School.	8,	U. of M.	18
7.	Nov. 3, at Ithaca, New York, Cornell,	22,	U. of M.	0
8.	Nov. 10, at Kansas City, University of Kansas,	12,	U. of M.	22
9.	Nov. 17, at Ann Arbor, Oberlin,	6,	U. of M.	14
10.	Nov. 24, at Detroit, Cornell,	4,	U. of M.	12
11.	Nov. 29, at Chicago, University of Chicago,	4,	U. of M.	6

Total scores U. of M., ... 248
Average per game, ... 22
Total scores for opponents, ... 84
Average per game, ... 7

'Varsity Foot-Ball Team.

Officers.

Charles Baird, ...	*Manager.*
Wm. L. M'Cauley, Princeton, '94, ...	*Coach.*
Keene Fitzpatrick, ...	*Trainer.*

Team.

		Age.	Height. Ft. In.	Weight Stripped Nov. 24.
Ends,	Senter, H. M.	22	5 10	156
	Price, G. D.	23	5 10½	140
	Hayes, R. W. E.	22	6 1	185
Tackles,	Hadden, H. G.	20	6 1	176
	Villa, G. R. F.	21	5 7	184
	Yont, J. G.	22	6 0	186
	Reynolds, J. B.	22	5 8	157
Guards,	Henninger, F. H.	21	5 9 ¼	177
	Carr, B. M.	23	5 11	195
	Ninde, D. B.	21	5 11	165
	Rundell, W. S.	25	5 11¼	185
Center,	Smith, C. H.	21	5 8	220
Quarters,	Baird, J. (Capt.)	20	5 6	141
	Greenleaf, G. F.	20	5 6	130
Halves,	Ferbert, G. H.	20	5 7 ½	147½
	Dyer, H. L.	22	5 11	167
	Richards, J. DeF.	20	5 8	150½
	Dygert, G. B.	23	5 8	166
	Leonard, H. B.	22	5 7 ¾	167
	Freund, J. D.	20	5 8 ½	150
	LeRoy, J. A.	21	5 9	163
Full-Back,	Bloomingston, J. A.	21	5 8	164½

Average weight of team, 170 pounds.
Average weight of line, 178 pounds.
Average weight of backs, 155½ pounds.

Above W. G. McCauley, Michigan football coach and Charles Baird, undergraduate manager.

November 17 our eleven met the eleven from Oberlin College on our home grounds, and in the presence of an enthusiastic crowd of over two thousand easily won by a score of 14 to 6. Boothman, Oberlin's ten second sprinter, is responsible for her only score, Oberlin during most of the game being on the defensive, and her line going to pieces toward the end of the game. This is the third time Oberlin has been beaten in two years. Our eleven was crippled by the absence of Captain Baird, but put up a splendid game. A. A. Stagg, of Chicago, acted as umpire.

The second game was with Cornell, at Detroit, November 24. This was to be the game of the year, and great preparations were made for it. Football songs were composed and rehearsed, yell masters were appointed, and over fifteen hundred students went to Detroit to cheer the boys, hoping to see the eleven score against our old opponent. It was a glorious game, every man on the eleven playing the game of their lives. Cornell was clearly outplayed. Michigan's game in spite of the fact that frequent fumbles lost us the ball at critical points, was superior to Cornell's both in offensive and defensive work. Cornell was weakened by the loss of Ohl and Rogers, but the game our eleven put up would have won from almost any team. At the end of the first half the score stood, Michigan 6, Cornell 4. In the second half Cornell was desperate but could not prevent the final score, Michigan 12, Cornell 4. The following was the line-up for Michigan: Senter, left end, Villa, left tackle, Carr, left guard, Smith, center, Henninger, right guard, Hadden, right tackle, Price, right end, Baird, quarterback, Ferbert. left halfback, Bloomington, right halfback, Dyer, fullback. A crowd of 4,000 saw the game.

The final game was played in Chicago on Thanksgiving Day with Stagg's Chicago University team. Though a victory, the score 6 to 4 was a disappointing one. Michigan looked upon Chicago as an easy team, and nearly lost the game. The boys were still crippled from the Cornell game, but at the latter part of the game braced up and won. It was also claimed that Stagg had secured our signals and made use of the knowledge, hoping to win the game by any means, however questionable.

THE MICHIGAN ALUMNUS.

Nov. 3d, at Ithaca, Cornell defeated the team 22–0. This was a pleasant surprise, notwithstanding the general feeling that Michigan would score. It augured well for the Detroit game. Cornell has a light, active team, unable to touch Michigan's line, but making her gains between ends and tackles. On the other hand, Michigan gained wholly through the line by quick openings and bucking. Scarcely a yard was made around the ends. Her interference was wretched, the backs being slow and not running hard.

With three days' practice, the men left for Kansas City, where they defeated University of Kansas 22–12 on Nov. 10. This was a disappointment, for a larger score and shut-out was expected. The first half was a walk-over for Michigan, the score being 16–6. Kansas made a touch-down on a fluke. In the second, honors were even—a touch-down and goal for each. Kansas earned hers by hitting the line, especially at centre. The three centre men, whom no team up to this time could touch, were opened up time and again for good gains. The long trip from Ann Arbor to Kansas City undoubtedly had a depressing effect on the men, causing them to play a somewhat listless game.

1895 Lettermen

J. Baird
J. A. Bloomingston
B. M. Carr
E. Denby
T. L. Farnham
G. H. Ferbert
G. F. Greenleaf
F. M. Hall
F. W. Henninger (Capt)
J. W. Hollister
W. H. Holmes
J. H. Hooper
W. R. Morley
J. DeF. Richards
H. M. Senter
G. R. F. Villa

1895 Season Won 8, Lost 1, Tied 0

			Date	Place	Attendance
Michigan 34,	Michigan M.A.	0	Oct 5	Ann Arbor	
Michigan 42,	Detroit A.C.	0	Oct 12	Ann Arbor	
Michigan 64,	Western Reserve	0	Oct 19	Ann Arbor	400
Michigan 40,	Lake Forest	0	Oct 26	Ann Arbor	700
Michigan 42,	Oberlin	0	Nov 2	Ann Arbor	
Michigan 0,	Harvard	4	Nov 9	Cambridge	
Michigan 12,	Purdue	10	Nov 16	Ann Arbor	1,000
Michigan 20,	Minnesota	0	Nov 23	Detroit	3,500
Michigan 12,	Chicago	0	Nov 28	Chicago	10,000

Michigan.	Position.	Lake Forest.
Senter	Left end	Johnson.
Villa	Left tackle	Woolsey.
Hooper	Left guard	Thom.
Carr	Center	Duncan.
J. Johnson	Right guard	Smolt.
Henninger (c)	Right tackle	Fullenweider.
Greenleaf	Right end	Seger (c).
Richards	Quarter	Wood.
Ferbert	Left half	Livy.
Holmes	Right half	Lee.
Bloomingston	Full back	Peel.

Touchdowns—Villa 4, Bloomingston, 2, Henninger. Goals—Bloomingston, 6. Referee—R. A. Hayner. Umpire–Gus Freund. Linemen—Jackson and Hollister. Substitutes—Denby for Carr, Dicken for Greenleaf, McNary for Seger. Attendance, 400.

On November 9, Michigan met Harvard at Boston and the whole West hung breathless on the result. Twelve years ago the two Universities met at Cambridge in a tie game each gaining a solitary touchdown, and the announcement that this year this tie would be played off resulted in bringing together at Ann Arbor the best foot ball players of the West, anxious to be on the team which it was confidently believed would force recognition from the sturdy collegians of the East. Not a college eleven in the West but looked upon the Michigan team which left Ann Arbor on Nov. 6 for Boston as their champions in this peculiar sense. The greatest care was used in selecting the nineteen men who should make the trip, and it was only on the evening previous to departure that the following list was announced: Center, Carr, Denby; guards, Hooper, Hall, Wambacker; tackles, Villa, Henninger, Yont; ends, Senter, Greenleaf, Farnum; quarter backs, Baird, Morley; halves, Hollister, Ferbert, Shields, Richards, Holmes; full back, Bloomingston. With them went Manager Baird, Coach McCauley, and Trainer Fitzpatrick. Fully two thousand howling students cheered the boys as they left Ann Arbor. Never has foot ball enthusiasm run so high. Saturday afternoon the best eleven Michigan ever had lined up on Soldiers' Field, Boston, against the Harvard rushers. The two teams were of nearly equal weight and each was determined to put up their best game. The day was the worst possible for the Michigan eleven. A steady downpour of rain soon covered the men with black mud and rendered the ball slippery and footing insecure. Harvard had played several times under just such circumstances, while the Michigan players had not met a wet day during the whole season. The unexpected happened. Our superb interference and end plays were seldom successful, the men slipping easily. But the game was an even one nevertheless. Neither side scored in the first half, the ball vacillating from one side to the other without much advantage to either eleven. Shortly after the opening of the second half Harvard scored. On Michigan's 20-yard line Bloomingston punted. Wrightington, who many of the onlookers say was plainly off-side at the time, blocked the ball. It bounded back and rolled over Michigan's line, Donald falling on it for a touchdown. No goal. This somewhat disheartened the Michigan men, who, however, braced up and played hard and heavy. After eighteen minutes play during which Harvard's line weakened perceptibly time was called on account of darkness. Final score, 4 0, in favor of Harvard. Witnesses of the game generally concede that if the game had lasted ten minutes longer, Michigan with her great strength and better training would have won.

The line up follows:

Michigan.	Position.	Harvard.
Senter	Left end	Cabot.
Villa	Left tackle	Stevenson.
Hooper	Left guard	Holt.
Carr	Center	Doucette.
Hall	Right guard	Shaw.
Henninger	Right tackle	Donald.
Greenleaf	Right end	Lowell.
Baird	Quarter	Borden.
Hollister	Left half	Wrightington.
Ferbert	Right half	C. Brewer.
Bloomingston	Full back	Dunlap.

Touchdown—Donald. Referee—J. M. Garfield. Umpires—Ward, of Princeton, and Kennedy, of Leland Stanford. Linesmen—Wood, of B. A. A., and Holt, of Michigan. Substitutes—Holmes for Hollister, Jaffrey for Shaw, Fairchild for Dunlap, Moulton for Cabot.

Michigan.	Position.	Oberlin.
Farnum	Left end	Behr.
Villa	Left tackle	McMurray.
Hooper	Left guard	Worcester.
Carr	Center	Pierce.
Henninger (c)	Right tackle	Gould.
Yont	Right guard	Churchill.
Greenleaf	Right end	Young.
Morley	Quarter back	Fulton.
Ferbert	Left half	Boothman (c).
Hollister	Right half	Fauver.
Bloomingston	Full back	Merrill.

Touchdowns—Henninger, Morley, Villa, Ferbert, Bloomingston, Farnum, Shields. Goals—Bloomingston, 7. Referee—Nate Williams of Yale. Umpire—Charley Stage of Adelbert. Linesmen and timekeepers—A. M. Burk of Oberlin, and R. C. Bourland of Michigan. Substitutes—Denby for Carr, Wambacker for Henninger, Henninger for Yont, Shields for Hollister, Mosier for Boothman. Attendance—700.

Michigan.	Position.	Purdue.
Senter	Left end	Marshall.
Yont	Left tackle	(c.) Robertson.
Hooper	Left guard	Kerchoff.
Denby	Center	Kercheval.
Hall	Right guard	Webb.
Henninger (c.)	Right tackle	Alward.
Greenleaf	Right end	Schmitz.
Holmes	Quarter back	Jamison.
Ferbert	Left half	Moore.
Hollister	Right half	Smith.
Bloomingston	Full back	Oesterlin.

Touchdowns—Marshall, Ferbert, Moore, Henninger. Goals—Bloomingston, 2, Jamison. Referee—Nate Williams of Yale. Umpire—J. P. Rafferty of Lehigh; linesmen and timekeepers, Freund of Michigan, and Bates of Purdue. Substitutes—Villa for Yont, Richards for Ferbert, Kingsbury for Marshall, Mulatte for Smith. Attendance—1,000.

THE MONTH IN FOOT BALL.

"Hippity hippity hop,
Michigan men on top.
Hippity hippity hoop,
Chicago in the soup."

In these few homely words is told the story of a great victory for the University of Michigan.

Ten thousand people crowded into the enclosure on Marshall Field on Thanksgiving morning to see the foot ball teams representing the Universities of Michigan and Chicago do battle for supremacy. Another thousand stood on neighboring house-tops, or in windows and nearly as many little urchins located themselves in the branches of trees or cut wide holes in the enclosing fence, to see "de big guys from Michigan" play ball.

The crowd was larger by at least four thousand than any crowd ever seen before at a Chicago foot ball game. The people came in tally-hos, coaches, and in drays of every conceivable kind and shape. Some came in cable cars and electric cars; others walked. But they all reached the grounds some time before the two elevens put in an appearance. So that when the players did finally jump over the ropes and run onto the field of play for their preliminary warming up, such a sight greeted their eyes as a western foot ball team has never before gazed upon. Grand stands alive with the maroon of Chicago and the yellow and blue of Michigan loomed up on either side of the field. Eight thousand pairs of eyes looked down upon them from these points of vantage while fully two thousand more viewed them from the ground just outside the ropes and from decorated tally-hos and coaches.

Contrary to what might have been expected in Chicago, the proportion of Michigan and Chicago adherents and "rooters" was a little in favor of the visitors. This is the way it seemed before the game began. When the game was finished everything was yellow and blue—Chicago men and Chicago colors were as scarce as Chicago touchdowns and Chicago goals.

Considering the state of the weather previous to the game, the grounds were in very fair shape. The three inches of snow and slush had been removed and a layer of sawdust spread about in its place. Beneath this sawdust there was ice and frozen ground but the total product of both ice and sawdust was a sound footing for the men and a tolerably soft surface to fall on.

Michigan.	Position.	Minnesota.
Farnum	Right end	Harrison
Henninger	Right tackle	Dalrymple
Hall	Right guard	Larson
Denby	Center	Fulton
Hooper	Left guard	Finlayson
Villa	Left tackle	Walker
Senter	Left end	Kehoe
Richards	Quarter back	Adams
Ferbert	Right half	Gilbert
Hollister	Left half	Loomis
Bloomingston	Full back	Parkyn

Referee—Herbert Alward, Chicago Athletic Association. Umpire—F. M. Gould of Amherst. Attendance—3,500.

Touchdowns—Ferbert, 2, Hall, Farnum. Goals—Bloomingston, 2. Substitutes—Greenleaf for Senter, Morley for Richards.

Chicago,	Position,	Michigan,
Robey	Right end	Farnum
C. Allen	Right tackle	Henninger
Ketman	Right guard	Hall
P. Allen	Center	Carr
Ruhlkoetter	Left guard	Hooper
Williamson	Left tackle	Villa
Flint	Left end	Senter
Ewing	Quarter back	Richards
Nichols	Right half back	Ferbert
Gale	Left half tackle	Hollister
Neil	Full back	Bloomingston

Score—Michigan, 12; Chicago, 0.
Place and date—Marshall Field, Nov. 28, 1895.
Touchdowns—Richards, Bloomingston.
Goals kicked on touchdowns—Bloomingston (2).
Time—Thirty-five minute halves.
Referee—Gould [Amherst]; umpire, Upton [Harvard]; linesmen, Freund and Sincere.

Michigan, 0.
Harvard, 4.

FOOTBALL, 1896

Hughes St. Mgr.   Hogg   Villa Capt.   Caley   Richards   Wombacher   Drumheller   Greenleaf
Felver   Baker   Farnham   Bennett   Henninger   Duffy   Ward Coach   Hutchinson

Season of 1896

Record

Oct. 3, at Ann Arbor,	. .	Michigan 18, Normals	0
Oct. 10, at Ann Arbor,	. .	Michigan 44, Grand Rapids	0
Oct. 15, at Ann Arbor,	. .	Michigan 28, C. of P. & S.	0
Oct. 17, at Ann Arbor,	. .	Michigan 66, Lake Forest	0
Oct. 24, at LaFayette,	. .	Michigan 16, Purdue	. 6
Oct. 31, at Detroit,	. .	Michigan 40, Lehigh	. 0
Nov. 7, at Minneapolis,	. .	Michigan 6, Minnesota	4
Nov. 14, at Ann Arbor,	. .	Michigan 10, Oberlin	0
Nov. 21, at Ann Arbor,	. .	Michigan 28, Wittenberg	. 0
Nov. 26, at Chicago,	. .	Michigan 6, Chicago	. 7

Total score for Michigan,	. .	262
Average per game,	. .	26
Total for opponents,	. .	11
Average,	. . .	1

'Varsity Foot-Ball Team

Season of 1896

Officers

WARD HUGHES, '98, Manager	C. O. COOK, '97 E, Assistant
W. D. WARD, } Coaches W. L. McCAULEY,	JAMES ROBINSON, Trainer
H. M. SENTER, Captain	FRANK VILLA, Captain

Team

Ends,	SENTER, '98 M GREENLEAF, '99 M FARNHAM, '97 E HUTCHINSON, '97 E	Half Backs,	FERBERT, '97 CALEY, '99 L PINGREE, '00
Tackles,	VILLA, P. G. L HENNINGER, '97 E	Full Backs,	HOGG, '99 L DUFFY, '98 D
Guards,	CARR, '98 M BENNETT, '98 E BAKER, '98 E		
Center, WOMBACHER, '97			
Quarter Backs,	DRUMHELLER, '97 L FELVER, 98 E RICHARDS, '98		

ATHLETICS.

The Board of Control has adopted the rules recommended by the Chicago Conference, as published in the December *Alumnus*. Five thousand copies of the rules will be printed for distribution among the students. Purdue, Illinois, Minnesota, Wisconsin, and Chicago, have also accepted the rules, and Northwestern has rejected them, with the exception of Nos. 1, 3, 4, and 12. The vote of Michigan's Board of Control was unanimous in favor of adoption.

W. Douglas Ward, of Princeton, is the 'Varsity's head coach this season. He had the assistance of W. L. McCauley, the coach of last year, during October. Keene Fitzpatrick, who has so successfully trained Michigan's teams for the last two years, accepted the position of trainer at Yale, and the training of the football team has been done by James Robinson. Mr. Robinson has trained some of the most famous Princeton and Harvard elevens, and before coming to Ann Arbor was the trainer of the Manhattan Athletic Club. Mr. Fitzpatrick's place as instructor in the gymnasium has been taken by Dr. Charles H. Rabethge, who came with excellent recommendations from the Boston Y. M. C. A.

A feature of the '96 foot ball season has been the hearty interest taken in University Athletics. The subscriptions made at the annual mass meeting amounted to more than $1,000.

1896 Saw Wolverines Beaten.

In this year the great Herschberger was developed and Chicago won by a score of 7 to 6. When the score was telegraphed to Ann Arbor that evening they would not believe it here and not until the papers reached here the next morning were the rooters convinced that Michigan had lost.

Chicago scored all her points in the first half. A blocked kick forced Michigan to make a safety, making two points for Chicago. Later Herschberger kicked a field goal from the 45-yard line, which counted five points in those days. In the second half Ferbert, Villa and Henninger did great work, and the ball was carried by Michigan for the entire length of the field. Farnham, Villa, Carr, Bennett, Henninger, Ferbert, Pingree and Coley were prominent members of the '96 team.

1897 Season   **Won 6, Lost 2, Tied 1**

			Date	Place	Attendance
Michigan	24.	Eastern Mich	0	Oct 2	Ann Arbor	
Michigan	0.	Ohio Wesleyan	0	Oct 9	Ann Arbor	
Michigan	34.	Ohio State	0	Oct 16	Ann Arbor	
Michigan	16.	Oberlin	6	Oct 23	Ann Arbor	
Michigan	0.	Alumni	15	Oct 30	Ann Arbor	
Michigan	34.	Purdue	4	Nov 6	Ann Arbor	
Michigan	14.	Minnesota	0	Nov 13	Detroit	
Michigan	32.	Wittenberg	0	Nov 20	Ann Arbor	
Michigan	12.	Chicago	21	Nov 25	Chicago	9,000

The Friday following Thanksgiving representatives from the seven universities represented in the Chicago Conference, Minnesota, Wisconsin, Northwestern, Purdue, Illinois, Chicago and Michigan met in Chicago and proposed a number of changes in the rules governing athletics in the West. Committees were appointed to improve the rules for football and to determine the exact meaning of the term "college students." A brief summary of the proposed changes in the rules is as follows.

Existing athletic regulations are to be altered regardless of the eastern colleges.

A four year limit to be placed upon college athletes.

Preparatory students to be barred from college athletics.

Games with colleges not parties to the agreement to be regarded as "practice games"

[THE ALUMNUS invites an expression of views on the part of Alumni on these important questions. Our pages are always open to communications.—EDITOR.]

"Summer nines" to be discouraged.

Rough football to be further eliminated by the abolition of mass plays.

The rules will do away with the last vestige of professionalism, and football in particular will be benefitted. The rules governing the great college sports will be so changed as to eliminate all the objectionable features that a committee of experts are able to discover. Professor Stagg of the University of Chicago will be a member of this important committee, and two other members will be drafted and presented for approval to the members of the conference before January 1, 1898.

As a result of the Oberlin game played here in October, that institution has severed athletic relations with Michigan for three years. The board of control at Oberlin sent to the board here a long list of petty charges against the alleged ungentlemanly treatment received by their team and manager at the hands of the Michigan team and management. Our board of control investigated the charges very carefully, questioning the officials, players and manager, and came to the conclusion that there was no basis for the accusation of discourteous and unnecessarily rough treatment. The Oberlin board was not satisfied with this issue of the examination and ordered their athletic managers to make no dates with Michigan for three years. The sentiment about the Campus is in favor of letting the black list go on indefinitely as there seems to be a lack of a proper athletic spirit at Oberlin. Her team came up here expecting to win and could not take a square defeat in a sportsmanlike manner.

In the game with the Ohio Wesleyan, that team played their coach, Yost, after promising that he should not be allowed to play. In consequence of this breach of faith, the board of control ordered Michigan's athletic managers to make no further engagements with teams from Ohio Wesleyan.

ATHLETICS.

The football season closed with the Thanksgiving Day game in Chicago and for the second time in two years Michigan was defeated. Herschberger won the game for Chicago as he did last year by three place-kick goals. Michigan lined up a green team against eleven veterans, but scored two touchdowns to Chicago's one by the pluckiest kind of playing. Both Michigan's scores came in the second half when five regular players had been forced to retire. The game was played in the Coliseum before an audiences of nearly 10,000. It is probably the last indoor game Michigan will play. There is also a very strong chance that the games hereafter will be played the Saturday previous to Thanksgiving. President Harper, of Chicago says, this change must be made.

FOOTBALL. 1897

Hannon   Ayers

Hughes St. Mgr.   Lockwood   Pingree   Teetzel

Baker   Bennett   Hogg Capt.   Egan   Keena

Michigan's Line-Up.

POSITION	NAME	WEIGHT	HEIGHT	AGE	PREV. EXPERIENCE
	Brown	204	5-11	20	Chillicothe, G., H. S.
G.	Caley	195	6-½	24	Michigan University
G.	Franz	200	5-11½	19	Decatur, Ill, H. S.
G.	Allen	185	6-4	21	Michigan Reserves
T.	Steckle	172	5-8½	25	Michigan University
T.	White	175	5-10½	21	Class Team
T.	Avory	180	5-8½	18	Detroit High School
E.	Bennett	185	6-4½	22	Michigan University
E.	Snow	168	6-2	18	Detroit High School
E.	Teetzel	156	5-9	20	Michigan University
E.	Hicks	169	5-10½	21	Tecumseh H. S.
Q. B.	Street	160	5-10	24	Williams College
Q. B.	Talcott	150	5-8	19	Michigan Reserves
H. B.	Widman	162	5-6	19	Detroit High School
H. B.	Barrabee	164	5-6½	22	Michigan University
H. B.	Whitcomb	163	5-10	22	Phillips Exeter
F. B.	Weeks	168	6	21	Michigan Reserves
F. B.	McDonald	170	5-9½	24	Oberlin University

1898 Season — Won 11, Lost 0, Tied 0

			Date	Place	Attendance
Michigan	21	Eastern Mich.	0	Oct 1	Ann Arbor
Michigan	29	Kenyon	0	Oct 8	Ann Arbor
Michigan	39	Michigan State	0	Oct 12	Ann Arbor
Michigan	18	Western Reserve	0	Oct 17	Ann Arbor
Michigan	23	Case	5	Oct 19	Ann Arbor
Michigan	11	Alumni	2	Oct 31	Ann Arbor
Michigan	6	Northwestern	5	Nov 5	Evanston
Michigan	12	Illinois	5	Nov 12	Detroit	3,500
Michigan	22	Beloit	0	Nov 19	Ann Arbor
Michigan	12	Chicago	11	Nov 24	Chicago

Widman's great run, as reproduced in The Chicago Tribune, when a small Michigan substitute, Charles Widman '98, ran the field against the Chicago eleven to give Michigan a 12 to 11 victory.

"BUCK' HALL,
MICHIGAN'S HEAD COACH.

Widman Won 1898 Game.

While Herschberger had won the game the year before from Michigan he really lost it in this year. With the score standing 6 to 6, Herschberger, who was playing back, was foolishly drawn into the line to back up his own men and "Chuck" Widman, for Michigan, shot out from behind the Michigan bunch and made his famous 65-yard run for a touchdown and Snow kicked goal. Later Herschberger made a field goal which brought the score to 12 to 11 in favor of Michigan, and that is the way the contest ended. On Michigan's champion team of that year were such men as Caley, Widman, McLean, Snow, Franz, Cunningham, White and Bennett.

ATHLETICS.

The space devoted to this department is limited this month, but in the March number the athletic prospects, particularly regarding track work and base-ball, will be taken up at length.

From a financial standpoint the Athletic Association has never been in such excellent condition as it is today. At the commencement of the foot-ball season the Association was in debt over $1,400. A mass meeting was held, the result of which netted the Association in subscriptions $1,338.52. A special effort was made to increase the membership list, the result is the Association has the largest membership roll in its history. Last season, at the end of the year there were only 302 members, while this year the membership at the middle of the season is 462.

The foot ball season of 1896-'97 left us in debt $568.06—this year the foot-ball receipts exceeds its expenditures $1,316.17. At present the Association has a balance of $2,426.96 in the bank.

Officers.

Charles Baird, '94, ... Graduate Manager
L. D. Verdier, '01 L., . . . Student Manager
H. K. Crafts, '01, . . . Assistant Student Manager
W. C. Steckle, '01 M., . . . Captain

Coaches.

G. H. Ferbert, '97.   J. R. Duffy, '91.
F. W. Henninger, '97.   H. G. Hadden, '95.

Team.

Center,   W. R. Cunningham, '99 M.   Ends,   { D. D. Gill, '03 M , { N. W. Snow, '02.

Guards,   { R. J. Siegmund, '02 D . { R. R. France, '02 M.   Quarterback,   C. E. Street, '02 M.

Halfbacks,   { J. F. McLean, '00. { A. E. Richardson, '00 E..

Tackles,   { W. C. Steckle, '01 M.. { Hugh White, '02 L.. { C. G. McDonald, '00 L.   Fullbacks,   { L. J. Keena, '01. { E. M. Sweeley, '03.

Football Record for 1899.

Sept. 30, at Ann Arbor,	Hillsdale,	0	Michigan, 11
Oct. 7, at Ann Arbor,	Albion,	0	Michigan, 26
Oct. 14, at Ann Arbor,	Western Reserve,	0	Michigan, 17
Oct. 18, at Ann Arbor,	Notre Dame,	0	Michigan, 12
Oct. 21, at Ann Arbor,	Alumni,	0	Michigan, 0
Oct. 28, at Champaign,	Illinois,	0	Michigan, 5
Nov. 4, at Detroit,	Virginia,	0	Michigan, 38
Nov. 11, at Philadelphia,	Pennsylvania,	11	Michigan, 10
Nov. 18, at Ann Arbor,	Case School,	6	Michigan, 28
Nov. 25, at Ann Arbor,	Kalamazoo College,	0	Michigan, 24
Nov. 30, at Chicago,	Wisconsin,	17	Michigan, 5

Michigan.	Positions.	Albion.
White	le	Marshall
Wilson	lt	Exelby
Barkabus	lg	Agnew
Dickie, Larsen	c	Hamlin
Seigmund, Kram'r	rg	Davis
Steckle, McD'nl'd	rt	Moore
Snow, McNemur	re	Bechtel, Hayd'n Brails
Fitzgerald, Gr'dn'r	q	Frost
Mohr.		
Teetzel, McLean	lh	Robertson
Sweeley, Hernst'n	rh	Grosenbaugh
McAfee.		
Keena, Weeks	f	Church, Dunster

Score—Michigan, 26; Albion, o. Touchdowns—Teetzel, Sweeley, Fitzgerald, Wilson, Hernstein. Goals from touchdown—Snow, 1. Time of halves—20 minutes. Referee—Shipp. Umpire—John Duffy. Linesmen—Talcott and Marshall.

Michigan.	Position	Wes. Reserve.
Gill, White	le	Mook
Wilson, McDon'd	lt	McCleary
Barkabus	lg	Yaegle, Johnson
Dickie, Larsen	c	Donly
Seigm'n'd, Kramer	g	Clisby
Steckle, Juttner	rt	Laub, capt.
Snow	re	Bissel
Fitzgerald	g	Philips
McLean, Sweeley	lh	Stribinger
Hernstein, Weeks	rh	Haldy
Keena, Sweeley	f	Nedlin

Touchdowns: Steckle, Juttner, Sweeley. Goals from touchdown, Snow (2). Umpire and referee, Knight and Williams. Time of halves, 25 and 20 minutes.

Michigan.		Pennsylvania.
Juttner, White	le	Stehle
McDonald	lt	Snover
Seigmund, Bliss	lg	Hare
Cunningham	c	Overfield
France	rg	Teas
Steckle	rt	Wallace, Outland
Snow	re	Coombs
Street	q	Woodley
McLean	lhb	Kennedy
Leiblee	rhb	Outland, J.
		Gardiner
Sweeley, White	f	McCracken

Touchdowns—Hare (2), McLean (1), McDonald (1). Goal from touchdown—Overfield. Referee—W. H. Corbin, Yale. Umpire—Dr. W. A. Brooks, Harvard. Timekeeper—Laurie Bliss, Yale. Thirty five minute halves.

The game with Notre Dame on the 18th was the first time that Michigan showed any promise of ultimate development into a first-class team. The fact is that both coaches and players were scared. The outcome of the game was in great doubt, as Notre Dame has been regarded this season as but little below the three big college teams in strength. This element of uncertainty was productive of good results, and at times the 'Varsity showed championship form, particularly when the Notre Dame team had forced the ball to her 20 and 25-yard lines, which the Indiana team did several times. Then the 'Varsity rallied and held their opponents for downs. The game was an exhibition of straight, hard football, with plenty of kicking to be sure, but with practically no end runs and continued line bucking. Both teams suffered severely from fumbling and off side playing. Neither team played fast ball, and in this respect the Notre Dame eleven, with its longer season back of it, was surprisingly off color.

Michigan.	Position.	Notre Dame.
White	le	Farley
Juttner, Wilson	lt	Wagner
Kramer	lg	O'Malley
Cunningham	c	Winters
Seigmund	rg	McNulty
McDonald	rt	Hanley
Snow	re	Mullen
Street	q	McDonald
Hernstein, Mcl'n	lh	Glynn
Teetzel	rh	Hayes
Keena, Sweeley	f	Duncan, Mon'h'n

Touchdowns, Keena, McLean. Goals from touchdown, Snow (2). Time of halves, 25 and 20 minutes. Referee and umpire, Williams and Clarke. Timekeepers, Wood and Eggeman. Linesmen, Fleming and Talcott.

Michigan.		Illinois.
Snow	r.e.	Francis
McDonald	r.t.	Lundgren
Seigmund	r.g.	Briley
Cunningham	c.	McLane
Kramer	lg.	Lowenthal
Juttner, Wilson	l.t.	Clayton
Gill, Martin	l.e.	Stahl
Street	q.	Adsit
Hernstein, Weeks	r.h.	Lewis, Lundgren
McLean	l.h.	Hall, Wadsworth
Keena, Sweeley	f.	Johnson

Umpire—Brown of Cornell. Referee—Heffelfinger of Yale. Timekeepers—Verdier of Michigan and Alarco of Illinois. Halves—30 minutes. Touchdown—McDonald.

ATHLETICS

FOOTBALL.

Before the largest crowd of football enthusiasts ever gathered together west of the Alleghenies, the University of Michigan met defeat at the hands of the University of Wisconsin on Thanksgiving day at the west side baseball park, Chicago, by a score of 17 to 5. It was the first time that the two State Universities had met on the gridiron in six years and intervening time had only served to sharpen the friendly rivalry which existed between them. The gathering was distinctly one of college men and friends, and everyone who crowded the grandstand and bleachers gave evidence of his partisanship by the cardinal or the maize and blue which he carried. Long before the opposing teams came onto the field, every available seat had been taken, and the keen rivalry which smoldered in each bosom then burst forth with unbounded energy in the college yells and songs. With the entrance of the antagonists, pandemonium reigned until silenced by the referee's whistle, and then until the game was over everyone of the 10,000 spectators was oblivious to all but the struggling forms, and held his breath in expectancy of the outcome.

WISCONSIN.

Hyman	R. E.
Curtis	R. T.
Rogers	R. G.
L. Chamberlain	C.
Lerum	L. G.
Blair	L. T.
Cochems	L. E.
Tratt	Q. B.
Peele	R. H. B.
Larson	L. H. B.
O'Dea, Driver	F. B.

MICHIGAN.

Snow	L. E.
Steckle, White	L. T.
France	L. G.
Cunningham	C.
Siegmund	R. G.
McDonald	R. T.
Gill	R. E.
Street	Q. B.
Sweeley, Keena	L. H. B.
McLean	R. H. B.
Richardson	F. B.

Touchdowns—McLean, Larson, Hyman. Goals from touchdown—Tratt (2). Goal from field—O'Dea. Umpire—Bliss of Yale. Referee—Corbin of Yale. Linesman—Caldwell of Michigan. Alstead of Wisconsin. Timer—Weeks of Brown.

THE 'VARSITY SQUAD, 1900

ENDS: N. W. Snow, C. G. Redden
TACKLES: Hugh White, B. C. Shorts
GUARDS: T. R. Marks, S. G. Kelly
CENTER: H. R. Brown
QUARTERBACK: H. S. Weeks
HALFBACKS: A. A. Redner, W. W. Shaw, N. G. Begle
FULLBACK: E. M. Sweeley

Michigan 29, Hillsdale 0; Kalamazoo 11, 0; Case School—24, 6; Purdue 11, 6; Illinois 12, 0; Indiana 12, 0; Iowa—5, 28;
Notre Dame—7, 0; Ohio State University 0, 0; Chicago—6, 15.

FINANCIAL REPORT.

The report of the financial secretar of the Athletic Association for the perio beginning April 1, 1899, and endin January 1, 1900, has just been made, an contains interesting figures showin what athletics cost at the University c Michigan. The total amount disburse for expense of all kinds during tha period, which included a baseball, track tennis and football season, was $18,411.89. This is an increase of about $2,40 over what was spent last year. At th time the report was completed, Michi gan's share of the profits of the Pennsyl vania game had not been received, bu a settlement was made recently, and i amounted to about $1,200. This as us ual, makes the football season th money making season, although the last baseball season was surprisingly suc cessful, considering the fact that the year before saw a loss of $1,570.89. The receipts during the football season wer as follows: Season tickets, $483 games, $10,417.27; a total of $10,900.27. The expenses were about $9,501.09, and included among other items which go to show the cost of running football elevens, $1,802.50, for salaries to coaches, and $1,052.25, for a training table. This leaves a profit of some $1,500 on the season, where last year the balance was but $131.57. The baseball team made money. The net profit on all the games was $1,783.41, while the general expenses were $1,065.03, leaving a bal ance of $718.38 to the credit of that team.

NEW BLEACHERS FOR REGENTS' FIELD.

The athletic management has decided to erect at Regents' Field some new bleachers that will be movable. The first section is now being built as more or less of an experiment, and will be at the middle of the field along the south side line of the gridiron. It will be moved back in the spring so as not to in terfere with baseball. Should the plan prove to be perfectly feasible other sec tions will be built from time to time until Michigan is thoroughly provided with bleachers on her home grounds, as well as in Chicago.

COACH LEA'S BLUE LAWS.

Last week, for the first time perhaps in the history of Michigan football, the head coach posted in the Gymnasium a set of rules for the edification of the men who are trying for places on the team. There have been rules before of course, but nothing like the following:

1. Any man tackling high goes off the field.

2. Signal to be given once only. Any body missing it goes off the field.

3. Line-up after each down to be made fast. Anyone loafing to his place goes off the field.

4. Eleven men must be in every play. Those who don't get in and help must get off the field.

5. No individual on offense. Anyone leaving interference and trying to go it alone, goes off the field.

6. Every man to play low and go through low and keep low on defense in front of the play if there is no chance for a tackle. Anyone not doing so goes off the field.

7. The word "Can't" is not in the foot ball vocabulary. Any man feeling that way about any part of the game in detail is not wanted on the field and will please stay away. Only those wanted who say "I will" with teeth together and who never stop fighting. Otherwise they go off the field.

CHAMPAIGN DEFEATED.

The game with the University of Illi nois at Marshall Field in Chicago, Sat urday, October 27, resulted in a com plete victory for Michigan by a score of 10 to 0. Without going into details suf fice it to say that the Ann Arbor team was the superior in almost every particu lar, and won the game on its merits. The Illinois team had been overtrained and was overconfident, and many of its men were badly crippled and in no condition to play. With one slight exception all of our men came out of the contest un injured in any way. As the result of this game it seems more than likely that Michigan will win the western cham pionship, but the matter is still very un certain as Minnesota and Iowa are not yet placed.

Michigan.		Kalamazoo.
Brookfield.		
Redden	l.e.	Brown
Durant	l.t.	Burns
Barcabus	l.g.	Upjohn
Wilson	c.	Bixby
Bliss	r.g.	Lenau
White	r.t.	Millar
Snow	r.e.	Schau
McGinnis	q.	Gilkey
Reddner.		
Hernstein	l.h.	Clapp
Webber	r.h.	Long
Begle, Sweeley	f.b.	Koster

Referee and umpire, Teetzle and Whit ney. Touchdown, Sweeley and White. Goal, Webber.

Michigan.	Positions.	Indiana.
Redden	l.e.	McGovney
White	l.t.	Sparks
Marks	l.g.	Elfers
Brown	c.	Hurley
Kelley	r.g.	Pike
Shorts	r.t.	Davidson
Snow, M. Brown	r.e.	Smith
Begle, Webber	l.h.	Teeter
Woodward.		
Herrnstein	r.h.	Clevenger
McGinnis	q.	Foster
Sweeley	f.	Hawley

Score—Michigan, 12; Indiana, 0. Touchdowns—Woodward, Redden. Goals from touchdowns—Sweeley 2. Umpire —Alexander, Wisconsin. Referee—Kel ley, Dartmouth. Linesmen—Talcott, Michigan: Hubbard, Indiana. Time of halves—20 and 25 minutes.

IOWA'S VICTORY.

Discouraged at the opening of the season for the want of veteran material and then encouraged to a magnified degree over the wonders worked by Coach Lea with the material in hand, Michigan went into the game with Iowa on Nov. 10 with full confidence of winning, only to come out of it with the chagrin of overwhelming defeat. In the enthusiasm of the moment, just credit was not given to the strength of the new adversary for champion-hip honors, and the fact that Michigan's own strength had not been tested, caused not only the team itself, but every loyal supporter to see but one end, and that to the honor of Michigan.

Michigan.	Positions.	Iowa.
Redden	l.e.	Seiberts
H. White	l.t.	Warner
Marks	l.g.	Little
Wilson, Brown	c.	Ely
Shorts, Kelley	r.g.	Brockway
Boggs, Shorts	r.t.	Burrier
Snow (Capt.)	r.e.	Watters
McGinnis, Weeks	q.	Williams (Capt.)
Begle, Redner	l.h.	Edson
Woodard, Webber	r.h.	Norton
Sweeley	f.b.	Eby

Score—Michigan, 5; Iowa, 28. Touchdowns—Eby 2, Edson 2, Norton. Goal from place kick—Sweeley. Goals from touchdowns—Warner 3. Time of halves—35 minutes. Referee—Ralph Hoagland, Princeton. Umpire—Bow Wrenn, Harvard. Timekeepers—Knight, Princeton; Rheinhart, Lafayette. Linemen—Frank Carter, D. A. C.; Middleton, Iowa.

THE NOTRE DAME GAME.

Michigan went into the game with Notre Dame on Nov. 17, a little the worse for wear as a result of her encounter with the "horn-huskers," and came out with but little glory. The score of 7 to 0, however, cannot be taken as indicative of Michigan's true strength, or of the showing that she is likely to make against Chicago, for several of her best ground gainers and defensive players were on the sick list. Captain Snow, though in football togs, did not play, and Sweeley, Woodward and Boggs were missing. Then, too, the condition of the field, slippery from the thin coating of slush which covered it, made it impossible for the defensive team to stay the onslaught of the offensive charges. Add to this the spiritless condition of the men, who so lately had all hopes for championship honors shattered, and some idea can be gained of the causes which produced the low score. On the whole it was to be attributed to the poor playing of Michigan rather than to high grade work on the part of the Hoosiers. Nevertheless, the men from Notre Dame must be given credit for having put up a stiffer game than was expected after the decisive defeat by Wisconsin. The seven points scored were due to Michigan gaining gaining possession of the ball on a fumble by Diebold at Notre Dame's 10-yard line, and pushing it over for a touchdown. The additional two points were made just before the close of the first half, when on an attempt to punt out of danger, Salmon missed a low pass and fell on the ball for a safety touchdown. The feature of the game was easily the good punting of Webber, who seldom failed to out-distance his competitor.

OHIO, 0; MICHIGAN, 0.

Ann Arbor was invaded November 24 to even a greater extent than the wildest predictions had reached. Coming in three sections, two specials and the regular train, the excursion brought into town no less than 1,200 people, 900 from O. S. U. and Columbus and 300 from Toledo. Bedecked in cardinal and gray ribbons and flourishing gaudy Ohio banners, the enthusiasts took the town by storm. Among their number were over 200 co-eds, a worthy example for the girls at Michigan. Michigan students, not backward in hospitality, were on hand many hundred strong to welcome the visitors and to show them that we have a band. After taking a superficial survey of the University, the Buckeye rooters drifted out to the athletic field and their presence, drawing upon the stock of Michigan enthusiasm, brought many rooters for the maize and blue to the fore, and when the call of time came shortly after 2:30, there were over 3,000 persons on the stands and along the side lines at Regents' Field.

With the opening of the game a steady, driving fall of snow and sleet opened up, and when Captain Tilton won the toss he chose the east goal, with the storm at his back. From start to finish both teams were in the game. The field was in a decidedly poor condition, the mud failing to give any foothold whatever, and in consequence the play was inclined to be slow. But there all criticism ceases. The presence of thoroughly competent officials precluded any attempt at rough play, and the game stands with that with Iowa as one of the cleanest contests Michigan has figured in. In both instances, thanks are due to "Bob" Wrenn, of Harvard, who stands as the fairest, most competent umpire in the West.

Ohio stayed by straight football, save in a couple of instances, when the fake kick was used for short gains, but still long enough to bring the desired first down. McClaren and Westwater were their strong ground gainers, both of them being heavy and fast. The latter weighs 190 pounds and carried his weight well, literally tearing things up until a twisted knee forced him to retire in favor of Hager toward the close of the game. He rounded Redden for twenty-two yards in the first half immediately after McClaren had found an equal distance inside of Snow. Hardy at quarter played a splendid game, using good judgment in calling his plays, and being fast and accurate in passing.

CHICAGO, 15; MICHIGAN, 6.

Michigan's hopes for a successful closing of the 1900 football season by the defeat of her old time rival, Chicago, were shattered on Marshall Field, Thanksgiving day, by a score of 15 to 6 in favor of the Midway team. Downcast as had been the spirits of Michigan after the Iowa defeat, it was still felt that if Chicago, poor as she was, could but be laid low, the wearers of the maize and blue might yet look with pride at the year's athletic history. Again, however, the strength of the adversary had not been properly appreciated, for the two weeks' rest and genius of the great Stagg had worked wonders. Michigan on the other hand played one of the hardest games of the year on the preceding Saturday, and there revealed to Prof. Stagg, who sat in the bleachers, her weakest point. Afterwards speaking of the game he said that he noticed that the Michigan backs did not back up the tackles in defense as they ought. He saw that if he could but place a mass in tackle, continual hammering would give him the victory so much desired. In a word that explains the entire game, for from the moment time was called the "whoa-back" formation, as it has been called, was directed at left tackle, in particular, until towards the close of the game, so telling had the onslaught become that White was removed from the game, worn out. Then, too, the guards and center proved vulnerable points of attack, and Sweeley's kicking, which has been so splendid the entire season, was miserably poor. In fact had he been up to his form of the Iowa game, it is probable that the story would have been a different one.

For Michigan, Snow's playing stands out as the only brilliant feature. Once Feil got around his end for a 30-yard run, but outside of this Michigan's captain was all over the field, always in the right place, and tackled brilliantly.

On the whole, Michigan lacked the dash which characterized the work of the maroons but did not let up for an instant and fought every foot of ground until the referee's whistle ended the game. During the first half honors were about even. The score stood 6 to 5 in Michigan's favor. Both elevens played a plunging, linebucking game. In the second half the Maroons cut loose and scored two more touchdowns while they kept Michigan at a safe distance from their own goal line. Both scores were made by the same plunging tactics which marked the first half.

Michigan.		Chicago.
Redden	l.e.	Horton
White, Horgan	l.t.	Atwood
Marks	l.g.	Bodwell
Brown	c.	McNab
Kelley	r.g.	Flanagan
Shorts	r.t.	Feil
Snow	r.e.	Rich
Weeks	q.	Garry
Redner, Webber	l.h.	Henry
Shaw	r.h.	Sheldon
Sweeley	f.b.	Perkins

Score — Michigan 6, Chicago 15. Touchdowns—White, Perkins 3. Goals from touchdowns—Sweeley. Time of halves—35 minutes. Referee—"Pudge" Heffelfinger, Yale. Umpire—Wrenn, Harvard. Timekeeper—Stanford.

O. S. U.		Michigan.
Scott	l.e.	Redden
Coover	l.t.	White
Wharton	l.g.	Marks
J. Segrist	c.	Brown
Tilton	r.g.	Kelly
C. Segrist	r.t.	Shorts
Lloyd	r.e.	Snow
Hardy	q.	Weeks
Westwater	l.h.	Reddner
Hager		
McClaren	r.h.	Shaw
Kittle	f.b.	Sweeley

Score—O. S. U., 0; Michigan, 0. Umpire—Bob Wrenn, Harvard. Referee—Fred Hayner, Lake Forest. Linesman—"Jim" Knight, Princeton. Timekeepers—T. E. Minshall, O. S. U.; Chas. Sweet, Michigan. Length of halves—25 minutes. Attendance—3,000.

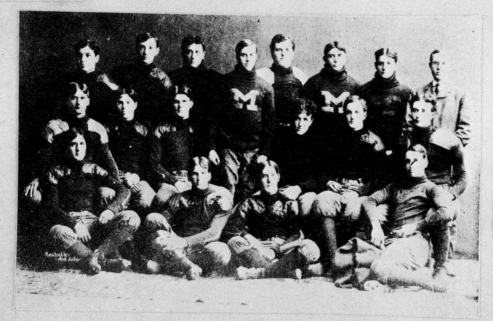

MICHIGAN'S FAMOUS "POINT-A-MINUTE" FOOTBALL TEAM, 1901

TOP ROW: WILSON, REDDEN, DICKIE, BARKENBUS, SWEELY, SHAW, CRAFTS (STUDENT MANAGER)
MIDDLE ROW: HERNSTEIN, HESTON, SHORTS, WHITE, CAPT., (STANDING), GREGORY, SNOW, McGUGIN.
BOTTOM ROW: REDNER, KNIGHT, GRAVER, "BOSS" WEEKS.

SEASON'S TOTAL: MICHIGAN, 550 POINTS; OPPONENTS, o.

	ALBION	50
1901	Sept. 28—Ann Arbor.	
	CASE,	57
Michigan	Oct. 5—Ann Arbor.	
vs.	INDIANA,	33
	Oct. 12—Ann Arbor.	
	NORTHWESTERN,	29
Michigan	Oct. 19—Ann Arbor.	
550	BUFFALO,	128
	Oct. 26—Ann Arbor.	
Opponents	CARLISLE,	22—0
0	Nov. 2—Detroit.	
	O. S. U.,	21—0
Won ... 11	Nov. 9—Columbus, O.	
	CHICAGO,	22—0
	Nov. 16—Ann Arbor.	
Lost 0	BELOIT,	89—0
	Nov. 23—Ann Arbor.	
	IOWA,	50—0
Tied ... 0	Nov. 28—Chicago.	
	LELAND STANFORD, JR.	49 0
	Dec. 25—Los Angeles, Cal.	

FOOTBALL PROSPECTS.

Coach Yost visited Ann Arbor a week before the Easter vacation, and devoted a couple of hours each day to coaching a number of the leading candidates for next year's team. The intent of the early practice is to get the men and coaches acquainted and to decide somewhat on the system of playing. As to the latter, it has practically been determined to follow the old '95 lines, which were similar to the modern Yale system. Yost's method of catching the ball, which is to catch it on the body, holding it at the bottom with one hand and pressing it toward the body with the other will be extensively practiced, as it practically insures an absence of fumbling. On the punts the coach has always been successful, so that one need not be surprised if some startling work is done in that line next year by the kickers. The old Michigan interference, bringing all the line men in, will be used, and the single and double man interference of Princeton dropped. While a number of elementary plays and formations were given during the week of practice, the work almost entirely consisted of passing and catching the ball, especial attention being devoted to the quarter and half-backs.

Of the more prominent men out were Weeks, Graves, Sackett and Smith, quarter; Southworth, Redner, Preussman, Hinks, Williams, Shaw, and Gooding, half-backs; Brown, Irquart, Redden, ends; Horegan, tackle; Carr, center and guard. A number of these are new men, but in nearly every instance great interest and plucky work was shown, making the result of the spring work satisfactory indeed.

It has practically been settled that Michigan will send a team to the coast during the holidays, playing Leland Stanford at Los Angeles on Christmas and the University of California at San Francisco on New Year's. Whether the trip be made is now entirely dependent upon the quality of team that is produced, so that the greatest interest of years is expected with the opening of the fall season, which will begin with early practice somewhere on the Detroit river.

MICHIGAN LINE-UP

Hernstein, Knight	Right End
Shorts	Right Tackle
Wilson	Right Guard
Gregory	Center
McGugin	Left Guard
White, Captain	Left Tackle
Redden	Left End
Weeks, Graver	Quarter
Sweely, Redner	Left Half B'k
Heston, Shaw	Right Half B'k
Snow	Full Back

'VARSITY 50. ALBION 0.

Michigan Trims the Methodists in the Biggest Score Seen on Regents' Field Since '96. Time Taken Out Once for Yost's Men.

Michigan.	Albion.
Knight, Hernstein, R.E.	Simons,
	T. Brail, Hunt, L.E.
Shorts, R.T.	Exely (Capt.), L.T.
Wilson, R.G.	Barry, L.G.
Gregory, Southworth, C.	Bentley, C.
McGugin, L.G., G. Brail Stewart, R.G.	
White (Capt.), L.T.	Bryan, R.T.
Weeks, Graver, Q.B.	Andrews,
	Darwin, Q.B.
Redden, L.E.	Bechael, R.E.
Sweeley, Redner	Priest, L.H
Preussman, R. H.	
Shaw, Heston, L.H.	Maddock, R.H.
Snow, Sweeley and	Church, F.
Reid, F.B.	

Touchdowns—Snow, White 3, Shaw 2, Sweeley, Heston, Shorts.
Goals from touchdown—Shaw 3, Sweeley, Graver.
Officials—Rhinehart (Lafayette), referee; Whitney (Amherst), umpire.
Time of halves—20 minutes.

Fielding Yost

1901

MICHIGAN 57, CASE 0.

Michigan.	Case.
Knight, and R. End.	Weatherby,
Hernstein,	Capt.
Woodward R. Tackle. Zimmerman,	
	Charlesworth.
Wilson R. Guard.	Grant
Gregory Center.	Cadle
McGugin L. Guard.	Kaufmann
White L. Tackle.	Swift
Redden L. End.	Muter
Weeks, Graver Quar.	Osborne
Sweely R. Half.	Sullivan
Shaw Heston L. Half.	Bargo,
	Davidson.
Snow Fullback	Willard,
	Emerson.

Touchdown—White, Sweely (2), Snow (2), Heston (4), Woodward.
Goals from touchdown—Shaw (6), Sweeley, Graver.
Referee—Merrill, Oberlin.
Umpire—Rinehart, Lafayette.
Time of halves—20 minutes.

Michigan.   Indiana.
Final score Michigan 33, Indiana, 0.
Redden ......L. End...... Rucker
White ......L. Tackle.. Gottschall
McGugin ....L. Guard...... Elfers
Gregory ......Center.... Wartsle
Shorts....R. Tackle... Davidson
 Woodward.
Herrnstein ....R. End ...... Smith
 Knight.
Weeks, Graver..Quar...F'ster, Ayers
Heston, Shaw..L. Half.... Clevinger
Sweeley ......R. Half...... Coval
Redner.   Lockridge, Foster.
Snow ......Fullback...... Darby
 Officials Hoagland, Princeton, um-
pire; Hinckney, Yale, referee.
Time of halves 25 and 20.
Touchdowns Shorts, 2, Snow 1, Hes-
t n 2. Shaw 1.
Goals from touchdowns Shorts 3.
Linesmen McGinnis and Beardsley.

Final score, Michigan, 29; North-
western, 0.
 The summaries:
 Michigan.   Northwestern.
Herrnstein ....R. End.........Daly
Shorts ......R. Tackle.....Paddock
Wilson ....R. Guard ....C. E. Dietz
Gregory ......Center .... Ward
McGugin ....L. Guard .....Ward
 Forrest.
White ......L. Tackle....Strathford
Redden ....L. End.......Elliott
Weeks Graver..Quar.......Johnson
Sweeley ......R. Half.....Fleager
 Redner.
Heston Shaw..L. Half....G. O. Dietz
Snow ....Back.....Smiley

Michigan 22
Carlisle 0

The Game in Detroit Today the Most Stubbornly Contested of the Season

Much Time Taken Out During the Halves for Injuries to Players. Indians Were Fierce Tacklers Yost Says Michigan Playek Best in Second Half. Rekden Was Severely Injured.

SNOW SELECTED.

Casper Whitney Gives Him a Place on the All-American—Only Western Player Honored.

Caspar Whitney has selected his All-American team and give Snow a place at end. Snow is the only western man selected, although Larsen and Curtis of Wisconsin are mentioned as substitutes. In sizing up the strength of the teams of the country Mr. Whitney places them in the following order:
 Harvard.
 Yale.
 Michigan.
 Wisconsin.
 West Point.
 Princeton.
 Cornell.
 Lafayette.
 Annapolis.
 Syracuse.
The other western colleges are away back and sitting down.

CASPER WHITNEY'S OPINION

In his ranking of the eastern and western teams, Mr. Whitney gives Michigan third place, following Harvard and Yale. Of the critic's remarks on football as played in the West, the following excerpts may prove of interest:—
 "Western men, as a rule, are more genuine than eastern men, dissemble less, are more stalwart in their actions and more faithful to their ideals. There is a real sense of the game for the game's sake among the faculty members of the leading middle western universities who meet annually to better their athletic conditions.
 "Michigan and Wisconsin in football are this year to the West, as is Harvard to the East, and between the western teams choice is difficult indeed, though Michigan has the remarkable total of 501 points scored to none against her. Each has a strong, heavy line and a good back field—especially Wisconsin, whose Larsen and Driver are just about as good as any in the country. In style of game, in running with the ball, and in punting these two teams stand well up towards the very head of American football; in handling of kicks and in highly developed team play, however, they are quite a bit inferior to the eastern leaders. In respect to ethics of the game, Michigan is easily the leader in the West, with Chicago and Iowa a good second and third."

U. OF B. UTTERLY ROUTED BY THE MICHIGANDERS.

Ann Arbor Football Eleven Piled Up the Amazing Score of 128 to 0.

22 TOUCHDOWNS AND 18 GOALS.

This Was All Done in 50 Minutes of Actual Play—Buffalo Boys Not in Condition.

In a game that savored more of a slaughter than an orthodox football match, Michigan defeated the much-touted team from the University of Buffalo, 128 to 0, yesterday afternoon on Regents' Field.
 Local experts in gridiron matters claim that this score is the highest ever tallied in an intercollegiate contest, and at any rate it far surpasses any score ever run up on the Ann Arbor grounds.
 With a victory over Columbia fresh to their credit the visitors were heralded as no mean adversaries, as they announced the intention of maintaining their untouched goal-line, still immaculate, as far as Michigan was concerned.
 Calculations miscarried, however. At no time were the visitors nearer than the 'Varsity's 20-yard line. At this critical stage in their chances Rice was called upon to try a place kick. The Buffalo center fumbled his pass, and the only opportunity to make good was denied the Buffalo aggregation.

MICHIGAN.   BUFFALO.
Herrnstein ....R. End........ DeCue
Shorts ....R. Tackle.....Smiley..
Wilson ......R. Guard.........Fish
Gregory ......Center...... Unbehaun
 Dickey.
McGugin ....L. Guard ...... Metzer.
 Forest.
White (Capt.)..L. Tack......Sims n
 Southworth.   Cannon
Redden ....L. End...Hasse (Capt)
            Lawton, Simpson
Weeks........Quarter........Rice..
 Graver.
Sweeley ......R. Half.......Wilson
Heston........L. Half........Wilson
 Redner.   Rollin
Snow ......Fullback...Mason, Espie
 Score—Michigan, 128; Buffalo, 0.
 Touchdowns—Sweely, 3, Shorts 1,
Redden 2, Heston 3, Snow 4, Redner
4, Herrnstein 5.
 Goals—Shorts, 18.
 Goals from field—None.
 Referee—Hayner, Lake Forest;
Hagland, Princeton.
 Linesmen—Cannon and Beardslee.
 Time of halves 30 and 20 minutes.

550-0

The Season Ended Brilliantly

By Winning From Leland Stanford the Michigan Team Proved Itself the Greatest Scoring Team the World Has Ever Seen.

(Paste this account in your Michigan Daily-News Football Yearbook.)

The greatest event of the Michigan vacation period was the football game at Pasadena on January first, when Michigan defeated Stanford University by the decisive score of 49-0. This score is said to be quite in proportion to the general superiority of Michigan over the great team of the far west, but it does not tell the story of Stanford's desperate but futile effort against defeat. The Associated Press dispatches were general in character, so the Michigan Daily-News will only give a detailed account of the game.

The game was played under the auspices of the Tournament of Roses Association and the conservative estimate places the attendance at eight thousand. "The enormous crowd sees the Michigan back-breakers make monkeys of the Stanford footballists," is the significant comment of the Los Angeles Daily Times.

To Stanford's honor let it be said, however, that her team played a plucky, clean game of orthodox football, and Michigan's superior physical condition and knowledge of the game were the factors which worked the wonder.

Technically speaking, Michigan lost no prestige in the Stanford game. The team successfully kept Stanford out of Michigan territory. Stanford was unable to break the record of fifteen yards as the longest gain made against Michigan during the year. None of the Michigan players were compelled to leave the field. Sweeley place-kicked the only goal from field for Michigan outside of Shorts' successful attempt in the Carlisle game, during the season. Michigan's sacred goal line was never in danger. In the gathering dusk, with ten minutes yet to play, Captain Fisher came to Captain White and said: "If you are willing, we are ready to quit," and, at the expense of one or two more goals, Michigan granted his request.

Stanford played six substitutes, while Michigan went through the game with the original eleven.

The officials were: Referee, David Brown; umpire, W. K. Peasley; linesmen, Phil Wilson and C. G. Roe; timers, "Jack" Sheehan and H. K. Crafts.

Michigan rushed the ball 503 yards, kicked 881 yards, ran back kicks 127 yards, first downs 12, penalized 1.

Time of halves, 35 and 27 minutes.

The line-up of the team was as follows:

MICHIGAN.	STANFORD.
Left End.	
Redden	Clark, Preston
Left Tackle.	
White (captain)	Traeger
Left Guard.	
McGugin	Roosevelt
Center.	
Gregory	Lee
Right Guard.	
Wilson	Thompson
Right Tackle.	
Shorts	McFadden
Right End.	
Sweeley	Cooper
Right Half.	
Herrnstein	Fisher (capt.)
Left Half.	
Heston	Slaker
Full.	
Snow	McGilvray, Allen
Quarterback.	
Weeks	Tarpey

REDDEN'S REINSTATEMENT

Curtis J. Redden, the Varsity end, who was barred from playing in the Michigan-Iowa game on the charge of professionalism made by Professor Stagg, has been reinstated by the Michigan Board of Control, the charges having been found without basis. Redden's father appeared before the Board of Control, and by his own testimony and the affidavits of the officials of the games, satisfactorily proved that while Redden had won the races for which eleven dollars had been offered as prizes, neither he nor his son had ever accepted the money. Redden himself testified that he did not receive the money personally, but had supposed when brought face to face with the charges of Professor Stagg that the money had been paid his father. Under the football rules of professionalism, Redden is cleared of the taint and has regained his amateur standing. The rule in substance is that any football or baseball player who is using or who has used his athletic knowledge or skill for gain, shall be prohibited from playing on the teams of the colleges parties to the agreement. Redden's reinstatement came in time for him to take the California trip.

The following comments taken from the Los Angeles Times, are indicative of the favorable impression made by the Michigan team:—

"It was at Ann Arbor University (sic) that President Roosevelt delivered one of his famed addresses on "The Strenuous Life." The eleven young men who stampeded over the eleven young men from Stanford heard that address and very evidently profited by it. They certainly gave their California opponents and spectators a touch of the real thing in strenuous living. The strength and speed of the Wolverines fairly took people's breath away. Not much had been expected in the way of a close contest, but as an exhibition it was something to marvel at. It was a rare treat for local experts and players, and doubtless some lessons were learned from the striking example of strenuousness.

"The Michigan men form a collection of superb specimens of all-round physical development. They sport calves like piano legs and arms to match—all as hard as rocks. The Stanford men, on the other hand, are just a trifle soft. The result is evidenced in the disability list. Only three of the Wolverines were injured at all. Heston, the ground-gaining half-back, sustained a black eye, skinned nose, and a leg wrench that made him limp. Snow and Redden were the others who showed the marks of battery, but their hurts were trivial. Four of the California boys were 'put out.'

"They have football heads, too, which is necessary. By a slow and tedious process their brains have been filled with a science of football—one set of ideas for the eleven component parts—and they have become an animated machine. Every football team that can do anything is so, but the Michiganders have been united by a controlling football head, into a more perfect body than has ever been seen on this Coast before, by long odds."

White - 1901

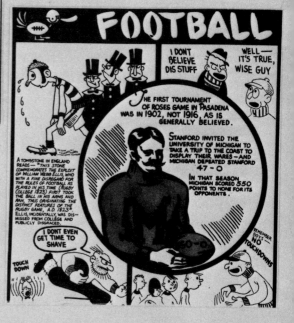

Yost's Soliloquy.

"First, Michigan scored the highest number of points ever rolled up in a season by a recognized team.

"Second, the lowest number of points scored against any one team by Michigan is higher than the lowest number of points scored against any other team this season.

"Third, the versatility of the team play. Ten men—all but the center—carry the ball in turns. This permits spreading the hard work and does not throw too much burden on any part of the team.

"Fourth, the rapidity of team play. In the Harvard-Yale game, the Harvard team executed 146 plays by actual count. In the Michigan-Iowa game, the Michigan team executed a total of 219 plays. This illustrates how fast they work.

"Fifth, the strength of Michigan's punting department. Sweeley is the best punter in the country. In the Harvard-Yale game, Kernan, for Harvard, made thirteen punts which averaged thirty-three yards. In the Michigan-Iowa game, Sweeley made thirteen punts and they averaged him $40\frac{1}{3}$ yards and it was with a wet, muddy ball at that.

"Sixth, the line defense. The Michigan full back on defense has been called upon to make a tackle but once this season.

"Seventh, in the last three games of the season, when all teams are on edge and when full thirty-five minute halves are played, the opposing teams made their first downs only seven times.

"Eighth, four of the opposing teams, viz., Albion, Case, Indiana and Beloit, never had possession of the ball on Michigan's territory, and Chicago had it there only once, when it was obtained on a punt.

"Ninth, only Northwestern and Buffalo got inside our 30-yard line, and in those two instances they got the ball on penalties for forward passes by Michigan.

"Tenth, the handling of punts. Only once during the season was a punt fumbled by Michigan men so that an opposing team secured the ball.

"Eleventh, only Yale in 1891, to my recollection, has been able to hold a similar record of a straight row of goose eggs for opponents during an entire season. A 'no score' record is almost an impossibility.

"Twelfth, only one man during the entire season was taken out of a game for injury, and he was back into the practice the Monday after the Saturday game.

"Thirteenth, an even distribution of weight throughout the team."

The New Ferry Field

BY CHARLES BAIRD, GRADUATE DIRECTOR OF ATHLETICS

FERRY FIELD is the name given to the present play ground of the University of Michigan. It comprises the ten acres of improved ground in the old Regent's Field, and the new plot of about twenty acres recently acquired through the generosity of Mr. Ferry.

The original athletic field was purchased by the Board of Regents about twelve years ago, dedicated to athletic uses, and placed under the control of the University of Michigan Athletic Association.

The University improved half of the field, put in a cinder track and erected a small grand stand. For about eight years practically no improvements were made on the field. However, about four years ago the Athletic Association became established on a sounder financial basis and the Athletic authorities of the University began to realize that large improvements on the field were necessary. First, the unimproved south half of the old field was filled, graded, and sown with grass seed. By careful attention this piece of ground has been developed into a level, beautiful field, and is now ready for continuous use. It is being used for baseball and football purposes.

The rapid growth of interest in football, and the greatly increased attendance necessitated the erection of large stands. The Athletic management foresaw that as soon as they were in use the new stands would soon pay for themselves. By practicing rigid economy the Athletic Association accumulated the necessary funds and the work was pushed with vigor. Following the example of the large Eastern universities, high, open bleachers were built, and, as the gridiron is laid out on the baseball field, the bleachers are movable, being placed and removed each season. In 1895 the original covered grand stand was burned and in the following year the Regents replaced it with another small covered stand which accommodated about 800 people. The large bleachers seat about 6,000. In addition to this, the Athletic Association has one thousand circus seats and materials for sloping platforms which will permit 8,000 more people to view a football game. Many lesser improvements have been made on the old field, and altogether over $10,000 has been expended in the development of this part of Ferry Field.

About one year ago the Honorable Dexter M. Ferry, of Detroit, purchased and gave to the University of Michigan the tract of land, about twenty acres in extent, lying between the Regents Field and Edwin Street. The ground with the house upon it cost seventeen thousand dollars, and the deed of gift specifically declares that it shall be used for athletic purposes only. Mr. Dexter M. Ferry, Jr., who has represented his father in attending to the matter of this noble gift, has shown great personal interest in the development of the new field. The University as a whole and the Athletic interests in particular, owe a debt of gratitude to the father and son for their generosity and interest in the welfare of the students. The Board of Regents promptly accepted the gift, formally named the entire playground Ferry Field in honor of the donor, and placed it under the jurisdiction of the Board of Control. When all the proposed improvements have been completed Michigan will have one of the finest athletic fields in the country. About thirty acres in area and rectangular in shape, it will extend South on State Street seventeen hundred and forty feet and have a frontage on Edwin Street of seven hundred and fifty feet. The work of improving the new ground is progressing as rapidly as possible. With the kindly co-operation of the Ann Arbor Railroad over ten thousand yards of sand and gravel will be placed in the low places and the entire field will be graded and made to slope gently from South to North. This will insure good drainage after the ground has been properly tiled. The surface will be covered with six inches of fine top-soil in order to secure a heavy turf. However, it will take several years to grow a firm sod.

The details of the surface improvements of Ferry Field have not yet been settled, but the general outline has been agreed upon. Before the final plans are drawn it is probable that a committee will visit the best fields of the country and secure information for guidance in making our own plans. The field will be enclosed by a substantial and handsome fence with ornamental entrance so as to avoid the unpleasant features of a blank wall. The gridiron will be located at the extreme North end of the grounds. The present bleachers will be moved and placed around the new gridiron, and new stands added from time to time as they are needed. Just south of the new gridiron will be placed the new 'Varsity baseball diamond, about this it is proposed to build a modern baseball grand stand. Other football and baseball fields will be laid out farther South. On the sides and in the corners tennis courts will be constructed.

At some favorable place on the field a serviceable club house will be erected. It will contain reception, dressing, and locker rooms, shower baths etc., and be equipped with all modern improvements.

All these improvements will cost money and take time for completion, so that it will probably be several years before the work is finished. However, a number of persons are deeply interested in the success of this work and it will be pushed as rapidly as possible.

In closing I wish to remind the readers that we should always be grateful to Mr. Ferry for his generous gift.

Smith, Carter, Jones, Gregory, McGugin, Baird, Fitzpatrick, Maddock, Lawrence, Weeks, Yost, Herrnstein, Cole, Redden, Heston, Sweeley, Graver.

1902

1902 Michigan vs. Michigan 664 Opponents 12 Won ... 11 Lost .... 0 Tied 0		
ALBION,	88	0
Sept. 20—Ann Arbor.		
CASE,	48	6
Sept. 27—Ann Arbor.		
M. A. C.,	119	0
Oct. 4—Ann Arbor.		
INDIANA,	60	0
Oct. 11—Ann Arbor.		
NOTRE DAME,	23	0
Oct. 18—Toledo.		
O. S. U.,	86	0
Oct. 25—Ann Arbor.		
WISCONSIN,	6	0
Nov. 1—Chicago.		
IOWA	107	0
Nov. 8—Ann Arbor.		
CHICAGO	21	0
Nov. 15—Chicago.		
OBERLIN	63	0
Nov. 22—Ann Arbor.		
MINNESOTA,	23	6
Nov. 27—Ann Arbor.		

Above—"Boss" Weeks, one of the greatest football players ever developed at Michigan. He was Captain of the '02 team which made 664 points to 12 for opponents.

Martin Heston

MICHIGAN, 88; ALBION, 0

First Game of the Season was Won Handily Yesterday by an Old-Time Score

Nearly 2,000 people braved the elements and sat in a chilling wind and rain to see the Varsity run back and forth across the white lines, pile up the score on Albion and make their debut for 1902 a notable one. It was the same old story that Michigan learned to love last year. A kick off, followed by two or three long runs, a line buck or so and then a touchdown. Fifteen times the ball was carried over that line and in all but four times it was followed by a kicked goal.

The Albion team was simply outclassed, but they were not discouraged to the point of losing for a single instant. They were game to the finish and fought their best battle throughout the entire game.

MICHIGAN TEAM WAS SCORED ON

BUT SHE WON FROM CASE BY 48 TO 6

An Account of the Game as Given in the Daily News—Case Has Been Michigan's Hordor

Case School of Applied Science has done what no other school has been able to do in two years. They sent a football team that found it possible to score on Michigan. It was a heartbreaking scene for Michigan rooters and a heart breaking incident for the members of the Michigan team. It took so little time for it to take place that the large crowd could not realize that at last Michigan's goal line had been crossed.

MICHIGAN 119, M. A. C. 0

Another Spectacular Game—Many Long Runs—Lawrence Kicks 19 Out of 20 Goals

In a game replete with brilliant plays of every description, which time and again brought the large crowd of rooters to its feet, Michigan yesterday piled up the almost unparalleled score of 119 points on the team from Michigan Agricultural College.

M. A. C. was helpless against our charging forwards and only a few times were they able to make the slightest gain. The score nearly equaled the famous mark of 128 made in the Buffalo game last year and in one respect is even more of a record, inasmuch as 71 points were made in the first half, 20 minutes in length. This is in all probability a world's record. Another notable performance was the magnificent goal kicking of Lawrence. He converted 19 of the 20 touchdowns into goals, missing the other by the smallest margin. In the games so far this season he has kicked 33 goals out of 34 attempted, a record seldom if ever surpassed.

CHAMPIONS

Michigan Earns Clear Title to Two Years Championship by Defeating Badgers in Hard Fought Game

Chicago, Ill., Nov. 1.—(Special.)—As soon as Michigan got the ball she dumbfounded Wisconsin by smashing through their impregnable line for 3 and 5 yards at a jump. Maddock making the most noticeable gains. Michigan, by consistent work, carried the pigskin without a single stop or once losing possession of the ball, and after ten minutes of play shoved Maddock over for the first touchdown. At this stage of the game it looked as if Michigan would run up a big score, and an offer made in the Wisconsin stand of even money that Michigan would score 28 points had no takers. Again Michigan started down the field for a touchdown. The Wolverine line-buckers carried the ball to the ten-yard line, where it was lost on a fumble. A second touchdown seemed certain, but Jones was badly hurt and when finally reinstated he was visibly handicapped by the injury and when Michigan had forced the ball to within a few inches of Wisconsin's goal line they were held for downs and Wisconsin punted out of danger. Sweeley was forced to punt and Fogg caught it just as Redden hit him like a thunderbolt, which caused him to fumble the ball and laid them both out. Fogg having to be carried off the field. Meanwhile Maddock picked up the fumbled ball and amid breathless excitement headed for the undefended goal line, but he was overtaken by a flying tackle and downed, the coveted place still 30 yards away. Time was called here, score 6 to 0.

At the end of the first half Ralph Hoagland predicted that Wisconsin would win yet, as Wisconsin had braced visibly and Michigan seemed slightly weakened after her tremendous efforts.

MICHIGAN 60; INDIANA 0

'Varsity Made a Great Score on the Hoosiers—Much Holding in Line and Many Bad Fumbles

The heavy team from the University of Indiana was completely snowed under by Yost's proteges at Ferry field yesterday afternoon by a score of 60 to 0. It was a fine game from a spectacular point of view. Wonderful dodging, sensational end runs, excellent line bucking and clever tackling, all went to make the game the best of the season thus far.

The features of the game were Lawrence's line bucks, Graver's work in running back punts and the backfield tackling of Clevenger, the Hoosier halfback.

Phil King, the Wisconsin coach, and Carl Driver, the famous Wisconsin fullback, viewed the game from the side lines for the purpose of getting a line on the Michigan play, in preparation for the Wisconsin-Michigan game on November 1.

Twelve hundred Ann Arbor school children saw the game as the guests of the Athletic association, and they proved to be most consistent rooters for Michigan.

The 'Varsity Band is improving every week and rapidly increasing in size, and proved yesterday that there is nothing like a good band to keep the rooters stirred up.

MICHIGAN 86, OHIO 0

O. S. U. Snowed Under—Their Great Hopes Pounded to Pieces in First Few Minutes of Play

What will we do,
What will we do,
We'll rub it into O. S. U.
That's what we'll do.

Thus sang the Michigan rooters yesterday afternoon in answer to the old Wah-hoo yell raised proudly by 2,000 wearers of the scarlet and gray.

And rub it in they did with both hands and feet by the absolutely unhoped for score of 86 to 0.

The Ohio rooters began to arrive at 9:30 a. m. and special train followed special train at short intervals until the whole city was thronged with the excursionists. They overran the campus in all directions and penetrated into every building including the Anatomical Laboratory.

Shortly after 1 o'clock the crowd began to stream out toward Ferry Field and by a quarter past two every inch of available room in the big stands and bleachers was occupied, the late comers being forced to stand up along the wire fences enclosing the field.

The O. S. U. rooters filled the whole east half of the south bleachers and part of the grand stand, while the supporters of Michigan swarmed on both sides of the field.

A STRENUOUS GAME

Played on Muddy Field—Michigan Made But Five in First Half—Maddock, Herrnstein and Jones Play Star Roles

On a field of wet clay that put the players at a great disadvantage, Michigan defeated the plucky Notre Dame team yesterday by a score of 23 to 0. The game was fraught with surprises, the most signal one being Michigan's failure to make over five points in the first half. The playing on both sides was fierce in the extreme, and the rooters experienced several breathless moments, as for example, in the first half when Notre Dame was held by Michigan for downs on the latter's six-yard line. Captain and Fullback Salmon played the star game for Notre Dame, while Maddock, Herrnstein and Jones did star work for Michigan.

There were several hundred dollars up at odds of 2 to 1 that Michigan would not score, even money that Michigan would make 30 points, and odds of 1 to 10 that Notre Dame would win.

MICHIGAN, 107; IOWA. 0

Yost's Men Swamp Dr. Knipe's Team by a Remarkable Score—Wolverines' Revenge is Now Complete

Michigan's revenge on Iowa is now complete. In 1900 Iowa won from Michigan by the score of 28 to 5. Last year the Wolverines partially redeemed themselves by rolling up 50 points to the Hawkeyes 0. And yesterday, just to show what they could do, Yost's whirlwinds swamped Dr. Knipe's men by the remarkable score of 107 to 0. It was an ideal football day and it was an ideal football game, from a Michigan partisan standpoint. As for Iowa, the less said the better. They were just simply Michiganized, to use a new word coined by the Ohio rooters after their little experience with the same dreaded football machine two weeks ago. [For abbreviated definition of the word Michiganized, see quotation from O. S. U. Lantern in another part of this issue.]

The feature of the day was the great number of spectacular plays executed by the Michigan men during each and every minute of the game. End run followed end run in rapid succession, and touchdown followed touchdown so fast that the fifteen or more telegraph operators on the press bench actually complained of not being able to keep up with the scoreboard.

There were 17 touchdowns made and one goal from the field, and it is remarkable that every single goal was kicked. Yesterday's work showed that Lawrence is not the only goal kicker on the Michigan team, as Graver and Sweeley did perfect work in that line. Herrnstein also has demonstrated his ability, thus giving Michigan four reliable goal kickers.

MICHIGAN SCORES BRILLIANT VICTORY

Stagg's Men Play a Plucky, Uphill Game, but Are Beaten by 21 to 0.

SWEELEY IS THE STAR

Wolverine Kicker Scores Two Goals From the Field—Sheldon's Good Work.

Michigan asserted its supremacy over Chicago yesterday in a telling manner. The final score was Michigan, 21; Chicago, 0. It was a clean, fast and hard game from start to finish. The field was in such condition that both teams showed their best work.

While Chicago was clearly outclassed by the whirlwind Ann Arbor eleven, at no time during the struggle was there any sign of the maroons losing their courage or spirits. Michigan's star kicker, Sweeley, kicked two good goals from field, one a hard one from the twenty-five yard line and another somewhat easier, seventeen yards from the Chicago goal.

BIG SCORE FOR MICHIGAN

Wolverines Win from Oberlin to the Tune of 63 to 0—A Hard Fought Battle—Many Brilliant Plays by Home Team

Yost's "scoring machine" did magnificent work yesterday afternoon when Michigan defeated Oberlin by the big score of 63 to 0. The Wolverine team was not only victorious in crushing the eleven from Ohio but was also successful in beating Cornell's score against the same aggregation by 6 points. The game was won by some of the most spectacular plays of the season and was one of the hardest fought battles of the year. The strength of Oberlin was a surprise to nearly everybody, but the Wolverines were equal to the emergency and made touchdown after touchdown in spite of the good work of their opponents.

YOST ANNOUNCES RETURN

Famous Coach at Last States Definitely That He Will Come Back to Michigan Next Fall

"Editor Michigan Daily-News:

"You may announce in your paper that I have definitely decided to coach Michigan again next year. Everything has been settled satisfactory, and I feel certain that I will at no time regret my decision, though it involves great sacrifice on my part, both pecuniary and otherwise. All I ask is that everybody shall give the team the loyal support it needs.

"Right here I want to say that Michigan will be up against an exceedingly stiff proposition next fall. As the acknowledged champions of the West in 1902, she will be the main object of attack of every university in the West. We must get together early in the season, and we must have united student support. The student body must realize that to bring out a championship team will be a harder job next year than it was either of the two preceding years. This will be due, of course, to the feeling of self-satisfaction which seems to possess all Michigan men. We will have to get out of the notion that winning is a matter of course—it will be a matter of the hardest kind of work, and the student body must back us up all the time.

"I do not care to make any definite statement as to the outlook for next year, except this: we are here to win

"FIELDING H. YOST."

CHAMPIONS OF THE WEST!

Maize and Blue Waves Triumphant—With Total of 644-12—Michigan's Claim is Undisputed

Michigan, the greatest football aggregation in America, put the finishing touches to a glorious season Thanksgiving Day in the greatest game ever seen in Michigan, before the largest crowd ever assembled in the state to witness the game. It was a game to settle the championship of the west, which Michigan claimed last year, but her title to which was then disputed. But this year there are none to dispute. One by one she has met her big rivals and easily vanquished them all.

And the credit belong to Yost. Yost is the greatest football coach in America. He has never coached a team which lost.

Michigan won yesterday because she knew more about football than her opponents, because she played faster, because she was more versatile, because she had team work, because she had Fitzpatrick to keep her men in condition to play an, because she had Yost, with his hurry up orders. She has met heavier teams than herself and vanquished them.

1903	CASE,	31	0
	Oct. 3 Ann Arbor.		
	BELOIT,	79	0
Michigan	Oct. 10 Ann Arbor.		
vs.	O. N. U.,	65	0
	Oct. 14 Ann Arbor.		
	INDIANA,	51	0
Michigan	Oct. 17 Ann Arbor.		
565	FER. INST.	88	0
	Oct. 21 Ann Arbor.		
	DRAKE,	47	0
Opponents	Oct. 24 Ann Arbor.		
6	ALBION,	76	0
	Oct. 28 Ann Arbor.		
	MINNESOTA	6	6
	Oct. 31 Minneapolis.		
Won ... 11	O. S. U.,	36	0
	Nov. 7 Ann Arbor.		
Lost.... 0	WISCONSIN,	16	0
	Nov. 14 Ann Arbor.		
	OBERLIN,	42	0
Tied.... 1	Nov. 21 Ann Arbor.		
	CHICAGO,	28	0
	Nov. 26 Chicago.		

Roberts, Gooding, McGugin, Baird, Curtis, Fitzpatrick.
Hammond, T., Graver, Maddock, Redden, Yost, Gregory, Schulte.
Norcross, Longman, James, Heston.

A Song of Michigan

'Tis of Michigan we sing,
With a merry, merry ring;
As we gaily march along,
We will sing a merry song,
Of Ann Arbor and her chimes,
And her happy, happy times.
And a joyous song we'll raise
To Ann Arbor and her praise.

VI
Wolverines, Wolverines
(To the tune of "Billy Boy.)

Oh! where are you going Wolverines,
Wolverines,
Oh where are you going on the choo
choos?
We are going to O-hi-o,
That the season's score may grow
By a score or two of counts from the
S. U.'s.

Oh why are you sure of the game,
Wolverines—
Oh why do you count on your win-
ning?

Ohio Normal

Columbia 5, Swarthmore 0.

Ann Arbor, Mich., October 14.—(Special.)—Yost's scoring machine worked finely in the first half of the game with the Ohio Normal university to-day, and 42 points were rolled up. In the second half, with the substitutes in, 23 points were scored in 14 minutes. The final score of 65 to 0 in favor of Michigan was very satisfactory for 34 minutes of play.

The team that opposed Michigan was a husky aggregation and they knew the game. They attempted a great variety of play in hopes of scoring. Wing shifts, criss-crosses, quarterback runs, revolves on tackles and the ordinary plays were tried, but only once was Michigan fooled. That was in the opening of the first half. On a wing shift with a run around right end, Michigan got tangled and McPherson gained seven yards before he was downed. However, Michigan's defense became alert and the trick plays did not work after this. In fact the Ohio men were thrown back for three times as much loss as they made gains and were forced to punt.

Michigan		Ferris Institute.
Redden	Left end	Arndt
Curtis	Left tackle	Smith
Schulte-Barnett	Left guard	Johnson
Ted Hammond	Center	Wiseman
Gooding	Right guard	Cole
Maddock-Eycke	R. tackle	Armstrong
Longman-Dunlap-		
Doty	Left end	Miller
James-Norcross	Quarterback	Failes
Norcross-		Harris
Bigelow	Left half	Mussell
Graver-Thomson	R. half	Hayes
Tom Hammond-		
Person	Full back	Warzinik

Touchdowns—Norcross 1, Maddock 3, Curtis 1, Hammond 3, Graver 3, Bigelow 1, Thomson 2, Person 1. Goals—Hammond 5, Curtis 5. Final score—Michigan 88, Ferris Institute 0. Umpire—Stripp. Referee—Hollister. Linesman—DePree. Time of halves—20 and 10 minutes.

FINAL FIGURES 51 TO 0

Gains Are Made by Opening of Holes Through the Line by Sheer Force.

[SPECIAL TO THE RECORD-HERALD.]

ANN ARBOR, Mich., Oct. 17.—Michigan rooters are happy to-night over the fact that Yost's men defeated Indiana by a larger score than Chicago was able to roll up against the hoosiers, the score being 51 to 0.

Heston was out of the game and there were no spectacular end runs, the gains being made by opening up holes on the tackles of the opponents. It was simply a fierce line bucking game by Michigan. James did not run the team with speed and there were several bad fumbles and mixups on signals by Michigan.

Hammond, Madock and Curtis were the stars on offense, all three doing sensational hurdles.

MICHIGAN.	Position.	CASE.
Redden	L. E.	Brandt, Swift
Shulte, Barnett	L. T.	Welfare
Curtis	L. G.	Charlesworth
Gregory	C.	Kauffmann
Gooding	R. G.	Dennis, Miller
Eycke, Bigelow,		
Drugeman		
Edmunds	R. T.	Cadle
Graver, Dunlap	R. E.	Gillie
Norcross	Q.	Orr
Heston Dickey	L. H. B.	Davidson
Longman, Graver	R. H. B.	Rook,
Dickey Weeks		Repner
Hammond	F. B.	Resch, Schroeder

Touchdowns—Heston, 3; Hammond, 2; Weeks, 1. Goals from touchdown—Graver, 1. Final score: Michigan, 31; Case, 0. Umpire—Hoagland, of Princeton. Referee—Gaston, of Washington and Jefferson. Head lineman—Brooks, of Detroit. Time of halves—20 minutes.

Drake

Ann Arbor, Mich., October 24.—(Special.)—Drake University came here today with the bulkiest and best team that Michigan has thus far met this year, and in 55 minutes were beaten by a score of 47 to 0. At that Drake men are satisfied with the showing, as they stated before the game that if Michigan did not roll up 50 points they would go home happy.

Today was the last view the rooters had, or will have, of the team play before Michigan goes against Minnesota in the critical game of the year, and opinions seem to differ as to the outcome of that coming contest.

"We can lick that bunch out there, but it may make some difference with Heston and Gregory in the game," said a Minneapolis dope writer who was sent here by his paper to give a critical analysis of Michigan's strength.

MICHIGAN 6 - MINNESOTA 6

The Wolverines And Gophers Struggle For Three Hours And The Result Is a Tie. Greatest Game In Western Football History.

COACH YOST is charged with coaching from the side lines in the Minnesota game. Yost does not deny the charge. "When I clapped my hands," he said, "I meant five yards through center. When I waved my arms it meant a fifty-yard run, and when I threw up my hat I called for a touchdown. And there you are."

Minnesota 6, Michigan 6.

With but one minute left for play, Minnesota shoved the ball over the Michigan line and tied the score in the greatest football game that has ever been played in Minneapolis.

Twenty thousand persons saw defeat averted at the last moment and from 20,000 throats came a roar of joy that echoed and reechoed while the crowd simply went mad in the revulsion of feeling.

Michigan, by a grand series of line bucking, scored a touch-down and goal twelve minutes before the end of the second half. Such play has seldom been seen, and as the ball sailed between Minnesota's goal posts there was little hope in the breasts of Minnesota men.

Teams Fight Hard.

For over an hour the teams had fought up and down the field in the fiercest kind of football, and neither side scored. Almost an hour had been consumed when Michigan scored and it was almost beyond the pale of reason to hope for anything.

Minnesota went back into the field and in eleven minutes of actual play fought her way down, yard by yard, until in sight of the coveted goal line.

It was now a fight against time and the sturdy Michigan line. The sun had long since gone down and darkness gradually fell on the field.

In the grandstand and bleachers it was a heart-breaking moment. Every second clipped off some of Minnesota's chances; Michigan saw victory almost within grasp, being slowly drawn away; the last stand was made but nothing could stop the Minnesota men. They hurled themselves into the line, crashed on the ends, fought and struggled with every ounce of strength and will to overcome their dual foe.

With the vast throng keyed to its highest pitch and nerves on the rawest edge, Harris sent Boeckmann against the line and the ball was over.

Score—Michigan 6, Minnesota 6.

Crowd Grows Wild.

The touch-down was the signal for the most abandoned demonstration. Roar after roar fairly shattered the air, frantic shrieks rose above the tumult of a thousand megaphones; hats and banners waved in indescribable confusion, while their owners indulged in every grotesque bodily manifestation of joy.

Old and young, staid and giddy, man and woman forgot everything, but the one fact—Minnesota had scored. From the very depths of despair, they had been brought in eleven short minutes to the highest point of hope, and the transition was almost too much for sanity.

Michigan was still one point ahead and one point was defeat, bitter and crushing. A sudden stillness fell over the crowd, the Minnesota and Michigan supporters, dumb with the idea that the supreme moment had arrived.

The ball had been pushed over to the right of the goal at an awkward angle, made doubly difficult by the fast gathering darkness. The players were shrouded beyond recognition and 20,000 pairs of eyes were riveted on the kicker out as he made his preparations.

Few persons saw the ball, but it fell true in the arms of a Minnesota man almost in front of the goal posts. Another short triumphant roar and every Minnesota man and woman on the field drew his breath hard as Rogers backed to kick.

The making ready seemed an aeon to the suspense racked watchers, every move took an hour. At last everything was ready and Captain Rogers booted he ball between the goal posts and the score was tied.

Then the pent-up excitement broke forth in one long delirium, the shout that went up made all previous efforts sound like peevish whimperings; the strain was over and maniacal joy reigned.

Everything that wasn't nailed down went high in the air, hats, canes, umbrellas and cushions. Dignity was cast to the winds.

THREE POINTS TO THE MINUTE

TWENTY MEN USED, INCLUDING MUCH GREEN MATERIAL.

Ann Arbor, Mich., October 8.—(Special.) Michigan and Albion started in to play two twenty-minute halves today, but darkness interfered when but 7 1-2 minutes had been played in the second half. In this 27 1-2 minutes Yost's whirlwinds scored 76 points. Fifty-two points were negotiated in the first half, and if the game had continued to the time scheduled Michigan would have touched the century mark. This romping for an avalanche of touchdowns was accomplished with Yost's green material. At the start of the game Gregory, Heston and Graver were the only veterans. Before the first half was finished Graver was taken out. At the conclusion of the half Ted Hammond went in at center to relieve Gregory. Before the second half was fairly started Heston went out, Norcross taking his place at half and Hal Weeks went to end. Edmunds was substituted for Bigelow and Bigelow for Tom Hammond. The final line-up would never have been recognized as a Michigan bunch by anyone who had seen last year's games.

THE OHIO GAME

The thousand excursionists who accompanied the Ohio State University eleven to Ann Arbor, Nov. 7, have reason to feel well satisfied with the game played by their team against Michigan. The size of the score would seem to indicate overwhelming superiority on the part of the Varsity at all stages of the contest. This was, however, far from being the case. Michigan's points were gained in the first half against a defense that increased in stubbornness after each touchdown. In the second half after a disastrous fumble by Michigan on Ohio's 5-yard line had thrown away what seemed an assured touchdown, the men from Columbus played the Varsity to a standstill. The watchfulness and speed of Captain Redden alone saved Michigan's goal line from being crossed. At the call of time Ohio had the ball on Michigan's 10-yard line, after having pushed the Varsity back almost the whole length of the field.

ALL-AMERICAN TEAM

1903	
Henry, Princeton	End
Hogan, Yale	Tackle
DeWitt, Princeton	Guard
Hooper, Dartmouth	Center
A. Marshall, Harvard	Guard
Knowlton, Harvard	Tackle
Rafferty, Yale	End
Johnson, Carlisle	Quarter
Heston, Michigan	Halfback
Kafer, Princeton	Halfback
Smith, Columbia	Fullback

THE LINE-UP:

Michigan		Ohio State
Redden	Left end	Heekin
Curtis	Left tackle	Lincoln / Case
Schulte	Left guard	Huntington
Gregory / Gooding	Center	Powell
Gooding / Edmunds	Right guard	Dietz
Maddock	Right tackle	Marker / Thrower
Hammond	Right end	Walker
James / Norcross	Quarter	Wallace / Foss
Heston, Person / Weeks	Left half	Thrower / Marker
Graver	Right half	Jones / Swan
Longman	Fullback	Lawrence / Case

Touchdowns—Graver 5, Curtis 1. Goals—Hammond 6.

MICHIGAN'S FIRST TOUCHDOWN AGAINST CHICAGO UNIVERSITY.

Michigan's Decisive Victory Over Chicago.

CHICAGO'S JONAH.

WHEN the great game of the Western football season was played at Minneapolis, and resulted in a six to six tie between the Minnesota and Michigan elevens, it was practically a foregone conclusion that we should have a split championship. You may pay your money and take your choice—Michigan or Minnesota. One has as good a right to the title as the other. Some believe Minnesota is a bit the better team, others pick Michigan; but any way the case may be argued it comes out even. Both teams have come through the season unbeaten; both have made magnificent records; both beat Wisconsin by nearly the same score, and the tie game now seems a just verdict. The Thanksgiving Day games, which ended the season, simply emphasized the tie at Minneapolis. Michigan surprised people, not that it beat Chicago, for that was expected, but because it did the trick so easily. Before the game Coach Yost said a one-point victory would satisfy him. Chicago proved to be as helpless an eleven of supposed class as ever faced a rival. Michigan walked over the Maroons, and that was all there was to it. There was not enough opposition on the part of Chicago to make the game interesting.

Minnesota's Victory Over Wisconsin.

While Michigan was busy humiliating the maroons, Minnesota was walloping the Badgers at Madison. Minnesota wanted to do better against Wisconsin than either Chicago or Michigan had done. The Gophers achieved that result in scoring three touchdowns where Michigan could score but one, and two goals from the field opposed to Chicago's three goals from the field. This game gave Minnesota an argument for the championship.

Of course for Chicago the Thanksgiving Day game was the big event of the football year; but it was not much of a football game. It was believed that Chicago had a possible chance against Michigan, but when the game started this idea was speedily dispelled. With the Maroons it looked very much like a case of quitting. I heard alumni and students of the Midway School indignantly accuse their team of quitting. Certain it is that the University of Chicago team did not play the football that it has played this fall, that it is capable of playing and the football that Stagg has taught it to play. When a team finds itself helpless before another, it is disheartening and discouraging, and takes some of the fight out of

By SHERMAN R. DUFFY.

the men. The Chicago team didn't seem to be putting up much of a fight until the end of the game.

Chicago had a wobbly team all season. It has seemed to me to have profited more by the luck of the game than any team I ever saw. Northwestern was almost certain of scoring when an unlucky fumble spoiled the chance, and another one was never secured. The Purple had walked for over fifty yards to within Chicago's five-yard line. There is considerable luck in three drop goals from the field, admitting all the skill of it, and this is what Chicago did to Wisconsin, the Badgers ploughing their way for a touchdown.

Chicago's Splendid Material.

Why the Chicago team has been such a shaky proposition this season is a mystery. It is true that the season was successfully passed through up to the concluding game, with defeats of Purdue, Indiana, Illinois and Wisconsin, and a tie with Northwestern. Every man on the team is a good all-around athlete. There was the material present, it seemed to me, for the making of a great eleven. Early in the season the Maroons seemed logical candidates for the Western championship honors, but they early gave indications of streakiness in their play. The offense never worked well, and the defense was one day good, the next indifferent, and at times bad. Stagg did everything a coach could to get his men playing with the machine-like precision that makes Michigan win, but he could not. The reason of this I attribute to the lack of a good scrub eleven at Chicago University. Every man on the team knew that he was comparatively sure of his position, as there were no capable substitutes. This may have had something to do with the lazy play complained of so frequently at Marshall Field.

Michigan represents the most modern type of football America has ever seen. I never saw anything even to closely approach the wonderful playing of Michigan this year. While the team is not so good, individually, as last year, its team work is much better. The offense is simply marvelous, with such a bewildering array of shifts, men drawn back and all manner of intricate performances that are reeled off with absolute precision and with seldom a slip. One writer likens the Michigan-Chicago contest to a modern battleship attacking a wooden cruiser. Whether this is to be taken as meaning that Chicago's football is too old-fashioned to win any longer, or not, I do not know, but it is a good simile. Chicago was outcharged every time, the ends and tackles were boxed, and there was a series of romps around the Maroon ends. Heston again gave an exhibition of how to

smash lines, rolling, hurdling and smashing over the big Chicago players for first downs or better every time.

Eckersall, who has been starred very heavily this fall, often had the task of bringing down a man to save a clear field for a touchdown. He shone as a tackler and defensive player, but he had no opportunity to do any drop kicking. Michigan gave Chicago no opportunity to come close enough. Michigan made two goals from the field through the medium of Tom Hammond, and scored three touchdowns.

It was a snowy, cold and disagreeable day for a football game, but there were no absentees from the game on that account. Coach Stagg, who was ill, insisted on being brought to the game despite his doctor's orders and watched the game from a closed carriage. A few improvised snow ploughs were brought into use to scrape the field, and then the captains tossed up for the kickoff. Michigan won the toss and Chicago kicked off.

Longman caught the ball and brought it back to his 25-yard line. Then Heston was called upon. He smashed four yards on a straight buck. That was the start of the game, and a presage of what was to follow. When Michigan didn't batter down the line, it romped around the ends for ten, fifteen and twenty yard gains. Chicago showed none of that fighting spirit which has so many times electrified the populace by warding off attacks at the five-yard line. Michigan simply crushed the Maroons, broke down their defense, and rendered their attack absolutely nil. The Wolverines had found their prey, and toyed with it. There was surprise, indignation and sorrow in the eyes of the Chicago rooters. They refused to believe that Michigan was strong enough to overwhelm their team so completely if their team did its duty.

Michigan's Wonderful Showing.

Michigan's showing was the most wonderful ever seen on a Chicago gridiron. It is said to be a vastly superior team to that which defeated Minnesota. But only a few days ago Michigan was held to a 16 score by Wisconsin, and Minnesota Thanksgiving Day made three touchdowns against the Badgers. Minnesota likewise maintains its team is just as much better at the close of the season as Michigan's.

Yost has completed three years as coach at Ann Arbor, and has made the greatest record of any single coach this country has ever known. He has brought his team through these three years at the top of the list. This year he has a rival. He had none before. In the three seasons Yost has coached at Michigan, the Wolverines have scored 1,718 points against 18 by opponents. Equal that if you can anywhere. This season Michigan has scored 523 points, and has been scored against but once.

Announcement

OF THE

Athletic Association of the University of Michigan

1904-1905

The management of athletics at the University of Michigan is entrusted to the Athletic Association under the supervision of the Faculty Board of Control. The student members annually elect the officers of the Association, and the Regents appoint the Director, who supervises the business of the Association.

Any student or alumnus of the University may become a member of the Athletic Association upon the payment of three dollars. Members, and members only, are entitled to wear the Athletic Button, a badge of honor among loyal students. Members also have the privilege of purchasing tickets to the foot ball and base ball games at greatly reduced rates. These priveleges enable those who wish to attend the games to save more than the price of the ticket. Members exclusively are entitled to use the tennis courts.

The past year has been a glorious one in Athletics for Michigan. She took second place in base ball and won the championship of the west in tennis, track, and foot ball. For three years Michigan has had a foot ball team second to none in America. This fall the prospects are not so good; and only by the greatest efforts of loyal students, alumni, and friends can the present high reputation of Michigan be sustained. Will you not help us in this work?

We earnestly hope that you will recognize it as a duty to yourself and your University to join our Association and contribute your share to the promotion of Athletics at our University.

Reasons Why a Student Should Belong to the Athletic Association.

1st—It is the best medium for the the manifestation and maintenance of college spirit in athletics.

2nd—It is the chief agent through which students may foster athletics.

3rd—The Association affords an excellent opportunity whereby the students of all departments may meet on common grounds.

4th—Season tickets to base ball and foot ball games can be purchased by members at reduced rates.

Montgomery, Graham, Carter, Fitzpatrick, Schulz, Yost, Schulte, Curtis.
Cole, Hammond, T., Longman, Heston, Baird.
Hammond, H., Clark,
Stuart, Norcross, Weeks, H.

1904	Case,	33— 0
Michigan vs.	Oct. 1—Ann Arbor.	
	O. N. U.	48— 0
	Oct. 5—Ann Arbor.	
	Kalamazoo,	95— 0
	Oct. 8—Ann Arbor.	
Michigan 567	P. and S.,	72— 0
	Oct. 12—Ann Arbor.	
	O. S. U.,	31— 6
	Oct. 15—Columbus.	
	Am. Col. M. & S.,	72— 0
Opponents 22	Oct. 19—Ann Arbor.	
	West Va.,	130— 0
	Oct. 22—Ann Arbor.	
Won 10	Wisconsin,	28— 0
	Oct. 29—Madison.	
Lost 0	Drake,	36— 4
	Nov. 5—Ann Arbor.	
Tied .. 0	Chicago,	22—12
	Nov. 12—Ann Arbor.	

Michigan (33.)	Case (0).
Garrels ....L. E.	Brandt ....R. E.
Curtis ....L. T.	Swift ....R. T.
Scutte ....L. G.	Walling ....R. G.
T. Hammond, Berchier.C.	Roberts, Wyman ....C.
Schultz ....R. G.	Bradford ....L. G.
Beechler, Cuull...R. G.	Welfare ....L. T.
Tom Hammond,	Parrott ....L. E.
Patrick ....R. E.	Orr ....Q. B.
Norcross, Becker...Q. B.	Gillie, Steiner...R. H. B.
Heston, Clark...L. H. B.	Thomas, Baker.
Stuart, Norcross,	Ransom ....L. H. B.
Depree ....R. H. B.	Dewey, Ripner....F. B.
Longman ....F. B.	

Touchdowns—Longman (3), Heston, Curtis, Rheinschild. Goals from touchdowns—Tom Hammond (3). Umpire—Hoagland of Princeton. Referee—Ryan of Detroit A. C. Linesmen—Post Detroit and Hollister of Cleveland. Time of halves—Twenty minutes.

Michigan	Kalamazoo.
R. E. ....Clark, Puffer	
Tom Hammond Smith, Post...L. E.	
R. T....Tom Hammond, Williams ....L. G.	
Graham Young	
R. G....Carter, Beechler Moore, Rooks....R. G.	
Schulte Carson, Moore....R. T.	
L. G....Schultz, Ted Giddings (capt.)..R. E.	
Hammond Phelps, Carlton....Q. B.	
L. T....Curtis Patrick Arndts ....L. H. B.	
L. E...Garrels, Reinschild Kimmerley...R. H. B.	
Q. B...Norcross, Becker Clapp ....F. B.	
H. B....Magoffin,	
Weeks, Stuart, Dupree	
L. H. B....Heston	
F. B...Harry Hammond	

Score—Michigan, 95, Kalamazoo, 0. Touchdowns—Harry Hammond [5], Heston [6], Clark, Weeks, Patrick [2], Schulte; total, 16. Goals—Tom Hammond, 15. Referee Fishleigh. Umpire Hollister. Time of halves—25 minutes, 20 minutes.

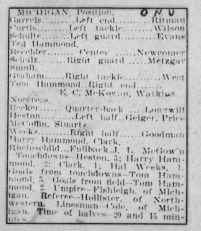

MICHIGAN. Position.	O. N. U.
Garrels........Left end....Rilman	
Curtis........Left tackle....Wilson	
Schulte....Left guard....Evans	
Ted Hammond,	
Beechler........Center ....Newcomer	
Schulz....Right guard ....Metzgar	
Small,	
Graham....Right tackle....West	
Tom Hammond..Right end....	
E. C. McKown, Watkins,	
Norcross,	
Becker.....Quarter-back ....Longwill	
Heston....Left half..Geiger, Price	
McCoffin, Stuart,	
Weeks......Right half....Goodman	
Harry Hammond, Clark,	
Rheinschild....Fullback..J. L. McGow'n	

Touchdowns—3: Harry Hammond, 2; Clark, 1; Hal Weeks, 1. Goals from touchdowns—Tom Hammond, 5. Goals from field—Tom Hammond, 2. Umpire—Fishleigh, of Michigan. Referee—Hollister, of Northwestern. Linesman—Cole, of Michigan. Time of halves—20 and 15 minutes.

The Summary.	
MICHIGAN	P. & S.
	O'Leary.
Garrels........Left end......Cremin	
Curtis,	
Patrick....Left tackle......Wagner	
Schultz....Left guard......Jones	
Schulte-Ted	
Hammond....Center ....Blair	
Carter....Right guard......James	
T. Hammond..Right tackle......Shock	
Clark........Right end....Hutchinson	
	Griffin	
Norcross........Quarter......O'Neill	
Heston........Left half........Mount	
H. Hammond	
Magoffin ...Right half...Livingston	
Hal Weeks....Fullback......Conroy	

Touchdowns—Tom Hammond, 2; Heston, 2; Curtis, 1, Clark, 1; Harry Hammond, 1; Norcross, 1. Goals from touchdowns—Tom Hammond, 12. Umpire, Cole, of Michigan. Referee—Fishleigh, of Michigan. Linesman—Montgomery, of Michigan. Time of halves—15 and 7 1-2 minutes.

GOT 3. 2 POINTS PER MINUTE

MICHIGAN'S BEST RECORD WAS EQUALED YESTERDAY.

SCORING MACHINE ROLLED UP 72 POINTS IN ALL.

NORCROSS WAS BRIGHT STAR OF BRILLIANT CLUSTER.

Ann Arbor, Mich., October 12.—(Special.)—Michigan defeated the College of Physicians and Surgeons of Chicago today by a score of 72 to 0 in exactly 22 1-2 minutes of play, and thus the great speed rate accomplished in that famous "128-to-0" Buffalo game was exactly equaled. In the Buffalo game the teams played 40 minutes. Today, in 22 1-2 minutes, the men of Yost also scored at the rate of 3 1-5 points a minute.

PASS CENTURY MARK

Michigan Rolls Up a Total of 130 Points Against West Virginia.

GAME WHIRLWIND OF RUNS

Playing of Norcross, Curtis, Heston and Clark Is a Feature.

Michigan (130).	West Virginia (0).
Weeks, Gatre......L. E.	McDonald, Ernest..R. E.
Curtis, Patrick....L. T.	Leahy.............R. T.
Schulte ....L. G.	Backman ....R. G.
Schulz ....C.	Yeardley ....C.
Carter, T.Hammond.R. G.	Post ....L. G.
Graham, Patrick...R. T.	Hall ....L. T.
Harry Hammond...R. E.	Wilson ....L. E.
Norcross, Becker..Q. B.	Martin ....Q. B.
Heston, Depree...L. H. B.	Hinman ....R. H. B.
Stuart ....R. H. B.	Sexton, Byers....L. H. B.
Magoffin ....R. H. B.	Elson ....R. H. B.
Clark ....F. B.	

Touchdowns—Magoffin (2), Curtis (5), Schulte (2), Carter, Clark (5), Norcross (5), Patrick, Graham, Becker, Harry Hammond. Umpire—Lewis, University of West Virginia. Referee—Hollister of Beloit. Time of halves—Twenty-five and twenty minutes.

THE ALL-AMERICA FOOTBALL TEAM
BY WALTER CAMP.
FIRST ELEVEN

Name.	Position.	College.
SHEVLIN	End	Yale
COONEY	Tackle	Princeton
PIEKARSKI	Guard	Pennsylvania
TIPTON	Centre	West Point
KINNEY	Guard	Yale
HOGAN	Tackle	Yale
ECKERSALL	End	Chicago
STEVENSON	Quarter	Pennsylvania
HURLEY	Half	Harvard
HESTON	Half	Michigan
SMITH	Full	Pennsylvania

SECOND ELEVEN	THIRD ELEVEN
WEEDE, Pennsylvania	GLAZE, Dartmouth
THORPE, Columbia	BUTKIEWICZ, Penn.
GILMAN, Dartmouth	SHORT, Princeton
RORABACK, Yale	TORREY, Pennsylvania
TRIPP, Yale	THORPE, Minnesota
CURTIS, Michigan	DOE, West Point
GILLESPIE, West Point	ROTHGEB, Illinois
ROCKWELL, Yale	HARRIS, Minnesota
REYNOLDS, Pennsylvania	HOYT, Yale
HUBBARD, Amherst	VAUGHN, Dartmouth
MILLS, Harvard	BENDER, Nebraska

SCORE ON YOST'S MEN

Drake's Players Prove a Surprise Against Michigan's Substitutes.

LOSERS MAKE A PLACE KICK

**William Heston
Halfback**

MICHIGAN WINS IN STUBBORN BATTLE

Chicago Proves Stronger Than Anticipated—Final Score, 22 to 12.

"SUBS" PLAY GRITTY GAME

Surprise Rooters by Grand Rally —Wolverines' Offense Too Much for Maroons.

[BY A STAFF CORRESPONDENT.]
ANN ARBOR, Mich., Nov. 12.—Michigan defeated Chicago on Ferry field to-day by the score of 22 to 12, and ended its fourth season under Coach F. H. Yost, in which time not a defeat has been suffered.

No battle on Ferry field was ever so fiercely waged, the maroons exhibiting strength wholly unexpected by the Michigan cohorts. Chicago suffered early in the game from the forced retirement of three of her greatest stars, Bezdek, Parry and Catlin. Stripped of these giants, the maroons only buckled down tighter to their work, and at one stage early in the second half the desperation of Chicago put it only four points behind the wolverines, whose supporters for the first time realized that the team was in danger.

One mighty shout of encouragement was given Michigan's warriors and they quickly answered with another touchdown.

Just Before the Kick-off at the Chicago-Michigan Football Game for the Western Championship. November 12, 1904. Attendance 13,500. Score, Michigan 22, Chicago 12.

GOT 65 POINTS

Michigan Made Good Start in Game With Ohio Wesleyan at Ann Arbor on Saturday.

NEW MEN ALL SHOW WELL

Not a First Down Made by Visitors—Michigan Stuck to Straight Football.

Ann Arbor, Mich., September 30.—(Special.)—Michigan started off the season today at a terrific pace, beating Ohio Wesleyan by 65 to 0 in 33½ minutes of actual play.

Taking into consideration that it was baseball weather, and not football temperature, the short halves, and the fact that such "M" men as Longman, Denny Clark, Schulte, Schultz, Hal Weeks and Harry Hammond were not available, the score was a beaut. And taking into consideration the work of the reserves who helped out Norcross, Curtis, Tom Hammond, Stuart and Octy Graham, it is enough to make a Michigan man shake hands with his fellows and himself and feel certain that "we're going to have another team."

MICHIGAN.		OHIO WESLEYAN
Garrels	Left end	Schweitzer
Curtis	Left tackle	Hutchinson, Smith
Love	Left guard	Cole
Clement	Center	Plaisted
Graham	Right guard	Hart
Patrick	Right tackle	Kennedy
Lyke		
Stuart	Right end	Doward, Ridgeway
Norcross	Quarterback	Bettenoom
Barlow		
Dunlap, Pierce	Left halfback	Rike
Workman, Rumney	Left halfback	Stroup
Hammond, Chandler	Fullback	Euegert

Touchdowns—Norcross 1, Hammond 4, Workman 2, Garrels 1, Rumney 1, Love 1. Goals for touchdowns—Hammond 5, Curtis 5. Umpire—Hollister of Michigan. Referee—Inglis of Columbus. Time of halves—15½ minutes and 15 minutes.

Schultz

When the football season of 1905 began, Coach Yost deviated from his usual custom and gave the newspaper reporters a tip. "Keep your eye on Schultz," he said, "That man is going to be the greatest center playing football this year." And as usual, the coach was right.

Adolph Schultz entered the engineering department in the fall of 1904. He had previously played on the Ft. Wayne high school team and when he appeared on Ferry Field, the coach thought he saw in the tall German youth the possibility of a great linesman. He was played at guard in the early games and afterward changed to center where he became a fixture. During the past season he easily outclassed every center to whom he was opposed. The manner in which he outplayed the veteran Kemp in the Wisconsin game was almost pathetic. Football critics were almost unanimous in placing him on the All-Western team.

As a football player Schultz's most valuable asset is his imperturbable disposition. Nothing ever excites him and consequently his errors of judgment in a game are few. His strength enables him to handle his opponents almost as he pleases. For a big man his speed is remarkable. It was his sprint and tackle from behind of an Oberlin man running with the ball that saved Michigan from the humiliation of being scored on by a minor college eleven. No greater praise can be bestowed upon "Germany" than to chronicle the simple fact that during two years of football, he has never asked to have time taken out for himself.

VANDERBILT DISPLAYS GREAT STRENGTH, BUT LOSES, 18-0.

Wolverines Rely on Their Line Hitters, Curtis, Hammond, and Reinschild, Who Do Brilliant Work—Blake and Hamilton, Southern Ends, the Best Yost's Men Have Faced—Northerners Cheer When Chicago-Indiana Game Is Posted.

Ann Arbor, Mich., Oct. 14.—[Special.]—Vanderbilt was all that Michigan expected, and a little more. The Commodores held Yost's full regular team to 18 points in two twenty minute halves. They fought fiercely from whistle to whistle. Their defense was excellent, and was beaten down only by the hard work of Michigan's best line hitters, Curtis, Hammond, and Reinschild. Their offense, however, was impotent against the Michiganders' defense, the best seen this year on Ferry field. Blake and Hamilton were two of the best ends ever put in against Yost. Their work was wonderful. No conspicuous gains were made by Michigan at end until Hammond got around for the twenty in the second half.

Rooters Cheer Vanderbilt.

The Michigan rooters gave Vanderbilt's yell as often as their own. The Wolverine band played "Dixie" as often as it did the "Yellow and Blue." The wildest cheering in the game arose when the first half score of the Chicago-Indiana game was announced. Vanderbilt's players did not know what had happened when the Michigan bleachers rose en masse and loudly handed Chicago the "Gee-hee, gee-haw" yell. Michigan's delight knew no bounds.

Coach Yost and Trainer Fitzpatrick said they were pleased with their team's showing against such a foe as Vanderbilt proved to be. The Vanderbilt coach, McGugin, could not get here in time for the game.

1905 Season			Won 12, Lost 1, Tied 0		
			Date	Place	Attendance
Michigan 65,	Ohio Wesleyan	0	Sep 30	Ann Arbor	
Michigan 44,	Kalamazoo	0	Oct 4	Ann Arbor	
Michigan 36,	Case	0	Oct 7	Ann Arbor	
Michigan 23,	Ohio Northern	0	Oct 11	Ann Arbor	
Michigan 18,	Vanderbilt	0	Oct 14	Ann Arbor	
Michigan 31,	Nebraska	0	Oct 21	Ann Arbor	
Michigan 79,	Albion	0	Oct 25	Ann Arbor	
Michigan 48,	Drake	0	Oct 28	Ann Arbor	
Michigan 33,	Illinois	0	Nov 4	Champaign	
Michigan 40,	Ohio State	0	Nov 11	Ann Arbor	
Michigan 12,	Wisconsin	0	Nov 18	Ann Arbor	17,000
Michigan 75,	Oberlin	0	Nov 25	Ann Arbor	
Michigan 0,	Chicago	2	Nov 30	Chicago	

Michigan (48)		Drake (0)	
Garrels	L. E.	Gilbert	R. E.
L. T. Curtis	L. T.	Nelson	R. T.
Schulte	L. G.	Conoway	R. G.
Schultz	C.	Palas	C.
Graham	R. G.	Hoffman	L. G.
Rheinschild	R. T.	Hasbrouck	L. T.
Stuart, Newton	R. E.	Keeney	L. E.
Barlow	Q. B.	Taylor	Q. B.
Marcille	L. H. B.	Burcham	R. H. B.
Hammond, Kanaga	R. H. B.	Woodrow, McCoy, Jefferson	L. H. B.
Weeks, Love	F. B.	Kintz	F. B.

Touchdowns—Hammond (2), Schulte, Weeks (3), Garrels, Barlow. Goals from touchdown—Curtis (8). Umpire—Hollister of Michigan. Referee—Wendell of Michigan. Linesman—Holbrook of Leland Stanford. Time of halves—Twenty-five minutes.

MICHIGAN ROLLS UP A SCORE OF THIRTY-ONE POINTS

Wolverines Win First Big Game by Decisive Score of 31 to 0—Cornhuskers Hold Varsity to Tie in First Half---Tom Hammond Kicks Two Goals From Field---Denny Clark Injured---Whole Michigan Team Starred in Yesterday's Game.

After being held to a tie during the first thirty-five minutes of play, Michigan's whirlwind football eleven took a decided brace in the second period, snowing under the game Nebraska bunch to the tune of 31 to 0. The varsity put up far and away the best game of the season and the way the team tore through Nebraska's defense in the second half made Coach H. U. Yost the happiest man in Ann Arbor. Not a man loomed up best for Michigan—the whole team starred. There was not a man on the team who did not play rings around his opponent, and the vast improvement in team-work looks well for a championship team.

TOM HAMMOND, WHOSE GOOD RIGHT FOOT STARTED NEBRASKA ON THE DOWNWARD PATH.

UBSTITUTES SCORE FORTY POINTS ON OHIO STATE

Barlow's Run of One Hundred and Fifteen Yards the Feature of a Spectacular Game --Coach King Watched Play

The most brilliant run ever seen on Ferry field and the longest run ever made anywhere, a sprint by Al Barlow from five yards behind Michigan's goal line to Ohio State's goal, a total distance of 115 yards, was the one feature of yesterday's game with Ohio State, which resulted finally in a victory for Michigan by a score of 40 to 0. Two forty-yard runs for touchdowns made by Garrels complete what was undoubtedly the most spectacular game ever seen in Ann Arbor.

Although H. U. Yost took no chances by playing any of his quasi-cripples, and consequently the varsity presented a largely substituted line-up. Michigan at times displayed flashes of better football than they have shown before this season. Then, at times their work was hardly above criticism. A long run or a series of short gains bringing the ball close to their opponents' goal, only to be followed by a fumble or some other serious loss, was no unfrequent occurrence. In one way, however, the varsity's work was inferior to that which they have done earlier this season. While such teams as Nebraska, Illinois, Drake, Case and Kalamazoo have been able to amass a total of only three first downs against Michigan for the season, Ohio State yesterday negotiated the required distance five different times, three of them coming in rapid succession. The penalties which the eagerness of Michigan's forwards brought about were also costly. Michigan gave Ohio State fifty-five yards in this way, most of the penalties being for off-side play.

CLARKE IS HEARTBROKEN

DETROIT BOY REALIZES WHAT MISPLAY COST TEAM.

Claims Official Did Not Hear Him Call "Down."

Chicago, Ill., November 30.—(Special.) —Of the thousands of persons who saw today's game, none felt as badly over the outcome as Denny Clark who blames himself because an attempt to run back a punt resulted in the loss of the game, when, by playing it safe he might have held the game to a tie. Clark came in from the field heartbroken. He refused to go in to dinner and took the first train back to his home in Detroit. He cried almost continuously from the moment that he was taken out of the game until he left his team-mates.

All Clark would say was: "As soon as I crossed the goal line and saw a chance of being tackled, I called 'Down.' The official was up the field and did not hear it and the safety resulted, as I was thrown back over the line."

MICHIGAN LOST TO CHICAGO

DESPERATE STRUGGLE RESULTED 2 TO 0

Measly Safety Was the Undoing of the Gladiators From the University of Michigan.

GAME FIERCELY FOUGHT

Both Elevens Put Up a Grand Contest, Barring Fumbling on Part of Wolvernies ---Garrels the Bright Star.

By JOE S. JACKSON.

Chicago, November 30.—(Special.)—By the smallest possible score in football, 2 to 0, and before the greatest crowd in the history of the game in the west, close to 27,000 persons, Michigan this afternoon lost the western championship to Chicago. It was a bitter blow both to team and to Yost, marking the first defeat Ann Arbor school has sustained in five years, and the first championship that the Michigan coach has ever been beaten out of.

It was the irony of fate that Michigan should finish her season with more points to her credit and less against her than any team in the country, and yet, on the two points that were made, she should lose the sectional title. In this feature, as well as in the extremely small amount of ground gained by the two teams, the contest was a remarkable one.

The smallness of the figures, and the fact that the defeat came through a mistake made at a critical time, take none of the sting from the defeat. In justice to the victorious team, it is entirely correct to say that Michigan followers, puzzled somewhat by the play of the first half, had resolved by the time the second period was well advanced, that a scoreless tie at the finish would be the result, and would be a satisfactory one. The fact that the two points made could as easily as not have been avoided, adds to, rather than detracts from, the force of the blow.

The two points that were made came with the second period a little better than half gone, the game, up to that time, having been very evenly contested. Chicago had secured the ball, and, as had happened a dozen times earlier, Eckersall, through failure of his team mates to advance it, was called upon to punt. Chicago at the time was on Michigan's 45-yard line. Barlow and Clark were playing back to take the kick, but the ball, low and well driven, went between them. Clark went behind the line after the ball, with two Chicago players down on him. There was hardly a chance to get away, and he could have played it safe and avoided a score by merely touching the ball down behind the line. He shook off the two tacklers, however, and tried to run the ball back. He was a yard or so over the line on the field when Catlin reached him, and threw him back, forcing him over his own goal line. The result was a safety, two points, and the game, Chicago contenting itself from that time on with kicking out of danger when it could not advance, being satisfied to win by two points, if possible.

Curtis - 1906

The 1906 Football Team

L. C. Hull, Jr.	Student Manager (Appointed)
C. A. Lohmiller	Student Manager (Resigned)
Fielding H. Yost	Coach
John S. Curtis	Captain
Charles Baird	Graduate Director

The Team

J. S. Curtis (Captain)	End, Tackle
W. D. Graham	Guard
J. C. Garrels	Full Back
P. P. Magoffin	Half Back
H. S. Hammond	End
H. E. Patrick	Tackle
J. L. Loell	Center, End, Tackle
W. L. Eyke	Tackle
C. H. Clement	Center
F. B. Newton	End, Tackle
H. A. Workman	Quarterback
M. P. Rumney	Halfback
S. J. Davidson	Guard
H. S. Bishop	Quarter, Halfback

Games 1906

October	3.	Reserves at Ann Arbor	Michigan	26	Opponents	0
October	6.	Case at Ann Arbor	Michigan	28	Opponents	0
October	10.	Reserves at Ann Arbor	Michigan	21	Opponents	0
October	13.	Reserves at Ann Arbor	Michigan	28	Opponents	0
October	20.	O. S. U. at Columbus	Michigan	6	Opponents	0
October	27.	Illinois at Ann Arbor	Michigan	28	Opponents	0
November	3.	Vanderbilt at Ann Arbor	Michigan	10	Opponents	4
November	10.	Alumni at Ann Arbor	Michigan	0	Opponents	0
November	17.	Pennsylvania at Philadelphia	Michigan	0	Opponents	17

Reserves

F. T. Wirtmire	Ben Harris	G. Gukenberger
A. F. Wright	K. S. Simpson	T. V. Bird
A. R. Chandler	F. N. Featherstone	H. K. Holland
I. N. Steckle	A. C. Fullinwider	H. P. Eastman
W. J. Embs	J. E. Kelly	G. B. Wheeler
C. J. Schenk	C. P. Davey	R. B. Ortmer
A. V. Evans	W. M. Casey	M. S. Crumpacker
E. D. Kanaga	J. K. Watkins	C. H. Spaancм
J. R. Langley	R. G. Chapman	Wm. Wasmund
H. A. Treat	J. H. Guenther	B. Coleman

Hard Fought Contest Wo[n] in Last Few Minutes [of] Play---Score 6-0---Loe[ll] Plays Star Game.

Columbus, O., Oct. 20.—After bei[ng] held scoreless until the last few minut[es] of play, the Michigan football tea[m] rallied and by a terrific onslaught ca[r]ried the ball within striking distance [of] Ohio's goal, when Garrels scored a fie[ld] goal from the 35-yard line. Two min[utes later Gibson downed a high pa[ss] for a punt behind his own goal line f[or] a safety, making the final score 6 to [2].

After the first half had ended wit[h] the score 0 to 0, the maize and blu[e] supporters were encouraged, for the[ir] team had kept Ohio State on the de[f]ensive during nearly the entire hal[f]. When, however, in the second hal[f] Michigan would carry the ball well int[o] Ohio's territory, only to lose it withou[t] scoring, they began to fear. Twenty [-] five minutes had passed and the scor[e] was 0 to 0 with only five minutes o[f] play left and visions of a second Chi[-] cago surprise became more and mor[e] prominent.

At this juncture Michigan carried the ball from their own 50-yard line t[o] Ohio's 20, Garrels, Curtis, Steckle an[d] Magoffin negotiating the distances b[y] straight football. Here, with 8 yards t[o] gain on the third down, Garrels droppe[d] to the 35-yard line where, for the fourt[h] time, he tried for a field goal. His ai[m] was true, and as the "Four" was marke[d] on the score board pandemonium brok[e] loose in the Michigan section, for th[e] game was won. The safety which add[ed] to the total came about one minute before the call of time. Ohio State had been penalized 15 yards and Gib[-] son dropped back to his 2-yard line t[o] punt. The pass was high and he re[-] covered beyond the goal line, where the ball was declared dead.

Pennsylvania.		Michigan.
Levene	L. E.	Loell
Draper	L. T.	Eyke
Gallagher	L. G.	Davison
Dwyer	C.	Clement
Zeigler	R. G.	Graham
Gaston-Lavery	R. T.	Newton
Scarlett	R. E.	Hammond
Lawrence	Q. B.	Workman
Folwell	L. H.	Magoffin
Greene	R. H.	Bishop-Rumney
Hollenbeck	F. B.	Garrels

Summary: Touchdowns—Green 2, Folwell. Goals from touchdowns—Hollenbach 2. Referee—Langford, of Trinity. Umpire—Kelly, of Princeton. Head linesman—Fultz. Attendance—30,000.

Total Michigan weight—1,951 pounds.
Total Pennsy weight—1,939 pounds.
Average Michigan weight—177 4-11 pounds.
Average Pennsy weight—176 3-11
Average weight of "M" linesmen—184 pounds.
Average weight of Penn linesmen—177 5-7 pounds.
Average weight of Michigan backs—168 1-3 pounds.
Average weight of Penn backs—180 1-3 pounds.

Coach Yost: "Penn outplayed Michigan. I always maintained that we had a very weak team this year, and down in my heart would have been the most surprised man in the world had we won. The east may perhaps ridicule Michigan now; but we hope to vindicate our west in the Pennsylvania game at Ann Arbor next year."

Trainer Fitzpatrick: "We must take our defeat gracefully and admit we were outplayed. We must look to the future. The team this year was by no means up to the normal Michigan standard."

Manager Baird: "Michigan will not grovel, but will take its defeat gracefully. This will only add to Michigan spirit."

MICHIGAN SCORES OFTEN ON FARMERS

Varsity, on Rampage, Rolls Up 46 Points—Yost Is Pleased by Team's Work.

Although the Farmers looked fully as strong as the Case team which but a week ago held the varsity to nine points, they were utterly unable to cope with the determined work of Michigan yesterday and the Wolverines walked off with the second game of the season by the one-edged score of 46 to 0. The visitors were played off their feet from whistle to whistle, the concentrated attack of the varsity proving more than they could solve. Incidentally the varsity showed an incredible reversal of form over the work in the Case game, and in running up the biggest score a Michigan team has boasted since the middle of the season of 1905—the year of the last of the great teams—the work was spectacular.

1907			
Michigan	9	Case	0
Michigan	46	M.A.C.	0
Michigan	22	Wabash	0
Michigan	22	O.S.U.	0
Michigan	8	Vanderbilt	0
Michigan	0	Pennsylvania	6

Season Summary
Games won, 5; Lost 1; Tied, 0.
Points for Michigan, 107; For Opponents 6.

CAPTAIN

McGoffin - 1907

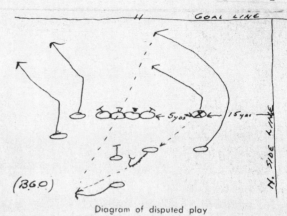

Diagram of disputed play

Top row: Fitzpatrick (Trainer), Loell, Graham, Lehr, Allerdice, Chandler, Featherstone, Kelly, Thornburg (Student Manager), Yost (Coach). Middle row: Crumpacker, Reinschild, Schulz, Magoffin (Captain), Embs, Casey, Hammond, Watkins. Bottom row: Miller, Witmire, Wasmund, Rumney, Sullivan, Evans.

STATISTICS OF MICHIGAN TEAM

NAME	POSITION	CLASS	WEIGHT	AGE	HOME
Mason Pittman Rumney	L. E.	'08 E	160	23	Detroit
William John Embs	L. T.	'10 L	190	22	Escanaba
William Mallory Casey	L. G.	'09	196	21	Cedar Falls, Iowa
Adolph George Schulz	C.	'08 E	225	23	Fort Wayne, Ind.
Walter DeWitt Graham	R. G.	'08 E	225	22	Chicago
Walter Morris Rheinschild	R. T.	'08 L	185	22	Los Angeles, Cal.
Harry Stevens Hammond	R. E.	'08 E	180	22	Chicago
William Stevens Wasmund	Q.	'09	163	20	Detroit
Paul Parker Magoffin	L. H.	'08	178	21	Washington, D.C.
Prentiss Porter Douglass	R. H.	'09 L	175	21	Monmouth, Ill.
David Way Allerdice	H.	'10 E	170	20	Indianapolis, Ind.
Clarence Emanuel Lehr	H.	'10	175	20	Escanaba
James Joy Miller	H.	'10 E	160	21	Detroit
John Lewis Loell	Full	'10	178	21	Escanaba

The Summary.

MICHIGAN.		VANDERBILT.
Rumney	Left end	V. Blke.
Embs	Left Tackle	McLin
Casey	Left Guard	Sherill
Schultz	Center	Stoc.
Graham	Right Guard	Kitz
Rheinschild	Right Tackle	Hassloc.
Hammond	Right End	B. Blak.
Wasmund	Quarterback	Coxfel.
Magoffin	Left Half	Campbel
Douglas, Allerdice	Right Half	Craig
Loell	Fullback	Morton.

Score: Michigan, 8; Vanderbilt, 0.
First half—Michigan, 8; Vanderbilt, 0.
Goals from placement—Graham 2.
Referee—Bradley Walker, Virginia.
Umpire—Neil Snow, Michigan.
Head linesman—Elder, Penn State.
Times of halves—Thirty-five minutes.

YOST TAKES MEDICINE BUT IS SORE ON MURPHY'S DECISION

Coach's Trick Play, Called Illegal by Referee, Is Canceded by Penn Leaders Foxiest Thing Developed Under New Rules.

BY SEWARD CRAMER.

Ann Arbor, Mich., November 16.—"There is a time when the worm will turn" and "There's a time when butternuts will burn." That is the kick Michigan lands tonight without being unsportsmanlike.

For weeks Coach Yost has been working on a trick play that was a corker, and so fearful of it was he that he would not allow the officials to be informed of it, even. It was a beauty and went through. It was on the play that Captain Magoffin made the touchdown that was disallowed.

"Nothing ever looked so good to me in all my life as to see those two goal posts and nobody to stop me," said Magoffin, and then he added, "nothing ever looked so sour as when I saw that official call the play back."

Yost is the best loser that ever happened. Michigan lost the game with Harvard in 1896 by calling short time. It is charged that Minnesota gained a tie score in 1893 in a rubbered out time. And that Denny Clark did not make a safety in the Chicago game of 1905 and the officials and dopesters have agreed that Yost's contentions at Philadelphia last year that a lineman could not carry a ball from his position correct. And Yost smiled all the while but he is hot tonight.

He would not say anything for publication except to doff his hat to Pennsy for their superior offense on straight old line football, but he gave Referee Murphy a calling in the presence of several men after the game.

The play was a shift and a bewildering one. "Germany" Shultz went to right end. Magoffin was directly back of Embs. Hammond was out at the left end to draw the attack on him. Watkins was ten yards back of Rheinschild. Wasmund was in a direct line with Embs and Magoffin. Allerdice was wau outside of Rumney, the left end. The ball was passed to Wasmund, who hurled it over to Allerdice. In the meantime Magoffin got through tackle and Schultz had gone down the end. Allerdice threw it far over the line and Magoffin made a beautiful catch and ran to the goal. Now then comes the point. From the position of Allerdice and where Magoffin caught it the ball must have gone at least twelve yards to the left of the center or where the ball was snapped back.

Nelly the umpire, said so, but McCarthy, the referee, said nay. Coach Torrey of Penn admitted tonight that on this play the score of the game should have been six to six. It was conceded that it was the most spectacular, perplexing and foxiest play developed under the new rules. The Michigan rooters are sore, but Yost, Fitzpatrick, Baird and the team simply smile and say, "They tell us the decision and we abide by it. No use of kicking. The less said the better."

ALL-AMERICAN

Adolph Schulz Center 1907

1908 Season	Won 5, Lost 2, Tied 1		
		Date	Place
Michigan 16	Case 6	Oct. 3	Ann Arbor
Michigan 0	Michigan State 6	Oct. 10	East Lansing
Michigan 12	Notre Dame 6	Oct. 17	Ann Arbor
Michigan 10	Ohio State 6	Oct. 24	Columbus
Michigan 24	Vanderbilt 6	Oct. 31	Ann Arbor
Michigan 62	Kentucky 0	Nov. 7	Ann Arbor
Michigan 0	Pennsylvania 29	Nov. 14	Ann Arbor
Michigan 4	Syracuse 28	Nov. 21	Syracuse

"GERMANY" SHULTZ
Captain

Halfback Scores Three Goals From Placement Against Notre Dame— Catholics Make Only Touchdown of Game on Long Run by Vaughn.

Wolverines Have Better of First Half, But Visitors Rip Them Up in Second —Capt. Schulz, Who Is Unable to Play, Is Much Missed.

Ann Arbor, Mich., October 16.— In spite of the fact that two veterans were out of the game, Schulz and Watkins, Michigan was able to beat Notre Dame here this afternoon by the score of 12 to 6. Allerdice's toe being responsible for the three field goals that netted Michigas her majority. Three times the Wolverines worked the ball to the 30-yard line and in the three attempts Allerdice easily booted the leather over the bars. This happened twice in the first half and once in the last two minutes of play in the second.

Notre Dame scored the only touchdown of the contest after 20 minutes of vicious playing in Michigan's territory. At the same time it was the most spectacular feature of the afternoon. Vaughn, the star fullback of the Notre Dame team, secured the ball on the 50-yard line in a common fullback play and ran 50 yards through seven Michigan men for a touchdown. Had Michigan been without Allerdice, this would have been the only score of the game and the Wolverines would have been defeated for the first time by the Indiana eleven.

MICHIGAN.	NOTRE DAME.
Embs .... L. E. .... Burdick
Casy .... L. T. ...... Edwards, Kelly
Crumpacker .... L. G. .... Payne
Brennan .... C. ..... Miller, Capt.
Primeau .... R. G. .... Dolan
Benbrook .... R. T. .... Dimmick
Ranney .... R. E. .... Wood
Wasmund .... Q. B. .... Hamilton
Douglas ..... L. H. Dwyer, McDonald
Allerdice .... R. H. .... Ruel
Davison .... F. B. .... Vaughn

Touchdown—Vaugh. Goal from touchdown—Hamilton. Goals from field—Allerdice 3. Umpire—Starbuck of Cornell. Referee—Hoagland of Princeton. Field judge—Kilpatrick of Wisconsin. Head linesman—Kidder of Penn state. Time of halves—30 min. Score—Michigan 12, Notre Dame 6.

"DAVE"
ALLERDICE
Captain Elect

RILEY

OHIO STATE GOES DOWN TO DEFEAT

Buckeyes Clearly Outplayed— Splendid Teamwork of Varsity Eclipses Individual Playing.

(Special to The Michigan Daily.)

Columbus, O., Oct. 24.—In an intensely exciting game today Michigan defeated O. S. U. by the score of 10 to 6. Only Captain Schulz's presence in the line saved Michigan from a more gory battle. For a long time the little crowd of Michigan rooters was on needles for fear of defeat. Allerdice had scored from field after thirteen minutes of play, but exactly thirteen minutes later Gibson, Ohio's fullback, broke away for an eighty-five yard run through the field for a touchdown. Douglas followed close on his heels, gaining constantly, and made a beautiful flying tackle just as the ball was shoved over the goal line. This, with a kicked goal, ended the scoring of the first half and the local fans began to offer their money upon Ohio. The worst of it was that seventeen minutes of play elapsed in the second before the Wolverines could score. Allerdice tried three times for a goal from field without success. Then Ranney got the ball from Dave on a perfectly executed forward pass and carried it to the Ohio ten-yard line, from which place Allerdice took the ball over for Michigan's lone touchdown.

Despite the closeness of the game, it is conceded that Michigan outplayed the Buckeyes. During practically all of the game the varsity was on the offensive and the line was practically impregnable for the first time this year. The game was won on the merits of team work, not the briliancy of one mans booting. The team played splendidly, but was up against tough luck a good deal of time.

"STUB"
CRUMPACKER

"SAM" DAVIDSON

DOUGLAS

Michigan Withdraws From Conference

In November of 1907, the Board of Regents adopted a resolution establishing the Board in Control of Intercollegiate Athletics, and defining its membership and responsibilities. This was by no means the first such group in Michigan athletic history, as 1890 saw the first lasting attempt at athletic organization with the formation of the Athletic Association of the University of Michigan.

Perhaps the most pressing problem to face this new group was the question of Michigan's position in the Western Conference. As a result of the "Angell Conferences" held in 1906, there were numerous changes being considered within the Conference, some of which Michigan could not accept. Thus, it was voted that Michigan's delegates (members of the new Board) to the January 1908 Conference meeting should be instructed to work for the passage of rules which would secure a seven-game schedule in football, authorize a training table, repeal the retroactive features of the three-year rule and permit interdepartment graduates "to play three years." At the January 15, 1908 meeting of the Board, the Chairman reported that at the Conference meeting, none of the changes in the rules urged by Michigan had been made. The Board voted to withdraw from the Conference. (It was also voted that Michigan should retain for the control of her athletics all of the Conference rules except those against which she had made formal protest, specifically the retroactive feature of the three-year rule, the limitation of football games to five instead of seven and the rule against the training table.)

PENNSYLVANIA, 29; MICHIGAN, 0

For the third time in as many years the Varsity suffered defeat at the hands of Pennsylvania Saturday November 14 on Ferry Field.

Michigan		Pennsylvania
Embs............	Left End	Braddock, Crooks
Casey...........	Left Tackle	Draper
Benbrook........	Left Guard	Dietrich
Schulz ....}	Center	Marks
Brennan .)		Cozzens
Riley...........	Right Guard	Lamberton, Pike
Crumpacker.....	Right Tackle	Gaston
Linthicum......	Right End	Scarlett
Wasmund.......	Quarterback	Keinath, Miller
Douglas........	Left Halfback	Means
Allerdice......	Right Halfback ..}	Manier, Somers
Davison........	Fullback ....}	Hollenback, Reagan

Summaries: Touchdowns—Hollenback 2, Manier, Means, Draper. Goals from touchdown—Scarlett 4. Time of halves—35 minutes.

Officials: Referee—Langford (Trinity). Umpire—Edwards (Princeton). Field judge—McCarty (Brown). Head linesman—Lerum (Wisconsin).

SYRACUSE, 28; MICHIGAN, 4

Disheartened by the absence of Allerdice and the ill-luck that seems to have followed the team throughout the season, the Varsity was unable to put up a stubborn defense against Syracuse and was defeated by the score of 28 to 4. Michigan scored first, early in the game, when after a touchdown had not been allowed. Davison kicked goal from the 15 yard line. From this time on luck seemed to break against the Varsity and after carrying the ball down the field nearly to Syracuse's goal line an unsuccessful forward pass would be recovered for a long gain by a Syracuse man. Schulz played the game of his career and was the whole line. Michigan's ends again proved to be below the class of eastern ends and Syracuse tore off end run after end run. Linthicum, at Allerdice's place at half, played a good consistent game and with Douglas and Davison showed up strongly on offense. Schulz was the defense as usual and, in the opinion of many who saw the game earned his right to selection as All-American center by his marvelous work in both the Syracuse and Pennsy games.

1909		
Michigan.........3;	Case........	0
Michigan.........33;	O.S.U.......	6
Michigan.........6;	Marquette......	5
Michigan.........44;	Syracuse......	0
Michigan.........3;	Notre Dame....	11
Michigan.........12;	Pennsylvania....	6
Michigan.........15;	Minnesota.....	6

Season Summary
Games won, 6; Lost, 1; Tied, 0.
Points for Michigan, 116; For Opponents 34

1909 TEAM

Gallup (student mgr.), Wells, Edmunds, Smith, Benbrook, Casey, Bartelme (athletic dir.), Fitzpatrick trainer.

Miller, Clark, Watkins, Allerdice capt., Yost coach, Magidsohn, Conklin.

Ranney, Pattengill, Wasmund, Green, Freeney.

Oct. 9

MICHIGAN		CASE
Rogers	L. E.	Wilcox
Edmunds	L. T.	Emerson
Benbrook	L. G.	Hinman
Watkins	C.	Abbott
Smith	R. G.	Barret
Wells	R. T.	Kipka, Brau
Wasmund	Q. B.	Regan
		McLaughlin
Bertrand,		
Magdisohn	L. H	Roby
Allerdice	R. H.	Twitchell
Lawton	F. B.	Heller, Forsythe

Summary: Score, Michigan, 3; Case 0. Goal from field—Allerdice. Referee—Eldridge. Umpire—Giddings. Field Judge—Kenny. Head Linesman—Sullivan. Times of halves—30 minutes.

BAFFLED BUT NOT BEATEN

In a Trying Game, the Varsity Defeats Marquette by a Close Score.

(From Staff Correspondent.)

Milwaukee, Wis., Oct. 23.—Michigan won from Marquette 6 to 5, each side scoring a touchdown in the first half. Allerdice won the game by kicking goal. Michigan was outplayed both on offensive and defensive and Allerdice's punting was the only thing that saved Michigan from defeat.

Oct. 16

MICHIGAN SWAMPS OHIO STATE ON FERRY FIELD BY SCORE OF 33 TO 6

DAVE ALLERDICE MAKES SPECTACULAR 45-YARD RUN FOR TOUCHDOWN; KICKS THREE GOALS FROM PLACEMENT.

Maize and Blue Men Show Big Improvement; Win by "Straight Foot Ball" and Relentless Attacks on Opponents.

By HAROLD TITUS.

ANN ARBOR, Mich., Oct. 16.—Yost's men defeated the snappy Ohio State university eleven by a score of 33 to 6 on Ferry Field this afternoon.

Michigan scored four touchdowns, and the good toe of Dave Allerdice three times sent the ball spinning between goal posts and over the bar from placement.

The Ohioans made but one touchdown, and this smacked strongly of flukishness.

Michigan won the game by straight foot ball, driving at the ends, striking off tackle and crashing into the line. The on-side kick was used with poor success. Wasmund called for the forward pass three times. Allerdice succeeded in tossing the pigskin but once, and when he did pass it a Buckeye player pulled the ball to earth.

Oct. 23

MICHIGAN HUMBLES SYRACUSE ELEVEN BY FURIOUS ATTACK

Men of Yost, Playing Like Hurry-up Coach's Heroes of Other Days, Take Sweet Revenge on Easterners —Prospects Bright for Future Games and Wolverine Rooters Rejoice—Benbrook, Allerdice and Wasmund Star—Team Works as Machine.

BY E. A. BATCHELOR.

Ann Arbor, Mich., October 30.—There is joy in Ann Arbor tonight, and, what is better yet, there is a promise of more joyous days to come. Playing real Michigan football for the first time in lo, these many years, the Yost machine today literally ground the Syracuse eleven to bits and distributed the fragments over the surface of Ferry field. In figures the result was 43 to 0, but in fact it was far more impressive than is indicated by this collection of numerals.

It was not so much what Michigan did as her manner of doing it, that set the hearts of loyal Wolverine rooters bounding for pure delight. In every department of the game the Yost outfit showed by far its best form of the season, and in almost every department the work was better than has been seen on the Ann Arbor battleground for four long years.

On a certain day last autumn Yost took a bunch of crippled, discouraged men down to Syracuse and saw them maltreated by the husky home eleven. It was a sad ending to a sad season, for the Maize and Blue got the wrong end of a 28 to 4 score. From that moment it has been one of the prime objects in every Michigan man's life to wipe the slate clean. Today came the opportunity, and the slaking of a burning thirst for vengeance.

MICHIGAN OVERWHELMED BY NOTRE DAME ELEVEN

Varsity Unable to Withstand Onslaught of the Catholics----Err in Judgment at Crucial Time ----Score 11 to 3.

Notre Dame defeated Michigan 11 to 3, the Wolverines losing because of the bad judgment of Wasmund in calling for a place kick near the close of the second half, the score 5 to 3 against Michigan, with the goal but ten yards away and with but one yard to go to secure a first down. Allerdice's attempt was blocked, the ball rolled to midfield, was secured by Notre Dame and a minute later Ryan made the Catholics' final touchdown. Borleske received a broken collar bone in the early part of the game and will be out for the rest of the season.

Nov. 6

PENN GOES DOWN TO DEFEAT AT THE HANDS OF MICHIGA.

For the First Time in History of Games Betwee. Wolverines and Red and Blue Westerner Leave Battlefield Victorious—Magidsoh. Scored Two Touchdowns in Rapid Succes. sion in First Half—Penn's Score Was Mad. by Hutchinson.

Nov. 13

PENN'S STUDENTS KEEP POLICEMEN BUSY

The first bit of excitement preceding the game itself came when the Pennsylvania undergraduates massed in front of the north gate. The management was very slow in throwing back the iron barriers, and the students utilized their spare time cheering the Quaker players, who were then eating lunch in the training house.

They sang Pennsylvania songs and cheered every member of the team in turn. Finally they became so exasperated at the delay that they began to rush the gate, and the whole force of policemen was necessary to restrain them. As a last resort they shunted into the street and torough the south gate.

The rush of undergraduates into the cheering section was followed by the Michigan delegation, which rapidly filled up its section.

But by far the most spectacular feature of the preliminaries was the arrival of the entire crew of the battleship Michigan. There were nearly 400 in this delegation. They were dressed in thir navy uniforms and led by their band, which is considered the finest in the naval service.

The battleship crew entered the field at the northeast gate and lined up in front of the cheering section. Tremendous applause greeted their arrival on the part of the Pennsylvania students. Then the Michigan delegation got busy and gave cheers for the Navy, followed by a corresponding roar from the Pennsylvania undergraduates. Then the jackies spread out across half the length of the gridiron and gave a carefully rehearsed cheer for Michigan.

At ten minutes to 2 o'clock the Michigan eleven raced out on the field. The Wolverine eleven ran into a position directly in front of the battleship crew. Captain Allerdice stepped out and accepted a magnificent flag of blue and gold, while the Michigan band played "Maryland, My Maryland." This was followed by the Michigan eleven giving three rousing cheers for the sailors.

Next there appeared on the field the University of Michigan undergraduate band. As the Michigan sailors stepped into the stand their band struck up "Harrigan, That's Me," to which the Michigan sailors sang a delightful parody.

Then the Michigan undergraduate band struck up a martial air which drew forth much cheering. During all this excitement the Pennsylvania eleven entered the field almost unnoticed.

As the Penn team ran on the field its band struck up "Hail, Pennsylvania," which the students sang with bared heads.

All American

Albert Benbrook
Guard
1909

Captain Allerdice, Whose Punting Has Been a Feature of Michigan's Games.

Nov. 20

CHAMPIONS OF THE WEST

MICHIGAN RESUMES OLD TITLE AFTER DECISIVE VICTORY OVER GOPHERS

MICHIGAN		MINNESOTA
Conklin, Ranney	L. E.	Videl, Chain
Casey	L. T.	Walker
Benbrook	L. G.	Molstad
Smith	C.	Farnum
Edmunds.		Powers.
Watkins	R. G.	Ostrand
Wells	R. T.	McCree
Pattengill	R. E.	Rademacher
Miller	Q. B.	McGovern.
		Atkins
Magidsohn	L. H.	Rosenwald
Allerdice	R. H.	Stevens.
		Ostrand
Freeney, Greene	F. B.	Pickering

Summary: Score First half, Michigan 6; Minnesota 6; final score, Michigan 15, Minnesota 6. Touchdowns Allerdice, Magidsohn, Walker. Goals from touchdowns—Allerdice 2, Farnum Goal from field—Allerdice. Referee Beavers, West Point. Umpire—Hinkey, Yale. Field Judge—Endsle ,Purdue Head Linesman—Porter, Cornell. Time of halves—35 minutes.

The Varsity Foot Ball Team
1910

CHARLES GORDON SPICE	Student Manager
ALBERT A. BENBROOK	Captain
FIELDING H. YOST	Coach
DR. ALVIN C. KRAENZLEIN	Trainer
P. G. BARTELME	Director of Outdoor Athletics

THE TEAM

STANLEY BORLESKE	Left End
W. EDMUNDS	Left End
FREDERICK L. CONKLIN (captain-elect)	Left Tackle
ALBERT A. BENBROOK (captain)	Left Guard
ARTHUR CORNWELL	Center
THOMAS BOGLE	Right Guard
CLEMENT P. QUINN	Right Guard
W. EDMUNDS	Right Tackle
F. C. COLE	Right Tackle
STANFIELD M. WELLS	Right End
NEIL McMILLAN	Quarter Back
JOE MAGIDSOHN	Left Half
VICTOR R. PATTENGILL	Right Half
DON GREENE	Right Half
GEORGE THOMSON	Full Back
GEORGE LAWTON	Full Back

SCORES FOR 1910

October 8—Case at Ann Arbor	Michigan 3—Case	3
October 15—M. A. C. at Ann Arbor	Michigan 6—M. A. C.	3
October 22—Ohio State at Columbus	Michigan 3—O. S. U.	3
October 29—Syracuse at Syracuse	Michigan 11—Syracuse	3
November 12—Pennsylvania at Philadelphia	Michigan 0—Pennsylvania	0
November 19—Minnesota at Ann Arbor	Michigan 6—Minnesota	0

1910

Kilpatrick, Yale	End
McKay, Harvard	Tackle
Benbrook, Michigan	Guard
Cozens, Pennsylvania	Center
Fisher, Harvard	Guard
Walker, Minnesota	Tackle
Wells, Michigan	End
Sprackling, Brown	Quarter
Wendell, Harvard	Halfback
Pendleton, Princeton	Halfback
Mercer, Pennsylvania	Fullback

CASE HOLDS MICHIGAN

Ohio School Springs Surprise by Getting a 3-to-3 Tie at Ann Arbor.

Michigan (3).		Case (3).
Daniels	L. E.	Brandt R. E.
Edmunds	L. T.	Prochaska R. T.
Benbrook	L. G.	Weller R. G.
Cole	C.	Abbott C.
Lawton	R. G.	Doane L. G.
Wells	R. T.	Rosendale L. T.
Pattengill	R. E.	Kipkin L. E.
McMillan	Q. B.	Goss Q. B.
Magidsohn	L. H. B.	Twitchell R. H. B.
Green	R. H. B.	Roby, Slater L. H. B.
Wenner	F. B.	Heller, Freeman F. B.

Goals from field—Heller, Lawton. Umpire—Dr. Robbins (Neb.). Referee—C. E. Eldridge (Mich.). Head linesman—Branch Rickey (Ohio Wesleyan). Time of quarters—10 minutes.

Michigan Wins by Scoring Touchdown Just Before Final Whistle, 6-3.

FARMERS COUNT ON GOAL

Opponents' Early Lead Causes Wolverines to Brace and Sweep Down the Field.

Michigan (6).		M. A. C. (3).
Borleske	L. E.	Montfort R. E.
Edmunds	L. T.	Pattison, Culver R. T.
Benbrook (captain)	L. G.	Leonardson R. G.
Bogle	C.	McWilliams C.
Conklin	R. G.	Baldwin L. G.
Wells	R. T.	Campbell L. T.
Pattengill	R. E.	Stone L. E.
McMillan	Q. B.	Ribbett Q. B.
Magidsohn	L. H. B.	Hill R. H. B.
Green	R. H. B.	Cortright (capt.) L. H. B.
Thompson	F. B.	Exelby F. B.

Touchdown—Green. Goal from touchdown—Conklin. Goal from field—Hill. Umpire—Jenkins. Referee—Hoaglund, Princeton. Head linesman—Rickey, Ohio Wesleyan. Field judge—Robbins, Nebraska.

OPINIONS OF COACHES.

COACH YOST.

We ought to have won. I think we have something on them. Still, I am well satisfied with the work of the team. Every man of them did splendid work and Michigan ought to be proud of them. The Pennsy team is one of the strongest that has ever represented that institution, but we had it on them at almost every point.

COACH SMITH, PENNSYLVANIA.

Michigan had the better team. Yost's men outplayed us from start to finish. I thought that our team was the strongest in the east, and I still cling to this belief, but Michigan showed us some football I did not think the west boasted of. All of our men were not in the best of shape, but I do not think we could have played better.

Ohio State

Michigan's eleven left the field trophy-less at Columbus yesterday, having been held to a 3 to 3 score by the Ohio State aggregation. It was the second time since the season opened that the Wolverines were played to a standstill by an Ohio team; and it was the third time that they failed entirely to show the class expected of them.

The Varsity's work was ragged in the extreme. The spectacle of backs wandering around the field seeking their proper places in the offensive formations while other players argued over the plays and signals, was all too frequently presented. Much of the play of the maize and blue representatives was characterized by a distressing listlessness. All of the men got together and played hard football part of the time, and a few of the men worked their hardest all of the time, but all of the men didn't fight as a determined unit all of the time.

Conklin's right boot gave Michigan her only score. On the only opportunity the husky guard was given, he booted the ball between the posts for the count that enabled the Wolverines to get away in the lead. The air route was resorted to only after many fruitless efforts to cross the Buckeye goal line; and while the Wolverines were within striking distance on several occasions after that, they kept on plugging for the touchdown they could not get.

Michigan (6).		Minnesota (0).
Borleske	L. E.	Frank R. E.
Conklin	L. T.	Young, Smith R. T.
Benbrook	L. G.	Robinson R. G.
Cornwell	C.	Morrell C.
Bogle	R. G.	Bromley L. G.
Edmunds	R. T.	Walker L. T.
Wells	R. E.	Pickering L. E.
McMillan	Q. B.	McGovern Q. B.
Magidsohn	L. H. B.	Rosenwald R. H. B.
Pattengill	R. H. B.	Stevens, Erdahl L. H. B.
Lawton	F. B.	Johnston F. B.

Score by periods.
Michigan .... 0 0 0 6—6
Minnesota .... 0 0 0 0—0
Touchdown—Wells. Goal from touchdown—Conklin. Umpire—Hinkey, Yale. Referee—Lieutenant Hackett, Army. Field judge—Ensley, Purdue. Head linesman—Starbuck, Cornell. Time of periods—Fifteen minutes.

THE CASE WITH MICHIGAN.

Michigan's cancellation of the Michigan-Notre Dame football game, which was to have been played at Ann Arbor last Saturday, has been the cause of much discussion here the past week. The trouble centered on our intention to play Dimmick and Philbrook, Michigan claiming that both these men were ineligible because of the fact that they had played out their time as collegiate football players. A review of the athletic career of both of these men shows that in 1904-'05 they were preparatory students in Tullatin academy and competed on teams there. The following year both men were students at Pearson's academy, an institution apart from Whitman college. In September, 1907, they registered at Whitman college, taking two freshman studies and three or four preparatory studies. Dimmick remained at Whitman until February, 1908, and Philbrook until June of the same year. Whitman college is not named in the list of conference colleges issued in September, 1907. Because of it is only reasonable to presume these men as participating in preparatory athletics prior to their coming to Notre Dame. On these grounds we maintain that Philbrook and Dimmick are eligible and will continue to hold these grounds. Last January when this game was arranged, Manager Curtis inquired as to whether we would be allowed to play these men in the game this fall, and Director of Athletics Bartelme gave his assurance that there would be no trouble on that score. Mr. Bartelme also assured Coach Longman to the same effect. The reason for Notre Dame's desire that this matter be settled was brought about by various reports which originated from the Michigan camp last fall, after the Notre Dame game, concerning the eligibility of these men.

The fact that Michigan sent down the names of Cole and Clarke as being eligible for this game leads to the one conclusion that they should consider Dimmick and Philbrook eligible, for Clarke and Cole, according to conference rules are ineligible, as Cole played the seasons of '05, '07, and '08 at Oberlin, and Clarke too has played his allotted time according to conference rule.

CASE PROVES EASY VICTIM FOR VARSITY

By Score of 24 to 0, Michigan Annexes Curtain Game of Football Season on Ferry Field.

GAME WITNESSED BY OVER 3,500.

Victors had Game All Through and Goal was Never in Danger.

Michigan answered the first curtain call of the 1911 football season yesterday with Case, old time and always respected opponents, the victims, 24 to 0. Four times "Bottles" Thomson finding himself across their line for a touch-down and four times Captain Conklin followed with tallies over the cross bar. From the opening call of play, it was Michigan all the way, and the lighter men Case met with complete failure in their attempt to furnish grounds for heart failure among the 3,500 who witnessed. A fast strong line, fair backfield work, and little if any of the fumbling that has marred the early games of late years were the big factors in the final result.

The Varsity Football Team
1911

WILLIAM J. LEARMONTH	Student Manager
FREDERIC L. CONKLIN	Captain
FIELDING H. YOST	Coach
ANDREW W. SMITH	Assistant Coach
CURTIS G. REDDEN	Assistant Coach
DR. ALVIN C. KRAENZLEIN	Trainer
PHIL G. BARTELME	Director of Out-door Athletics

THE TEAM

FREDERIC L. CONKLIN (captain)	Tackle and End
GEORGE C. THOMPSON (captain elect)	Full Back
THOMAS BOGLE	Guard and Tackle
STANFIELD M. WELLS	End and Half
CLEMENT P. QUINN	Guard and Tackle
NEIL McMILLAN	Quarter Back
MILLER H. PONTIUS	End
JAMES B. CRAIG	Half
GEORGE C. PATERSON	Center
HOWARD S. KAYNER	Tackle and Guard
OTTO C. CARPELL	Half
ALLAN E. GARRELLS	Guard and End
HERBERT H. HUEBEL	Half
RICHARD C. MEEK	Full Back
FRANK A. PICARD	Quarter Back
ROY H. TORBET	Half

24 Case	0	9 Vanderbilt	8	0 Cornell	6
15 M.A.C.	3	6 Syracuse	6	11 Pennsylvania	9
19 Ohio State	0			6 Nebraska	6

Michigan 90; Opponents 38
Won 5; Tied 2; Lost 1

FARMERS FALL BEFORE ATTACK OF WOLVERINES

Michigan Wins Decisively in The Last Quarter, Coming From Behind With an Overwhelming Rush.

15 TO 3 SCORE TELLS TALE.

Aggies Fight Desperately but Weight, Condition an Skill Tip The Balance.

As The Coaches Look at it.

Coach Yost. "I can't say that I am tickled but am pleased with the general result. I think that the score fairly represents the relative ability of the two teams. The line was fair. Maybe is was because we were up against a better team than we anticipated that the line did not come up to what we expected it would. Craig is a half back from now on I thought in the first half that I would need to look for another full back but I have changed my mind."

Coach Macklin. "Our men did all that I expected them to. I am satisfied. They could not stand up against the heavier team and that is the reason we lost."

Wolverines Capture Fiercely Fought Contest with Score of 9 to 8; Battle Featured by See-Saw of Points

CRAIG STARS FOR MICHIGAN

Snappy Half Tears off Sensational 80 Yard Run and Displays Best Form of Year.

OHIO BRAVES FALL BEFORE WOLVERINES

Varsity's Superior Endurance Turns Tine of Hard Battle at Critical Stage of Game. Score 19 to 0.

WHAT THE COACHES SAY.

We were defeated—that's all. As to the Michigan team, I have nothing to say. I have all that I can do to attend to my own. Possibly my boys were out-weighed.
Vaughn.

It was a fairly well fought game Ohio was plucky; they fought when their line was being torn to pieces. We made lots of mistakes and our play was far from being satisfactory. There was some improvement over last week but there is room for a lot more.
Yost.

Played to a standstill by the Vanderbilt eleven yesterday afternoon, Michigan was lucky to escape a tie and come out of it on the right end of a 9 to 8 score. The southern Yellow Jackets nearly stung the Wolverines, and but for a misdirected punt-out, they would have been in line to total 9 for themselves. As it was there was not a moment when they were not threatening to turn the slender margin the other way, and in the last minute of the game they played better football than Michigan.

Michigan	Position	Vanderbilt
Conklin(Capt)	L.E.	K. Morrison
Bogle	L.T.	Freeland Covington
Quinn	L.G.	Metzger
Paterson	C.	Morgan
Garrels	R.G.	C. Brown
Pontius	R.T.	T. Brown
Wells	R.E.	E. Brown
McMillan	Q.	R. Morrison (Capt.)
Craig	L.H.	Hardage
Thomson	F.B.	Sikes
Carpel	R.H.	Collins, Curlin

Officials—Referee, Bradley Walker, Virginia; Umpire, Eckersall, Chicago; Field Judge, Lieut. Nelley, West Point; Head Linesman, Heston, Michigan.

EASTERN MEN PLAY VARSITY TO TIE SCORE

Mediocre Playing of Michigan Combined With Many Injuries, Results in Drawn Battle; Score 6-6.

CRAIG IS SERIOUSLY INJURED.

Speedy Back May Possibly be out of the Game for the Remainder of the Season.

Playing a ragged game of football against a team trained to the minute and fighting like demons, Michigan deprived herself of a clear record and was forced to agree to a tie with Syracuse on Saturday. The result was a surprise and disappointment to even the most pessimistic of the Wolverine followers and Michigan must show a sudden reversal for the better if they are to trim Cornell next Saturday.

WHAT THE COACHES SAID

Cummings:—"Yes, I'm satisfied. I agree with the officials—it was a nice, clean game."

"I think Michigan displayed the finest spirit I've seen on a college field, today, when the lone Syracuse rooter was applauded. It was the real college stuff."

"The prettiest thing in the game was the way Cassell heeled the Syracuse punt-out. It certainly saved the game for us."

Redden:—"Injuries were the primary cause of Michigan's poor showing. Injuries to McMillan, Craig, Pontius and Quinn played havoc with the team. Garrells was injured, too, though I had intended substituting Smith for him, anyway.

"If we had played the whole game like we did the first ten or the last five minutes, though, we would have beaten Syracuse 30 to 0. We gained enough ground to do it. We gained 10 yards to their one. The boys make a touchdown and then let up—think they've got the game on ice. We'll never have a team till the players get over that spirit."

CORNELL WAS LUCKY TO WIN

MICHIGAN LOST TO THE RED TEAM ON FLUKE.

THOMSON'S PUNT BLOCKED AND EASTERNER FELL ON THE BALL.

ITHACA, N. Y., Nov. 13.—Michigan lost a heart-breaking game to Cornell on Percy field Saturday afternoon by a score of 6 to 0. For two quarters the two elevens had battled fiercely, and neither side seemed to have an advantage, although Michigan kept the ball in the Red territory much of the time. Towards the close of the third quarter, Thomson had dropped behind his own own goal line for a punt out. The left wing of the Michigan line gave way, and Thomson's kick was blocked, a Cornell man falling on the ball as it bounded over the last white chalk line.

MICHIGAN.		CORNELL.
Conklin (capt.)	L. E	Eyrich
Quinn	L. T	Munk (capt.)
Kaynor	L. G	O'Rourke
Paterson	C	J. S. Whyte
Garrels	R. G	Munns
Bogle	R. T	Champalgn
Pontius, Meek	R. E	Fritz
Picard	Q	Butler
Carpell	L. B	O'Connor,
Wells	R.	Collins
	B.	R. B. Whyte
Thomson	F.	Underhill

Final score: Cornell 6, Michigan 0. First quarter: Michigan 0, Cornell 0; second quarter: Michigan 0, Cornell 0; third quarter: Michigan 0, Cornell 6; fourth quarter, Michigan 0, Cornell 6. Touchdowns—Fritz. Goals from touchdowns—Butler. Referee—Dave Fultz, Brown. Umpire—A. H. Sharpe, Yale. Field judge—Louis Tinkey, Yale. Head linesman—W. C. Booth, Princeton. Time of quarters—15 minutes.

Captain Mercer's Spectacular Dashes Through Mud and Snow Thrill Crowd of 17,000.

QUAKERS UNLUCKY

Jourdet Scores Touchdown On Brilliant Play at Start But It Is Disallowed.

By Telegraph from a Staff Correspondent. Ann Arbor, Mich., Nov. 18.—Old Penn succumbed to a combined attack of Michigan football and Michigan weather in her annual game with the Middle Western University this afternoon on Ferry Field. The Maize and Blue aided by the blizzard which raced down from the west carrying with it snow, nosed out a victory in the final period, the score reading 11 to 9. A crowd of 17,000 saw the game.

The spurt of the Wolverines, when even her stanchest rooters appeared to have lost hope, caught the Red and Blue jaded after the battle against eleven huskier men, the wind, the snow and the soft treacherous footing. Penn was leading at the time, but Michigan mustered her last forces and pushed across another touchdown, carrying with it victory.

The blizzard was true in intensity to all the storms of its kind for which Michigan and the Great Lakes Region are famed. Three hours before the game started the wind began and it blew a gale. Then when the game came near the wind brought along a flurry of snow. This was increased as the game progressed and the field was covered with a thin white mantle, which interfered with the speed of Penn and her fleet backs.

Michigan (11)	Position	Penn (9)
Conklin, (Capt)	L.E.	Young Stuart
Quinn	L.T.	Dillon
Kaynor	L.G.	Wolferth
Paterson	C.	Morris
Garrells	R.G.	Findheisen
Bogle	R.T.	Bell
Torbet, Carpell	R.E.	Jourdet
McMillan	Q.	Minds
Craig	L.H.	Thayer, Marshall, Barr
Meek	F.B.	Mercer (Capt)
Wells, Huebel	R.H.	Kennedy

Touchdowns—Wells, Craig, Mercer. Goals from touchdowns—Conklin 1, Minds 1. Goal from drop kick—Marshall 1.

Officials—Referee, Pendleton, Bowdoin; umpire, Sharpe, Yale; field judge, Eckersall, Chicago; headlinesmna, Booth, Princeton. Time of quarters 15 minutes.

Nebraska (6)		Michigan (6)
Chauner	L.E.	Conklin (Capt)
Shonka (Capt)	L.T.	Quinn
Pearson	L.G.	Kaynor
Elliot	C.	Paterson
Hornberger	R.G.	Garrells, Almendinger
Harmon	R.T.	Bogle
Lofgren	R.E.	Herrington, Carpell
Warner	Q.B.	McMillan
D. Frank	L.H.	Craig
E. Frank	R.H.	H. Smith
Gibson	F.B.	Thomson

Referee—Stuart, Michigan.
Umpire—Hickey, Yale.
Field Judge—Ver Weibe, Harvard.
Head Linesman—Williams, Indiana.
Touchdowns—Conklin, Purdy.
Goals from Touchdown—Conklin, O. Frank.
Time of Quarters—15 minutes.

Thompson - 1912

MICHIGAN 34.   CASE 0.
Pontius, Pierson,
Wyman ....L. E...........Callender
Cole, Mussen ......L. T...........Rosendale
Clem Quinn ......L. G...........Parsons
Paterson ....C...........Whelan
Almendinger ......R. G...........Randall
Raynsford,
McHale ....R. T...........Whitehouse
Barr......... .....R. E......Francy (capt.)
Huebel, Boyle,
Bushnell ....Q...........Goss
Craig, Hughitt.....L. H......Parshall, Powell
Thomson (capt.)
Cyril Quinn ......F...........Marsh
Carpell, Torbet,...R. H...........Kenyon
Collett ....R. H...........Parshall
  Score—First quarter: Michigan 14, Case
0. Second: Michigan 7, Case 6. Third:
Michigan 0, Case 0. Fourth: Michigan 13,
Case 0. Total: Michigan 34, Case 0.
Touchdowns—Thomson 2, Huebel, Craig,
Bushnell. Goals from touchdown—Patter-
son 4. Time of quarters—15 minutes. Of-
ficials—Referee, Hoagland, Princeton; um-
pire, Halnes, Yale; head linesman, Per-
rine, Iowa.

35 Case 0   14 Ohio State 0   21 Pennsylvania ...27
55 M.A.C. 7   7 Syracuse 18   20 Cornell 7
                    7 South Dakota .. 6
            Michigan 159; Opponents 65
                 Won 5; Tied 0; Lost 2

OHIO STATE HUMBLED BY WARRIORS FROM MICHIGAN

YOST'S MEN RUN UP HIGH SCORE AGAINST AGGIES

Michigan Wins Annual Contest 55 to 7—Intercepted
Forward Pass and 85-Yard Run by B. Miller
Gives M. A. C. Only Chance to Count.

MICHIGAN, 7; SYRACUSE, 18

Syracuse upset all expectations of the
dopesters by defeating Michigan by a score
18-7. The condition of the field literally
covered with pools of water after an all
night's rain, probably contributed to the
outcome, as far as Michigan was concerned. But somehow or other it didn't
seem to affect Castle, the wonderful Syracuse back.

Michigan started the scoring by carrying
the ball down the field for a touchdown,
in the first three minutes of play. The
points including one for goal, remained
this way until the end of the second quarter, when Syracuse scored a touchdown
but failed to kick the goal. The third and
fourth quarters added six more points each
to the Syracuse total. These arose in both
cases after Michigan had lost the ball on
fumbles. Several other times Michigan
threatened to score, but in each instance
was held for downs within a few yards of
the Syracuse goal.

VICTORY WRESTED FROM WOLVERINES IN LAST QUARTER

Marshall's Dash Through Entire Maize and Blue
Eleven Cinches Game That Looked Lost
to Sons of Penn.

ONE TIME MICHIGAN HOLDS LEAD OF TWENTY-ONE POINTS

Yost's Men Go to Pieces in Closing Stages and Are
Powerless to Stop Rush of Enemy—
Score Is 27 to 21.

CORNELL, 7; MICHIGAN, 20

In the last football contest of the season
Michigan defeated Cornell by a score of
20 to 7. Contrary, perhaps, to expectations
the game was characterized by a display of
football tactics far above mediocre. Both
institutions were represented on Ferry
Feld by line-ups more capable than their
previous records would indicate.

Michigan.		Cornell.
Torbet................	L.E.	Eyrich
Cole.................	L.T.	Geyer
Quinn...............	L.G.	Munns
Paterson............	C.	Whyte
Allmendinger / Raynsford	R.G.	Champaign
Musser..............	R.T.	Nash
Pontius.............	R.E.	O'Hearn
Huebel.............	Q.	Butler (Capt)
Craig / Collette	L.H.	O'Connor / Taber
Hughitt............	R.H.	Bennett
Thomson (Capt.).....	F.B.	Hill

Referee—Hackett, West Point; Head Linesman
—Pendleton, Bowdoin.

Philadelphia, November 9.—The
Pennsylvania worm turned.

Three touchdowns by Michigan
before the Quakers scored a point
ought to have beaten the sons of
Old Penn today, or at least ought
to have discouraged them. Three
touchdowns did nothing of the sort..
On the contrary, the early advantage secured by the Wolverines
only seemed to furnish the inspiration that the Red and Blue had
lacked previously. With apparently certain defeat, and that by an
overwhelming score, staring them
in the face, the Pennsylvania men
began to fight, and they kept on
fighting until the final whistle
blew.

Four touchdowns, the last of
which was scored in the final minute of play by Quarterback Marshall, who ran 50 yards through
the entire Ann Arbor team, gave
Penn a victory that will live forever in the memories of those who
witnessed the contest as the finest
exhibition of gameness ever witnessed on the gridiron.

Had the result and the manner
of its achievement been reversed,
Philadelphia would have been no
place for a sane man tonight; as
it is, they have turned out the
fire department, the militia and the
police reserves to keep the Penna.
students from making a bonfire of
the city hall, and that even more
sacred edifice, the Broad street station of the Pennsylvania railroad.

MICHIGAN.

Player.	Position.	Age.	Weight.	Year.
Raynsford	L.E.	22	170	Second
Musser	L.T.	22	200	Second
Traphagen	L.G.	21	178	First
Paterson, Capt.	C.	22	210	Third
Allmendinger	R.G.	23	198	Second
Pontius	R.T.	22	190	Third
Lyons	R.E.	21	170	First
Hughitt	Q.B.	20	144	Second
Craig	L.H.	20	158	Third
Torbet	F.B.	24	172	Third
Galt	R.H.	22	162	First

Average age—21½ years.   Average weight line—188.
Average weight—177½.   Average weight backfield—159.

1913 Season   Won 6, Lost 1, Tied 0

				Date	Place
Michigan 48,	Case	0		Oct 4	Ann Arbor
Michigan 14,	Mount Union	0		Oct 11	Ann Arbor
Michigan 7,	Michigan State	12		Oct 18	Ann Arbor
Michigan 33,	Vanderbilt	2		Oct 25	Nashville
Michigan 43,	Syracuse	7		Nov 1	Ann Arbor
Michigan 17,	Cornell	0		Nov 8	Ithaca
Michigan 13,	Pennsylvania	0		Nov 15	Ann Arbor

CAPT. PATERSON

MICHIGAN'S FOOTBALL SQUAD, 1913.

Top Row:—Cole, ass't coach; Bennett, ass't coach; Bentley, Traphagen, Lyons, James, Benton, Tessin, Quinn, McHale, "Steve" Farrell, trainer, Meade, "Germany" Schultz, ass't coach, Redden, ass't coach.
Middle Row:—Fielding H. Yost, head coach, Hughitt, Musser, Craig, Torbet, Paterson, captain, Pontius, Allmendinger, Raynsford, Bushnell.
Bottom Row:—Bastian, Cochran, Catlett, Watson, Galt, Lichtner.

MICHIGAN.		CASE.
Torbet-Tessin	L. E.	Boley-Allen
Musser- Raynsford	L. T.	Zellner
Lichtner-Morse	L. G.	Perkins
Paterson-Lichtner	C.	Whelan
Allmindinger- Cochran	Mitchell- R. G.	Byers-Diver
Pontius-Millard	R. T.	Horslet-Callender
Lyons-James	R. E.	Kenyon
Hughitt-Galt	Q. B.	Parshall
Catlett-Watson- Roehm	L. H.	Jenkins
Galt-Diehl	R. H.	Whitacre
Bentley-Quinn	F. B.	Bentley
Touchdowns—Bentley 2, Hughitt 2, Lyons, Watson 1, Paterson 1. Goals from touchdown—Paterson 6. Score end first half—34 to 0. Time of quarters—15 minutes. Referee—Hougland, Princeton. Umpire—Henry Kenyon. Head linesman—Conklin, Michigan.		

MICHIGAN.		M. A. C.
Torbet	L. E.	Schulz
Musser	L. T.	G. E. Smith
Traphagen- Lichtner	L. G.	Leonardson
Paterson (capt.)	C.	Vaughn
Allmenanger	R. G.	McCurdy-Kurtz- Worth-Pohan
Raynsford	R. T.	(capt.) Giffor
Lyons	R. E.	Hennig
Hughitt-Roehm	Q. B.	Gauthier
Catlett-Bastian	L. H.	H. Blakemiller-Miller
Bentley	R. H.	Blacklock
Pontius	F. B.	Julian
Touchdowns—Julian 1, Gauthier 1, Bastian 1. Goals from touchdown—Paterson 1. Time of quarters—12 minutes. Referee—Hougland, Princeton. Umpire—Knight, Dartmouth. Head linesman—Drew.		

DESPERATE RALLY IN CLOSING MINUTES BY WOLVERINES IS SHORT

Aggies Thwart Attack of Maize and Blue and at Whistle Have Enemy in Own Territory—Michigan's Only Score Comes Late in Final Period, Following Fumble by Gauthier—Macklin's Backfield Crushes Heavier Line of Opponents.

Special to The Free Press.

ANN ARBOR, MICH., OCTOBER 18.—Fourteen real football players, entirely surrounded by about 1,000 frenziedly happy rooters from Michigan Agricultural college, journeyed back to Lansing tonight with the first victory over the Wolverine in the history of the game securely tucked away in their vest pockets by a score of 12 to 7.

The combat which resulted in the near-insanity of the Aggie rooters occurred on Ferry field this afternoon before a throng which numbered nearly 8,000 persons, over half of whom were attendants of the University of Michigan, and securely convinced that their football team was going to be an easy winner over their old foe, the Farmer.

The result is that tonight Ann Arbor is enshrouded in a pall of gloom which is none the less thick because they were beaten by a superior eleven.

Ann Arbor Men Play With Dash and Vim That Make Them Seem Like New Team.

BY E. A. BATCHELOR.

NASHVILLE, Tenn., October 25.—There is no other tonic quite so beneficial to a football team as a good beating properly applied.

Michigan proved this today when an eleven constituted in the main like the one which last Saturday allowed the M. A. C. huskies to walk all over it, peeled the hide off the fiery Vanderbilt Commodores and gave them a beating in terms of 33 to 2. It was the most decisive victory that the Wolverines ever have scored over this respected and formidable foe.

Reprinted with permission from the **Detroit Free Press**

MICHIGAN 43, SYRACUSE 7.

MICHIGAN (43).		SYRACUSE (7).
Lichtner	L. E.	Robbins
Tessin		Woodruff
		Hilfinger
Musser	L. T.	McElligott
Traphagen		Armstrong
Cochran	L. G.	White
Paterson	C.	Shafelt, Ransier
Alldemlinger		
McHale	R. G.	Rabbit
Pontius		Propst
Raynsford	R. T.	Trigg
Lyons, James	R. E.	Track, Ferber
Hughitt, Bushnell	Q.	Seymour
Craig, Catlet		Castle
Bastis	L. H.	Johnson
Galt, Bentley	R. H.	Rose, Kingsley
Quinn, Mead		Forsyth
Benton	F. B.	Wakefield

Referee—Haines, Yale. Umpire—Hinkey, Yale. Head linesman—Lach, Brown. Time of quarters, 15 minutes. Touchdowns—Craig 4, Hughitt 3, Travis. Goals from touchdown—Paterson 5, Castle 1. Safety—Seymour. Score end of first half—Michigan 25, Syracuse 0.

Referee Eckersall Explains Why Penn Didn't Make Safety

Ann Arbor, Mich., November 15.—Near the end of the game many of the spectators thought that Michigan should have been given an additional two points for what appeared to be a safety made by Pennsylvania.

Michigan punted, and a Penn man touched the ball, which then rolled over the goal line and was recovered by another Quaker. Referee Eckersall ruled that the momentum impetus which sent the ball over the line did not come from the man who touched it in the field of play, but from the kicker, and that it therefore was a touchback instead of a safety. The rules say that when the ball crosses the goal line from impetus furnished by one of the defending side and is there recovered by one of the defending side, a safety shall be scored.

Jimmy Craig came within an ace of securing the ball on this occasion, in which event it would have been a touchdown.

$2,000 Worth of Ticket Money Sent Back—No Seats

ANN ARBOR, Mich., Nov. 19—Director Bartelme today refunded almost $2,000 to people who had written for seats for the Pennsy game. Most of the disappointed people are Detroiters. All of the $2 seats, 15,253 in number, have been sold, and most of the 680 boxes have been reserved.

FINAL SCORE—MICHIGAN 17, CORNELL 0.

MICHIGAN.		CORNELL.
Lichtner-Raynsford	L. E.	Ross
Musser	L. T.	Guyer-Collyer
Traphagen	L. G.	(capt.) Munns
Paterson (capt.)	C.	Conf
Allmendinger	R. G.	Hyland
		Mallory
Pontius-Cochran	R. T.	Williamson
Lyons-James	R. E.	Mehaffey
Hughitt	Q. B.	Shuler
Craig-Bushnell	L. H.	Barrett
Galt	R. H.	Fritz
Torbet-Quinn	F. B.	Shelton-Lahr

Final score—Michigan 17, Cornell 0. First quarter—Michigan 7, Cornell 0. Second quarter—Michigan 7, Cornell 0. Third quarter—Michigan 17, Cornell 0. Touchdowns—Craig, Hughitt. Goals from touchdown—Paterson 2. Goal from placement—Paterson. Referee—Pendleton, Bowdoin. Umpire—Hinkey, Yale. Head linesman—O'Keeson, Lehigh. Time of quarters—minutes.

Camp's All-America Eleven

Hogsett, Dartmouth	End
Ballin, Princeton	Tackle
Pennock, Harvard	Guard
Des Jardien, Chicago	Center
Brown, Navy	Guard
Talbot, Yale	Tackle
Merrilat, Army	End
Huntington, Colgate	Quarter
Craig, Michigan	Halfback
Brickley, Harvard	Halfback
Mahan, Harvard	Fullback

MICHIGAN RUSHES BOWL OVER PENN IN WEST BY 13 TO 0

Red and Blue Linemen Waver Before Driving Attack of Wolverines in First Half When Jimmie Craig Races for Touchdown on Two Occasions

25,000 SEE STRUGGLE END IN RAIN

Old Penn's eleven met with its second defeat of the 1913 football season, yesterday afternoon. Coach "Hurry Up" Yost and his Michigan warriors giving the Red and Blue a 13 to 0 defeat in the annual gridiron battle at Ann Arbor. Failure of the Quaker line to live up to its reputation caused the defeat for the plunging backs of the Wolverines broke through the Red and Blue first line of defense like battering rams.

James Craig
Halfback
1913

CAPT. RAYNSFORD

Player	Position	Age	Height	Weight	Year
L. H. Benton	L.E.	24	5.11	165	1
Lewis Reimann	L.T.	22	5.11	184	1
Frank McHale	L.G.	23	5.11	212	2
James Raynsford (Capt.)	C.	23	6.	187	3
Robert Watson	R.G.	21	5.9	174	2
Wm. Cochran	R.T.	21	5.8	224	2
Karl Staatz	R.E.	22	6.	178	2
M. F. Dunne	R.E.	20	6.	164	1
E. F. Hughitt	Q.B.	21	5.8	146	3
John Maulbetsch	L.H.	22	5.8	168	1
Lamar Splawn	F.B.	21	5.11	167	1
John J. Lyons	R.H.	21	6.	180	2
C. E. Bastian	R.H.	22	5.10	178	2

Average age—21.
Total weight—1985.
Average weight—180 5-11.
Average weight of line—174 6-7.
Average weight of back field—165 1-4.

Substitutes

Thos. H. Bushnell	Q.B.
E. W. James	End
Lawrence Roehm	H.B.
John Bland Catlett	F.B.
E. L. Bentley	H.B.
John K. Norton	L.G.
F. J. Millard	L.G.
Walter Niemann	C.
R. R. Huebel	Q.B.
J. L. Whalen	R.E.
F. L. Rehor	L.G.
H. M. Zieger	Q.B.
S. R. McNamara	Q.B.
F. D. Quail	R.G.
C. O. Skinner	C.
M. H. Galt	H.B.
F. C. Morse	C.

1914

Michigan	58	DePauw	0
Michigan	69	Case	0
Michigan	27	Mount Union	7
Michigan	23	Vanderbilt	3
Michigan	3	M.A.C.	0
Michigan	6	Syracuse	20
Michigan	0	Harvard	7
Michigan	34	Pennsylvania	3
Michigan	13	Cornell	28

Season Summary
Games won, 6; Lost, 3; Tied, 0;
Points for Michigan 233; For Opponents 68.

CORNER STONE OF STADIUM IS LAID

Laying the literal corner stone of the new stadium on Ferry field, Engineer Weeks' men, yesterday, poured concrete for the foundation footing of the tallest support, that in the southeast corner, which will be 63 feet high. The filling with concrete of the foundation holes will be commenced tomorrow, and will be completed in about ten days.

Work will probably start on the super-structure in another week. The 100-foot derrick, which is being erected just behind the site of the big stand for use in elevating the concrete, has reached half its height.

From 15 to 20 carpenters will be added this week to the total force of about 30 men now employed.

MICHIGAN (58)		DePauw (0)
Staatz, Dunne	L.E.	Woodruff
Reimann, Benton		
Finkbeiner	L.T.	Northway
Quail, Norton		
Morse	L.G.	Sefton
Raynsford, capt.		
Niemann	C.	Meredith
Millard, Whalen		
Graven	R.G.	Cochran
Cochran, Hildner	R.T.	Dunn
Lyons, E. James		
D. James	R.E.	Sharpe
Hughitt, Zieger	Q.B.	Anderson, Bittle
Maulbetsch, Cohn	L.H.G.	Thomas, capt.
Splawn, Catlett		
Mead	F.B.	Ade, Harvey
Bastian, Roehm		
Bentley	R.H.B.	Thomas, Pence

The line-up:
Touchdowns—Maulbetsch 2, Splawn 2, Hughitt 2, Lyons, Cohn. Goals from touchdown—Hughitt 6, Bastian, Mead. Goal from drop kick—Splawn.

Score:

	First Quarter	Second Quarter	Third Quarter	Fourth Quarter
Michigan	7	23	21	7
DePauw	0	0	0	0

Officials: Referee — Kennedy, Chicago. Umpire—Lynch, Brown. Head linesman—Knight, Michigan.
Time of quarters—12, 10, 12 and 10 mins.

MICHIGAN		CASE
Dunne	L.E.	Howard
Reimann	L.T.	Cullen
Quail	L.G.	Mitchell
Raynsford (capt.)	C.	Kretchman
Whalen	R.G.	Hellencamp
Cochran	R.T.	Conant
Lyons	R.E.	Allan
Hughitt	Q.B.	Post
Maulbetsch	L.H.	Anderson
Roehm	R.H.	Black
Splawn	F.B.	Fiber

Score by quarters:

Michigan	21	20	21	7 — 69
	0	0	0	0 — 0

Touchdowns—Roehm 2, Maulbetsch 2, Lyons, Catlett 2, Hughitt 2. Goals from touchdown—Hughitt 5.

Substitutions—Benton for Whalen, Capt. Marshall for Post; Catlett for Splawn; Bastian for Roehm; Staatz for Dunne; Benton for Bastian, Millard for Whalen, Hildner for Lyons; Ovington for Kretch; Finkbeiner for Reimann; Zieger for Hughitt; Mead for Catlett; Niemann for Raynsford; House for Howard; Splawn for Mead; E. W. James for Staatz; Graven for Hildner; Cohn for Maulbetsch; Ben James for E. James; Morse for Millard; Norton for Benton.

Referee—Ralph Hoagland, of Princeton. Umpire—J. D. Henry, of Kenyon. Head linesman—William Knight, of Michigan. Time of quarters—10 minutes.

Michigan (27)		Mt. Union (7)
Staatz	LE	Stambaugh
Reimann	LT	Beck (C)
Watson	LG	Peterson, McLain, Peterson
Raynsford (C)	C	Thorpe
Whalen	RG	Bletzer
Cochran	RT	Marlowe
Lyons	RE	West
Hughitt, McNamara, Zieger	QB	Wilson
Maulbetsch	LH	Geltz
Splawn	FB	Lovell
Roehm, Catlett	RH	Thompson

Score	1	2	3	4	Final
Michigan	10	10	7	0	27
Mount Union	0	0	0	7	7

Touchdowns—Maulbetsch 2, Splawn, Wilson; goals from touchdown—Hughitt 2, Splawn, Bletzer; goals from field—Splawn 2; officials: Referee—W. C. Kennedy, Chicago; umpire—Leigh Lynch, Brown; Head Linesman—William Knight, Michigan; time of quarters—12, 10, 12, and 4 minutes. (Last quarter shortened six minutes by referee on account of darkness.)

MICHIGAN		VANDERBILT
Staatz	L.E.	Putnam
Reimann	L.T.	Cody
Quail	L.G.	Beckleheimer
Raynsford (capt.)	C.	Huffman
Watson	R.G.	Brown
Cochran	R.T.	Warren
Lyons	R.E.	Cohen
Hughitt	Q.B.	Curry
Maulbetsch	L.H.	(capt.) Sikes
Roehm	R.H.	Morrison
Splawn	F.B.	Carman

Score by quarters:

Michigan	7	9	0	7 — 23
Vanderbilt	3	0	0	0 — 3

Touchdowns—Hughitt 1, Maulbetsch 2. Goals from touchdown—Hughitt 2. Goals from field—Cody 1, Splawn 1. Substitutions—Liscomb for Beckleheimer; Putnam for Carman; Chester for Putnam; McHale for Watson; Catlett for Roehm; James for Lyons; Benton for Quail; Hildner for Staatz, Carman for Cody; Bastian for Splawn; Whalen for Reimann; Skinner for Raynsford; Royer for Brown; Zieger for Hughitt. Referee—Bradley Walker, Virginia. Umpire—J. C. Holterness, of Lehigh. Head linesman—William Heston, of Michigan. Time of quarters—15 minutes.

MICHIGAN.   M. A. C.
Staatz ....L. E......Blake Miller
Reimann ....L. T.........Smith
Rehor ....L. G........Straight
Raynsford (capt.)...C.........Vaughn
McHale ....R. G.....Vandervoort
Cochran ....R. T......Blacklock
Lyons ....R. E.......Chaddock
Hughitt ....Q. B....Dutch Miller
Maulbetsch ....L. H........Deprato
Bushnell ....R. H.......H. Miller
Splawn ....F. B.....(capt.) Julian

Score by quarters:
                     1   2   3   4 Tot
Michigan ....
M. A. C. 0   0   0   0 0

Substitutions—Roehm for Bushnell; Ren
ton for Staatz; Huebel for Hughitt, Hugh
itt for Huebel; Watson for Reimann; Ca
lett for Roehm, James for Lyons, Rehor
for Benton, Roehm for Catlett, Catlett for
Splawn; Huebel for Hughitt. Goal from
field—Splawn. Referee—Hackett, of West
Point. Umpire—Holderness, of Lehigh.
Field judge—Haines, of Yale. Head lineman—Gardner, of Cornell. Time of quarters 15 minutes.

Over 800 Wolverines Buy Tickets for Big Battle at Cambridge

ANN ARBOR, Mich., Oct. 19.
Athletic Director Bartelme today reported that 800 tickets
to the Harvard game had already been sold to Michigan students and alumni from the
local office. The Pennsylvania
and Cornell pasteboards are going even more rapidly and the
indications are that the Ferry
field stands will be taxed to
their capacity for both the big
games this fall.
The stadium stand is now
practically completed, although
the paint is not yet dry on
some of the west sections. The
new structure will be dedicated
at the time of the Pennsylvania
game.

MICHIGAN.   PENN.
Benton ............L.E.........Hopkins
Reimann ...........L.T.........Henning
McHale ............L.G.........Norwald
Raynsford, capt. ..R.G......Journeay, capt.
Watson ............R.G.........Dorizas
Cochran ...........R.T.........Harris
Staatz ............R.E........Urquhart
Hughitt ...........Q.B.........Merrill
Maulbetsch ........L.H.........Vreeland
Splawn ............F.B.........Tucker
Bastian ...........R.H.........Mathews

Score:
              1st Q. 2nd Q. 3rd Q. 4th Q.
Michigan ..   0   20   14   0—34
Pennsylvania   3   0   0   0— 3
Touchdowns—Maulbetsch 2, Hughitt,
Catlett and Benton. Goals from touch-
down—Hughitt 4. Goal from field—Ma-
thews.
Substitutions — Michigan, Staatz for
Lyons, Catlett for Bastian, Huebel for
Splawn, Bushnell for Catlett. Pennsyl-
vania, Withrow for Norwald, Wrag for

MICHIGAN (13).   CORNELL (28).
Benton ............L.E.........Shelton
Reimann ...........L.T.........Gallogly
McHale ............L.G.........Munsick
Raynsford, capt. ..C............Cool
Watson ............R.G........Anderson
Cochran ...........R.T.........Allen
Staatz ............R.E....O'Hearn, capt.
Hughitt ...........Q.B.........Barrett
Maulbetsch ........L.H........Schuler
Splawn ............F.B..........Hill
Bastian ...........R.H.........Collyer

Score by periods:
Michigan 6   7   0   0—13
Cornell 0   6   13   9—28
Touchdowns—Phillippi (2), Collyer, Bar-
rett, Maulbetsch, Staatz. Goals from
touchdown—Hughitt, Barrett. Goals from
field—Barrett. Substitutions: Michigan—
Catlett for Bastian, Dunne for Benton.
Cornell—Tilley for Munsick, Phillippi for
Hill, Jameson for Gallogly, Phillippi for
Schuler, Hill for Phillippi, McCutcheon for
Anderson, Anderson for Tilley, Collins for
Barrett, Schuler for Collyer. Officials:
Referee—Joseph Pendleton, Bowdoin. Um-
pire—Lewis Hinckey, Yale. Field judge—
E. C. Holderness, Lehigh. Head linesman
—Lieut. N. A. Prince, West Point. Time
of quarters—15 minutes.

YOST HAS THE RIGHT DOPE ON T. HARDWICK

Calls Him "World's Greatest Foot Ball Player" Before Contest Begins; His Touchdown Beats Michigan But Maulbetsch Outplays Him.

By HAP CHURCH.
(From a Staff Correspondent.)

BOSTON, Mass., Oct. 31—
"Tacks" Hardwick, the man
man whom Yost said before
the game was the best foot ball
player in America today, was the
Harvard man who scored the seven
points against Michigan. Although really an end, Hardwick is
a wonderful back, and next to
Maulbetsch, was the star of the
game. Hardwick was repeatedly
stopped by the Wolverine forwards, however, and did not come
any where near Maulbetsch's total
of ground gained.
He is probable as remarkable an
all around player as the game ever
saw, in Yost's opinion, and his

work proved it. He caught punts,
kicked them, played the star ground
gaining game for his team, and
tossed forward passes without a miss.
Despite the prevalence of the idea
that the west plays open foot ball and
the east the conservative kicking
game, Harvard alone gained on forward passes, and Michigan outgained
the crimson on kicks. Harvard made
the perfect tosses for a total gain of
forty yards. Michigan's one attempt
was high, and slipped off the finger
tips of the intended receiver into
Logan's arms.

COCHRAN TO LEAD TEAM NEXT YEAR

John Maulbetsch
Halfback

MICHIGAN SCORING, 1914.
                Touch- Goals from Goals from To-
Player.   downs. Touchdowns. Field.   tal.
Maulbetsch...   12   0   0   72
Hughitt.....   6   22   0   58
Splawn......   4   1   5   40
Catlett.....   3   0   0   18
Roehm.......   2   0   0   12
Fenton......   1   0   0   6
Staatz......   1   0   0   6
Lyons.......   1   0   0   6
Dunne.......   1   0   0   6
Cohn........   0   2   0   8
Bastian.....   0   1   0   1
Mead........   0   1   0   1
                ---   ---   ---   ---
Totals....   32   25   5   232

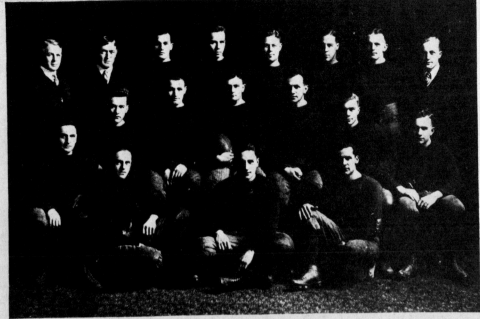

UNIVERSITY OF MICHIGAN FOOTBALL TEAM, 1915

TOP ROW: BARTELME, DIRECTOR OF ATHLETICS; FARRELL, TRAINER; DUNNE, WESKE, REHOR, SMITH, WHALEN, COMPTON, STUDENT MGR.
MIDDLE ROW: ROEHM, STAATZ, MILLARD, COCHRAN, CAPT., NORTON, WATSON, CATLETT.
BOTTOM ROW: NIEMANN, BASTIAN, MAULBETSCH.

1915			
Michigan	39	Lawrence	0
Michigan	35	Mt. Union	0
Michigan	28	Marietta	6
Michigan	14	Case	3
Michigan	0	M.A.C.	24
Michigan	7	Syracuse	14
Michigan	7	Cornell	34
Michigan	0	Pennsylvania	0

Season Summary
Games won, 4; Lost, 3; Tied, 1.
Points for Michigan, 130; Opponents 81.

Michigan's
200th Win   Oct. 9

YOST'S BACKS PLOUGH THRU MOUNT UNION

Maulbelsch, Smith and Benton Hammer Visitors' Line for Long Gains; Roehm Plays Quarterback.

SHOWERS OF PASSES FAIL FOR VISITORS

Nov. 6

MICHIGAN.		CORNELL.
Benton, Dunne	L. E.	Shelton, Fischer
Watson	L. T.	Gilles, Jewett
Millard	L. G.	Miller
Niemann	C.	Cool
Cochran (capt.)	R. G.	Anderson
Norton	R. T.	Jameson
Staatz	R. E.	Eckley, Zander
Roehm	Q.	Barrett
Maulbetsch	L. H.	Collins
Catlett, Bastian	R. H.	Shiverick
Smith	F. B.	Mueller

Score by quarters:

	1	2	3	4	
Michigan	0	0	7	0	7
Cornell	14	7	0	13	34

Touchdowns—Barrett 2, Collins 2, Shiverick, Roehm. Goals from touchdowns—Barrett 4, Cochran. Time of quarters—15 minutes. Referee—Hackett, Army. Umpire—Holderness, Lehigh. Field Judge—Eckersall, Chicago. Head linesman—Obeson, Lehigh.

Oct. 23

AGGIES BATTER THE WOLVERINES FOR RECORD SCORE OF 24 TO 0

Michigan (0).		M. A. C. (24).	
Benton	L. E.	Flenning	R. E.
Watson	L. T.	Blacklock	R. T.
Millard	L. G.	Vandevoort	R. G.
Norton	C.	Frimodig	C.
Cochran (C.)	R. G.	Straight	L. G.
Reiman	R. T.	Smith	L. T.
Whalen	R. E.	Butler	L. E.
Roehm	Q. B.	Hubel	Q. B.
Maulbetsch	L. H. B.	Hewitt	R. H. B.
Eberwein	R. H. B.	Blake	L. H. B.
Bastian	F. B.	Deprato	F. B.

Substitutes—Michigan: Rehor for Reiman, Catlett for Eberwein, Raymond for Bastian. M. C. A.: Springer for Huebel, Miller for Hewitt, Miller for Blake, Beatty for Miller.

Michigan	0	0	0	0	0
M. A. C.	3	3	9	14	24

Touchdowns—Deprato (3). Goals from touchdown—Deprato (3). Goals from field—Deprato. Umpire—Holderness, Lehigh. Referee—Hackett, Army. Field judge—Haines, Yale. Head linesman—Lynch, Brown. Time of periods—Fifteen minutes.

FOR NERVE YOU CAN'T BEAT OUT THIS GAMBLER

Returns to "Rim" U. of M. Students After Being Exposed in Bribery Charge.

Special to The Free Press.

Ann Arbor, Mich., Oct. 14.—As a reminder of the famous Reinger bribery charges of last fall, when Michigan students stormed the pool room operated by Joe Reinger in this city following charges that he was plotting to bribe Hughitt and Maulbetsch to "throw" the Cornell-Michigan game that he might win large wagers. Reinger today made public charges against the eastern man responsible for his trouble last year.

According to the statement made by Reinger, H. P. Bailey, of Summerville, Mass., is the man who made public the fatal letter which caused the trouble. Now Reinger charges that Bailey is operating a football pool proposition which is taking a large amount of money away from the students here.

Officials and those who are the local agents for the pool scout the charge made by Reinger that Bailey cleared $1,500 on his pool here last Saturday. Reinger claims that Bailey is a professional gambler from the east and that he is operating his pool in all parts of the country. It is stated that investigation of Reinger's charges is to be made by the officials.

Following the disclosures of last year, Reinger retired from the pool room business.

Reprinted with permission from the **Detroit Free Press**

MAULBETSCH IS HONORED WITH ATHLETIC TROPHY

Named as Most Valuable All-'Round Player; Wallie Niemann Second Highest

In addition to being chosen the leader of next year's eleven, "Johnny" Maulbetsch has been doubly honored by being named the most valuable player on the 1915 Varsity. The Heston-Schulz trophy has just been awarded to "Maullie" by vote of Head Coach Yost, first assistant coach "Germany" Schulz, and trainer Farrell.

```
          1916
Michigan........30; Marietta......0
Michigan........19; Case.........3
Michigan........54; Carroll.......0
Michigan........26; Mt. Union.....0
Michigan.........9; M.A.C.........0
Michigan........14; Syracuse......13
Michigan........66; Washington U..7
Michigan........20; Cornell.......23
Michigan.........7; Pennsylvania..10
          Season Summary
Games won, 7; Lost, 2; Ties, 0.
Points for Michigan, 245; For Opponents 56
```

UNIVERSITY OF MICHIGAN SQUAD

No.	Player	Position	Prep. School	Age	Wt.	Y
2.	Cedric C. Smith	Fullback	Bay City H. S.	21	194	
3.	John F. Maulbetsch	Left Half	Ann Arbor H. S.	23	155	
4.	Clifford M. Sparks	Quarter	Jackson, H. S.	19	153	
5.	Willard L. Peach	Right End	Western State Normal	21	178	
6.	Elton E. Wieman	Left Tackle	Los Angeles H. S.	19	183	
7.	Maurice F. Dunne	Left End	Loyola Academy	21	166	
8.	Clifford C. Gracey	Left Guard	Cass City H. S.	25	205	
9.	Phil T. Raymond	Right Half	Arthur Hill H. S.	22	172	
10.	Joseph A. Hanish	Fullback	Grand Rapids Union	20	180	
11.	N. J. Brazell	Left Half	Tacoma, Wash., H. S.	21	165	
12.	J. Orton Goodsell, Jr.	Right Guard	Arthur Hill H. S.	19	218	
14.	James L. Whalen	Left Tackle	Savannah, N. Y., H. S.	23	186	
16.	Walter A. Niemann	Center	Hermansville H. S.	22	160	
17.	Clarence O. Skinner	Right Guard	Lansing H. S.	21	218	
19.	Harold M. Zeiger	Quarter	Pueblo H. S.	20	142	'17
20.	Frank A. Willard	Center	Topeka H. S.	22	205	'18
21.	Harry B. McCallum	Left Tackle	Keewatin Academy	20	190	'18
22.	George C. Dunn	Left Guard	Maywood, Ill.	24	218	'18
23.	Albert C. Martens	Right End	Provaso H. S.	22	159	'17
24.	James H. Sharpe	Right Half	Sault Ste. Marie H. S.	20	165	'18
25.	Fred L. Rehor	Right Guard	Hastings H. S.	22	268	'17
27.	Alan W. Boyd	Left Guard	Shortridge, Ind., H. S.	19	205	'18
28.	Sidney B. Eggert	Left Half	Shortridge South H. S.	21	162	'19
31.	Richard F. Weske	Right Tackle	New London, Conn., H. S	22	177	'18
33.	Alvin E. Loucks	Right Half	Grand Rapids Union	21	170	'18

Oct. 11

```
MICHIGAN.                    CARROLL.
Dunne ..........L. E...........Mohlke
Weimann ........L. T...........Howard
Boyd ...........L. G............Moore
Niemann ........C............Shepard
Goodsell .......R. G..........Halloran
Weske ..........R. T...........Burns
Peach ..........R. E..........Atwood
Sparks .........Q. B......Kutchenberg
Maulbetsch .....L. H..........Haugen
Brazell ........R. H...........Keller
Raymond ........F. B..........Taugher
  Score by quarters:     1  2   3   4
Michigan ................ 20 14  13  7-54
Carroll ................. 0  0   0   0-0
```

Touchdowns—Sparks 2, Maulbetsch, Brazell, Hanish, Zeiger, Dunne, Raymond. Goals from touchdowns—Maulbetsch 6. Substitutions: Michigan—Martens for Peach; Hanish for Raymond; Zeiger for Brazell; Smith for Hanish; Willard for Niemann; Patrick for Zeiger; Zeiger for Sparks; Biber for Goodsell; Skinner for Maulbetsch; Loucks for Dunne; Dunn for Skinner; McCallum for Weimann. Carroll—Mund for Howard; Howland for Burns; Fisher for Haugen; Robb for Mohlke. Officials: Referee Snyder, Harvard. Umpire Kennedy, Chicago. Head linesman—Samson Springfield. Time of quarters—12, 12, 10, 6.

Oct. 21

```
MICHIGAN.                    M. A. C.
Dunne ..........L. E..........Ramsey
Wieman .........L. T.........Straight
Boyd ...........L. G..........Coryell
Niemann ........C...........Frimodig
Rehor ..........R. G......Vandervoort
Weske ..........R. T.......Blacklock
Peach ..........R. E........Henning
Sparks .........Q. B..........Huebel
Maulbetsch .....L. H...........Jacks
Raymond ........R............Fick
Smith ..........F. B..........Butler
  Score by quarters:     1  2   3   4
Michigan ................ 3  0   0   6-9
M. A. C. ................ 0  0   0   0-0
```

Touchdown—Maulbetsch. Field goal—Sparks. Referee Hackett, Army. Umpire Holderness, Lehigh. Field judge—Haines, Yale. Linesman Lynch, Brown. Time of quarters Fifteen minutes. Substitutions—Michigan: Gracey for Boyd, Patrick for Raymond, Eggert for Maulbetsch. M. A. C.: McClellan for Vick, Nelson for Henning, Henning for Nelson, Ede for Coryell, Baker for Butler, Coryell for Straight.

Nov. 4

```
MICHIGAN (66).          WASHINGTON (7).
Dunne ..........L. E............Kling
Weimann ........L. T..........Hackman
Boyd ...........L. G.........Grossman
Niemann ........C.............Weiz
Rehor ..........L. G..........Kurrus
Weske ..........R. T..........Busick
Peach ..........R. E.......Pemberton
Zeiger .........Q...........Reichel
Maulbetsch .....L. H....Schwartzenberg
Raymond ........R. H..........Dawson
Smith ..........F. B..........Foelch
  Score by periods:
                     1   2   3   4   T
Michigan ........... 6  20  20  20-66
Washington ......... 0   7   0   0-7
```

Summary: Touchdowns — Maulbetsch, 4; Kling, Zeiger, 2; Raymond, Brazell, Hanish, 2. Goals—Maulbetsch 4; Rehor, 2; Dawson. Substitutions—Michigan: Hanish for Smith, Glen Dunn for Boyd, Goodsell for Rehor, Martins for M. Dunne, Whalen for Weimann, Rehor for G. Dunn, Skinner for Niemann, Boyd for Goodsill, Brazell for Maulbetsch, Loucks for Peach, Eggert for Raymond, Willard for Skinner. Washington: Nelson for Hackman, Benway for Reichert, Hackman for Nelson, Meyer for Kurrus, Stout for Dawson, Caffee for Pemberton, McRoberts for Meyers, Moore for Caffee, Peters for Hackman, Brooks for Moore, Roberts for McRoberts. Referee—Haines, Yale; umpire—Holderness, Lehigh; head linesman—Sampson, Iowa. Time of periods 15 minutes.

Nov. 11

```
MICHIGAN.                    CORNELL.
Dunne ..........L. E.........Ryerson
Weimann ........L. T.........Gillies
Gracey .........L. G..........Miller
Neimann ........C............Carry
Rehor ..........R. G........Anderson
Weske ..........R. T.........Jewett
Peach ..........R. E.........Eckley
Zeiger .........Q. B.......Shiverick
Maulbetsch .....L. H........Hoffman
Raymond ........R. H..........Speed
Smith ..........F. B.........Mueller
```

Touchdowns—Maulbetsch, Smith, Dunne, Mueller (2). Goals after touchdowns—Maulbetsch 2, Shiverick 2. Field goals—Shiverick 3.

```
  Score by quarters:
Michigan ............ 0  14  6   0-20
Cornell ............. 6   6  7  10-23
```

Substitutions—Cornell: Taylor for Jewett, Bard for Miller, Dixon for Taylor, Jewett for Dixon, Brown for Carry, Haucke for Hoffman, Zander for Ryerson. Michigan: Boyd for Gracey, Gracey for Boyd, Sparks for Raymond.

EARLY SLIP GIVES PENN BIG CHANCE

ANN ARBOR, Mich., Nov. 18.—It takes just about no time at all to tell the story of the Michigan-Pennsylvania game. So far as actual results go it was all over just after the start of the second period, though the score, which then chalked up 10 for Penn and none for Michigan, was later changed to read Penn 10, Michigan 7. It was Berry's touchdown and Berry's goal that did the trick, but behind the score is one of the finest, hardest fought battles ever seen on Ferry field.

There is little one can criticize in the play of the Michigan eleven, and practically no alibi. It went into the game crippled by the loss of Gracey at guard, and hampered by injuries to Sparks and Peach, but so excellent was the work of Boyd and Martens, who replaced Peach, that except for the fact that Sparks at times did not look himself, it is difficult to tell if a clean hospital sheet would have told in the score.

```
MICHIGAN.                    PENN.
Dunne ..........L. E.........Urquhart
Weimann ........L. T.........Matthews
Boyd ...........L. G.........Henning
Neimann ........C............L. Wray
Rehor ..........R. G.......Ertresvaag
Weske ..........R. T..........Little
Peach ..........R. E..........Miller
Sparks .........Q. B............Bell
Maulbetsch .....L. H...........Derr
Raymond ........R. H..........Light
Smith ..........F. B...........Berry
```

Line-up:

```
  Score by quarters:
Michigan ............ 0  0  0  7-7
Pennsylvania ........ 7  3  0  0-10
```

Touchdowns—Berry, Smith. Goals from touchdowns—Derr, Maulbetsch. Field goals—Berry. Referee—Holderness, Lehigh. Umpire—Haines, Yale. Field judge—Okeson, Lehigh. Head linesman—Cooney, Princeton. Substitutions: Michigan—Martens for Peach; Zeiger for Sparks. Pennsylvania—Berry for Matthews; A. Wray for L. Wray. Time of quarters 15 minutes.

Board of Regents Votes Unanimously for Return of Michigan to Conference Games

PASS VETO POWER NECESSARY TO SENATE COUNCIL; ACTION WILL NOT AFFECT 1917 FOOTBALL SCHEDULE; ALUMNI FAVOR MOVE

ATHLETIC ASSOCIATION TO DISCONTINUE ALL-FRESH TEAMS AND TRAIN-ING TABLE

By R. T. McDonald

Michigan has voted to go back to the Conference.

The Regents yesterday afternoon voted for a return to the western con-ference, passing the veto power necessary to the Senate council, a body composed entirely of faculty men. The vote for the return was unanimous.

Michigan has been out of the conference since 1908. The biggest reason for the break was the desire of the Big Nine to install the retro-active three year clause which hit Michigan hardest because at that time it had a number of track and football stars who would have been made ineligible by that rule. The Wolverine was the strongest school in the body and as the motion was passed, Michigan decided to cease being one of the body. Since then the three year action has been enforced here, and many of the other changes proposed by the conference have been followed by Michigan.

The action of the Regents will make it impossible for the Wolverine to maintain All-fresh teams. It will also abolish the training table and faculty supervision over athletics automatical-ly goes into effect following the order of the Regents.

Agitation Starts Last Fall

Yesterday's action was the result of concerted working by students and alumni organizations for more than two months. Agitation on the pro-posed return started last fall immedi-ately after the poor football season. When it became definitely known that

> It is the sense of the board of regents that athletic competition with the members of the west-ern intercollegiate conference will be for the best interests of the University of Michigan, therefore be it
>
> Resolved, that the action of the board in control of athletics shall be reported to the Senate council of the University and that the Senate council is here-by vested with power of veto over the actions of the board in control of athletics.

Princeton refused to play home and home games with Michigan the agita-tion took on added impetus.

The board in control of athletics in February added to the movement by voting for the return, 8-1. Since then there have been two meetings of the Regents, both unfruitful of action.

SETTLED!

The conference question which has occupied the thoughts of Michigan men ever since the fall of 1905 was set-tled yesterday. It is no longer a question. In voting to reopen the competition with our old rivals in the west the Regents took a step which will be welcomed by a majority of alumni and undergraduates, a step which cannot but be of benefit to Mich-igan athletics, and to the University in every way.

As for our rivals in the East, Michi-gan has cemented friendly athletic re-lationships with Pennsylvania and Cornell, friendships which should not be affected by the Regents' action, al-though from now on our competition will naturally be for the most part with Michigan's natural opponents in the West.

Time has wiped out the old ani-mosities which may have existed be-tween Michigan and the conference colleges. We re-enter the conference today not arrogantly, nor as a prodigal, but with a free conscience, an open heart, and a firm conviction that the step will be of benefit both to Michi-gan and to our rivals.

The Regents came up to bat yester-day and knocked a homer!

OFFICIAL LINE-UP

No.	Name	Position	Age	Weight
4.	A. G. Goetz	End	20	183
6.	J. O. Goodsell	Tackle	20	198
15.	F. W. Culver	Guard	20	190
12.	O. P. Lambert	Center	24	161
7.	W. P. Fortune	Guard	19	188
31.	R. F. Weske	Tackle	23	185
3.	A. W. Boyd	End	20	182
11.	A. B. Weston	Quarterback	21	147
13.	C. M. Sparks	Halfback	20	159
5.	J. A. Hanish	Halfback	21	167
2.	E. E. Wieman	Fullback	21	194
8.	G. W. Froemke	Halfback	22	150
9.	Harold Rye	Halfback	21	157
10.	A. J. Cohn	Halfback	20	178
16.	T. C. Garrett	Fullback	20	150
17.	W. R. Cruse	Halfback	22	166
18.	L. B. Genebach	Halfback	19	145
19.	J. R. St. Clair	End	23	165
22.	C. C. Morrison	Tackle	21	160
24.	C. P. Beath	Center	20	176
26.	H. A. Wellford	Quarterback	21	140
27.	C. A. Moulthrop	Halfback	19	156
28.	Lee Bonar	End	25	161
30.	O. H. Cartwright	End	21	160

ERNEST J. ALLMENDINGER, ALL-AMERICAN GUARD, 1917

41	Case	0	14 Univ. of Detroit	3	42 Cornell 0
17	Kalamazoo Nor.	3	20 Nebraska	0	0 Pennsylvania ...16
69	Mount Union	0	62 Kalamazoo Col.	0	12 Northwestern 21
			27 M.A.C.	0	

Michigan 304; Opponents 53
Won 8; Tied 0; Lost 2

YOST MEN NEARLY DEFEATED BY KALAMAZOO NORMAL

Michigan.		Kalamazoo.
Goetz	L.E.	Houston
Culver	L.T.	Chapel
Boyd	L.G.	Stockdale
Goodsell	C.	Johnson
Fortune	R.G.	Miller
Weske	R.T.	Allen (C.)
Cartwright	R.E.	Millar
Sparks	Q.	Berman
Hanish	R.H.	Angell
Cohn	L.H.	Dunlap
Wieman	F.B.	Olsen

Score by quarters:

Michigan	3	0	7	7—17
Kalamazoo Normal	0	0	7	7—14

Summaries

Substitutions—Michigan: Cress fo
Goetz, Rye for Hanish, St. Clair fo
Cartwright, Hendershot for Cres
Lindstrom for Fortune, Genebach fo
Sparks, Goodsell for Lindstrom, Bar
nard for Rye. Kalamazoo Normal
Thomas for Angell, Cudmore fo
Stockdale.

Touchdowns—Wieman 2, Berma
Houston. Goals kicked—Wieman
Olsen. Field goals—Wieman.

Walter Kennedy (Chicago), refere
Dalrimple, umpire.

Nov. 3

Nov. 10

Oct. 27

MICHIGAN BURIES CORNELL, 42 TO 0

Michigan.	Position	Cornell
Goetz	L. E.	Colvin
Goodsell	L. T.	Ackernecht
Culver	L. G.	Strauss
Lamber	C.	Trobride
Fortune	R. G.	Swanson
Weske	R. T.	Harriman
Boyd	R. E.	Harris
Weston	Q.	Nethercott
Sparks	L. H.	Cross
Hanish	R. H.	Hoffman
Wieman	F. B.	Pendleton

Officials—Eckersall, Chicago, referee; Holder-
ness, Lehigh, umpire; Haines, Yale, field judge;
Evans, Williams, head linesman. Time of quar-
ters—15 minutes.
Michigan, 42; Cornell, 0.
Touchdowns—Weston 3, Sparks, Hanish, Cohn.
Goals from touchdown—Wieman 6.

MICHIGAN.		NEBRASKA.
Goetz	L. E.	Rhodes
Goodsell	L. T.	Munn
Culver	L. G.	Kositzky
Lambert	C.	Cook
Fortune	R. G.	Wilder
Weske	R. T.	Shaw (capt.)
Boyd	R. E.	Hooka
Weston	Q. B.	Schellenberg
Froemke	L. H.	McMahon
Hanish	R. H.	Dobson
Wiemann	F. B.	Day

Score by quarters:

	1	2	3	4
Michigan	7	7	3	3—20
Nebraska				0

Touchdowns—Froemke, Welmann. Goals
from touchdowns—Weimann 2. Goals from
place kick—Weimann 2. Umpire—Fultz, of
Brown. Field judge—Durfee, of Williams.
Referee—Snyder, of Harvard. Time of
quarters—15 minutes.
Substitutions—Deteau for Munn, Cruse for
Froemke, Munn for Deteau, Young for
Munn, Deteau for Young, Rye for Cruse,
Genebach for Rye. Bonar for Goetz, Kelley
for Schellenberg, Morrison for Fortune.

Wolverines Trample Aggies and Even Up Old Grid Scores, 27-0

Ann Arbor, Mich., Oct. 20.—Michigan
secured a slight bit of revenge for the
two defeats administered them by M.
A. C. the last few seasons when it
trounced the Aggie eleven, 27 to 0, this
afternoon on Ferry field.

Throughout the game Michigan's superiority was demonstrated in the
yards gained by the rushes of the
Wolverines' backs, who went off tackle
or through guard for gains varying
from one to thirty yards at a consistent
pace. But the fight of the farmer team
showed itself when the ball was in the
shadow of the goal posts, and several
times Michigan was held with a touchdown but a few yards away.

Weimann and Weston were the big
guns for the Wolverine offense. Weston
scoring one touchdown on a beautiful
run through a broken field, and Weimann toting the ball over three times,
once shaking off five tacklers in a
thirty-yard dash to the goal line. Weimann held his own with Hammes on
punts and missed but one try at goal
after a touchdown, the second one he
has missed all season. The line-up:

Michigan (27).		M. A. C. (0).
Goetz	L. E.	Bussett, R. E.
Goodsell	L. T.	Franson, R. T.
Boyd	L. G.	Bailey, R. G.
Lambert	C.	Archer, C.
Culver	R. G.	Leffler, L. G.
Weske	R. T.	Correll, L. T.
Cartwright	R. E.	Ramsey, L. E.
Weston	Q. B.	Kellogg, Q. B.
Cohn	L. H. B.	Oas, R. H. B.
Genebach	R. H. B.	Turner, L. H. B.
Weimann	F. B.	Hammes, F. B.

Michigan	6	0	7	14—27
M. A. C.	0	0	0	0—0

Touchdowns—Weston, Weimann (3). Goals
from touchdown—Weimann 3. Umpire—Hol-
derness, Lehigh. Referee—Haines, Yale.
Head linesman—Kennedy, Chicago.
Substitutions—Rye for Genebach, Harris for
Cartwright, McCool for Oas, Oas for McCool,
Crane for Cohn, Froemke for Crane, St. Clair
for Harris, Fortune for Culver, Hendershot
for Goetz, Barnard for Rye, Miller for Bailey,
Wellford for Barnard, Weddorf for Wellford,
Garrel for St. Clair.

Nov. 17

Folwell's Team Whips Michigan Eleven, 16 to 0

Howard Berry's Three Field Goals and Touchdown Resulting From Blocked Punt, the Nemesis of Yostmen.

PENNSYLVANIA.		MICHIGAN.
VanGinkel	L. E.	Goetz
Maynard	L. T.	Goodsell
Cleary	L. G.	Culver
Wray	C.	Lambert
Dieter	R. G.	Fortune
Thomas	R. T.	Weske
Miller	R. E.	Boyd
Bell	Q. B.	Weston
Straus	L. H.	Cohn
Light	R. H.	Hanish
Berry	F. B.	Wieman

Penn	0	0	6	10—16
Michigan	0	0	0	0—0

Field goals—Berry 3. Referee—Tufts,
Brown. Umpire—Fultz, Brown. Field
judge—Okeson, Lehigh. Head linesman—
Cooney, Yale. Substitutions—Penn—Rose-
nead for Straus, Quigly for Bell; Michigan
—Genebach for Weston, Sparks for Gene-
bach, Cruse for Cohn. Touchdown—Cleary.
Goal from touchdown—Berry.

WOLVERINES ARE BADLY OUTPLAYED

7 Case 0   15 Syracuse 0   21 M.A.C. 6
3 Chicago 0   14 Ohio State 0

Michigan 96; Opponents 6
Won 5; Tied 0; Lost 0

University of Michigan Football Squad Statistics

Player.	Position.	Weight	Hight	Year.	High School.
Cohn	Half Back	185	6.00	Second	Spokane
Goetz	Guard	185	6.00	Second	Sault Ste. Marie
Morrison	Tackle	173	6.01	Second	Peabody-Pittsburgh, Pa.
Knode	Quarter	149	5.08	First	Martinsburg, W. Va.
Dunne	End	179	6.00	First	Loyola Academy
Perrin	Half Back	160	5.09	First	Escanaba
Stekette	Full Back	179	5.10	First	Grand Rapids-Central
Vick	Center	182	5.08	First	Toledo Scott High
Freeman	Guard	180	5.11	First	Exeter Academy
Barnes	End	179	6.00½	First	Washington-Tech High
Genebach	Half Back	145	5.08	Second	Battle Creek
Cruse	Half Bach	164	5.09	Second	Detroit Eastern
Walker	Half Back	142	5.06	Second	Detroit
Lindstrom	Guard Tackle	172	5.10½	Third	Marquette
Karpus	Back	162	5.08	First	Grayling
Jordon	Quarter	155	5.10	First	Detroit-Cass Tech
Van Wagoner ..	Center	183	5.09	First	Pontiac
Hunt	Lineman	170	5.09		
Wilson	Lineman	166	5.08	First	Grand Rapids-Central
Boville	End	161	5.10	First	Detroit-Central
Scheidler	Guard	173	5.10		

Michigan Keeps Slate Clean by Downing Ohio State, 14-0

Columbus, O., Nov. 30.—[Special.]—Michigan's first appearance on Ohio field in years resulted in a 14 to 0 victory for Yost's men, thereby strengthening the Wolverines' claims on the conference championship.

The Buckeye team staged a decided comeback in today's game, holding the Yostmen for three quarters. Michigan's two touchdowns came in the last quarter on a blocked punt by Goetz and his recovery behind the goal line and a forward pass over the line, executed by Steketee and Dunne.

Michigan [14].	Ohio State [0].
R. E......Bovill	McDonald........L. E.
Hendershot	
R. T...Czys.. Morrison	Hoffman........L. T.
R. G........Freeman	Bixley, Gillam....L. G.
C..........Vick	Friedman ....C.
L. G........Fortune	Sneddon,
	Churches ......R. G.
L. T.........Goetz	McClure, Addison.R. T.
L. E........Dunne	Styler, Elgin,
	Howell ....R. E.
Q. B..........Knode	Wiper.........Q. B.
R. H. B...Perrin	Davies........L. H. B.
Van Wagoner	
L. H. B...Conn, Csner	Rife..........R. H. B.
F. B........Steketee	Matheny, Taylor.F. B.
Touchdowns—Goetz,	Dunne. Goals from
touchdowns—Steketee [2]. Referee—Snyder,
Harvard. Umpire—Schommer, Chicago. Head
lineman—Thurber, Colgate.

MICHIGAN AVENGES 1905 DEFEAT; WINS 13 TO 0 VICTORY FROM CHICAGO TEAM; STEKETEE'S KICKING FEATURE OF GAME

CHICAGO'S TERRITORY SEES MOST OF YESTERDAY'S BATTLE

GOETZ RUNS 50 YARDS FOR FIRST TOUCHDOWN

Game Is Largely a Punting Contest Between Steketee and Elton Stek Wins

Stagg field, Chicago, Nov. 9.—Michigan avenged a defeat of 13 years' standing, when the Wolverines took the University of Chicago football team into camp this afternoon by a score of 13 to 0, in a rather loosely played but hard fought game on this field. In 1905, the Maroons defeated the Maize and Blue warriors in one of the greatest football battles in the history of the game. As a result of that, today's clash was a thing of 12 years planning by Coach Yost, the Michigan mentor, and the outcome fully repaid the labor and worry of the "Hurry Up" Coach.

Score—Michigan 13, Chicago 0.	
Michigan	Chicago
Karpus .......R.E........Schwab
Morrison ......R.T.......McGuire
Freeman ......R.G.......McQuaig
Vick ....C..........Reb.
Adams .......L.G........Miller
Goetz ........L.T.......Stegman
Dunne , ...L.E.......Halliday
Knode ....Q..........Neff
Cohn ........R.H.......Eubank
Steketee .....F.B.......Hermes
Perrin .......L.H........Elton

Substitutions:

For Michigan—Walker for Perrin, Perrin for Walker, Henderson for Freeman, Cruze for Cohn, Boville for Karpus, Jordan for Perrin.

For Chicago — Eubanks for Neff, Tays for Hermes, McCraig for Miller, Schwab for Bradley, Fouche for Eubanks.

Officials—Referee, Birch, Earlham; umpire, White, Illinois; field judge, Robinson, Indiana; headlinesman, Ellicott, Northwestern.

ALL AMERICAN TEAM

1918	
Robeson, Rutgers	End
Hilty, Pittsburgh	Tackle
Alexander, Syracuse	Guard
Day, Georgia Tech.	Center
Perry, Annapolis	Guard
Usher, Syracuse	Tackle
Hopper, Pennsylvania	End
Murray, Princeton	Quarter
Davies, Pittsburgh	Halfback
Roberts, Annapolis	Halfback
Steketee, Michigan	Fullback

**Frank Steketee
Fullback
1918**

MICHIGAN LINE-UP

Left End ....Peach (10)
Left Tackle ....Goetz (1) (Capt.)
Left Guard ....Fortune (7)
Center ....Johnson (16)
Right Guard ....Wilson (14)
Right Tackle ....G. Dunn (2)
Right End ....R. J. Dunne (22)
Quarter ....Sparks (5)
Left Half ....Cruse (3)
Right Half ....Weston (11)
Fullback ....Vick (19)

Substitutes:

Knode (6), Froemke (8), Rye (9), McGrath (12), Cress (15), Eades (17), Henderson (18), Schumacher (20), Loucks (21), Barnes (23), Czysz (24), Hammels (25), Campbell (28), Timchac (29), Breakey (30), Stewart (31), Van Wagoner (32), Hamilton (33), Culver (34), Cary (35), Weadock (36).

34 Case	0	3 Ohio State	13	7 Illinois	29
26 M.A.C.	0	16 Northwestern	13	7 Minnesota	34
		0 Chicago	13		

Michigan 93; Opponents 102
Won 3; Tied 0; Lost 4

BIG TEN PLACES SERVICE MEN IN INELIGIBLE CLASS

BY WALTER ECKERSALL.

Western conference service athletes who failed to register at some college before they entered the service will not be eligible for competition this fall.

This was the edict handed down yesterday by the faculty committee of the Western Intercollegiate Conference Athletic association at its June meeting at the Auditorium.

At a special meeting of the committee on Dec. 7, 1918, it was voted to allow students' time spent in the service to count the same as if they were in college. This resolution, the committee ruled, applied only to those students who had registered and then were sent to some training camp or overseas.

Oct. 18

MICHIGAN		M. A. C.
Peach	L.E.	Ramsay
Goetz	L.T.	Coryell
Van Wagoner	L.G.	Vandervoort
Johnson	C.	Archer
Wilson	R.G.	Miller
G. Dunn	R.T.	Franson
Rye	R.E.	Bassett
Sparks	Q.	Springer
Weston	L.H.	Schewel
Froemke	R.B.	Hammes
Vick	F.H.	Snider
Michigan		0 6 7 13 26
M. A. C.		0 0 0 0 0

Touchdowns—Weston 2, Czysz, Dunne. Goals from touchdowns—Sparks 2. Referee—Durfee (Williams). Umpire—Kennedy (Chicago). Head linesman—Burroughs (Illinois). Substitutions—Michigan: Hammels for G. Dunn, Fortune for Van Wagoner, J. Dunne for Peach, Czysz for Fortune, Schumacher for Wilson, Cress for Johnson, Knode for Froemke, Loucks for Glenn Dunn, Culver for Cress, McGrath for Rye, Campbell for Loucks, Tinchak for McGrath; M. A. C.: Bos for Vandervoort, Hutchings for Bassett, Thompson for Hutchings. Time of quarters 15 minutes.

Steketee Lost to Ann Arbor Football Team

Ann Arbor, Mich., Aug. 27.—Frank Steketee, all-American fullback, has been declared ineligible because of poor class work, and Coach Yost will have to do without the services of his star kicker this fall. Steketee was one of the best kickers who ever played for Michigan and he will be missed when the big games roll around in November. Owing to war time conditions freshmen were permitted to play on the varsity eleven last season and Steketee in his first year in the university not only on his varsity letter but was placed on Walter Camp's all-American team. Steketee's home was in Grand Rapids.

1919

Ann Arbor, Mich., Oct. 25—Packed stands on Ferry Field saw Michigan go down to defeat before Ohio State this afternoon for the first time in the history of their football relations.

The score was 13 to 3 and the story of the game largely is the story of Capt. Chick Harley, 165-pound Buckeye halfback. After Ohio had gained a 7-3 halftime lead, Harley turned in the decisive score with a 42-yard run around his own right end for a touchdown. Ohio State made six first downs, Michigan two.

MICHIGAN (3)		OHIO (13)
R. Durne	L.E.	Meyers
Goetz	L.T.	Huffman
Fortune	L.G.	Pixley
Johnson	C.	Holtkamp
Peach	R.G.	Trott
Wilson	R.T.	Spiers
Rye	R.E.	Flower
Sparks	Q.	Stinchcomb
Cruse	L.H.	Bliss
Weston	R.H.	Harley
Vick	F.B.	Willaman
Michigan		0 3 0 0 3
O.S.U.		7 0 6 0 13

Touchdowns—Flower, Harley. Goal from touchdown—Harley. Field goal—Sparks. Referee—Birch (Earlham). Umpire—Schrommer (Chicago). Field judge—Thurber (Colgate). Head linesman—Prugh (Ohio Wesleyan). Substitutions—Michigan, Czysz for Peach, Peach for Rye, Hammels for Peach, G. Dunn for Czysz, Czysz for Wilson, Froemke for Cruse, Ohio, Davies for Bliss, Wieche for Pixley, Taylor for Willaman, Slyker for Flower, MacDonald for Meyers.

Nov. 8

CHICAGO WINS OVER MICHIGAN

Stagg Gets 13-0 Verdict, Giving Maize and Blue Its Worst Beating.

First Time in Yost's Regime Any Man Has Held Post 2 Years in Succession.

Nov. 15

MICHIGAN DEALT STAGGERING BLOW BY ZUPPKE'S MEN

ILLINI ELEVEN GOES THROUGH LINE FOR FOUR TOUCHDOWNS

"M" MEN AGAIN SELECT GOETZ

Captain of Wolverine Eleven Once More is Honored by Teammates.

Nov. 22

GOPHER ATTACK SMOTHERS YOSTS IN 34 TO 7 GAME

Oct. 9

WOLVERINES WIN FROM SCIENTISTS IN FIRST BATTLE

FIVE TOUCHDOWNS SCORED BY YOSTMEN, PLAYING STRAIGHT FOOTBALL

MICHIGAN ROLLS UP THIRTY-FIVE POINTS

Case Held Scoreless by Excellent Maize and Blue Defense; Steketee Makes 75-Yard Run

OCT. 16

THE LINE-UPS

Michigan	Position	M. A. C.
Cappon	L.E.	Basset
Goetz (capt.)	L.T.	Bos
Dunne	L.G.	Matson
Vick	C.	Morrison
Wilson	R.G.	Radewald
Wieman	R.T.	Leffler
Goebel	R.E.	Gingrich
Dunn	Q.B.	Springer (capt.)
Usher	L.H.	Johnson
Perrin	R.H.	Wilcox
Nelson	F.B.	Hammes

Referee — Durfee (Williams). Umpire—Dr. Lambert (O. S. U.). Head linesman—Olds (Ypsi Normal). Substitutions: Michigan—Petro for Dunne, Fortune for Petro, Planck for Vick, Johns for Wilson, Gilmore for Wieman, Banks for Dunn, Searle for Usher, Cohn for Perrin, Steketee for Nelson. M. A. C.—Willman for Bassett, Bassett for Willman, Swanson for Radewald, Parks for Leffler, Thorpe ofr Parks, Leffler for Thorpe, Gingrich for Thompson, Brady for Johnson, Schwei for Wilcox, Johnson for Hammes.

35 Case	0	6 Illinois	7	14 Chicago	0
35 M.A.C.	0	21 Tulane	0	3 Minnesota	0
		7 Ohio State	14		

Michigan 121; Opponents 21
Won 5; Tied 0; Lost 2

Oct. 23

MICHIGAN FIGHT HOLDS ILLINOIS ELEVEN TO ONE TOUCHDOWN; DUNN PLAYS BRILLIANT GAME FOR VARSITY

Illinois' powerful eleven nosed out the Wolverines, 7 to 6, in a game filled with thrills and good football yesterday afternoon on Ferry field. The failure to kick the goal after the sole Michigan touchdown cost Michigan a tie.

The Illini outplayed the Yost men throughout the game, particularly on the offensive. Their touchdown came as a result of a long steady march down the field ending with a pretty forward pass, Walquist to Carney for the score.

Jack Dunn was the Wolverine hero of the contest. Intercepting a pass on his own 25-yard line, the little quarterback ran the length of the field for a touchdown. The blocking of the Michigan interference was the most spectacular feature of the whole game.

Reprinted with permission from the **Michigan Daily**

MICHIGAN, 7; OHIO STATE, 14

Because Captain Huffman of Ohio State broke through the Michigan line in the fourth quarter of the Michigan-Ohio game, played at Columbus on November 6, and blocked Steketee's punt behind the goal line, the Ann Arbor team was defeated 14 to 7. Huffman flashed on the ball for the winning touchdown as it bounded away from his upraised arms and Michigan lost her second Conference game.

FIELD GOAL ONLY TALLY IN BATTLE WHICH BRINGS FORTH COURAGEOUS EFFORTS FROM COMBATING TEAMS

PERRIN'S BRILLIANT 50-YARD DASH ONE OF FEATURES OF GAME; EVERY MAN ON WOLVERINE TEAM PERFORMS WELL; STEKETEE MARKED FROM START

MINNESOTA PLAYS BEST FOOTBALL OF SEASON; YOSTMEN CONTEND WITH AERIAL ATTACKS

Captain Goetz and Wieman Prove Main Stays in Line and Block Plays When Foe Is Twice Within Eight-Yard Line; Breaks Favor Michigan

(Special to The Daily)

Minneapolis, Nov. 20.—Battling as never before the Michigan eleven this afternoon stemmed the slashing line attacks of the Gophers and withstood the aerial efforts of Williams' men so valiantly that the Wolverines won by the narrow margin of a field goal from Steketee's toe.

The Minnesota team played the best football that it has exhibited this season. Several times the advances of the Gophers were stopped by the Yostmen in the nick of time, particularly when Michigan held on the 3-yard line. Oss, who was on the receiving end of several passes, was the star of the day as his line bucking was also excellent. The triple shift of the Gophers worked well in midfield but lacked the punch to put across a touchdown.

Reprinted with permission from the **Michigan Daily**

Oct. 30

TULANE		MICHIGAN
Wiegan	L.E.	Cappon
Payne	L.T.	Goetz
Fitz	L.G.	Dunne
Reed	C.	Vick
Killinger	R.G.	Petro
Blanchard	R.T.	Johns
Wight	R.E.	Goebel
Richardson	Q.B.	Banks
Dwyer	L.H.	Steketee
Nagel	R.H.	Usher
McGraw	F.B.	Nelson

Tulane	0	0	0	0
Michigan	0	7	7	7—21

Touchdowns—Banks, Perrin 2. Goals from touchdowns—Steketee, Dunn, Goebel. Substitutions: Michigan—Jack Dunn for Banks; Paper for Usher; Perrin for Steketee; Fortune for Petro; Banks for Dunn; Cohn for Nelson; Lehman for Cappon. Tulane—B. Brown for Nagel; Pardie for Killinger; Lewis for Payne; Dolerno for Fitz; Smith for Dwyer. Time of quarters—15 minutes. Referee—Harvey Snyder (Harvard). Umpire—John Schoomer (Chicago). Hear linesman—Anthony Haines (Yale).

Dunne - 1921

44 Mount Union	0	30 M.A.C.	0	7 Wisconsin	7
64 Case	0	0 Ohio State	14	38 Minnesota	0
		3 Illinois	0		

Michigan 186; Opponents 21
Won 5; Tied 1; Lost 1

YOST ASSUMES NE[W] DUTIES THIS FAL[L]

Is Director of Athletics in Additio[n]
to Coaching Varsity
Gridders

VARSIY COACHES TO TEACH THEORY OF VARIOUS SPORT[S]

Fielding H. Yost, for 21 years hea[d] coach and builder of Wolverine grid iron machines, assumes a double dut[y] this fall as director of intercollegiat[e] athletics and head of the staff of gri[d] coaches. In his new role as directo[r] of athletics, Yost will have charge o[f] the athletic offices and will look aft er the interests of Michigan in a[ll] matters pertaining to intercollegiat[e] competition. In assuming his new du ties Coach Yost will hold a position somewhat analogous to that held b[y] Hugo Bedzek at Penn State, where Bedzel is director of athletics and ac tively engaged as head coach.

In addition to his duties as director of athletics, Coach Yost will assist in the new four year course in Physi cal Education, Hygiene, and Athletics which leads to a bachelor's degree and fits the graduates to be coaches and athletic directors. Although Michigan is not the first of the larger institu tions in the Middle West to establish a school of this nature, its courses wi[l]l cover all the branches of major sports in addition to the academic work required, and with the present st[a]ff of coaches Director Yost will have a corps of men who are the equal of any in the country.

The first year courses in the new school will include theory and prac tice in football, basketball, baseball and track, while the later years will allow the students in the school to specialize more extensively in the branches which they are best adapted to. Other electives in addition to the major sports will be offered in the sophomore, junior and senior years. During the summer session of 1922 special courses will be given by Coaches Yost, Farrell, Mather and Fisher for high school and prep school coaches in all of the major branches of sports.

Oct. 22

SCORE BY QUARTERS					
---	1st	2nd	3rd	4th	FINAL
MICHIGAN -	0	0	0	0	0
OHIO - - -	0	7	0	7	14

Oct. 15

CONTEST WITH FARMERS OFFERS MICHIGAN REAL TEST FOR O. S. U.

AGGIES STRONG FIRST HALF; WEAK IN SECOND

Kipke and Goebel Star, Helping to Overcome Absence of Steketee and Dunne

Michigan football followers had the first opportunity to see the Wolver ines in action against a team of near ly equal defensive ability yesterday afternoon when the Wolverine eleven took M. A. C.'s measure on Ferry field by defeating the Aggies 30 to 0 in the first hard game of the 1921 schedule.

Eighteen thousand or more specta tors watched the rejuvenated Farmer eleven fight to the last ditch, during the first half of the battle, in a vain attempt to check the Michigan of fense.

MICHIGAN		M. A. C.
Kirk	L.E.	Gingrich
Cappon	L.T.	Thorpe
Van Orden	L.G.	Matson
Vick	C.	Morrison
Wilson	R.G.	Swanson
Muirhead	R.T.	Bos
Goebel	R.E.	Johnson
Banks	Q.B.	Archibald
Kipke	L.H.	Wilcox
Uteritz	R.H.	Brady
Usher	F.B.	Graves

Summary—Touchdowns, Kipke 2, Dean 1, Goebel 1.
Drop-kicks, Knode 1.
Goals after touchdown, Goebel 3.

In a game featured by adverse breaks in luck and the loss of Harry Kipke, Michigan was defeated by the Ohio State eleven yesterday afternoon in the opening Conference game of the season. The largest crowd which has ever witnessed a game on the Ferry field gridiron filled the new stadium to its full capacity of 42,000, while 3,000 more were accommodat ed through the general admission.

Michigan Line Strong

Both teams opened the game cau tiously, each fearing to open up with new plays. Michigan received the kickoff, but chose to resort to a kick ing game. All doubt as to the strength of the Wolverine line was removed when during the first quarter Michi gan's forward wall held Ohio at bay, while the Wolverine backs tore wide gaps through the Buckeye defense. Uteritz received a long punt from Stuart on Michigan's 49 yard line and on the next play Kipke made his fam ous run through the Ohio team to the Buckeye 18 yard line, where he was stopped by the last Ohio defender of the Scarlet and Grey goal. This play probably cost Michigan the game, for the speedy Kipke was injured and was unable to continue in the game. Roby carried the ball to the Buckeye 10 yard line, where the Wolverines with fourth down and two yards to go, chose to attempt a place kick which went short of the posts.

NOV. 19

RUNS ACCOUNT FOR WOLVERINES' VICTORY OVER MINNESOTA, 38-0

POWERFUL DEFENSE BREAKS UP FAMOUS MINNESOTA SHIFT

SPECTATORS BAFFLED BY BRILLIANT PLAYS

Michigan Line and Backfield Prove Mystery to Northmen and Score at Will

Michigan ended her 1921 gridiron season in a blaze of glory yesterday afternoon when the powerful Wolverine machine completely overwhelmed the Gophers by the score of 38 to 0. Not since the fall of 1913 has a Yost eleven displayed such power as did the Michigan team yesterday against Minnesota.

Coach Yost treated the crowd with his tricks when in play after play the Wolverine backs sped down the field to the astonishment of the bewildered Gopher eleven. Michigan plays were executed with such a smoothness that the Northmen were baffled at all times.

Reprinted with permission from the **Michigan Daily**

HOW THEY LINED UP TODAY.

Michigan		Minnesota
Dean	L. E.	Cole
Johns	L. T.	Conklin
Petro	L. G.	Grose
Vick	C.	Aas
Wilson	R. G.	Tierney
Muirhead	R. T.	Johnsen
Goebel	R. E.	Wallace
Uteritz	Q.	Brown
Kipke	L. H.	McCreery
Roby	F. B.	Gilstad
Cappon	R. H.	Martineau

SUMMARY

Touchdowns—Uteritz 2, Cappon, Banks, Goebel. Goals after touchdowns—Goebel 5. Field goal—Dean.

Officials—Referee, H. B. Hackett, Army. Umpire, J. J. Schommer, Chicago. Field judge, F. H. Young, Illinois Wesleyan. Head linesman, H. D. Ray, Illinois.

Oct. 29

MICHIGAN COMES BACK AND WINS OVER ILLINOIS

Steketee's Toe Brings Victory; Cappon and Roby Batter Illini Line

Michigan came back at Urbana Saturday afternoon.

The Wolverines, with Cappon shifted from tackle to the backfield, showed unexpected strength and handed the Illini their third consecutive Conference defeat, by a score of 3 to 0.

Frank Steketee displayed a big reversal of form over his kicking in the Ohio State game and booted the placement goal in the second period which was the only scoring of the day. This kick was made possible by a succession of line plunges by Roby and Cappon in which these two Wolverines tore the Illinois line into shreds and battered down a defense which fought back very inch of the way.

It was a great game to watch. Michigan rooters were not sure of their team, for, with Harry Kipke, the brilliant Lansing star, out of the contest, many feared Yost's backfield would be a weak spot. Cappon came through brilliantly, however, his work stamping him as a real contender for all-Conference honors in the backfield.

Big Day for Holland.

Douglas Roby shared premier honors with Cappon, both these lines smashing stars hailing from the same city—Holland. Michigan's marches down the field, and there were several of them, were one long succession of alternating plunges, first Cappon and then Roby carrying the leather.

Reprinted with permission from the **Michigan Daily**

SUMMARY

MICHIGAN		ILLINOIS
Kirk	L.E.	Carney
Johns	L.T.	Olander
Dunne	L.G.	Mohr
Vick	C.	Vogel
Wilson	R.G.	Anderson
Muirhead	R.T.	Drayer
Goebel	R.E.	Sabo
Uteritz	Q.B.	Walquist
Cappon	L.H.	Peden
Steketee	R.H.	Durant
Roby	F.B.	Crangle

Substitutes: Illinois—Wilson for Carney; Woodward for Crangle; Greene for Olander; Gammage for Mohr; Relckle for Wilson. Michigan—Swan for Wilson. Goal from placement—Steketee, Michigan.

Umpire, Eckersall, Chicago; Referee, Haines; Field judge—McGovern; Head linesman—Kiritz.

VICK SELECTED ON MYTHICAL ELEVEN BY WALTER CAMP

PLAYS STERLING GAME IN LAST YEAR ON VARSITY SQUAD

PLACED AT CENTER IN CHOICE OF HONOR TEAM

Makes Tenth Man to Be Picked from Among Yostmen for High Award

**Henry Vick
Center**

THE MICHIGAN SQUAD

No.	Name	Position	Height	Weight	Class	Home
1	Goebel, P. G. (Captain)	End	6 ft. 3 in.	185	'23E	Grand Rapids
2	Johns, J. E.	Guard	6 ft.	172	'23E	East Lansing
3	VanderVoort, E. R.	Tackle	6 ft. 1 in.	198	'24	Lansing
4	Roby, D. F.	Halfback	5 ft. 10 in.	180	'23	Holland
5	Cappon, E. C.	Fullback	5 ft. 10 in.	185	'23E	Holland
6	Kipke, H. G.	Halfback	5 ft. 9 in.	155	'24	Lansing
7	Kirk, Bernard	End	5 ft. 10 in.	170	'23	Ypsilanti
8	Knode, R. T.	Quarterback	5 ft. 9 in.	155	'23	Baltimore, Md.
9	Neisch, L. E.	End	6 ft. 1 in.	180	'25	Detroit
10	Slaughter, E. R.	Center	5 ft. 10 in.	190	'25E	Louisville, Ky.
11	Muirhead, S. N.	Tackle	6 ft	175	'24	Detroit
12	Blott, J. L.	Center	6 ft.	185	'24	Girard, Ohio
13	Rosatti, R. F.	Guard	6 ft.	190	'23A	Norway
14	Blahnik, J. G.	Tackle	6 ft. 1 in.	175	'25	Menominee
15	Dunleavy, George	Halfback	6 ft.	178	'25	Gary, Ind.
16	Gunther, J. E.	Fullback	5 ft. 10 in.	177	'23	Goshen, Ind.
17	Henderson, W. P.	End	5 ft. 11 in.	170	'23Ed	Detroit
18	Keefer, J. M.	Halfback	5 ft. 9 in.	155	'25	Dayton, Ohio
20	Heath, M. W.	Guard	6 ft.	185	'23	Albion
21	Steele, H. O.	Guard	5 ft. 10 in.	175	'25	Sioux City, Iowa
22	Steger, Herbert	Halfback	5 ft. 10 in.	170	'25	Oak Park, Ill.
23	Swan, D. M.	Guard	5 ft. 10 in.	185	'24E	Detroit
24	Van Orden, W. J.	Guard	5 ft. 11 in.	210	'23	Ann Arbor
25	Uteritz, I. C.	Quarterback	5 ft. 7 in.	140	'23	Oak Park, Ill.
26	Curran, L. B.	End	5 ft. 10 in.	165	'23E	Louisville, Ky.
27	Garfield, S. M.	Tackle	6 ft. 1 in.	185	'23	Albion
29	Chamberlain, R. W.	Tackle	6 ft. 1 in.	175	'23	Lakewood, Ohio
30	Rankin, D. N.	Halfback	5 ft. 10 in.	170	'24	Shelby
31	Murray, J.	Guard	5 ft. 9 in.	165	'25	Saginaw
34	White, H. S.	Tackle	6 ft. 2 in.	208	'25L	Ashton
35	Tracy, F. S	Quarterback	5 ft. 8 in.	140	'24	Chicago, Ill.

Season Summary
Games won, 5; Lost, 1; Tied, 1.
Points for Michigan, 187; For Opponents 21
1922
Michigan........48; Case...........0
Michigan.........0; Vanderbilt......0
Michigan........19; Ohio State......0
Michigan........24; Illinois........0
Michigan........63; M.A.C..........0
Michigan........13; Wisconsin......6
Michigan........16; Minnesota......7

CAPTAIN PAUL GOEBEL

Paul Goebel, Michigan's football captain, is playing his third year as right end on the Varsity squad. Goebel is considered one of the best flank men who has appeared in the Big Ten in recent years. Although he has been handicapped all season by an injured leg, he has started each game in his regular position and stayed in as long as his leg would hold out.
Goebel's home is in Grand Rapids, where he starred at end on the Central High School team before entering Michigan. Paul is now a senior in the Engineering College.

With the preliminary games aside, the Wilce machine concerted its efforts for the important dedication game in the Stadium with Michigan, October 21. Before a throng of more than 70,000 persons—the largest which ever saw a football game in the West and which included many Homecoming alumni—Michigan cleanly defeated the Buckeyes, 19 to 0. From the early moments of the game, when Captain Goebel of the Wolverines toed over a field goal, until the final whistle, Michigan cleanly had the advantage. Only at the outset of the second half did Pixley and his mates seem to have a chance, and this was short-lived. On the other hand, Yost's brilliant eleven gathered 16 more points. Kipke at half was the outstanding star of the contest, his all-round play lifting him upon a high eminence. Goebel and Kirk were also bugbears for the Buckeyes.

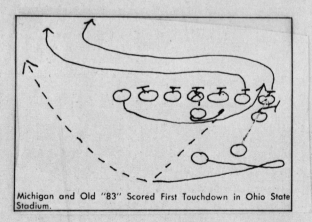

Michigan and Old "83" Scored First Touchdown in Ohio State Stadium.

Wolverines Beat Illinois, 24-0

Ann Arbor, Mich., Oct. 28.—Beating down the stubborn defense of Bob Zuppke's men, Michigan won its second western conference football game of the season here today, downing Illinois, 24 to 0.

Although balked at many stages in the game by the Illinois line, Yost's machine took advantage of every opportunity, carrying the battle into Illinois territory repeatedly during the second and third periods.

The visitors threatened the Michigan line but once. That was in the final period when Zuppke's men smashed their way from midfield to win 18 yards of the Wolverine goal in line plunges and end runs by Happenney and McIlwain. Here the Michigan defense held.

In the opening period the Yostmen were almost helpless before the Illini, the Wolverines' revamped line not being able to clear the path for the backs.

Illinois failed to make a first down until the final period, when six were registered. Michigan made eight first downs during the game.

Top Row: Vick (Coach), Wieman (Coach), Steger, Murray, Henderson, Vander Voort, Muirhead, Blahnik, Van Orden, Goebel, Chamberlain, Gunther, Rosatti, Heath, Neisch, Steele, Dunleavy, Sturzenegger (Coach).
Middle Row: Johns, Uteritz, Keefer, Slaughter, Blott, Yost and Little (Coaches), Kipke, Cappon, Roby, Lipscher, Kirk.
Bottom Row: Foster, Carter, Rankin, Knode.

KIPKE WILL CAPTAIN 1923 MICHIGAN TEAM

Ann Arbor, Mich., Nov. 27.—Harry G. Kipke of Lansing, Mich., star halfback of the Michigan 'varsity football eleven, was elected captain of the 1923 squad at a meeting of the "M" men today. Kipke, one of the best halfbacks Michigan has produced, has one more year to play.

Michigan's undefeated football team will make no claim to sole possession of the Western conference championship, being perfectly willing to share honors with Iowa, another undefeated eleven, it was announced by Coach Fielding H. Yost today. Some Michigan supporters had urged that Michigan claim first position on points.

Coach Yost will continue indefinitely as head of the Michigan football coaching staff, despite his added burdens as head of the university's athletic department, he announced today. He will be unable to devote as much time to the squad next year, however, as was the case this season, and much of the duties will fall upon Assistant Coach George Little, who is serving his first year in the Maize and Blue coaching department.

CAMP NAMES THREE MICHIGAN PLAYERS ON ALL-AMERICAN

KIPKE CHOSEN AS HALFBACK ON NOTED CRITIC'S FIRST ELEVEN

KIRK MAKES SECOND TEAM, UTERITZ THIRD

More Wolverines Receive Honor Than Any Other School in Country; 24 Colleges Represented

Walter Camp, noted football critic, gave the Wolverines unusual honor last week when he named three Michigan men on his all-American selection. Harry Kipke, captain-elect of the Varsity, was given one of the half back positions on the first team. Bernard Kirk won an end berth on the second team and Irwin Uteritz was selected to pilot the third team which was picked by Camp.

**Harry Kipke
Halfback**

KIRK DIES FROM HURTS RECEIVED IN AUTO CRASH

NAMED ON CAMP'S MYTHICAL ELEVEN BEFORE HIS DEATH

FORMER TEAM MATES ACT AS PALLBEARERS

Knocked Unconscious When Maching Skids Into Telephone Pole; Dies 6 Days Later

Bernard Kirk, '23, end on the Varsity football team in 1921 and 1922, died of meningitis at the Beyer Memorial hospital in Ypsilanti, December 23. Meningitis, the immediate cause of death, was brought on by a fracture of his skull sustained in an automobile accident December 17.

Kirk was in an automobile with Cyrenus Darling, '25M, and Harold E. Covert, '21, and the party was driving to Kirk's home in Ypsilanti, when the car struck a sign-post that had fallen across the road, and skidded into a telephone pole. Kirk, who was immediately knocked unconscious, was rushed to the Beyer Memorial hospital, where he recovered consciousness 12 hours later.

36 Case	0	37 M.A.C.	0	26 Quantico Marines	6
3 Vanderbilt	0	9 Iowa	3	6 Wisconsin	3
23 Ohio State	0			10 Minnesota	0

Michigan 150; Opponents 12
Won 8; Tied 0; Lost 0

MICHIGAN SQUAD

No.	Name	Position	Height	Weight	Prep School	Ye...
1	Kipke, Captain	Half	5' 9"	158	Lansing High	'2...
2	Blott	Center	6'	185	Girard, Ohio	'2...
3	Miller	Full	5' 10"	170	Grand Rapids Central	'2...
4	Muirhead	Tackle	6'	180	Detroit Northern	'2...
5	Uteritz	Quarter	5' 8"	150	Oak Park	'2...
6	Van Dervoort	Tackle	6' 1"	198	Lansing High	'2...
7	Steele	Guard	5' 10"	175	Sioux City	'2...
8	Neisch	End	6' 1"	178	Detroit Eastern	'24
9	Steger	Half	5' 10"	170	Oak Park	'2...
10	Marion	End	5' 9"	180	Detroit Northwestern	'24
11	Herrnstein	Half	5' 11"	157	Chillicothe, Ohio	'2...
12	Grube	Half	5' 10"	155	Arthur Hill, Saginaw	'26
13	Witherspoon	End	5' 11"	170	Detroit Northwestern	'25
14	Vick	Half	5' 8"	155	Scott High, Toledo	'26
15	Babcock	Tackle	5' 11"	180	Royal Oak, Mich.	'26
16	Curran	End	5' 10"	165	Louisville, Ky.	'24
17	Hawkins	Guard	6'	185	Arthur Hill, Saginaw	'26
18	Heston	Half	5' 11"	170	Detroit	'26
19	Kunow	Tackle	6'	204	Detroit Eastern	'25
20	Ingle	Guard	6' 2"	190	Ann Arbor High	'25
21	Donnelly	Tackle	5' 11"	185	Cadillac	'24
22	Brown	Center	5' 10"	178	Ypsilanti	'26
24	Parker	Half	5' 8"	150	Hastings	'26
25	Palmer	End	6' 1"	170	Grand Rapids Central	'26
26	Rockwell	Quarter	5' 9"	160	Jackson	'25
27	White	Guard	6' 2"	195	Reed City, Mich.	'24
28	Swan	Guard	5' 10"	175	Detroit Central	'24
29	Wall	Center	5' 11"	170	Birmingham	'24
30	Slaughter	Guard	5' 10"	190	Louisville, Ky.	'25
31	Ferenz	End	5' 10"	163	Flint	'26
32	Baker	Quarter	5' 7"	148	Kalamazoo Central	'26

THE FIRST GAME

Michigan, 36; Case, 0

MICHIGAN defeated Case in the opening game of the 1923 season Saturday, October 6, by a score of 36 to 0, the points being made through five touchdowns, one field goal and three goals after touchdown.

As a curtain-raiser for one of the heaviest schedules Michigan has ever faced, the game was highly satisfactory; the weather was bright and clear and the stands well filled with spectators. But there was nothing in the exhibition to give the spectators any inkling of what the team's strength may proved to be against opponents of the same caliber. Case was plucky and never gave up, several times checking the Michigan offensive and forcing their opponents to punt; but they displayed little or no offensive strength, and their one slim chance for a score was an attempted drop-kick from the 40-yard line which went very wide of the mark.

MICHIGAN		VANDERBILT
Marion	le	Bomar
Muirhead	lt	Reeves
Slaughter	lg	Lawrence
Blott	c	Sharpe
Steele	rg	Kelley
Vandevoort	rt	Walker
Curran	re	Wakefield
Uteritz	qb	Kuhn
Kipke	lh	Meiers
Steger	rf	Reece
Miller	fb	Ryan

Score by quarters—
Michigan .... 0 3 0 0—3
Vanderbilt ...... 0 0 0 0—0
Field Goals—Blott.
Substitutions: Michigan—Grube for Miller; Vick for Steger.
Referee — McDonald (Brown); umpire — Springer (Penn.); field judge — Page (Ohio Wesleyan); headlinesman — Finley (Virginia)

Oct. 13

COMMODORES IN FIRST DEFEAT ON GRID SINCE 1920

McGugin's Men Keep Goal Line Uncrossed; Vandy Ends Prove Strong

History nearly repeated itself at Ferry field Saturday afternoon when 11 football warriors representing Vanderbilt, a team which had not tasted defeat since 1920 battled the Yostmen in one of the hardest conflicts ever staged on Wolverine soil.

Held to a scoreless tie in 1922, Michigan nearly suffered the same fate again Saturday. Vanderbilt's goal line is still uncrossed but Jack Blott, standing on the Commodore 19-yard line in the second quarter, booted a field goal which gave Michigan its 3-0 victory.

Vanderbilt has no need to be ashamed of its team which was glorious in defeat. With a strong forward wall supported by two exceptional flankers in Bomar and Wakefield and aided by the great punting of Tom Ryan, Vanderbilt thrust back the Wolverines time after time and while the southerners exhibited little in the matter of offense the team was one of the best drilled on defense which has ever played at Ferry field.

Oct. 20

MICHIGAN		OHIO STATE
Marion	l. e.	Seiffer
Muirhead	l. t.	Oberlin
Slaughter	l. g.	Steel
Blott	c.	Young
Steele	r. g.	Schulist
Vandervoort	r. t.	Pectcoff
Curran	r. e.	Wilson
Uteritz	q. b.	Marts
Kipke	l. h.	Wendler
Steger	r. h.	Workman
Miller	f. b.	DeVoe

Score by quarters:
Michigan .... 0 3 7 13—23
Ohio State ...... 0 0 0 0— 0
Touchdowns—Steger 2; Kipke 1. Field goals—Blott.
Points after touchdowns—Blott 2 (place kicks).
Substitutions: Michigan — Hawkins for Steele, Steele for Slaughter, Rockwell for Kipke, Grube for Miller, Hernstein for Steger, White for Steele, Vick for Grube, Witherspoon for Marion, Brown for White. Ohio State—Cunningham for Seiffer, Gorrill for Wilson, Judy for Marts, Watts for Young, Nichols for Steel, Marts for Judy, Young for Watts, Snyder for Wendler, Kuttler for Nichols, Southern for DeVoe, Honaker for Snyder.
Referee—Eckersall (Chicago).
Umpire—Schommer (Chicago).
Field judge — Young (Illinois Wesleyan).
Head linesman—McCord (Illinois).

BLOCKED DROP KICK WINNER FOR YOSTMEN

Kipke and Blott Prove Great Factors in Toe Victory of Undefeated Wolverines.

SCORE IS 9 TO 3

IT WAS a game full of the popularly called "breaks" which Michigan won November 3rd at Iowa City by the score of 9 to 3. The ability of Blott to take advantage of the breaks when taking such advantage spelled scores, represents the margin of victory over the team which tied Michigan last year for the Conference championship.

Nov. 10

A STRONG FINISH

MICHIGAN		MARINES.
Marion	L.E	Farrell
Muirhead	L.T.	Liversedge
Slaughter	L.G.	Cercek
Blott	C.	Bailey
Hawkins	R.G.	McHenry
Babcock	R.T.	Hunt
Neisch	R.E.	Skinner
Uteritz	Q.	Goettge
Kipke	L.H.	Heny
Steger	R.H.	Ryckman
Miller	F.B.	Neale

Score:

Michigan	0	7	7	12—26
Marines	6	0	0	0— 6

Touchdowns—Michigan: Uteritz (on quarterback sneak), Miller (on short plunge at 21-yard pass to Steger), Rockwell (from fake 18-yard placement), Parker (on 24-yard run after intercepting pass). Marines: Neal (on short plunge after plunges and pass from first kickoff to Marine 30-yard line). Goals from touchdowns—Uteritz (15-yard placement), Uteritz (15-yard placement).

Steger Never in a Losing Battle

CHICAGO, Nov. 27.—Herbert J. Steger, captain-elect of the Michigan football team, never has played in a losing game of football.

During the four years that he played halfback and fullback on the championship Oak Park High School here, the school was undefeated. Michigan has had an unsullied record for the two years that Steger has been its star halfback.

The first time the new captain was put in a varsity game his signal was called and he ran 60 yards for a touchdown.

Nov. 17

WISCONSIN NEVER BEAT A YOST TEAM!

Michigan Has Big Edge in Past Grid Battles With Badgers

Michigan and Wisconsin football teams will renew a rivalry of more than 30 years' standing when the two teams clash at Madison Saturday, the first Badger and Wolverine teams clashing in 1892.

The game Saturday will be the tenth encounter between the two teams, Michigan having won six games, Wisconsin two, while one game resulted in a tie.

The two games won by Wisconsin were played before Yost came to Michigan and a Yost coached eleven has never yet tasted defeat at the hands of Wisconsin although the game in 1921 resulted in a tie, score, 7 to 7.

Michigan	Position	Wisconsin
Marion	LE	Irish
Muirhead	LT	Below
Slaughter	LG	Bieberstein
Blott	C	Teckmeyer
Hawkins	RG	Nichols
Babcock	RT	Bentson
Curran	RE	Nelson
Rockwell	QB	Schneider
Kipke	LH	Williams
Steger	RH	Harris
Vick	FB	Taft

Score by quarters:

Michigan	0	6	0	0—6
Wisconsin	3	0	0	0—3

Touchdown—Rockwell. Field goal—Below.

Slaughter Makes Spectacular Play In Badger Tussle

The final play of the Michigan-Wisconsin football game brought out a situation never presented in the great fall game before, in the opinion of Fielding H. Yost, who has personally watched about as much football as anyone.

The play was the tackling of a runner with the ball 50 yards ahead of the line of scrimmage by a guard. In a last desperate attempt Taft had dropped back, waited as long as he could, and then sent the ball skimming through the air in one of the longest passes of the day. Three Wisconsin men and Herrnstein jumped for the ball and it finally settled in the arms of Harris. He staggered 10 yards from the impact of the other men and before he could regain his equilibrium, Ediff Slaughter of Louisville, Ky., got one hand on him and then bore him to earth just as Colonel Mumma, field judge, sounded the end of the game.

The ball had been put in play on the Wisconsin 32-yard line and Slaughter brought his man to earth on the Michigan 15-yard line, 53 yards ahead of the line of scrimmage.

Yost says it is the first time in history that a guard made a tackle that far ahead of the line of scrimmage.

Nov. 24

VARSITY STAYS UNDEFEATED FOR SECOND SEASON, TAKING LAST CONTEST FROM GOPHERS

MICHIGAN		MINNESOTA
Neisch	L. E.	Eklund
Muirhead	L. T.	Gross
Slaughter	L. G.	Gay
Brown	C.	Cooper
Hawkins	R. G.	Abramson
Babcock	R. T.	Cox
Curran	R. E.	Merrill
Rockwell	Q. B.	Graham
Kipke	L. H.	Martineau
Steger	R. H.	Lidberg
Vick	F. B.	Asher

Michigan	0	7	3	0—10
Minnesota	0	0	0	0— 0

ALL-AMERICAN

Jack Blott
Center

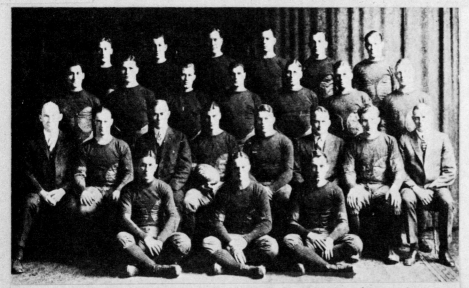

PARKER   BABCOCK   KUNOW   DEWEY   DOMHOFF   GREGORY
FLORA   HAWKINS   STEELE   SLAUGHTER   EDWARDS   GRUBE   STAMMAN
Coach WIEMAN   MARION   Coach YOST   STEGER   BROWN   Coach LITTLE   MILLER   Trainer HOYT
FRIEDMAN   ROCKWELL   HERRNSTEIN

1924 Varsity Football Team

OFFICERS

Herbert F. Steger	Captain
George E. Little	Coach
J. Glenn Donaldson	Manager-Elect

PERSONNEL

R. George Babcock	Tackle	Edgar Madsen	Center, End
Robert J. Brown	Center	Phillip E. Marion	Back, End
R. Sidney Dewey	Guard	James K. Miller	End, Back
Victor Domhoff	Quarter	H. Frederick Parker	Back
Thomas L. Edwards	Tackle	Ferdinand A. Rockwell	Back
William R. Flora	End	Edliff R. Slaughter	Guard
Bruce R. Gregory	Back	Carl P. Stamman	Back
Charles W. Grube	End	Harold O. Steele	Guard
Harry Hawkins	Guard, Tackle	Herbert F. Steger	Back
William H. Herrnstein, Jr.	Back	Ben Friedman	Back
Walter Kunow	Tackle		

A. M. A.

Merle C. Baker	Elmer E. Langguth
William D. Coventry	John H. Lovette
Russell W. Davis	Kent C. McIntyre
Harlan Froemke	Paul C. Samson
William H. Heath	William E. Ullmann
	John H. Witherspoon

Results of Season

Michigan	55	Miami	0
Michigan	7	M.A.C.	0
Michigan	14	Illinois	39
Michigan	21	Wisconsn	0
Michigan	13	Minnesota	0
Michigan	27	Northwestern	0
Michigan	16	Ohio State	6
Michigan	2	Iowa	9

MICHIGAN 55   MIAMI 0

THE first game of the 1924 season showed that the team had great possibilities, and that the coaches were well on their way to finding men who could fill the places left vacant by the graduation of such men as Kipke, Blott, Uteritz, and Muirhead. With Captain Steger, Steele, Slaughter, and Miller as the only veterans, their task was a difficult one. Brown, Rockwell, Babcock, and Marion had had some Conference experience but were not what may be termed veterans. The green team gained at will against the Ohioans.

Active as Usual

Coach Yost has taken active charge of the kickers on the Michigan squad this year. The above picture was snapped of the coach as he was showing some of his punters the proper method of applying the boot to the pigskin.

JUST IN TIME

Michigan	Pos.	M. A. C.
Marion	L.E.	Schultz
Edwards	L.T.	Eckert
Slaughter	L.G.	Hultman
Brown	C.	Eckerman
Steele	R.G.	Hackett
Kunow	R.T.	Haskins
Grube	R.E.	Robinson
Rockwell	Q.	Lyman
Steger (C)	L.H.	Lioret
Herrnstein	R.H.	Richards
Miller	F.B.	Neller
Michigan	0 0 7—7	
M. A. C.	0 0 0 0—0	

Touchdown—Steger on 20-yard run after 28-yard pass from Parker. Goal from touchdowns—Rockwell (placement).

Substitutions Michigan—Parker for Herrnstein; Herrnstein for Parker; Gregory for Herrnstein; Samson for Edwards; Parker for Gregory; Heath for Miller. M. A. C. Garver for Hultman; Hultman for Robinson; Beckley for Richards; Richards for Lyman; Spickerman for Eckert; Lyman for Richards; Eckert for Spickerman; Schmyser for Lioret; Kipke for Schultz; Goede for Schmyser; Garver for Hultman; Voget for Eckerman; Fremont for Lyman.

Referee—Sisler, (Illinois). Umpire —Knight, (Dartmouth). Field Judge —Bay, (Illinois). Head Linesman— Costello, (Georgetown).

RANGE THRILLS HUGE CROWD BY RACING TO 5 TOUCHDOWNS

BY JAMES CRUSINBERRY.

Champaign, Ill., Oct. 18.—[Special.]—Michigan never knew Red Grange, e Illinois wildcat, until today. Now Michigan knows him well.

This great runner of Bob Zuppke's football team ran all over Michigan the first quarter of their grid battle today at the new Illinois stadium and ushed the Ann Arbor boys before they realized they were in a contest. The al score was 39 to 14 in favor of the boys of Illinois, but was 27 to 0 a e end of the first period when Grange raced down the field four times for uchdowns.

Grange had torn Michigan to pieces before the game had gone more than teen seconds because he received the first kickoff from Capt Steger of e Wolverines, and from his own 5 yard line ran and dodged and tore his ay 95 yards for a touchdown. Right then and there Michigan knew it was against something it hadn't seen football before.

Three More Long Runs.

Three more times in that first pe-ed Grange got loose for long runs r touchdowns. His second one came ter about five minutes of play and as 67 yards in length. The joyful lini rooters were hardly through eering that thrilling play before the d headed Wheaton lad got loose gain for another, 56 yards in length, d before the quarter was ended he ok the ball on the Michigan 44 yard ne and dashed through the whole am for a fourth touchdown.

In that first period he made four as nsational open field runs as have en seen in years.

It is doubtful if anything near its qual has been seen in the West since e days of Walter Eckersall. Going to the game, Michigan was figured have an equal chance to win. The ur startling runs in the first quarter y young Grange made Illinois a 1 o 1 shot. He carried the ball for total of 262 yards on those four plays nd Michigan was a crushed and aten foe.

The second quarter had hardly be-un when Coach Zuppke called his star rom the game to save him for other es to come later in the season, hough he was back in the fray for he entire second half, but content to ake one touchdown, the final run for being only 11 yards. He did a lot plunging and passing in the sec-nd half, but never again got loose r a long and thrilling dash.

Reprinted with permission from the **Michigan Daily**

RED'S RECORD AGAINST WOLVERINES READS LIKE A FAIRY STORY

CHAMPAIGN, Ill., Oct. 18.—This is the record of Harold [Red] Grange, sensational 22 year old Illinois half back, perhaps the outstanding gridiron star in America last season, in today's Michigan-Illinois game:

Scored five touchdowns—four in less than 12 minutes of play.

Broke away for successive runs of 95, 67, 56, and 44 yards for touchdowns.

Scooped up the ball on the very first kick off and raced 95 yards, dodging through Michigan's tacklers for a touchdown.

Carried the ball in twenty-one plays and gained the astonishing distance of 409 yards.

Threw most of Illinois' forward passes and also held the ball for Britton on the points for goal after touchdowns.

MICHIGAN 21   WISCONSIN 0

SHOWING strength and a comeback spirit that startled the entire Conference, Michigan defeated Wisconsin the following Saturday, 21-0. The team was completely reorganized with Captain Steger at quarter, Rockwell at half, Miller at end, and Marion at full. Michigan's running and passing game was at its best with Friedman, a new man doing the hurling and Captain Steger the receiving. A long pass from Friedman to Steger put the ball on the two-yard line. Here Wisconsin held for four downs. Wisconsin punted out, but on the next play, Michigan passed again, this time going over. Rockwell made several beautiful runs around end and off tackle.

The Michigan-Wisconsin Game, Oct. 25, 1924

Gopher Eleven To Banquet Michigan Team and Coaches

Michigan gridders and coaches will be the guests of Minnesota players and athletic staff at the annual "Jug" Dinner to be held Saturday night after the game, at the Minnesota Union.

And in the center of the table, decorated with the colors of the victor in the afternoon's football battle, will repose the little brown jug, most famous and unusual trophy in American athletics.

MICHIGAN 13   MINNESOTA 0

THE third Conference game played with Minnesota at Minneapolis resulted in another victory for Michigan. Captain Steger who had injured his foot in the Wisconsin game was forced to view the contest from the side-lines, Slaughter acting as Captain. The game developed into a fight between the tricky, overhead game of the Wolverines against the heavy, line-smashing tactics of Ascher and Liedberg. Several times the Gophers ploughed down the field only to lose the ball on downs or by an intercepted pass as soon as they neared the Wolverine goal line. The Little Brown Jug, the traditional emblem of rivalry between the two schools, was carried ack triumphantly to Ann Arbor.

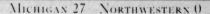

"Fight like Steger."

**Edliff Slaughter
Guard
1924**

Brown Is Elected Captain of 1925 Michigan Eleven

Robert Brown of Ypsilanti was elected captain of the 1925 Michigan football team at a meeting of the letter men held this noon. Brown has played at center for the past two seasons, taking Jack Blott's place last year and filling the position in a capable manner.

Brown is a great defensive player and a good passer and extremely popular with his teammates. He has one more year in which to represent the Wolverines.

MICHIGAN 27   NORTHWESTERN 0

NORTHWESTERN was unable to cope with the driving attack of the Wolverine backs and the baffling passes thrown by Friedman. Though the Purple put up a hard fight, they were outclassed and could neither stop the Maize and Blue nor gain against her. Northwestern's outstanding player, "Moon" Baker, was unable to gain but a few yards. Three of Michigan's touchdowns were gained by passes, the Wolverines presenting one of the most effective aerial games in the 1924 Conference.

MICHIGAN 16   OHIO STATE 6

SCORING a touchdown in the first quarter and holding Michigan scoreless for three quarters, the Buckeyes were finally defeated by the score of 16—6. Despite the Ohioian's long stand, the Wolverines were not to be denied, and when their overhead and running attack got under way, gained two touchdowns by the combined passing of Friedman and the sensational line smashing of Marion. Rockwell kicked a field goal in the last quarter, and later a pass from Steger to Flora placed the ball on the Buckeye fifteen yard line where it was taken over in three plays by Friedman, Marion and Rockwell.

MICHIGAN 2   IOWA 9

THE second defeat of the season came when the heavy Iowa team succeeded in breaking up the Wolverine passing attack, Michigan completing but two out of attempted passes. A touchdown by Scantlebury in the first quarter and a place kick by Hancock in the final period completed Iowa's scoring, while Michigan gained her point when Edwards blocked a kick and an Iowa player recovering was tackled behind his own goal line. The line worked unusually well, holding the Hawkeyes time and again. Rockwell by his sensational field running, and Marion, with his line plunging, succeeded in working the ball down the field four successive times, only to lose it when Michigan attempted to pass over Iowa's goal line.

Between halves, taps were sounded, a salute was fired, and the flag placed at half mast as a tribute to Edgar "Farmer" Madsen, substitute center and end on the Varsity team, who died from pneumonia the Thursday preceding the game.

Michigan concluded the season with four victories and two defeats: she won more games than any team in the Conference, but still had to be content with third place in the Conference rating.

The Squad — Michigan

Playing Number	Name	Wgt.	Position	Home City	Yrs. Prior Varsity Exp.
11	Hoffman, Leo	147	Q	Richmond Hill, N. Y.	0
14	Babcock, R. G.	181	T	Royal Oak, Mich.	2
15	Garber, Martin	152	H	Enid, Okla.	0
16	Gilbert, Lewis	159	H	Kalamazoo, Mich.	0
17	Babcock, S.	157	H	Detroit, Mich.	0
18	Baer, Ray	181	G	Louisville, Ky.	0
19	Brown, Robt. (Capt.)	183	C	Ypsilanti, Mich.	2
20	Coventry, W. D.	172	C	Duluth, Minn.	1
21	Cowell, Wayne	162	F	Coldwater, Mich.	0
22	Dewey, Sid	197	G	Monroe, Mich.	1
23	Domhoff, Victor	169	Q	Toledo, Ohio	1
24	Gregory, Bruce	160	H	Ann Arbor, Mich.	1
25	Edwards, Tom	180	T	Central Lake, Mich.	1
26	Grinnell, Henry	184	T	Grosse Isle, Mich.	0
27	Friedman, Ben	174	Q	Cleveland, Ohio	1
28	Grube, Charles	174	E	Saginaw, Mich.	2
29	Gabel, Norman	192	T	Detroit, Mich.	0
30	Hawkins, Harry	198	G	Saginaw, Mich.	2
31	Flora, William	185	E	Muskegon, Mich.	1
32	Herrnstein, Wm.	163	H & E	Chillicothe, Ohio	2
33	Heston, LeRoy	180	H	Ann Arbor, Mich.	0
34	Fuller, Fred	173	H	Jackson, Mich.	0
35	Kelly, Earl	167	H	Cadillac, Mich.	0
36	Koplin, Barney	169	E	South Orange, N. J.	0
38	Levi, Waldeck	190	G	Ann Arbor, Mich.	1
40	Lovette, John	190	F	Saginaw, Mich.	1
41	McIntyre, Kent	168	G	Detroit, Mich.	1
42	Miller, James	162	Q	Adrian, Mich.	0
43	Molenda, John	187	F	Detroit, Mich.	0
45	Nickerson, M. E.	187	E	Oak Park, Ill.	0
46	Oade, James	186	T	Lansing, Mich.	0
47	Oosterbaan, B.	182	E	Muskegon, Mich.	0
48	Palmeroli, John	183	G	Highland Park, Mich.	0
49	Palmer, Lowell	181	E	Grand Rapids, Mich.	1
50	Parker, H. F.	165	H	Hastings, Mich.	2
51	Puckelwartz, Wm.	152	Q	Chicago, Ill.	0
52	Rankin, Don	172	F	Shelby, Mich.	0
53	Schoenfeldt, John	184	C	Detroit, Mich.	0
54	Skidmore, Stanley	169	Q	Battle Creek, Mich.	0
55	Stamman, Carl	165	E	Toledo, Ohio	1
56	Thisted, Carl	185	C	Great Falls, Mont.	0
57	Webber, Howard	194	G	Mt. Clemens, Mich.	0
58	Webber, Walter	181	F	Mt. Clemens, Mich.	0
59	Welling, Arthur	168	E	Grand Haven, Mich.	0
61	Witherspoon, John	169	F	Detroit, Mich.	1

63	Indiana	0	3	Illinois	0	2 Northwestern	3
39	Michigan State	0	54	Navy	0	10 Ohio State	3
21	Wisconsin	0				35 Minnesota	0

Michigan 227; Opponents 3
Won 7; Tied 0; Lost 1

Yost's Twenty-Fifth Year

Fielding H. Yost is starting his twenty-fifth year as coach of the Michigan football team. Like every other coach he hopes for a successful year and from now until the end of the season he will strive with all the resources at his command to produce a winner. But it is safe to say that now, today, with practice just starting and the first game several weeks away, the Yost season is already a success.

Why? Because Yost is not one of the win-at-any-price fellows. His outlook is broader than that of the man who strives for nothing but victories, at whatever cost achieved. He builds character, he trains the athletes under him as intelligent gentlemen should be trained, and they benefit accordingly, no matter whether the team always wins or not. It might be mentioned, incidentally, that in the 24 years of Yost's coaching at Ann Arbor, the Michigan football teams have scored 5,673 points against 806 for their opponents, proving that the Yost methods pay in material ways.

Why is the athletic prestige of the University of Michigan so high? Largely because of Yost. No scandal has ever been connected with Yost's teams, which means that the reputation of the institution which they represent has been enhanced.

Yost wants victory. He seeks it with brain and with brawn, but his vision is broad, and to his natural heritage of true and honest sportsmanship there has come, through the years, a philosophical realization of the bigger things that are really and enduringly worth while in life. That is why he is the greatest football coach in America and that is why Michigan football teams are successful always and would be if they never won a game.

Oct. 10

Michigan		Indiana
Oosterbaan	L.E.	Lanman
Hawkins	L.T.	Clifford
Lovette	L.G.	Bishop
Brown (Capt.)	C.	Zaicher
Edwards	R.G.	Bernoske
Oade	R.T.	Fisher
Flora	R.E.	Nessell
Friedman	Q.B.	Salmi
Gilbert	R.H.B.	Marks, (Capt)
Gregory	L.H.B.	Byers
Molenda	F.B.	Prucha

Summaries: Touchdowns—Gregory (2), Oosterbaan (2), Gilbert, Flora, Molenda, Babcock, Friedman. Goals after touchdown Friedman (8), Stamman.

Substitutes, Michigan. Stamman for Molenda, Grube for Oosterbaan, Puckelwartz for Friedman, Dewey for Lovette, Parker for Gilbert, Oosterbaan for Grube. Molenda for Stamman, S. Babcock for Parker, Palmerole for Hawkins, Gable for Oade, Grinnell for Edwards, Schoenfeldt for Brown, Hoffman for Friedman, Miller for Gregory, H. Webber for Oosterbaan. Indiana. Kelso for Lanman, Watson for Lanman, Corum for Byers, McConnell for Prucha.

Referee, Eckersall, Chicago. Umpire, Kennedy, Chicago. Field Judge, Ray, Illinois. Head Linesman, Huston, Parsons.

Oct. 3

LINE-UP AND SUMMARY

MICHIGAN		STATE
Grube	L. E.	Drew
Hawkins	L. T.	Spiekerman
Lovette	L. G.	Rummell
Thisted	C.	Vogel
Edwards	R. G.	Hackett
Babcock	R. T.	Haskins
Flora	R. E.	Lyman
Friedman	Q.	Fouts
Fuller	L. H.	Boehringer
Gregory	R. H.	Smith
Molenda	F. B.	Van Buren

Score by periods:
Michigan .... 13 0 26 0—39
State .... 0 0 0 0—0

Touchdowns—Friedman 1, Gregory 1, Oosterbaan 2, R. G. Babcock 1, Gilbert 1. Goals from touchdowns—Fuller, 1; Gilbert 2. Substitutions—Michigan: Gilbert for Fuller, Stamman for Molenda, Oosterbaan for Grube, Grinnel for Edwards, S. Babcock for Gregory, Dewey for Lovette, Oade for Edwards, Puckelwartz for Friedman, Baer for Dewey, Nickerson for George Babcock, Schoenfeldt for Thisted, Palmer for Flora, Fuller for Babcock, McIntyre for Hawkins, Palmeroli for Baer, Webber for Stamman, Coventry for Schoenfeldt, Grube for Oosterbaan, Miller for Fuller. Michigan State College: Ruhl for Boehringer, Eberbach for Vogel, Grim for Edmunds, Boehringer for Van Buren, Garver for Rummell, Valentine for Hackett, Edmunds for Drew, Anderson for Edmunds, Lyman for Grim, Van Buren for Smith, Ames for Eberbach, McCoss for Van Buren, Wolfinger for Fouts, Wenner for Spiekerman, George for Ruhl, Collett for Lyman, Cole for Anderson, and Kiebler for Boehringer. Referee — Hackett (West Point). Umpire — Kennedy (Chicago). Head linesman—Gardner (Illinois). Field Judge—Nells (West Point).

THE VICTORS
Louis Elbel

Hail! to the victors valiant
Hail! to the conquering heroes.
Hail! Hail! to Michigan and best,—
Hail! to the victors valiant,
Hail! to the conquering heroes.
Hail! Hail! to Michigan the champions of the West.

OCT. 17

MICHIGAN (21)	
Flora	RE
G. Babcock, Baer	RT
Edwards	RG
Brown	C
Lovette, Dewey	LG
Hawkins	LT
Oosterbaan	LE
Friedman	QB
Gregory, Herrnstein	RH
Gilbert, S. Babcock	LH
Molenda, Stamman	FB

WISCONSIN (0)	
Burrus, Blackman, Long	RE
Straubel, Kasiska	RT
Von Bremer	RG
Wilson, Wilkie	C
Larson	LG
Nelson, Leitl	LT
Polaski, Cameron	LE
Crofoot	QB
L. Harmon	RH
D. Harmon	LH
Radke, McAndrews	FB

Touchdowns—Gregory, Friedman, Oosterbaan. Goals from touchdowns Friedman (3). Referee—Masker, Northwestern. Umpire—Haines, Yale. Field Judge—Hedges, Dartmouth. Head Linesman—Ray, Illinois.

NOV. 14

MICHIGAN (10)	
Flora	RE
Hawkins, G. Babcock	RT
Lovette	RG
Brown	C
Baer, Gabel	LG
Edwards	LT
Oosterbaan, Grube	LE
Friedman	QB
Gregory, S. Babcock, Herrnstein	RH
Gilbert	LH
Molenda, Stamman	FB

OHIO STATE (0)	
Rowan, Gorrill	RE
Reed	RT
Hess	RG
Klein, Ullery	C
Meyers, Young, Bradley	LG
Nichols, Slaugh, Uridil	LT
Cunningham	LE
Wendler, Blanchard	QB
Clark	RH
Grim	LH
Karow, Willaman	FB

Touchdown—Molenda. Goal after touchdown—Friedman. Goal from field —Friedman. Referee—Masker, Northwestern. Umpire—Schommer, Chicago. Field Judge—Moloney, Notre Dame. Head Linesman—Lipski, Chicago.

YOST LONGS FOR LIVE WOLVERINE

"Wolverine, wolverine—who's got a real live, fighting Wolverine?" This is the query being broadcast to all corners of Michigan by Coach Fielding H. Yost, Michigan's veteran football teacher.

The only live Wolverines in the state, so far as can be learned, are in the Detroit Zoological Gardens. Not until a live specimen is cavorting around Ferry Field will the coach be fully content.

Red Grange Is Stopped By Michigan Tacklers

Never Once Threatens Wolverines' Goal Zuppke Secondary Defense Breaks Up Yost's Air Attack.

By H. G. SALSINGER.

URBANA, Ill., Oct. 24.—Benny Friedman, standing on the Illinois 24-yard line a few moments before the close of the first half, kicked a field goal from placement and by the virtue of this kick Michigan defeated Illinois by a score of 3 to 0.

For nearly two hours the two teams ploughed through the mud of the stadium, under leaden skies and with or against a strong, cold penetrating wind.

What was to have been one of the most spectacular, colorful and flashy gridiron battles of the year, was converted into a monotonous routine of plunging, tackling, kicking and erratic passing.

It was Homecoming Day at Illinois and the occasion was dedicated to Harold (Red) Grange but the sorrel crowned phantom of the Illini never got loose. He failed completely on this day that was set aside for him. The uncertain footing, and a better Michigan defense than he had seen before, stopped him. Several times Grange got through, inside or outside end, but he was always smothered in the Michigan secondary zone. His best play of the afternoon came at the start of the second half when he caught Gilbert's kickoff, standing on the Illinois 10-yard line and ran the ball back to the Illinois 41-yard line.

Statistics

URBANA, Ill., Oct. 24.—Statistics on today's game show that Michigan made six first downs and Illinois five.

Michigan completed two forward passe, threw six that were incompleted and two of them were intercepted.

Illinois completed one forward pass, three were incompleted and seven were intercepted.

PURPLE ASTOUNDS HAUGHTY YOSTMEN

Lewis' Kick in First Period Beats Wolverines, 3 to 2, in Surprise Game of Nation's Football Realm—Wet Ball Puts Stop to Michigan's Vaunted Passing Attack All Through Contest.

BY M. F. DRUKENBROD.

Chicago, Ill., Nov. 7.—Chicago's mud and a Northwestern team today left a blot on the record of a proud Michigan team, a Michigan lineup unscored on and undefeated this season until this afternoon.

The Yostmen lost to Northwestern three to two in one of the greatest upsets of the season. The game was played in the mud at Grant park, a gridiron which was almost a swamp land today. It was a test at plowing and sliding, certainly not football.

The outcome was determined less than five minutes after the intial kickoff, when Lewis, a Northwestern sophomore, made a place kick with the ball held for him on Michigan's 12-yard line.

The three points which resulted sufficed to bring an unexpected victory to the Evanston team.

Michigan's scoring was brought about in the third period when Lewis intentionally grounded the ball behind his own goal line rather than risk a punt from his precarious position with a leaden, soggy and slippery ball.

MICHIGAN WINS BIG TEN TITLE

MINNESOTA FALLS BEFORE CRUSHING WOLVERINE ATTACK

	W	L	T	Pts.	Opts
BIG TEN STANDING					
Michigan	5	1	0	227	3
Northwestern	3	1	0	81	69
Wisconsin	3	1	1	131	49
Illinois	2	2	0	98	59
Iowa	2	2	0	121	74
Chicago	2	2	1	44	76
Minnesota	1	1	1	176	91
Ohio State	1	3	1	55	45
Purdue	0	3	1	119	39
Indiana	0	3	1	102	115

MICHIGAN tried the "old 83" play against Minnesota Saturday, but the referee wasn't tipped off by the quarterback what was coming. He got in the way of the man who was to receive the pass just as he got started and they fell down and rolled over together. The ball was passed to where the player should have been. A Minnesota player picked it up and made about 30 yards. When "old 83" goes blooey it goes very blooey indeed. It looked as if the trick would have been successful at that if the referee had been somewhere else, but there is no rule to penalize this kind of interfrne.

COACH YOST of the Michigan team was hilarious following the one-sided victory over the strong Minnesota team at Ferry field last Saturday and in the dressing room after the game after slapping each player on the back in none too gentle form said: "That's the best Michigan team I've ever coached," which is saying quite a mouthful for one who has had charge of the Maize and Blue for 25 years.

STADIUM APPROVED

REGENTS AUTHORIZE BUILDING OF NEW FOOTBALL STRUCTURE; LEAVING DETAILS TO BOARD

70,000 Seats Will Meet Approval; New Athletic Body Will Handle Problem

FIGHT MEN OF MICHIGAN

Wm. Achi Jr., '14—'17L

Fight men of Michigan,
Down them in your might.—
Rush them off the field,
And for Michigan, Oh! fight, fight,
fight, fight,
Win men of Michigan,
Comrades brave and true,
Shoulder to shoulder fight
For the Maize and Blue.

VARSITY

J. Fred Lawton, '11   Earl B. Moore, '12

Men of Michigan on to victory,
Every man in every play:—
Michigan expects her Varsity to win to-day.
Rah! Rah! Rah! Rah! Rah!
Win for Michigan!—

Chorus

Varsity, down the field.
Never yield, raise high our shield.
March on to victory for Michigan
And the Maize and Blue.—Oh, Varsity,
We're for you,
Here for you, to cheer for you,
We have no fear for you,
Oh Varsity!

Glenn Warner - Knute Rockne - Babe Ruth - Christy Walsh - T.A.D.Jones - F.H Yost
Coachmen's Dinner
New York — Nov. 30th, 1925

ALL AMERICAN TEAM

1925	
Oosterbaan, Michigan	End
Chase, Pittsburgh	Tackle
Diehl, Dartmouth	Guard
McMillan, Princeton	Center
Hess, Ohio State	Guard
Weir, Nebraska	Tackle
Thayer, Pennsylvania	End
Grange, Illinois	Quarter
Oberlander, Dartmouth	Halfback
Wilson, Washington	Halfback
Nevers, Stanford	Fullback

THE MICHIGAN SQUAD

No.	Name	Position	Weight	Experience
17	BABCOCK, S.	Half	155	1
18	BAER, R.	G. or T.	186	1
14	BLACK, D.	F. or H.	170	0
19	BODEN, M.	End	171	0
20	COOK, A.	Half	165	0
21	COWELL, G.	H. or F.	170	0
64	CRAGIN, R.	Center	169	0
62	DAHLEM, A. G.	Q. or H.	147	0
22	DEWEY, S.	Guard	192	2
23	DOMHOFF, V.	Q. or H.	175	1
31	FLORA, WM.	End	182	2
27	FRIEDMAN (Capt.)	Quarter	182	2
29	GABEL, N.	G. or T	195	1
16	GILBERT, L.	Half	157	1
24	GREENWALD, H. T.	Half	156	0
26	GRINNELL, H. S.	Tackle	188	0
28	HARRIGAN, FRANK	Half	180	0
30	HEATH, W. H.	T. or F.	178	0
33	HESTON, L. G.	End	175	0
11	HOFFMAN, L.	Q. or H.	152	0
32	HUGHES, A. M.	F. or H.	164	0
34	KELLY, J. J.	Q. or H.	160	0
40	LOVETTE, J.	Guard	185	1
41	MC INTYRE, K. C.	Guard	166	0
36	MEESE, F. E.	G. or T.	174	0
42	MILLER, J. F. JR.	Half	165	1
43	MOLENDA, J.	Full	195	1
44	NICHOLSON, G. A.	G. or T.	197	0
45	NICKERSON, M.	Tackle	187	0
49	NYLAND, H. Z. JR.	End	170	0
46	OADE, J.	Tackle	177	1
47	OOSTERBAAN, B. G.	End	192	1
48	PALMEROLI, J.	G. or T.	188	0
50	POMMERENING, O.	G. or T.	176	0
51	PUCKELWARTZ, W.	Quarter	157	1
52	RICH, G.	H. or F.	180	0
15	ROSE, H.	Tackle	178	0
53	SCHOENFELD, J.	Center	191	0
55	STIENECKER, C.	Center	193	0
59	SQUIER, G.	Guard	192	0
60	TOTZKE, H. G.	Half	166	0
61	TRUSKOWSKI, J.	Center	190	0
57	WEBER, H.	Guard	194	0
58	WEBER, W.	Full	188	1
63	WHITTLE, J. D.	Quarter	146	0

1926

Michigan	42	Okla. A&M.	3
Michigan	55	M.S.C.	3
Michigan	20	Minnesota	0
Michigan	13	Illinois	0
Michigan	0	Navy	10
Michigan	37	Wisconsin	0
Michigan	17	Ohio State	16
Michigan	7	Minnesota	6

Season Summary
Games won, 7; Lost, 1; Tied, 0.
Points for Michigan, 191; For Opponents 38

LINEUP OF TEAMS

Michigan (55)	Pos.	M.S.C. (3)
Oosterbaan	l.e.	Christensen
Baer	l.t.	Wenner
Palmeroli	l.g.	Ross
Gabel	r.t.	Hitchings
Truskowski	c.	Barret
Squier	r.g.	Gordon
Flora	r.e.	Hornbeck
Friedman (capt.)	q.b.	Boehringer
Miller	l.h.	Kiebler
Rich	r.h.	McCosh
Molenda	f.b.	Smith (capt.)

Substitutions—Greenwald for Miller; Grinnel for Gabel; Babcock for Rich; Harrigan for Flora; Totzke for Greenwald; McIntyre for Palmeroli; lenda; Weber for Cowell; Schoenfeldt for Truskowski; Rose for Baer; Dewey for McIntyre; Molenda for Miller; L. Hoffman for Rich; Puckelwartz for Friedman; Truskowski for Schoenfeldt; Baer for Rose; Babcock for Weber; Nicholson for Dewey; Dahlem for Babcock; Boden for Harrigan; Pommerening for Gabel; Heston for Boden; Oade for Pommerening; Danziger for McCosh; Armstrong for Ross; Froebel for Barret; Grimm for Christensen; Kanitz for Wenner; Anderson for Hornbeck; Danziger for McCosh; Arnold for Ross; Hornbeck for Christensen; Grimm for Hornbeck; O'Connor for Anderson.

Touchdowns—Molenda (2), Friedman, Oosterbaan, Flora, Greenwald, Babcock, Puckelwartz. Points after touchdown—Friedman (5), Molenda (2). Goal from field—Smith. Referee—Daniels (Loyola); umpire—Young (Illinois Wesleyan); field judge—Ghee (Dartmouth); head linesman—Ward (Ohio State).

BUILDING PERMIT

This card must be tacked on building. any person willfully destroying this card before completion of this building will be prosecuted to the full extent of the law.

Date _____ Permit No. _____

HAS BEEN ISSUED FOR THE ERECTION OF

Location _____

MICHIGAN BOND ISSUE TO BE SOLD THIS YEAR

Entire $1,500,000 Will Be Raised for New Stadium.

ANN ARBOR, Mich., Oct. 30.—So great has been the demand for the University of Michigan's new stadium bonds, authorized only recently by the Board in Control of Athletics, that there is now every prospect that the entire issue of 3,000 for $500 each can be entirely sold out before the close of the 1926 foot ball season.

One of the most valuable rights that go with each bond is the privilege of buying two tickets for each foot ball games at Ann Arbor for the next 10 years beginning with 1927. This privilege holds good regardless of when the bond is retired in one year or 10 years.

Columbus, O., Nov. 13— One lone point determined he winner in one of the greatest and most spectacular ames in the history of Big Ten football when Michigan ept its conference slate clean and eliminated its old val, Ohio State, from Big Ten title hopes by a score of 7-16 before a record breaking throng of 90,411 frenzied ooters here this afternoon.

Only a Victor Hugo could do justice to the thrilling rama of the two teams seesawing from one goal to the ther with the conference title hanging in the balance.

Ohio scored 10 points in the first 12 minutes of play, ut Michigan tied the count at 10-all before the end of he half on a touchdown pass from Benny Friedman to Benny Oosterbaan. Friedman's point after touchdown nd his field goal from Ohio's 43-yard line in the last ninute of the half. Both teams scored in the second half.

NAVY 10 MICHIGAN 0

Wolverine Mentor Smiles In Defeat

Fielding H. Yost

MICHIGAN		OHIO
Oosterbaan	L.E.	R. Bell
Baer	L.T.	Raskowski
Dewey	L.G.	Hess
Truskowski	C.	Klein
Lovette	R.G.	Meyer
Gabel	R.T.	Uridil
Flora	R.E.	Rowan
Friedman (C)	Q.	Clark
Gilbert	L.H.	Kruskamp
Molenda	R.H.	Grim
W. Weber	F.B.	(C) Karow

Score by periods:

Michigan	0	10	0	7—17
Ohio	10	0	0	6—16

"Michigan scoring: Touchdowns— Oosterbaan, Hoffman. Goals after touchdown—Friedman 2 (place kicks). Field goal—Friedman (place kick 43 yards).

"Ohio scoring: Touchdowns—Karow, Eby. Goal after touchdown—Clark (drop kick). Field goal—Clark drop kick 15 yards.

DICKINSON RATING

	Pts.
MICHIGAN	24
Northwestern	22
Purdue	19.38
Ohio	18.75
Minnesota	17.50
Wisconsin	17.08
Illinois	15
Iowa	10
Indiana	10
Chicago	10

Michigan's football team is entitled to an undisputed claim for the Conference championship, according to a wire received last night from Prof. Frank G. Dickinson of the University of Illinois, originator of the Dickinson rating system.

MICHIGAN END RACES 60 YARDS FOR SCORE ON GOPHER'S FUMBLE

WOLVERINES TIE FOR BIG TEN TITLE BY ELIMINATING GOPHERS, 7 TO 6

BIG TEN STANDINGS

	W	L	T	Pct.
Michigan	5	0	0	1.000
Northwestern	5	0	0	1.000
Ohio State	3	1	0	.750
Purdue	2	1	1	.666
Wisconsin	3	2	1	.600
Minnesota	2	2	0	.500
Illinois	2	2	0	.500
Indiana	0	4	0	.000
Iowa	0	5	0	.000
Chicago	0	5	0	.000

Fans Pay Half a Million to Watch Michigan Eleven

Gross football receipts at the University of Michigan this year were in the neighborhood of $504,654, Harry Tillotson, business manager of the athletic association, has estimated. This includes all of the money taken in at Michigan's home games and the Wolverine share of games played on foreign gridirons. Michigan's cut of the games played away from home has been estimated.

Taking out of this total the share of visiting teams and expenses of putting on the home games, a net profit of $326,159 still remains.

This year's record undoubtedly will be broken next season when Michigan will have its new football stadium with permanent seats for 75,000 spectators, whereas the present seating capacity of Ferry Field is around 48,000.

Hanson, Syracuse	End
Wickhorst, Navy	Tackle
Connaughton, Georgetown	Guard
Boeringer, Notre Dame	Center
Shively, Illinois	Guard
Smith, Brown	Tackle
Oosterbaan, Michigan	End
Friedman, Michigan	Quarter
Baker, Northwestern	Halfback
Kaer, S. California	Halfback
Joesting, Minnesota	Fullback

BEN FRIEDMAN
All-American Quarterback, 1926

1927 Season		Won 6, Lost 2, Tied 0			
			Date	Place	Attendance
Michigan	33, Ohio Wesleyan	0	Oct 1	Ann Arbor	17,483
Michigan	21, Michigan State	0	Oct 8	Ann Arbor	27,864
Michigan	14, Wisconsin	0	Oct 15	Madison	32,645
Michigan	21, Ohio State	0	Oct 22	Ann Arbor	84,401
Michigan	0, Illinois	14	Oct 29	Champaign	61,924
Michigan	14, Chicago	0	Nov 5	Chicago	53,042
Michigan	27, Navy	12	Nov 12	Ann Arbor	83,650
Michigan	7, Minnesota	13	Nov 19	Ann Arbor	84,243

1927 University of Michigan

No.	Name	Position	Wgt.	Yrs. Experience
4	CARTER, C. F.	End	172	0
5	CREGO, W. B.	T	190	0
6	DRABICKI, J. J.	FB	190	0
7	FLAJOLE, PAUL	G	140	0
8	KANITZ, G.	H	170	0
9	RODERICK, H.	End	170	0
10	SHANTZ, FRED B.	C	165	0
11	HOFFMAN, LEO	Q	152	1
12	SCHWARZE, BRUCE	H	160	0
14	SIMS, A. H.	H	165	0
15	SULLO, DOMINIC	G	198	0
16	GILBERT, LOUIS	H	160	2
17	BABCOCK, SAM	H	155	2
18	BAER, RAY	T	185	2
19	BODEN, M. H.	End	177	0
20	COOK, PAUL A.	H	160	0
21	BOVARD, A. J.	C	174	0
22	DANSBY, WILLIAM J.	FB	183	0
23	DOMHOFF, VICTOR	Q	170	2
24	GREENWALD, H. T.	H	158	1
25	FULLER, FRED	FB	170	0
26	GRINNELL, HENRY	T	187	1
27	GEORGE, EDWARD	G	160	0
28	HARRIGAN, FRANK	End	184	0
29	GABEL, NORMAN	T	198	2
30	GEISTERT, W. E.	H	159	0
31	TAYLOR, L. H.	End	180	0
32	KERR, DOUGLAS	End	169	0
33	HESTON, L. G.	End	180	1
34	McBRIDE, JENNINGS	Q	165	0
35	KETZ, W. H.	T	191	0
36	MEESE, FRANK	T	175	0
37	PARKER, ROY	G	170	0
38	POE, H. W.	G	185	0
39	POORMAN, E. B.	T	178	0
40	ROBBINS, J. S.	T	190	0
41	STRAUB, G. H.	Q	155	0
42	MILLER, JAMES F., Jr.	Q	165	2
43	GEMBIS, J. G.	FB	190	0
44	NICHOLSON, GEO., Jr.	G	195	0
45	NICKERSON, MAX	T	185	0
46	THISTED, C. E.	C	188	1
47	OOSTERBAAN, B.(Capt.)	End	186	2
48	PALMEROLI, JOHN	G	185	1
49	NYLAND, H., Jr.	End	163	0
50	POMMERENING, O. P.	T	178	0
51	PUCKELWARTZ, WM.	H	160	2
52	RICH, GEORGE	H	180	1
53	SHOENFELD, JOHN	C	195	1
54	WALDER, HAROLD	T	188	0
55	WHITTLE, JOHN	Q	153	0
56	WILLIAMS, R. J.	G	190	0
57	WEBER, H. A.	G	194	0
58	WOLFF, JOHN S., Jr.	G	185	0
64	CRAGIN, RAY	C	182	0

Official Program
OHIO WESLEYAN
UNIVERSITY
vs.
UNIVERSITY OF
MICHIGAN
NEW MICHIGAN STADIUM
ANN ARBOR
October 1, 1927

Today's Game Goes Down in History As The First To Be Held in the New Stadium

THE OFFICIAL FOOTBALL PROGRAM
is published and distributed at home games by The Board in Control of Athletics. Revenues from the Official Football Program are paid directly into the General Fund of the Board and utilized by the Board in the conduct of the University's program of Athletics and Physical Education

PHILIP C. PACK '18—PROGRAM MANAGER
Kermit K. Kline '28,—Ellis B. Merry '28
Student Assistants

PRICE TWENTY-FIVE CENTS

RECORD CROWD AT OPENER NEW STADIUM

Michigan and Ohio Wesleyan Battle on Rain-Soaked Gridiron

FANS NUMBER 50,000

State High School Students Are Guests of University

Threatening weather failed to dampen the ardor of the football crowd which began pouring into the city at an early hour today to watch Michigan and Ohio Wesleyan inaugurate the new Wolverine stadium.

With all high school students in the state invited to attend the game as guests of the University it was easy to believe that few had declined the invitation as the young visitors thronged to the stadium.

They were instructed to report at Yost Field House at 2 o'clock this afternoon where they were addressed by Dr. Clarence C. Little, president of the University. Following the president's brief remarks, the students, lead by the Varsity band, marched to the stadium.

A crowd of more than 50,000 the largest gathering for a football game in Ann Arbor was on hand to cheer the Wolverines and the Fighting Bishops.

Traffic became congested as early as noon today but state troopers augmenting the local police force handled the situation in a most capable manner.

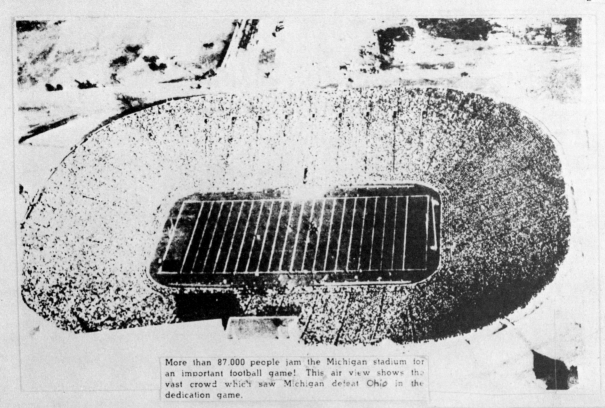

More than 87,000 people jam the Michigan stadium for an important football game! This air view shows the vast crowd which saw Michigan defeat Ohio in the dedication game.

Wisconsin Crosses Michigan Line in Second Period But Draws 15-Yard Penalty When Guilty of Holding

(By Associated Press)

Camp Randall, Madison, Wis., Oct. 15. — Michigan emerged triumphant from its first Western Conference football game of the season here this afternoon, defeating University of Wisconsin. The score was 14 to 0.

Returns Prize to Oosterbaan

BENNIE OOSTERBAAN, Michigan athletic star, is happy again. Oosterbaan has recovered the gold watch stolen from his fraternity house a few weeks ago.

Bennie owes the recovery of his watch to the honesty of a pawnbroker at Indianapolis. The pawnbroker discovered recently that he had Oosterbaan's watch and he notified the police. The watch was returned to its owner. Oosterbaan was given the watch by a New York newspaper which selected an All-American foot ball team.

ANN ARBOR DAYS

Russell Barnes   George H. Roderick

Chorus

Ann Arbor days,—Ann Arbor days,—
When our hearts were young and gay;
Dear old days,—college days,—
Worldly cares were far away.
All friendships were strong,—
And life a sweet song
In those wonderful Ann Arbor days.

A Ballad of the Yostmen

We love the plucky doughboy,
    and admire the flying ace;
We doff our hats to the French poilu
    and all his dauntless race,
But the thrill comes somewhat nearer
    and our deep love stands revealed
When on some autumn afternoon
    the Yostmen take the field.

The Yostmen are a sturdy lot; they're bone,
    and brains, and brawn.
If need be every mother's son would fight
    through night 'til dawn.
And each man looks for victory,
    nor seeks a selfish fame,
And watchers glow with vivid pride,
    when Yostmen play the game.

They came from east and north and west,
    but now their bosoms burn
With loyal love for Michigan,
    that mother fond but stern.
And we know that every man has pledged
    his heart, his strength, his all,
When the whistle blows and the game begins,
    and the Yostmen have the ball.

Watch! How they wage a noble strife.
    Our throats cannot but cheer
As down the field they rush and roar.
    None knows a craven fear!
And every blow and buffet given
    inspires the men like wine.
Ah, 'tis a glorious pile of legs when
    the Yostmen buck the line!

See how they sway and strain and strive,
    but never a coward's trick,
And who is best and who is less
    'twere difficult to pick.
And beneath each sweaty helmet
    thinks and thinks a manly soul,
'Til victory comes and mid huzzahs
    the Yostmen cross the goal.

(Written and read by Rev. Herbert A. Jump, Kiwanian, at a dinner given the University of Michigan football team.)

THE MICHIGAN ALUMNUS

Michigan Loses to Minnesota, 13-7

SPLINTERING the slender Michigan rapier under the blows of their battle-axes, Minnesota's team of northern giants achieved the first successful invasion of the new stadium, beating Michigan 13-7 in the final game of the 1927 season on November 19. By virtue of the result, the famous "Brown jug" goes back to Minneapolis for the first time since 1919.

WHEN one team beats another by two touchdowns to one, and both of the former come largely as the result of desperate forward passes flung after a running attack has been halted, the natural inference is a struggle close all the way. The following statistics tell a very different story: they reveal at once the enormous physical power of the Minnesota machine and the indomitable courage of a defense which held to two touchdowns a foe powerful enough to have scored twenty!

Total first downs—Minnesota, 18; Michigan, 2.
First downs by rushing—Minnesota, 15; Michigan, 0.
First downs by passes—Minnesota, 3; Michigan, 2.
Forward passes completed—Minnesota, 7 out of 19; Michigan, 3 out of 10.
Forward passes intercepted—Minnesota, 4; Michigan, 1.
Yards gained by rushing—Minnesota, 307; Michigan, 28.
Yards gained by passes—Minnesota, 96; Michigan, 58.
Yards lost by rushing—Minnesota, 39; Michigan, 15.
Total net advance of ball, including returns of kick-offs and punts—Minnesota, 487; Michigan, 77.
Average distance of punts—Minnesota, 32 yards; Michigan, 37 yards.

Surely any man given this set of figures would be justified in supposing the final score to have been something like 75 to 0!

Oosterbaan Named All-American for Third Year in Row

Selection of Benny Oosterbaan as All-American end for 1927 marks the third consecutive year that the Wolverine star has been named on the official team selected by Collier's.

Only five other players in the history of football have been picked three times as All-American. Eddie Mahan of Harvard and Red Grange of Illinois are the only other modern players thus named. Campbell of Harvard, Shevlin of Yale and Eckersall of Chicago are the only others who made the team on three occasions.

**Bennie Oosterbaan
End**

Collier's
ALL-AMERICA

Oosterbaan	End	Michigan
Raskowski	Tackle	Ohio State
Smith	Guard	Notre Dame
Charlesworth	Center	Yale
Crane	Guard	Illinois
Smith	Tackle	Pennsylvania
Nash	End	Georgia
Drury	Quarterback	Southern Cal.
Cagle	Halfback	Army
Welch	Halfback	Pittsburgh
Joesting	Fullback	Minnesota

(Copyright, 1927, Collier's Weekly)

The Michigan Squad

No.	Name	Position	Wgt.	Yrs. Experience	Home
4	CARTER, C. F.	End	170	0	Bay City, Mich.
5	McCORMICK, W.	Half	155	0	Ann Arbor, Mich.
6	AVERY, L.	Half	170	0	South Haven, Mich.
7	BARLEY, A.	Half	165	0	Marion, Ind.
9	COOKE, T. M.	Center	197	0	Chicago, Ill.
10	DUFF, R.	Guard	200	0	Canton, Ohio
11	DAHLEM, A. G.	Half	155	0	Jackson, Mich.
12	GRODSKY, I.	Half	170	0	New Haven, Conn.
13	WHITTLE, J. D.	Half	158	1	Chicago, Ill.
14	HOLMES, D. W.	Quarter	165	0	Canton, Ohio
15	GUNDRY, G.	Half	160	0	Grand Blanc, Mich.
16	SQUIER, G.	Guard	205	1	South Haven, Mich.
17	SIMRALL, J. O.	Quarter	155	0	Lexington, Ky.
18	BATOR, K., JR.	Half	178	0	Detroit, Mich.
19	HOZER, S.	Full	170	0	Muskegon, Mich.
20	ORWIG, J.	End	172	0	Ann Arbor, Mich.
21	BOVARD, A.	Center	178	1	Ann Arbor, Mich.
22	BERGMAN, M.	Tackle	178	0	Clarence, N. Y.
23	BIEDENWEG, C.	Half	165	0	Ft. Wayne, Ind.
24	BOVARD, T.	End	175	0	Ann Arbor, Mich.
25	BROWN, F. P.	Quarter	190	0	Elgin, Ill.
26	BROWN, W. A.	Center	200	0	Sandusky, Mich.
27	DRAVELING, L.	Tackle	200	0	Port Huron, Mich.
28	CORNWELL, F.	End	185	0	Grand Rapids, Mich.
29	DANSBY, W. J.	Full	182	0	Monroe, Mich.
30	GEISTERT, W.	Half	156	0	Grand Rapids, Mich.
31	DECKER, A. W.	Guard	200	0	Flint, Mich.
32	KERR, D.	End	170	0	Gary, Ind.
33	FISH, W.	Guard	180	0	Battle Creek, Mich.
34	McBRIDE, J.	Half	170	0	Oklahoma City, Okla.
35	STEINKE, A.	Guard	182	0	St. Joseph, Mich.
36	MEESE, E.	Tackle	200	0	Toledo, Ohio
37	PARKER, R.	Guard	170	0	Ann Arbor, Mich.
38	POE, H.	Guard	185	1	Toledo, Ohio
39	POORMAN, E.	Tackle	184	0	Chicago Heights, Ill.
40	BODEN, M.	End	175	0	Detroit, Mich.
41	STRAUB, H.	Quarter	158	0	Toledo, O.
42	GITMAN, W.	Tackle	190	0	Dayton, Ohio
43	GEMBIS, J.	Full	210	1	Vicksburg, Mich.
44	KANITZ, T.	Half	170	0	Milan, Mich.
45	MORGAN, R.	Guard	180	0	Toledo, Ohio
46	MOYER, C. P.	Tackle	201	0	Detroit, Mich.
48	SLATER, R.	Tackle	195	0	Webster Grove, Mo.
49	SMITH, H. A.	End	168	0	Algonac, Mich.
50	POMMERENING, O.	Tackle	176	1	Ann Arbor, Mich.
51	TOTZKE, J. H.	Half	170	0	Benton Harbor, Mich.
52	RICH, G. (Captain)	Full	180	2	Lakewood, Ohio
53	PATTON, R. J.	Center	200	0	Springfield, Ill.
54	KEENE, C.	Tackle	175	0	Buffalo, N. Y.
55	KUBICEK, L.	Tackle	194	0	Chicago, Ill.
56	WILLIAMS, R.	Guard	190	0	Detroit, Mich.
57	CRAGIN, R.	Center	188	0	Leominster, Mass.
58	HAGER, H.	Tackle	190	0	Lansing, Mich.
59	LYTLE, R.	Full	156	0	Valparaiso, Ind.
60	McCOY, E.	End	170	0	Detroit, Mich.
61	PARKER, C. F.	End	175	0	Wray, Colo.
62	SHERWOOD, M.	Center	170	0	Grand Haven, Mich.
63	SUKUPCHAK, P.	Half	163	0	Bridgman, Mich.
64	WHEELER, C. J.	Quarter	152	0	Bay City, Mich.
65	WIDMAN, J. C.	Half	160	0	Detroit, Mich.
66	TRUSKOWSKI, J.	End	188	1	Detroit, Mich.
67	HUGHES, A. M.	Full	174	0	Gary, Ind.

1928 Season — Won 3, Lost 4, Tied 1

				Date	Place	Attendance
Michigan	7,	Ohio Wesleyan	17	Oct 6	Ann Arbor	17,877
Michigan	0,	Indiana	6	Oct 13	Ann Arbor	25,896
Michigan	7,	Ohio State	19	Oct 20	Columbus	72,439
Michigan	0,	Wisconsin	7	Oct 27	Ann Arbor	58,259
Michigan	3,	Illinois	0	Nov 3	Ann Arbor	78,229
Michigan	6,	Navy	6	Nov 10	Baltimore	28,433
Michigan	3,	Michigan State	0	Nov 17	Ann Arbor	28,067
Michigan	10,	Iowa	7	Nov 24	Ann Arbor	53,572

OTTO P. POMMERENING

Pommerening is a home product, having been born in Ann Arbor, Michigan, January 26, 1904. He graduated from the Ann Arbor High School with 3 football letters to his credit. Stands 5 feet, 11 inches in height, and weighs 178 pounds. His athletic record in college consists of numerals and a letter in football. This year Pommerening is a senior and will graduate next June in an Engineering course.

Michigan Needs Him

Fielding H. Yost, who will return to the job of head coach of the University of Michigan football team. He is needed now more than for the past two years to weld green material into polished timber.

I'LL MAKE SOMETHIN' OUT OF YOU

PROSPECTS AT MICHIGAN WERE NOT ANY TOO BRIGHT THIS YEAR

FIELDING H. YOST

BACK AGAIN AS MICHIGAN'S FOOTBALL COACH

MICHIGAN	7
OHIO WESLEYAN	17

An inexperienced Michigan eleven lost the first opening game since 1888 to a strong and well seasoned Ohio Wesleyan team. The Bishops scored by a consistently smart offensive in each of the last three quarters on two touchdowns and a field goal. A forty-eight yard dash through the line when orthodoxy called for a punt was typical of Wesleyan's daring play.

Besides gaining through the line, Wesleyan used a short pass over the line after faking a punt which on one occasion culminated in a fifty-seven yard run for touchdown. Michigan's touchdown came in the third quarter when Holmes intercepted a pass in mid-field and ran until out of bounds on the Bishop's two yard line. Captain Rich plunged over on the third play. Pommerening's fine all around work which included covering punts and recovering fumbles from his tackle position was the bright spot of the Wolverines' play, while Breese starred for the visitors.

| MICHIGAN | 0 | INDIANA | 6 |

In the first conference game Michigan's fighting varsity battled on even terms with Indiana until the fourth quarter when the insistent Hoosier offensive finally pushed over a lone score. The Michigan performance was a distinct reversal of form from its previous mediocre game against Ohio Wesleyan.

In the first half Michigan displayed a plunging attack which smashed out five first downs, three of them in succession. A great improvement in Michigan's play was shown at the ends where Truskowski and Draveling broke up many Indiana plays. The speed of the Hoosier backfield led by Captain Bennett, who alone gained 151 yards, proved the margin of victory. Truskowski threw three successful passes for the Wolverines which totaled fifty yards, although several of his heaves suffered costly interceptions. John Totzke outpunted his opponents by an average of four yards.

| MICHIGAN | 7 | OHIO STATE | 19 |

Ohio State finally gained revenge for seven consecutive defeats at the hands of Michigan by giving the Wolverines their third defeat in as many contests.

Both teams scored in the first period following fumbles and Michigan had a temporary point advantage when Gembis succeeded in the try for goal. Draveling, Wolverine end, made the Michigan touchdown when he fell over the goal line on the ball after a Buckeye accidentally touched Wheeler's punt.

The long hoped for Michigan offensive again disappointed Michigan's followers. The defense stubbornly resisted Ohio's attack throughout the contest although it was inevitable that the Buckeyes would score since the ball was constantly in Michigan territory. As a last minute attempt to inject the missing spark in the Wolverine offense, a pony backfield was rushed in but its speed proved of little avail.

| MICHIGAN | 0 | WISCONSIN | 7 |

A minute and a half before the final gun, Cuisinier of Wisconsin grabbed a pass which had escaped Truskowski's straining fingers and scuttled through Michigan's defense for the only score of the game. With a few moments remaining, Michigan kicked off and soon gained the ball. Then a desperate passing attack rushed the ball down the field to Wisconsin's seventeen year line where the ball and game was lost as the gun sounded.

| MICHIGAN | 3 | ILLINOIS | 0 |

An unusual underhand pass from Truskowski to Dahlem followed by the latter's dash straight through the Illinois line put the ball on the eleven yard line from which point of vantage Gembis booted the ball through the goal posts for a victory. The undefeated Illini had confidently invaded Ferry field with nine veterans from last year's conference championship team and could not see how the downtrodden Michigan team could possibly resist the terrific smashing of their great backs.

Pommerening, Poe, Truskowski and their fellow linesmen turned back the Illinois backfield aces besides completely overshadowing the experienced Sucker line. Pommerening outdid Captain Butch Novack at Tackle position and Poe ran circles around Crane, Grantlant Rice's 1927 All-American guard.

| MICHIGAN | 6 | NAVY | 6 |

The fighting Wolverines came back in the last quarter to even terms with the Navy in one of the years' most thrilling contests. The Midshipmen scored at the start of the second half following the kickoff which was returned seventy-six yards by Bannon to the Michigan seven yard line.

The irresistible Michigan march began on her forty-eight yard line late in the third period and ended early in the fourth as Hozer plunged over. Hozer, substituting for Gembis who was ill, was the unexpected bulwark of Michigan's scoring offense. The Navy's last bid for victory in the form of her second attempted place kick failed.

Bovard's brilliant defensive play was often disastrous for the Navy backs; Poe also played a fine defensive game. Simrall, sophomore halfback, outkicked the highly touted Midshipman, Bowstrom.

Both teams suffered crushing set-backs early in the season and it was in a sense unique that they should tie each other and then proceed to comebacks that made Grantland Rice call them great.

| MICHIGAN | 3 | STATE | 0 |

Defensive play predominated throughout the game with Michigan State. When both teams found their offense unprofitable, a punting duel began in which Grove outpunted the three Michigan kickers. The only thrill of the game was furnished by the spectacular State aerial attack. Schau's zipping passes pierced the falling rain time and again for substantial gains and this threat kept the outcome of the game in constant doubt.

Again, as in the Navy contest, an untried fullback showed his worth. Hozer plunged over in the Navy game for the tying score, and in the State game Hughes was called from the bench to substitute at fullback where he booted the winning goal.

Geistert was the greatest ground gainer with fifty yards. Truskowski also stood out in the offense throwing a thirty yard pass and making thirty yards through the line in four tries. Michigan showed little to the Iowa scouts, because only eight different plays were used. The game was of particular interest to a Michigan crowd in that the two coaches, Wieman and Kipke, were both former Michigan Captains.

POMMERENING IS NAMED ON ALL-AMERICAN

Washington, Nov. 28.—(AP)—Lou Little, Georgetown football coach, names two Carnegie Tech and two New York University players on his All-American eleven selected for the Associated Press. No other team has more than one. Eight eastern players, two from middle western teams and one from the south comprise Little's selection, which follows:

Ends—Barrabee, New York University; and Rosenzweig, Carnegie.

Tackles—Nowak, Illinois; and Mooney, Georgetown.

Guards—Pommerening, Michigan; and Getto, Pittsburgh.

Center—Westgate, Pennsylvania.

Quarterback—Harpster, Carnegie.

Halfbacks—Strong, N. Y. U; and Mizell, Georgia Tech.

Fullback—Cagle, Army.

Wieman's Dismissal Shadowed By Controversy Begun Last Fall

Michigan's head football coach has been removed from the 1929 Wolverine football coaching staff according to an announcement made by Fielding H. Yost, director of athletics, yesterday afternoon. Coach Wieman has emphatically reiterated his statement of Monday night that he has no intention of resigning his position at the University.

According to a newspaper report based on an interview with a member of the Board in Control of Athletics, the breakup in the athletic adminisration had its inception in trouble between Yost and Wieman during the 1928 football season. Yost, after stating that he would again assume active coaching duties, announced that Wieman was in complete charge of the team on the eve of the first game.

The Wolverine eleven made its most disastrous start in history, losing its first four games to Ohio Wesleyan, Indiana, Ohio State, and Wisconsin.

FOOTBALL ONLY SPORT TO SHOW FINANCIAL GAIN FOR FISCAL YEAR

Michigan's board of athletic control will turn its attention to getting out of debt when the proposed 18-hole golf course is finished, says the annual report of the board. The statements for the fiscal year ended Sept. 1 are favorable.

Football again proved the sustaining sport of the athletic department, showing a profit for the fiscal year of about $550,000. Football during the season just closed, not a part of the fiscal year report, paid to Michigan $418,316.43. The total attendance for the year was 393,568.

Michigan Squad

No.	Name	Position	Age	Height	Weight	Exp.	Class	Home
4	Jones, Wm.	E	18	6' 1½"	176	0	'32	Bay City, Mich.
5	Hodgson, H.	B	20	5' 11"	160	0	'32	River Forest, Ill.
6	Hayden, E.	T	18	5' 11½"	200	0	'32	Chicago, Ill.
7	Miller, W.	T	19	6' 2"	190	0	'32	Wilmette, Ill.
8	Bauer, C. J., Jr.	G	21	5' 8"	200	0	'31	Saginaw, Mich.
9	Hayes, N. R.	E	24	6' 0"	182	0	'30	Grosse Isle, Mich.
10	Renner, J.	E	20	5' 10"	175	0	'30	Youngstown, Ohio
11	Dahlem, A.	B	21	5' 8"	152	1	'30	Jackson, Mich.
12	Andreae, G.	B	20	5' 11"	175	0	'31	Yale, Mich.
14	Holmes, D. W.	B	20	5' 11"	165	1	'31	Canton, Ohio
16	Heston, W.	B	20	5' 9"	165	0	'32	Detroit, Mich.
17	Simrall, J. O. H., Jr.	Q	19	5' 10"	163	1	'31	Lexington, Ky.
18	Wills, R.	B	23	5' 8"	154	0	'31	Ann Arbor, Mich.
20	Williams, E.	B	19	5' 10"	165	0	'31	Yale, Mich.
21	Bovard, A.	C	22	5' 11"	195	2	'30	Ann Arbor, Mich.
22	Bergman, M. E.	T	24	5' 10½"	178	0	'30	Clarence, N. Y.
23	Christensen, V.	E	22	5' 10"	184	0	'32	Ann Arbor, Mich.
24	Anderson, J. G.	Q	20	5' 9"	150	0	'32	Ann Arbor, Mich.
25	Brown, F. P.	B	21	6' 0"	188	0	'30	Elgin, Ill.
26	Brown, W. A.	C	21	5' 11"	200	0	'31	Sandusky, Mich.
27	Draveling, L.	E	21	6' 1"	205	1	'31	Port Huron, Mich.
28	Cornwell, F. M.	E	22	5' 10½"	180	1	'31	Grand Rapids, Mich.
29	Ricketts, G.	E	18	6' 2"	178	0	'32	Covington, Ky.
30	Holland, K. D.	Q	19	5' 9"	150	0	'32	Evanston, Ill.
31	Hudson, R.	B	21	5' 8½"	195	0	'32	Girard, Ohio
32	Daniels, X. N.	E	22	6' 0"	168	0	'31	Detroit, Mich.
33	Dierberger, W.	E	19	6' 1"	170	0	'32	Great Falls, Mont.
34	McBride, J.	B	20	5' 7"	180	0	'30	Oklahoma City, Okla.
35	Steinke, A.	G	21	6' 0"	184	1	'31	St. Joseph, Mich.
36	Goodenow, T.	C	24	5' 10½"	170	0	'31	Endicott, N. Y.
37	Parker, R.	G	28	5' 9½"	168	0	'30	Ann Arbor, Mich.
38	Poe, H.	G	21	5' 11"	190	2	'30	Toledo, Ohio
39	Poorman, E.	T	20	6' 0"	185	1	'30	Chicago Heights, Ill.
40	Blowney, H. E.	T	20	5' 11"	190	0	'32	Toledo, Ohio
41	Straub, H.	Q	24	5' 8"	160	1	'30	Toledo, Ohio
42	Gitman, W.	B	21	5' 10"	190	0	'30	Dayton, Ohio
43	Gembis, J.	B	21	5' 11½"	200	2	'30	Vicksburg, Mich.
44	Wilson, D.	G	20	5' 7"	140	0	Show	Jefferson, Ia.
45	Morgan, R.	G	23	5' 11"	180	0	'31	Toledo, Ohio
46	Moyer, C.	G	20	6' 1"	197	0	'30	Detroit, Mich.
48	Grinnell, I.	G	19	6' 0"	195	0	'32	Detroit, Mich.
49	Miller, H.	B	18	5' 4"	125	0	'32	Ann Arbor, Mich.
50	Auer, H. J.	T	21	6' 0"	193	0	'31	Bay City, Mich.
51	Sukupckak, P.	B	21	5' 7"	163	0	'30	Bridgman, Mich.
52	Smith, I. C.	E	19	5' 11"	185	0	'32	Toledo, Ohio
53	Patton, R.	C	20	6' 1"	205	0	'31	Springfield, Ill.
54	Jones, M.	G	19	6' 0"	180	0	'32	Toledo, Ohio
55	Roach, T.	T	10	6' 0½"	190	0	'32	Grand Rapids, Mich.
56	Hewitt, W.	E	19	5' 10½"	175	0	'32	Bay City, Mich.
57	Morrison, M.	B	20	5' 9½"	210	0	'32	Royal Oak, Mich.
58	LaJuenesse, O.	B	21	5' 9½"	168	0	'32	Iron Mountain, Mich.
59	Lytle, R.	B	20	5' 8"	160	0	'31	Valparaiso, Ind.
60	Mosser, M. W.	E	20	6' 0"	168	0	'32	Detroit, Mich.
61	Richardson, K.	G	19	5' 11½"	190	0	'31	Ottawa, Ohio
62	Sherwood, M.	C	19	6' 0"	168	0	'32	Grand Haven, Mich.
63	Kurty, W. H.	B	23	6' 0"	173	0	'30	Detroit, Mich.
64	Wheeler, C. J.	B	21	5' 11"	154	1	'31	Bay City, Mich.
65	Widman, J. C.	B	21	5' 11"	165	0	'30	Detroit, Mich.
66	Truskowski, J. (Capt.)	E	22	6' 0"	190	2	'30	Detroit, Mich.
67	Hughes, A. M.	B	22	5' 10½"	175	0	'30	Gary, Ind.
68	Samuels, T.	G	20	6' 0"	196	0	'31	Canton, Ohio
69	Sikkenga, J.	E	18	5' 10"	180	0	'32	Muskegon, Mich.
70	Sorensen, T.		19	5' 11"	197	0	'32	Marquette, Mich.
71	Wolff, J. S.	G	21	5' 9"	185	0	'30	Detroit, Mich.
72	Heath, C.	T	22	6' 0"	190	0	'30	Cedar Rapids, Ia.

1929 Season — Won 5, Lost 3, Tied 1

Date	Result	Place	Attendance
Sep. 28	Michigan 39, Albion 0	Ann Arbor	16,412
Sep. 28	Michigan 16, Mount Union 0	Ann Arbor	16,412
Oct. 5	Michigan 17, Michigan State 0	Ann Arbor	30,494
Oct. 12	Michigan 16, Purdue 30	Lafayette	18,484
Oct. 19	Michigan 0, Ohio State 14		85,088
Oct. 26	Michigan 14, Illinois 12	Champaign	53,403
Nov. 9	Michigan 14, Harvard 14	Ann Arbor	85,042
Nov. 16	Michigan 7, Minnesota 6	Minneapolis	58,160
Nov. 23	Michigan 0, Iowa 0	Ann Arbor	50,639

LINEUP

Michigan	Pos.	Purdue
Truskowski	LE	Caraway
Hayden	LT	Vanbibber
Poe	LG	Sears
Bovard	C	Miller
Steinke	RG	Buttner
Roach	RT	Sleight
Draveling	RE	Werner
Simrall	QB	White
Hudson	LH	Harmeson
Dahlem	RH	Welch
Gembis	FB	Yunovitch

Score by Quarters

Michigan .... 0 0 16 0—16
Purdue .... 0 6 0 24—30

Substitutions

Hewitt for Draveling; Heston for Dahlem; Poorman for Roach; Trimble for Sears; Christian for Buttner; Mackle for Werner; Sherbeck for Miller; Woerner for Mackle; Wheeler for Dahlem; Smith for Bovard; Auer for Hayden; Morrison for Gembis; Priest for Wheeler; Trimble for Sears; Christian for Buttner; Chasey for Welch; Yunovitch for Harmeson.

Officials—Referee Ghee; Umpire Haines; Field Judge Hackett; Head Linesman, Gardiner. Touchdowns—Welch, Yunovitch (3) Caraway, Gembis Truskowski. Goals after touchdown—Gembis; Field goal—Gembis.

Doubleheader

MT. UNION COLLEGE
ALLIANCE, OHIO
Versus
UNIVERSITY OF MICHIGAN

ALBION COLLEGE
ALBION, MICHIGAN
Versus
UNIVERSITY OF MICHIGAN

NEW MICHIGAN STADIUM
Ann Arbor
Sept. 28, 1929
INAUGURAL OF THE 1929 SEASON

THE OFFICIAL PROGRAM

is published and distributed at home games by The Board in Control of Athletics. Revenues from the Official Football Program are paid directly into the General Fund of the Board and utilized by the Board in the conduct of the University's program of Athletics and Physical Education.

TWENTY-FIVE CENTS

SCORES BY QUARTERS

	1st	2nd	3rd	4th	Final
Michigan	0	0	16	0	16
Purdue	6	0	0	24	30

SCORES BY QUARTERS

	1st	2nd	3rd	4th	Final
Michigan	0	0	0	0	0
Ohio State	0	7	0	0	7

SCORE BY QUARTERS

	1st	2nd	3rd	4th	Final
Michigan	0	0	0	0	0
Illinois	0	0	14	0	14

SCORE BY QUARTERS

	1st	2nd	3rd	4th	Final
Michigan	0	0	0	7	7
Minnesota	0	6	0	0	6

Michigan Triumphs Over Harvard

Great Game Marks Crimson's First Invasion of Middle West—Margin of Victory is 14-12

IT WAS a game which will live long in football annals, that battle staged in the Michigan stadium between the teams of Harvard and Michigan.

For Michigan it was a well-earned victory, a victory which came after 48 years of waiting—waiting which had never been granted even the solace of a single score made against a Harvard eleven.

For Harvard it was a bitter disappointment, but a disappointment tempered by the knowledge that a Crimson Varsity, coming into the Middle West for the first time in history, had waged a brilliant, fighting battle.

The score—unimportant save that it represented a Michigan triumph—was 14 to 12.

DeBAKER   LaJEUNESSE   WILLIAMSON   MILLER   DANIELS   COX   HEWITT
ROBERTS   PURDUM   MORGAN   HUDSON   AUER   SAMUELS   MORRISON   HIGHFIELD
CORNWELL   DRAVELING   YOST   SIMRALL   KIPKE   WHEELER   HOZER
NEWMAN   EASTMAN   DOUGLASS   HESTON   TESSMER

1930 Season		Won 8, Lost 0, Tied 1			
			Date	Place	Attendance
Michigan	33	Denison	0	Sep 27	Ann Arbor	12,760
Michigan	7	Eastern Mich.	0	Sep 27	Ann Arbor	12,760
Michigan	0	Michigan State	0	Oct 4	Ann Arbor	22,571
Michigan	14	Purdue	13	Oct 11	Ann Arbor	38,851
Michigan	13	Ohio State	0	Oct 18	Columbus	68,459
Michigan	15	Illinois	7	Oct 25	Ann Arbor	63,191
Michigan	6	Harvard	3	Nov 8	Cambridge	43,913
Michigan	7	Minnesota	0	Nov 15	Ann Arbor	54,944
Michigan	16	Chicago	0	Nov 22	Ann Arbor	42,078

Newman Shifts and Dodges

CAPTAIN

ROY HUDSON, of Michigan

Varsity Held Scoreless by State

Michigan State		Michigan
Fogg	LE	Hewitt
Brunette	LT	Auer
Gross	LG	Cornwell
Meiers	C	Morrison
Streb	RG	LaJeunesse
Ridler	RT	Samuels
Vandermeer	RE	Daniels
Grove	QB	Tessmer
Monnett	LH	Heston
Breen	RH	Simrall
Eliowitz	FB	Hudson

Score by quarters—
Michigan State 0   0   0   0—0
Michigan 0   0   0   0—0

Substitutions: Michigan State—Handy for Streb; Streb for Handy. Michigan—Williamson for Hewitt; Purdum for Auer; Auer for Purdum; Hozer for LaJeunesse; LaJeunesse for Hozer; Hozer for LaJeunesse; Morgan for Morrison; Oehmann for Cornwell; Cornwell for Oehmann; Oehmann for Cornwell; Newman for Tessmer; Tessmer for Newman; Newman for Tessmer; DeBaker for Heston; Heston for DeBaker; Cox for Simrall; Goldsmith for Hudson; Eastman for Goldsmith; Wheeler for Eastman.

HARVARD FALLS 6 to 3

After a vacation of a week the well rested Michigan aggregation secured full and complete revenge for all previous gridiron defeats suffered at the hands of Harvard by defeating the Crimson eleven for the second time in their two game series, last year in the stadium by the score of 14-12 and this time at Soldiers Field in Cambridge by the close score of 6-3 in a hotly contested game.

The first half was played with no score being made by either team; the Wolverines nearly scored, however, late in the first quarter when they pushed the ball to Harvard's eight-yard line. On the next play an official, who unfortunately had not been warned to look out for this particular combination, got in the way of a run by Wheeler which looked like a sure gain but resulted in a seven-yard loss through this unfortunate incident, blasting Michigan's scoring chance. The second and third periods witnessed no serious threat by either team to score, except for Barry Wood's tries for a field goal. Morrison blocked the first kick when the ball thumped resoundingly against his chest and was recovered by Ivan Williamson, the right end. The second one sailed along the ground, much too low to clear the goal posts. As the period drew to a close, a long pass from Wood to Huguley gained 42-yards, at a time when the Wolverines expected not more than a twenty-yard pass, bringing the ball to Michigan's ten-yard line. Two running plays netted a loss of two yards, leaving Harvard on the twelve-yard stripe, third down, and touchdown to go as the period ended.

Wood tried to circle the end but was thrown for a three yard loss by Stan Hozer. But he would not be denied. For the third time he tried the drop-kick, and in true proverbial manner, succeeded.

To quote an eastern writer, "The Wolverine is a cruel, cunning animal of the weasel family. It is quick; it is merciless. It strikes with shocking rapidity and accuracy. Newman and his cohorts were like eleven wolverines in their actions. Rarely did they strike but they sunk their fangs into a vulnerable spot. And the chief fang was a crushing, sweeping wide play around end or off-tackle with John Wheeler, the destructive Wolverine."

According to eastern newspapers Wheeler was entirely unheralded in the east. But it was Wheeler who circled left end for five yards at a clip in two plays, for twelve yards in another, ably spelled by Newman and "Solly" Hudson, the fullback. The Wolverines rushed viciously down to the Crimson 32-yard stripe; then Wheeler was hit for a two-yard loss.

Back into a huddle these sturdy battlers came, then back into the line together. The ball came singing back to Newman, who had not thrown a pass this period. He faded toward his own goal and toward right end and then let the ball fly straight down the field where Hudson was galloping with all his speed. He passed two Harvard defenders, looked over his shoulder as he neared the ten-yard line, reached up, caught the pass as if a part of a perfect mechanism, and raced on across the goal line. Newman missed the try for point and the scoring for the game was over.

WHEELER GETS PERFECT INTERFERENCE AGAINST HARVARD

Courtesy of the Detroit News

THE MICHIGAN SQUAD, 1931

TOP ROW, LEFT TO RIGHT—J. Heston, Clohset, Auer, Samuels, Cooke, McGuire, Hazen, Ellerby, Frisk, W. Miller, Kirby, Cantrill, Kelley, Stone, McCrath, Goldsmtl.

MIDDLE ROW, LEFT TO RIGHT—Wistert, Horner, Savage, Bernard, LeJeunesse, Oehman, Winston, Maldman, Savage, Morrison, Sikkenga, Markovsky, Shick, Douglass, Kowalik, Conover, Chapman, Petoskey, Damm.

BOTTOM ROW, LEFT TO RIGHT—Hewitt, Westover, Hayes, Kutsche, Cox, DeBaker, Hudson, Newman, Tessmer, Holland, Schmidt, Renner, Stinespring, Everhardus, Fay, Williamson, H. Heston.

THE MICHIGAN SQUAD

No.	Name	Class	Position	Weight	Age	*Experience	Home
4	SAVAGE, CARL	'33	T	188	20	0	Flint
5	OEHMANN, WARD	'33	G	170	20	0	Washington, D. C.
6	BREMEN, GEORGE K.	'33	HB	185	20	0	Detroit
7	MILLER, WALLACE	'33	T	195	22	1	Wilmette, Ill.
8	HAZEN, FRANCIS	'32	T	182	19	0	Bellingham, Wash.
9	WESTOVER, LOUIS	'34	HB	160	19	0	Bay City
10	ELLERBY, HAROLD	'34	E	180	19	0	Birmingham
11	WISTERT, FRANCIS	'34	E	196	19	0	Chicago, Ill.
12	CLOHSET, FRED	'33	T	185	20	0	Bay City
13	HUDSON, ROY, CAPT.	'32	FB	185	23	2	Girard, O.
14	HOLLAND, KIRK	'32	HB	150	21	0	Evanston, Ill.
16	HESTON, WILLIAM	'32	HB	165	21	2	Detroit
17	PETOSKEY, FRED	'34	E	175	20	0	Saginaw
18	STONE, CHARLES	'34	E	170	19	0	Detroit
19	EASTMAN, HARRY	'32	HB	168	22	1	Detroit
20	DE BAKER, CHARLES	'33	HB	165	20	1	Muskegon
21	HESTON, JOHN P.	'34	HB	170	20	0	Detroit
22	FRISK, LESLIE	'33	T	178	24	0	Rock Island, Ill.
23	KUTSCHE, ARTHUR	'33	QB	155	20	0	Monroe
24	TESSMER, ESTIL	'33	QB	165	21	1	Ann Arbor
26	DAMM, RUSSELL	'33	T	186	20	0	Muskegon
27	BERNARD, CHARLES	'34	C	215	19	0	Benton Harbor
28	CANTRILL, CECIL	'33E	T	195	20	0	Lexington, Ky.
29	DOUGLASS, LESLIE	'32	G	185	24	1	Gary, Ind.
30	WINSTON, J. LEO	'33	C	155	20	0	Washington, D. C.
31	EVERHARDUS, HERM	'34	HB	175	18	0	Kalamazoo
32	DANIELS, NORMAN	'32	E	175	24	2	Detroit
34	CHAPMAN, HARVEY	'34	T	178	19	0	Detroit
35	FAY, STANLEY	'34	HB	175	21	0	Detroit
39	WILLIAMSON, IVAN	'33	E	180	20	1	Toledo, O.
40	MELDMAN, LEONARD	'34	T	175	18	0	Detroit
41	MARCOVSKY, ABE	'33	G	163	18	0	Pittsburgh, Penn.
42	McCRATH, L. E.	'32	T	215	22	0	Grand Rapids
43	SCHMID, HERBERT	'34	HB	182	21	0	Grand Rapids
45	KOWALIK, JOHN	'34	G	190	21	0	Chicago, Ill.
46	NEWMAN, HARRY	'32	QB	174	21	1	Detroit
48	McGUIRE, DONALD	'34	E	183	21	0	South Haven
49	MILLER, ROBERT	'33	E	180	20	0	Highland Park
50	AUER, HOWARD	'32E	T	198	23	2	Bay City
51	HORNER, WILLIAM	'33E	E	155	21	0	Jackson
52	CONOVER, JAMES	'34E	G	202	19	0	Ann Arbor
54	SINGER, OSCAR	'34	G	185	19	0	Jackson Hgts., N. Y.
55	COX, RODERICK	'33	FB	196	20	1	Birmingham
56	HEWITT, WILLIAM	'32	E	185	21	2	Bay City
57	MORRISON, MAYNARD	'32	C	210	22	2	Royal Oak
58	LAJEUNESSE, OMER	'32	G	185	23	1	Iron Mountain
60	YOST, FIELDING H.	'32	E	168	19	0	Ann Arbor
61	COOKE, THOMAS	'33	T	195	22	0	Chicago, Ill.
62	KELLEY, BETHEL	'34	E	164	18	0	Bardstown, Ky.
63	RENNER, WILLIAM	'34	HB	165	21	0	Youngstown, O.
64	STINESPRING, HARRY	'34	QB	140	18	0	Chicago, Ill.
66	HOZER, STANLEY	'32	E	187	26	2	Muskegon
68	SAMUELS, TOM	'32	T	190	21	1	Canton, O.
69	SIKKENGA, JAY	'32	G	182	20	0	Muskegon Hgts.
72	GOLDSMITH, DUVAL	'33	T	200	24	0	Christiansburg, Va.

*Experience refers to letters won.

FRANCIS WISTERT, '34 of Chicago, Ill. Prepared at Carl Schurz where he was a team-mate of Stinespring and Kowalik of the Michigan squad. He is 19 and stands 6'3" in his sox. A likely end candidate.

1931 Season			Won 8, Lost 1, Tied 1		
			Date	Place	Attendance
Michigan 27,	Central Mich.	0	Oct 3	Ann Arbor	13,169
Michigan 34,	Eastern Mich.	0	Oct 3	Ann Arbor	13,169
Michigan 13,	Chicago	7	Oct 10	Ann Arbor	17,284
Michigan 7,	Ohio State	20	Oct 17	Ann Arbor	58,026
Michigan 35,	Illinois	0	Oct 24	Champaign	33,496
Michigan 21,	Princeton	0	Oct 31	Princeton	14,797
Michigan 22,	Indiana	0	Nov 7	Ann Arbor	26,410
Michigan 0,	Michigan State	0	Nov 14	Ann Arbor	35,844
Michigan 6,	Minnesota	0	Nov 21	Ann Arbor	37,251
Michigan 16,	Wisconsin	0	Nov 28	Ann Arbor	9,190

MICHIGAN'S STAFF

Left to Right—End Coach Bennie Oosterbaan; Line Coach Jack Blott; Head Coach Harry Kipke; Director and Coach Emeritus Fielding H. Yost; Backfield Coach Walter Weber; Backfield Coach Franklin Cappon.

Two All-Americans and two former captains are on this All-Michigan coaching staff.

ALL-AMERICAN

**Maynard Morrison
Center
1931**

OCT. 17

The summaries:

Michigan		Ohio State
Hewitt	LE	Nasman
Auer	LT	Bell
LaJeunesse	LG	Varner
Morrison	C	Smith
Kowalik	RG	Gailus
Samuels	RT	Haubrich
Williamson	RE	Gillman
Newman	QB	Cramer
J. Heston	LH	Hinchman
Fay	RH	Holcomb
Hudson	FB	Vauchnich

Michigan	0	0	0	0 — 7
Ohio State	7	0	6	7 —20

Touchdowns—Carroll 2, Williamson, Cramer. Goals after touchdown—Haubrich, Goldsmith, Peppe.

Substitutions—Michigan: Everhardus for Heston, Goldsmith for Samuels, Tessmer for Newman, Hozer for Kowalik, Cantrill for LaJeunesse, DeBaker for Everhardus, Wistert for Goldsmith, Newman for Tessmer, Samuels for Wistert, Heston for Everhardus, Petoskey for Williamson, Wistert for Auer, Kowalik for Hozer, Bernard for Morrison. Ohio State: Carroll for Holcomb, Keefe for Hinchman, Baumgarten for Haubrich, Haubrich for Baumgarten, Holcomb for Carroll, Peppe for Haubrich, Delich for Peppe, Kile for Gailus, Grady for Holcomb, Welever for Vauchnich, Russ for Nasman.

Officials—Referee, Frank Birch, Earlham; Umpire, John Schommer, Chicago; field judge, Fred Young, Illinois Wesleyan; head linesman, Arlie Mucks, Wisconsin.

OCT. 24

The summary:

ILLINOIS		MICHIGAN
Frink	LE	Petoskey
Jackson	LT	Wistert
May	LG	Hozer
Hedtke	C	Morrison
Nusspickel	RG	LaJeunesse
Hyink	RT	Auer
Marriner	RE	Williamson
Walser	QB	Tessmer
Berry	LH	Fay
Evans	RH	Heston
Murray	FB	Hewitt

Illinois	0	0	0	0 — 0
Michigan	7	7	0	21 —35

Touchdowns—Fay 2, Heston, Kowalik, Newman. Points after touchdown—Petoskey 2, Newman 3.

Substitutions—Illinois: Gorenstein for Nusspickel, Horsley for Walser, Schalk for Murray, Jensen for May, Cook for Evans, O'Neill for Jackson, Schustek for Marriner, Carson for Berry, Bailey for Frink, Kennedy for Hyink, Munch for Horsley, Straw for Hedtke. Michigan: Kowalik for Hozer, Samuels for Wistert, Cantrill for LaJeunesse, Goldsmith for Auer, Bernard for Morrison, Everhardus for Heston, Yost for Petoskey, Newman for Tessmer, Daniels for Williamson, DeBaker for Fay, Marcovsky for LaJeunesse, Westover for Everhardus.

Referee—Col. Hackett (West Point). Umpire—Anthony Haines (Yale). Field judge—Dr. J. H. Nichols (Oberlin). Head linesman—Fred Young (Illinois Wesleyan).

NOV. 14

MUD PRODUCES TIE

Michigan		Michigan State
Petoskey	LE	Fase
Auer	LT	Buss
LaJeunesse	LG	Gross
Morrison	C	Meirs
Hozer	RG	Handy
Samuels	RT	Brunette
Williamson	RE	Vandermeer
Hudson	QB	Kowatch
Heston	LH	Monnett
Fay	RH	Jones
Hewitt	FB	Eliowitz

Michigan	0	0	0	0 — 0
M. S. C.	0	0	0	0 — 0

Substitutions—Michigan: Kowalik for Hozer, Cantrill for LaJeunesse, Wistert for Samuels.

Referee—Gardner, Cornell; Umpire—Lipp, Chicago; Field judge—Hackett, West Point; Head linesman—Wyatt, Missouri.

NOV. 21

Michigan		Minnesota
Petoskey	LE	Robinson
Auer	LT	Gay
LaJeunesse	LG	Munn
Morrison	C	Stein
Hozer	RG	Dennerly
Samuels	RT	Boland
Williamson	RE	Teeter
Hudson	QB	Somers
Fay	LH	Ubl
Heston	RH	Haas
Hewitt	FB	Manders

Michigan	6	0	0	0 — 6
Minnesota	0	0	0	0 — 0

Touchdown—Hewitt.

Substitutions: Michigan—Daniels for Petoskey. Minnesota—Wells for Gay, Swartz for Haas, Koski for Dennerly, Champlin for Somers, Haas for Swartz, Griffith for Champlin, Dennerly for Koski, Krezowski for Teeter, Dillner for Robinson, Greenberg for Stein.

Referee, James Masker, Northwestern; Umpire, H. G. Hedges, Dartmouth; Field judge, George Simpson, Wisconsin; Head linesman, J. J. Lipp, Chicago.

THE 1932 MICHIGAN SQUAD

No.	Name	Class	Position	Weight	Age	Varsity Exp.	Home
4	SAVAGE, CARL M.	'33	T	188	21	1	Flint, Mich.
5	MELDMAN, LEONARD	'34	FB	175	19	1	Detroit, Mich.
6	BORGMANN, WILLIAM	'35	G	180	18	0	Ft. Wayne, Ind.
9	WESTOVER, LOUIS	'34	HB	168	20	1	Bay City, Mich.
11	WISTERT, FRANCIS	'34	T	196	20	1	Chicago, Ill.
12	CLOHSET, FRED	'33	T	185	21	1	Bay City, Mich.
14	OTTOMAN, LOUIS J.	'35	E	163	19	0	Chicago, Ill.
16	REGECZI, JOHN	'35	FB	180	19	0	Muskegon Hts., Mich.
17	PETOSKEY, FRED	'33	E	175	20	1	St. Charles, Mich.
18	FUOG, RUSSELL	'35	G	185	21	0	Chicago, Ill.
19	JACOBS, BENJAMIN	'35	QB	155	19	0	Sault Ste. Marie, Mich.
20	DeBAKER, CHARLES	'33	HB	165	21	2	Fruitport, Mich.
21	HESTON, JOHN P.	'34	HB	170	20	1	Ann Arbor, Mich.
22	FRISK, LESLIE L.	'33	T	178	25	2	Rock Island, Ill.
24	PALMEROLI, PETER	'35	FB	170	22	0	Highland Park, Ill.
26	DAMM, RUSSELL	'33	T	186	21	1	Muskegon, Mich.
27	BERNARD, CHARLES	'34	C	215	20	1	Benton Harbor, Mich.
28	CANTRILL, CECIL, JR.	'33	T	195	20	1	Lexington, Ky.
29	HILDEBRAND, WILLARD	'34	T	187	19	0	Saginaw, Mich.
30	ANTELL, GUNNARD	'34	E	168	21	0	Negaunee, Mich.
31	EVERHARDUS, HERMAN	'34	HB	175	19	1	Kalamazoo, Mich.
32	McCLINTIC, WILLIAM	'35	C	216	17	0	Detroit, Mich.
34	CHAPMAN, HARVEY	'34	T	178	20	1	Detroit, Mich.
35	FAY, STANLEY E.	'34	HB	175	22	1	Detroit, Mich.
39	WILLIAMSON, I. (Capt.)	'33	E	180	21	2	Toledo, O.
40	SHEA, SYLVESTER	'34	E	178	22	1	Detroit, Mich.
41	MARCOVSKY, ABE	'33	G	163	18	2	Pittsburgh, Pa.
42	MADDEN, FRANCIS L.	'35	T	234	20	0	Lockport, N. Y.
43	OLIVER, RUSSELL D.	'35	FB	190	21	0	Pontiac, Mich.
45	KOWALIK, JOHN	'33	G	190	22	0	Chicago, Ill.
46	NEWMAN, HARRY	'33	QB	174	22	2	Detroit, Mich.
48	FORD, GERALD	'35	C	187	18	0	Grand Rapids, Mich.
49	MILLER, ROBERT E.	'33	T	180	20	1	Highland Park, Mich.
50	SINGER, OSCAR A.	'34	G	186	19	1	Jackson Hts., N. Y.
51	STEWART, THOMAS	'34	HB	170	19	0	Detroit, Mich.
52	AUSTIN, THOMAS D.	'34	T	200	20	0	Columbus, O.
54	PONTO, HILTON A.	'34	G	170	21	0	Ann Arbor, Mich.
55	COX, RODERICK	'33	FB	196	21	2	Birmingham, Mich.
57	ZENDZIAN, FRANK P.	'35	HB	170	22	0	Providence, R. I.
61	WARD, WILLIS	'35	E	185	19	0	Detroit, Mich.
62	KELLY, BETHEL B.	'34	E	164	18	1	Beardstown, Ky.
63	RENNER, WILLIAM	'34	HB	165	21	1	Youngstown, O.
64	SHAW, LEE C.	'35	QB	150	18	0	Coldwater, Mich.
72	JACOBSON, TAGE	'35	T	193	18	0	Detroit, Mich.

Squad Roster and Playing Numbers Copyrighted 1932
Reproduction in This or Another Arrangement Prohibited

Michigan's Old '83' Is Banned By New System

Coach Harry Kipke Must Find Substitute for Old Favorite

Play Is Described

Famed Trick Play Fooled All Foes for More than 30 Years

By MERLE OLIVER

If Michigan's Wolverines uncork a new and startling trick play next fall it will have to be designated as "Young 83," for according to the experts "Old 83," the time honored deception invented by Fielding H. Yost, is doomed by rule changes made since the close of the 1931 football season. It is no secret that Head Coach Harry Kipke plans to work out a play to replace the old thriller.

The new rules declare the ball dead if any part of the ball carrier's body other than his hands or feet touch the ground. In "Old 83" the quarterback dropped to one knee while concealing the pigskin, and this no longer is allowed.

Reprinted with permission from the **Detroit Free Press**

Still Another Big Ten Championship!

Michigan's 1932 football team finished last fall's schedule without a defeat, amassing a total of 123 points against 13 for all opponents combined.

Not only Big Ten Champions, but also, under the Dickinson System, rated as United States National Champions.

THE 1932 SCORES

Michigan	26	Michigan State	0
Michigan	15	Northwestern	6
Michigan	14	Ohio State	0
Michigan	32	Illinois	0
Michigan	14	Princeton	7
Michigan	7	Indiana	0
Michigan	12	Chicago	0
Michigan	3	Minnesota	0

Ford, Gerald, '35 Lit., came to Michigan with a reputation of having been one of the best high school centers ever developed in western Michigan, and indicated on both the freshman team and again in spring practice that he had not been over-rated. He matriculated from Grand Rapids South High where he held down the pivot position for three years, besides having been a basketball guard for a season and a weight man on the track team for three years. He played well on the freshman team and forged ahead so far in spring practice as to win the Chicago Alumni trophy, given each year to the candidate who develops most, is attentive to duty and attends practice regularly. Ford will be understudy to Charles Bernard this season and is likely to see much service. He is 18 years old, weighs 187 pounds and is 6 feet tall. He plans to enter law after finishing school.

Two Passes

LINEUPS

MICHIGAN		OHIO STATE
Petoskey	LE	Ferrall
Wistert	LT	Monahan
Marcovsky	LG	Varner
Bernard	C	R. Smith
Cantrill	RG	Gailus
Damm	RT	Rosequist
Williamson	RE	Gillman
Newman	Q	Cramer
Everhardus	LH	Hichman
Fay	RH	Carroll
Regeczi	F	Vuchinich

Scoring:
Michigan ...... 7 7 0 0—14
Ohio State .... 0 0 0 0— 0

STATISTICS

	Michigan	Ohio
First Downs	7	8
by rushing	2	6
by passing	4	1
by penalties	1	1
Yards gained by rushing	76	172
Yards lost by rushing	28	18
net gain	48	156
Forwards attempted	6	11
Completed	4	1
Intercepted	2	0
Return of intercepted passes	7	0
Yards gain on passes	84	50
Yards gain on laterals	0	0
Total yards on punts	521	501
Average on punts	35	36
Yards return on punts	65	97
Penalties, yards lost	45	15

Oct. 15

Petoskey Scores On 56-Yard Run

Regeczi Out-kicks Indian Booters; Newman Runs Punt Back 73 Yards In Spectacular Play

By JOHN W. THOMAS

With their scoring punch greatly improved by a rebuilt backfield, the Wolverines moved forward yesterday in their march to a Big Ten championship, sweeping aside the feeble threat of the Illini, 32 to 0, before 30,000 people.

Michigan outclassed Illinois with a new running offense built around Ted Petoskey and Herman Everhardus, intermixed with Harry Newman's usual accurate passing. Michigan's line, 18-pounds heavier to a man, cut wide swaths for Coach Harry Kipke's duet of ground-gaining stars, through Coach Bob Zuppke'seleven.

Petoskey Makes 197 Yards

Petoskey made 197 yards from the line of scrimmage, including one gallop of 56 yards for a touchdown, while Herm Everhardus netted 105 yards. The new fullback carried the ball 23 times, while the speedy halfback took the pigskin only 18 times.

Reprinted with permission from the **Michigan Daily**

MICHIGAN

Player	T	G	L	N	A
Newman	12	18	12	6	
Petoskey	15	67	2	65	4.
Everhardus	4	15	4	11	2.
Regeczi	4	27	1	26	6.
Westover	0	0	0	0	

PRINCETON

Kadlic	4	4	4	0	
Bales	20	41	8	33	1.
Purnell	1	0	3	-3	-.
James	36	100	7	93	2.
Wardell	0	0	0	0	
Craig	1	4	0	4	4.
McPortland	0	0	0	0	

T is times carried ball; G is ga[ ] L is loss; N is net.

LINEUPS

Michigan		Princet[ ]
Ward	LE	Fairm[ ]
Wistert	LT	Cep[ ]
Kowalik	LG	Billin[ ]
Bernard	C	Hinm[ ]
Marcovsky	RG	Garre[ ]
Damm	RT	Fortu[ ]
Williamson	RE	Dela[ ]
Newman	Q	Kad[ ]
Everhardus	LH	Ba[ ]
Regeczi	RH	Purn[ ]
Petoskey	F	Jam[ ]

Score by Quarters:
Michigan .... 0 2 6 6—
Princeton .... 0 7 0 0—

Oct. 29

3=0 Victory Wins Championship

Champions of The West

FINAL STANDING

	W	L	T	Pct.
Michigan	6	0	0	1.000
Purdue	5	0	1	1.000
Wisconsin	4	1	1	.800
Ohio State	2	1	2	.667
Minnesota	2	3	0	.400
Northwestern	2	3	1	.400
Illinois	2	4	0	.333
Chicago	1	4	0	.200
Indiana	1	4	1	.200
Iowa	0	5	0	.000

Minnesota Vanquished By Star Quarterback's Kick From Fifteen-Yard Line; Quick Passes Are Help

Invitation To Game In Rose Bowl Seen

Gopher Aerial Attack Is Ineffective; Wolverines' Rushing Game Fails To Work; Fumbles Costly

By JOHN W. THOMAS
(Special to the Daily)

MEMORIAL STADIUM, MINNEAPOLIS, Minn., Nov. 19.—Two quick passes set the ball in position for Harry Newman to kick a field goal winning for Michigan their sixth straight conference victory, 3 to 0, and their eighth game of their undefeated season. Michigan's great quarterback, by bringing victory to the Wolverines here this afternoon, not only clinched an undisputed Western Conference title, but allowed the Maize and Blue to make a strong bid for the Rose Bowl invitation.

Reprinted with permission from the **Michigan Daily**

Stan Fay Elected Football Captain For 1933 Season

How Dickinson Rates Top Elevens

Team	Won	Lost	Tied	Points
Michigan	8	0	0	28.47
S. Calif.	9	0	0	26.81
Pittsburgh	8	0	2	26.49
Purdue	7	0	1	26.33
Colgate	9	0	0	25.00
Ohio State	4	1	3	23.60
Notre Dame	7	2	0	20.44
Army	8	2	0	20.00

Rice Names Newman For All-American

Williamson, Petoskey Win Honorable Mention For End Positions

Quarterback Is 18th Wolverine Selected

Bernard Considered At Center; Wistert Among Tackle Candidates

Harry Newman, brilliant quarterback on Michigan's championship football team, was selected by Grantland Rice as a member of the 1932 All-America team announced yesterday in Collier's magazine.

Newman is the eighteenth Wolverine to be honored as an All-American. Maynard Morrison, center on the 1931 squad, was the last to be so chosen.

Captain Ivan Williamson and Ted Petoskey were among those whom Mr. Rice considered in making his selection for the end position, while Francis Wistert was on the list as a candidate for tackle. Charles Bernard was among those from whom the center was chosen.

THE YELLOW AND BLUE

Sing to the colors that float in the light;
Hurrah for the Yellow and Blue!
Yellow the stars as they ride thro' the night,
And reel in a rollicking crew;
Yellow the fields where ripens the grain,
And yellow the moon on the harvest wain:—Hail!
Hail to the colors that float in the light;
Hurrah for the Yellow and Blue!

Blue are the billows that bow to the sun
When yellow robed morning is due;
Blue are the curtains that ev'ning has spun,
The slumbers of Phoebus to woo;
Blue are the blossoms to memory dear,
And blue is the sapphire and gleams like a tear;—Hail!
Hail to the ribbons that nature has spun;
Hurrah for the Yellow and Blue!

Here's to the college whose colors we wear,
Here's to the hearts that are true!
Here's to the maid of the golden hair,
And eyes that are brimming with blue!
Garlands of bluebells and maize intertwined,
And hearts that are true and voices combine;—Hail!
Hail to the college whose colors we wear;
Hurrah for the Yellow and Blue!

**Harry Newman
Quarterback**

HARRY NEWMAN, 1932 All-American quarterback, won national fame for his performance on the gridiron last fall. In addition to winning this place on Grantland Rice's team, he won the Chicago *Tribune* Trophy as the most valuable player, the gold football emblem of the All-Players All-American Board, the medal replica of the Douglas Fairbanks trophy, Collier's All-America football and a number of minor awards.

Newman is the eighteenth Michigan man to be placed on All-America teams since Heston first won a place in 1903.

Reprinted with
permission from
The Michiganensian

Unexpected Move Gives Pittsburgh Rose Bowl Game

Trojans' Bid To Eastern Team Accepted; Success In Difficult Season Cited As Reason For Choice

Michigan Marches On To Title Honors With Smashing 13 To 0 Win Over O.S.U. Before 93,000

Attendance Figure Announced; 85,000 Attended Contest

Reports of the attendance at the game here Saturday were grossly exaggerated according to Harry Tillotson, business manager for the athletic association, who said today that about 85,000 persons saw the contest.

During the game it was announced that the attendance was 93,508, but Mr. Tillotson said today that the paid attendance was 84,403. The largest crowd ever to attend a game here numbered 86,000 in 1927 when Ohio State opposed the Wolverines in the first game at the stadium.

Ohio Gains Only 24 Yards On Running Attack; Are Held to 3 First Downs

Renner Tallies Late In Second Quarter

Reprinted with permission from the **Michigan Daily**

Band Director Explains Alma Mater Omission

A crowded between-halves program was responsible for the Varsity Band's failure to play "The Yellow and Blue" at yesterday's game, it was explained last night by Prof. Nicholas D. Falcone, director.

"Each band is alloted a certain period for its formations between halves, and the Ohio State band took three minutes more than the period assigned it, cutting into our time," the bandmaster declared. "Even though we had allowed ourselves plenty of time for the lengthy "STEVE" formation and our others, we were hampered by the three minutes being cut from our time."

When the Buckeye band had gone through its formations the "Fighting Hundred" was forced to take its seats after the "STEVE" and script "OHIO" formations, omitting the alma mater in what one former student referred to as "the cardinal sin of omission" for Homecoming Week-end.

1933 Season			Won 7, Lost 0, Tied 1			
				Date	Place	Attendance
Michigan	20.	Michigan State	6	Oct 7	Ann Arbor	22,090
Michigan	40.	Cornell	0	Oct 14	Ann Arbor	27,431
Michigan	13.	Ohio State	0	Oct 21	Ann Arbor	82,606
Michigan	28.	Chicago	0	Oct 28	Chicago	19,458
Michigan	7.	Illinois	6	Nov 4	Champaign	20,405
Michigan	10.	Iowa	6	Nov 11	Ann Arbor	22,130
Michigan	0.	Minnesota	0	Nov 18	Ann Arbor	51,137
Michigan	13.	Northwestern	0	Nov 25	Evanston	23,940

Wolverines Stand Off Last Quarter Threats Of Illinois To Win By One Point, 7-6

Michigan Smashes Way To Conference Championship In 13-0 Win Over Wildcats

The 1933 Michigan Squad

No.	Name	Class	Position	Weight	Age	Varsity Exp.
4	SAVAGE, CARL M.	'34	G	200	22	2
5	REMIAS, STEVE	'36Ed	FB	175	19	0
6	BORGMANN, WILLIAM F.	'35	G	180	20	1
7	KIDSTON, JAMES A.	'36	FB	170	19	0
8	STETSON, PARKER F.	'36	HB	160	21	0
9	WESTOVER, LOUIS W.	'34E	QB	167	21	2
10	BEARD, CHESTER C.	'35	G	178	19	1
11	WISTERT, FRANCIS M.	'34	T	205	21	2
12	RAYMOND, HENRY T.	'36	HB	165	20	0
14	PAULSON, HERBERT C.	'35Ed	HB	168	20	0
15	FRANKOWSKI, WALLACE	'35	E	173	22	1
16	REGECZI, JOHN M.	'35Ed	FB	185	21	1
17	PETOSKEY, FRED L.	'34Ed	E	182	22	2
18	FUOG, RUSSELL J.	'35Ed	C-G	195	22	1
19	JACOBS, BENJAMIN P.	'35	QB	155	20	1
20	TRIPLEHORN, HOWARD	'36	HB	165	20	0
21	HESTON, JOHN P.	'34Ed	HB	170	21	0
23	DAUKSZA, ANTONE	'36E	QB	163	20	0
24	TESSMER, ESTEL S.	'34Ed	QB	170	23	2
25	WELLS, ROBERT L.	'34E	G	167	20	0
27	BERNARD, CHARLES J.	'34	C	215	22	2
29	HILDEBRAND, WILLARD	'35	T-G	187	20	1
30	BOLAS, GEORGE	'36	QB	158	19	0
31	EVERHARDUS, HERMAN	'34	HB	174	21	2
32	STONE, EDWARD ADAM	'36	T	172	21	0
33	RATTERMAN, LAWRENCE F.	'34	QB	160	21	1
34	CHAPMAN, HARVEY E.	'35	E	180	21	2
35	FAY, STANLEY E. (Capt.)	'34Ed	HB	175	23	2
36	NELSON, WINFRED	'36Ed	HB	175	22	0
37	RUDNESS, GEORGE	'36Ed	HB	153	20	0
38	SOODIK, ELI	'34Ed	C	165	20	2
40	SHEA, SYLVESTER C.	'34	E	178	23	2
41	McGUIRE, DONALD T.	'34	T	190	23	1
42	VIERGIVER, JOHN D.	'35Ed	T	220	20	0
43	OLIVER, RUSSELL D.	'35	FB	190	23	1
44	SWANSON, ROBERT G.	'34	T	187	21	0
45	KOWALIK, JOHN F.	'34Ed	G	190	23	2
48	FORD, GERALD	'35	C-G	195	20	1
49	SCHMIDT, HERBERT T.	'35	FB	190	23	1
50	SINGER, OSCAR A.	'34	G	180	21	2
52	AUSTIN, THOMAS D.	'35	T	200	21	1
53	JOHNSON, ERNEST C.	'36Ed	E	170	19	0
54	PONTO, HILTON A.	'34Ed	G	175	21	1
55	LEWIS, D. KING	'36	HB	175	18	0
56	HUNN, DAVID S.	'36	QB	160	19	0
61	WARD, WILLIS F.	'35	E	183	20	1
62	MALASHEVICH, MICHAEL	'36Ed	E	196	20	0
63	RENNER, WILLIAM W.	'34	HB-QB	165	23	2
64	SHAW, LEE CHARLES	'35	QB	150	19	1
66	TOMAGNO, CHELSO	'36Ed	E	177	21	0
67	JAMES, RICHARD	'36E	QB	162	19	0
68	PATCHIN, ARTHUR B.	'35	FB	175	22	0
70	SEMEYN, ROY A.	'36E	T	198	26	0
72	JACOBSON, TAGE O.	'35E	T	210	20	1

Charles Bernard Center

Francis Wistert Tackle

LEADING TEAMS FOR 1933

	W	L	T	Rating
Michigan	7	0	1	28.52
Nebraska	8	1	0	24.61
Minnesota	4	0	0	23.87
Pittsburgh	8	1	0	23.01
Ohio State	7	1	0	22.79
So. Calif.	10	1	1	22.61
Princeton	9	0	0	22.50
Oregon	9	1	0	22.16
Army	9	1	0	22.16
Purdue	6	1	1	21.88
Stanford	9	1	1	20.34

Four U-M Gridders Included In Rice's Football Selections

Selecting his annual All-American football team for Collier's magazine, Grantland Rice placed two Michigan gridiron luminaries of the past season, Charles Bernard, center, and Frances Wistert, tackle, on his first team.

Bernard, one of the greatest of a great group of Michigan centers, was a unanimous choice on everybody's All-American eleven. Wistert, regarded as one of the two best tackles in Michigan football history, rates his selection because of his outstanding offensive and defensive line play throughout the season, coupled with his ability to drop back into the backfield and throw long distance passes. 'Whitey,' being a modest young man, laughingly discounts this acknowledgement by saying that Grantland Rice is a fraternity brother of his.

Ted Petoskey, Wolverine star end of three years, who was last year chosen by the "All-American Board" last year, was named on the second All-American team this season by Mr. Rice. While Petoskey was one of the outstanding ends in the country, one of the most apparent reasons for his relegation to the second squad was that it would not have been proper for three Michigan to make the same All-American team, and Bernard and Wistert couldn't properly be kept off.

Herman Everhardus, main offensive threat of a championship team, was honored by Mr. Rice, who placed him in his third team backfield.

To Our Patrons:

With the personal habits and tastes of those who attend football games at the Michigan Stadium the Board in Control of Athletics frankly concedes that, generally speaking, it has no concern. When, however, indulgence in such habits and tastes results in conduct disgusting or offensive to other patrons, the Board does feel a very deep concern.

A very large percentage of those who attend the games do not look upon the occasion as one calling for throwing off all restraint in the use of intoxicating liquors. Unfortunately a certain percentage, relatively small, do seem to look upon attendance at a football game as an excuse for drinking in manner and extent beyond the limits of propriety and decency.

We wish to take this opportunity to give general notice that ushers and officers are being instructed to receive complaints regarding the offensive use of liquor in and about the stands. We shall not hesitate to revoke the license conferred by the ticket and to eject from the stadium grounds anyone against whom a reasonable complaint is made.

It is more than probable that you who receive this communication are not one of those directly affected by it. At the same time you will be interested in knowing that this effort is being made for your protection. We earnestly request the cooperation of all our patrons.

Board in Control of Athletics
University of Michigan

Fielding H. Yost
Secretary.

University of Michigan

SQUAD LIST

No.	Name	Class	Position	Height	Years on Squad	Weight
5	REMIAS, STEVE	'36	FB	5'11"	1	190
6	BORGMANN, WILLIAM F.	'35	G	5'10"	2	198
9	RIECK, JOHN A.	'37	E	5'11"	0	161
10	BEARD, CHESTER C.	'35	G	5'9"	2	191
11	SEARS, HAROLD W., JR.	'37	G	5'8"	0	202
14	MEYERS, EARL J.	'37	E	5'11½"	0	188
15	PILLINGER, HARRY J.	'36	Q	5'8½"	0	155
16	REGECZI, JOHN M.	'35	FB	6'	2	186
17	PATANELLI, MATTHEW L.	'37	E	6'1"	0	202
18	FUOG, RUSSELL J.	'35	C	5'11"	2	193
19	JACOBS, PHILLIP H.	'37	HB	5'10½"	0	160
20	TRIPLEHORN, HOWARD	'36	HB	5'10½"	1	166
21	BARNETT, DAVID G.	'37	HB	5'11"	0	165
23	LIFFITON, JACK K.	'37	FB	5'11"	0	180
24	AMRINE, ROBERT O.	'37	HB	6'	0	189
25	GARBER, JESSE G.	'37	G	5'8½"	0	187
26	CARR, CARL W., JR.	'37	T	6'2"	0	189
27	WRIGHT, HARRY T.	'37	T	6'2¼"	0	242
29	HILDEBRAND, WILLARD H.	'35	G-T	6'	2	195
30	BOLAS, GEORGE	'36	Q	5'7"	1	162
31	EVERHARDUS, CHRIS	'37	HB	6'1"	0	169
32	STONE, EDWARD ADAM	'36	T	6'	1	185
34	GRAPER, ROBERT	'37	E	6'1½"	0	188
35	AUG, VINCENT J.	'37	HB	5'11½"	0	175
36	NELSON, WINFRED	'36	HB	5'10"	1	176
37	RUDNESS, GEORGE	'36	HB	5'8"	1	160
38	SOODIK, ELI	'35	G	5'7"	2	168
40	MUMFORD, JOHN	'37	FB	5'10½"	0	180
41	SCHUMAN, STANTON J.	'37	C	5'9"	0	189
42	VIERGEVER, JOHN D.	'36	T	6'1"	1	233
43	OLIVER, RUSSELL D.	'35	FB	5'10½"	2	181
45	OYLER, THOMAS T.	'37	E	5'11¼"	0	190
48	FORD, GERALD	'35	C	6'	2	198
49	ELLIS, JOSEPH O.	'37	Q-HB	6'	0	178
50	BRANDMAN, CHARLES	'37	Q	5'6"	0	162
52	AUSTIN, THOMAS D. (Capt.)	'35	T	6'1"	2	207
53	JOHNSON, ERNEST C.	'36	E	6'	1	181
54	FISHER, JOE	'36	T	5'11"	0	197
55	PEDERSON, ERNEST A.	'37	G	5'10½"	0	175
60	SWEET, CEDRIC C.	'37	FB	6'	0	192
61	WARD, WILLIS F.	'35	E	6'1"	2	185
62	SAVAGE, MICHAEL	'36	E	6'3"	1	210
63	RENNER, WILLIAM W.	'35	Q	5'10½"	2	159
64	JENNINGS, FERRIS	'37	Q	5'10"	0	137
66	HANSHUE, CLOYCE E.	'37	G	5'11"	0	202
67	JAMES, RICHARD H.	'36	Q	5'9"	1	164
68	BISSELL, FRANK	'37	G	5'8"	0	162
70	LETT, FRANKLIN	'37	E	6'	0	197
72	JACOBSON, TAGE O.	'35	T	6'1"	2	199

1934 Season — *Won 1, Lost 7, Tied 0*

				Date	Place	Attendance
Michigan	0.	Michigan State	16	Oct 6	Ann Arbor	25,644
Michigan	0.	Chicago	27	Oct 13	Chicago	18,013
Michigan	9.	Georgia Tech	2	Oct 20	Ann Arbor	20,901
Michigan	6.	Illinois	7	Oct 27	Ann Arbor	34,822
Michigan	0.	Minnesota	34	Nov 3	Minneapolis	59,362
Michigan	0.	Wisconsin	10	Nov 10	Ann Arbor	21,963
Michigan	0.	Ohio State	34	Nov 17	Columbus	62,893
Michigan	6.	Northwestern	13	Nov 24	Ann Arbor	19,196

Big 10 Standings

1934				
Minnesota	5	0	0	1.000
Ohio State	5	1	0	.833
Illinois	4	1	0	.800
Purdue	3	1	0	.750
Northwestern	2	3	0	.400
Wisconsin	2	3	0	.400
Chicago	2	4	0	.333
Indiana	1	3	1	.250
Iowa	1	3	1	.250
Michigan	0	6	0	.000

Ford, Gerald (Jerry) '35, Grand Rapids, Mich. Age 2[illegible] years, weight 201 pounds, 6 feet tall. Plays center. Played [illegible] years at Grand Rapids South under Coach Cliff Gettings. Has won 2 "M" awards in football and freshman numerals. Has also won freshman basketball numerals.

Warmbein Leads Attack With Two Touchdowns

Wolverines Never Have Scoring Chance and Are Kept Constantly on Defensive by Spartans' Accurate Forward Passes.

By JOHN THOMAS.

ANN ARBOR, Mich., Oct. 6.—Kurt Warmbein, 160-pound halfback scored two touchdowns to climax Michigan State's well-deserved victory over the once mighty Wolverines here this afternoon, 16 to 0, and gave the Spartans their first win over Michigan since 1915.

Warmbein's runs in the fourth quarter were the punch needed by State. Quarterback Russ Reynolds used the junior from St. Joseph Mich., as the director of State's powerful passing attack that made 94 yards and five first downs and then sent him with the ball for the touchdowns.

First in 19 Years

MICHIGAN.		STATE.
Savage	L. E.	Zarza
Viergever	L. T.	Zindel
Hildebrand	L. G.	Dahlgren
Ford	C.	Buzoltis
Borgman	R. G.	Wagner
Austin	R. T.	Reavely
Ward	R. E.	Klewicki
Oliver	Q.	Reynolds
Triplehorn	L. H.	Warmbein
Patanelli	R. H.	Colina
Remias	F. B.	McCrary

Score by periods:

Michigan	0	0	0	0—0
State	0	0	3	13—16

Touchdowns — State, Warmbein (2).

Field goal—State, Sebo.

Points after touchdown — State, Sebo.

Substitutions — Michigan: Ends, Patanelli; tackles, Jacobson; guards, Hanshue, Beard; center, Fuog; quarterback, Jennings; fullback, Regeczi; halfback, Aug.

State: Ends, Allman; tackles, Brakeman, Sleder; guard, Wilson; centers, Vanderburg; halfbacks, Sebo, Ageh, Williamson; fullback, Wiseman.

Officials—Referee, Col. H. B. Hackett (West Point); umpire, Lionel Gardiner (Illinois); field judge, R. J. Eichenlaub (Notre Dame); head linesman, Dr. E. P. Maxwell, (Ohio State).

Chicago Wins, 27-0, to Gain First Michigan Conquest Since 1919

Look Out, Zuppke!

MICHIGAN		GEORGIA TECH
Patanelli	L.E.	Katz
Viergever	L.T.	Williams
Hildebrand	L.G.	Wilcox (D.)
Ford	C	Preston
Borgmann	R.G.	Wilcox (J.)
Austin (C)	R.T.	Dean
Savage	R.E.	Boulware
Jennings	Q	Roberts
Aug	L.H	Martin
Regeczi	R.H	Perkerson
Sweet	F.B.	Phillips (C)

Score by periods:

Georgia Tech	0	0	0	2—2
Michigan	0	0	0	0—0

Georgia Tech scoring: Safety, Thompson. (substitute for Katz).

Michigan scoring: Touchdown, Jennings; point from try after touchdown, Hildebrand; safety, Patanelli.

Summary: Officials: Referee— J. T. Clinton (Yale). Umpire—C. A. Reed (Springfield). Linesman—J. C. Hennessy (Brown). Field Judge—George Vergara (Notre Dame). Time of periods— 15 minutes.

Oct. 20 (only win)

Varsity Carries $810.15 Worth Of Equipment Into Each Game

By FRED DE LANO

According to Henry Hatch the 11 men that start for Michigan Saturday against Minnesota will be carrying, besides the good wishes of thousands of Wolverine grid fans, $810.15 worth of Michigan football equipment.

Henry Hatch, who for 15 years has taken care of the athletic equipment at the Field House is the man who outfits the squad with their uniforms, each of which is worth $73.65 at present prices. The shoes are the most expensive articles of a player's equipment, costing the Athletic Association $12.50 a pair.

The shoulder pads go for $12.00 and the helmets cost $10.50 apiece. Michigan's pants cost $9.50 a pair and the hip pads $9.00. Four dollars are paid out for each pair of knee pads and three more for each of the yellow and blue jerseys. Hose cost the department $1.25, undershirts, supporters, and ankle wraps fifty cents each with the sweat socks selling for forty cents.

Michigan Concludes Its Most Disastrous Season With Seventh Loss, 13-6

Jerry Ford Named Most Valuable of Michigan Players

Ford Will Play With East In New Year's Tilt

Wolverine Center To Leave With 22 Man Squad On Dec. 19 For Coast

Gerald Ford, selected by his teammates as the most valuable man on Michigan's 1934 football team, has accepted an invitation to play with the eastern stars in the annual East-West charity game New Year's Day in San Francisco.

FORD

Ford, another of Michigan's mighty centers, received his offer from Dick Hanley Monday. Hanley and Andy Kerr, Northwestern and Colgate mentors, coach the eastern aggregation and each selects 11 players from his section of the country.

"I HATE YOU"

The University of Michigan Squad
1935

FIRST ROW—Cooper, Rinaldi, Muzyk, Brandman, Ziem, Barclay, Lutomski, Gray, Bissell, Campbell, Pillinger, Walder, Babbin, Lincoln.

SECOND ROW—Oyler, Barnett, Smithers, Garber, Pederson, Lillie, Renner (Capt.), Barasa, Hinshaw, McClintic, Ellis, Nelson, Cushing, Sweet, Remias.

THIRD ROW—Kramer, Schuman, Wright, Johnson, Savage, Greenwald, Patanelli, Aug, Viergever, Warns, Murray, Farmer, Sobsey, Shakarian, Luby, Carr, Valpey, Everhardus, Hanshue, Levenson.

Will Coach at Yale

Jerry Ford, star center on the Michigan football team last fall, has accepted an offer from Yale University to serve as line coach of the junior varsity next fall. At present Ford is helping Harry Kipke with the Wolverine squad in spring practice. He will report at Yale in the fall.

New Drum Major's Strut Endangered By Oversize Shako

Michigan's new drum major, Robert Fox, '38, showed 'em how it should be done at the football game yesterday, but his shako—the towering helmet which graces the heads of all drum majors—nearly fell off.

The hat was too big in the first place, George Hall, '36BAd., explained. "We had to sort of tie it on." But when Fox was strutting his stuff and whisking his baton every which way during the half, the strings came untied. And by the time he had led the band back to the Michigan side for the Alma Mater song, the shako was well down over his eyes.

It was only his ears which kept it up at all, and as soon as the Fighting Hundred broke formation, he jerked it off and sighed.

Fox vied for honors with Tony Mariottes, Michigan State sophomore, who drum majored the eighty-odd musicians from East Lansing. Neither dropped his baton when tossing it over the goal posts, but the concensus had it that Fox outfoxed his "opponent." Except for one thing: Mariottes had boots.

Fox received a bad break, however, when he was introduced as "Robert Hall" as he led the band onto the field before the game.

University of Michigan
SQUAD LIST

Name and Class	Pos.	Hgt.	Wgt.	Experience Symbol	Home
Remias, Steve, '36	F	5' 11"	183	B	Chicago, Ill.
Olds, Frederic C., '38	G	5' 11"	186	--	East Lansing
Rieck, John, '37	E	5' 11"	158	D	Detroit, Mich.
Gray, Charles, '38	Q	5' 6"	140	E	Lombard, Ill.
Babbin, George, '37	H	5' 6"	166	E	Pentwater
Valpey, Arthur L., '38	E	6' 2"	188	E	Detroit
Kramer, Melvin G., '38	T	6' 0"	194	—	Toledo, Ohio
Ellis, Joseph O., '37	H	6' 0"	181	B, E	Eagle River, Wis.
Meyers, Earl J., '37	H	6' 0"	183	E	Detroit
Pillinger, Harry J., '36	H	5' 9"	165	C, E	Whitehall
Cooper, Robert E., '38	F&Q	6' 0"	188	—	Detroit
Barasa, Joseph L., '38	Q	5' 9"	161	E	Chicago, Ill.
Lillie, Walter I., '38	G	5' 11"	187	E	Grand Haven
Barclay, William C., '38	Q&H	5' 11"	153	F	Flint
Barnett, David G., '37	H&E	5' 10"	169	D, E	Detroit
Campbell, Robert D., '38	H	5' 10"	175	E	Ionia
Amrine, Robert Y., '37	C	6' 0"	179	B, E	London, Ohio
Garber, Jesse G., '37	E	5' 8½"	185	E	New York, N. Y.
Carr, Carl W., '36	T	6' 2"	196	D	Saline, Mich.
Wright, Harry T., '37	C	6' 2¾"	242	E, D	Mt. Clemens
Greenwald, Edward U., '38	T	6' 3"	203	E	Whiting, Ind.
Bolas, George A., '36	Q&H	5' 8"	161	B, C, E	Chicago, Ill.
Everhardus, Chris, '37	H	6' 1"	172	B	Kalamazoo
Shakarian, George, '38	C	6' 0½"	177	E	Dearborn
Ritchie, C. Stark, '38	H	5' 10"	170	E	Battle Creek
Hinshaw, Joseph M., '37	H	5' 9½"	192	E	Bloomfield Hills
Aug, Vincent, '37	H	6' 0"	177	B, E	Cincinnati, Ohio
Nelson, Winfred, '36	H	5' 10"	170	E, D	Greenville
Lutomski, Harry J., '38	F	5' 9"	187	E	Detroit
Mumford, John, '37	F	5' 10½"	181	E, D	Birmingham
Schuman, Stanton J., '37	C&G	5' 9"	191	D, E	Winnetka, Ill.
Viergever, John D., '36	T	6' 1"	228	A, E	Algonac
Smithers, John A., '38	H	5' 11"	188	E	Elkhart, Ind.
Luby, Earle B., '38	C	5' 11½"	199	E	Chicago, Ill.
Oyler, Thomas T., '37	C	5' 11½"	190	D, E	Cincinnati, Ohio
Ziem, Fred C., '38	C	5' 10"	167	E	Pontiac
Brandman, Charles, '37	Q	5' 7"	175	C, E	Findlay, Ohio
Murray, Charles A., '37	T	6' 1"	218	E	Butte, Mont.
Lincoln, James H., '38	E	6' 0"	193	E	Harbor Beach
Johnson, Ernest C., '36	E	6' 0½"	182	C	Grand Rapids
Cushing, Frederick, '38	G	5' 11"	191	—	Birmingham
Pederson, Ernest A., '37	G	5' 10½"	184	D, E	Grand Blanc
Stabovitz, Chester C., '37	E	5' 11"	180	D, E	Chicago, Ill.
Sweet, Cedric C., '37	F	6' 0"	197	B, E	Fremont
Rinaldi, Joseph M., '38	E	5' 11"	195	E	Elkhart, Ind.
Savage, Michael, '36	E	6' 3"	218	A	Dearborn
Muzyk, Alexander F., '37	E	6' 1"	180	E	Pittsburgh, Pa.
Jennings, Ferris G., '37	Q	5' 10"	144	B	Ann Arbor
Renner, Wm. W. (Capt.), '36	Q	5' 10½"	159	B	Youngstown, Ohio
Hanshue, Cloyce E., '37	E	5' 11"	200	B, E	Kalamazoo
Patanelli, Matthew L., '37	E	6' 1½"	203	B, E	Elkhart, Ind.
Bissell, Frank S., '37	G	5' 8"	164	B, E	Hyannisport, Mass.
Warns, James, '37	E	6' 5"	198	—	Ann Arbor, Mich.
Farmer, Douglas A., '38	G	6' 0"	181	F	Hinsdale, Ill.
Sobsey, Solomon, '38	E	6' 0"	186	E	Brooklyn, N. Y.

KEY TO EXPERIENCE SYMBOLS

A—Varsity letterman, 2 years

B—Varsity letterman, 1 year

C—Varsity squad, 2 years (no letters)

D—Varsity squad, 1 year (no letter)

E—Freshman letterman

F—Freshman squad (no numerals)

1935 Season				Won 4, Lost 4, Tied 0	
			Date	Place	Attendance
Michigan	6,	Michigan State	25	Oct 5	Ann Arbor	32,315
Michigan	7,	Indiana	0	Oct 12	Ann Arbor	18,533
Michigan	20,	Wisconsin	12	Oct 19	Madison	14,381
Michigan	19,	Columbia	7	Oct 26	New York	24,901
Michigan	16,	Pennsylvania	6	Nov 2	Ann Arbor	30,751
Michigan	0,	Illinois	3	Nov 9	Champaign	28,136
Michigan	0,	Minnesota	40	Nov 16	Ann Arbor	32,029
Michigan	0,	Ohio State	38	Nov 23	Ann Arbor	53,322

Attendance For Year Reaches 255,000 Mark

In figures disclosed yesterday by Ralph W. Aigler, faculty chairman of the Board in Control of Athletics, it was estimated that the University of Michigan's football team played to crowds totaling 255,000 this season. Home games drew 185,000 fans.

Michigan drew some of its largest crowds in defeat. Michigan State opened the grid season here with a smashing 25-6 victory over the Wolverines before 32,500 partisan rooters. Minnesota and Ohio State handed Michigan two of the worst defeats in Michigan grid annals before crowds of 35,000 and 65,000 respectively, and Illinois eked out a win over the Wolverines at Champaign in a game that attracted 25,000.

The Michigan Coaching Staff

Left to right—Walter Weber, backfield coach; Franklin Cappon, line coach; Bennie Oosterbaan, end coach; Clifford Keen, assistant line coach; Harry Kipke, head coach; Ray Courtright, freshman coach; Carl Savage, assistant coach; William Borgmann, assistant coach; Ray Fisher, freshman coach.

MEN OF THE MAIZE AND BLUE

W. A. P. John   A. J. Gorney

Chorus

Men of the Maize and Blue
We place our trust in you;
Bravest of all and best,
Lift up your gleaming crest;
Conquer for Michigan,
Fight for your colors true,
Go at them man to man
For good old Michigan,
Men of the Maize and Blue!

COLLEGE DAYS

Donald A. Kahm   Earl V. Moore

Chorus

I'll ne'er forget my college days
Those dear sincere old college days
I'll ne'er forget my Michigan
'Twas there long friendships first began.
At Michigan all hearts are true
All loyal to the Maize and Blue,
There e'er will be a golden haze
Around those dear old college days.

University of Michigan
FOOTBALL SQUAD
1936

No.	Name and Class	Pos.	Hgt.	Wgt.	Experience Symbol	Home
5	Loiko, Alex, '39	HB	6'1¼"	188	F	Hamtramck
6	Olds, Fredric C., '38	G-T	5'11"	185	—	E. Lansing
8	Mark, Martin, '39	G	5'9"	180	F	New York, N.Y.
9	Gray, Charles, '38	QB	5'6"	140	V	Lombard, Ill.
11	Valpey, Arthur L., '38	E	6'2½"	190	*	Detroit
12	Kramer, Melvin G., '38	T	6'	196	*	Toledo, Ohio
13	Hook, R. Wallace, Jr., '39	HB	5'9"	170	F	Grand Rapids
14	Paquette, Donald M., '39	HB	6'1½"	190	F	Superior, Wis.
15	Ochs, Lilburn M., '38	HB	5'9"	175	—	Univ. City, Mo.
16	Cooper, Robert E., '38	QB	6'	187	X	Detroit
17	Barasa, J. Laurence, '38	QB	5'8½"	160	X	Chicago, Ill.
19	Marzonie, George A., '38	G	5'9"	178	—	Flint
20	Barclay, William C., '38	QB	5'11"	160	*	Flint
21	Barnett, James A., '39	G	5'8½"	168	F	Detroit
23	Campbell, Robert D., '38	HB	5'9½"	174	*	Ionia
24	Stanton, Edward C., '39	FB	6'	183	F	Charleston, W. Va.
25	Garber, Jesse G., '37	G	5'9"	190	*	Brookline, Mass.
26	Jordan, Forrest R., '39	G	6'2"	195	F	Clare
27	Jordan, John D., '39	C	6'2"	228	F	Evanston, Ill.
29	Greenwald, Edward, '38	T	6'3"	203	X	Whiting, Ind.
30	Piotrowski, Robert P., '39	HB	5'10½"	157	—	Manistee
31	Everhardus, Chris, '37	HB	6'1"	170	**	Kalamazoo
32	Floersch, Harold J., '39	E	6'2"	185	—	Wyandotte
33	Ritchie, C. Stark, '38	HB	5'11"	180	*	Battle Creek
34	Nickerson, Norman J., '39	FB	6'¼"	182	—	Detroit
35	Phillips, Edward J., Jr., '39	HB	5'10"	177	F	Bradford, Pa.
36	Heikkinen, Ralph L., '39	G	5'8"	187	F	Ramsay
37	Levine, Louis, '39	QB	5'10½"	180	F	Muskegon
40	Curren, Robert B., '39	FB	5'11"	190	F	Warren, Pa.
41	Rosenthal, Seymour C., '39	T	6'2½"	200	F	Blue Island, Ill.
42	Smick, Dan, '39	E	6'4"	198	F	Hazel Park
43	Smithers, John A., '38	HB	5'11"	188	*	Elkhart, Ind.
44	Luby, Earle B., '38	T	5'11½"	195	*	Chicago, Ill.
45	Brennan, John C., '39	T	6'1"	199	F	Racine, Wis.
48	Leadbeater, Arthur, '38	HB	5'10½"	180	—	Belleville, N.J.
49	Ziem, Fred C., '38	G	5'10"	162	V	Pontiac
50	Belsky, Jerome, '39	G	6'	190	F	Woodcliff, N.J.
51	Gedeon, Elmer J., '39	E	6'3"	180	F	Cleveland, Ohio
52	Lincoln, James H., '38	T	6'	190	*	Harbor Beach
53	Shakarian, George, '38	C	6'½"	180	X	Dearborn
54	VandeWater, Clarence, '39	G	5'11"	185	F	Holland
55	Pederson, Ernest A., Jr., '38	G	5'10½"	190	*	Grand Blanc
56	Stabovitz, Chester C., '37	E	5'11"	180	V	Chicago, Ill.
60	Sweet, Cedric C., '37	FB	6'	200	**	Fremont
61	Rinaldi, Joe M., '38	C	5'11"	190	*	Elkhart, Ind.
62	Siegel, Don J., '39	T	6'4"	199	F	Royal Oak
63	Frost, Kenneth D., '39	HB	5'9"	170	F	Willoughby, O.
64	Jennings, Ferris G., '38	QB	5'10"	140	*	Ann Arbor
65	Purucker, Norman B., '39	HB	5'10"	168	F	Poland, Ohio
66	Janke, Fred C., '39	T	6'½"	200	F	Jackson
67	Patanelli, Matthew, '37 (Capt.)	E	6'1"	200	**	Elkhart, Ind.
68	Bissell, Frank S., '37	G	5'8"½	165	**	Hyannisport, Mass.
70	Farmer, Douglas A., '38	FB	6'	183	—	Hinsdale, Ill.
72	Maurer, George J., '39	FB	5'11"	180	F	Toledo, Ohio

KEY TO EXPERIENCE SYMBOLS
*—Varsity Letters   F—Freshman numerals, 1935
V—Varsity reserve award, 1935   X—Varsity squad, 1935

1936 Season			Won 1, Lost 7, Tied 0		
			Date	Place	Attendance
Michigan	7,	Michigan State	21	Oct 3	Ann Arbor	45,656
Michigan	3,	Indiana	14	Oct 10	Ann Arbor	19,110
Michigan	0,	Minnesota	26	Oct 17	Minneapolis	41,209
Michigan	13,	Columbia	0	Oct 24	Ann Arbor	23,835
Michigan	6,	Illinois	9	Oct 31	Ann Arbor	29,901
Michigan	7,	Pennsylvania	27	Nov 7	Philadelphia	30,501
Michigan	0,	Northwestern	9	Nov 14	Ann Arbor	28,295
Michigan	0,	Ohio State	21	Nov 21	Columbus	56,277

Band Provides Bright Momen In M.S.C. Wi

Providing the only bright spot an otherwise dreary afternoon Michigan football fans, the Univ sity Band, newly garbed in milit: coats and showing almost as ma formations as both football tear proved that Michigan need not ashamed when the band goes to Ph adelphia November 7 for the Qual game.

Heralded in by the trumpet sectio which was in perfect harmony, t members of the maize and blue ba stepped out on the field before t game to the tune of the Victors a proceeded to twine in and about t grey clad State organization.

Between the halves, the ba showed the training which it has u dergone unnoticed by the stude body. Highlight was the featur "Music Goes Round and Round" three revolving crosses were formec

The band is drilled every afternoc from 5 to 6 p.m. and from 7 to p.m. every Wednesday. Captain W: ter Ferris, drill master, Bob Fox, '3 drum major, a junior and two sop: omore members then make out blu prints which are exact in every deta These prints are then mimeographe and copies handed out to all mer bers on Saturday morning.

Harmonically, the band is directe by William D. Revelli who is begin ning his second year in the capaci of band head. Revelli directed th nation's outstanding high school bar at Hobart, Indiana for ten years.

For Scrapbooks

Buckeyes Win, 21-0 As Michigan Closes Unsuccessful Year

No Disgrace

NORTHW'ST'N		MICHIGAN
Kovatch	L.E.	Patanelli
Gibson	L.T.	Siegel
Devry	L.G.	Garber
Wegner	C.	Rinaldi
Reid	R.G.	Bissell
Burnett	R.T.	Lincoln
Zitko	R.E.	Smick
Vanzo	Q.B.	Barclay
Heap	L. H.	Hook
Jefferson	R.	Smithers
Geyer	F.B.	Sweet
NORTHWESTERN	0 3 0 6—9	
MICHIGAN	0 0 0 0—0	

Patanelli Is Named On Italian-American Team

DES MOINES, Nov. 30.—(AP)— Capt. Matt Patanelli, University of Michigan end, has been placed on the Italian-American all star football team, an honorary selection by the National Italian American Civic League's athletic council.

MICHIGAN		OHIO STATE
Patanelli	L.E	Wend
Siegel	L.T	Hamric
Garber	L.G	Smit
Rinaldi	C.	Wol
Marzonie	R.G	Zarna
Lincoln	R.T	Schoenbaum
Smick	R.E	Cumiskey
Barclay	Q.B	Dye
Ritchie	L.H	Booth
Phillips	R.H	Wedebrook
Sweet	F.B	McDonald
Ohio State	0 6 9 6—2	
Michigan	0 0 0 0—0	

BOTTOM ROW, LEFT TO RIGHT: Laskey, Mulholland, Belsky, Sukup, Trosko, Ulevitch, Piotrowski, Campbell, Barclay, Marzonie, Hook, Ziem, Renda, Heikkinen, Pederson, Ritchie, Warren.
CENTER ROW: Cooper, Kinsey, Tinker, VandeWater, Valek, Bilbie, Siegel, Gates, Luby, Farmer, Rinaldi, Kuhn, Sobsey, Jordan, Brennan, Kramer, Penvenne, Olds.
TOP ROW: Nickerson, Frutig, Smick, Hutton, Lincoln, Shaw, Floersch, Nielsen, Savilla, Janke, Smith, Steen, Nicholson, Kodros, Valpey, Gedeon, Levine, Curren, Purucker.

1937 MICHIGAN ROSTER 1937

Key to Experience Symbols

No.	Name and Class	Position	Height	Weight	Age	Symbol	Home City
2	BENNETT, Arthur L., '40	G	5'9"	170	18	F	Schenectady, N. Y.
3	VIAL, A. Burgess, '40	G	6'0"	164	18	F	LaGrange, Ill.
4	BOWERS, Charles L., '40	E	5'11"	165	19		Pontiac, Mich.
6	KINSEY, John H., '40	FB	6'0"	194	19	F	Plymouth, Mich.
7	PENVENNE, Paul F., '40	FB	6'1½"	190	19	F	Lenox, Mass.
9	LASKEY, Derwood D., '40	HB	5'9"	155	19	F	Milan, Mich.
11	VALPEY, Arthur L., '38	E	6'2"	201	22	**	Detroit, Mich.
12	KRAMER, Melvin G., '38	T	6'0"	200	22	V	Toledo, Ohio
13	HOOK, R. Wallace, Jr., '39	HB	5'9"	175	20	*	E. Grand Rapids, Mich.
14	HUTTON, Thomas G., '40	C	5'11"	174	19	F	Bay City, Mich.
15	SUKUP, Milo F., '40	HB	5'7½"	176	20	F	Muskegon Hgts., Mich.
16	MARZONIE, George A., '38	G	5'9"	185	21	*	Flint, Mich.
17	RENDA, Hercules, '40	HB	5'4"	152	20	F	Jochin, W. Va.
19	TROSKO, Fred, '40	HB	5'9"	154	20	F	Flint, Mich.
20	BARCLAY, William C., '38	QB	5'11"	163	21	**	Flint, Mich.
21	NIELSEN, Paul, '40	E	6'0"	182	20	F	Ann Arbor, Mich.
22	GATES, David W., '40	G	5'10"	174	18	F	Plymouth, Mich.
23	CAMPBELL, Robert D., '38	HB	5'9½"	170	22	*	Ionia, Mich.
24	STANTON, E. Cramon, '39	FB	6'0½"	183	20	*	Charleston, W. Va.
25	ZIEM, Frederick C., '38	G	5'10"	161	21	*	Pontiac, Mich.
26	JORDAN, Forrest R., '39	G	6'2"	203	23	V	Clare, Mich.
27	KUHN, Dennis A., '40	T	6'2"	207	22		River Rouge, Mich.
29	SAVILLA, Roland, '40	T	6'3½"	195	21	V	Gallagher, W. Va.
30	PIOTROWSKI, Robert P., '39	HB	5'11"	157	20	V	Manistee, Mich.
32	FLOERSCH, Harold J., '39	E	6'2½"	188	23	V	Wyandotte, Mich.
33	RITCHIE, C. Stark, '38	HB	5'11"	173	21	**	Battle Creek, Mich.
34	NICKERSON, Norman J., '39	FB	6'1¼"	192	23	V	Detroit, Mich.
36	HEIKKINEN, Ralph I., '39	G	5'9"	180	20	V	Ramsay, Mich.
37	LEVINE, Louis, '39	QB	5'11"	186	20	*	Muskegon Hgts., Mich.
40	CURREN, Robert B., '39	FB	6'0"	198	21	V	Warren, Pa.
41	BILBIE, James N., '39	T	6'1"	200	20		South Lyon, Mich.
42	SMICK, Dan, '39	E	6'4"	198	20	*	Hazel Park, Mich.
43	SMITH, William A., '40	T	6'2"	203	19	*	Brooks Field, Texas
44	LUBY, Earle B., '38	T	6'0"	204	21	**	Chicago, Ill.
45	BRENNAN, John C., '39	G	6'2"	201	22	*	Racine, Wis.
49	FRUTIG, Edward C., '40	E	6'1"	176	19	F	River Rouge, Mich.
50	BELSKY, Jerome, '39	G	6'0"	184	19	X	Woodcliff, N. J.
51	GEDEON, Elmer J., '39	E	6'3"	192	20	*	Cleveland, Ohio
52	LINCOLN, James H., '38	T	6'0"	191	21	*	Harbor Beach, Mich.
53	KODROS, Archie J., '40	C-G	5'8"	191	19	F	Alton, Ill.
54	VANDE WATER, Clarence H., '38	G	5'10"	183	21	*	Holland, Mich.
55	PEDERSON, Ernest A., '38	G	5'11"	185	22	*	Grand Blanc, Mich.
56	VALEK, Vincent, '40	E	6'2"	170	19		Holly, Mich.
59	MULHOLLAND, Harry K., '40	FB	5'11"	191	19	F	Bay City, Mich.
60	STEEN, Kenneth, '40	T	6'2"	196	20	F	Detroit, Mich.
61	RINALDI, Joseph, '38 (Captain)	C	5'11"	190	21	**	Elkhart, Ind.
62	SIEGEL, Donald J., '39	T	6'4"	205	23	*	Royal Oak, Mich.
63	FROST, Kenneth J., '39	HB	5'9"	170	20	X	Willoughby, Ohio
64	TINKER, Horace C., '40	C	5'10"	173	20	*	Battle Creek, Mich.
65	PURUCKER, Norman B., '39	HB	5'10"	170	20	V	Poland, Ohio
66	JANKE, Fred C., '39	FB	6'1"	208	20	*	Jackson, Mich.
67	NICHOLSON, John E., Jr., '39	E	6'4"	186	20	X	Elkhart, Ind.
69	ROGERS, Joseph C., '40	E	6'3"	190	18	F	Royal Oak, Mich.
70	FARMER, Douglas A., '38	FB	6'1"	182	21	V	Hinsdale, Ill.
71	ULEVITCH, Herman H., '40	G	5'8"	188	19	F	Cleveland, Ohio
72	SOBSEY, Solomon, '39	E	6'0"	189	22		W. New York, N. J.
75	OLDS, Fred C., '39	GT	6'0"	192	21	X	East Lansing, Mich.
77	COOPER, Robert E., '38	HB	6'0"	185	21		Detroit, Mich.

Key to Experience Symbols

* —Stars Show Number of Letters Won   F —Freshman Numerals, 1936
V —Varsity Reserve Squad, 1936   X —Varsity Squad, 1936

Oct. 2

Mich. State (19)	Pos.	Michigan (14)
Nelson	LE	Nicholson
Speelman	LT	Siegel
Gortat	LG	Olds
Miknavitch	C	Kodros
Dudley	RG	Marzonie
Swartz	RT	Savilla
Gaines	RE	Valpey
Diebold	QB	Farmer
Ciolek	LH	Ritchie
Coolidge	RH	Renda
Haney	FB	Stanton

Score by periods:

Michigan State .... 0 0 13 6—19
Michigan .... 0 0 7 7—14

Michigan State scoring: Touchdowns—Ciolek, Nelson 2. Point after touchdown—Pearce (sub for Coolidge) (placekick).

Oct. 9

Mr. Don Heap

MICHIGAN		NORTHWEST.
Nicholson	L.E.	Kovatch
Siegel	L.T.	Cutlich
Brennan	L.G.	Wells
Kodros	C.	Wegner
Heikkinen	R.G.	Calvino
Smith	R.T.	Voigts
Smick	R.E.	Diehl
Farmer	Q.B.	Vanzo
Trosko	L.H.	Heap
Renda	R.H.	Jefferson
Stanton	F.B.	Ryan

Officials—Frank Birch (Earlham), referee; John Schommer, (Chicago), umpire; J. S. Getchell (St. Thomas), field judge; Jay Wyatt (Missouri), head linesman.

Michigan .... 0 0 0 0—0
Northwestern ...... 0 0 7 0—7

Touchdowns — Diehl, (pass from Heap).

Point after touchdown—Ryan, (placekick).

Oct. 23

Iowa	Pos.	Michigan
Lannon	LE	Gedeon
Harris	LT	Siegel
Brady	LG	Brennan
Anderson	C	Rinaldi
Allen	RG	Heikkinen
F. Gallagher	RT	Smith
Prasse	RE	Nicholson
Kinnick	QB	Farmer
Eicherly	LH	Trosko
W. Gallagher	RH	Barclay
McLain	FB	Stanton

Score by periods:

Iowa	0	0	6	0—6
Michigan	0	7	0	0—7

Iowa scoring: Touchdown, Kinnick.

Michigan scoring: Touchdown, Stanton. Point after touchdown: Trosko (placement).

OCT. 30

Trosko Passes For Initial Score And Tallies Point To Break The Deadlock

Recovered Fumble Gives Illini Score

By IRVIN LISAGOR
(Daily Sports Editor)

CHAMPAIGN, Ill., Oct. 30.—With characteristic calm, little Fred Trosko booted a placekick squarely across the goal posts late in the third quarter today to give Michigan a 7-6 victory over Illinois and to spoil Coach Bob Zuppke's 25th anniversary party before 29,000 homecomers in Memorial Stadium.

A few minutes prior to his payoff boot, Trosko had pitched a 39 yard pass to John Nicholson, Wolverine end, who gathered it in on the run and galloped untouched for about 15 more yards and a touchdown which put Michigan back into a ball game they seemed determined to lose.

Illinois tallied by marching 69 yards from the second half kickoff, culminating the drive by Ken Zimmerman's fumble which rolled across the Varsity goal and which Willard Cramer, Illini guard, pounced on for the score. Jack Berner's attempted conversion sailed wide of the bar.

Reprinted with permission from the **Michigan Daily**

Oct. 16

Michigan-Minnesota Game Summaries

Starting Lineups:

Minnesota	pos.	Michigan
Reed	LE	Gedeon
Shultz	LT	Siegel
Bell	LG	Brennan
Elmer	C	Kodros
Twedell	RG	Heikkinen
Midler	RT	Savilla
King	RE	Smick
Gmitro	QB	Farmer
Uram	LH	Trosko
Moore	RH	Renda
Buhler	FB	Stanton

Score By Periods:

Michigan	6	0	0	0	6
Minnesota	0	13	13	13	39

Touchdowns, Michigan: Gedeon. Minnesota: Gmitro 2, Spadaccini, Buhler, Van Every, Matheny.

Points after touchdowns: Bell 2, Faust.

Substitutions: Michigan: Ends, Valpey for Smick; tackles, Janke for Siegel, Smith for Savilla; guards, Pederson for Brennan, Vanderwat for Heikkenen; center, Rinaldi f Kodros; quarterback, Campbell f Farmer; halfbacks, Piotrowski f Renda, Hook for Trosko, Ritchie f Hook, Lasky for Piotrowski; fullbac Nickerson for Stanton.

Minnesota: ends, Nash for Kin Ohlgren for Nash, Mariucci for Oh gren; tackles, Kilbourne for Schult R. Johnson for Kilbourne, Pedersc for Midler; guards, Filbert for Be Twedell for Filbert, Wells for Kafk Rork for Twedell; center, Kulbits for Elmer; quarterback, Spadaccini for Gmitro, Faust for Spadaccin halfbacks, Matheny for Moore; full back, Christianson for Buhler, Be fiori for Christianson.

7-6

After Four Years!

MICHIGAN		ILLINOIS
Nicholson	L.E.	Klemp
Segal	L.T.	Reeder
Brennan	L.G.	Hodges
Rinaldi	C	McDonald
Heikkinen	R.G.	Fay
Smith	R.T.	Lundberg
Smick	R.E.	Castelo
Farmer	Q.	Berner
Trosko	L.H.	Zimmerman
Barclay	R.H.	Wehrli
Stanton	F.B.	Carson

Michigan	0	0	7	0—7
Illinois	0	0	6	0—6

Touchdown — Cramer (substitute for Lundberg), Nicholson. Point after touchdown—Trosko. Missed point after touchdown—Berner.

Nov. 6

Chicago (12)	Pos.	Michigan (13)
Fitzgerald	LE	Nicholson
Petersen	LT	Janke
Fink	LG	Brennan
Pierce	C	Kodros
Kelley	RG	Heikkenen
Johnson	RT	Smith
Wasem	RE	Smick
Hamity	QB	Farmer
Sherman	LH	Purucker
Valorz	RH	Barclay
Goodstein	FB	Stanton

Score by periods:

Chicago	0	6	6	0—12
Michigan	0	0	0	13—13

Nov. 20

O.S.U. 21, Michigan 0

First downs:	M	O.S.
By rushing	1	6
By passing	3	1
Through penalties	0	0
Total	4	7
Yards gained from scrimmage:		
By rushing	63	225
By passing	37	101
Yards lost rushing	55	31
Net yardage gained, pass and running	45	295
Passes:		
Attempted	12	12
Completed	4	4
Intercepted	4	3
Yards lost by penalties	35	35
No. of penalties	4	7

Nov. 13

Fourth Victory

MICHIGAN		PENN
Nicholson	L.E.	Gustafsor
Janke	L.T.	Polill
Brennan	L.G.	Fiedle
Kodros	C.	O'Neil
Heikkinen	R.G.	McNamar
Smith	R.T.	Shin
Smick	R.E.	Schueneman
Farmer	Q.	Coulte
Ritchie	L.H.	Burk
Purucker	R.H.	Mille
Kinsey	F.B.	Connel

Michigan	0	7	0	0—
Pennsylvania	0	0	0	0—

Michigan scoring—Touchdown Purucker. Point after touchdown: Marzonie (sub for Heikkinen), placement.

Referee—J. R. Trimble. Umpir —C. G. Eckles. Linesman—H. Vo Kersburg. Field judge— C. M Waters.

HOW MICHIGAN FARED IN 1937

Michigan	14;	Michigan State	19
Michigan	0;	Northwestern	7
Michigan	6;	Minnesota	39
Michigan	7;	Iowa	6
Michigan	7;	Illinois	6
Michigan	13;	Chicago	12
Michigan	7;	Pennsylvania	0
Michigan	0;	Ohio State	21

FINAL STANDINGS, WESTERN CONFERENCE 1937
(Conference Opponents Only)

	W	T	L	P	OP	Pct.
Minnesota	5	0	0	100	22	1.000
Ohio State	5	0	1	99	10	.833
Indiana	3	0	2	33	25	.600
Wisconsin	2	1	2	59	40	.500
Purdue	2	1	2	40	41	.500
Northwestern	3	0	3	35	33	.500
Michigan	3	0	3	33	91	.500
Illinois	2	0	3	39	39	.400
Chicago	0	0	4	12	100	.000
Iowa	0	0	5	22	71	.000

HERBERT O. "Fritz" Crisler takes charge of Michigan's football team this year as one of the Big Ten's most notable products in the coaching field. A graduate of the University of Chicago in 1922, he starred in three sports there. Under A. A. Stagg he was named an all-Western and all-American end in football, and was also an all-Conference guard in basketball and the Maroons' leading hurler on the diamond.

Academic honors were Crisler's as an undergraduate, too. He received the Western Conference Medal as an outstanding scholar-athlete, and qualified for Phi Beta Kappa, highest scholastic honor society, although deprived of membership by a technicality.

An assistant to Stagg while still an undergraduate, Crisler remained with him and as assistant basketball and baseball coach until 1925 when he became head baseball coach and assistant director of athletics. In 1930 he went to Minnesota as head football coach and director of athletics, where he remained for two years before going to Princeton in 1932 as football coach.

As a head coach his Minnesota team won 10, lost 7 and tied 1 while his Princeton teams in six seasons won 35, lost 9 and tied 5.

"We're short a couple of suits this week!"

1938 MICHIGAN ROSTER 1938

No.	Name and Class	Position	Height	Weight	Age	Experience	Home
5	FABYAN, August E. '41	HB	5'8"	165	19		Muskegon Heights, Mich.
6	KINSEY, John '40	FB	6'0"	194	20	R	Plymouth, Mich.
7	KOHL, Harry E. '41	QB	5'6"	147	18		Dayton, Ohio
9	LASKEY, Derwood '40	HB	5'9"	155	20	R	Milan, Mich.
10	LUTHER, William '41	HB	5'11"	165	19		Toledo, Ohio
14	HUTTON, Thomas '40	C	5'11"	185	20	JV	Bay City, Mich.
15	SUKUP, Milo '40	G	5'8"	176	21		Muskegon Heights, Mich.
16	WICKTER, Larry '41	FB	5'10"	170	19		Toledo, Ohio
17	VIAL, A. Burgess '40	FB	5'9"	175	20	JV	LaGrange, Ill.
18	PARFET, William '40	E	6'1"	190	20		Golden, Colo.
19	BENNETT, Arthur J. '40	G	5'8"	170	19	JV	Schenectady, N.Y.
21	PHILLIPS, Edward J. '39	FB	5'10"	180	22	*	Bradford, Pa.
22	MEHAFFEY, Howard '41	FB	6'0"	177	24		Pittsburgh, Pa.
26	JORDAN, Forrest '39	G	6'2"	200	24	R	Clare, Mich.
27	KUHN, Dennis '40	T	6'2"	207	23	R	River Rouge, Mich.
29	SAVILLA, Roland '40	T	6'1"	206	22	*	Gallagher, W. Va.
30	PERSKY, Lester '41	QB	5'10"	170	19		Cleveland Heights, Ohio
31	STEKETEE, Jack N. '41	C	6'0"	185	19		Detroit, Mich.
32	FLOERSCH, Harold '39	E	6'3"	188	24	RR	Wyandotte, Mich.
33	VALEK, Vincent '40	E	6'2"	170	20		Holly, Mich.
34	NICKERSON, Norman J. '39	E	6'1"	192	24	RR	Detroit, Mich.
36	HEIKKINEN, Ralph '39	G	5'10"	180	21	*	Ramsey, Mich.
38	SMICK, Danny '39	E	6'4"	205	21	**	Hazel Park, Mich.
39	KITTI, Walter '41	QB	5'10"	170	20		Calumet, Mich.
40	CZAK, Edward '41	G	5'11"	180	19		Elyria, Ohio
41	VOLLMER, William E. '41	T	6'0"	200	23		Manistee, Mich.
43	SMITH, William A. '40	T	6'2"	210	20	*	Riverside, Cal.
46	LEVINE, Louis '39	QB	5'11"	188	21	**	Muskegon Heights, Mich.
49	FRUTIG, Edward '41	E	6'0"	176	19		River Rouge, Mich.
50	KELTO, Reuben '41	C	6'1"	195	19		Bessemer, Mich.
51	GEDEON, Elmer J. '39	E	6'4"	192	21	**	Cleveland, Ohio
53	KODROS, Archie '40	C	5'8"	190	20	*	Alton, Ill.
54	NIELSEN, Paul '40	E	6'0"	182	21		Ann Arbor, Mich.
55	TROSKO, Fred '40	HB	5'9"	154	21	*	Flint, Mich.
56	OLDS, Frederick '40	G	6'0"	192	22	*	East Lansing, Mich.
57	FORD, Thomas G. '41	C	6'1"	185	20		East Grand Rapids, Mich.
58	PURUCKER, Norman B. '39	HB	5'11"	180	21	*	Youngstown, Ohio
59	MULHOLLAND, Harry '40	FB	5'11"	195	20	R	Bay City, Mich.
61	MEGREGIAN, Michael '41	HB	5'8"	190	20		Detroit, Mich.
62	SIEGEL, Don '39	T	6'4"	210	24	**	Royal Oak, Mich.
63	FRITZ, Ralph '41	G	5'9"	198	19		New Kensington, Pa.
64	TINKER, Horace '40	C	5'10"	173	21	R	Battle Creek, Mich.
65	BRENNAN, John C. '39	G	6'2"	200	23	**	Monroe, Mich.
66	JANKE, Fred '39 (Capt.)	T	6'1"	205	21	**	Jackson, Mich.
67	NICHOLSON, John '40	E	6'4"	190	21	*	Elkhart, Ind.
69	EVASHEVSKI, Forest '41	C-QB	6'1"	198	20		Detroit, Mich.
70	PADDY, Arthur '41	G	5'7"	160	20		Benton Harbor, Mich.
71	ULEVITCH, Herman '40	G	5'8"	188	20	JV	Cleveland, Ohio
72	SCOTT, Virgil '40	G	5'11"	175	19		Hazel Park, Mich.
73	FLORA, Robert L. '41	T	6'1"	213	22		Muskegon, Mich.
74	BENNETT, Richard C. '41	HB	5'10"	170	20		Springfield, Ill.
76	HOOK, Robert M. '41	T	6'3"	205	19		East Grand Rapids, Mich.
77	MEYER, Jack '41	QB	5'9"	195	20		Elyria, Ohio
79	HOOK, R. Wallace, Jr. '39	FB	5'11"	176	21	*	East Grand Rapids, Mich.
80	ZIELINSKI, Ernest P. '40	E	6'1"	185	20		Bay City, Mich.
83	KROMER, Paul S. '41	HB	5'10"	160	19		Lorain, Ohio
85	RENDA, Hercules '40	HB	5'4"	163	21	*	Jochin, W. Va.
88	STRONG, David A. '40	HB	5'10"	155	22		Helena, Mont.
96	CHRISTY, Edward '41	FB	5'10"	185	21		Gary, Ind.
98	HARMON, Tom '41	HB	6'0"	194	18		Gary, Ind.

* Number of Football Letters Won   R Varsity Reserve Awards   JV Junior Varsity Award, 1937

1938 Record			
Michigan	14	Michigan State	0
Michigan	45	Chicago	0
Michigan	6	Minnesota	7
Michigan	15	Yale	13
Michigan	14	Illinois	0
Michigan	19	Pennsylvania	13
Michigan	0	Northwestern	0
Michigan	18	Ohio State	0
Michigan	131	Opponents	33

Michigan, Won 6, Lost 1, Tied 1

Michigan Helmet Goes Back to '38

Reprinted with permission from The 1969 Football Guide

Michigan's famed winged football helmet dates back to 1938 when Fritz Crisler arrived from Princeton with his penchant for detail and style.

"Michigan had a plain black helmet and we wanted to dress it up a little," Fritz recalls. "We added some color (maize and blue) and used the same basic helmet I had designed at Princeton."

There was one other consideration. Fritz thought this unique helmet could be helpful to his passers when they tried to spot their receivers downfield. There was a tendency to use different colored helmets just for receivers in those days, but I always thought that would be as helpful for the defense as for the offense," Fritz explained.

Michigan Stadium Can Seat 85,753 And Not One More

If your favorite radio announcer tells you Saturday that there are 93,000 spectators at the Michigan-Michigan State football game, don't believe him.

If your favorite newspapers tell you Sunday that you were one of 89,000 spectators who watched the Michigan - Michigan State game, don't believe him.

Because with every permanent, temporary and box seat filled in the Wolverine stadium, the capacity is 85,753. Those are the exact figures, and by actual count, the exact number of seats.

There are 72,929 permanent seats in the stadium. In addition there are 2,776 box seats. When all of the temporary seats are erected around the top of the stadium (as will be the case Saturday) it adds 10,048 to the seating capacity.

The permanent seats are divided into two sections. There are 23,889 end zone seats and 49,040 side seats of which 25,600 are between the goal lines.

Reprinted with permission from the **Michigan Daily**

Alert Wolverines End Four Year Era Of Spartan Victory

Coach Crisler Offers Prizes As Incentive

It became known yesterday just how much Coach Fritz Crisler wants a good defense against Yale.

He has offered a brand new autographed football to the lineman making the most tackles Saturday as well as to the back who intercepts the greatest number of passes.

The autographs will be those of the coaching staff and the entire Michigan team.

| Michigan | 2 | 0 | 6 | 7—15 |
| Yale | 6 | 7 | 0 | 0—13 |

Michigan scoring: Touchdowns—Purucker, Nicholson. Point from try after touchdown, Brennan (placement).

Yale scoring: Touchdowns—Moody 2. Point from try after touchdown—Humphrey (placement). Safety—Siegel.

LINE-UPS

Nelson	LE	Valek
Ketzko	LT	Janke (c)
Rockenbach	LG	Brenna
Alling	C	Kodros
Abdo	RG	Heikkinen
Bremer	RT	Smith
Kinek	RE	Nicholson
Bruckner	QB	Evashevski
Pingel	LH	Purucker
Szasz	RH	Troske
Haney	FB	Phillips

Score By Periods

| MICHIGAN STATE | 0 | 0 | 0 | 0— 0 |
| MICHIGAN | 0 | 7 | 0 | 7—14 |

Michigan scoring: Touchdowns, Kromer (sub for Purucker) 2.

Point after touchdown, Valek (place kick); Kromer (run after blocked place-kick.

Michigan State subs: Ends, Diehl, Bennett. Tackles, Pearson, Gargett, Maliskey. Guards, Masny, Griffeth. Center, McShannock. Backs, Kovacich, Rossi, Pearce, Ciolek, Hill.

Michigan subs: Ends, Frutig, Nielsen, Smick. Tackles, Siegel. Guards, Olds, Fritz. Centers, Tinker. Backs, Kromer, Kitti, Harmon, Hook and Meyer.

Tough One To Lose!

The Lineups

Michigan (6)		Minnesota (7)
Valek	LE	Mariucci
Janke	LT	Pederson
Brennan	LG	Bell
Kodros	C	Elmer
Heikkinen	RG	Twedell
Savilla	RT	Schultz
Nicholson	RE	Nash
Evashevski	QB	Faust
Purucker	LH	Moore
Harmon	RH	Buhler
Phillips	FB	Christiansen
Michigan	0 0 0 6—6	
Minnesota	0 0 0 7—7	

Michigan scoring — Touchdown, Kromer, (sub for Harmon). Minnesota scoring—Touchdown, Moore. Point from try after touchdown—Faust (placement).

Substitutions:

Michigan: Ends—Smick, Frutig, Gedeon; Tackles—Smith, Siegel, Jordan; Guards—Fritz, Olds, Sukup; Quarterbacks—Meyer, Kitti, Levine; Halfbacks—Kromer, Trosko, Hook, Laskey, Strong.

Minnesota: Ends—Bill Johnson, Bjorcklund; Guards—Bob Johnson, Rork; Center—Kulbitski; Halfbacks—Franck, Van Every, Jamnik.

Referee, Frank Lane, Detroit; Umpire, W. D. Knight, Dartmouth; Field Judge, Fred Gardner, Cornell; Head Linesman, Lee Daniels Loyola.

TEAMMATES BATTLE FOR BALL: Louie Levine shown in the middle of the above picture, nearly spoiled Ed Czak's catch of a pass for a Michigan touchdown against Chicago Saturday. Czak at the right finally made the catch, although in the above picture the ball has slipped through his hands and is rolling on his chest. Both Levine and Czak appear to have their eyes closed. Solly Sherman, Chicago quarterback at the left and Robert Meyer (No. 17) Chicago halfback, failed to break up this touchdown pass hurled by Dave Strong. Michigan ran up the biggest total a Wolverine team ever scored in the stadium in beating Chicago, 45 to 7.

Ohio State 0, Michigan 18

Finally the day of days had arrived; Michigan had come to town. Filled not only with traditional rivalry, but also with high spirits, a crowd of 75,000 people jammed the stadium to witness the battle.

With effectiveness rarely seen by Ohio fans, Michigan completely unseated the Buck's chances for a Big Ten title. Michigan, for the first time in five years, came from behind, and defeated a Buck team.

The Bucks had more first downs and net yardage than the Wolves in the first half, but lost their stamina. A score was inevitable. Michigan again scored in the fourth period, when Harmon passed to Frutig on the Buck's 18. Another pass with the same combination, scored the second tally. The Bucks attempted to score with an aerial attack but it failed. Two plays later, Michigan romped unscathed for another touchdown.

Reprinted with permission from the Ohio State Makio

Michigan Rated Sixth By Dickinson System

CHICAGO, Dec. 5.—(AP)—Elmer Layden's once-beaten Notre Dame eleven was given top national ranking today for the 1938 football season by Dr. Frank G. Dickinson, University of Illinois professor and originator of the rating system bearing his name. The Irish were rated at 27.72 points.

Undefeated Duke rated second 27.10 points and Tennessee, also unbeaten, was third at 26.68. Michigan was sixth with 23.02.

		W	L	T	
1	Notre Dame	8	1	0	27.72
2	Duke	9	0	0	27.10
3	Tennessee	10	0	0	26.68
4	Southern Calif	8	2	0	23.71
5	Oklahoma	10	0	0	23.69
6	Michigan	6	1	1	23.02
7	Minnesota	6	2	0	22.71
8	Texas Christian	10	0	0	22.67

THE 1938 A.P. ALL-AMERICA

First Team	Position	Second Team
Jerome Holland, Cornell	END	Bowden Wyatt, Tennessee
Joseph Beinor, Notre Dame	TACKLE	Insull Hale, Texas Christian
RALPH HEIKKINEN, Michigan	GUARD	Sidney Roth, Cornell
Charles Aldrich, Texas Christian	CENTER	Dan Hill, Jr., Duke
Edward Bock, Iowa State	GUARD	Francis Twedell, Minn.
Alvord Wolff, Santa Clara	TACKLE	Torrance Russell, Auburn
Walter Young, Oklahoma	END	Earl Brown, Notre Dame
David O'Brien, Texas Christian	BACK	George Cafego, Tennessee
James Hall, Mississippi	BACK	William Patterson, Baylor
John Pingel, Michigan State	BACK	Victor Bottari, California
Marshall Goldberg, Pittsburgh	BACK	Sidney Luckman, Columbia

RUSHING

Player, Position	Times Carried	Yards Gained	Yards Lost	Net Gain	Ave. Gain
Kromer, LH	103	334	47	287	2.70
Harmon, RH	77	405	7	398	5.17
Purucker, LH	55	296	22	274	5
Trosko, RH	43	210	36	174	4
Phillips, FB	24	63	3	60	2.5
Hook, FB	23	114	1	113	5
Mehaffey, FB	21	96	0	96	4.5
Strong, LH	18	70	13	57	3.16
Luther, LH	7	10	3	7	1
Christy, FB	5	26	0	26	5.2
Evashevski, QB	4	19	1	18	4.5
Gedeon, LE	3	7	1	6	2
Renda, RH	2	47	0	47	23.5
Kitti, RH	2	11	2	9	4.5
Valek, LE	2	7	0	7	3.5
Laskey, RH	2	3	0	3	1.5
Meyer, QB	1	0	1	-1	-1
Smick, LE	1	6	0	6	6
TOTALS—					
Michigan	393	1724	140	1584	4.03
Opponents	307	999	169	830	2.7

SCORING

Player and Position	Touch-Downs	Conv. Att.	Conv. Made	Field Goals	Saf'ty	Pts.
Kromer, LH	6	1	1	0	0	37
Harmon, RH	3	1	0	0	0	18
Purucker, LH	2	1	0	0	0	12
Trosko, RH	2	0	0	0	0	12
Evashevski, QB	1	0	0	0	0	6
Nicholson, RE	1	0	0	0	0	6
Mehaffey, FB	1	0	0	0	0	6
Czak, LE	1	0	0	0	0	6
Sukup, RG	1	0	0	0	0	6
Frutig, LE	1	0	0	0	0	6
Strong, LH	1	0	0	0	0	6
Brennan, LG	0	7	4	0	0	4
Meyer, QB	0	4	2	0	0	2
Siegel, RT	0	0	0	0	1	2
Smick, RE	0	3	1	0	0	1
Valek, LE	0	3	1	0	0	1
TOTALS—						
Michigan	20	20	9	0	1	131
Opponents	6	6	4	0	0	40

PASS RECEIVING

Player and Position	Number Caught	Yards Gained	Player and Position	Number Caught	Yards Gained
Kromer, LH	9	72	Nicholson, RE	3	30
Evashevski, QB	8	83	Valek, LE	2	45
Mehaffey, FB	4	52	Kitti, RH	2	32
Trosko, RH	4	34	Czak, LE	2	34
Purucker, RH	3	41	Meyer, QB	1	14
Phillips, FB	3	27	Smick, RE	1	13
Gedeon, LE	3	23	Levine, QB	1	7
Frutig, LE	4	72	Harmon, RH	1	-9

RETURN OF PUNTS AND INTERCEPTED PASSES

Player and Position	Punts Ret'rnd.	Yards Ret'rnd.	Ave. Ret'rn.	Passes Inter.	Yards Ret'rnd.
Kromer, LH	20	246	12.3	1	16
Purucker, LH	17	171	10	2	7
Strong, LH	5	23	4.6	1	3
Luther, LH	2	29	14.5		
Harmon, RH	2	11	5.5	2	23
Kitti, RH	1	8	8		
Evashevski, QB	1	5	5	2	10
Trosko, RH	1	5	5	1	5
Renda, RH				2	60
Hook, FB				1	22
Frutig, LE				1	10
Fritz, LG				1	7
Levine, QB				1	3
Meyer, QB				1	2
TOTALS—					
Michigan	49	498	10.2	16	165
Opponents	47	276	5.8	7	27

PASSING

Player and Position	Number Attemp.	Number Com.	Pct.	Had Inter.	Yards Gained
Harmon, RH	45	21	.466	1	310
Trosko, RH	25	9	.360	2	109
Kromer, LH	25	11	.440	1	103
Strong, LH	17	7	.412	1	96
Purucker, LH	9	2	.221	2	16
Phillips, FB	1	1	1.000	0	4
TOTALS—					
Michigan	122	51	.418	7	638
Opponents	116	57	.390	16	774

1938 BIG TEN

	W	L	T
Minnesota	4	1	0
Michigan	3	1	1
Purdue	3	1	1
Northwestern	2	1	2
Ohio State	3	2	1
Wisconsin	3	2	0
Illinois	2	3	0
Iowa	1	3	1
Indiana	1	4	0
Chicago	0	4	0

PUNTING

Player and Position	Number Kicks	Yards Kicked	Had Blocked	Ave. Kick
Kromer, LH	34	1191	0	35
Purucker, LH	22	781	0	35.5
Strong, LH	6	224	0	37
Trosko, RH	4	162	0	40.5
Hook, FB	1	34	0	34
Luther, LH	1	33	0	33
TOTALS—				
Michigan	68	2425	0	35.6
Opponents	82	2765	3	33.7

MICHIGAN ROSTER, 1939

No.	Name and Class	Pos.	Hgt.	Wgt.	Age	Exp.*	Home
7	KOHL, Harry E. '41	QB	5'6"	150	19	R	Dayton, Ohio
10	LUTHER, William A. '41	HB	5'11"	165	20	F	Toledo, Ohio
15	WILSON, John L. '42	C	5'9"	188	18	F	Monroe, Mich.
16	WICKTER, Larry D. '41	FB	5'11"	175	19	F	Toledo, Ohio
17	FUNK, William '42	HB	5'10"	160	21	F	Athens, Mich.
18	LAINE, John T. '42	G	5'11"	185	19	F	Puritan, Mich.
19	NELSON, David '42	HB	5'8"	165	18	F	Detroit, Mich.
24	GALLES, James '42	G	5'11"	180	19	F	Chicago, Ill.
26	JORDAN, Forrest R. '40	G	6'2"	202	24	R	Clare, Mich.
27	KUHN, Dennis '40	T	6'2"	207	24	R	Ann Arbor, Mich.
28	ZIMMERMAN, Robert '42	FB	5'10"	180	18	F	Chicago, Ill.
29	SAVILLA, Roland '40	T	6'2"	206	22	M	Gallagher, W.Va.
31	BOSZA, Joseph J. '42	E	6'0"	170	23	—	Pittsburgh, Pa.
33	KENNEDY, Theodore, Jr. '42	E	6'2"	190	19	F	Saginaw, Mich.
34	CUNNINGHAM, Leo P. '42	G	6'0"	184	18	—	Revere, Mass.
35	WEBER, Marwood A. '42	HB	5'10"	164	18	F	Saginaw, Mich.
36	FRAUMANN, Harlin E. '42	E	6'3"	190	19	F	Pontiac, Mich.
38	BUTLER, Jack W. '42	G	6'0"	185	19	F	Port Huron, Mich.
39	KITTI, Walter L. '41	HB	5'10"	170	20	R	Calumet, Mich.
40	CZAK, Edward W. '41	E	5'11"	180	20	R	Elyria, Ohio
41	VOLLMER, William E. '41	T	6'1"	200	23	R	Manistee, Mich.
42	SALVATERRA, Arnold '42	HB	5'11"	173	20	F	Bellaire, Ohio
43	SMITH, William A. '40	T	6'2"	217	21	M	Riverside, Calif.
45	GRISSEN, James '42	FB	5'11"	180	19	F	Holland, Mich.
48	MELZOW, William '42	G	5'11"	185	19	F	Flint, Mich.
49	FRUTIG, Edward C. '41	E	6'1"	186	20	M	River Rouge, Mich.
53	KODROS, Archie (Capt.) '40	C	5'8"	202	21	MM	Alton, Ill.
54	NIELSEN, Paul '40	E	6'0"	185	22	R	Ann Arbor, Mich.
55	TROSKO, Fred '40	HB	5'9"	154	22	MM	Flint, Mich.
56	OLDS, Frederick C. '40	G	6'0"	192	22	MM	East Lansing, Mich.
57	FORD, Thomas G '41	C	6'2"	193	20	R	E. Grand Rapids, Mich.
58	KELTO, Reuben '41	T	6'1"	195	19	R	Bessemer, Mich.
59	SUKUP, Milo '41	G	5'8"	182	22	M	Muskegon Hgts., Mich.
60	CALL, Norman '42	HB	6'1"	170	18	F	Norwalk, Ohio
61	PURCELL, George A. '42	E	6'3"	200	20	F	Marshall, Mich.
62	OSTROOT, George '42	T	6'4"	215	19	F	Viborg, So. Dak.
63	FRITZ, Ralph '41	G	5'9"	198	20	M	New Kensington, Pa.
64	TINKER, Horace '40	C	5'10"	173	22	M	Battle Creek, Mich.
65	MORROW, Ned '41	G	5'10"	185	21	—	Elkhart, Ind.
66	INGALLS, Robert D. '42	C	6'3"	200	20	F	Marblehead, Mass.
67	NICHOLSON, John E., Jr. '40	E	6'4"	190	22	MM	Elkhart, Ind.
68	WISTERT, Albert A. '42	T	6'2"	205	18	F	Chicago, Ill.
69	EVASHEVSKI, Forest '41	QB	6'1"	198	21	M	Detroit, Mich.
70	PADDY, Arthur '41	G	5'7"	160	21	R	Benton Harbor, Mich.
71	ROBERTS, Harris W. '42	QB	6'0"	185	20	F	Shaker Hgts., Ohio
73	FLORA, Robert L. '41	T	6'1"	212	23	R	Muskegon, Mich.
74	THOMAS, Robert '42	G	5'11"	176	20	F	Muskegon, Mich.
76	GANNATAL, Paul '41	HB	6'0"	198	25	—	Detroit, Mich.
77	MEYER, Jack '41	QB	5'9"	195	21	M	Elyria, Ohio
78	ROGERS, Joseph C. '41	E	6'3"	193	21	F	Royal Oak, Mich.
80	ZIELINSKI, Ernest '41	T	6'1"	195	22	R	Bay City, Mich.
83	KROMER, Paul '41	HB	5'10"	160	20	M	Lorain, Ohio
85	RENDA, Hercules '40	HB	5'4"	163	22	MM	Jochin, W.Va.
86	WESTFALL, Robert B. '42	FB	5'7"	178	19	F	Ann Arbor, Mich.
88	STRONG, David A. '40	HB	5'8"	185	23	M	Helena, Mont.
96	CHRISTY, Edward '41	FB	5'10"	185	22	R	Gary, Ind.
98	HARMON, Tom '41	HB	6'0"	194	19	M	Gary, Ind.

* Experience Symbols:

M—Indicates number of Varsity letters won   R—Indicates Reserve award, 1938   F—Indicates Freshman award, 1938

1939 Record

Michigan	26	Michigan State
Michigan	27	Iowa
Michigan	85	Chicago
Michigan	27	Yale
Michigan	7	Illinois
Michigan	7	Minnesota
Michigan	19	Pennsylvania
Michigan	21	Ohio State

1939 BIG TEN FOOTBALL

Team	W	L	T	
Ohio State	5	1	0	.8
Iowa	4	1	1	.8
Purdue	2	1	2	.6
Michigan	3	2	0	.6
Northwestern	3	2	1	.6
Illinois	3	3	0	.5
Minnesota	2	3	1	.4
Indiana	2	3	0	.4
Wisconsin	0	5	1	.0
Chicago	0	3	0	.0

First Half Enough

Mich. State (13)		Michigan (
Blackburn	LE	Nichols
Handler	LT	Savi
Rockenback	LG	Fr
Batchelor	C	Kodros
Griffeth	RG	Suk
Bruckner	RT	Smi
Kinek	RE	Frut
H. Klewicki	QB	Evashevs
Crosthwaite	LH	Krom
Pearce	RH	Harmo
Asher	FB	Westfa

Score by periods:

Michigan State .....0 0 7 6—1
Michigan ....7 19 0 0—2

Michigan State scoring: touch
downs, Batchelor, Wyman Davis (su
for Crosthwaite). Point from tr
after touchdown, Bruckner (place
ment). Michigan scoring: touch
downs, Kromer, Harmon, Evashevsk
2. Point from try after touchdown
Harmon (placement) Melzow (su
for Sukup) (placement).

Harmon, Tom, played under possibly more pressure than any other halfback in the Big Ten last year, and he came through. Called the nation's outstanding interscholastic athlete while at Horace Mann High, Gary, Ind., where he was an all-state gridder and national scoring leader under Doug Kerr, Tom was constantly placed in the spotlight. But he did not crack and his versatile play as a hard running back who had old-timers recalling even Willie Heston, as a passer, as a blocker and as a defensive player easily earned him several all-Big Ten berths at halfback and general all-American mention. A sincere athlete who lives for football, Tom has pledged himself to a great year and his physical assets make him one of the finest halfback prospects in the country for the year. Tom also earned a berth on Michigan's basketball team last year. He spent his summer as a life guard on a Gary beach.

Evashevski, Forest, who acquired the title of Michigan's "One Man Gang" last year, won all-Conference recognition at quarterback as a sophomore in 1938, though he had never been in the backfield until two wee before the opening of the season. At Detroit Northweste he was a center and tackle under Sam Bishop and w listed as a center prospect as a freshman at Michigan Evy's exceptional speed for his size and his ever-willing ness to block and to tackle made him a logical choice fe quarterback, however, where he was a key man last ye with his play leading and his line backing. As a sign caller, although an absolute novice, his first game la fall was termed by critics "the finest piece of quarterbac ing by a sophomore in many years." Also a baseba catcher, Evy is a high ranking student in a pre-Busines Administration course. He ran a day camp for young A Arbor boys during the summer.

Blocking By Evashevski Is Invaluable; Rogers, Frutig Shine On Defense

Michigan Makes Bid For Big Ten Crown

By MEL FINEBERG

Michigan hitched its football wagon to Tom Harmon's star and trampled Iowa rudely underfoot 27-7 before a slim but gasping crowd of 27,518 yesterday afternoon at the stadium.

The Hoosier Hammer was the entire offensive show in Michigan's Conference opener. He scored all of the Wolverine's four touchdowns, one of them on a 95-yard runback of an intercepted pass, and successfully converted on three of them. His offensive play completely over-shadowed the bruising line-backing and blocking of Forest Evashevski, the defensive play of Joe Savilla, ends Joe Rogers and Ed Frutig, the passing of Iowa's Nile Kinnick. It was a Harmon day and nobody could take anything away from him.

Reprinted with permission from the **Michigan Daily**

Harmon-izing

IOWA		MICHIGAN
Prasse (c)	LE	Frutig
Walker	LT	Savilla
Tollefson	LG	Fritz
Diehl	C	Kodros
Snider	RG	Sukup
Enich	RT	Smith
Norgaard	RE	Rogers
Gallagher	QB	Evashevski
Kinnick	LH	Trosko
Dean	RH	Harmon
Green	FB	Westfall

Score by periods:

IOWA	7 0 0 0—	7
MICHIGAN	7 13 7 0—	27

Iowa scoring: Touchdowns, Dean. Point from try after touchdown, Kinnick (dropkick).

Michigan scoring: Touchdowns, Harmon 4; Point from try after touchdown, Harmon 3 (placements).

A Scholarly Lesson

MICHIGAN		CHICAGO
Czak	LE	R. E. Miller
Ostroot	LT	Wilson
Olds	LG	Jensen
Ingalls	C	Wheeler
Sukup	RG	Wallace
Smith	RT	Lounsbury
Fraumann	RE	Richardson
Kohl	QB	Jampolis
Renda	LH	Letts
Call	RH	Wasem
Zimmerman	FB	Davenport

Score by periods:

MICHIGAN	21	34	6	24—85
CHICAGO	0	0	0	0—0

Michigan scoring: Touchdowns, Zimmerman, Renda, Czak, Harmon (sub for Call) 2, Evashevski (sub for Kohl), Trosko (sub for Renda), Westfall (sub for Zimmerman) 2, Strong (sub for Trosko) 2, Nelson (sub for Harmon). Points from try after touchdown: Melzow (sub for Sukup) 4, Harmon (sub for Call) 3, Grissen (sub for Trosko), Evashevski (sub for Kohl), Trosko (sub for Renda), (all conversions by placement). Field goal—Harmon (sub for Renda), (by placement.)

Elis Battered By Harmon For 21 Points

"BILL" RENNER   "SPIKE" NELSON   "CHUCK" HOYT   "DUCKY" POND   "EARLY" NEALE   "IVY" WILLIAMSON   "GERRY" FORD

THE YALE COACHES, 1939

Fighting Illini Score Stunning Upset, 16-7

Michigan	0 7 0 0—	7
Illinois	0 9 0 7—	16

Touchdowns: Harmon; Illinois, Rettinger, Smith. Point after touchdown—Strong (run); Illinois, Brewer (placement). Field goal: Illinois, Brewer (placement). Officials: Referee, Masker (Northwestern); Umpire, Hedges (Dartmouth); Field Judge, Gardner (Cornell); Head Linesman, Taylor (Wichita).

On The Down Beat

Minnesota (20)		Michigan (7)
Mariucci	LE	Rogers
Pedersen (c)	LT	Savilla
Paschka	LG	Fritz
Bjorcklund	C	Kodros (c)
Kussisto	RG	Sukup
Vant Hull	RT	Wm. Smith
Ohlgren	RE	Nicholson
Mernik	QB	Ingalls
Van Every	LH	Kromer
Franck	RH	Harmon
Sweiger	FB	Westfall

Score by periods:

Minnesota . . . . . . 7 0 6 7—20
Michigan . . . . 0 0 0 7— 7

Minnesota scoring: Touchdowns, Van Every, Franck, Bruce Smith (substitute for Franck). Points from try after touchdown, Mernik, Pedersen (placements).

Michigan scoring: Touchdown, Kromer. Point from try after touchdown, Harmon (placement).

Ann Arbor, Mich., Nov. 25— One final burst of Michigan brilliance broke through the sullen skies that hung over the stadium today and when the last bit of lightning had struck in the last 50 seconds of play the Wolverines had beaten the new conference champions, Ohio State, 21-14.

A crowd of 78,815 watched Michigan overcome a 14-0 first period deficit and went wild in the last minute when Fred Trosko of the Wolverines scored from Ohio's 23-yard line on a fake place kick in which Tom Harmon was the bait with his supposed try for a field goal. Michigan had previously scored on a 16-yard run by Harmon and a pass from Harmon to Forest Evashevski.

Harmon Gets Another All-American Position

Another All-American berth for Michigan's Tom Harmon! After being picked by Bill Stern in Life Magazine and by the International News Service, Harmon was yesterday named captain and halfback of the Movietone News mythical team. The other backs were Nile Kinnick of Iowa, George Cafego of Tennessee and Bill Kimbrough of Texas A. and M.

1939

STATISTICS, 1939 TEAM
RUSHING

Player and position	Games	Times Carried	Yards Gained	Yards Lost	Net Gain	Ave. Gain
Strong, QB	8	7	118	13	105	15.
Harmon, LH	8	130	956	72	884	6.8
Kromer, RH	4	30	68	27	41	1.5
Evashevski, QB	7	3	0	2	-2	-.6
Westfall, FB	8	82	372	4	368	4.49
Zimmerman, FB	7	29	48	17	31	1.
Christy, FB	3	1	1	0	1	1.
Nelson, RH	4	5	30	0	30	6.
Renda, RH	4	9	25	3	22	2.5
Trosko, RH	8	26	89	18	71	3.
Call, LH	7	4	10	-1	9	2.3
Luther	4	2	3	0	3	1.5
Ingalls, QB	7	3	3	0	3	1.
Rogers, E	8	4	3	1	2	.5
Frutig, RE	7	1	9	0	9	9.

PASSING

Player and Position	Number Attempt.	Number Com.	Pct.	Had Inter.	Yards Gained
Harmon, LH	94	37	.394	8	583
Trosko, RH	9	2	.250	4	19
Kromer, RH	16	4	.250	0	65
Nelson, RH	2	1	.500	1	-3
Strong, RH	3	1	.333	0	49

PASS RECEIVING

Player and Position	Number Caught	Yards Gained	Player and Position	Number Caught	Gained
Kromer, RH	3	92	Czak, RE	5	73
Evashevski, QB	14	134	Harmon LH	4	110
Frutig, LE	4	80	Westfall, FB	3	40
Nicholson, RE	1	13	Rogers, RE	2	21
Zimmerman, FB	2	30	Trosko, RH	1	7
Strong, RH	1	-3			

RETURN OF PUNTS AND INTERCEPTED PASSES

Player and Position	Punts Rtd.	Yards Rtd.	Ave. Ret.	Passes Inter.	Yds. Rtd.
Kromer, RH	14	75	5	1	1
Strong, RH	9	57	6.3	1	2
Harmon, LH	1	10	10	3	98
Trosko, RH	6	69	11.5	3	11
Renda, LH	1	35	35	0	0
Evashevski, QB	0	0	0	2	14
Kodros, C	0	0	0	3	24
Westfall, FB	0	0	0	4	38
Nelson RH	2	80	40	0	0

PUNTING

Player and Position	Number Kicks	Yards Kicked	Had Blocked	Ave. Kick
Kromer, RH	16	662	0	38.8
Smith, RT	15	506	0	33
Strong, RH	6	240	0	40
Trosko, RH	10	372	1	37
Harmon, LH	2	110	0	55
Westfall FB	1	43	0	43

SCORING

Player and Position	Touchdowns	Conv. Atts.	Conv. Made	Field Goals	Safeties	Total Points
Harmon, LH	11	22	15	1	0	8.
Kromer, RH	3	0	0	0	0	1
Trosko, RH	5	4	3	0	0	3
Evashevski, QB	4	1	1	0	0	2
Strong, RH	2	1	1	0	0	1
Melzow, RG	0	6	5	0	0	
Westfall, FB	2	0	0	0	0	12
Zimmerman, FB	1	0	0	0	0	6
Renda, RH	1	0	0	0	0	6
Czak, RE	2	0	0	0	0	12
Nelson, LH	1	0	0	0	0	6
Grisson, LH	0	1	1	0	0	1

TEAM STATISTICS

	Michigan	Opponents
First Downs from Rushing	60	49
First Downs from Passing	23	24
First Downs by Penalties	2	2
Total First Downs	85	75
Yards Gained from Rushing	1704	970
Yards Gained from Forward Passes	573	756
Yards Gained from Penalties	119	196
Total Yards Gained (Net)	2219	1648
Forward Passes Attempted	120	141
Forward Passes Completed	50	55
Forward Passes Intercepted by	17	13
Lateral passes Attempted	5	6
Lateral Passes Completed	5	6
Number of Punts	56	68
Ave. Length of Punts (from scrimmage)	37.4	38.9
Punt Returns (ave. dist.)	9.3	7.2
Kickoff Returns (ave. dist.)	27	23
Fumbles by	21	20
Opponents Recovered by	13	13
Number of Penalties	22	16
Yards Penalized	196	119

MICHIGAN ROSTER, 1940

Name and Class	Pos.	Hgt.	Wgt.	Age	Exp.	Home
MANALAKAS, George S. '41	HB	5'9"	160	21	F	Detroit, Mich.
DAY, Frank S. '43	HB	5'8"	165	20	F	Detroit, Mich.
WISTERT, Albert A. '42	T	6'2"	212	19		Chicago, Ill.
DENISE, Theodore '43	G	5'11"	187	21	F	Lansing, Mich.
MELZOW, William '42	G	5'11"	185	20	M	Flint, Mich.
NELSON, David M. '42	HB	5'8"	165	19	R	Detroit, Mich.
LAINE, John T. '42	G	5'11"	185	20	—	Puritan, Mich.
ZIMMERMAN, Robert O. '42	F	5'10"	180	19	M	Chicago, Ill.
KENNEDY, Ted, Jr. '42	C	6'2"	185	19	—	Saginaw, Mich.
CUNNINGHAM, Leo P. '42	G	6'0"	188	20	—	Revere, Mass.
SMEJA, Rudy M. '43	E	6'1"	200	19	—	Chicago, Ill.
KARWALES, John J. '43	E	6'1"	180	20	F	Chicago, Ill.
WOYTEK, Louis K. '43	C	5'9"	170	20	—	Johnson City, N.Y.
LOCKARD, Harold C. '43	HB	5'9"	180	20	F	Canton, Ohio
SMITH, Robert B. '43	T	6'3"	210	20	F	Riverside, Calif.
ANDERSON, Harry F. '43	C	5'11"	210	19	F	Chicago, Ill.
BUTLER, Jack W. '42	T	6'0"	193	21	R	Port Huron, Mich.
HALL, Clarence S. '43	E	6'0"	192	19	R	Raynham, Mass.
GRISSEN, James '42	FB	5'11"	185	21	R	Holland, Mich.
CALL, Norman D. '42	HB	6'1"	170	20	R	Norwalk, Ohio
SENGEL, Rudolph J. '43	T	6'2"	217	19	—	Louisville, Ky.
SHARPE, Philip E. '43	E	6'2"	185	19	F	Lakewood, Ohio
KELTO, Reuben A. '41	T	6'1"	195	21	M	Bessemer, Mich.
SUKUP, Milo F. '41	G	5'8"	190	23	MM	Muskegon Heights, Mich.
WISE, Clifford C. '43	HB	5'11"	170	20	—	Spring Lake, Mich.
FRITZ, Ralph A. '41	G	5'9"	202	22	MM	New Kensington, Pa.
MADAR, Elmer F. '43	HB	5'11"	180	19	—	Detroit, Mich.
INGALLS, D. Robert '42	C	6'3"	200	21	M	Marblehead, Mass.
FRAUMANN, Harlin E. '42	E	6'3"	190	21	R	Pontiac, Mich.
EVASHEVSKI, Forest '41	QB	6'1"	198	22	MM	Detroit, Mich.
SELTZER, Holbrooke S. '41	G	5'9"	165	22	—	Chicago, Ill.
MEGREGIAN, Michael '42	QB	5'8"	180	22	—	Detroit, Mich.
FLORA, Robert L. '41	T	6'2"	215	24	M	Muskegon, Mich.
GANNATAL, Paul H. '41	HB	6'0"	185	25	—	Detroit, Mich.
ROGERS, Joseph C. '41	E	6'3"	200	21	M	Plymouth, Mich.
KREJSA, Robert C. '43	HB	5'10"	190	21	F	Shaker Heights, O.
HILDEBRANDT, George '43	G	5'11"	185	22	F	Hamburg, N.Y.
KROMER, Paul S. '41	HB	5'10"	165	21	MM	Lorain, O.
CZAK, Edward W. '41	E	5'11"	180	21	M	Elyria, O.
WESTFALL, Robert B. '42	F	5'8"	175	21	M	Ann Arbor, Mich.
FRUTIG, Edward C. '41	E	6'1"	180	20	MM	River Rouge, Mich.
KOHL, Harry E. '41	HB	5'6"	150	20	R	Dayton, O.
CEITHAML, George F. '43	QB	6'0"	190	19	F	Chicago, Ill.
KOLESAR, Robert C. '43	G	5'10"	198	19	F	Cleveland, O.
HARMON, Tom '41	HB	6'0"	195	20	MM	Gary, Ind.

EXPERIENCE SYMBOLS

M—Indicates number of Varsity letters won in football.
R—Indicates Reserve award in football, 1939.
F—Indicates Freshman Award in football, 1939.

1940 Record

Michigan	41	California	0
Michigan	21	Michigan State	14
Michigan	26	Harvard	0
Michigan	28	Illinois	0
Michigan	14	Pennsylvania	0
Michigan	6	Minnesota	7
Michigan	20	Northwestern	13
Michigan	40	Ohio State	0

1940 WESTERN CONFERENCE FOOTBALL STANDINGS

Team	W	L	T	Pct.
Minnesota	6	0	0	1.000
Michigan	3	1	0	.750
Northwestern	4	2	0	.667
Ohio State	3	3	0	.500
Wisconsin	3	3	0	.500
Indiana	2	3	0	.400
Iowa	2	3	0	.400
Purdue	1	4	0	.200
Illinois	0	5	0	.000

MICHIGAN		MICHIGAN STATE
Rogers (Fraumann)	LE	(McRae) Smith
Wistert	LT	(Johnson) Oals
Fritz (Melzow)	LG	(Kutchins) Griffin
Ingalls (Kennedy)	C	(Vierra) (Kennedy) Bator
Sukup (Kolesar)	RG	(Abbe) Kip
Kelto (Butler) (Flora)	RT	(Switzer) Karr
Frutig (Czak)	RE	(Friedlund) Blackburn
Evashevski (Ceithaml)	QB	(Martin) (Miller) Sherman
Harmon (Kromer)	LHB	(Wil Davis) (Miller) Sherman
Nelson (Krejsa) (Kromer)	RHB	(Kirgis) Wm. Davis
Westfall (Lockard)	FB	(Balfe) Pawlowski

MICHIGAN	7	7	7	0—21
MICHIGAN STATE	0	7	7	0—14

Touchdowns—Harmon 3, Pawlowski 2.
Points after touchdown—Harmon 3, Pawlowski 2.
Officials: Referee, Clarno (Bradley); Umpire, Dilweg (Marquette); Field Judge, Graves (Illinois); Head Linesman, Finsterwald (Ohio State).

MICHIGAN		ILLINOIS
Rogers (Fraumann) (Smeja)	LE	(Kozul) (Marlain) Phillips
Wistert (Butler) (Sengel)	LT	(Johnson) Dillon
Fritz (Melzow)	LG	(Hurley) Siebold
Ingalls (Kennedy) (Hall)	C	(Kolens) (Checley) Wilford
Sukup (Kolesar) (Cunningham)	RT	Riggs
Kelto (Flora) (Denise)	RG	(Pawlowski) Turk
Frutig (Czak) (Sharpe)	RE	(Engel) O'Neill
Evashevski (Ceithaml) (Kohl)	QB	Ehni
Harmon (Call) (Kromer)	LHB	(Easterbrook) Wehba
Nelson (Lockard)	RHB	(Miller) Astroth
Westfall (Zimmerman) (Krejsa)	FB	(Bernhardt) Pfeifer

MICHIGAN	12	9	7	0—28
ILLINOIS	0	0	0	0—0

Touchdowns by Nelson, Harmon, Frutig, Westfall.
Points after touchdown—Harmon (placement).
Goal from field—Harmon (placement).
Officials: Referee, Getchell (St. Thomas); Umpire, Krieger (Ohio Univ.); Field Judge, Eichenlaub (Notre Dame); Head Linesman, Simpson (Wisconsin).

MICHIGAN		PENNSYLVANIA
Rogers (Fraumann)	LE	(Shane) (McKettian) Kuzzkick
Wistert (Butler)	LT	(Moding) (Donaldson) Leu
Fritz (Melzow)	LG	(Hartwig) Menke
Ingalls (Kennedy)	C	(Butler) Fix
Sukup (Kolesar)	RG	(Hunt) Brehl
Kelto (Flora)	RT	(Donaldson) V...
Frutig	RE	(Martin) Watt
Evashevski (Ceithaml) (Kohl)	QB	(Wexler) (Chandler) D...
Harmon	LHB	(Nolan) Kern
Nelson (Lockard) (Kromer) (Call)	RHB	(Welsh) Dight...
Westfall	FB	(Chizmadia) (Stiff) (Rainwater) V...

MICHIGAN	7	0	7	0—14
PENNSYLVANIA	0	0	0	0—0

Touchdowns—Harmon, Frutig.
Points after touchdown—Harmon 2 (placement).
Officials: Referee, Layden (Notre Dame); Umpire, Schommer (Chicago); Field Judge, Barnum, W... consin); Head Linesman, Graves (Illinois).

MICHIGAN		NORTHWESTERN
Frutig	LE	(Motl) Smith
Wistert (Butler)	LT	Bauman
Fritz	LG	(Burke) Lokan
Ingalls (Kennedy)	C	Hornitz
Kolesar (Melzow)	RG	(Heavy) Zerieb
Kelto (Flora)	RT	(Kiefer) Aartt
Rogers (Fraumann)	RE	(Hasse) Boeheck...
Evashevski (Ceithaml)	QB	(Fills) Richards
Harmon	LHB	(deCorevont) (Sques) Habrzettoo
Lockard (Kromer)	RHB	(Kepford) Chandler
Westfall	FB	(Clawson) Botten

MICHIGAN	14	6	0	0—20
NORTHWESTERN	0	6	0	7—13

Touchdowns—Westfall 2, Harmon, Motl, Habnstein.
Points after touchdown—Harmon 2 (placement); Enlitz (placement).
Officials: Referee, Getchell (St. Thomas); Umpire, Simpson (Wisconsin); Field Judge, Hasse, Marquette); Head Linesman, Lipp (Chicago).

FIRST MICHIGAN TEAM TO FLY: When the University of Michigan football team flew 5,124 miles to Berkeley, Calif., and return for the first game of the season in September with California, it marked the first time that a Wolverine athletic aggregation ever took to the air.

The above picture shows the Michigan squad just before its departure. Three chartered planes conveyed the Wolverine party of 53 to the west coast. The trip was made without incident, except that some of the boys became air-sick. Coach Fritz Crisler predicts many such trips in the future.

Columbus, O., Nov. 23—Michigan's thundering football forces roared all over the Ohio stadium today before winding up one of the greatest years in Wolverine gridiron history. With brilliant Tom Harmon leading the way, Michigan defeated the Buckeyes, 40-0, before 73,480 spectators.

All in all, the dazzling Harmon drove over the Ohio goal three times to smash Red Grange's former Western Conference three-year touchdown record of 31, passed to teammates for two of the other Wolverine tallies, place kicked four points after touchdown, and maintained a punting average of 50 yards per kick.

MICHIGAN   **OHIO STATE**

MICHIGAN		OHIO STATE
Rogers, Czak	L.E	McCafferty, Anderson, J.
Wistert, Butler	L.T	Dixon, Da
Fritz, Melzow	L.G	Tobik, Bruckner, The
Ingalls, Kennedy	C	Vickroy, Bell, Wh
Kolesar	R.G	Rosen, Howard, Nish
Kelto, Flora, Senzel	R.T	Stephenson, Piccinini, Ma
Frutig, Fraumann	R.E	Newlin, Hershberger, C
Evashevski, Ceithaml, Kohl	Q	Sinzione, Sexton, S
Harmon, Nelson	L.H	Horvath, Strausbaugh, Fish
Kromer, Call, Lockard	R.H	Sweeney, Wynn, Kinc
Westfall, Zimmerman, Krejsa	F	Nichols, Langho

Michigan	13	7	13	7—40
Ohio State	0	0	0	0— 0

Touchdowns—Harmon 3, Kromer, Evashevski, Frutig. Points after touchdown—Harmon 4 (placement). Officials—Referee, Masker (Northwestern); Umpire, Finsterwald (Syracuse); Field Judge, Rupp (Lebanon Valley); Head Linesman, Haines (Yale).

Something To Judge By
TOM HARMON'S THREE-YEAR MICHIGAN FOOTBALL RECORD

	Rushing		Passing				Punting		Kick-off and Punt Returns		Scoring					Touchdown Passes	Min. Played
1938	Tries	Net Gain	Att'd	Comp.	Had Int.	Gain	No.	Dist.	No.	Yards	T.D.	P.A.T.	F.G.	Pts.		
MICHIGAN STATE	4	27	1	0	0	0	0	0	0	0	0	0	0	0	0	16
CHICAGO	6	99	1	0	0	0	0	0	1	10	1	0	0	6	0	24
MINNESOTA	13	54	5	1	0	13	0	0	0	0	0	0	0	0	0	56
YALE	12	66	12	6	1	147	0	0	0	0	0	0	0	0	1	60
ILLINOIS	9	43	5	3	0	38	0	0	1	1	1	0	0	6	0	21
PENNSYLVANIA	11	46	3	2	0	10	0	0	0	0	0	0	0	0	1	22
NORTHWESTERN	6	22	10	5	0	52	0	0	0	0	0	0	0	0	0	32
OHIO STATE	16	41	8	4	0	50	0	0	0	0	1	0	0	6	1	58
SOPHOMORE TOTALS	77	398	45	21	1	310	0	0	2	11	3	0	0	18	3	289
1939																
MICHIGAN STATE	6	32	16	7	1	47	0	0	1	17	1	1	0	7	2	41
IOWA	18	112	6	2	2	46	0	0	4	3	0	27	0	0	0	56
CHICAGO	7	127	5	2	0	44	0	0	2	3	1	18	0	0	1	15
YALE	19	206	6	2	1	21	0	0	3	3	0	21	0	0	0	58
ILLINOIS	18	72	20	5	3	35	0	0	1	0	0	6	0	0	0	60
MINNESOTA	10	47	19	7	1	118	0	0	0	1	0	1	0	0	1	60
PENNSYLVANIA	29	202	5	1	0	26	0	0	2	1	0	13	0	0	1	56
OHIO STATE	23	86	17	11	0	151	2	110	4	85	1	3	0	9	1	60
JUNIOR TOTALS	130	884	94	37	8	488	2	110	5	102	14	15	1	102	6	406
1940																
CALIFORNIA	16	131	9	5	0	39	3	73	4	184	4	4	0	28	1	34
MICHIGAN STATE	28	120	11	5	3	50	4	148	5	50	3	3	0	21	0	58
HARVARD	21	109	18	5	4	60	6	216	5	31	3	2	0	20	1	47
ILLINOIS	21	58	4	2	1	49	5	197	4	22	1	1	1	10	1	55
PENNSYLVANIA	28	142	8	3	0	51	12	442	1	8	1	2	0	8	1	60
MINNESOTA	29	58	15	10	1	81	7	306	0	0	0	0	0	0	1	60
NORTHWESTERN	23	95	7	2	0	25	10	364	3	62	1	2	0	8	0	60
OHIO STATE	25	139	22	11	2	151	3	150	3	81	3	4	0	22	2	59
SENIOR TOTALS	191	852	94	43	11	506	50	1896	25	438	16	18	1	117	7	433
THREE-YEAR TOTAL	398	2134	233	101	20	1304	52	2006	32	551	33	33	2	237	16	1128

All-America 1940

~~MAS~~ DUDLEY HARMON holding the John W.
~~nan~~ Memorial Trophy, awarded to him after he was
voted the outstanding college player of the year.

Maxwell Club Names Harmon Nation's Best

PHILADELPHIA. Nov. 25.—(P)—
Tommy Harmon, Michigan's great
halfback was chosen by the Maxwell
Memorial Club today as the nation's
No. 1 football player for 1940.

He will receive the award at the
Club's annual dinner here on Dec. 17.

Nile Kinnick, of Iowa, received the
award last year. Davey O'Brien, of
Texas Christian, was honored in
1938 and Clint Frank, of Yale, in 1937.

STATISTICS, 1940 TEAM
RUSHING

Player and Position	Games	Times Carried	Yards Gained	Yards Lost	Net Gain	Ave. Gain
Krejsa, LH	3	4	24	0	24	6
Nelson, RH	5	21	101	6	95	4.5
Harmon, LH	8	191	977	125	852	4.46
Westfall, FB	8	190	834	26	808	4.25
Lockard, RH	8	26	89	5	84	3.23
Wise, LH	3	8	20	1	19	2.5
Call, RH	3	4	11	3	8	2
Evashevski, QB	8	1	2	0	2	2
Zimmerman, FB	1	4	7	0	7	1.75
Rogers, RE	8	4	11	6	5	1.25
Kromer, RH	8	10	12	20	—8	—.8

PASSING

Player and Position	Number Attempt.	Number Completed	Pct.	Had Inter.	Yards Gained
Westfall, FB	1	1	1.000	0	10
Harmon, LH	94	43	.457	11	506
Wise, LH	3	1	.333	0	8

PASS RECEIVING

Player & Position	Number Caught	Yards Gained	Player & Position	Number Caught	Yards Gained
Frutig, LE	12	181	Rogers, RE	5	55
Westfall, FB	2	28	Kromer, RH	4	60
Evash'ski, QB	5	73	Nelson, RH	2	15
Call, RH	1	10	Fraumann	2	19
Lockard, RH	1	7	Ceithaml	1	5
Krejsa, RH	1	5			

RETURN OF PUNTS AND INTERCEPTED PASSES

Player and Position	Punts Rtd.	Yards Rtd.	Ave. Ret.	Passes Inter.	Yards Rtd.
Harmon, LH	19	234	12.3	4	30
Kromer, RH	6	122	20.3	1	0
Wise, LH	3	35	11.6		
Nelson, RH	2	18	9		
Lockard, RH	1	26	26		
Westfall, FB	1	17	17	2	14
Frutig, LE				1	26
Sukup, RG				1	4
Kennedy, C				1	2
Ingalls, C				2	9
Zimmerman, FB				1	0
Kolesar, RG				1	5
Evashevski, QB				2	0

PUNTING

Player and Position	Number Kicks	Yards Kicked	Had Blocked	Aver. Kick.
Harmon, LH	42	1557	0	37
Kromer, RH	1	47	0	47
Wise, LH	2	52	0	26

SCORING

Player and Position	Touch-Downs	Conv. Atts.	Conv. Made	Field Goals	Safeties	Total Pts.
Harmon, LH	16	28	18	1	0	117
Westfall, FB	3	0	0	0	0	18
Frutig, LE	3	0	0	0	0	18
Evashevski, QB	2	0	0	0	0	12
Nelson, RH	2	0	0	0	0	12
Kromer, RH	1	0	0	0	0	6
Wise, LH	1	0	0	0	0	6
Melzow, RG	0	1	1	0	0	1

COACH CRISLER
and
CAPT. EVASHEVSKI

Illness Over, Fielding Yost Back At Work

Fielding "Hurry-Up" Yost, Michigan's famed athletic director, yesterday demonstrated one of the traits that earned him his nick-name years ago. Returning in the morning from Nashville, Tenn., where for several days he has been confined to a hospital bed, he went immediately to work at his office in the administration building.

Yost, who will retire next month, looked exceptionally well and, as he pitched into all the back work which had piled up in his absence, told reporters that he had "never felt better in his life."

"They gave out the information in Nashville that I had suffered a heart attack, but this information did not come from the hospital. According to the physicians there I was suffering from a gall bladder attack. They told me I could start playing golf again, but there is a lot of work to be done before July 1."

MICHIGAN FOOTBALL ROSTER

No.	Name and Class	Pos.	Hgt.	Wgt.	Age	
10	LOCKARD, Harold C. '43	HB	5'9"	186	20	
11	WISTERT, Albert A. '43	T	6'2"	206	20	
14	MORRISON, Robert L. '44	HB	5'10"	160	20	
15	BROWN, James J. '44	HB	5'9"	156	20	
16	WHITE, Paul G. '44	HB	6'1"	184	19	
18	SOWERS, Ray B. '44	HB	6'0"	193	21	
19	KENNEDY, Chas. F. '44	HB	6'1"	180	71	
22	HARRIGAN, John F. '44	QB	5'8"	165	19	F
23	NELSON, David M. '42	HB	5'7"	156	20	F
24	GREENE, John J. '44	QB	6'0"	191	20	
26	HASLAM, Charles J. '44	QB	6'1"	190	19	F
27	SHEMKY, Robert W. '44	E	6'0"	177	18	F
28	MADAR, Elmer F. '43	QB	5'10"	170	20	
29	DAWLEY, Fred M. '44	QB	5'8"	178	20	
31	LONG, Don R. '44	E	6'0"	170	19	
33	KENNEDY, Ted '42	C	6'2"	190	20	M
34	MILLER, Austin S. '44	FB	5'7"	169	19	F
36	STENBERG, Robert P. '44	FB	5'7"	168	20	F
38	MacCONNACHIE, Wm. M. '44	E	6'1"	181	20	
39	BOOR, Donald P. '44	FB	5'11"	185	21	F
41	CHADY, Otto E. '43	E	6'1"	191	20	
42	THOMAS, Alfred S. '42	HB	5'10"	162	21	
45	KUZMA, Thomas G. '44	HB	6'1"	196	19	F
46	ROBINSON, Don W. '44	HB	5'11"	167	19	F
48	CALL, Norman D. '42	HB	6'1"	170	21	M
54	PRITULA, William '44	C	6'0"	198	19	F
55	McFADDIN, Robert L. '44	C	6'0"	173	19	
60	AMSTUTZ, Ralph H. '44	G	5'11"	168	19	F
61	TROGAN, Angelo E. '44	G	5'8"	202	21	F
62	FRANKS, Julius S. '44	G	6'0"	187	19	F
64	LAINE, John T. '43	G	6'0"	196	21	R
65	MELZOW, William '42	G	5'11"	190	21	M
66	INGALLS, Robert D. '42	C	6'3"	190	22	MM
67	PREGULMAN, Mervin '44	G	6'3"	207	19	F
68	KOLESAR, Robert C. '43	G	5'10"	193	20	M
69	ANDERSON, Harry F. '43	G	6'0"	192	20	R
71	CASWELL, Harry H. '44	T	6'2"	190	20	F
72	KUYPER, William E. '44	T	6'0"	201	18	
73	DENISE, Theodore E. '43	T	5'11"	188	22	R
74	MacDOUGALL, William J. '43	T	6'3"	190	20	
75	HILDEBRANDT, Geo. H. '43	T	5'11"	181	23	R
76	FLORA, Robert L. '42	T	6'2"	216	25	MM
77	SECONTINE, Vincent C. '44	T	6'0"	193	19	F
78	KELTO, Reuben W. '42	T	6'1"	198	22	MM
79	CUNNINGHAM, Leo P. '42	T	6'0"	187	21	R
80	FREIHOFER, Walter B. '44	E	5'11"	180	19	F
81	FLYNN, Terrance R. '44	E	6'0"	188	20	—
82	KARWALES, John J. '44	E	6'1"	190	21	
83	SMEJA, Rudy M. '43	E	6'2"	185	20	R
84	FRAUMANN, Harlin E. '42	E	6'3"	190	22	M
85	SHARPE, Philip E. '43	E	6'2"	188	20	R
86	WESTFALL, Robert B. '42	FB	5'8"	186	21	MM
87	ROGERS, Joseph C. '42	E	6'3"	184	22	MM
88	PETOSKEY, Jack E. '44	E	5'11"	167	19	F
89	CEITHAML, George F. '43	QB	6'0"	184	20	M

M Indicates number of Varsity letters won in football.
F Indicates Freshman Numeral winner in 1940. R Indicates Reserve Award winner

SERVING HIS LAST YEAR: This is Fielding H. Yost's last year as athletic director at the University of Michigan. Now 70 he will be forced to retire in June under a compulsory university ruling.

His last year in the service of his beloved "Meechegan" which he has served as football coach and athletic director since 1901, has been one of his most strenuous. He was honored with a testimonial banquet, attended by 2,000 of his admirers and was the recipient of gifts from Michigan State, Illinois and Ohio State at football games this fall and is the only non-Michigan football player ever to be awarded an "M" ring by the Detroit alumni.

Yost is shown above at his desk in the Michigan administration building, still working hard daily on plans for the fulfillment of his program of "athletics for all." He attends athletic banquets in all parts of the country. They may force him to retire yet today he is still the dynamic force back of Michigan athletics that gained for him the title of "Hurry-Up" Yost.

Michigan's 1941 Record

19	MICHIGAN	Michigan State College	7
6	MICHIGAN	University of Iowa	0
40	MICHIGAN	University of Pittsburgh	0
14	MICHIGAN	Northwestern University	7
0	MICHIGAN	University of Minnesota	7
20	MICHIGAN	University of Illinois	0
28	MICHIGAN	Columbia University	0
20	MICHIGAN	Ohio State University	20

The Final 1941 Conference Standings

	Won	Lost	Tied	Points	Opponents Points
Minnesota	5	0	0	124	32
MICHIGAN	3	1	1	60	34
Ohio State	3	1	1	101	89
Northwestern	4	2	0	116	57
Wisconsin	3	3	0	117	153
Iowa	2	4	0	53	77
Purdue	1	3	0	21	42
Indiana	1	3	0	53	60
Illinois	0	5	0	13	114

Oct. 5

Wet Victory!

	Iowa	Mich.
First downs	9	6
Yds gained rushing	147	129
Fwd. passes attempted	11	4
Fwd. passes completed	3	0
Yds. by fwd. passing	46	0
Yds. lost att. passes	32	0
Punt Ave. (from scrim.)	30.5	31
Total yds., kicks returned	73	80
Yds. lost by penalties	55	15

* * *

THE LINEUPS

IOWA	Pos.	MICHIGAN
Parker	LE	Fraumann
Walker	LT	Wistert
Curran	LG	Kolesar
Diehl	C	Ingalls
Anderson	RG	Melzow
Urban	RT	Kelto
Burkett	RE	Rogers
Couppee	QB	Ceithaml
Youel	LH	Kuzma
Mertes	RH	Lockard
Green	FB	Westfall

MICHIGAN	6	0	0	0—6

Oct. 12

THE LINEUP

Pittsburgh		Michigan
Gervelis	LE	Fraumann
Kindelberger	LT	Wistert
Mitchell	LG	Kolesar
Heister	C	Ingalls
Fite	RG	Pregulman
Benghouser	RT	Kelto
Hinte	RE	Rogers
West	QB	Ceithaml
Stetler	LH	Kuzma
Dutton	RH	Lockard
Ross	FB	Westfall

Michigan	6	0	14	20—40

Michigan Scoring: Touchdowns, Kuzma 2, Lockard, Boor, Robinson, Nelson. Points after touchdown: Ingalls 2, Melzow 2.

Oct. 19

Wildcats Tamed

THE LINEUPS

Michigan		Northwestern
Fraumann	LE	Colberg
Wistert	LT	Bauman
Kolesar	LG	Burke
Ingalls	C	Johnson
Pregulman	RG	Kiefer
Kelto	RT	Samarzia
Rogers	RE	Wallis
Ceithaml	QB	Kruger
Kuzma	LH	de Correvont
Lockard	RH	Kepford
Westfall	FB	Benson

Michigan	7	0	0	7—14
Northwestern	0	7	0	0— 7

Michigan Scoring: Touchdowns, Fraumann, Rogers. Points after touchdown, Melzow (for Kelto) 2 placements.

Northwestern Scoring: Touchdown, Graham (for de Correvont). Point after touchdown, Erdlitz (for Kruger) placement.

Oct. 26

Team Loses Again To Bierman Jinx

Rogers Suffers Spinal Injury In Battle; Frickey Scores Lone Gopher Marker

By HAL WILSON
(Daily Sports Editor)

Sometimes when the fire and desire to win burns too brightly, smoke gets in your eyes.

Thus it was for Michigan yesterday as Minnesota's mighty gridiron machine, rolling relentlessly toward another national championship, outmanned the Wolverines, 7-0, before a record capacity crowd of 85,753 in the Stadium.

Fighting with a frenzy born of seven consecutive defeats at the cleats of these Golden Giants from the Northland, Michigan's highly-keyed gridmen had three wonderful opportunities to score—but couldn't quite do it. Minnesota's poised gang of Gophers made just one outstanding scoring threat—and capitalized. That was the game.

Statistics show that Michigan drove for 13 first downs to Minnesota's 11, while the Gophers held a slight advantage in net yards by rushing, 179 to 135, and a scant margin in the yards gained by passing department, 87 to 85.

Outweighed 16 Pounds To Man

But they don't tell the manner in which the Wolverines poured everything they had into the terrific battle with the massive Golden Giants who outweighed them 16 pounds to a man.

Concrete evidence of the fierceness with which the clash, number one grid attraction in the nation, was waged is found in the hospital lists. Most serious casualty and a vital blow to the Wolverine grid team for the remainder of the season is the permanent loss of husky Joe Rogers, senior end, who suffered a spinal injury early in the first period. He was rushed to the hospital immediately for treatment and Dr. George Hammond, team physician, declared that Joe, a regular at his right flank position for two years, had incurred three fractures in the transverse processes of the lumbar vertebrae that have terminated his collegiate grid career.

Nov. 15

A Sub Field Day

THE LINEUPS

Michigan		Columbia
Fraumann	LE	Kelleher
Wistert	LT	Maack
Kolesar	LG	Demartini
Ingalls	C	Ruberti
Pregulman	RG	MacMichael
Kelto	RT	Makofske
Sharpe	RE	Siegal
Ceithaml	QB	Wood
Kuzma	LH	Governali
White	RH	Germann
Westfall	FB	McIlvennan

MICHIGAN	14	7	7	0—28

Touchdowns—Kuzma, Westfall 3. Points after touchdown—Melzow 4 (placements).

Ann Arbor, Mich., Nov. 22—Once-beaten Ohio State and Michigan football machines, primed to the limit for this traditional battle, rocked the vast Wolverine stadium and its 84,581 roaring occupants today with an explosion of offensive strength seldom equalled before winding up in a 20-20 deadlock.

The Buckeyes scored in the first, third and fourth quarters with Graf, Kinkade and Fisher getting the touchdowns. For Michigan, Kuzma, Fraumann and Westfall crossed the Ohio goal.

Michigan came from behind to tie the score at 7-7 at the half and then went ahead by a touchdown after eight minutes of the third quarter. Ohio soon tied the count by taking the kickoff on their 29-yard line and rolling without interruption to a score.

The Buckeyes then moved ahead, 20-14, on a 52-yard pass play from Graf to Fisher but Michigan came back after the kickoff to drive all the way for a final score with Capt. Bob Westfall finally going over.

An Upset That Almost Proved Fatal

	OHIO STATE	MICHIGAN
First Downs	15	19
Yards Gained Rushing (net)	179	271
Forward Passes Completed	6	7
Yards by Forward Passing	124	104
Yards Lost, Attempted Forward Passes	0	0
Forward Passes Intercepted by	2	0
Yards Gained Run-Back of Intercepted Passes	11	0
Punting Average (from scrimmage)	37	37
Total Yards, All Kicks Returned	83	70
Opponents' Fumbles Recovered	1	0
Yards Lost by Penalties	5	35

THE LINEUPS

Ohio State		Michigan
Fox	LE	Fraumann
Daniell	LT	Wistert
Howard	LG	Kolesar
Vickroy	C	Ingalls
Cheroke	RG	Pregulman
Stephenson	RT	Kelto
Shaw	RE	Sharpe
Hallabrin	QB	Ceithaml
Fisher	LH	Kuzma
Kinkade	RH	White
Graf	FB	Westfall

OHIO STATE ... 7 0 7 6—20
MICHIGAN ... 0 7 7 6—20

Ohio State scoring: Touchdowns, Graf, Kinkade, Fisher; points after touchdown, Hallabrin 2 (placekicks.)

Michigan scoring: Touchdowns, Kuzma, Fraumann, Westfall; points after touchdown, Melzow (for Kolesar) 2 (place-kicks).

Westfall Named On UP All-American Eleven

Bobby Westfall, Michigan's football captain who has been acclaimed as the best fullback in the nation, received another honor yesterday when he was named on the first team of the United Press All-American eleven.

Al Wistert, Wolverine tackle, was named on the second team and Bob Ingalls was selected as third team center. Guard Merv Pregulman and halfback Tom Kuzma received honorable mention.

1941 Team Statistics

	Michigan	Opponent
First Downs from Rushing	91	46
First Downs from Passing	14	31
First Downs by Penalties	2	5
Total First Downs	107	82
Yards Gained from Rushing	1870	942
Yards Gained from Forward Passes	418	712
Yards Gained from Penalties	166	305
Total Yards Gained (Net)	2454	1959
Forward Passes Attempted	75	119
Forward Passes Completed	33	54
Forward Passes Intercepted By	7	12
Yards Interceptions Returned	52	99
Number of Punts	54	70
Punts Returned By	29	27
Yards Punts Returned By	325	271
Punts Blocked By	3	0
Punt Returns (Average Distance)	11.2	10
Number of Kick-offs	32	11
Kick-offs Returned By	10	30
Yards Kick-offs Returned	179	492
Fumbles By	22	17
Opponents' Fumbles Recovered By	11	7
Number of Penalties	37	22
Yards Penalized	305	166
Total Points Scored	147	41

	Rushing			Passing				Receiving		Punt Returns		Punting		Scoring		
	Tries	Net Gain	Aver.	Att'd.	Comp.	Had Int.	Gain	Caught	Gain	No.	Yds.	No.	Aver.	TD	PAT	Total
Westfall, fb	156	688	4.41	1	1	0	10	1	2	1	5	0	0	7	0	42
Kuzma, hb	140	581	4.15	59	26	10	317	0	0	19	179	43	36.7	8	0	48
Nelson, hb	29	184	6.31	6	3	0	31	0	0	8	122	7	32.0	1	0	6
White, hb	28	147	5.25	5	2	1	53	2	30	1	11	0	0	0	0	0
Lockard, hb	18	106	5.89	0	0	0	0	2	14	0	0	0	0	1	0	6
Ceithaml, qb	4	1	0.25	0	0	0	0	10	77	0	0	0	0	0	0	0
Boor, fb	20	70	3.50	0	0	0	0	1	19	0	0	0	0	1	0	6
Robinson, hb	16	63	3.94	4	1	1	7	0	0	0	0	4	39.5	1	0	6
Thomas, hb	6	21	3.50	0	0	0	0	0	0	0	0	0	0	0	0	0
C. Kennedy, hb	1	5	5.00	0	0	0	0	0	0	0	0	0	0	0	0	0
Wistert, t	2	4	2.00	0	0	0	0	8	90	0	0	0	0	2	0	12
Fraumann, e	0	0	0.00	0	0	0	0	2	50	0	0	0	0	1	0	6
Rogers, e	0	0	0.00	0	0	0	0	0	0	0	0	0	0	0	0	0
Sharpe, e	0	0	0.00	0	0	0	0	4	106	0	0	0	0	0	0	0
Smeja, e	0	0	0.00	0	0	0	0	2	19	0	0	0	0	0	0	0
Karwales, e	0	0	0.00	0	0	0	0	1	11	0	0	0	0	0	0	0
Melzow, g	0	0	0.00	0	0	0	0	0	0	0	0	0	0	0	12	12
Ingalls, c	0	0	0.00	0	0	0	0	0	0	0	0	0	0	0	3	3

The 1942 Record

9	MICHIGAN	Great Lakes	0
20	MICHIGAN	Michigan State	0
14	MICHIGAN	Iowa Pre-Flight	26
34	MICHIGAN	Northwestern	16
14	MICHIGAN	Minnesota	16
28	MICHIGAN	Illinois	14
35	MICHIGAN	Harvard	7
32	MICHIGAN	Notre Dame	20
7	MICHIGAN	Ohio State	21
28	MICHIGAN	Iowa	14

Air Corps Claims T.D. 'Ace' Harmon

Tommy Harmon, Michigan athlete turned businessman, has put his private affairs in order long enough to join the Army Air Corps.

Yesterday the former gridiron No. 1 man was granted permission by the War Department to enlist as an aviation cadet at the Detroit recruiting station. An Army captain said that Harmon would probably report at Santa Anita, Calif., next week for pre-flight training.

Harmon had applied for entrance into the Air Corps in November but the final O.K. was put off pending time for Tommy to fulfill a few business contracts and see that his parents were well settled in their new $18,000 Ann Arbor home he built for them.

Crisler Given New Position By War Board

The University took another big step Tuesday in its attempt to aid in the nation's defense program when the War Board announced the appointment of Michigan's Athletic Director, Fritz Crisler, as chairman of a Physical Education and Public Health Committee.

Crisler, who recently returned from a football coaches' meeting in Phoenix, Ariz., immediately took active steps in appointing members and organizing plans of the committee so as to increase the value of the Physical Education and Public Health Departments in the present crisis.

The plans of the committee are to make a study of present conditions, take an inventory of all equipment and buildings and to make recommendations for future undertakings.

Football Ticket Price Changed

$2.50 General Admission Is Home Game Charge

Adoption of a uniform ticket price of $2.50 plus federal tax per game for all except box seats in the huge Michigan stadium was announced yesterday by H. O. Crisler, Director of Athletics.

If there is no change in the tax, single game tickets will sell for $2.75 and box seats will go on sale at $3.00 plus tax. This new ticket price was approved by the Board in Control of Intercollegiate Athletics.

Season tickets for all seven home games will sell for $15.40 each. The second type of season tickets to go on sale, for the five games against college foes but not including the battles with the two service elevens from Great Lakes and Iowa, will be sold for $11.00.

1942 MICHIGAN FOOTBALL ROSTER

No.	Name and Class		Class	Pos.	Hgt.	Wgt.	Age*	Exp.¶	Home Town	High School Coach
10	AVERY, Charles B.		So.	HB	6'	170	19	F	Antigo, Wis.	George Svendsen
11	WISTERT, Albert A.		Sr.	T	6'2"	205	21	MM	Chicago, Ill.	E. J. Zahoric
14	KEENAN, William C.		So.	HB	5'11"	175	19	F	Cleveland, O.	Trevor Rees
16	WHITE, Paul G.		Jr.	HB	6'1"	184	20	M	River Rouge, Mich.	Frank Weeber
17	PETOSKEY, Jack E.		Jr.	E	5'11"	167	20	—	Dearborn, Mich.	Mac Whalen
18	WARDLEY, Frank L.		So.	HB	6'1"	180	20	F	Joliet, Ill.	H. J. Walser
26	VERNIER, Robert W.		So.	QB	5'11"	184	18	F	Toledo, Ohio	Harry Rice
28	KIESEL, George C. F.		So.	QB	5'10"	165	19	F	Detroit, Mich.	Sam Bishop
29	PERGAMENT, Milton		So.	QB	6'	185	21	F	Chicago, Ill.	George Ring
33	LUND, Donald A.		So.	FB	6'	193	19	F	Detroit, Mich.	Wayne Nester
36	STENBERG, Robert P.		Jr.	FB	5'7"	168	21	—	Chicago, Ill.	George Ring
38	WIESE, Robert L.		So.	FB	6'2"	193	19	F	Jamestown, N. D.	Ernie Gates
39	BOOR, Donald P.		Jr.	FB	5'11"	185	22	M	Dearborn, Mich.	Jack Rabe
40	MYLL, Clifton O.		So.	E	6'	175	19	—	St. Clair Shores, Mich.	C. Warden
42	YAAP, Warren E.		So.	HB	5'11"	165	19	F	Chicago, Ill.	R. C. Antonides
45	KUZMA, Tom G.		Jr.	HB	6'1"	196	20	M	Gary, Ind.	Arthur Rolfe
46	ROBINSON, Don W.		Jr.	HB	5'11"	168	20	M	Detroit, Mich.	Herb Smith
48	WISE, Clifford C.		Jr.	HB	5'11"	170	22	M	Jackson, Mich.	J. L. Marks
49	CHAPPIUS, Robert R.		So.	HB	6'	174	19	F	Toledo, Ohio	Harry Rice
54	PRITULA, William		Jr.	T	6'	195	20	—	Detroit, Mich.	Floyd Groves
56	BRIESKE, James F.		So.	C	6'2"	194	19	F	Harbor Beach, Mich.	T. G. Pipple
57	KUYPER, William E.		Jr.	T	6'	201	19	—	Boston, Mass.	Paul J. King
58	MOONEY, Phillip K.		So.	C	6'	182	18	F	Marion, Ind.	O. C. Naugle
60	AMSTUTZ, Ralph H.		Jr.	G	5'10"	167	20	S	Oak Park, Ill.	Don Harshbager
61	TROGAN, Angelo E.		Jr.	G	5'8"	202	22	—	Saginaw, Mich.	Howard Hanson
62	FREIHOFER, Walter B.		Jr.	G	6'	185	20	—	Indianapolis, Ind.	Robert Nipper
63	FRANKS, Julius		Jr.	G	6'	187	20	—	Hamtramck, Mich.	Frank Cobb
64	HARTRICK, James G.		So.	G	5'8"	175	19	F	Royal Oak, Mich.	Bob French
65	GAGE, Robert J.		So.	T	6'	185	20	—	Reading, Mich.	H. E. Pierce
66	GANS, William		Sr.	G	5'9"	165	21	—	Poland Mines, Pa.	Louis Haley
67	PREGULMAN, Mervin		Jr.	C	6'3"	207	19	M	Lansing, Mich.	John Middlesworth
68	KOLESAR, Robert C.		Sr.	G	5'10"	193	21	MM	Cleveland, O.	G. G. Kozak
69	ROHRBACH, William R.		Jr.	G	5'8"	185	21	—	E. Aurora, N. Y.	Judson Hulbert
70	BRYAN, Fred J.		Jr.	E	6'2"	200	19	—	Melvindale, Mich.	Carl Newton
72	KARWALES, John J.		Jr.	T	6'	190	21	M	Chicago, Ill.	Bob Dougherty
73	OREN, Robert A.		So.	E	6'4"	197	19	F	Evart, Mich.	Richard Larimer
74	GRITIS, Peter		Jr.	T	5'10"	200	21	—	Chicago, Ill.	H. T. Dixon
75	GREENE, John J.		Jr.	T	6'	193	22	—	Pittsburgh, Pa.	J. L. Marks
76	BALDWIN, William W.		So.	T	6'4"	208	20	F	Lansing, Mich.	John Middlesworth
77	SECONTINE, Vincent C.		Jr.	T	6'	191	20	—	Detroit, Mich.	Charles Jenks
78	DERLETH, Robert J.		Jr.	T	6'1"	203	20	—	Marquette, Mich.	C. C. Rushton
79	CADY, Donald J.		So.	T	6'2"	190	18	F	Saginaw, Mich.	Carl Nordberg
80	GREY, William		So.	E	6'1"	172	19	—	Arlington, Va.	Dan Ahearn
81	VAN SUMMERN, John S.		Jr.	E	5'10"	180	20	—	Kenmore, N. Y.	Dick Offenhamer
82	KENNEDY, Charles F.		Jr.	HB	6'1"	180	22	S	Van Wert, Ohio	Glen Livingston
83	SMEJA, Rudy M.		Sr.	E	6'2"	187	21	M	Chicago, Ill.	E. L. Moore
84	SHEMKY, Robert W.		Jr.	E	6'	178	19	S	Crystal Falls, Mich.	Wm. Waytolonis
85	SHARPE, Philip E.		Sr.	E	6'2"	185	21	M	Lakewood, O.	R. J. Northcote-Green
87	CHADY, Otto E.		Sr.	E	6'1"	191	21	—	Highland Park	C. E. Horning
88	MADAR, Elmer F.		Sr.	E	5'10"	170	21	M	Detroit, Mich.	Charles Jenks
89	CEITHAML, George F.		Sr.	QB	6'	184	21	MM	Chicago, Ill.	E. L. Moore

* Age given is that of September 7, 1942.

¶ Experience symbols: M—indicates number of Varsity letters won in football; S—indicates secondary winners in 1941; F—indicates freshman.

"They must've lost more men to the draft than they let on!"

Sturdy Iowans Crush Michigan Eleven 26-14

By BUD HENDEL
(Daily Sports Editor)

The Iowa Seahawks proved their right to football greatness in Michigan Stadium yesterday before a crowd of 34,124 fans who sat stunned by the show of unimpeachable gridiron power taking place before them.

Striking through the air with the devastating efficiency of their own Navy dive-bombers and rolling along the ground with all the bone-crushing force of an Army tank, the Seahawks overcame a 14 point deficit to whip a dead-tired but fighting Michigan eleven, 26-14, and take another step forward in their quest for the mythical national championship.

Yesterday's defeat was the worst suffered by Coach Fritz Crisler's Michigan squad since the 20-7 licking absorbed at the hands of Minnesota in 1935 and it marked the ninth straight year that the Maize and Blue has fallen before a Bernie Bierman coached team.

Big Ten Eye-Opener

Northwestern		Michigan
Motl	LE	Madar
Karlstad	LT	Wistert
Kapter	LG	Kolesar
Hudson	C	Pregulman
Burke	RG	Franks
Vincent	RT	Pritula
Hasse	RE	Sharpe
Kean	QB	Ceithaml
Graham	LH	Robinson
Buffmire	RH	White
Hirsch	FB	Wiese

NORTHWESTERN	0	3	0	13—16	
MICHIGAN	7	11	6	7—31	

Northwestern Scoring: Touchdowns, McNutt (for Kean) Vodick (for Buffmire). Points after touchdown: Pick (placement) Field goal: Pick.

Michigan Scoring: Touchdowns, Wiese, White 2, Kuzma (for Robinson), Pregulman. Points after touchdown: Brieske 4.

MICHIGAN HOPES SKYROCKET WHEN ELMER MADAR (88) OF THE WOLVERINES MAKES A BEAUTIFUL CATCH OF THIS TOSS FROM BOB CHAPPUIS TO SCORE IN THE SECOND QUARTER. THE PLAY GAVE THE WOLVERINES A TWO-TOUCHDOWN LEAD.

Next Year — Maybe

Michigan		Minnesota
Sharpe	LE	Hein
Wistert	LT	Wildung
Kolesar	LG	Perko
Pregulman	C	Nollander
Franks	RG	Billman
Pritula	RT	Mitchell
Madar	RE	Mulready
Ceithaml	QB	Sandberg
Kuzma	LH	Daley
White	RH	Frickey
Lund	FB	Kulbitski

MICHIGAN	7	0	0	7—14	
MINNESOTA	0	10	6	0—16	

Michigan Scoring: Touchdowns—Kuzma 2. Points after touchdown—Brieske 2 (placements).

Minnesota Scoring: Touchdowns—Daley, Frickey. Points after touchdown—Garnaas. Field goal—Garnaas.

Michigan Substitutions: Guards, Friehofer; Center, Brieske; Backs, Robinson, Wardley, Chappuis, Boor.

Minnesota Substitutions: Ends, Anderson, Baumgartner; Guard, Bicanich; Center, Solheim; Backs, Garnaas, Kula, Kelley.

Great Day for Subs

Illinois		Michigan
Grierson	LE	Madar
Genis	LT	Wistert
Agase	LG	Kolesar
Wenskunas	C	Pregulman
Wilson	RG	Franks
Kasap	RT	Pritula
Engel	RE	Sharpe
Florek	QB	Ceithaml
Griffin	LH	Kuzma
Correll	RH	White
Smith	FB	Boor

ILLINOIS	0	7	0	7—14	
MICHIGAN	7	7	7	7—28	

Failure To Extract Penalty Proves Costly

Field Goal Made After Half Should Have Ended; Clock Illegally Stopped By Official

By Mill Marsh

Coach Fritz Crisler, his assistants and the Michigan football players are all true sportsmen. They were a grim lot and tight-lipped after returning from Minnesota where they succumbed to the Gophers Saturday, 16 to 14, for the ninth consecutive time.

The record books will read 16-14, yet if the official timer had not illegally stopped the clock with six seconds of the first half remaining, the Wolverines would have won the contest, 14-13. Crisler and his players are making no alibis nor are they issuing any comments whatever on the inefficiency of the game officials.

The illegal stopping of the clock and the failure of the officials to inflict a five-yard penalty for delaying the game, cost Michigan the victory, as it was in the last two seconds of the first half that Quarterback Bill Garnaas of the Gophers drop-kicked the field goal which ultimately supplied Minnesota with its margin of victory. Actually, the winning field goal was kicked between the first and second half.

Here was the picture:

After taking the ball away from Michigan on downs on the Gopher 46 near the end of the second quarter, Minnesota rushed to the Michigan two-yard line. On the next play Julie Franks tackled Bill Daley of the Gophers for a loss to the six.

Irish Suffer Worst Defeat Since 1916

Great Power and Deception Mark Rough Offensive Play by Both Teams

By BUD HENDEL
Special to The Daily

SOUTH BEND, Nov. 14.—Michigan and Notre Dame bridged the 33 year gap in their football relations today with an explosive display of offensive fireworks that had a howling mob of 57,000 spectators screaming in the aisles of Notre Dame Stadium as a sensational third period Wolverine scoring splurge gave Michigan a stunning 32-20 victory.

Keyed to a fighting pitch, the Wolverines unleashed a savage third quarter ground attack that netted them three quick decisive touchdowns and sent them soaring far ahead of the Ramblers in the wildest grid contest staged this season.

Not since 1916, when Army walloped them by a score of 30 to 10, have the Irish been administered such an authoritative drubbing. Twice, Michigan came from behind before it finally overtook the embattled Irish, once in the opening period and again in their amazing third quarter touchdown bonanza.

Reprinted with permission from the **Michigan Daily**

Michigan (32)		Notre Dame (20)
Sharpe	L.E.	Dove
Wistert	L.T.	Rymkus
Kolesar	L.G.	McBride
Pregulman	C.	Ziemba
Franks	R.G.	Wright
Pritula	R.T.	Neff
Madar	R.E.	Murphy (C)
Ceithml (C)	Q.B.	Bertelli
Kuzma	L.H.	Livingstone
White	R.H.	C. Miller
Wiese	F.B.	Clatt

Michigan	7	6	19	0—	32
Notre Dame	7	7	0	6—	20

Touchdowns: Notre Dame—Dove, C. Miller, 2. Michigan—Ceithml, Robinson, White, Kuzma, 2.

Points after touchdown: Notre Dame—Bertelli, 2. Michigan—Brieske, 2.

Substitutions: Notre Dame—Left end, Yonaker; left tackle, White; lef guard, Filley; center, Coleman, Brock; right guard, Tobin; right tackle, Czarobski; right end, Limont; quarterback, J. Creevy; left half, R. Creevy, T. Miller; right half, Earley; full back, Cowhig. Michigan—Left guard, Friehofer; right tackle, Derleth; left half, Robinson; right half, Brieske.

Officials: Referee — William Blake (Loras); Umpires—H. G. Hedges (Dartmouth); Field Judge—R. H. Rupp (Lebanon Valley); Head Linesman—Roy Knipschild (Chicago).

Coaches: Frank Leahy (Notre Dame); Fritz Crisler (Michigan).

Julius Franks Named By Rice On All-America

Julius Franks today became the 24th Michigan football player to be picked on Collier's All-America eleven. His selection by Grantland Rice and the All-America advisory Board is great tribute to the Wolverine guard.

Buckeyes Complete Three Passes For Touchdown Scores

By Mill Marsh

Ohio State knew what it wanted. And it went out and got it.

The Buckeyes wanted the Big Ten football championship and they clinched the crown Saturday at Columbus by thrashing Coach Fritz Crisler's Wolverines, 21 to 7.

Michigan also was pennant-bound before it ran into an alert and inspired Ohio eleven. The Wolverines could have shared the title with Wisconsin's surprising Badgers by beating the Buckeyes and then taking care of Iowa this week.

As it now stands, the Iowa game is a sort of an anti-climax to one of the dizziest football campaigns that the Big Ten has ever known.

By beating Iowa the best that the Wolverines can do is to tie Illinois for third spot in the final standings behind Ohio, the Big Ten champs, and Wisconsin which finished second.

BROWN'S BUCKEYES WERE AROUSED

Coach Paul Brown's Buckeyes definitely deserve the conference championship. They were an inspired eleven Saturday, just as Michigan was an inspired eleven the previous week in beating Notre Dame.

The results of Saturday's encounter at Columbus bear out the opinion of experts that a collegiate football squad cannot be kept at its peak for two weeks in succession.

Paul Brown's charges were fired up Saturday. Just as Crisler's squad, trailing, 14-13 at halftime, was fired up against the Irish last week in scoring 19 points in the third quarter.

It took Ohio State only seven plays Saturday to achieve its victory. Four of these seven plays were pass plays.

All three Buckeye touchdowns were scored through the air. The markers were scored against Michigan's pass defense which has been vulnerable all season.

Reprinted with permission from the **Ann Arbor News**

Michigan's Team Statistics for 1942

	Michigan	Opponents
Total First Downs	159	101
Rushing	113	59
Passing	35	38
Penalties	11	4
Net Yards Gained Rushing	2019	1055
Number of Rushes	519	379
Net Yards Gained Passing	835	1115
Total Yards Gained*	3171	2513
Forward Passes Attempted	159	158
Forward Passes Completed	59	75
Forward Passes Intercepted By	14	11
Yards Interceptions Returned	255	109
Number of Punts	49	67
Punts Returned By	39	15
Punts Blocked By	2	1
Yards Punts Returned	522	159
Number of Kick-offs	42	31
Kick-offs Returned By	24	38
Yards Kick-offs Returned	434	747
Fumbles By	23	17
Opponents' Fumbles Recovered By	9	10
Number of Penalties	36	42
Yards Penalized	343	317
Total Points Scored	221	134

* Includes rushing, passing and penalty gains.

SIX MARINES, FOUR GOBS AND A CIVILIAN: They will comprise the starting lineup for the University of Michigan in its grid opener Saturday with Camp Grant at Rockford, Ill.

Reading from left to right the above line includes Art Renner, Marines; Mervin Pregulman, Navy; George Kraeger, Navy; Fred Negus, Marines; Johnny Gallagher, Marines; Bob Hanzlik, Marines and Rudy Smeja, deferred engineering student.

The above backfield from left to right includes Capt. Paul White, Marine trainee; Bob Wiese and Bill Daley of the Navy and Elroy Hirsch, Marine.

Negus, Gallagher, Hanzlik and Hirsch are former Wisconsin players; Bill Daley was a star at Minnesota for three years. White, Wiese, Pregulman and Smeja are lettermen from last year's Wolverine squad while Kraeger and Renner were Wolverine freshmen a year ago.

AP Poll (1943)

1. Notre Dame
2. Iowa Pre-Flight
3. MICHIGAN
4. Navy
5. Purdue
6. Great Lakes
7. Duke
8. Del Monte P
9. Northwestern
10. March Field

The 1943 Record

26	MICHIGAN........................Camp Grant at Rockford, Ill.	0
57	MICHIGAN........................Western Michigan at Ann Arbor	6
21	MICHIGAN........................Northwestern at Evanston	7
12	MICHIGAN........................Notre Dame at Ann Arbor	35
49	MICHIGAN........................Minnesota at Ann Arbor	6
42	MICHIGAN........................Illinois at Champaign	6
23	MICHIGAN........................Indiana at Ann Arbor	6
27	MICHIGAN........................Wisconsin at Ann Arbor	0
45	MICHIGAN........................Ohio State at Ann Arbor	7
302		73

(Michigan and Purdue tied for the Conference Championship)

'Ole 98' Is Safe

Lt. Thomas Harmon, U. S. bomber pilot shown above, was reported safe at a South American airport today following the crash of his bombing plane in the jungles.

Thousands of Michigan grid fans joined with his parents, Mr. and Mrs. Louis Harmon and his coach, Fritz Crisler, in saying: "Thank God."

MICHIGAN FOOTBALL ROSTER, 1943

Pos.	Name	Service Status *	Pos.	Age	Wgt.	Hgt.	Home Town
10	NUSSBAUMER, Robert J.	M	HB	19	160	5'11"	Oak Park, Ill.
14	DREYER, Walter O.	M	HB	20	158	5'9"	Milwaukee, Wis.
15	STURGES, Ray E.	R	G	17	169	5'11"	Detroit, Mich.
16	WHITE, Paul G.	M	HB	21	181	6'1"	River Rouge, Mich.
17	PETOSKEY, Jack	N	E	21	168	5'11"	Dearborn, Mich.
18	HOLGATE, James G.	M	HB	23	167	6'	Milwaukee, Wis.
19	BROWN, James J.	N	HB	22	155	5'9"	St. Ignace, Mich.
22	POWERS, Jerome E.	M	HB	20	180	6'3"	Green Bay, Wis.
24	WINK, Jack S.	M	QB	21	185	5'10"	Milwaukee, Wis.
26	PONSETTO, Joe L.	R	QB	17	175	6'	Flint, Mich.
27	MACK, High R., Jr.	NR	QB	20	180	5'11"	Birmingham, Mich.
28	KIESEL, George C.	M	QB	20	172	5'10"	Detroit, Mich.
29	ALIBER, James J.	N	QB	18	185	5'11"	Detroit, Mich.
33	LUND, Donald A.	R	FB	20	180	6'	Detroit, Mich.
34	MAVES, Earl C.	M	FB	20	180	5'10"	Stanley, Wis.
36	STENBERG, Robert P.	M	FB	22	168	5'7"	Milwaukee, Wis.
38	WIESE, Robert L.	N	FB	20	190	6'2"	Jamestown, N.D.
40	HIRSCH, Elroy L.	M	HB	20	182	6'1"	Wausau, Wis.
42	HILKENE, Bruce L.	ER	E	17	180	6'1"	Indianapolis, Ind.
43	LeROUX, Arthur N.	R	T	19	190	6'	Muskegon Hts., Mich.
45	DALEY, Wm. E.	N	FB	23	206	6'2"	St. Cloud, Minn.
46	CULLIGAN, W. L.	N	HB	19	160	5'10"	Detroit, Mich.
49	ALBERTI, Larry R.	N	HB	20	162	6'1"	Chicago, Ill.
51	NEGUS, Fred W.	M	C-T	21	196	6'2"	Martins Ferry, Ohio
53	CRANDELL, John S.	N	C	19	170	5'10"	Ann Arbor, Mich.
54	KAVIEFF, Sheldon M.	N	E	20	180	5'11"	Detroit, Mich.
56	BRIESKE, James F.	N	C	20	194	6'2"	Harbor Beach, Mich.
61	GALLAGHER, John M.	M	G	21	176	5'9"	Eau Claire, Wis.
62	KRAEGER, George W.	N	G	20	190	6'1"	Indianapolis, Ind.
63	AMSTUTZ, Ralph H.	R	G	21	164	5'10"	Oak Park, Ill.
65	FISCHER, Robert H.	M	G	20	176	5'10"	Benton Harbor, Mich.
66	TRUMP, Jack	M	G	20	202	5'10"	Battle Creek, Mich.
67	PREGULMAN, Mervin	N	C-T	20	207	6'3"	E. Lansing, Mich.
68	MANNING, Richard E.	N	G	23	178	5'11"	Ecorse, Mich.
69	ROHRBACH, Wm. R.	R	G	22	185	5'8"	East Aurora, N.Y.
70	BRYAN, Fred J.	N	T	20	192	6'2"	Melvindale, Mich.
71	MROZ, Vincent P.	M	E	21	191	6'2"	E. Chicago, Ind.
72	BAUMAN, Clement L.	N	T	19	200	6'3"	Dayton, Ohio
73	KENNEDY, Robert W.	N	T	18	198	6'	Riverside, Ill.
75	GREENE, John J.	R	T	23	193	6'	Pittsburgh, Pa.
76	WHEELER, Lewis	N	T	21	215	6'4"	Roosevelt, N.Y.
77	HANZLIK, Robert L.	M	T	19	195	6'1"	Chippewa Falls, Wis.
80	RENNER, Arthur W.	M	E	19	172	6'2"	Sturgis, Mich.
81	COOK, Thomas C.	M	E	20	178	6'	Detroit, Mich.
82	OLSHANSKI, Henry S.	M	E	20	180	6'1"	Wausau, Wis.
83	SMEJA, Rudy M.	R	E	22	187	6'2"	Chicago, Ill.
84	SCHWARTZ, Alan E.	R	E	17	173	6'1"	Detroit, Mich.
85	CRANE, Fenwick J.	M	E	20	201	6'3"	Pleasant Ridge, Mich.
86	WELLS, Rex C.	M	G	21	178	6'1"	Twin Falls, Idaho
87	JOHNSON, Farnham J.	M	E	19	188	6'	Appleton, Wis.
88	RENNEBOHM, Robert B.	M	E	20	183	5'11"	LaCrosse, Wis.
89	MYLL, Clifton O.	N	E	20	180	6'	St. Clair Shores, Mich.

* M, indicates Marine trainee; N, Navy trainee; R, Ready for call to service. The abbreviation, ER, indicates member of the Army enlisted reserve; NR indicates Naval Reserve.

Bill Daley Puts On Great One-Man Show

Former Gopher Scores Twice And Sets Up Another Tally; Merv Pregulman Stars On Line

By Mill Marsh

There is plenty of work ahead this week for the Michigan gridders if they hope to stop the Fighting Irish from Notre Dame. Despite the 21 to 7 triumph over Northwestern in the Big Ten opener at Evanston Saturday, the Wolverines were far from being impressive and had it not been for the individual exploits of Big Bill Daley the game could very easily have gone the other way.

Big Bill was terrific on the seven plays that were needed to score all three Michigan touchdowns. On the first Michigan play from scrimmage, Daley powered his way 37 yards across the Wildcat goal. A short time later he reeled off 19 more yards to make it first down on the Northwestern eight. He moved it up to the three and Elroy Hirsch went over for the score.

MICHIGAN WAS OUTPLAYED IN THIRD PERIOD

Michigan was definitely outplayed in the third period and the Wildcats were getting wilder by the minute after Otto Graham had crashed over from the 12-yard line to score in the fourth period.

But Big Bill again took charge and at the same time took most of the fight out of the Wildcats by lugging the ball on a quick-opening play through center and kept rambling for 64 yards without interference to smash his way over for the third Michigan score.

On this run, Daley bumped two tacklers out of the way and simply out-ran Otto Graham, the Wildcat safety man.

Michigan gained only 226 net yards by rushing and Big Bill accounted for 216 which gives some idea as to what he meant to the Michigan eleven Saturday.

INDIVIDUAL GAINING

Michigan

	Tries	Gain	Ave.
Daley	26	216	8.3
Hirsch	14	19	1.4
White	12	-8	
Lund	1	2	2.0

Northwestern

	Tries	Gain	Ave.
Graham	14	-4	
Frickey	8	39	4.9
Buffmire	5	17	3.4
Schwall	16	54	3.2

Hirsch Sneaks into Game Just to Tally for M

By the Associated Press

ANN ARBOR, Nov. 13—The injured Elroy (Crazy Legs) Hirsch was so determined to score against his old Wisconsin mates today that he rushed in while Coach Fritz Crisler wasn't looking and kicked the extra point after Michigan's fourth touchdown.

Bob Nussbaumer had just passed 34 yards to Earl Maves for the score, and when Crisler looked up again he saw No. 40 trotting out from the bench.

"Who's that, anyway?" called Crisler to Line Coach Clarence Munn. "By gosh, it's Hirsch. How did he get in there?"

"He just ran out there," replied Munn.

With Howie Wikel holding the ball, Hirsch booted one right down the middle for the extra point. Then he trotted out again, injured shoulder and all.

"I just had to score against Wisconsin," he explained to his coaches, who were having a hard time suppressing a grin.

Wolverines Unable To Stop Bertelli, Miller And The 'T'

By Mill Marsh

Michigan's football season isn't over, despite the 35 to 12 thumping which the Wolverines absorbed at the hands of Notre Dame Saturday.

The season may be over for many of the 90,000 spectators who saw the well-oiled "T" formation of Coach Frank Leahy of Notre Dame humble the Wolverines Saturday with an attack that struck swiftly and surely on the ground as well as in the air.

The Wolverines with five Big Ten games yet to play are still undefeated in the Big Ten. They have a victory over Northwestern, with Minnesota, Illinois, Indiana, Wisconsin and Ohio State still to be met.

There is no game this week. That gives Coach Fritz Crisler two weeks in which to rally his forces for the combat with Minnesota on Oct. 23, a team which we have not beaten in nine long years.

After the Minnesota game Crisler is apt to lose some of his present talent, including the seniors on the squad.

He will have to carry on against the Illini, Hoosiers, Badgers and Buckeyes with what he has left and what he can develop in the meantime.

MICHIGAN HAS NO ALIBIS TO OFFER

It is useless to alibi or find excuses for the worst defeat that a Crisler-coached Michigan team ever suffered here Saturday. The Fighting Irish from South Bend were just too good for our boys. Leahy's "T" formation which sputtered and faltered last year in the 32-20 victory of the Wolverines at South Bend, was hitting on all 11 cylinders Saturday and if Notre Dame is not the greatest team in the country today, it will do until a better one can be uncovered.

Back of a seasoned line the light-footed Creighton Miller and Angelo Bertelli were terrific Saturday. Bertelli pitched two touchdown passes and bucked over a third. Miller tallied twice and personally rang up 155 yards by rushing.

All last week Coach Fritz Crisler worked his coaching staff from early in the morning until late at night, trying to figure out a way to stop the "T" attack of Notre Dame. His scouts were right when they reported that Notre Dame was 20 per cent stronger this year than last. He likewise was right in announcing as late as Friday that his team was 20 per cent weaker than a year ago.

DALEY WAS GREAT EVEN IN DEFEAT

All Michigan had in the way of an offense Saturday was Big Bill Daley, who still rates as one of the greatest football players of the year with his 145 yards by rushing Saturday that raised his total in four games to 540 yards.

Give Big Bill that Notre Dame line which was in front of Angelo Bertelli, Creighton Miller, Jim Mello and Julius Rykovich Saturday and it is doubtful if any team in the land could have stopped him.

Big Bill, taking his cue from another Minnesota great, Bronko Nagurski, provides his own interference. His most spectacular run Saturday was a 20-yard sweep around end in which he stiff-armed three tacklers, eluded another and powered his way to the Wolverine 28-yard line.

Sharp Wolverines Bury Gophers Under Record Score Of 49-6

By Mill Marsh

Tackle Mervin Pregulman and Fullback Bill Daley, who were terrific in the 49-6 defeat of the Golden Gophers from Minnesota Saturday, are expected to make their final Michigan gridiron bow this week at Illinois.

Big Bill accompanied the beaten Gophers back to Minneapolis Saturday, but will return Thursday after visiting his mother a few days at St. Cloud. Both Pregulman and Daley will leave immediately after the Illinois game for their new naval base. Also leaving the squad after Saturday are Jack Petoskey, end; John Crandall, reserve center; James J. Brown, reserve halfback, and Dick Manning, reserve guard.

Capt. Paul White, Bob Stenberg and Leonard Naab, Marines, played their final game Saturday in the rout of the Gophers. They, with Jim Holgate, who was kept out of Saturday's game with an injury, move to Parris Island this week.

1943

Ann Arbor, Nov. 22—Coach Fritz Crisler's Michigan gridiron machine ended a 10-year title drought this afternoon by routing Ohio State 45-7 and tying with Purdue for the 1943 Western Conference football championship.

It was the eighth victory in nine games for the Wolverines and the second largest point total in the series with the Buckeyes since 1897. The Crisler machine completly routed the Bucks civilian eleven by piling up 426 yards and 23 first downs to 68 yards and two first downs. In writing the grand finale of the 1943 season the Maize and Blue gridders were sparked by hard-driving Bob Wiese. Wally Dreyer, a pony back and stocky Earl Maves as well as Don Lund, reserve back.

Buckeyes Routed In Final Game, 45 To 7; Crisler's First Title

First for Fritz

OHIO STATE		MICHIGAN
Dugger	LE	Smeja
Willis	LT	Hanzlik
Neff	LG	Gallagher
Appleby	C	Negus
Hackett	RG	Wells
Thomas	RT	Derleth
Souders	RE	Renner
Williams	QB	Wiese
Sensanbaugher	LH	Nussbaumer
Parks	RH	Dreyer
Davis	FB	Lund

Ohio State ...... 0 0 7 0— 7
Michigan ....13 0 13 19—45

Ohio State Scoring: Touchdown, Parks. Point after touchdown, Stungis (for Williams) (placekick).

Michigan Scoring: Touchdowns, Wiese 2, Dreyer, Nussbaumer, Mroz (for Smeja), Lund, Maves (for Dreyer). Points after touchdown, Wells 2, Hirsch (for Nussbaumer) (placekicks).

	MICH.	OPP.
Total First Downs	131	6
Rushing	114	5
Passing	14	1
Penalties	3	
Net Yards Gained—Rushing	2648	94
Number of Rushes	524	35
Net Yards Gained—Passing	621	45
Total Yards Gained *	3269	140
Forward Passes Attempted	74	11
Forward Passes Completed	36	3
Forward Passes Intercepted By	22	1
Yards Interceptions Returned	263	14
Number of Punts	36	6
Punts Returned By	55	14
Punts Blocked By	0	
Yards Punts Returned	454	223
Number of Kick-offs	52	26
Kick-offs Returned By	11	41
Yards Kick-offs Returned	923	622
Fumbles By	28	20
Opponents' Fumbles Recovered By	10	9
Number of Penalties	40	20
Yards Penalized	413	155
Total Points Scored	302	73

* Includes rushing, passing and penalty gains.

MICHIGAN INDIVIDUAL STATISTICS FOR 1943

	RUSHING			PASSING				RECEIVING		PUNT RET.		PUNTING		SCORING				
	Tries	Net Gain	Ave.	Att'd	Comp.	Had Int.	Gain	C'ght	Gain	No.	Yds.	No.	Ave.	TD	CA	CM	FG	TP
Daley, FB	120	817	6.80	4	1	0	24	0	0	6	119	1	40.0	9	5	3	0	57
Nussbaumer, HB	55	379	6.60	14	5	5	78	3	23	5	50	0	0.0	6	0	0	0	36
Wiese, FB	77	343	4.40	1	1	0	10	3	32	0	0	26	38.8	5	0	0	0	30
Hirsch, HB	70	313	3.80	22	9	2	213	1	38	17	189	2	61.5	11	4	2	0	68
Lund, FB	48	260	5.10	0	0	0	0	0	0	0	0	1	27.0	1	0	0	0	6
Dreyer, HB	42	237	5.50	0	0	0	0	2	53	3	23	0	0.0	3	0	0	0	18
Maves, FB	24	169	7.00	0	0	0	0	1	34	1	-1	0	0.0	2	0	0	0	12
White, HB	50	154	3.10	5	2	1	58	1	14	1	9	0	0.0	2	0	0	0	12
Stenberg, FB	2	13	6.50	0	0	0	0	1	6	1	4	0	0.0	0	1	1	0	1
Renner, E	0	0	0.00	0	0	0	0	2	56	0	0	0	0.0	0	0	0	0	0
Johnson, E	0	0	0.00	0	0	0	0	4	109	0	0	0	0.0	1	0	0	0	6
Olshanski, E	0	0	0.00	0	0	0	0	1	9	0	0	0	0.0	0	0	0	0	0
Crane, E	0	0	0.00	0	0	0	0	1	11	0	0	0	0.0	0	0	0	0	0
Pregulman, T	0	0	0.00	0	0	0	0	0	0	0	0	0	0.0	0	24	21	0	21
Culligan, HB	1	2	2.00	4	2	0	51	0	0	0	0	0	0.0	1	0	0	0	6
Holgate, HB	3	3	1:00	1	0	1	0	1	33	0	0	0	0.0	0	0	0	0	0
Brown, HB	2	12	6:00	5	1	0	6	0	0	0	0	0	0.0	0	0	0	0	0
Hilkene, E	0	0	0.00	0	0	0	0	1	18	0	0	0	0.0	0	0	0	0	0
Wink, QB	2	-6	-3.00	15	8	1	161	0	0	0	0	0	0.0	0	0	0	0	0
Rennebohm, E	0	0	0.00	0	0	0	0	1	13	0	0	0	0.0	0	0	0	0	0
Smeja, E	0	0	0.00	0	0	0	0	2	53	0	0	0	0.0	1	0	0	0	6
Mroz, E	0	0	0.00	0	0	0	0	3	74	0	0	0	0.0	1	0	0	0	6
Wells, G	0	0	0.00	0	0	0	0	0	0	0	0	0	0.0	0	9	7	0	7
Wikel, HB	9	33	3.60	2	1	0	20	0	0	0	0	1	37.0	1	0	0	0	6

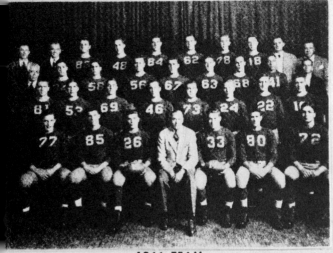

1944 TEAM

Front Row: Lazetich, Hilkene, Ponsetto' co-captain, H. O. Crisler (coach), Lund' (co-captain), Renner, Bauman.

Second Row: Greer, Wahl, Weyers, Culligan, LeRoux, Yerges, Mehaffey, Chubb.

Third Row: Hatch (equipment custodian), T. Peterson, Watts, Lintol, Burg, Swift, Chiaverini, Derricotte.

Fourth Row: Roberts (trainer), Martineau (backfield coach), Freihofer, Weisenburger, Rifenburg, Sickels, Brielmier, Bentz, Oosterbaan (end coach), Munn (line coach).

' Co-captains named after Capt. Wiese was transferred by Navy.

Michigan's 1944 Football Record

Michigan	12	Iowa Pre-Flight	7	at Ann Arbor
Michigan	14	Marquette	0	at Milwaukee
Michigan	0	Indiana	20	at Ann Arbor
Michigan	28	Minnesota	13	at Minneapolis
Michigan	27	Northwestern	0	at Ann Arbor
Michigan	40	Purdue	14	at Ann Arbor
Michigan	41	Pennsylvania	19	at Philadelphia
Michigan	14	Illinois	0	at Ann Arbor
Michigan	14	Wisconsin	0	at Ann Arbor
Michigan	14	Ohio State	18	at Columbus
Ttl. Pts.	204		91	

The 1944 Western Conference Standings

	Won	Lost	Tied	%	Pts.	Opp. Pts.
Ohio State	6	0	0	1.000	153	54
MICHIGAN	5	2	0	.714	137	65
Purdue	4	2	0	.667	143	87
Minnesota	3	2	1	.600	134	116
Indiana	4	3	0	.571	119	79
Illinois	3	3	0	.500	122	105
Wisconsin	2	4	0	.333	66	110
Northwestern	0	5	1	.000	40	114
Iowa	0	6	0	.000	20	204

AP Poll (1944)

1. Army
2. Ohio State
3. Randolph Field
4. Navy
5. Bainbridge
6. Iowa Pre-Flight
7. Southern Cal.
8. MICHIGAN
9. Notre Dame
10. 4th AAF

Sept. 23

Wolverines Win Despite Errors

Derricotte, Rifenburg, Ponsetto Do Scoring In 14-0 Victory Over Hilltoppers; Eight Fumbles Hurt

TEAM STATISTICS

	Marq'te	Mich.			
First Downs	11	18	Punts, Number	8	5
Rushing	6	16	Returned by	4	6
Passing	3	2	Blocked by	0	0
Penalties	2	0	Punts, Av. Yards	38	45
Net Yards Rushing	68	230	Kickoffs, Number	1	3
Yards Lost	28	25	Returned by	1	3
Net Yards Forwards	90	67	Kickoffs, Av. Yards	60	56
Total Net Yardage	158	297	Yards Kicks Returned	108	77
Forwards Attempted	24	8	Punts	33	51
Forwards Completed	10	4	Kickoffs	75	26
Intercepted By	0	2	Fumbles	4	8
Yards Interceptions Return	0	2	Ball Lost	1	5
			Penalties	3	3
			Yards Lost On Penalties	25	20

Michigan Win Made Via Overland Route

By Dave Tefft

The Little Brown Jug was back in Ann Arbor today following a round-trip journey to Memorial Stadium, Minneapolis, Minn.

And Coach H. O. "Fritz" Crisler knows he has a real football team to send against Northwestern's Wildcats here next Saturday.

Those are the two most-important aftermath facts of Saturday's 28-13 victory which the Wolverines scored over the Golden Gophers of Minnesota to mark (1)—Michigan's second successive win over Minnesota; (2)—the Wolverines' second victory in 12 starts against the Gophers; (3)—the 20th win in the 35-game series; (4)—the worst defeat inflicted on a Minnesota team at Minneapolis since 1926, and (5)—the first time a Crisler-coached Michigan team has won at Minneapolis.

Most interesting phase of the game itself, from an analytical standpoint, was not the victory but the way it was won. Michigan virtually beat Dr. George Hauser's Golden Gophers at their own game as the Wolverines smashed their way to four touchdowns via an overland route that was gunned straight at, and through, Minnesota's bragged-up pre-war line.

Oct. 14

27-0 Victory Over Northwestern Indicates Probable Replacements For Men To Be Transferred Soon

TEAM STATISTICS

	Mich.	N.W.
First Downs	20	8
By rushing	18	3
By passing	1	5
By penalty	1	0
Net yards, rushing	435	23
Yards lost	0	19
Forwards attempted	10	16
Completed by	2	7
Intercepted by	7	1
Net yards, forwards	22	103
Totals yards gained	457	126
Punts, number of	2	6
Returned by	2	2
Punts, average yards	41	38
Kickoffs, number of	4	2
Returned by	2	
Kickoffs, average	43	42
Yards kicks returned	61	67
Punts	15	10
Kickoffs	43	57
Fumbles	2	2
Ball lost	1	1
Penalties	4	3
Yards lost	30	15
Touchdowns	4	0
Conversions	3	0

INDIVIDUAL GAINS

Michigan

	Tries	Gain	Loss	Net
Weise	21	122	0	122
Nussbaumer	14	135	0	135
Culligan	4	20	0	20
Ponsetto	1	9	0	9
Derricotte	13	71	0	71
Chubb	3	14	0	14
Aliber	1	4	0	4
Lund	3	8	0	8
Renner	1	0	0	0
Rifenburg	1	2	0	2
Weisenburger	6	35	0	35
Bentz	3	11	0	11
Peterson	1	4	0	4

NORTHWWESTERN

	Tries	Gain	Loss	Net
Yungwirth	6	3	13	
Conners	6	20	0	20
Funderburg	2	3	0	3
Roper	3	6	0	6
Schadler	1	0	6	
Akpeter	4	10	0	10
Doyle	1	3	0	3

Oct. 7

1944

Columbus, O., Nov. 25—The Buckeyes defeated Michigan, 18-14, before 71,958 gasping and stuttering fans here this afternoon in one of the most dramatic football battles of recent years.

Showing the stuff of which champions are made. Ohio State, trailing 14-12, staged a 51-yard march to send Les Horvath, All-American quarterback, across from the 1-yard line in the final four minutes.

Michigan had just staged a tremendous 83-yard drive. Bill Culligan scoring from the 1. The Wolverines kickoff went out of bounds and Ohio got the ball on its own 49 to start its winning march.

Ohio scored first, a 56-yard first quarter march with Ollie Cline counting. Ralph Chubb brought an intercepted pass back to the Buckeye 25, and then drove to the 1, with Culligan scoring. Ponsetto's kick made it 7-6 at the halftime.

Ohio State regained the lead when Center Gordon Appleby recovered Chubb's fumble on the Michigan 22. Horvath drove over seven plays later. Again the point was missed. Then Culligan and Ponsetto made it 14-12. Only three minutes and 16 seconds remained when Horvath scored again to bring Ohio the conference title.

Michigan's Team Statistics for 1944

	MICH.	OPP.
Total First Downs	139	104
Rushing	123	78
Passing	12	23
Penalties	4	3
Net Yards Gained—Rushing	2553	1423
Number of Rushes	527	430
Net Yards Gained—Passing	492	609
Total Yards Gained *	3342	2336
Forward Passes Attempted	79	124
Forward Passes Completed	24	42
Forward Passes Intercepted By	15	14
Yards Interceptions Returned	198	103
Number of Punts	47	60
Punts Returned By	25	30
Punts Blocked By	1	1
Yards Punts Returned	184	331
Number of Kick-offs	39	24
Kick-offs Returned By	22	29
Yards Kick-offs Returned	433	687
Fumbles By	33	30
Opponents' Fumbles Recovered By	19	18
Number of Penalties	34	32
Yards Penalized	304	297
Total Points Scored	204	91

* Includes rushing, passing and penalty gains.

MICHIGAN INDIVIDUAL STATISTICS FOR 1944

	RUSHING			PASSING				RECEIVING		PUNT RET.		PUNTING		SCORING				
	Tries	Net Gain	Ave.	Att'd	Comp.	Had Int.	Gain	C'ght	Gain	No.	Yds.	No.	Ave.	TD	CA	CM	FG	TP
Nussbaumer, hb	78	502	6.43	1	0	0	0	0	0	4	44	0	0	4	0	0	0	24
Derricotte, hb	88	493	5.60	17	7	0	125	0	0	11	69	0	0	4	0	0	0	24
Wiese, fb	103	467	4.53	0	0	0	0	0	0	0	0	24	41	7	0	0	0	42
Chubb, hb	74	324	4.10	1	0	1	0	0	0	3	25	0	0	2	2	1	0	13
Culligan, hb	60	303	5.00	39	12	8	245	0	0	4	38	0	0	4	0	0	0	24
Lund, fb	64	228	3.56	0	0	0	0	0	0	0	0	17	32.4	2	0	0	0	12
Weisenburger, hb	27	133	4.92	7	2	0	27	0	0	0	0	5	42.2	2	0	0	0	12
Bentz, hb	10	75	7.50	0	0	0	0	0	0	1	16	0	0	0	0	0	0	0
Ponsetto, qb	11	29	2.63	9	2	1	70	1	28	1	1	0	0	0	28	23	0	23
Aliber, qb	3	8	2.66	1	0	0	0	0	0	0	0	0	0	0	0	0	0	0
Rifenburg, e	4	10	2.50	0	0	0	0	8	232	0	0	0	0	3	0	0	0	18
Peterson, fb	3	5	1.66	0	0	0	0	0	0	0	0	0	0	0	0	0	0	0
Hilkene, e	1	2	2.00	0	0	0	0	3	54	0	0	0	0	1	0	0	0	6
Renner, e	1	1	1.00	0	0	0	0	4	84	0	0	0	0	1	0	0	0	6
Yerges, qb	0	0	0.00	4	1	0	25	0	0	0	0	0	0	0	0	0	0	0

MICHIGAN FOOTBALL ROSTER

No.	Name	Service Status	Pos.	Age	Wgt.	Hgt.
5	OTT, John A.	C	HB	17	180	6:00
6	COLEMAN, Horace	C	HB	21	180	5:10
8	*BENTZ, Warren W.	N	HB	19	167	5:11
9	FONDE, Henry	N	HB	21	165	5:8
12	DOTY, Howard R.	C	QB	17	165	5:9
14	*YERGES, Howard F., Jr.	N	QB	20	175	5:10
16	*PONSETTO, Joe L. Jr. Capt.	N	QB	19	190	6:00
28	HUTTER, George	N	QB	20	173	5:10
33	CHIAMES, George J.	C	FB	17	180	5:10
36	FOLTZ, James H.	M	FB	20	185	5:9
39	DWORSKY, Daniel	C	FB	17	206	6:00
40	*NUSSBAUMER, Robert	D	HB	19	165	5:11
42	TENINGA, Walter H.	C	HB	17	180	5:10
45	ELLIOTT, Peter R.	N	HB	18	187	6:00
46	MUELDER, Wesley W.	N	HB	19	165	5:11
48	*WEISENBURGER, Jack	C	HB	19	176	6:1
51	KAVANAUGH, Russell L.	C	C	17	175	6:1
54	SAULS, Reginald	M	HB	19	175	5:11
55	SWANSON, Robert	C	C	17	180	6:04
56	MOMSEN, Anton, Jr.	C	C	17	205	6:2
58	*WATTS, Harold M.	N	C	20	176	5:10
60	*WEYERS, John	N	G	20	180	5:11
62	*FREIHOFER, Cecil	C	G	19	187	6:00
63	SMITH, Jack E.	N	G	20	195	6:00
64	NAKAMURA, Frank	C	G	22	185	5:06
65	TOMASI, Dominic	C	G	17	180	5:10
66	*LINTOL, John F.	N	G	21	187	6:1
68	WILKINS, F. Stuart	C	G	17	187	5:10
69	SOBOLESKI, Joseph R.	D	G	20	182	5:11
72	JOHNSON, C. Robert	C	T	17	192	6:2
73	REHBERGER, James	N	T	19	210	6:3
74	PRASHAW, Michael	C	T	23	200	6:00
75	CALLAHAN, Robert F.	D	T	22	200	6:00
76	WAHL, R. Allen	C	T	17	210	6:3
77	JOHNSON, George	N	T	19	190	6:2
78	HINTON, Eugene	C	T	17	233	6:2
79	PRATT, William	D	T	21	200	6:1
81	ANDERSEN, John M.	C	E	17	185	6:5
82	GRENKOSKI, Edward	C	E	17	165	6:00
83	HERSHBERGER, Donovan	C	E	17	180	6:1
85	McNEILL, Edward D.	C	E	17	190	6:1
86	BRUNSTING, Louis A., Jr.	C	E	17	175	6:2
87	YOUNGBLOOD, Dennis E.	M	E	20	185	6:00
88	RABBERS, Norman	M	E	20	165	6:00
89	KUICK, Stanley J.	C	E	17	195	6:4

C indicates Civilian; N indicates Navy; M indicates Marines
D indicates Dischargee; (*) indicates Letterman from 1944

Michigan's Team Statistics for 1945

	Mich.	Opp.
Total First Downs	136	112
Rushing	96	81
Passing	31	24
Penalties	9	7
Net Yards Gained — Rushing	1832	1652
Number of Rushes	468	452
Net Yards Gained — Passing	983	807
*Total Yards Gained	3165	2869
Forward Passes Attempted	128	124
Forward Passes Completed	51	54
Forward Passes Intercepted By	17	12
Yards Interceptions Returned	106	61
Number of Punts	60	65
Punts Returned By	33	26
Punts Blocked By	3	1
Yards Punts Returned	246	239
Number of Kick-offs	36	25
Kick-offs Returned By	18	41
Yards Kick-offs Returned	577	392
Fumbles By	16	20
Opponents' Fumbles Recovered By	5	5
Number of Penalties	40	47
Yards Penalized	410	395
Total Points Scored	187	99

*Includes rushing, passing and penalty gains.

The 1945 Football Record

27	MICHIGAN	Great Lakes	2
7	MICHIGAN	Indiana	13
40	MICHIGAN	Michigan State	0
20	MICHIGAN	Northwestern	7
7	MICHIGAN	Army	28
19	MICHIGAN	Illinois	0
26	MICHIGAN	Minnesota	0
7	MICHIGAN	Navy	33
27	MICHIGAN	Purdue	13
7	MICHIGAN	Ohio State	3
187			**99**

OLD TIME POWER

GREAT LAKES (2)		MICHIGAN (27)
Baker	L. E.	McNeill
Stall	L. T.	G. Johnson
Foley	L. G.	Tomasi
Wilkins	C.	Watts
Bland	R. G.	Lintol
Kane	R. T.	Hinton
O'Connor	R. E.	Hershberger
Terlep	Q. B.	Ponsetto
Sullivan	L. H.	Teninga
Aschenbrenner	R. H.	Bentz
Motley	F. B.	Dworsky

SCORING.

GREAT LAKES	2	0	0	0—2
MICHIGAN	14	0	13	13—27

Touchdowns: Michigan—McNeill (2), Teninga, Yerges. Points after touchdown: Michigan — Ponsetto (2), Callahan, place kicks. Safety: Michigan—Ponsetto.

SUBSTITUTES.

GREAT LAKES—Ends: Jesko, Jones, Grant, Bailey. Tackles: Wendt, Widset, Sinofsky. Guards: Lamoure, Harvey. Centers: Adair, Alban. caBks: Ottele, Salatore, Parker, Byler, Bye, Chandler, Deere, Nadherny and McClerry. MICHIGAN — Ends: Grenkoski, Brunsting, Swanson, Youngblood. Tackles: Prashaw, Callahan, C. Johnson, Pratt. Guards: Wilkins, Soboleski, Freihofer, Smith, Weyers, Nakamura. Centers: Kavanaugh, Momsen, Anderson. Backs: Yerges, Doty, Hunter, Weisenburger, Coleman, Fonde, Elliott, Foltz, Dworsky, Chiames, Ott and Mueller.

Michigan . . 40
Mich. State . 0

MICHIGAN STATE	Position	MICHIGAN
Barbas	L E	Hershberger
Goldsmith	L T	G. Johnson
Black	L G	Smith
Sullivan	C	Watts
Lamssies	R G	Wilkins
Eshbaugh	R T	Hinton
Massuch	R E	McNeill
Siler	Q	Ponsetto
Ludwig	L H	Teninga
Aronson	R H	Fonde
Breslin	F B	Dworsky

Referee—Layden (Notre Dame); Umpire—Krieger (Ohio State); Field Judge—Farrell (Minnesota); Head Linesman—Morrow (River Falls Teachers).

Michigan State	0	0	0	0— 0
Michigan	7	13	7	13—40

Touchdowns: Michigan—Dworsky, Hershberger, Nussbaumer, Teninga (2), Mueller. Conversions—Ponsetto (4).

Substitutions: Michigan—Ends: Renner, Swanson, Youngblood, Grenkoski, Brunsting, Kuick. Tackles: Prashaw, Callahan, Wapl, Johnson, Pratt. Guards: Soboleski, Freihofer, Nakamura. Center: Momsen, Kavanaugh. Quarterback: Yerges, Hutter, Doty. Halfbacks: Weisenburger, Nussbaumer, Elliott, Coleman, Ott, Mueller, Saul. Fullback: Chiames, Foltz. Michigan State—Ends: Ziegler, Huey, Gunerson. Tackles: Strola, Tepton. Guards: Godfrey, Arnson, Dusseau. Center: Vezmar, Wenger. Quarterback: Conti, Hatfield. Halfbacks: Contos, Hendricks, Maskill, Foster, Bogart. Fullback: Jones.

Time of game, two hours and 11 minutes. Official attendance—33.200.

	Mich. State	Michigan
Total first downs	5	16
By rushing	2	14
By passing	2	2
By penalties	1	0
Net yards rushing	37	274
Yards lost	34	23
Number of rushes	32	57
Net yards forwards	48	128
Forwards attempted	14	10
Forwards completed	7	5
Behind lines	4	0
Passing intercepted by	0	2
Yards interceptions returned	0	3
Punts, number	5	3
Average distance	43	49
Returned by	1	4
Blocked by	0	0
Kickoffs, number	2	6
Returned by	6	2
Kickoffs average	47	46
Yard kicks returned	75	127
Punts	0	88
Kickoffs	0	0
Fumbles	3	8
Penalties	7	47
Yards penalized	25	110

500th Wolverine Football Game

Game-Ending Play Astonishes Fans As Hoosiers Win

Michigan-Indiana Story In Figures

TEAM STATISTICS	Mich.	Ind.
First downs	13	14
By rushing	10	11
By passing	3	3
Net yards rushing	183	157
Yards lost	15	24
Forwards attempted	12	15
Completed by	3	6
Intercepted by	1	0
Net yards, forwards	87	120
Total yards gained	270	297
Punts, number of	5	5
Returned by	2	2
Average distance	36	23
Blocked by	1	0
Kickoffs, number of	2	3
Returned by	2	1
Average distance	58	57
Yards kicks returned	63	47
Punts	16	14
Kickoffs	47	23
Fumbles	2	2
Ball lost	0	0
Penalties	3	3
Yards penalized	25	25

	Mich.	Ind.
Touchdowns	1	2
Conversions	1	1

INDIVIDUAL RECORDS
Michigan

	T	G	Lost	Net
Ponsetto	2	4	0	4
Teninga	7	31	2	29
Bentz	2	2	5	-3
Dworsky	7	31	0	31
Nussbaumer	2	7	0	7
Foltz	8	35	0	35
Weisenburger	1	3	0	3
Fonde	6	40	0	40
Coleman	1	1	0	1
Elliott	8	36	0	36

Indiana

	T	G	Lost	Net
Raimondi	4	14	0	14
Taliaferro	19	98	9	89
Lysohir	7	23	0	23
Adams	1	0	3	-3
Sebek	0	15	0	15
Graomes	7	25	0	25
Miller	3	13	8	5

By Dave Tefft

Well, it looks like that revenge and Indiana business will have to wait another year.

While the Hoosiers today were boasting their second successive win over Michigan, a 13-7 effort, about all Fritz Crisler's crew could do was begin thinking about Michigan State here next Saturday between moments of answering questions about the astonishing play that ended Saturday's contest against Indiana.

To reverse chronological order it might be as well to get that last play out of the way first and then consider the ball game. The play came in the last 50 seconds of the tilt with Michigan in possession of the ball, after a great drive from the Wolverine eight, on Indiana's four-yard line. Three downs had been exhausted.

Crisler then sent in a substitute. That move brought forth much logical criticism since it meant a five-yard penalty against Michigan for too many time-outs. Then came the shocker. At fourth down and nine to go, trailing by six points, Michigan went into a place-kick formation with Jack Weisenburger holding and Bob Nussbaumer, who doesn't kick anyway, back. While the crowd of 24,500 persons "oh-ed and ah-ed" the ball was snapped to Weisenburger who still had a knee to ground. That technically ended the play but Weisenburger flicked the pigskin to Nussbaumer who tried to sneak down the short side close to the sideline but got exactly nowhere.

That play admittedly was called by Crisler, over considerable argument. Crisler also admitted after the game that he pulled a 'boner.'

85,000 SEE MICHIGAN OVERPOWER GOPHERS

Bierman's Men Fade in Final

Wolverines Close With Three Markers

By BOB MURPHY

ANN ARBOR, Nov. 3—Using everything but such unconventional football equipment as brass knuckles and blackjacks, Michigan's Wolverines and the Golden Gophers from Minnesota put on a slashing, gouging, dynamiting fray here today before a colorful crowd of 85,000 fans.

At the end of the autumn afternoon the men of Michigan led, 26-0, and seemed to be spoiling for some Gopher to suggest the score shouldn't have been larger.

All-America Backs Tally on Long Runs

STATISTICS

	ARMY	MICH.
First downs	16	11
Yards rushing	380	143
Yards passing	72	95
Passes attempted	9	17
Passes completed	5	8
Passes intercepted	1	2
Punting average	39	35
Opp. fumbles recovered	2	2
Yards penalized	41	15

BY WILFRID SMITH
Free Press-Chicago Tribune Wire

NEW YORK—Michigan sent its football boys on a man's errand Saturday afternoon in Yankee Stadium but before Army's national champions proved their experience and skill with a 28-7 victory, 70,000 fans thrilled to the Wolverines' battle against the Cadets' power and speed.

In winning their twelfth consecutive game and third of the season, Army had to go all out all the way.

Army's stars were its 1944 All-America players, Glenn Davis and Felix (Doc) Blanchard.

Blanchard ran off Michigan's left tackle 69 yards for Army's second touchdown in the second quarter and Davis sprinted 70 yards around Michigan's left flank for the final score in the last period.

* * *

WITHOUT either one of these superb backs, Michigan might well have contained the Cadet attack and turned the football trick of the year. It was no parade for Army, and the score belies the ferocity of the competition.

Michigan, trailing 14 to 0, at the start of the second half, took the kickoff and drove 75 yards to the Cadet goal. In possession again, the Wolverines were checked on a march for the tying touchdown by a fumble.

From this point there was no doubt of the final result, but Michigan's youngsters fought to the end. They made six first downs in the last 15 minutes to one for Army.

Michigan Wolverines Stage Rally To Defeat Buckeyes 7-3 Before 85,132

STATISTICS.

	OhioS.	Mich.
First downs	11	11
Yds. gained rush.	143	105
Forwards attempted	6	12
Forwards completed.	1	4
Yds. forwards	35	63
Forwards intercepted	2	2
Yds. gained run-back		
intercepted passes	28	5
Punting avg. scrim.	31.8	29.7
Total yds. kicks ret.	33	56
Oppo. fumbles recov.	1	2
Yds. lost penalties	14	15

Ann Arbor, Mich., Nov. 24.—(AP.) — Michigan's dogged Wolverines, coming from behind for a capacity crowd of 85,132 fans, punched over a fourth period touchdown for a 7 to 3 victory over Ohio State here today after tackle Max Schnitaker had put the Buckeyes ahead, 3 to 0, with a 17-yard field goal in the third period.

The hard-earned victory gave Michigan second place in the final big ten standings behind unbeaten Indiana, which won the title by pasting Purdue, 26 to 0.

Less than seven minutes of play remained when Michigan sent halfback Henry Fonde diving through Ohio State's right tackle from the one-yard line for the winning touchdown. The 18-years-old Navy trainee had made the opportunity himself by going 25 yards with a pass from Pete Elliott.

OHIO STATE		MICHIGAN
Crane	le	McNeill
Thomas	lt	Johnson
McGinnis	lg	Tomasi
Lininger	c	Momsen
Amling	rg	Wilkins
Schnittker	rt	Hinton
Watson	re	Renner
Priday	qb	Yerges
Daugherty	lh	Elliott
Fisher	rh	Nussbaumer
Cline	fb	Dworsky
Michigan	0 0 0 7—7
Ohio State	0 0 3 0—3

Ohio State scoring: Field goal, Schnittker (placement). Michigan scoring: Touchdown, Fonde (sub for Nussbaumer; point after touchdown, Chiames (sub for Dworsky).

Substitutes—Ohio State—end, Steinberg; tackles, Dixon, Maltinsky, Fazio, Winters; guards, Roe, Redd; center, O'Dea; backs, Ehrsam, Krall, Verdova, Sarringhaus, Gandee. Michigan—ends, Ford, Hershberger; tackles, Derleth, Prashaw, Callahan; guards, Lintol, Soboleski, Smith; center, Teninga; backs, Muelder, Bentz, Fonde, Chiames.

MICHIGAN		NAVY
Hershberger	L. E.	Duden
Johnson	L. T.	Kiser
Tomasi	L. G.	Carrington
Watts	C.	R. Scott
Wilkins	R. G.	Deramee
Hinton	R. T.	Coppedge
Renner	R. E.	Dramlett
Dworsky	Q. B.	Smith
Teninga	L. H.	C. Scott
Nussbaumer	R. H.	Minisi
Weisenb'g'r	F. B.	Jenkins
Navy	6 7 14 6—33
Michigan	0 7 0 0— 7

Touchdowns—Bramlett, C. Scott, Weisenburger, Minisi, Bartos, Williams.

Points after touchdown — Currence (3); Chiames.

U-M Gridders Place Sixth In Last Poll

Army Listed In First Spot With Only One Dissenting Vote Cast

1-Army (115)	1,159
2-Alabama (1)	942
3-Navy	941
4-Indiana	720
5-Oklahoma Aggies	651
6-Michigan	378
7-St. Mary's	320
8-Pennsylvania	218
9-Notre Dame	217
10-Texas	163

MICHIGAN INDIVIDUAL STATISTICS FOR 1945

	RUSHING			PASSING				RECEIVING		PUNT RET.		PUNTING		SCORING				
	Tries	Net Gain	Ave.	Att'd	Comp.	Had Int.	Gain	C'ght	Gain	No.	Yds.	No.	Ave.	TD	CA	CM	FG	TP
Teninga	66	317	4.80	27	10	2	124	3	78	5	78	2	32	5	0	0	0	30
Elliott	89	316	4.80	52	19	6	393	1	15	3	78	3	35.7	2	0	0	0	12
Nussbaumer	50	172	3.44	1	1	0	2	3	117	6	53	0	0	3	0	0	0	18
Wiesenburger	64	264	4.12	5	2	0	66	0	0	1	21	38	35.3	2	0	0	0	12
Fonde	51	192	3.86	1	0	0	0	11	148	6	63	0	0	3	0	0	0	18
Dworsky	67	289	4.31	1	1	0	9	0	0	0	0	0	0	3	0	0	0	18
Ponsetto	12	13	1.08	28	14	0	282	0	0	0	0	0	0	0	12	10	0	10
Yerges	7	24	2.42	11	5	1	87	0	0	0	0	2	0	0	0	0	0	12
Foltz	31	116	3.74	0	0	0	0	0	0	0	0	0	0	0	0	0	0	0
Coleman	11	61	5.54	0	0	0	0	1	28	1	7	0	0	0	0	0	0	0
Bentz	7	9	1.28	0	0	0	0	2	15	0	0	1	0	1	0	0	0	6
Chiames	9	39	4.33	0	0	0	0	0	0	0	0	0	0	3	2	2	0	2
Muelder	3	11	3.66	2	0	0	0	0	0	0	0	0	0	1	0	0	0	6
McNeill	0	0	0.00	0	0	0	0	7	179	0	0	0	0	2	0	0	0	12
Hershberger	0	0	0.00	0	0	0	0	6	112	0	0	0	0	1	0	0	0	6
Callahon	0	0	0.00	0	0	0	0	0	0	0	0	0	0	4	2	0	0	2
Ford	1	2	0.50	0	0	0	0	2	59	0	0	0	0	1	0	0	0	6
Renner	1	9	0.11	0	0	0	0	8	116	0	0	0	0	3	0	0	0	18
Robinson	0	0	0.00	2	2	0	56	0	0	0	0	0	0	0	0	0	0	0
Hutter	1	8	8.00	0	0	0	0	0	0	0	0	0	0	0	0	0	0	0

MICHIGAN FOOTBALL ROSTER—1946

No.	Name	Service Status	Pos.	Hgt.	Wgt.	Age	Home Town	H. S. Coach
14	WISNIEWSKI, IRVIN C........	D	E	6:3	190	21	Toledo (Woodward)	E. Vonderberg
15	KUICK, DONALD O.	C	HB	6:1	173	17	Midland, Mich.	Stan Kuick
16	WHITE, PAUL C.**	D	HB	6:0	180	24	River Rouge, Mich.	Frank Weeber
18	CHUBB, RALPH L.*	D	HB	5:11	182	22	Ann Arbor	Laverne Taylor
19	FONDE, HENRY*	D	HB	5:8	162	22	Knoxville, Tenn.	S. W. Jones
24	YERGES, HOWARD**	D	QB	5:10	172	21	Pt. Pleasant, W. Va.	George Hood
25	VERNIER, ROBERT W.*	D	QB	5:11	183	22	Toledo, O.	Harry Rice
33	YEDINAK, MICHAEL	D	FB	5:7	182	22	Flint, Mich.	
38	WIESE, ROBERT L.***	D	FB	6:2	193	23	Jamestown, N.D.	Ernest Gates
39	DWORSKY, DANIEL *	C	FB	6:0	198	18	Sioux Falls, S.D.	Howard Wood
40	CULLIGAN, WILLIAM L.* ..	D	HB	5:10	158	22	Detroit (Cooley)	Herbert Smith
41	DERRICOTTE, GENE*	D	HB	5:11	172	20	Defiance, O.	
42	ELLIOTT, CHALMERS W.	D	HB	5:10	170	21	Bloomington, Ill.	Howard Saar
44	TRAUGOTT, ALAN S.	D	HB	5:11	180	22	Indianapolis (Shortridge)	R. Nipper
45	ELLIOTT, PETER R.*	D	HB	6:0	186	19	Bloomington, Ill.	Howard Saar
46	ROBINSON, DONALD W.** ..	D	QB	5:11	168	24	Detroit (Cooley)	Herbert Smith
48	WEISENBURGER, JACK E.** ..	C	FB	6:1	178	18	Muskegon Hts, Mich.	Oscar Johnson
49	CHAPPUIS, ROBERT*	C	HB	6:0	183	23	Toledo (DeVilbiss)	Harry Rice
53	KAMPE, KURT	D	G	5:9	181	23	Detroit (Cooley)	Herb Smith
55	WHITE, J. T.	D	C	6:2	189	26	River Rouge, Mich.	Frank Weeber
56	BRIESKE, JAMES F.	D	C	6:2	201	23	Harbor Beach, Mich.	Truman Pippel
57	CALLAHAN, ROBERT F.	D	C	5:11	198	23	St. Louis (Beaumont)	B. Franklin
58	WATTS, HAROLD M.***	D	C	5:10	173	21	Birmingham, Mich.	
59	KEELER, WALTER	D	C	6:00	190	21	Bay City, Mich.	
60	PHILLIPS, ELMER	D	G	5:10	185	20	Big Bend, W. Va.	
61	HENEVELD, LLOYD A.	D	G	6:0	180	22	Holland, Mich.	M. R. MacKay
62	SICKELS, QUENTIN*	D	G	6:2	194	19	Benton Harbor, Mich.	Carlton Roels
63	FREIHOFER, WALTER	D	G	6:0	180	21	Indianapolis (Shortridge)	R. Nipper
64	KRAEGER, GEORGE W.*	D	G	6:1	178	23	Indianapolis (Shortridge)	R. Nipper
65	TOMASI, DOMINICK T.*	C	G	5:8	180	18	Flint, Mich. (Northern)	Guy Huston
66	LINTOL, JOHN F.	D	G	6:1	185	21	Detroit (Holy Redeemer)	D. Wolfe
67	BURG, GEORGE*	D	G	5:11	187	21	Winnetka, Ill.	F. Achenbach
68	WILKINS, F. STUART*	D	G	5:10	183	18	Canton, O. (Lincoln)	J. Farrell
69	SOBOLESKI, JOSEPH R.	D	G	6:0	187	20	Grand Rapids (Cath. Cent.)	Killoran
72	PRITULA, WILLIAM*	D	T	5:11	189	24	Pittsburgh (Chadsey)	F. C. Groves
73	DERLETH, ROBERT**	D	T	6:3	206	24	Marquette, Mich. (Barage)	
74	BALLOU, ROBERT	D	T	6:0	192	21	Springfield, Vt.	Conn. W. Fowler
75	HILKENE, BRUCE L.**	D	T	6:2	193	22	Indianapolis (Shortridge)	R. Nipper
76	BROWN, RICHARD S.	D	T	6:1	203	21	Detroit (Redford)	F. J. Hojnacki
77	CRANE, FENWICK J.	D	T	6:3	195	23	Pleasant Ridge, Mich.	
78	CARPENTER, JACK C.	D	T	6:0	226	23	Kansas City, Mo.	E. A. Markey
79	HONIGSBAUM, FRANK	D	T	6:3	198	19	Troy, N.Y.	E. Picken
80	RENNER, ARTHUR W. (C)***	D	E	6:2	172	22	Sturgis, Mich.	Robt. Miller
81	MANN, ROBERT	D	E	5:10	167	21	New Bern, N.C.	
82	BAHLOW, EDWARD H.	D	E	6:2	196	26	Springfield, Ill.	Bill Roellig
83	HERSHBERGER, DONOVAN P.*	D	E	6:1	183	19	Freeport, Ill.	W. Fulkerson
85	McNEILL EDWARD D.*	C	E	6:1	185	18	Toledo (Libbey)	Bill Orwig
87	FORD, LEONARD G.*	C	E	6:4	207	20	Washington, D.C.	T. McIntyre
88	MADAR, ELMER F.	D	E	5:10	172	25	Detroit (Northeastern)	C. Jenks
89	RIFENBURG, RICHARD*	D	E	6:3	191	20	Saginaw (Arthur Hill)	Bill Kelly

C—Civilian, D—Dischargee, *—Letters

The Official Watch for Timing Today's Game is Longine—The World's Most Honored Watch

Sept. 28

Wolves' Last Period Buries Indiana, 21-0

Oct. 5

IOWA		MICHIGAN
Phillips	L. E.	Ford
Kay	L.T.	Hilrene
Benda	L.G.	Tomasi
Laster	C.	J. T. White
Day	R.G.	Sickels
Cozad	R. T.	Carpenter
Guzowski	R.E.	Renner
King	Q.B.	Yerges
Sullivan	L.H.	Derricotte
Smith	R.H.	P. White
Hoerner	F.B.	Wei'burger

Iowa	0	0	7	0—7
Michigan	7	7	0	0—14

Iowa scoring: Touchdown—Herb Shoener (sub for Guzowski). Point after touchdown—Sullivan (placement).

Michigan scoring: Touchdowns — Chappuis 2. Points after touchdown—Brieske (sub for J. T. White) 2 (placements).

The 1946 Western Conference Standings

	W	L	T	Pct.	Pts.	Opp. Pts.
Illinois	6	1	0	.857	133	58
MICHIGAN	5	1	1	.785*	165	46
Indiana	4	2	0	.667	76	67
Iowa	3	3	0	.500	63	44
Minnesota	3	4	0	.429	51	108
Northwestern	2	3	1	.416*	89	87
Ohio State	2	3	1	.416*	112	144
Wisconsin	2	5	0	.286	78	137
Purdue	0	5	1	.083	68	144

* By Conference agreement ties are counted as a half-game won and a half game lost in computing percentage standings.

Rose Bowl Tie-Up Officially Accepted

Michigan's 1946 Football Record

MICHIGAN	21	Indiana	0
MICHIGAN	14	Iowa	7
MICHIGAN	13	Army	20
MICHIGAN	14	Northwestern	14
MICHIGAN	9	Illinois	13
MICHIGAN	21	Minnesota	0
MICHIGAN	55	Michigan State	7
MICHIGAN	28	Wisconsin	6
MICHIGAN	58	Ohio State	6
	233		73

Yost, Michigan's Football Pioneer, Dies

Succumbs After Prolonged Illness

Achieved National Fame as Coach Of 1901-1905 'Point-A-Minute' Teams

By JACK MARTIN

Fielding Harris (Hurry Up) Yost died yesterday afternoon at his Ann Arbor home.

The man who has done more than anyone else to put the University of Michigan on the athletic map passed away suddenly after an acute gall-bladder attack.

Although he had undergone several illnesses during the past few years and only recently returned from a Battle Creek hospital to his home, his death came as a shock to all his relatives. He had been active around his house as late as Monday. No arrangements have been made as yet, but the funeral will probably be Friday.

"Mr. Michigan" is survived by his wife, Mrs. Eunice Yost, his son, Fielding, Jr., two brothers and a sister. One brother, Ellis, lives in Mt. Pleasant, while the other, Nicholas, resides in Fairview, W. Va. His sister, Mrs. Charles Berry, lives in Morgantown, W.Va.

The man who was to become a guiding spirit of American football was born 75 years ago in Fairview, W.Va. He received his high school education at Fairmont. During his boyhood, Yost was called upon to act as the local marshal for his hometown coal community, a good background for the rugged gridiron days to come.

Reprinted with permission from the **Michigan Daily**

The name of Fielding Yost has been revered throughout the sports world for half a century. To Wolverine followers, especially, he is a traditional, a familiar, and a well-loved figure. His 'point-a-minute' elevens in the early 1900's first established Michigan's football reputation. As athletic director Yost's personal efforts brought into being the greater part of the University's present outstanding athletic plant.

OCT. 12

'Army Day'

	Mich.	Army
Total first downs	12	12
By rushing	7	5
By passing	5	6
By penalties	0	1
Net yards rushing	141	152
Yards lost	4	49
No. of rushes	43	42
Net yards forwards	95	211
Forwards attempted	17	15
Forwards completed	8	12
Behind line	0	0
Passes intercepted by	0	3
Yds. intercptns retd	0	18
Punts, number	8	5
Average distance	45	33.3
Returned by	4	7
Blocked by	0	0
Kickoffs, number	2	5
Returned by	5	2
Kickoffs, average	46.5	53.4
Yds. kicks ret'd	114	96
Punts	28	57
Kickoffs	86	39
Fumbles	0	3
Balls lost	0	2
Penalties	4	2
Yards penalized	50	10

Blanchard powers over for an Army touchdown.

OCT. 19

NWESTERN		MICHIGAN
Gorski	L. E.	McNeill
Ivy	L. T.	Hilkene
Difrancesca	L. G.	Tomasi
Sarkisian	C.	J. T. White
Hirsch	R. G.	Kraeger
Sawle	R. T.	Pritula
Wiltgen	R. E.	Madar
Burson	Q. B.	Yerges
Asch'brenner	L. H.	Derricotte
Schwall	R. H.	P. White
Everist	F. B.	Wiese

Michigan	7	0	0	7—11
Northwestern	0	14	0	0—11

Touchdowns: C. Elliott 2, Schwall, Murakowski. **Points after** touchdown: Brieske 2, Schwall 2.

OCT. 26

Fumbles
'M'-Illini Statistics

	Michigan	Illinois
Total first downs	18	9
By rushing	14	6
By passing	4	1
By penalties	0	2
Net yards rushing	190	112
Yards lost	30	14
Net yards forwards	142	39
Forwards attempted	21	6
Forwards completed	11	1
Passes intercepted by	0	2
Number punts	4	7
Average distance	30.5	31.4
Fumbles	12	1
Ball lost	1	1
Penalties	4	1
Yards penalized	30	8

NOV. 2

Rolling Again

MICHIGAN		MINNESOTA
McNeill	L. E.	Hein
Hilkene	L. T.	Widseth
Tomasi	L. G.	Olsonoski
White	C.	Tonnemaker
Sickels	R. G.	Nomellini
Pritula	R. T.	Carroll
Madar	R. E.	Gagne
Weis'burger	Q. B.	Sandberg
Derricotte	L. H.	Faunce
Chubb	R. H.	Heffelfinger
Dworsky	F. B.	Elliott

Michigan	0	7	7	7—21
Minnesota	0	0	0	0— 0

Michigan scoring: Touchdowns—C. Elliott (sub for P. White 2. Mann (sub for Ford).

Points after touchdowns — Brieske (sub for J. White) 3 (placements).

OSU Slaughtered, 58-6, in Lost Cause

Nov. 9

77,134 See Chappuis Show Way

8 Different Players Score for Wolverines

STATISTICS
	MICHIGAN	STATE
First downs	23	8
Yards rushing	293	42
Yards passing	207	165
Passes attempted	21	11
Passes completed	9	7
Passes intercepted	1	0
Punting average	43.5	39.8
Opp. fumbles recovered	3	1
Yards penalized	40	30

MICHIGAN (55)   MICH. STATE (7)
Mann   LE   Sobczak
Hilkene   LT   Zito
Tomasi   LG   LeClair
J. White   C   McCarra
Sickels   RG   Conner
Pritula   RT   Baldwin
Madar   RE   Balge
P. Elliott   QB   Gilpin
Chappuis   LH   Waldron
C. Elliott   RH   Chandnois
Wiesenburger FB   Waters
Michigan   14 11 13 11—55
Michigan State   0   0   7   0— 7

Michigan scoring: Touchdowns — Chappuis, P. Elliott, Derricotte, Madar, P. White, Robinson, Weisenburger, Momsen. Points after touchdowns—Brieske 6 (placement), Ford (pass).

Michigan State scoring: Touchdown — Waters. Point after touchdown—Mazza (placement).

Michigan's Team Statistics for 1946
	Mich.	Opp.
Total First Downs	148	110
Rushing	97	57
Passing	40	31
Penalties	2	4
Net Yards Gained—Rushing	1844	1028
Number of Rushes	428	330
Net Yards Gained—Passing	1322	875
*Total Yards Gained	3166	1903
Forward Passes Attempted	151	116
Forward Passes Completed	63	51
Forward Passes Intercepted By	22	22
Yards Interceptions Returned	348	235
Number of Punts	43	58
Punts Returned By	40	18
Punts Blocked By	1	0
Yards Punts Returned	465	147
Number of Kick-offs	35	33
Kick-offs Returned By	24	37
Yards Kick-offs Returned	777	822
Fumbles By	25	21
Opponents Fumbles Recovered By	17	7
Number of Penalties	31	21
Yards Penalized	314	155
Total Points Scored	233	73

*Includes rushing, passing and penalty gains.

COLUMBUS, O., Nov. 23—Coach Fritz Crisler in the dressing room declared his Wolverines had played their greatest game of the season, including Army, but he added that he did not mean "to imply that we can necessarily beat Army." He elbowed his way around the locker room, grabbing his players by the hand and congratulating them.

* * *

Michigan captured second place in the conference but captured first in the attendance totals. Today's Ohio crowd, 78,387, was tops for the Buckeyes, and it boosted Michigan's over-all total to 651,387, an all time record.

MICHIGAN (58)   OHIO STATE (6)
Mann   LE   Souder
Hilkene   LT   Amlin
Tomasi   LG   Gaud
White   C   Adam
Kreager   RG   Dea
Carpenter   RT   Csu
Madar   RE   Cran
Yerges   QB   Spence
Derricotte   LH   Jame
Weisenberger RH   Verdov
Wiese   FB   Whisle
Michigan   7 20 14 17—58
Ohio State   0   0   0   6— 6

Michigan scoring: Touchdowns — Fonde (sub for C. Elliott) 2, Mann (sub for McNeill) 2, Chappuis, P. White (sub for C. Elliott), Rifenberg (sub for McNeill), Culligan (sub for Chappuis). Points after touchdowns—Brieske (sub for Hilkene) 7. Field goal—Brieske (sub for Hilkene).
Ohio scoring: Touchdown — Swinhart (sub for James).

STATISTICS
	MICHIGAN	OHIO S.
First downs	22	4
Yards rushing	209	47
Yards passing	300	78
Passes attempted	29	18
Passes completed	16	4
Passes intercepted	5	2
Punting average	30	43
Opp. fumbles recovered	2	1
Yards penalized	35	10

MICHIGAN INDIVIDUAL STATISTICS FOR 1946

	RUSHING			PASSING				RECEIVING		PUNT RET.		PUNTING		SCORING				
	Tries	Net Gain	Ave.	Att'd	Comp.	Had Int.	Gain	C'ght	Gain	No.	Yds.	No.	Ave.	TD	CA	CM	FG	TP
Chappuis	116	501	4.31	92	52	7	734	2	49	9	89	3	34.5	4	0	0	0	24
C. Elliott	30	153	5.10	6	4	0	77	3	59	2	14	0	0	4	0	0	0	24
Derricotte	42	167	3.97	33	11	6	233	1	9	15	209	7	41	2	0	0	0	12
Wiese	70	241	3.44	1	0	0	0	2	15	0	0	16	40	1	0	0	0	6
Weisenburger	45	175	3.88	1	0	0	0	0	0	0	0	10	37.5	1	0	0	0	6
P. White	32	80	2.50	2	1	0	21	7	169	3	32	0	0	5	0	0	0	30
Dworsky	28	100	3.57	0	0	0	0	1	5	0	0	0	0	1	0	0	0	6
Culligan	12	53	4.41	6	1	1	40	0	0	0	0	0	0	2	0	0	0	12
Mann	9	114	12.76	0	0	0	0	14	285	0	0	0	0	5	0	0	0	30
Fonde	13	42	3.23	0	0	0	0	4	41	4	17	0	0	3	0	0	0	18
Ford	6	78	13	1	0	0	0	11	203	0	0	0	0	2	1	1	0	13
P. Elliott	4	10	2.50	3	1	1	17	1	27	0	0	0	0	1	0	0	0	6
Brieske	0	0	0	0	0	0	0	0	0	0	0	0	0	0	32	29	1	32
Robinson	9	21	2.33	16	7	2	148	0	0	0	0	0	0	1	0	0	0	6
Madar	2	44	22	0	0	0	0	7	80	0	0	0	0	1	0	0	0	6
Yerges	4	0	0	11	4	1	52	10	129	0	0	0	0	2	0	0	0	12
Rifenburg	4	17	4.25	0	0	0	0	3	48	0	0	0	0	1	0	0	0	6
Hilkene	0	0	0	0	0	0	0	0	0	0	0	0	0	0	(Safety)			2
McNeill	0	0	0	0	0	0	0	3	46	0	0	0	0	0	0	0	0	0
Renner	0	0	0	0	0	0	0	6	43	0	0	0	0	0	0	0	0	0
Chubb	12	29	2.41	0	0	0	0	2	2	0	0	0	0	0	0	0	0	0

1947 ROSTER

No.	Name	Pos.	Ht.	Wt.	Age	Class
1	Wistert, Alvin	T	6:3	218	31	Jr.
5	Kuick, Donald O.	HB	6:2	178	19	So.
8	Elliott, Chalmers W.*	HB	5:10	158	22	Jr.
9	Fonde, Henry *		5:8	158	23	Sr.
3	Ghindia, John	QB	5:10	175	22	So.
4	Yerges, Howard ***	QB	5:9	178	22	Sr.
5	Kiesel, George *	QB	5:11	185	24	Sr.
3	Peterson, Thomas R.*	FB	5:9	183	21	So.
38	Kempthorn, Richard J.	FB	6:0	190	19	So.
40	Lentz, Charles W., Jr.	HB	5:9	160	20	So.
41	Derricotte, Gene A.**	HB	5:11	175	21	Jr.
42	Teninga, Walter H.	QB	5:10	186	20	So.
45	Elliott, Peter R.**	QB	6:0	187	20	Jr.
48	Weisenburger, Jack E.***	FB	6:1	178	20	Sr.
49	Chappuis, Robert R.**	HB	6:0	184	24	Sr.
55	White, John T.*	C	6:3	185	27	Sr.
56	Brieske, James F.**	C	6:2	195	24	Sr.
59	Dworsky, Daniel **	C	6:0	208	20	Jr.
60	Ballou, Robert *	G	6:2	200	22	Jr.
61	Heneveld, Lloyd A.	G	6:0	190	23	So.
62	Sickels, Quentin B.**	G	6:2	195	19	Jr.
63	Kampe, Kurt	G	5:8	180	24	Sr.
64	Strauss, Richard	G	6:1	204	19	So.
65	Tomasi, Dominic **	G	5:10	180	19	Jr.
67	McClelland, Donald B.	G	6:0	190	19	So.
68	Wilkins, Stuart F.**	G	5:10	186	19	Jr.
69	Soboleski, Joseph R.**	G	5:11	193	21	Sr.
72	Pritula, William **	T	5:11	180	25	Sr.
75	Hilkene, Bruce L. (C) ***	T	6:2	192	21	Sr.
76	Kohl, Ralph A.	T	6:2	223	22	So.
77	Johnson, George W.*	T	6:1	188	21	Jr.
78	Dendrinos, Peter C.	T	6:2	210	21	So.
81	Mann, Robert **	E	5:11	167	22	Sr.
82	Hollway, Robert C.	E	6:3	195	19	So.
83	Hershberger, Donovan P.*	E	6:1	185	20	Jr.
84	Wisniewski, Irvin C.	E	6:3	194	21	Jr.
85	McNeill, Edward D.**	E	6:1	190	19	Jr.
87	Ford, Leonard **	E	6:5	208	21	Jr.
89	Rifenburg, Richard **	E	6:3	195	21	So.

* Lettermen

Michigan's 1947 Record

MICHIGAN	55	Michigan State	0
MICHIGAN	49	Stanford	13
MICHIGAN	69	Pittsburgh	0
MICHIGAN	49	Northwestern	21
MICHIGAN	13	Minnesota	6
MICHIGAN	14	Illinois	7
MICHIGAN	35	Indiana	0
MICHIGAN	40	Wisconsin	6
MICHIGAN	21	Ohio State	0
MICHIGAN	345		53

ROSE BOWL GAME

MICHIGAN	49	Southern California	0

Bob Chappuis Hits Pay Dirt For Three Wolverine Scores

By Mill Marsh

All the nice things that had been said and printed about this year's Michigan football team came true in the Wolverine stadium Saturday afternoon as Coach Fritz Crisler's team crushed Biggie Munn's Spartans from Michigan State, 55 to 0.

This week it is Stanford that will face one of the most versatile Michigan teams ever fielded. Stanford lost its opener to Idaho 19-16. There is every reason to believe that Michigan will roll over Stanford in the same manner as it did Michigan State.

Stanford is a big team but it is doubtful if the giants from the Pacific coast can cope with Michigan's speed.

It was Michigan's speed, perhaps more than anything else that enabled the Wolverines to roll for eight touchdowns on offense and keep the Spartans from crossing midfield until late in the game.

Bob Chappuis, the Big Nine's leading offensive star last season, took up where he left off as he spearheaded the Wolverines to victory with three touchdowns. Other touchdowns were made by Jack Weisenburger, "Bump" Elliott, Lenny Ford, Dan Dworsky and Dick Kempthorn.

Reprinted with permission from the **Ann Arbor News**

The Wolverines gave West Coast gridiron circles a Rose Bowl preview on October 4th as they rolled over an out-manned Stanford delegation, 49-13, in their first meeting since the initial Rose Bowl contest of 1902. A deadly precision attack netted the Wolverines 28 points in the first nine minutes of play as Chappuis, Mann, Bump Elliott, Weisenburger, Rifenburg, and of course Brieske figured in the scoring.

Gene Derricotte spearheaded the second quarter offense as he plunged over twice to make the halftime score 42-0. The brilliant punt returning of El-liott and Derricotte kept the Indians with their backs to the wall as the Michigan defense shone.

Stanford's quick-opening T clicked in the second half as the Indians pushed across two touchdowns to stave a shutout. Wally Tenninga counted for the last Wolverine tally on an aerial to Don Kuick.

Reprinted with permission from The Michiganensian

	M	S
Total first downs	10	13
Total yards gained	460	321
Yards gained, rushing	208	193
Yards gained, passing	252	128
Number of rushes	42	45
Forward passes attempted	17	27
Forward passes completed	8	11
Passes intercepted by	3	4
Number of punts	2	8
Average distance of punts	44.5	33.5
Total yards all kicks returned	136	119
Number of fumbles	3	5
Number of penalties	3	3

Kicker Jim Brieske, "Mr. Automatic," kicks while Gene Derricotte holds.

Oct. 11

Line-ups

Michigan	Pos.	Pittsburg
Ford	LE	Skladan
Wistert	LT	Forsyth
Soboleski	LG	Barkouski
Dworsky	C	Redno
Sickels	RG	Razzan
Dendrinos	RT	Plof
McNeill	RE	McPea
Elliott	QB	Matiel
Derricotte	LH	Ceccon
C. Elliott	RH	Robinson
Kempthorn	FB	DeMatte

Score by periods:
Michigan .....0 20 21 28—6
Pittsburgh ...0 0 0 0—
Touchdowns: Mann (M) 2
Weisenburger (M); C. Elliot
(M); Kuick; Derricotte (M)
Teninga (M) 2; Peterson (M)
Ford. Conversions: Brieski (M
8.

Nov. 15

Qualify for Trip to Rose Bowl

Hail! Hail!

WISCONSIN [6]		MICHIGAN [40]
Rennebohm	L. E.	Mann
Loepfe	L. T.	Hilkene
George	L. G.	Tomasi
Wilson	C.	White
Knauff	R. G.	Wilkins
Otterback	R. T.	Pritula
Zoelle	R. E.	Rifenburg
Wink	Q. B.	Yerges
Girard	L. H.	Chappuis
Self	R. H.	C. Elliott
Bendrick	F. B.	Weisenburger

Wisconsin ....0 6 0 0—6
Michigan ....13 7 6 14—40
Touchdowns—Wisconsin: Embach; Michigan:
Yerges [2], Derricotte, Weisenburger, Rifen-
burg, Peterson.
Points after touchdowns—Michigan: Brieske
[4].
Substitutions: Wisconsin—Ends, Bennett, Ol-
shanski, Hanley, Toepfer; tackles, Elliott, Shea,
Donnellan, Hoehn; guards, Collias, Currier,
Price, Surber, O'Neill; center, Kelly; backs,
Wink, Evans, Embach, Bendrick.
Michigan—Ends, Ford, McNeill, Hershberger,
Wisniewski, Hollway; tackles, Wistert, Kohl,
Johnson, Dendrinos; guards, Sobeleski, Bickels;
centers, Dworsky, Brieske, Erben; backs, P.
Elliott, Derricotte, Kempthorn, Teninga, Kuick,
Kiesel.
Coaches—Harry Stuhldreher, Wisconsin; Fritz
Crisler, Michigan.
Referee — Russell Rupp [Lebanon Valley].
Umpire—Dewitt Gibson [Northwestern]. Field
judge—George Rennix [Minnesota]. Head lines-
man—Cleo Diehl [Northwestern].

Minnesota Scares All

Gophers Amaze Packed Stadium

MICHIGAN	MINNESOTA
55—Mich. State. 0	7—Washington..
49—Stanford ...13	28—Nebraska ...7
69—Pitt 0	37—Northwestern 7
49—N'western ..21	13—Illinois 4
13—Minnesota .. 6	6—Michigan ...13
245	31 91

By WATSON SPOELSTRA

ANN ARBOR, Mich., Oct. 25.—
Mighty Michigan, cast in the role
of a front runner all season
showed the mark of a champion
today by coming from behind to
defeat Minnesota, 13 to 6, in an
epic football game before a sell-
out 85,938 crowd.

Minnesota was magnificent
in defeat. A three or four-
touchdown underdog, the
gigantic Gophers stopped the
Michigan attack for all but two
scant instances. In these inter-
ludes Michigan went 40 yards
by air and 21 yards on the
ground each in one play for
the touchdowns that won the
game.

It was Michigan's fifth victory
and it sent Fritz Crisler's embattled team with an unbeaten
record into the show down Western Conference game at Illinois
next Saturday.

Expensive Sale:

Scalper Pays $106 Fine On $1.20 Profit

Stanley Vetowich, 41, of Dear-
born—who refused an offer of $5
apiece for three tickets to last Saturday's Indiana-Michigan football
game with the muttered remark
that he'd "eat 'em first"—probably
wishes he had.

Instead, he ended up in munici-
pal court and was fined $106.40
after finally reducing his price and
selling the ducats at a measly
profit of 40 cents each—in full view
of two Ann Arbor police detectives
who were posted at the Stadium
gates for the specific purpose of
snaring ticket-scalpers.

The $106 fine—the largest drawn
for such an offense this year—was
imposed by Judge Jay H. Payne,
before whom Vetowich entered a
plea of guilty.

Michigan Closes Unbeaten Season By Beating Ohio 21-0

Elliott Named Big Nine's Most Valuable Gridder

'Bump' Becomes Fourth Michigan Man To Be Chosen for Chicago Tribune Trophy

Crisler of Michigan Is Voted Coach of the Year

Chappuis Second in Vote For '47 Heisman Trophy

'Most Valuable' Award to Lujack

'M'--Notre Dame Get Bowl Bids

CLEVELAND, Oct. 16—(A)— Notre Dame and the University of Michigan tonight were extended bids to the first Great Lakes Bowl game which the Knights of Columbus plan to hold here in December.

A "substantial guarantee" was offered the two schools in telegrams sent to Frank Leahy, Notre Dame mentor, and Herbert O. (Fritz) Crisler, coach of the Wolverines.

Councilman Stephen Suhajcik, president of the committee in charge of the event, declared that "although we have set Dec. 6 as the tentative date for the Great Lakes Bowl game, we could change that date to suit Notre Dame and Michigan."

Proceeds of the Bowl contest will be used for athletic promotion in Cleveland, Suhajcik said.

(Fritz Crisler could not be reached for comment last night. However an unofficial source stated that since the Western Conference (which, of course, includes Michigan) already has post-season commitments with the Pacific Coast Conference, the possibility of such a contest is slight.

1947 AP All-America

Position, Player, College	Age	Hgt	Wgt	Home Town
E Paul Cleary, Southern Calif.	25	6-1	195	Santa Ana, Calif.
T Bob Davis, Georgia Tech	20	6-4	225	Columbus, Ga.
G Steve Suhey, Penn State	25	5-11	210	Cazenovia, N. Y.
C Charles Bednarik, Penn.	22	6-3	220	Bethlehem, Pa.
G William Fischer, Notre Dame	20	6-2	230	Chicago, Ill.
T Richard Harris, Texas	19	6-3	212	Wichita Falls, Tex.
E William Swiacki, Columbia	22	6-2	198	Southbridge, Mass.
B John Lujack, Notre Dame	22	6-0	180	Connellsville, Pa.
B Robert Chappuis, Michigan	24	6-0	184	Toledo, O.
B Ray Evans, Kansas	24	6-1½	191	Kansas City, Kas.
B Doak Walker, So. Methodist	20	5-11	175	Dallas, Tex.

Second And Third Selections

SECOND TEAM	Position	THIRD TEAM
Robert Mann, Michigan	End	Barney Poole, Mississippi
Zyg. Czarobski, Notre Dame	Tackle	John Ferraro, So. California
Leo Nomellini, Minnesota	Guard	Joseph Steffy, Army
Richard Scott, Navy	Center	Jay Rhodemyre, Kentucky
Rod Franz, California	Guard	Mike Dimitro, UCLA
Malachi Mills, VMI	Tackle	George Connor, Notre Dame
Ike Owens, Illinois	End	Lenny Ford, Michigan
Chalmers Elliott, Michigan	Back	Clyde Scott, Arkansas
Charles Conerly, Mississippi	Back	Anthony Minisi, Penn.
Harry Gilmer, Alabama	Back	Bobby Layne, Texas
Charles Justice, N. Carolina	Back	Jack Cloud, William & Mary

MICHIGAN'S 1947 TEAM STATISTICS
(Nine Games of Regular Season)

	MICH.	OPPO.
Total First Downs	154	90
Rushing	103	61
Passing	46	28
Penalties	5	2
Net Yards Gained—Rushing	2149	1159
Number of Rushes	429	371
Net Yards Gained—Passing	1565	764
° Total Yards Gained	3714	1923
Forward Passes Attempted	155	145
Forward Passes Completed	77	61
Forward Passes Intercepted By	26	16
Yards Interceptions Returned	314	101
Number of Punts	34	63
Punts Blocked By	1	0
Yards Punts Returned	738	110
Kick-offs Returned By	11	37
Yards Kick-offs Returned	189	767
Fumbles By	26	34
Opponents Fumbles Recovered By	14	14
Number of Penalties	27	21
Yards Penalized	245	191
Total Points Scored	345	53

° Includes Rushing, Passing, Penalty Gains

	RUSHING			PASSING				RECEIVING		PUNT RET.		PUNTING		SCORING				
	Tries	Net Gain	Ave.	Att'd	Comp.	Had Int.	Gain	C'ght	Gain	No.	Yds.	No.	Ave.	TD	CA	CM	FG	TP
CHAPPUIS	113	419	3.7	86	48	5	976	1	10	8	88	3	42	5	0	0	0	30
ELLIOTT	68	438	6.4	1	0	0	0	16	318	9	155	0	0	9	0	0	0	54
WEISENBURGER	101	682	6.7	6	2	1	35	1	19	1	5	25	33.2	7	0	0	0	42
DERRICOTTE	28	169	6.0	11	6	0	79	1	21	14	347	2	88	5	0	0	0	30
FONDE	25	91	3.6	1	1	0	25	4	74	3	18	0	0	3	0	0	0	18
TENINGA	14	17	1.2	25	11	6	283	2	29	9	112	4	35.1	2	0	0	0	12
PETERSON	35	118	3.3	1	1	0	32	0	0	0	0	1	0	1	0	0	0	6
MANN	15	129	8.6	0	0	0	0	12	302	0	0	0	0	4	0	0	0	24
FORD	6	15	2.5	0	0	0	0	3	111	1	16	0	0	2	0	0	0	12
KUICK	2	7	3.5	0	0	0	0	5	125	1	25	0	0	1	0	0	0	6
KEMPTHORN	11	46	4.1	0	0	0	0	0	0	0	0	0	0	1	0	0	0	6
YERGES	4	−3	−1.5	1	0	0	0	11	117	0	0	0	0	2	0	0	0	12
N. JACKSON	2	−4	−2	0	0	0	0	0	0	1	3	0	0	0	0	0	0	0
LENTZ	3	23	7.6	2	0	1	0	0	0	1	13	0	0	0	0	0	0	0
P. ELLIOTT	1	4	4.0	8	5	1	70	2	45	0	0	0	0	0	0	0	0	0
RIFENBURG	0	0	0	0	0	0	0	6	156	0	0	0	0	0	0	0	0	0
McNEILL	0	0	0	0	0	0	0	3	115	0	0	0	0	0	0	0	0	0
HOLLWAY	0	0	0	0	0	0	0	1	4	0	0	0	0	0	0	0	0	0
WISNIEWSKI	0	0	0	0	0	0	0	4	73	1	5	0	0	0	0	0	0	0
HERSHBERGER	0	0	0	0	0	0	0	5	92	0	0	0	0	0	0	0	0	0
BRIESKE	0	0	0	0	0	0	0	0	0	0	0	0	0	0	50	45	0	45
DWORSKY	0	0	0	0	0	0	0	0	0	0	0	0	0	1	0	0	0	6

Michigan Is Runner-Up In Final Voting

Team	1st Pl. Votes	Pts.
1—Notre Dame	107	1,410
2—Michigan	25	1,289
3—S. Methodist		975
4—Penn State	1	853
5—Texas		757

New Honors Are Heaped on Chappuis

Bob Named Top Player in Rose Bowl

PASADENA, Calif.—Bob Chappuis, Michigan's All - American halfback, won additional honors Friday when he was named the outstanding player of the 1948 Rose Bowl game.

Chappuis' selection was made by the Helms Athletic Foundation after its annual poll. The choice was made just before the Wolverine ace and his teammates departed for the trip home.

MICHIGAN TROUNCES USC 49-0

Wolverines Score 7 Touchdowns

Michigan, the mystifying and mighty football champions of the Big Nine, treated University of Southern California to its season's most humiliating defeat yesterday. 49-0, before 93,000 stunned fans in the 34th annual Rose Bowl game at Pasadena.

Summer temperatures failed to slow Coach Fritz Crisler's flawless ball handlers who led the bewildered Trojans, 21-0, at the half and who closed out the debacle by snowing the Pacific Coast grid champions under three touchdowns in the final period.

CHAPPUIS STARS—

Bob Chappuis, Michigan's All-American halfback, was unhampered by an injured thigh of two days ago as he threw two touchdown passes and scampered into Troy territory all afternoon.

1948 ROSE BOWL STATISTICS

SOUTHERN CALIFORNIA
versus
MICHIGAN

(Played January 1, 1948, at Pasadena, California)

SCORE: Michigan 49   Southern California 0

ATTENDANCE: 93,000

	Michigan	U.S.C.
Total First Downs	21	10
Rushing	13	7
Passing	8	2
Penalties	0	1
Net Yards Gained—Rushing	268	91
Number of Rushes	47	44
Net Yards Gained—Passing	223	42
* Total Yards Gained	501	173
Forward Passes Attempted	25	11
Forward Passes Completed	15	6
Forward Passes Intercepted By	1	1
Yards Interceptions Returned	7	12
Number of Punts	4	8
Punts Returned By	6	1
Punts Blocked By	0	0
Yards Punts Returned	53	4
Number of Kick-offs	7	1
Kick-offs Returned By	1	7
Yards Kick-offs Returned	3	117
Fumbles	2	4
Opponents Fumbles Recovered By	2	1
Number of Penalties	4	1
Yards Penalized	40	10

* Includes Rushing, Passing, Penalty Gains

Four Rose Bowl Records Set, Three Equaled

Michigan's mighty Wolverines set four Rose Bowl game records and equaled three others in handing S.C. its worst drubbing in the school's history. Here they are:

1—Record for net yards gained by a team, 491 yards. The former mark was 320 yards set by Illinois a year ago.

2—Record for most passes completed, 17. The old mark was 16 by Navy against Washington in 1924.

3—Record for point conversions. Set by Jim Brieske, who kicked seven straight. The former record was four, shared by Ernie Smith of Southern California in 1933, Hugh Morrow of Alabama in 1946 and Don Maechtle of Illinois in 1947.

4—Record for individual total offense. Set by Bob Chappuis with 279 yards, with 188 by passing and 91 by rushing. The former mark was 151 yards by Stanford's Bobby Grayson against Columbia in 1934.

5—Tied total point record the great Michigan Wolverines of 1902 set when they walloped Stanford, 49-0, in the inaugural New Year's Day game.

6—Tied record for most conversions in one quarter. Brieske kicked three in the fourth period to equal a mark set by Johnny Campbell of Alabama against Washington State in 1931.

7—Tied record for most points in a Rose Bowl game by a player. Jack Weisenburger scored three times to equal a mark set by Elmer Layden, fullback of Notre Dame's immortal Four Horsemen in the 1925 contest against Stanford.

Michigan Band Stages New Stunts in Bowl

'Crisler Coached' Says Sports Writer

Michigan's colorful marching band, composed of 128 precision drilled members, staged a brilliant array of high stepping antics during the pre-game and halftime ceremonies that never before have been seen in either the Rose Bowl or Michigan Stadiums.

One sportswriter remarked that "The band's maneuvers are so well executed, it looks like they were drilled by Coach Crisler." This is fine tribute to Conductor William D. Revelli, who rejuvenated the marching style with some high-kicking, about-face swivel steps that made the fans sit up and take notice.

Led by flashy drum major, Noah Knepper, the Wolverine music makers struck up several varsity songs before the initial period of play. During halftime ceremonies, they saluted SC with 'Hi Neighbor' and then quickly started forming the different seasons of the year.

First of the drills was a tribute to March as a large shamrock was formed with all the members dancing a jig. Next stunt changed the formation into an umbrella for April showers, then into a bell signifying June weddings.

An exploding firecracker was followed by a large fish while the band played "Three Little Fishes" as its concluding number.

SPECIAL POLL

Wolverines Placed Above Notre Dame By 2 To 1 Margin

Nation's Sport Writers Give Crisler Team 226 Of 357 Votes; Twelve Classify Squads 'Even'

MAN OF YEAR

That's Crisler of Michigan

DES MOINES — (AP) — Fritz Crisler, coach of Michigan's unconquered Rose Bowl team, is football's man of the year for 1947.

Selection of the Wolverine coach by the Football Writers Association of America was announced by Bert McCrane, secretary of the organization.

Crisler polled 75 votes, seven more than Lynn Waldorf, University of California coach.

THE COACHING STAFF
BENNIE G. OOSTERBAAN

Bennie G. Oosterbaan, head coach of the 1948 Wolverines, brings to his new position the accumulated knowledge of a score of years on the Michigan coaching staff. A pupil of the late Fielding H. Yost, he was one of the greatest athletes ever to engage in athletics in the Western Conference. Oosterbaan is the only Wolverine among thirty All-Americans, to win top honors three times in a row — as end in 1925-26-27. His feats are almost legendary, not only on the gridiron, but on the basketball court and the baseball diamond as well. A graduate of the University in 1928, Oosterbaan has been a member of the coaching staff since that time. First as freshman coach, then

as end coach, and finally as backfield mentor and No. 1 assistant to Fr[...] Crisler, he has a wealth of experience to bring to his new position.

A nine-letterman, he entered the University from Muskegon, Mich[...] gan, where he was twice All-American interscholastic basketball cent[...] state record maker in the discus, and one of the best high school foo[...] ball players ever developed in the state. Although he never played baseb[...] in high school, he became one of the stand-out players in the Big T[...] under Ray Fisher. He played first base and led the conference in batting o[...] season. As a basketball player he was chosen on the collegiate All-Americ[...]

Oosterbaan was a great offensive end. He also was a great defensi[...] player. As a coach he has that same idea of balance, the same kind [...] balance that made the Crisler-coached teams some of the best in the lan[...] Michigan teams of the past decade have been offensive-minded, singl[...] wing with a smattering of T-formation. But Michigan teams under Crisl[...] always knew what to do defensively; they have been well balanced — a[...] it is in that school Oosterbaan has reached his greatest heights. He [...] married and has one daughter, Anne.

Michigan Coach To Quit Post, Become Athletic Director

ANN ARBOR, Mich., March 16 —(AP)—H. O. (Fritz) Crisler, who guided Michigan to the apex of football glory, today ended his coaching career.

Even as he announced his retirement from the football bench, the handsome, greying, 49-year-old mentor named as his immediate successor Benny G. Osterbaan, his backfield assistant.

Crisler will remain the university's athletic director.

Resignation Surprise

He startled the sports world with his announcement shortly before midnight, attributing his decision the "exacting demands" of his position as head of the department of physical education, athletic director and head football coach.

The Michigan coach discounted the suddenness of the announcement by saying he had been considering the move "for some time."

His withdrawal as head coach and the appointment of Osterbaan was discussed and approved, he said, by the Michigan athletic board in control just prior to his announcement.

Michigan's 1948 Record		
MICHIGAN	13	Michigan State
MICHIGAN	14	Oregon
MICHIGAN	40	Purdue
MICHIGAN	28	Northwestern
MICHIGAN	27	Minnesota
MICHIGAN	28	Illinois
MICHIGAN	35	Navy
MICHIGAN	54	Indiana
MICHIGAN	13	Ohio State
WESTERN CONFERENCE and NATIONAL CHAMPIONS		

'Bump' Elliott Ruled Ineligible

U-M Loses Star Back on Big Nine Decision; Aigler Denounces Action

BY TOMMY DEVINE
Free Press Staff Writer

CHICAGO—The Big Nine has ruled Chalmers (Bump) Elliott, star University of Michigan football players, ineligible for play during the 1948 grid season.

The decision had a two-fold effect:

1—It dimmed Michigan's hope of retaining its Western Conference football championship.

2—The ruling brought forth a scathing and unprecedented denunciation of his fellow faculty representatives by Prof. Ralph Aigler, of Michigan.

Elliott was the storm center of the bitterest eligibility controversy in Big Nine history. The case last December was taken out of the hands of the three-member eligibility committee and given to the entire faculty group of nine men.

• • •

IT WAS BASED on Elliott's play as a Marine trainee at Purdue during the football season of 1943 and 1944. He played three games during the '43 campaign and six with the Boilermakers the following season.

Bump then was given an overseas assignment and sent to China. He enrolled at Michigan after his discharge from service in 1946, playing that year and throughout the Wolverines' unbeaten campaign of 1947.

UNIVERSITY OF MICHIGAN
1948 ROSTER

No.	Name	Pos.	Ht.	Wt.	Age	Class	Home Town
1	Wistert, Alvin*	T	6:3	218	32	Jr.	Chicago, Ill.
6	Van Summern, Robert	HB	6:0	187	21	Jr.	Kenmore, N.Y.
8	Koceski, Leo R.	HB	5:10	163	19	So.	Canonsburg, Pa.
9	Souchek, Donald O.	HB	5:9	180	21	Jr.	Onekama, Mich.
22	Raymond, Harold	G	5:9	172	22	Sr.	Flint, Mich.
23	Ghindia, John	QB	5:10	175	23	Jr.	Ecorse, Mich.
24	Small, Irwin	QB	5:8	160	20	Jr.	Tarrytown, N.Y.
26	Bartlett, William H.	QB	5:9	180	22	Jr.	Muskegon, Mich.
28	Palmer, Peter	QB	5:11	190	19	So.	Indianapolis, Ind.
30	Dufek, Donald	FB	5:11	185	19	So.	Evanston, Ill.
32	Straffon, Ralph A.	FB	5:8	185	21	So.	Croswell, Mich.
33	Peterson, Tom R.*	FB	5:9	185	22	Jr.	Racine, Wis.
36	Jackson, Norman	FB	6:0	185	20	Jr.	Canton, O.
38	Kempthorn, Dick*	FB	6:0	195	20	Jr.	Canton, O.
40	Lentz, Charles W.	HB	5:9	162	21	Jr.	Toledo, O.
41	Derricotte, Gene A.*	HB	5:11	178	22	Sr.	Defiance, O.
42	Teninga, Walter H.*	HB	5:10	179	21	Jr.	Chicago, Ill.
45	Elliott, Peter*	QB	6:0	188	21	Sr.	Bloomington, Ill.
46	Jennings, William A.	HB	5:9	168	21	Jr.	Negaunee, Mich.
49	Ortmann, Charles H.	HB	6:1	183	19	So.	Milwaukee, Wis.
53	Erben, Robert	C	5:11	190	21	Jr.	Akron, O.
55	Farrer, Richard	C	6:0	195	20	So.	Trenton, O.
56	Kreager, Carl	C	6:4	216	19	So.	Detroit, Mich.
58	Padgen, John	C	5:11	190	19	So.	Calumet City, Ill.
59	Dworsky, Dan*	C	6:0	210	21	Sr.	Sioux Falls, S.D.
60	Powers, John	G	5:9	178	20	So.	Tulsa, Okla.
61	Heneveld, Lloyd*	G	6:0	190	24	Jr.	Holland, Mich.
62	Sickels, Quentin*	G	6:2	195	21	Sr.	Benton Harbor, Mich.
63	Fitch, Alan	G	5:10	185	20	Jr.	Detroit, Mich.
64	Jackson, Allen	G	6:0	180	21	Jr.	Dearborn, Mich.
65	Tomasi, Dominic* (C)	G	5:10	180	20	Sr.	Flint, Mich.
66	Wolter, James R.	G	6:0	195	19	So.	Ypsilanti, Mich.
67	McClelland, Donald B.*	G	6:0	190	20	Jr.	Calumet, Mich.
68	Wilkins, F. Stuart*	G	5:10	186	20	Sr.	Canton, O.
69	Soboleski, Joseph*	T	5:11	195	22	Sr.	Grand Rapids, Mich.
70	Eizonas, John	T	6:1	238	21	Jr.	Detroit, Mich.
72	Wahl, Allen*	T	6:2	210	20	So.	Oak Park, Ill.
73	Atchison, James	T	6:1	195	21	Jr.	Cleveland, O.
74	McWilliams, Richard	T	6:3	248	20	So.	Cleveland, O.
76	Kohl, Ralph A.*	T	6:2	220	23	Sr.	Cleveland, O.
77	Ohlenroth, William	T	6:0	205	19	So.	Chicago, Ill.
78	Dendrinos, Peter C.*	T	6:2	212	22	Jr.	Muskegon Hts., Mich.
79	Hess, John	E	6:2	195	19	So.	Grand Rapids, Mich.
80	Sutherland, George	E	6:0	185	20	So.	Montclair, N.J.
82	Hollway, Robert C.*	E	6:3	200	20	Jr.	Ann Arbor, Mich.
83	Hershberger, Donn*	E	6:1	190	21	Jr.	Freeport, Ill.
84	Wisniewski, Irwin*	E	6:3	193	22	Jr.	Lambertville, Mich.
85	McNeill, Edward*	E	6:1	194	20	Sr.	Toledo, O.
86	Clark, Oswald	E	6:2	200	22	Jr.	Montclair, N.J.
88	Allis, Harry	E	6:0	190	20	So.	Flint, Mich.
89	Rifenburg, Dick*	E	6:3	197	22	Jr.	Saginaw, Mich.

*Lettermen.

ALVIN WISTERT One of three brothers to earn letters at tackle at Michigan. His two brothers, Francis and Albert, 1933 and 1942, respectively, were chosen All-Americans at their positions. Alvin looks like a regular, probably on offense as well as defense, although he teamed with the latter unit last fall. The Rose Bowl game was perhaps his finest performance at Michigan although he turned in some good earlier season games. He's nearing 32, and he probably wouldn't have returned to school if it hadn't been for the GI Bill. Four years overseas with the Marines failed to dampen his zest for football, and despite his age he's a hard-working, fiery type of player. He's 6'3" tall, weighs 218 and very rugged to run into.

OCT. 2

OREGON		MICHIGAN
Garza	LE	Rifenburg
Dotur	LT	Soboleski
Moland	LG	Tomasi
Ecklund	C	Dworsky
Chrobot	RG	Wilkins
Stanton	RT	Kohl
Wilkins	RE	McNeill
Van Brocklin	Q	Elliott
McKay	LH	Ortmann
Bell	RH	Koceski
Sanders	F	Peterson

Score by quarters:

Michigan	0 7 7 0—14
Oregon	0 0 0 0— 0

Touchdowns—Michigan: Rifenburg, Peterson.

M-Oregon Statistics

	Mich.	Oregon
Total first downs	14	16
By rushing	8	7
By passing	6	9
By penalties	0	0
Number of rushes	40	48
Total yards	157	171
Yards lost	25	34
Net yards rushing	132	137
Net yards forwards	217	194
Forwards attempted	16	24
Forwards complete	8	13
Behind line	0	2
Passes intercepted by	1	2
Yards intercepted returned	12	9
Punts, number	5	7
Average distance	39.6	36.1
Returned by	4	4
Blocked by	0	0
Kickoffs average	55.6	60
Yards kicks returned	56	61
Punts	56	14
Kickoffs	0	47

---

oct. 9

MICHIGAN

L. E.—Rifenburg, Clark, Holloway.
L. T.—Soboleski, Wistert.
L. G.—Tomasi, Sickels.
C.—Dworsky, Erben, Farrer.
R. G.—Wilkins, Heneveld, McClelland.
R. T.—Kohl, Wahl, Ohlenroth.
R. E.—McNeill, Allis, W'n'ski, H'berger.
Q.—Elliott, Peterson, Bartlett, Palmer.
L. H.—Ortmann, Lentz.
R. H.—Koceski, Teninga, Vansummern.
F. B.—Peterson, Kempthorn, Staffon.

PURDUE

L. E.—Heck, Jeffery, Bland.
L. T.—O'Reilly, Karras, Considine.
L. G.—Horvath, Murray, Afflis.
C.—Sprang, Carnaghi.
R. G.—Gibron, Scallish, Weizer.
R. T.—Barbolak, Kalapos, Beletic.
R. E.—McCaffrey, Scheer, Sebastian.
Q.—Demoss, Gorgal, Hartman, Punzelt.
L. H.—Szulborski, Schmidt, Gorgal.
R. H.—Adams, Manich, Samsen, Conlin.
F. B.—Agnew, Milito, K'estes, Campfield.

Purdue	0 0 0 0— 0
Michigan	13 6 7 14—40

Touchdowns: Koceski, Peterson 2, Rifenburg, Teninga, Lentz. Points after touchdowns: Allis 4.

400th WIN

No. 19 in Row OCT. 23

MICHIGAN

LE—Rifenburg, Clark, Sutherland.
LT—Soboleski, Wistert.
LG—Tomasi, Heneveld.
C—Erben, Dworsky, Farrer.
RG—Wilkins, Sickels.
RT—Kohl, Wahl.
RE—McNeill, Allis.
Q—Elliott.
LH—Ortmann, Derricotte, Lentz.
RH—Koceski, Teninga.
FB—Peterson, Kempthorn.

MINNESOTA

LE—Grant, Soltau.
LT—Nomellini, Jaszewski.
LG—Fritz, Bailey, Kissell.
C—Beson, Tonnemaker.
RG—Widseth, Lundin.
RT—Ekberg, Carroll, Mealey.
RE—Hein, Bierman, Gagne.
Q—Malosky, Thiele, Anonsen.
LH—Faunce, Bye, Lawrence, Sturdevant, H. Elliott.
RH—McAlister, Warner, Hausken, Gagne, Pullens.
FB—Kuzma, Bill Elliott, Beiersdorf.

MICHIGAN	0 13 7 7—27
MINNESOTA	0 7 7 0—14

Michigan Scoring: Touchdowns, Peterson (2) Rifenburg, Koceski. Points after touchdowns, Allis (sub for McNeils) 3, (placements.)

Minnesota Scoring: Touchdowns, Nomellini, Faunce. Points after touchdowns, Soltau (sub for Grant) 2 (placements.)

Bucks Fall, 13-3; Wolverines Cop 23 Straight Wins

Coach Bennie Oosterbaan Finishes His First Season Unbeaten, Untied

By MURRAY GRANT
(Special to The Daily)

COLUMBUS, O.—Michigan wrote finis to one of the most glorious pages in football annals today as they vanquished a stubborn and, at times, brilliant Ohio State eleven, 13-3 at the Ohio Stadium to capture their second straight Big Nine title.

Playing before 82,754 fans, the second largest crowd ever to see a football game in Columbus, the Wolverines struck with characteristic suddenness for two scores in the second and fourth periods to overcome a 3-0 lead the Buckeyes had built up.

Oosterbaan Is Named As Football Coach Of Year

NEW YORK - (AP) - Bennie G. Oosterbaan, serving his first year as head coach at Michigan, was voted "coach of the year" today in the World Telegram's annual poll.

Oosterbaan, who led the Wolverines through a perfect season to a second straight Western conference championship, succeeds Fritz Crisler, who received the honor last year.

The former All America Michigan end graduated to the head coaching post when Crisler decided to serve exclusively as Michigan athletic director after the successful 1947 season. Oosterbaan had been serving as assistant coach of the Wolverines.

The Michigan mentor received 61 first place votes in the nation wide poll of football coaches.

Lynn Waldorf of California was second with 33 votes and Bob Voights of Northwestern, whom Waldorf meets in the Rose Bowl, was third with 22. Waldorf won the honor in 1935.

AP Poll (1948)
1. MICHIGAN
2. Notre Dame
3. N. Carolina
4. California
5. Oklahoma
6. Army
7. Northwestern
8. Georgia
9. Oregon
10. S.M.U.

Game Statistics Michigan-Ohio

TEAM STATISTICS

	Mich.	O. S.
FIRST DOWNS (Total)	9	11
By rushing	3	9
By passing	4	5
By penalties	2	0
RUSHING (Number of)	36	51
Yards gained	106	164
Yards lost	52	34
Net yards gained, rushing	54	130
FORWARD PASSING		
Number attempted	16	20
Number completed	7	3
Number had intercepted	0	2
Net yds gained, passing	116	73
TOTAL PLAYS		
(Rushes and passes)	52	71
Total net yards gained	170	201
PUNTS (Number)	9	10
Average, yards	42	36.5
Had blocked	0	0
KICK RETURNS		
Punt returns, number	4	4
Punt returns, yards	43	15
Kickoff returns, number	2	3
Kickoff returns, yards	50	49
Interception returns (Number)	2	0
Yards returned	34	0
FUMBLES (Number)	3	3
Ball lost, fumbles	2	1
PENALTIES (number)	1	4
Yards penalized	15	54
FINAL SCORE	13	3
Touchdowns	2	0
Conversions	1	0
Field goals	0	1
Field goals attempted	1	1
Safeties	0	0

Attendance 82,754

SCORE BY PERIODS

Michigan	0	7	0	6	13
Ohio State	3	0	0	0	3

Michigan scoring: Allis, Peterson. Points after touchdown: Allis.
Ohio scoring: Field goal: Hague.

Michigan (28)
Left End—Rifenburg, Clark.
Left Tackle—Soboleski, Wistert.
Left Guard—Tomasi, Heneveld.
Center—Erben, Dworsky.
Right Guard—Wilkins, Sickels.
Right Tackle—Kohl, Wahl.
Right End—McNeill, Allis.
Quarterback—Elliott.
Right Halfback—Koceski, Teninga.
Left Halfback—Ortmann, Derricotte.
Fullback—Peterson, Kempthorn.

Illinois (20)
Left End—Klimek, Maechtle, Smith.
Left Tackle—Button, Prymuski.
Left Guard — Gottfried, Martignago, Cahill.
Center—Vohaska, Levanti, Massrangeli, Seliger.
Right Guard—Elegert, Archer.
Right Tackle—Tate, Brown.
Right End—Valek, Kersulis, Dimit.
Quarterback—Krueger, Gallagher, Stewart.
Right Halfback — Eddleman, Malinski, Patterson, Willis.
Left Halfback—Piazza, Pierce, Lazier.
Fullback—Steger, Schmidt.

Illinois	0	7	6	7	20
Michigan	0	7	14	7	28

Illinois scoring: Touchdowns — Patterson, Klimek, Kreuger. Points after touchdown—Maechtle 2 (placement).
Michigan scoring: Touchdowns—McNeill, Rifenburg, Teninga, Allis. Points after touchdown—Allis 4 (placement).

MICHIGAN
LE — Rifenburg, Clark, Hershberger, Hess, Sutherland.
LT—Soboleski, Wistert, Atchison.
LG—Tomasi, Heneveld, Jackson, Raymond.
C—Erben, Dworsky, Farrar, Kraeger.
RG—Wilkins, Sickels, McClelland, Fitch.
RT—Kohl, Wahl, Ohlenroth.
RE—McNeil, Allis, Wisniewski, Hollway.
QB—Elliott, Bartlett, Palmer, Ghindia, Small.
RHB—Koceski, Teninga, Van Summern, Souchek.
LHB—Ortmann, Derricotte, Lentz.
FB—Peterson, Kempthorn, Dufek, Straffon.

NAVY
LE—Harrison, Carson, Ridderhof.
LT—Renneman, Emerson.
LG—Schiweck, Weir.
C—Lawrence, Parsons.
RG—Hunt, Cooper, Mandeville.
RT—Beeler, J. Hunt.
RE—Ryan, McElroy, Wilson.
QB—Baysinger, Horne, Sinclair.
RHB—Greene, Powers.
LHB—Williams, Earl, Arnold.
FB — McCully, Marquardt, Hawkins, Bannerman.
Officials: Referee—Rupp (Lebanon Valley), umpire—Krieger (Ohio U.), field judge—Larson (Wisconsin), Morrow (River Falls Teachers).
Attendance—85,938.
Score by Quarters:

Navy	0	0	0	0	0
Michigan	7	7	14	7	35

Scoring: Touchdowns—Ortmann, Peterson, Teninga, Rifenburg (2). Points After Touchdown—Allis (4).
Time of Game—2 hours and 18 minutes.

Consensus All-America Table

NAME SCHOOL	United Press	Associated Press	Int. News Service	N. Y. News	Chicago Tribune	N. Y. Sun	Collier's	Look	Sporting News	N.E.A.	Central Press	Totals
ENDS												
Dick Rifenburg, Michigan	1	1	1	1		1		1	1	1	1	9
Leon Hart, Notre Dame	1		1	1	1	1		1	1		1	8
Barney Poole, Mississippi		1	1		1		1					3
Art Weiner, N. Carolina					1		1		1			2
Sam Tamburo, Penn State			1				1					2
George Brodnax, Georgia Tech							1					1
Dale Armstrong, Dartmouth										1		1
TACKLES												
Leo Nomellini, Minnesota	1	1	1	1	1	1	1	1	1	1	1	11
Al Wistert, Michigan	1			1	1		1	1		1		6
Al De Rogatis, Duke					1							1
Paul Lea, Tulane			1									1
Jim Turner, California			1									1
Al Niemi, Washington State			1									1
GUARDS												
Bill Fischer, Notre Dame	1	1	1	1					1	1	1	7
Paul Burris, Oklahoma	1	1		1		1		1			1	6
Bill Healy, Georgia Tech			1	1				1	1	1	1	6
Joe Henry, Army					1	1		1				3
Rod Franz, California		1					1					2
Marty Wendell, Notre Dame					1							1
CENTERS												
Chuck Bednarik, Penn	1	1	1	1	1		1	1	1	1	1	10
Alex Sarkisian, Northwestern					1							2
BACKS												
Doak Walker, Southern Methodist	1	1	1	1	1	1	1	1	1	1	1	11
Jack Jensen, California	1		1	1	1		1	1	1	1	1	9
Charley Justice, North Carolina	1	1	1	1	1		1		1	1	1	9
Emil Sitko, Notre Dame			1		1	1		1	1			4
Clyde Scott, Arkansas			1		1	1	1					3
Jack Mitchell, Oklahoma					1					1		2
Bobby Stuart, Army		1										1
Lou Kusserow, Columbia									1			1
John Rauch, Georgia Tech						1						1
Jack Cloud, William and Mary						1						1
Stan Heath, Nevada	1											1
Pete Elliott, Michigan			1									1
George Taliaferro, Indiana			1									1
Bobby Gage, Clemson			1									1
Norm Van Brocklin, Oregon			1									1
Art Murakowski, Northwestern		1										1

MICHIGAN'S 1948 TEAM STATISTICS
(Nine Games of Regular Season)

	MICH.	OPPO.
Total First Downs	134	100
Rushing	80	46
Passing	45	51
Penalty	9	3
Net Yards Gained—Rushing	1467	789
Number of Rushes	406	373
Net Yards Gained—Passing	1375	1059
Scoring Passes	15	3
*Total Yards Gained	3095	2086
Forward Passes Attempted	186	167
Forward Passes Completed	77	74
Forward Passes Intercepted by	21	7
Yards Interceptions Returned	126	21
Number of Punts	54	67
Punts Blocked by	2	0
Yards Punts Returned	392	138
Kickoffs Returned by	12	45
Yards Kickoffs Returned	207	642
Fumbles by	35	33
Opponents Fumbles Recovered by	18	19
Number of Penalties	26	27
Yards Penalized	281	318
Total Points Scored	252	44

*Includes Rushing Passing, Penalty Gains.

	RUSHING			PASSING				RECEIVING		PUNT RET.		PUNTING		SCORING				
	Tries	Net Gain	Ave.	Att'd	Comp.	Int.	Gain	Cgh't	Gain	No.	Yds.	No.	Ave.	TD	CA	CM	FG	TP
PETERSON	109	330	3.03	9	4	2	118	3	16	0	0	0	0	9	2	1	0	55
KOCESKI	67	257	3.84	2	0	0	0	22	419	5	52	6	35.5	5	0	0	0	30
DERRICOTTE	13	28	2.15	14	6	2	65	0	0	11	79	0	0	0	0	0	0	0
RIFENBURG	15	102	6.80	1	0	0	0	22	508	0	0	0	0	8	0	0	0	48
TENINGA	36	99	2.75	28	12	0	153	2	14	12	139	48	39.8	4	0	0	0	24
ELLIOTT	16	21	1.31	14	7	0	77	5	90	0	0	0	0	0	0	0	0	0
McNEILL	1	1	1.0	0	0	0	0	7	90	1	12	0	0	1	0	0	0	6
ORTMANN	92	237	2.58	87	41	2	856	1	12	10	87	0	0	2	0	0	0	12
LENTZ	12	43	3.58	7	5	0	79	0	0	2	18	0	0	1	0	0	0	6
VAN SUMMERN	13	46	3.54	1	1	0	18	1	12	2	5	0	0	0	0	0	0	0
DUFEK	14	54	3.86	0	0	0	0	0	0	0	0	0	0	1	0	0	0	6
KEMPTHORN	10	47	4.70	1	0	0	0	0	0	0	0	0	0	1	0	0	0	6
STRAFFON	1	-4	4.00	0	0	0	0	0	0	0	0	0	0	0	0	0	0	0
BARTLETT	1	-5	-5.0	0	0	0	0	0	0	0	0	0	0	0	0	0	0	0
JENNINGS	1	-4	-4.0	3	1	0	9	0	0	0	0	0	0	0	0	0	0	0
JACKSON	5	11	2.2	0	0	0	0	0	0	0	0	0	0	1	0	0	0	6
WISNIEWSKI	0	0	0	0	0	0	0	6	57	0	0	0	0	0	0	0	0	0
ALLIS	0	0	0	0	0	0	0	6	141	0	0	0	0	3	35	29	0	47
GHINDIA	0	0	0	0	0	0	0	1	7	0	0	0	0	0	0	0	0	0
SOUCHEK	0	0	0	0	0	0	0	1	9	0	0	0	0	0	0	0	0	0
ERBEN	0	0	0	0	0	0	0	0	0	0	0	1	0	0	0	0	0	0

MICHIGAN FOOTBALL TEAM ROSTER, 1949

No.	Name	Pos.	Hgt.	Wgt.	Class	Age
11	*Wistert, Alvin (C)	T	6:3	223	Sr.	33
15	Wilcox, John	HB	5:8	160	Sr.	21
16	*Van Summern, Robert	HB	5:11	187	Sr.	22
17	Ryan, Prentice	HB	5:8	164	Sr.	22
18	*Koceski, Leo R.	HB	5:10	165	Jr.	20
19	Peterson, Donald	HB	5:10	175	So.	20
23	*Ghindia, John V.	QB	5:10	180	Sr.	24
24	Putich, William	QB	5:9	165	So.	18
25	Burns, Jerry	HB	5:8	155	Sr.	20
26	*Bartlett, William	QB	5:9	180	Sr.	22
28	Palmer, Peter	QB	5:11	190	Jr.	19
30	*Dufek, Donald	FB	5:11	185	Jr.	20
32	Straffon, Ralph	FB	5:8	188	Jr.	22
33	*Peterson, Thomas	FB	5:9	185	Sr.	23
36	Jackson, Norman	FB	6:0	185	Sr.	21
38	*Kempthorn, Richard	FB	6:0	195	Sr.	21
39	Contino, Amato	FB	5:9	190	So.	20
40	*Lentz, Charles W.	HB	5:10	165	Sr.	20
41	Osterman, Russell	HB	5:11	170	Jr.	21
42	*Teninga, Walter H.	HB	5:10	180	Sr.	22
46	Ely, Roger	QB	5:11	175	So.	18
48	Eldridge, James E.	HB	5:10	175	So.	18
49	*Ortmann, Charles	HB	6:1	190	Jr.	20
50	Robinson, Otho	G	5:9	220	Jr.	23
51	Beel, Joseph G.	G	5:8	190	So.	18
52	Flynn, Leo M.	T	6:2	188	Jr.	21
53	*Erben, Robert F.	C	5:11	190	Sr.	22
54	Smale, Harry	C	6:0	195	Jr.	20
55	*Farrer, Richard D.	C	6:0	195	Jr.	21
56	Kreager, Carl A.	C	6:4	220	Jr.	20
57	Sauls, Reginald	C	5:10	184	Jr.	22
58	Padjen, John	G	5:9	180	Jr.	22
59	*Momsen, Anton (1945)	C	6:2	205	Jr.	21
60	Powers, John E.	G	5:10	176	Jr.	21
61	*Heneveld, Lloyd A.	G	6:0	190	Sr.	25
62	Smith, Gilbert	G	5:11	180	So.	19
63	Fitch, Alan	G	5:10	185	Jr.	20
64	*Jackson, Allen M.	G	6:0	185	Jr.	21
65	Stapp, William	G	5:9	178	Jr.	21
66	Wolter, James	G	6:0	190	So.	22
67	*McClelland, Donald	G	6:0	190	Sr.	21
68	Kinyon, Peter	G	5:11	190	So.	19
69	McWilliams, Richard	T	6:3	248	Jr.	21
70	Dunne, Arthur L.	T	6:4	211	So.	19
71	Tandjourian, Rostom	T	6:0	180	Jr.	21
72	*Wahl, Robert A.	T	6:2	212	Jr.	21
73	*Atchison, James L.	T	6:1	195	Jr.	22
75	Stribe, Ralph	T	6:0	198	So.	20
76	Johnson, Thomas	T	6:2	225	So.	18
77	*Ohlenroth, William	T	6:1	205	Jr.	20
78	*Hinton, Gene (1946)	T	6:2	225	So.	21
79	Hess, John H.	T	6:2	195	Jr.	20
80	Sutherland, George	E	6:0	185	Jr.	21
81	Dingman, Robert	E	6:1	185	So.	18
82	*Hollway, Robert C.	E	6:3	200	Sr.	21
83	Popp, Leslie	E	6:1	180	Jr.	20
84	*Wisniewski, Irvin	E	6:3	195	Sr.	23
85	Kelsey, Thomas	E	6:2	190	Sr.	21
86	*Clark, Oswald V.	E	6:1	200	Sr.	23
87	Skala, James	E	6:2	190	So.	18
88	*Allis, Harry D.	E	6:0	190	Jr.	21
89	Grenkoski, Edward	E	6:0	180	Jr.	20
90	Pickard, Fred	E	6:0	185	So.	20
91	Ray, David	E	5:11	178	So.	18
96	Cerecke, Charles	G	5:11	190	Jr.	19

*—Lettermen

Sept. 24 — Michigan 7, Michigan Sta...
Oct. 1 — Michigan 27, Stanford 7
Oct. 8 — Army 21, Michigan 7
Oct. 15 — Northwestern 21, Michigan...
Oct. 22 — Michigan 14, Minnesota 7
Oct. 29 — Michigan 13, Illinois 0
Nov. 5 — Michigan 20, Purdue 12
Nov. 12 — Michigan 20, Indiana 7
Nov. 19 — Michigan 7, Ohio State 7
Totals — Michigan 135, All Opponents...

Close Call

STATISTICS

	MICH.	MICH. S
First downs	12	
Yards rushing	89	9...
Yards passing	115	8...
Passes attempted	18	1...
Passes completed	8	...
Passes intercepted by	4	...
Punting average	38.9	3...
Opp. fumbles rec.	1	...
Yards penalized	15	16...

MICHIGAN (7)

LEFT ENDS—Allis, Clark.
LEFT TACKLES—Wistert, Johnson.
LEFT GUARDS—Heneveld, Jackson.
CENTERS—Erben, Momsen.
RIGHT GUARDS—McClelland, Wolte...
RIGHT TACKLES—Wahl, Athison.
RIGHT ENDS—Wisniewski, Holloway.
QUARTERBACKS — Bartlett, Putic...
Ghindia.
LEFT HALFBACKS—Ortmann, Tening...
RIGHT HALFBACKS — Koceski, Va...
Summern.
FULLBACKS—Kempthorn, Dufek, Pete...
son.

MICHIGAN STATE (3)

LEFT ENDS—Gilman, R. Carey.
LEFT TACKLES — Esbaugh, Colema...
Stevens.
LEFT GUARDS—Bagdon, Yocca.
CENTERS—Wenger, Gasser, Stein, Lum...
den.
RIGHT GUARDS—Mason, Tobin, W...
liams.
RIGHT TACKLES—Fusi, Cappaert, N...
stie.
RIGHT ENDS — Minarik, W. Care...
Dibble.
QUARTERBACKS — Ciolek, Glick, ...
Smith.
LEFT HALFBACKS — Grandelin...
Thomas, H. Smith, B. Crane.
RIGHT HALFBACKS—Chandnois, Spe...
gel, Poloncak.
FULLBACKS — Waters, Blenkhorn, ...
Crane.

Score by periods:

Michigan	0	7	0	0—
Michigan State	3	0	0	0—

Touchdown: Wisniewski. Field Goa...
G. Smith. Point after touchdown: Allis.

Take 25th Straight

PALO ALTO, Cal., Oct. 1...
(AP)—Mighty Michigan steam-
rollered over a willing but outclassed Stanford football team
today by a 27-7 count.

A crowd of 88,000 fans, the
largest of the season here, saw
the Wolverines' wingback attack pulverize Stanford's defense for three touchdowns in
the third quarter, after being
held to a 7-0 lead at half time.

Michigan, undefeated since October, 1946, when Illinois turned
the trick, racked up its 25th consecutive victory since then.

25 Game Streak Blasted by Army

Wolverine Passing Offense Snuffed Out by 'Tragic' Injury to Ortmann

By PRES HOLMES
(Sports Co-Editor)

It had to end sometime.

Michigan's still-mighty Wolverines went down to defeat at the hands of a relentless Army team yesterday, 21-7, to clip The String at 25 victories in a row. The Cadets win stretched their undefeated streak to 14 games.

*　*　*　*

THE SPIRITED WOLVERINES received the opening kick off and looked for all the world as if they were going to march up and down the field at will, as Leo Koceski took the kick and raced to the Michigan 45 before he was stopped to start things off.

On the first play from scrimmage Charlie Ortmann threw a long pass which was knocked down out of the waiting hands of end Harry Allis by two Army defenders. The next play was one that will be talked about whenever armchair quarterbacks gather to figue out why Michigan lost.

Ortmann, the Wolverines' ace passer who set the Western Conference pasing record last season, was kicked in the head and suffered a slight concussion. He was carried off the field on a stretcher and taken to Health Service. X-Rays showed negative results but he remained there overnight for observation.

*　*　*

WITHOUT a passer who could consistently hit his target, on the long passes in particular, Michigan had to rely almost solely on its ground game, which was superb, but just not enough.

The Wolverines outgained the Cadets on the ground, grinding out a net of 187 yards to 171 for Army. It's the forward passing statistics which all but explain why the Wolverines couldn't sustain more than one touchdown drive.

Michigan passers threw the ball 23 times and completed only three—two in the first half, one in the last—for a total of 16 yards.

MICHIGAN'S SURGE BEATS MINNESOTA

ANN ARBOR, Mich., Oct. 22—Halfback Chuck Ortman led a rejuvenated Michigan football team to a smashing 14-7 win over powerful Minnesota today.

The tow-headed star from Milwaukee almost single handed blasted possible national championship hopes of the unbeaten Minnesota squad. The golden gophers had been favored to take Michigan, the Big Ten title and go to the Rose Bowl.

Ortmann passed with a rare accuracy and ran with a shiftiness that bewildered the Minnesota defenses. He reeled off 115 of Michigan's total ground gain of 126 yards and completed 9 of 17 passes for 92 of Michigan's 102 aerial yards.

The sellout crowd of 97,239 homecoming fans screamed approval.

The kid who suffered a concussion two weeks' ago when army snapped Michigan's 25-game winning streak and played with little spark when Michigan lost to Northwestern last week, kept the Minnesota team on its heels for most of the afternoon.

Bowl-Bound Buckeyes Tie Varsity

The little quirks of fate are the factors which make this game of college football the thrilling thing it is.

Over in Evanston earlier this season reliable Harry Allis sliced a placement a wee bit off line and Northwestern won that game. It was just a one-point victory, but that one point (that one slightly sliced boot) was as important as a million.

In the season's finale three over-anxious Wolverines tensely intent on blocking an Ohio State placement, were off-side. While they were off-side the State kicker missed the placement and Ohio was still behind and Michigan still was headed for a championship which would have been unique in Conference history. A clear-cut title would have made this the first time that a Big Ten school ever had won three such championships in succession in the entire life of the Conference.

But that off-side gave Ohio another chance to tie the game — and that is just what happened. A little thing, but most awfully important.

ILLINOIS
LE—Klimek, Schlosser.
LT—Button, Siegert.
LG—Cahill, Gottfr'd, Lynch, Martignago.
C—Levanti, Vohaska.
RG—Studley, Brown.
RT—Ulrich, Tate, Mueller.
RE—Jones, Kersulis, Valentino.
QB—Steger, Krueger, Vukelich.
LH—Dougiass, Clark, Stevens.
RH—Raklovits, Stewart, Karras.
FB—Ellis, Schmidt.

MICHIGAN
LE—Allis, Clark, Popp.
LT—Johnson, Wistert, McWilliams.
LG—Heneveld, Jackson.
C—Erben, Momsen, Farrer, Sauls.
RG—McClelland, Wolter, Powers.
RT—Atchison, Wahl.
RE—Wisniewski, Holloway.
QB—Ghindia.
LH—Ortmann, Lentz, D. Peterson.
RH—Teninga, Van Sum'rn, T. Peterson.
FB—Dufek, Kempthron.

Score by periods:

Illinois	0	0	0	0—	0
Michigan	0	7	0	6—	13

Touchdown: Allis, T. Peterson. Points after touchdown: Allis.

STATISTICS

	U-M	IND.
First downs	21	6
Yards rushing	202	10
Yards passing	165	120
Passes attempted	25	17
Passes completed	9	9
Passes intercepted by	3	3
Punting average	41.5	34.4
Opp. fumbles recovered	2	1
Yards penalized	40	16

Indiana	0	7	0	0—	7
Michigan	0	7	13	0—	20

Michigan scoring: Touchdowns—Teninga, Van Summern, Don Peterson. Points after touchdown—Allis 2 (placement).

Indiana scoring: Touchdown—Sebek. Point after touchdown—Hinkle (placement).

AP Poll (1949)
1. Notre Dame
2. Oklahoma
3. California
4. Army
5. Rice
6. Ohio State
7. MICHIGAN
8. Minnesota
9. L.S.U.
10. Coll. of Pacific

1949 Look ALL AMERICA

FOOTBALL TEAM

MICHIGAN'S 1949 TEAM STATISTICS
(Nine Games of Regular Season)

	Michigan	Opponents
Total First Downs	135	94
Rushing	98	55
Passing	34	37
Penalty	3	2
Net Yards Gained: Rushing	1607	1048
Passing	854	888
*Total Yards Gained	2769	2257
Number of Rushes	469	406
Forward Passes Attempted	199	148
Forward Passes Completed	66	55
Touchdowns Scored on Forward Passes	5	2
Forwards Intercepted by	25	12
Yards Interceptions Returned	227	66
Number of Punts	62	66
Total Distance of Punts	2355	2166
Average Distance of Punts	38.0	32.8
Punts Blocked by	2	1
Punts Returned by	41	31
Yards Punts Returned	391	236
Kickoffs Returned by	17	31
Yards Kickoffs Returned	386	462
Fumbles by	33	17
Opponents' Fumbles Recovered by	12	16
Penalties	33	31
Yards Penalized	261	258
Total Points Scored	135	85

* Includes Rushing, Passing, Penalty Gains.

1st TEAM

LEON HART	Notre Dame	End
WADE WALKER	Oklahoma	Tack
EDWARD BAGDON	Michigan State	Gua
CLAYTON TONNEMAKER	Minnesota	Cent
RODNEY FRANZ	California	Gua
ROBERT WAHL	Michigan	Tack
JAMES WILLIAMS	Rice	End
ARNOLD GALIFFA	Army	Back
DOAK WALKER	Southern Methodist	Back
ROBERT WILLIAMS	Notre Dame	Back
EMIL SITKO	Notre Dame	Back

2nd TEAM

HARRY GRANT	Minnesota	End
JAMES MARTIN	Notre Dame	Tackle
STANLEY WEST	Oklahoma	Guard
JOE WATSON	Rice	Center
JOHN SCHWEDER	Pennsylvania	Guard
ROBERT GAIN	Kentucky	Tackle
ARTHUR WEINER	North Carolina	End
ROBERT CELERI	California	Back
LYNN CHANDNOIS	Michigan State	Back
EDWARD PRICE	Tulane	Back
RICHARD KEMPTHORN	Michigan	Back

MICHIGAN INDIVIDUAL STATISTICS FOR 1949

	RUSHING			PASSING				RECEIVING		PUNT RET.		PUNTING		SCORING				
	Tries	Net Gain	Ave.	Att'd	Comp.	Int.	Gain	Cgh't	Gain	No.	Yds.	No.	Ave.	TD	CA	CM	FG	TP
ALLIS (e)	9	14	1.55	0	0	0	0	23	338	0	0	0	0	2	20	15	0	27
BARTLETT (qb)	3	-6	-2.00	0	0	0	0	0	0	0	0	0	0	0	0	0	0	0
CLARK (e)	1	1	1.00	0	0	0	0	1	7	0	0	0	0	0	0	0	0	0
DUFEK (fb)	122	392	3.21	4	1	0	15	3	24	0	0	0	0	5	0	0	0	30
GHINDIA (qb)	4	-7	-1.75	7	1	2	11	8	77	0	0	0	0	0	0	0	0	0
HOLLOWAY (e)	0	0	0	0	0	0	0	1	11	0	0	0	0	0	0	0	0	0
KEMPTHORN (fb)	42	157	3.74	4	1	0	12	1	26	0	0	0	0	2	0	0	0	12
KOCESKI (hb)	54	247	4.57	6	1	0	20	5	55	5	34	6	35.0	3	0	0	0	18
LENTZ (hb)	5	5	1.00	8	2	3	19	0	0	17	169	0	0	0	0	0	0	0
ORTMANN (hb)	105	329	3.13	126	45	3	627	0	0	2	28	3	30.0	1	0	0	0	6
PETERSON, D (hb)	29	152	5.24	1	1	0	12	3	56	0	0	0	0	2	0	0	0	12
PETERSON, T. (fb)	29	72	2.48	1	0	0	0	3	43	0	0	0	0	1	0	0	0	6
POPP (e)	2	6	3.00	0	0	0	0	2	17	0	0	0	0	0	0	0	0	0
PUTICH (qb)	2	-11	-5.50	8	5	0	45	0	0	0	0	0	0	0	0	0	0	0
SKALA (e)	0	0	0	0	0	0	1	1	0	0	0	0	0	0	0	0	0	0
STRAFFON (fb)	2	8	4.00	0	0	0	0	0	0	0	0	0	0	0	0	0	0	0
TENINGA (hb)	32	131	4.10	32	8	4	62	1	4	16	160	53	38.8	2	0	0	0	12
VAN SUMMERN (hb)	27	113	4.19	2	1	0	31	3	39	1	0	0	0	1	0	0	0	6
WISNIEWSKI (e)	1	4	4.00	0	0	0	0	11	126	0	0	0	0	1	0	0	0	6
TOTALS	469	1607	3.43	199	66	12	854	66	854	41	391	62	38.0	20	20	15	0	135

Crisler Acts As Chairman Of Meeting

Films Of Games May Be Shown On Sunday Nights Following Grid Contests

By Charles Chamberlain

CHICAGO –(P)– The powerful Big Ten, whose athletic policies usually keynote the trend for the nation's other major conferences, has barred live television of all its 1950 football games.

In the first concerted move to prohibit on-the-spot video, the Big Ten concluded that the entire future of intercollegiate athletics is endangered by TV.

The decision of athletic directors figures to cost the Western conference and its member schools an estimated $500,000 in TV revenue rights that could have been sewed up in 1950.

Some of this, however, may be recovered by the new policy of allowing complete films of games to be televised the following day. Movies of Saturday's contests could not be released before 6 p.m. on Sundays.

NCAA Observes

Significantly, the three-man TV study committee of the NCAA sat in on the Big Ten parley.

Athletic director Tom Hamilton of Pittsburgh, a member of the group which is making a survey to submit to the annual NCAA convention next January at Dallas, said:

"We obtained much information to consider in our recommendation to the NCAA. We will check all sections of the country before the 1950 football season, during it and after it."

At its 1950 convention in New York, the NCAA instructed members to limit commitments to one year.

Fritz Crisler, Michigan athletic director, said that a midwest report made by Ted Payseur of Northwestern showed that TV "did not affect attendance last year" when all Big Ten schools except Iowa, Indiana and Purdue televised.

MICHIGAN VARSITY SQUAD

14	Oldham '53	B	18	5'8"	166
15	Howell '53	B	18	5'8"	160
16	Witherspoon '53	B	18	5'11"	178
17	Stinson '53	B	19	5'9"	175
18	Koceski '51	B	21	5'10"	165
23	Scarr '53	B	18	6'2"	180
24	Putich '52	B	19	5'9"	165
25	Burns '51	B	22	5'8"	155
26	Billings '53	B	18	5'11"	180
27	Topor '53	B	19	6'0"	215
28	Palmer '51	B	20	5'11"	190
30	Dufek '51	B	21	5'11"	185
32	Straffon '51	B	23	5'8"	188
33	Hurley '53	B	18	5'10"	183
35	Rescorla '53	B	19	6'0"	180
36	Jackson, N. '51	B	22	6'0"	185
37	Tinkham '53	B	18	5'10"	170
39	LeClaire '53	B	19	6'0"	190
40	Nulf '53	B	18	5'9"	174
44	Hill '53	B	18	6'0"	172
46	Peterson '52	B	21	5'10"	175
48	Eldridge '52	B	19	5'10"	175
49	Ortmann '51	B	21	6'1"	190
52	Dingman '52	E	19	6'1"	185
53	Melchiori '53	C	19	6'0"	182
54	Smale '51	G	21	6'0"	195
55	Farrer '51	C	22	6'0"	195
56	Kreager '51	C	21	6'4"	220
58	Padjen '51	C	23	5'9"	180
59	Momsen '51	C	22	6'2"	207
60	Powers '51	G	22	5'11"	175
62	Strozewski '53	f	19	6'0"	200
63	Smith '52	G	19	5'11"	190
64	Jackson, A. '51	G	22	6'0"	185
65	Kelsey '52	G	22	6'2"	190
66	Wolter '52	G	23	6'0"	190
67	Timm '53	C	18	5'11"	185
68	Kinyon '52	G	19	5'11"	190
69	McWilliams '51	G	22	6'3"	248
70	Zatkoff '53	B	18	6'2"	208
71	Tandourjian '51	T	22	6'0"	180
72	Wahl '51	f	22	6'3"	217
73	Bartholomew '53	T	18	6'3"	198
74	Rahrig '53	C	18	6'0"	230
75	Stribe '52	G	21	6'0"	198
76	Johnson '52	T	19	6'2"	225
77	Ohlenroth '51	T	21	6'1"	205
78	Hinton '52	T	22	6'2"	225
79	Hess '51	T	20	6'2"	195
80	Osterman '51	B	22	5'11"	170
81	Aartila '53	E	18	6'0"	175
82	Reeme '53	E	21	6'2"	195
83	Popp '51	E	21	6'1"	180
84	Green '53	E	18	6'0"	175
85	Perry '53	E	17	6'0"	178
86	Clark '51	E	24	6'1"	200
87	Skala '52	E	19	6'2"	190
88	Allis '51	E	22	6'0"	190
89	Pickard '52	E	22	5'11"	180
91	Ray '52	E	19	5'11"	178

Michigan's 1950 Record

MICHIGAN	7	Michigan State	14
MICHIGAN	27	Dartmouth	7
MICHIGAN	6	Army	27
MICHIGAN	26	Wisconsin	13
MICHIGAN	7	Minnesota	7
MICHIGAN	0	Illinois	7
MICHIGAN	20	Indiana	7
MICHIGAN	34	Northwestern	23
MICHIGAN	9	Ohio State	3
	136		108

1951 ROSE BOWL GAME

Michigan	14	California	6

WESTERN CONFERENCE AND ROSE BOWL CHAMPIONS

MSC Warns on Painting of U-M Campus

EAST LANSING — Michigan State College students were warned not to retaliate for last week's prank painting of the campus.

The caution came from MSC Police Chief Arthur Brandstatter.

Large blue and gold "M's" and "U of M's" were painted on four locations at MSC.

* * *

"MICHIGAN STATE students are urged to stop this attempt of both student bodies to see which can put the most paint on a campus," Brandstatter declared.

Seven or eight students from the University of Michigan were picked up in early morning on the MSC campus the day before the defacing, but without paint or brushes, the chief said.

No trace of the pranksters has been found.

MICHIGAN		MICHIGAN STATE
Perry	LE	R. Carey
Johnson	LT	Coleman
Powers	LG	Yocca
Padjen	C	Tamburo
Kelsey	RG	Tobin
Wahl	RT	Horrell
Allis	RE	Minarik
Putich	QB	W. Carey
Ortmann	LH	Grandelius
Koceski	RH	Vogt
Dufek	FB	Crane

Score by Periods:
Michigan ...... 0 0 7 0 — 7
Michigan State .. 7 0 0 7 — 14

Officials — Referee: Rollie Barnum (Wisconsin); Umpire: John Wilson (Ohio State); Field Judge: M. J. Delaney (St. Viator); Head Linesman: John R. McPhee (Oberlin); Fifth Official: A. T. Skover (Detroit).

Touchdowns:
Michigan: Pickard.
Michigan State: Grandelius, Crane.
Conversions:
Michigan: Allis.
Michigan State: R. Carey.
Substitutions:

MICHIGAN
Ends: Clark, Pickard, Popp, Timm.
Tackles: Hess, Ohlenroth.
Guards: Kinyon, McWilliams, Jackson.
Centers: Momsen, Farrer.
Quarterbacks: Palmer, Billings.
Halfbacks: Howell, Peterson, McAuliffe.
Fullbacks: Zatkoff.

MICHIGAN STATE
Ends: King, Dibble, Dekker.
Tackles: Strola, Stevens, Kozikowski.
Guards: D. Thomas, Kuh.
Centers: Bolthouse, Weaver.
Quarterback: Jones.
Halfbacks: Pisano, Jesse Thomas, Wilson, Dorow, Benson.
Fullbacks: Timmerman, Panin.
Time of Game: 2 hours, 25 minutes.
Official Attendance: 97,239.

Wolverines Block Punts To Upset Buckeyes, 9-3

Michigan Gains Probable Rose Bowl Shot Without Making First Down on Wind Swept, Snow Blanketed Gridiron at Columbus

Columbus, O., Nov. 25.—(AP)—Michigan's wily Wolverines wrapped up the Western Conference championship and a probable Rose Bowl bid today, blocking two attempted punts to defeat Ohio's favored Buckeyes 9 to 3 on a snow-covered, storm-swept gridiron.

Michigan failed to make a first down in fighting its way into the king row, but turned a pair of breaks into the nine points needed to give it the title.

Playing on a field on which several inches of snow hid the yard lines and made ball-handling treacherous, Michigan was able to gain only 27 yards by rushing. Ohio's vaunted offense was held to 16 yards on the ground and a total of 41 as the Bucks picked up 25 yards on three successful passes in 18 attempts.

A 28-mile wind swept across the Buckeye Stadium and the athletes played like they were wearing boxing gloves as Michigan took advantage of a weird set of circumstances to annex the title and take the favored role for the Rose Bowl invitation.

Michigan had to couple a victory over Ohio State with a Northwestern win over Illinois today, and both came to pass.

Chuck Ortmann, Michigan's brilliant halfback, was the difference in today's climatic contest. Known mostly for his fine passing, Ortmann's nine aerial attempts today failed to find a mark, but his unerring kicking kept the Buckeyes deep in their own territory.

Eleven times in 24 attempts, Ortmann punted out of bounds inside the Ohio 15-yard line, and the Buckeyes failed to fight their way out of the hole at any time.

Bucks Score First

Ohio drew first blood in the opening five minutes, when Vic Janowicz booted a field goal through the swirling snow flakes from 22 yards out.

The break on that one came the first time Michigan had the ball. Joe Campanella, Ohio tackle, blocked Ortmann's attempted quick kick from the six-yard line, and Bob Momsen fell on it there. Janowicz was thrown for a loss and an intentional grounding penalty moved the ball back to the 35, but Janowicz hit Tom Watson with a pass to the 22. From that point the Ohio halfback booted his three-pointer to wind up the Buckeye scoring.

Late in the same period, Ortmann booted out of bounds on Ohio's three, from which point Michigan's Captain, R. Allen Wahl, broke through to block Janowicz' kick, the ball rolling out of the end zone for an automatic safety.

A bit of quick thinking and another blocked kick gave Michigan its winning touchdown in the second period. Ortmann had punted out on Ohio's eight, with less than a minute to go, and Ohio attempted to run line plays to use up the time rather than kick from its own end zone.

Brooms Needed

After each play, however, Michigan called time out. Ohio was forced to kick with 20 seconds to play. Tony Momsen, brother of Ohio's Bob, rushed through the line, blocked Janowicz' kick in the slippery footing, and fell on the ball in the end zone for the score.

Harry Allis booted the extra point and Michigan was on its way to the Big Ten title and the Tournament of Roses.

The last half was a scoreless duel, with Janowicz and Ortmann continuing their punting exchanges.

Ortmann booted 24 times for a 30-yard average, and Janowicz kicked 21 times for a 32-yard average.

Both were phenomenal marks in view of the slippery going and the heavy wind. So heavy was the snow that at times it was impossible to see the players from the pressbox, and when measurements for first downs were necessary brooms were used to sweep off the gridiron to find the yard markers.

Although 82,300 tickets—third largest amount ever sold for an Ohio game—were disposed of before the contest, only 50,503 braved the elements to see the game.

Only two weeks ago Ohio State was rated the No. 1 team in America, but today after successive defeats by Illinois and Michigan, the Buckeyes find themselves as also-ran in their own conference.

Chuck Gandee was Ohio's top ground gainer, with 15 yards in 11 tries, while Ralph Straffon, substitute fullback, topped the Wolverines on the ground with 14 yards in 12 tries.

All of Straffon's running was in the closing periods, when Michigan used ground plays to runout the clock and relied on Ortmann's fine punting to keep the Buckeyes from scoring.

Carl Kreager Today

Carl Kreager is not in the Michigan football record book, but he should be.

Kreager was the center on Michigan's 1950 football team, the one that defeated Ohio State 9-3 in the famed 'Snow Bowl' and went on to a Rose Bowl victory. The triumph in Columbus was achieved amid the worst blizzard in Ohio since 1913. Temperatures were near 10 degrees.

In that game Chuck Ortmann set a Big Ten record that has not been equalled. He punted 24 times and just as remarkable was the snapping ability of Kreager who centered the ball perfectly to Ortmann despite the impossible weather conditions.

Kreager also centered the ball on Michigan's successful extra point conversion. His coach, Bennie Oosterbaan, still considers Kreager's performance one of the finest he has ever seen in college football.

Today, Kreager is president of Builder-Developer, Fine Bilt Homes, Inc., in Okemos. Carl and his wife of 26 years, Donna Marie, have three children; Kathleen 23, Kurt 21, and Brad 15.

FIVE OUT OF FIVE

Wolverines Overcome Bears in Last Quarter

Monday quarterbacks today, Tuesday, were still calling the plays by which California could have but did not beat Michigan, as the Golden Bears bowed to the Wolverines, 14-6, in the Rose Bowl 1951 football classic yesterday with five and one-half minutes left to play before 98,939 happy and disappointed fans—mostly the latter.

Bed-Rock Level

It was Don Dufek, a 185-pound fullback from Chicago, who dropped Coast football to bed-rock by leading Michigan to the fifth straight triumph for the Midwest as the five year pact between the Western and Pacific Coast Conferences came to an end. Oh, he had plenty of help from Chuck Ortmann's passing, Fred Pickard's receiving, Harry Allis' converting and QB Bill Putich's signal calling.

But it was Dufek who packed the ball or caught passes for nine of the 15 plays his team employed in a rousing 80-yard touchdown rally that tied California and gave the Wolverines the lead when Allis converted. And it was still Dufek who in three carries boosted his team's lead to 13-6 with three minutes to go and gave Allis another conversion opportunity to write down the final score: Michigan 14, California 6.

MICHIGAN
LE—Perry, Clark, Pickard
LT—Johnson, Zatkoff, B. Witter.
LG—Kinyon, McWilliams, Strozewski.
C—Kreager, Momsen, Podien.
RG—Wolter, Kelsey, Timmi, Jackson.
RT—Wahl, Ohlenroth, Stribe.
RE—Allis, Green, Popp.
Q—Putich, Palmer, Topor.
LH—Ortmann, Osterman.
RH—Koceski, Bradford, Peterson.
F—Dufek, Straffon.

CALIFORNIA
LE—Fitzgerald, Minahen, Ward, Bartlett.
LT—Karpe, Gulvin.
LG—Laster, Solari, Mering.
C—Harris, Groger, Cadenasso.
RG—Bagley, Richter, Wardlaw, Ely.
RT—Kreuger, Curran.
RE—Cummings, Beal, Parker.
Q—Marinos, Ogden, Van Heuit.
LH—Monachino, Pappa, Robison.
RH—Schabarum, West, LemMon.
F—Olszewski, Baham, Richter.

SCORE BY QUARTERS

Michigan	0	0	0	14—14
California	0	6	0	0—6

Michigan scoring: Touchdowns—Dufek, 2. PAT—Allis, 2.
California scoring: Touchdown—Cummings.

Here They Come—The Rose Bowl Champs, 1951—Back To The Dressing Room

1951 ROSE BOWL CHAMPIONSHIP
January 1, 1951
Pasadena, California

MICHIGAN   14   CALIFORNIA   6

Team Statistics

	Michigan	California
First Downs	17	12
Yards Gained Rushing	145	175
Forward Passes	21	8
Forwards Completed	15	4
Yards Gained by Passes	146	69
Passes Intercepted By	0	2
Number of Punts	2	4
Average Distance of Punts	32.5	35.7
Fumbles	2	2
Opponents Fumbles Recovered	2	2
Penalties	2	6
Yards Lost by Penalty	20	50

Individual Statistics
RUSHING

MICHIGAN	TC	Net Gain	Ave.	CALIFORNIA	TC	Net Gain	Ave.
Dufek, fb	23	113	4.9	Olzewski, fb	16	58	3.6
Koceski, hb	7	19	2.9	Schabarum, hb	15	57	3.8
Ortmann, hb.	5	6	1.2	Monochino, hb	12	47	3.9
Putich, qb	3	4	1.3	Marinos, qb	3	6	2.0
Bradford, hb	1	2	2.0	Robison, hb	2	10	5.0
				Ogden, qb	1	4	4.0

PASSING

	Att.	Co.	In.	Ga.		Att.	Co.	In.	Ga.
Ortmann, hb	19	15	1	146	Marinos, qb	7	4	0	69
Putich, qb	1	0	1	0	Schabarum, hb	1	0	0	0
Dufek, fb	1	0	0	0					

SCORE BY QUARTERS

Michigan	0	0	0	14	14
California	0	6	0	0	6

Michigan Scoring: Touchdowns, Dufek 2. Point After Touchdown, Allis 2.
California Scoring: Touchdown, Cummings.
Crowd: 98,939.

MICHIGAN'S 1950 TEAM STATISTICS
(Nine Games of Regular Season)

	Michigan	Opponen
Total First Downs	112	100
Rushing	68	64
Passing	40	34
Penalty	4	2
Net Yards Gained: Rushing	1265	1278
Passing	980	750
°Total Yards Gained	2539	2326
Number of Rushes	398	439
Forward Passes Attempted	184	151
Forward Passes Completed	73	56
Touchdowns Scored on Forward Passes	4	7
Forwards Intercepted By	16	14
Yards Interceptions Returned	225	140
Number of Punts	79	88
Total Distance of Punts	2578	3326
Average Distance of Punts	32.88	37.8
Punts Blocked By	7	3
Punts Returned By	45	30
Yards Punts Returned	292	200
Kickoffs Returned By	28	28
Yards Kickoffs Returned	394	342
Fumbles By	39	32
Opponents Fumbles Recovered By	16	21
Penalties	25	39
Yards Penalized	298	294
Total Points Scored	136	108

°Includes Rushing, Passing, Penalty Gains.

MICHIGAN'S INDIVIDUAL SCORING FOR 1950

	RUSHING Tries	Net Gain	Ave.	PASSING Att'd	Comp.	Int.	Gain	RECEIVING Cgh't	Gain	PUNT RET. No.	Yds	PUNTING No.	Ave.	SCORING TD	CA	CM	FG	TP
ALLIS (e)	1	23	23.00	0	0	0	0	9	117	0	0	0	0	3	19	14	0	32
BILLINGS (hb)	0	0	0	0	0	0	0	0	0	0	0	3	39.30	0	0	0	0	0
BRADFORD (hb)	25	135	5.40	0	0	0	0	0	0	0	0	0	0	1	0	0	0	6
CLARKE (e)	0	0	0	0	0	0	0	1	10	0	0	0	0	0	0	0	0	0
DUFEK (fb)	151	589	3.90	1	0	0	0	8	140	1	0	0	0	7	0	0	0	42
ELDRIDGE (hb)	3	2	.66	1	1	0	5	0	0	0	0	0	0	0	0	0	0	0
HILL (hb)	5	5	1.00	1	0	0	0	0	0	0	0	0	0	0	0	0	0	0
HOWELL (hb)	12	41	3.41	0	0	0	0	0	0	4	23	0	0	0	0	0	0	0
KOCESKI (hb)	26	94	3.61	0	0	0	0	2	10	9	47	15	36.00	1	0	0	0	6
MOMSEN (c)	0	0	0	0	0	0	0	0	0	1	12	23	31.30	1	0	0	0	6
OLDHAM (hb)	15	46	3.06	0	0	0	0	1	11	5	52	0	0	0	0	0	0	0
ORTMANN (hb)	76	110	1.44	101	41	7	595	2	9	10	73	38	32.00	3	0	0	0	18
PALMER (qb)	2	-4	-2.00	3	2	0	33	0	0	0	0	0	0	0	0	0	0	0
PERRY (e)	3	37	12.33	0	0	0	0	21	345	9	53	0	0	1	0	0	0	6
PETERSON (hb)	23	97	4.21	23	8	0	114	1	-2	1	8	0	0	1	0	0	0	6
PICKARD (e)	0	0	0	0	0	0	0	13	155	0	0	0	0	1	0	0	0	6
PUTICH (qb)	18	-36	-2.00	54	21	7	233	11	142	1	8	0	0	1	0	0	0	6
RESCORLA (fb)	4	-1	-.25	0	0	0	0	0	0	0	0	0	0	0	0	0	0	0
SKALA (e)	0	0	0	0	0	0	0	2	33	0	0	0	0	0	0	0	0	0
STRAFFON (fb)	34	127	3.73	0	0	0	0	2	13	0	0	0	0	1	0	0	0	6
TINKHAM (fb)	0	0	0	0	0	0	0	0	0	0	0	0	0	0	0	0	0	0
WITHERSPOON (hb)	0	0	0	0	0	0	0	0	0	2	8	0	0	0	0	0	0	0
Safety (WAHL) (t)°																		2
TOTALS	398	1,265	3.17	184	73	14	980	73	983	45	292	79	32.88	20	19	14	0	136

° Blocked punt which rolled out of end zone

14—Oldham '53	B	19	5:9	166
15—Howell '53	B	19	5:8	160
16—Witherspoon	B	19	5:11	177
18—Hickey '55	B	18	5:8	160
19—Bradford '53	B	19	5:6	155
23—McDonald '55	B	18	6:0	175
24—Putich '52	B	20	5:9	170
25—Newbrough '55	B	18	5:11	173
26—Billings '53	B	19	5:11	180
27—Topor '53	B	20	6:1	215
28—Zanfagna '54	B	21	5:10	175
30—Baer '55	B	18	5:11	180
33—Hurley '53	B	19	5:10	185
35—Rescorla '53	B	20	6:0	180
37—Tinkham '53	B	19	5:10	170
38—Balzhiser '54	B	18	6:1	185
39—LeClaire '53	B	20	6:0	190
40—Canty '54	B	19	5:11	170
41—Eaddy '55	B	17	5:11	165
44—Kress '54	B	19	5:11	175
46—Peterson '52	B	22	5:11	175
49—Evans '55	B	18	5:11	187
52—Vanderzyde '54	C	19	6:0	190
53—O'Shaughnessy '54	C	19	5:11	190
54—Melchiori '53	C	20	6:0	185
55—Morlock '53	C	20	6:1	200
56—Drake '55	T	25	5:10	225
57—Ludwig '55	C	17	6:2	190
58—Snider '55	C	18	6:0	185
59—Bowers '55	C	18	6:2	238
60—Wagner '55	G	18	5:11	198
61—Dugger '53	G	19	5:10	180
64—Beison '54	G	19	6:0	200
65—Kelsey '52	G	23	6:2	195
66—Wolter '52	G	23	6:0	190
67—Timm '53	G	19	5:11	185
68—Kinyon '52	G	20	5:11	190
69—Williams '54	G	20	5:9	183
70—Zatkoff '53	C-T	19	6:2	210
72—Balog '54	T	19	6:3	210
73—Bartholomew '53	T	19	6:3	200
74—Rahrig '53	C	19	6:0	230
75—Stribe '53	T	21	6:1	200
76—Johnson '52	T	20	6:2	227
77—Walker '55	E	17	5:11	198
78—Pederson '53	T	19	6:2	215
79—Bennett '54	T	19	6:2	195
80—Osterman '52	E	22	5:11	170
81—Topp '54	E	19	6:2	185
82—Dingman '52	E	19	6:0	180
83—Stanford '54	E	19	6:0	170
84—Green '55	E	19	6:0	180
85—Perry '53	E	18	6:0	178
86—Knutson '54	E	18	6:4	210
87—Schlicht '55	B	18	6:4	210
88—Veselenak '55	E	18	6:2	190
89—Pickard '52	E	23	6:2	190
90—Dutter '54	E	19	6:2	190
91—Ray	E	20	5:11	180

Michigan's 1951 Record

MICHIGAN	0	Michigan State	25
MICHIGAN	13	Stanford	23
MICHIGAN	33	Indiana	14
MICHIGAN	21	Iowa	0
MICHIGAN	54	Minnesota	27
MICHIGAN	0	Illinois	7
MICHIGAN	7	Cornell	20
MICHIGAN	0	Northwestern	6
MICHIGAN	7	Ohio State	0
TOTALS	135	TOTALS	122

SEPT. 29

MICHIGAN
LE—Perry, Greene, Stanford, Ray, Schlicht.
LT—Johnson, Bartholomew, Bennett, Wolter, Timm.
LG—Wolter, Timm.
C—O'Shaughnessy, Zatkoff.
RG—Kinyon, Pleson, Dugger.
RT—Stribe, Pederson, Walker, Balog.
RE—Pickard, Osterman, Dingman.
QB—Putich, Billings, Topor.
LH—Oldham, Tinkham, Witherspoon, Eaddy.
RH—Howell, Bradford.
FB—Peterson, Le Claire, Rescorla.

MICHIGAN STATE
LE—R. Carey, Luke, Dekker.
LT—Coleman, Klein.
LG—Garner, Kush, Kuh.
C—Tamburo, Creamer, Hughes.
RG—Kaparal, Seer.
RT—McFaddin, Horrell.
RE—W. Carey, Dohoney.
QB—Dorow, Wilson, Thrower, Jones.
LH—McAuliffe, Bolden, Yewcic, Corless.
RH—Pisano, Fills, Vogt, Duckett.
FB—Benson, Timmerman, Panin, Slonac.

| Michigan | 0 | 0 | 0 | 0—0 |
| Michigan State | 0 | 6 | 13 | 6—25 |

Touchdowns: Dorow, McAuliffe, Bolden and Pisano. Point after touchdown: R. Carey.

Oct. 6

STANFORD		MICHIGAN
Storum	LE	Perry
Vick	LT	Johnson
Manoogian	LG	Kinyon
Garner	C	O'Shaugnessy
Bonetti	RG	Wolter
Broderick	RT	Stribe
McColl	RE	Pickard
Kerkorian	QB	Putich
Hugasian	LH	Tinkam
Crist	RH	Howell
Meyers	FB	Witherspoon

| STANFORD | 0 | 20 | 0 | 3—23 |
| MICHIGAN | 6 | 0 | 7 | 0—13 |

Stanford Scoring: Touchdowns, Kerkorian, Meyers 2; Conversions, Kerkorian 2. Field Goal, Kerkorian.
Michigan Scoring: Touchdowns, Perry, Putich. Conversion, Rescorla.

Oct. 27

In High Gear

STATISTICS

	Michigan	Minnesota
First Downs	16	20
Rushing Yardage	224	125
Passing Yardage	203	249
Passes Attempted	9	33
Passes Completed	8	16
Passes Intercepted	6	0
Punting Average	34	40.5
Fumbles Lost	3	2
Yards Penalized	50	20

| MICHIGAN | 14 | 14 | 14 | 12—54 |
| MINNESOTA | 7 | 13 | 7 | 0—27 |

MICHIGAN: Touchdowns—Bradford (2), Putich, Perry (3), Pickard, Stanford. Conversions—Rescorla 6.
MINNESOTA: Touchdowns — Engel, Lindgren, Swanson. Conversions—Cappelletti 4.

'M' Downs Ohio

ANN ARBOR, Nov. 24 — Michigan's Wolverines won the complete admiration of a gigantic crowd of 95,000 in the big stadium here this afternoon by defeating the favored Buckeyes from Ohio State, 7-0, in the finale of the Western Conference football season.

Michigan's Record Worst in 15 Years

MICHIGAN'S 1951 TEAM STATISTICS

	Michigan	Opponents
Total First Downs	117	139
Rushing	83	88
Passing	29	48
Penalty	5	3
Net Yards Gained: Rushing	1226	1590
Passing	891	1031
Total Yards Gained	2497	2989
Number of Rushes	454	492
Forward Passes Attempted	146	168
Forward Passes Completed	58	76
Touchdowns Scored on Forward Passes	7	4
Forward Passes Intercepted by	21	17
Yards Interceptions Returned	324	84
Number of Punts	73	67
Total Distance of Punts	2510	2298
Average Distance of Punts	34.4	34.2
Punts Blocked By	0	2
Punts Returned By	34	30
Yards Punts Returned	292	205
Kickoffs Returned By	20	29
Yards Kickoffs Returned	367	598
Fumbles By	39	23
Penalties	45	43
Yards Penalized	368	380
Total Points Scored	135	122

Includes Rushing, Passing, Penalty Gains.

All-Time Michigan Team

Left End	Bennie Oosterbaan	1925–26–27
Right End	Edward Frutig	1940
Left Tackle	Albert Wistert	1942
Right Tackle	Mervin Pregulman	1943
Left Guard	Julius Franks	1942
Right Guard	Ed R. Slaughter	1924
Center	Adolph Schulz	1907
Quarterback	Bennie Friedman	1926
Left Halfback	Tom Harmon	1939–40
Right Halfback	William Heston	1903–04
Fullback	Bob Westfall	1941

MICHIGAN'S INDIVIDUAL SCORING FOR 1951

	RUSHING			PASSING				RECEIVING		PUNT RET.		PUNTING		SCORING				
	Tries	Net Gain	Ave.	Att'd	Comp.	Int.	Gain	Cgh't	Gain	No.	Yds	No.	Ave.	TD	CA	CM	FG	TP
BILLINGS (qb)	0	0	0.0	0	0	0	0	0	0	0	0	66	34.4	0	0	0	0	0
BRADFORD (hb)	64	348	5.4	0	0	0	0	2	26	0	0	0	0.0	2	0	0	0	12
EADDY (hb)	9	-27	-.3	3	1	0	23	0	0	0	0	0	0.0	0	0	0	0	0
HOWELL (hb)	17	85	5.0	0	0	0	0	0	0	0	0	0	0.0	0	0	0	0	0
KRESS (hb)	0	0	0.0	1	0	1	0	0	0	0	0	0	0.0	0	0	0	0	0
McDONALD (qb)	2	-35	-17.5	16	7	3	96	0	0	0	0	0	0.0	0	0	0	0	0
OLDHAM (hb)	12	-5	-.4	3	2	0	9	1	1	3	8	0	0.0	0	0	0	0	0
PERRY (e)	15	39	2.6	4	0	0	0	16	395	22	232	0	0.0	5	0	0	0	30
PETERSON (hb)	132	549	4.2	13	6	3	184	5	20	0	0	8	.4	4	0	0	0	24
PICKARD (e)	0	0	0.0	0	0	0	0	11	215	0	0	0	0.0	2	0	0	0	12
PUTICH (qb-hb)	115	268	2.3	77	32	7	380	2	8	11	74	0	0.0	4	0	0	0	24
RESCORLA (fb)	5	7	1.4	0	0	0	0	0	0	0	0	0	0.0	0	20	15	0	15
STANFORD (e)	0	0	0.0	0	0	0	0	2	61	0	0	0	0.0	2	0	0	0	12
TOPOR (qb)	29	-15	-.5	26	9	2	71	9	81	0	0	0	0.0	1	0	0	0	6
WITHERSPOON (hb)	29	35	1.2	0	0	0	0	7	78	0	0	0	0.0	0	0	0	0	0
ZANFAGNA (qb)	0	0	0.0	3	1	1	0	1	4	0	0	0	0.0	0	0	0	0	0

LOWELL PERRY — The versatile Ypsilanti, Mich., athlete, one of the finest ends in college football, presents an interesting paradox. Playing for the institution credited with fathering the famed "platoon system" Perry is one of the top examples of an all-around college player. Gifted with two of the best pass-grabbing hands in football, he also is a dangerous broken field runner, and one of the country's top safety men on defense. Offensively, he is a good blocker, carries the ball well on "end-around" plays. On defense, in addition to his punt catching abilities, he is extremely dangerous against passes, being the type of player who can go all the way in a broken field. Two years ago he picked off 21 passes for 345 yards and one touchdown, and averaged 12 yards on three end-around plays and ran back nine punts for 53 yards. Last year he led Michigan scoring with 30 points on five touchdowns, gaining 395 yards on 16 pass receiving attempts and threw several passes himself. He picked up 63 yards on 15 end-around attempts although closely watched by the defense. An injured ankle handicapped him throughout the latter part of the season but he was always one of the most dangerous players on the field. Perry was named on the coaches all Big Ten as an offensive end, was selected on the Chicago Tribune's All-Midwestern, placed on at least one All-American second team and received honorable mention on the Associated Press All-American selection. Son of an Ypsilanti dentist, Perry was a high school quarterback and a star in basketball and track. A track man at Michigan he earned his letter as a high jumper and broad jumper, was fast enough to run with the 220 and 440 men and would have been a likely candidate for the Olympic team in the hop-step and jump had he decided to concentrate on the event. He is 6' tall, weighs 180 pounds and is 19. Last year he played 351 minutes in all 9 games.

Michigan's 1952 Record

MICHIGAN	13	Michigan State	2
MICHIGAN	7	Stanford	14
MICHIGAN	28	Indiana	13
MICHIGAN	48	Northwestern	14
MICHIGAN	21	Minnesota	0
MICHIGAN	13	Illinois	22
MICHIGAN	49	Cornell	7
MICHIGAN	21	Purdue	10
MICHIGAN	7	Ohio State	27
TOTALS	207	TOTALS	134

Football Ticket Price Increases To $4.00

The price of football tickets for Michigan's home games is going up. Beginning this fall reserved seats will cost $4.00, an increase of forty cents over the 1951 admission.

Athletic Director H. O. Crisler stated that the Board in Control of Intercollegiate Athletics approved the move in order to help meet greatly expanded operational costs of the University's athletic and physical education plant. He pointed out that costs have risen more than 200 per cent in the past twelve years, while ticket prices for football games have increased only 20 per cent.

The Athletic Ticket Department is following the pattern of former years as it prepares for the 1951 Varsity season. Approximately 100,000 information folders and application cards have been mailed to alumni in selected areas and previous attendants at Wolverine games.

Reprinted with permission from the **Michigan Alumnus**

SEPT. 27

1952 MICHIGAN VARSITY SQUAD

No.	Name	Pos.	Age	Ht.	Wt.	Class	Home Town
14	*Oldham, Donald L.	HB	20	5:9	167	Sr.	Indianapolis, Ind.
15	*Howell, Frank	HB	20	5:8	165	Sr.	Muskegon Hts., Mich.
16	Witherspoon, Thomas W.	HB	20	5:11	185	Sr.	Detroit, Mich.
17	Branoff, Tony	HB	18	5:11	180	Fr.	Flint, Mich.
18	Hickey, Edward L.	HB	19	5:8	160	So.	Anaconda, Mont.
19	Knickerbocker, Stanley	HB	19	5:10	165	So.	Chelsea, Mich.
23	*McDonald, Duncan B.	QB	19	6:0	175	So.	Flint, Mich.
26	*Billings, Bill E.	QB	20	5:11	180	Sr.	Flint, Mich.
27	*Topor, Ted P.	QB	20	6:1	212	Sr.	East Chicago, Ind.
28	*ZanFagna, Donald M.	QB	22	5:10	180	Jr.	Providence, R. I.
30	Baer, Fred N.	FB	19	5:11	180	So.	LaGrange, Ill.
32	Gagalis, Peri	FB	20	5:11	190	So.	Ann Arbor, Mich.
33	Hurley, Robert	FB	19	5:10	185	Jr.	Alamosa, Colo.
35	*Rescorla, Russell G.	FB	20	5:11	180	Sr.	Grand Haven, Mich.
37	*Tinkham, David J.	FB	20	5:10	178	Sr.	E. Grand Rapids, Mich.
38	Balzhiser, Richard E.	FB	19	6:1	185	Jr.	Wheaton, Ill.
39	*LeClaire, Laurence E.	FB	21	6:0	190	Sr.	Anaconda, Mont.
42	Kress, Edward S. (Ted)	HB	20	5:11	175	Jr.	Detroit, Mich.
44	Cline, J. Daniel	HB	19	5:10	168	So.	Brockport, N. Y.
49	Evans, Donald K.	HB	19	5:11	185	So.	Chagrin Falls, Ohio
50	Shomsky, Joseph G.	G	19	5:10	190	So.	Flint, Mich.
51	Muellich, George C.	T	18	6:2	185	So.	Bowling Green, Ohio
53	*O'Shaughnessy, Richard E.	C	20	5:11	190	Jr.	Seaford, N. Y.
54	Melchiori, Wayne F.	C	21	6:0	185	Sr.	Stambaugh, Mich.
55	Wine, Raymond L.	C	18	6:2	195	Fr.	Port Huron, Mich.
56	Drake, Donald D.	C	25	5:11	220	So.	Ypsilanti, Mich.
58	VanderZeyde, Raymond	C	20	6:0	190	Jr.	East Chicago, Ind.
61	*Dugger, Donald R.	G	20	5:10	178	Jr.	Charleston, W. Va.
62	*Strozewski, Richard J.	T	21	6:0	200	Sr.	South Bend, Ind.
63	*Matheson, Robert K.	G	20	5:10	190	Sr.	Detroit, Mich.
64	*Beison, Richard A.	G	20	6:0	200	Jr.	East Chicago, Ind.
65	Cachey, Theodore J.	G	20	5:11	185	Jr.	Chicago, Ill.
66	Chomicz, Casimir A.	G	19	6:1	195	Fr.	Detroit, Mich.
67	*Timm, Robert F.	G	20	5:11	185	Sr.	Toledo, Ohio
68	Kamhout, Carl R., Jr.	T	19	6:2	205	So.	Grand Haven, Mich.
69	Williams, Ronald M.	G	21	5:9	185	Jr.	Massilon, Ohio
70	*Zatkoff, Roger	T	20	6:2	210	Sr.	Hamtramck, Mich.
71	Geyer, Herbert Ronald	T	19	6:2	215	So.	Toledo, Ohio
72	*Balog, James T.	T	20	6:3	210	Jr.	Wheaton, Ill.
73	*Bartholomew, Bruce A.	T	20	6:3	200	Jr.	Detroit, Mich.
74	Shields, Kenneth H.	T	18	6:3	215	Fr.	Detroit, Mich.
75	*Stribe, Ralph C., Jr.	T	22	6:1	205	Sr.	Detroit, Mich.
77	Walker, Arthur D.	T	18	5:11	198	So.	South Haven, Mich.
78	*Pederson, Bernhardt L.	T	20	6:2	215	Sr.	Marquette, Mich.
79	*Bennett, Don	T	20	6:2	195	Jr.	Chicago, Ill.
80	Rex, Richard U.	E	19	6:1	185	Fr.	Pearl Beach, Mich.
81	Topp, E. Robert	E	20	6:2	190	Jr.	Kalamazoo, Mich.
82	*Dingman, Robert W.	E	21	6:0	180	Sr.	Saginaw, Mich.
83	*Stanford, Thad C.	E	20	6:2	190	Jr.	Midland, Mich.
84	*Green, Merritt II (Capt.)	E	20	6:0	180	Sr.	Toledo, Ohio
85	*Perry, Lowell P.	E	19	6:0	180	Sr.	Ypsilanti, Mich.
86	*Knutson, Eugene P.	E	19	6:4	210	Jr.	Beloit, Wis.
87	Bowns, Stanley	E	18	6:0	190	Fr.	Flint, Mich.
88	Veselenak, John J.	E	19	6:2	190	So.	Flint, Mich.
89	Bates, James V.	E	19	6:0	195	So.	Farmington, Mich.
90	Dutter, George S.	E	20	6:2	190	Jr.	Fort Wayne, Ind.
92	Ritter, Charles A.	T	19	6:0	210	So.	Cassopolis, Mich.
93	McIntyre, John	T	21	6:0	190	Jr.	Monroe, Mich.
94	Rahrig, Don	G	21	5:11	195	Jr.	Toledo, Ohio
96	Pella, G. Roy	T	20	6:2	205	Sr.	Sudbury, Ont.

*Lettermen

Family Feud

MICHIGAN		MICHIGAN STATE
Perry	L. E.	Duckett
Strozewski	L. T.	Serr
Timm	L. G.	Kush
O'Shaughnessy	C.	Tamburo
Beison	R. G.	Breniff
Stribe	R. T.	Klein
Stanford	R. E.	Dekker
Topor	Q. B.	Yewcic
Kress	L. H.	McAuliffe
Howel	R. H.	Pisano
Baer	F. B.	Panin

Michigan State .... 7 13 7 0—27
Michigan .... 13 0 0 0—13

Touchdowns—Michigan: Kress, Perry; Michigan State: McAuliffe, Bolden [2], Wells. Points after touchdown—Michigan: Rescorla; Michigan State: Slonac [3].

Substitutions—Michigan: Ends, Green, Bates, Dingman, Knutson, Topp; tackles, Zatkoff, Bennett, Balog, Walker; guards, Dugger, Williams, Matheson, Cachey; centers, none; quarter backs, Zanfagna, Billings; half backs, Oldham, Tinkham, Witherspoon, Branhoff; full backs, Rescorla, LeClaire, McDonald. Michigan State—Ends, Bobo, Luke, Dohoney, Quinlan; tackles, Fowler, Frank, Cutler, Hallmark; guards, Bullough, Morgan, Schieswohl, Adams; quarter backs, none; half backs, Wilson, Bolden, Boyd, Corless, Ellis, Vogt, Wells; full backs, Timmerman, Slonac, Lekenta, Benson.

Coaches — Bennie Oosterbaan, Michigan; Clarence [Biggie] Bunn, Mich. State. Referee —George Rennix [Minnesota]. Umpire—Dewitt Gibson [Northwestern]. Field judge—Corby Davis [Indiana]. Head linesman—Archie Morrow [River Falls]. Back judge—Joel Burghalter [Heidelberg].

Balzhiser, Kress Star in Runaway

Ted's 218 Yards Set Big Ten Mark

STATISTICS

	U-M	NW
First downs	19	10
Rushing yardage	415	110
Passing yardage	57	197
Passes attempted	9	18
Passes completed	4	13
Passes intercepted	1	0
Punting average	31.6	31
Fumbles lost	2	2
Yards penalized	58	60

Michigan 11 20 0 11—18
Northwestern 0 0 0 11—11

Michigan scoring: Touchdowns—Kress 2, Green, Witherspoon, Balzhiser, Topor. Conversions—Rescorla 6.

Northwestern scoring: Touchdowns—Collier, C. Hren. Conversions—Kragseth 2.

NOV. 22

MICHIGAN [7]		OHIO STATE [27]
Perry	L. E.	Grimes
Strozewski	L. T.	Guthrie
Timm	L. G.	Takacs
O'Shaughnessy	C.	Krisher
Beison	R. G.	Reichenbach
Pederson	R. T.	Jacoby
Stanford	R. E.	Dugger
Topor	Q. B.	Borton
Kress	L. H.	Bruney
Branoff	R. H.	Watkins
Balzhiser	F. B.	Illay

Michigan 0 0 0 7— 7
Ohio State 0 14 7 6—27

Touchdowns—Michigan: Howell; Ohio State: Joslin, Borton, Grimes.
Points after touchdowns—Michigan: McDonald; Ohio State: Week [3].

Oct. 18 · Oct. 25

Gophers Skunked

MICHIGAN
LE—Perry, Dingman, Green
LT—Strozewski, Zatkoff, Walker
LG—Timm, Williams, Cachey, Vander Zeyde
C—O'Shaughnessy, Melchiori, Wine, Drake
RG—Beison, Dugger, Matheson, Rahrig
RT—Pederson, Balog, Geyer, Bennett
RE—Stanford, Topp, Knutson, Dutter
QB—Topor, McDonald, Billings
LH—Kress, Oldham, Cline, Tinkham, Evans
RH—Howell, Witherspoon, Branoff, Knickerbocker
FB—Balzhiser, Rescorla, LeClaire, Baer

MINNESOTA
LE—McNamara, McElroy, Soltau
LT—Hansen, Almer, Zachary, Canakes, Andrus
LG—Anderson, Kauffmann
C—Prescott, Stamschror, Helgeson
RG—Coates, Lindgren, Heidenreich
RT—Drill, Hagemeister, Holz, Foss
RE—Rutford, French, Kapotas
QB—Swanson, Schmitt, Cappelletti
LH—Giel, Klefsaas, Goode
RH—Meighen, Sullivan
FB—Baumgartner, Holme, Dargis, Wallin

MICHIGAN 7 7 0 7 — 21
MINNESOTA 0 0 0 0 — 0

TOUCHDOWNS
MICHIGAN—Balzhiser (2), Topor
CONVERSIONS
MICHIGAN—Rescorla (3)
Time of Game: 2 Hours, 20 Minutes
Official Attendance: 70,858

Nov. 8

Michigan ....14 7 7 21—49
Cornell .... 0 0 7 0— 7

Touchdowns — Michigan: Perry, Kress, Topor (2), Oldham, Dingman, Topp. Cornell: Whelan.
Points After Touchdown—Michigan: Rescorla (7). Cornell: Van Buren.

Oct. 11

Michigan ....0 7 14 7—28
Indiana ....0 6 0 7—13

Scoring—Touchdowns: Michigan—Topor, Branoff, Perry 2. Indiana—Gedman 2. Conversions: Michigan — Rescorla 1, McDonald 3. Indiana—D'Achile 1.

MICHIGAN'S 1952 TEAM STATISTICS

	Michigan	Opponents
Total First Downs	143	108
Rushing	91	51
Passing	46	51
Penalty	6	6
Net Yards Gained: Rushing	1852	1149
Passing	1246	1232
Total Yards Gained	3098	2381
Number of Rushes	462	375
Forward Passes Attempted	188	219
Forward Passes Completed	93	109
Touchdowns Scored on Forward Passes	11	6
Forward Passes Intercepted by	23	11
Yards Interceptions Returned	222	118
Number of Punts	48	62
Total Distance of Punts	1755	2144
Average Distance of Punts	36.5	34.5
Punts Blocked by	1	2
Punts Returned by	31	28
Yards Punts Returned	172	223
Kickoffs Returned by	24	36
Yards Kickoffs Returned	398	524
Fumbles by	39	32
Penalties	52	51
Yards Penalized	501	503
Total Points Scored	207	134

*Includes Rushing, Passing, Penalty Gains.

MICHIGAN'S INDIVIDUAL SCORING FOR 1952

	RUSHING			PASSING				RECEIVING		PUNT RET.		PUNTING		SCORING				
	Tries	Net Gain	Ave.	Att'd	Comp.	Int.	Gain	Cgh't	Gain	No.	Yds	No.	Ave.	TD	CA	CM	FG	TP
BAER (fb)	17	53	3.1	0	0	0	0	2	-5	0	0	0	0.0	0	0	0	0	0
BALZHISER (fb)	75	327	4.3	7	2	2	25	2	13	0	0	0	0.0	3	0	0	0	18
BILLINGS (qb)	2	29	14.5	0	0	0	0	0	0	0	0	40	36.7	0	0	0	0	0
BRANOFF (hb)	86	342	3.9	4	1	1	24	10	138	5	12	0	0.0	3	0	0	0	18
CLINE (hb)	11	54	4.9	8	3	1	66	0	0	3	18	0	0.0	0	0	0	0	0
DINGMAN (e)	1	12	12.0	0	0	0	0	3	75	0	0	0	0.0	1	0	0	0	6
GREEN (e)	0	0	0.0	0	0	0	0	0	0	0	0	0	0.0	1	0	0	0	6
HOWELL (hb)	46	223	4.8	0	0	0	0	1	1	1	13	0	0.0	2	0	0	0	12
HURLEY (fb)	20	68	3.4	0	0	0	0	2	3	0	0	0	0.0	0	0	0	0	0
KNICKERBOCKER (hb)	1	3	3.0	0	0	0	0	0	0	0	0	0	0.0	0	0	0	0	0
KRESS (hb)	135	623	4.6	85	45	7	559	6	40	0	0	8	29.6	6	0	0	0	36
McDONALD (qb)	2	0	0.0	17	7	2	90	0	0	0	0	0	0.0	0	3	0	0	3
OLDHAM (hb)	15	32	2.1	9	2	2	42	0	0	5	31	0	0.0	1	0	0	0	6
PERRY (e)	5	-4	-.4	0	0	0	0	31	492	11	66	0	0.0	5	0	0	0	30
RESCORLA (fb)	0	0	0.0	0	0	0	0	0	0	0	0	0	0.0	0	31	24	0	24
STANFORD (e)	0	0	0.0	0	0	0	0	12	200	0	0	0	0.0	0	0	0	0	0
TINKHAM (hb)	0	0	0.0	0	0	0	0	0	0	1	6	0	0.0	0	0	0	0	0
TOPOR (qb)	28	36	1.2	58	33	3	441	18	208	0	0	0	0.0	6	0	0	0	36
TOPP (e)	0	0	0.0	0	0	0	0	5	59	0	0	0	0.0	1	0	0	0	6
WITHERSPOON (hb)	14	38	2.7	0	0	0	0	0	0	0	0	0	0.0	1	0	0	0	6

Mr. Crisler Headed It

'Fine for Small Colleges,' Says He

(From AP and UP Dispatches)

ST. PETERSBURG, Jan. 15.— 'We think we'll have a better foot ball game than we ever had, especially among small colleges,' said Herbert O. (Fritz) Crisler, athletic director of the University of Michigan and chairman of the rules committee that killed the two-platoon system in foot ball.

By coincidence, Crisler is the man generally credited with starting the two-platoon system in 1941 when he was Michigan's foot ball coach. The success enjoyed by his Wolverine teams prompted other schools to convert to the mass-substitution method.

With one quick, dramatic blow, the two-platoon system was killed Wednesday by the Football Rules Committee of the National Collegiate Athletic Association.

RESENTMENT GROWS

It was no secret that resentment against the system and its costs, which had forced 50 small colleges to abandon foot ball, was building up to a high pitch among college presidents and administrators.

But the coaches, in a recent poll, had voted 4-1 to keep the system alive, and it was generally believed that if the coaches were to be overridden, it would be gradually and not by such a sudden reversion to the old style of play.

1953 MICHIGAN VARSITY SQUAD

No.	Name	Pos.	Age	Ht.	Wt.	Class	Home Town
12	Wheeler, Jack C.	FB	18	6:0	187	Soph.	Ypsilanti, Mich.
14	Ames, Robert T.	HB	19	5:10	172	Soph.	Algonac, Mich.
15	Corey, George R.	HB	20	5:10	175	Soph.	Baden, Pa.
16	Rentschler, David F.	HB	20	6:0	183	Soph.	Detroit, Mich.
17	*Branoff, Tony	HB	19	5:11	180	Soph.	Flint, Mich.
18	Hickey, Edward	HB	20	5:8	160	Sr.	Anaconda, Mont.
19	*Knickerbocker, Stanley	HB	20	5:10	165	Jr.	Chelsea, Mich.
22	Murray, Douglas	QB	19	5:11	170	Soph.	Muskegon, Mich.
23	*McDonald, Duncan	QB	20	6:0	175	Jr.	Flint, Mich.
24	Kenaga, Ray	QB	20	5:11	170	Jr.	Sterling, Ill.
27	Baldacci, Louis G.	QB	19	6:0	205	Soph.	Akron, O.
28	McKinley, G. William	QB	21	6:1	195	Soph.	Norwalk, O.
30	*Baer, Fred	FB	20	5:11	180	Jr.	LaGrange, Ill.
32	Gagalis, Peri	FB	21	5:10	190	Jr.	Ann Arbor, Mich.
33	Hurley, Robert	FB	20	5:10	180	Sr.	Alamosa, Colo.
35	Johnson, Earl, Jr.	FB	24	5:11	200	Soph.	Muskegon, Hts., Mich
38	*Balzhiser, Richard	FB	20	6:0	186	Sr.	Wheaton, Ill.
40	Cox, Larry G.	HB	20	5:11	175	Soph.	Dowagiac, Mich.
41	*Kress, Ted	HB	21	5:11	175	Sr.	Detroit, Mich.
42	Hendricks, Thomas, Jr.	HB	19	5:11	178	Soph.	Detroit, Mich.
43	Krahl, Joseph W.	FB	19	6:0	185	Jr.	Wheaton, Ill.
44	*Cline, J. Daniel	HB	20	5:10	168	Jr.	Brockport, N. Y.
46	Sriver, Robert	HB	19	5:11	178	Soph.	Mishawaka, Ind.
50	Kamhout, Carl	T	20	6:2	205	Jr.	Grand Haven, Mich.
51	Muellich, George	G	19	6:2	195	Jr.	Bowling Green, O.
52	Bowman, James	C	20	5:11	190	Jr.	Charlevoix, Mich.
53	*O'Shaughnessy, Dick (Capt.)	C	21	5:11	190	Sr.	Seaford, N. Y.
55	Morrow, John M., Jr.	C	20	6:2	220	Soph.	Ann Arbor, Mich.
56	Drake, Donald	C	26	5:11	215	Jr.	Ypsilanti, Mich.
58	VanderZeyde, Ray	C	21	6:0	192	Sr.	East Chicago, Ind.
59	Peckham, John	C	19	6:2	220	Soph.	Sioux Falls, S. D.
60	Marion, Robert	G	19	5:10	178	Soph.	Muskegon Hts., Mich.
61	*Dugger, Don	G	20	5:10	185	Sr.	Charleston, W. Va.
62	*Strozewski, Richard	T	22	6:0	205	Sr.	South Bend, Ind.
63	Shomsky, Joseph	G	20	5:10	193	Jr.	Flint, Mich.
64	*Beison, Richard	G	21	6:0	200	Sr.	East Chicago, Ill.
65	*Cachey, Ted	G	21	5:11	185	Sr.	Chicago, Ill.
66	Fox, James W.	G	19	6:0	185	Soph.	Saginaw, Mich.
67	Brown, Wilbur P.	G	19	5:11	180	Soph.	Toledo, O.
68	Ritter, Charles	G	20	6:0	210	Jr.	Cassopolis, Mich.
69	*Williams, Ronald	G	22	5:9	185	Sr.	Massilon, O.
70	VorenKamp, Richard	E	19	6:0	190	Soph.	Grand Rapids, Mich.
71	*Geyer, Ronald	T	20	6:2	220	Jr.	Toledo, O.
72	*Balog, James	T	21	6:3	210	Sr.	Wheaton, Ill.
73	Milligan, Robert	T	20	6:1	195	Jr.	Dearborn, Mich.
74	Shields, Kenneth	T	19	6:3	215	Soph.	Detroit, Mich.
75	Kolesar, William P.	T	19	6:0	190	Soph.	Mentor, O.
76	Meads, G. Edgar	G	19	6:0	190	Soph.	Oxford, Mich.
77	*Walker, Arthur	T	19	5:11	200	Jr.	South Haven, Mich.
78	Krahnke, Charles H.	T	19	6:0	205	Soph.	Charlevoix, Mich.
79	*Bennett, Don	E	21	6:2	195	Sr.	Chicago, Ill.
80	Kuchka, John M.	E	18	6:0	185	Soph.	Berwick, Pa.
81	*Topp, Robert	E	21	6:2	190	Sr.	Kalamazoo, Mich.
82	Gonser, Jerry I.	E	19	6:0	190	Soph.	Saline, Mich.
83	*Stanford, Tad	E	21	6:0	175	Sr.	Midland, Mich.
84	Williams, Gerald H.	E	19	6:2	188	Soph.	Flint, Mich.
85	Williams, Dave	E	20	6:4	195	Fr.	Dearborn, Mich.
86	*Knutson, Gene	E	20	6:4	210	Sr.	Beloit, Wis.
87	*Schlicht, Leo	E	20	6:4	210	Sr.	Madison, Wis.
88	Veselenak, John	C	20	6:2	190	Jr.	Flint, Mich.
89	Bates, James V.	E	20	6:0	195	Jr.	Farmington, Mich.
90	*Dutter, George	E	21	6:2	190	Sr.	Fort Wayne, Ind.
91	Wolgast, Pete	T	20	6:2	185	Jr.	Petoskey, Mich.

*Lettermen

1953

Michigan........50;	Washington.....0
Michigan........26;	Tulane.........7
Michigan........14;	Iowa...........13
Michigan........20;	Northwestern...12
Michigan........0;	Minnesota......22
Michigan........24;	Pennsylvania...14
Michigan........3;	Illinois.......19
Michigan........6;	Michigan State.14
Michigan........20;	Ohio State.....0

Season Summary
Games won, 6; Lost, 3; Tied, 0.
Points for Michigan, 163; Opponents, 101.

SEPT. 26

Washington		Michigan
Black	LE	Topp
Wardlow	LT	Strozewski
Noe	LG	Dugger
Lindskog	C	O'Shaughnessy
Bohart	RG	Beison
Chambers	RT	Balog
McClary	RE	Knutson
Lederman	Q	Baldacci
Kyllingstad	LH	Kress
Crook	RH	Branoff
Nugent	F	Balzhiser

SCORE BY QUARTERS

Washington	0	0	0	0—	0
Michigan	13	18	13	6—	50

Michigan scoring: TD—Branoff, 2. Kress, 2, Baldacci, Hurley, Hickey, Hill. PAT—Branoff, McDonald.

STATISTICS

	Wash.	Mich.
First downs	5	20
Rushing yardage	72	337
Passing yardage	61	134
Passes attempted	19	21
Passes completed	5	10
Passes intercepted	3	2
Punts	7	3
Punting average	36	27.6
Fumbles lost	3	0
Yards penalized	60	65

Michigan Swamps Washington, 50-0

Baldacci's Conversion Wins, 14-13

McDonald Sparks Late TD Drive

STATISTICS

	MICHIGAN	IOWA
First downs	21	14
Rushing yardage	120	225
Passing yardage	186	28
Passes attempted	23	15
Passes completed	15	3
Passes intercepted	3	4
Punting average	48	39
Fumbles lost	2	0
Yards penalized	23	19

| Iowa | 6 | 7 | 0 | 0—13 |
| Michigan | 0 | 0 | 7 | 7—14 |

Iowa: Touchdowns—Smith 2. Conversions—Wiegmann.
Michigan: Touchdowns—Topp, Knutson. Conversions—Baldacci 2.

Revenge

MICHIGAN

LE — G. Williams, Stanford, Schlicht
LT—Strozewski, Walker, Kolesar
LG—Dugger, R. Williams, Fox, Meads
C — O'Shaughnessy, Morrow, VanderZeyde
RG—Beison, Cachey, Bennett
RT—Balog, Geyer
RE—Topp, Veselenak, Dutter
QB—Baldacci, Kenaga
LH—Kress, Cline, Hendricks
RH—Branoff, Hickey, Corey
FB—Balzhiser, Hurley

OHIO STATE

LE—Hague, Dugger
LT—Swartz, Hilinski, Machinsky
LG—Takacs, Williams
C—Vargo, Thronton, Krisher
RG—Reichenbach
RT—Jacoby
RE—Joslin, Brubaker
QB—Borton, Leggett
LH—Cassady, Howell, Augenstein
RH—Watkins, Auer
FB—Rosso, Bond

SCORE BY PERIOD

| MICHIGAN | 0 | 13 | 7 | 0—20 |
| OHIO STATE | 0 | 0 | 0 | 0—0 |

Michigan scoring: Touchdowns, Balzhiser, Branoff, Cline. Conversions, Baldacci 2.

STATISTICS

	Michigan	OSU
First Downs	15	10
Rushing Yardage	285	95
Passing Yardage	19	107
Passes Attempted	12	21
Passes Completed	2	10
Passes Intercepted by	5	2
Punts	5	5
Punting Average	37	33
Fumbles Lost	1	1
Yards Penalized	74	10

MICHIGAN'S 1953 TEAM STATISTICS

	Michigan	Opponer
Total First Downs	129	118
Rushing	83	86
Passing	40	28
Penalty	6	4
Net Yards Gained: Rushing	1578	1488
Passing	1048	742
*Total Yards Gained	2681	2271
Number of Rushes	401	416
Forward Passes Attempted	169	164
Forward Passes Completed	73	68
Touchdowns Scored on Forward Passes	7	4
Forward Passes Intercepted by	19	21
Yards Interceptions Returned	181	204
Number of Punts	37	47
Total Distance of Punts	1378	1612
Average Distance of Punts	37.2	36.4
Punts Blocked by	2	0
Punts Returned by	31	19
Yards Punts Returned	245	189
Kickoffs Returned by	21	33
Yards Kickoffs Returned	414	620
Fumbles by	28	25
Penalties	41	55
Yards Penalized	422	599
Total Points Scored	163	101

*Includes Rushing, Passing, Penalty Gains.

MICHIGAN'S INDIVIDUAL SCORING FOR 1953

	RUSHING			PASSING				RECEIVING		PUNT RET.		PUNTING		SCORING				
	Tries	Net Gain	Ave.	Att'd	Comp.	Int.	Gain	Cgh't	Gain	No.	Yds.	No.	Ave.	TD	CA	CM	FG	TP
Kress (hb)	101	339	3.3	43	19	4	238	5	102	11	63	4	27.4	6	1	0	0	36
Branoff (hb)	101	501	4.9	5	3	2	113	11	151	8	90	17	32.8	6	7	3	0	39
Balzhiser (fb)	54	165	3.0	11	0	1	0	3	25	0	0	0	0.0	1	0	0	0	6
Baldacci (qb)	20	2	.1	51	21	6	302	8	57	2	-1	13	42.5	3	13	4	1	25
Hurley (fb)	47	282	6.0	5	4	0	20	0	0	0	0	0	0.0	1	0	0	0	6
Hickey (hb)	35	141	4.0	1	0	0	0	4	64	3	36	0	0.0	1	0	0	0	6
Cline (hb)	21	74	3.5	12	5	1	90	3	31	3	16	1	53.0	1	0	0	0	6
Hendricks (hb)	4	37	9.2	1	0	0	0	0	0	1	21	0	0.0	0	0	0	0	0
Corey (hb)	4	20	5.0	0	0	0	0	0	0	0	0	0	0.0	0	0	0	0	0
Topp (e)	2	6	3.0	0	0	0	0	23	331	1	12	0	0.0	2	0	0	0	12
McDonald (qb)	1	-10	-.1	39	18	2	266	0	0	0	0	2	29.0	0	3	3	0	3
Kenaga (qb)	0	0	0.0	2	0	1	0	1	13	0	0	0	0.0	0	0	0	0	0
McKinley (qb)	0	0	0.0	2	1	0	14	0	0	0	0	0	0.0	0	0	0	0	0
Knutson (e)	0	0	0.0	0	0	0	0	11	201	0	0	0	0.0	2	0	0	0	12
Veselenak (e)	0	0	0.0	0	0	0	0	2	17	1	8	0	0.0	1	0	0	0	6
Schlicht (e)	0	0	0.0	0	0	0	0	1	17	0	0	0	0.0	0	0	0	0	0
Stanford (e)	0	0	0.0	0	0	0	0	1	9	0	0	0	0.0	0	0	0	0	0
Geyer (t)	0	0	0.0	0	0	0	0	1	10	0	0	0	0.0	0	0	0	0	0
Hill (fb)	3	16	5.3	0	0	0	0	0	0	0	0	0	0.0	1	0	0	0	6

Alphabetical Listing
1954 MICHIGAN VARSITY

No.	Name	Pos.	Age	Ht.	Wt.	Class
	Baer, Fred	FB	21	5:11	188	Sr.
	Baldacci, Louis G.	QB	20	6:1	196	Jr.
	Baldwin, Paul T.	QB	19	6:0	200	Soph.
	Barr, Terry A.	HB	19	6:1	172	Soph.
	Basford, Michael J.	FB	19	5:11	177	Soph.
	Bates, James V.	C	21	6:0	198	Sr.
	Bowman, Jim	C	21	5:11	187	Sr.
	Branoff, Tony	HB	20	5:11	188	Jr.
	Brooks, Charles E	E	19	6:1	202	Soph.
	Brown, Wilbur P.	G	20	5:11	184	Jr.
	Cachey, Ted (Capt.)	G	21	5:10	178	Sr.
	Cline, J. Daniel	HB	22	5:10	175	Sr.
	Corey, George R.	HB	21	5:10	163	Jr.
	Corona, Clement L.	G	20	6:2	218	Soph.
	Crisler, Prescott A.	T	20	6:4	214	Soph.
	Davies, James H.	T	19	5:10	209	Soph.
	Drake, Donald	C	27	5:11	213	Sr.
	Fox, James W.	G	20	6:0	190	Jr.
	Gagalis, Peri	FB	22	5:11	204	Sr.
	Geyer, Ronald	T	21	6:2	225	Sr.
	Goebel, Jerry P.	C	18	6:3	214	Soph.
	Gonser, Jerry I.	E	20	6:0	187	Jr.
	Greenwood John C.	HB	19	5:10	172	Soph.
	Hendricks, Thomas	HB	20	5:11	181	Jr.
	Hickey, Edward	HB	21	5:8	173	Sr.
	Higgins, Michael E.	E	19	6:1	205	Soph.
	Hill, David J.	FB	22	6:0	188	Jr.
	Hill, Richard F.	G	19	5:11	188	Soph.
	Johnson, Earl	FB	25	5:11	196	Jr.
	Johnston, Donald	FB	19	6:0	184	Soph.
	Kamhout, Carl	G	21	6:2	203	Sr.
	Kenaga, Ray	QB	21	5:11	182	Sr.
	Knickerbocker, Stanley	HB	21	5:11	173	Sr.
	Kolesar, William	T	20	6:0	221	Jr.
	Krahl, Joseph	HB	20	6:0	186	Sr.
	Kramer, Ronald J.	E	19	6:3	210	Soph.
	Kuchka, John M.	G	19	6:0	187	Jr.
	Maddock, James A.	QB	19	6:0	187	Soph.
	Maentz, Thomas S.	E	19	6:2	205	Soph.
	Marion, Robert L.	G	20	5:10	192	Jr.
	Matulis, Charles F.	HB	19	5:9	165	Soph.
	McDonald, Duncan	QB	21	6:0	170	Sr.
	McKoan, Joseph H.	E	19	6:0	189	Soph.
	Meads, G. Edgar	T	20	6:0	199	Jr.
	Morrow, John M.	T	21	6:2	228	Jr.
	Nyren, Marvin R.	G	19	6:0	200	Soph.
	Orwig, James B.	T	19	6:0	191	Soph.
	Peckham, John	C	20	6:2	227	Jr.
	Preston, James O.	T	19	6:1	200	Soph.
	Rentschler, David F.	HB	21	6:0	192	Jr.
	Ritter, Charles	G	21	6:0	195	Sr.
	Rotunno, Michael J.	E	19	6:0	187	Soph.
	Shannon, Edward J.	HB	19	5:8	172	Soph.
	Shomsky, Joseph	G	21	5:11	193	Sr.
	Snider, Eugene	C	23	6:0	195	Soph.
	Sriver, Robert E.	HB	21	5:11	172	Jr.
	Steele, Dale E.	C	19	5:11	194	Soph.
	Steinmeyer, William B.	G	18	5:11	183	Soph.
	Uzis, Alfred R.	FB	19	5:11	192	Soph.
	Veselenak, John	E	21	6:2	192	Sr.
	VorenKamp, Richard J.	G	20	6:0	200	Jr.
	Walker, Arthur	T	20	5:11	218	Sr.
	Ward, David H.	E	19	6:1	192	Soph.
	Williams, Dave	T	21	6:4	191	Soph.
	Williams, Gerry	E	20	6:2	189	Jr.

*Letterman

1954			
Michigan	14	Washington	0
Michigan	7	Army	26
Michigan	14	Iowa	13
Michigan	7	Northwestern	0
Michigan	34	Minnesota	0
Michigan	9	Indiana	13
Michigan	14	Illinois	7
Michigan	33	Michigan State	7
Michigan	7	Ohio State	21

Season Summary
Games won, 6; Lost, 3; Tied, 0.
Points for Michigan, 139; For Opponents 87

Washington 14 - 0

Michigan played from a T-formation in a running-passing game that gave the Wolverines a 14 - 0 decision over the victory hungry Huskies. Baldacci opened the scoring by slicing over right tackle and dashing 21 yards for a touchdown after Art Walker recovered a Washington fumble. Although the Huskies played an effective game with Lederman hurling passes behind fine line work, Baldacci again bulled his way to the one yard line after taking a pass on the ten. A one yard plunge from a single-wing put the Wolverines on pay dirt and McDonald converted for the 14 - 0 margin.

Iowa 14 - 13

Fumbling twice, underdog Michigan spotted Iowa a 13 point lead early in the game. They fought back magnificently to score seconds before the end of the first period and again midway in the second in one of the most brilliant upsets of Michigan gridiron history. The first tally, set up by Ed Hickey's two consecutive eleven yard gains, climaxed a superbly directed drive by quarterback Jim Maddock. To highlight the game, Maddock completed a 29-yard pass to Ron Kramer for the final TD. Kramer then converted for the second time to provide the margin of victory. The second half was all Michigan as Iowa never advanced past the Wolverine's 42-yard line. The Wolverines drove deep into enemy territory in two sustained drives of 71 and 51 yards only to lose the ball each time within sight of the Iowa goal.

ART WALKER—Rated one of the top tackle prospects in the country at the beginning of last season, Walker received a knee injury jumping a hedge before practice opened which became aggravated the first few days of practice and bothered him all season. If he's in top shape again this fall he should be one of the outstanding linemen in the country. Although he was never at full capacity last year, he turned in some fine performances upon occasion and played in all but one contest, totaling 208 minutes of playing time. His longest periods of service were in his first two contests and then again in the season's finale against Ohio State where he showed to advantage for 41 minutes. Extremely quick and fast, Walker stands 5'11" and weighs 203 pounds. Two years ago he played 227 minutes and was ranked as one of the defensive stars of the nation. As a freshman he played 15 minutes and 40 seconds. He's 19 and is enrolled in the Lit school.

WOLVERINES TOP GOPHERS BY 34-0

Branoff Figures in 4 Scores as Michigan Notches Upset Triumph at Ann Arbor

Indiana 9 - 13

The Indiana game looked like one of the softest touches on the Maize and Blue schedule at the beginning of the season, but it proved to be Michigan's hardest game of the year. Decidedly the underdog, the Indiana eleven were determined and stubborn as they upset the Michigan Rose Bowl aspirations 13 - 9 in a tough, hard fought game. Covering 66 yards, the Wolverines scored as soon as they got possession of the ball in the opening period. Three completed passes to Kramer highlighted this sustained drive. This early success made it look like the Wolverines were going to win hands down, but Indiana was yet to be heard from. Indiana recovered a fumble on the Michigan 27, and the Hoosier quarterback, Florian Helinski, was given his first opportunity to shine. Following two running plays, Helinski passed for a first down down to the Wolverines 4-yard line. Four plays later he was over the stripe. Michigan took up the fight again and succeeded in moving as deep in the Indiana 20. Here Helinski climaxed a pass-studded 67-yard drive by throwing a 20-yard touchdown pass to halfback Milt Campbell. Helinski then ended the Indiana scoring for the day by kicking the extra point.

ILLINOIS 14 - 7

Once more on the victory march, Michig... defeated Illinois 14-7 for a Big Ten 4-1 recor... The win was the first the Maize and Blue ha... been able to gain from Illinois since 1949.

The Illini got off to an early lead with a seri... of long gains scoring after a sustained 72-ya... drive. The Wolverines initial touchdown cam... on the first play of the second quarter as L... Baldacci picked up the final yardage. The 6... yard drive, completed in nine plays, was beaut... fully directed by quarterback Jim Maddock wit... Lou Baldacci doing most of the work from th... fullback spot.

With less than two minutes remaining in th... first half, Michigan took over possession of th... ball after an Illinois punt rolled dead on the 11... In just six plays, sparked by the running and... passing of Dan Cline, the Michigan eleven had... scored. On a brilliantly executed transconti... nental play Cline received the pitch-out, sped t... the left behind a mass of blockers, looked straight... down-field where the Michigan ends had draw... pass defenders, and then threw a long pass to... Maddock who stood all alone along the right... sideline. Maddock scampered over for the score... just twenty seconds before the end of the half.

Illinois moved within striking distance three... times in the last half but their backs proved in... effective within the Michigan 20.

Three Michigan players about to pounce on the loose ball after Ron Kramer (upper left) blocked a punt by Illini back Abe Woodson. The ball was downed by Michigan on the Illinois 15-yard line.

MICHIGAN STATE 33 - 7

Playing before a capacity crowd, Michigan routed the Michigan State Spartans in the season's final home game. After losing four previous encounters with Michigan State College, the Wolverines finally found themselves in possession of the famed Paul Bunyan trophy.

The Maize and Blue took a two-touchdown lead after defensive play was combined with the offensive punch as needed. The first rally came late in the second quarter following an interception of a Spartan pass by center Gene Snider. After eight plays and 64 yards later, Baldacci plowed over for the first of his two touchdowns. The key play of this drive was a fourth down Maddock-to-Maentz pass, good for the first down.

The clincher came when Cline fired a touch-down pass to Baldacci who grabbed the ball on the State 46-yard line and galloped the rest of the way for the score. Preceeding this, the Spartans scored their lone touchdown of the game after intercepting a Michigan pass.

Throughout the game, the outstanding performance of end Ron Kramer sparked Michigan's offense and defense. A few plays after his opening kickoff of the second half, Kramer broke through the Spartan line and blocked a punt. Snatching the ball out of the air, he lumbered into the end zone for the score. Michigan scored again on Ed Shannon's plunge, after Baldacci had picked up a punt that was partially blocked by Kramer.

Michigan's final score came after a superb 68-yard punt was returned by Tom Hendricks.

Walker Makes 'Look' All-America

OHIO STATE   7 - 20

	Michigan	Opponents
Total First Downs	123	110
Rushing	89	77
Passing	31	31
Penalty	3	2
Net Yards Gained: Rushing	1414	1427
Passing	889	743
*Total Yards Gained	2640	2499
Number of Rushes	452	380
Forward Passes Attempted	136	164
Forward Passes Completed	54	68
Touchdowns Scored on Forward Passes	5	3
Forward Passes Intercepted by	8	18
Yards Interceptions Returned	100	235
Number of Punts	41	52
Total Distance of Punts	1513	1617
Average Distance of Punts	36.9	31.1
Punts Blocked by	4	0
Punts Returned by	27	25
Yards Punts Returned	268	210
Kickoffs Returned by	23	24
Yards Kickoffs Returned	360	451
Fumbles by	21	27
Penalties	46	35
Yards Penalized	329	337
Total Points Scored	139	87

*Includes Rushing, Passing, Penalty Gains.

In the final and most important game of what turned out to be a highly successful '54 football season, the Michigan Wolverines bowed to the dauntless and unbeatable Ohio Buckeyes, 20-7, at Columbus. Consequently, Michigan finished in a tie for second place in the Western Conference.

The Wolverines, who outplayed Ohio State for three frustrating quarters, marched 68 yards after the opening kickoff to score before the Buckeyes had their hands on the ball. Dan Cline swept left end, ran seven yards for the touchdown, which terminated the initial drive.

From then on Michigan had plenty of scoring opportunities, but none of them materialized. OSU'S defense proved tough to crack as they stopped Michigan drives on three interceptions and two fumbles.

After Michigan had failed to score on a fourth and one foot situation, Ohio State took over the ball and proceeded to march 99 2 3 yards for the score which ultimately sent them to the New Year's Day classic in Pasadena.

Reprinted with permission from the Michigan Alumnus

MICHIGAN'S INDIVIDUAL SCORING FOR 1954

	RUSHING			PASSING				RECEIVING		PUNT RET.		PUNTING		SCORING				
	Tries	Net Gain	Ave.	Att'd	Comp.	Had Int.	Gain	Cgh't	Gain	No.	Yds.	No.	Ave.	TD	CA	CM	FG	TP
Baer (fb)	107	439	4.1	1	0	0	0	1	4	0	0	0	4.0	3	0	0	0	18
Cline (hb)	97	340	3.5	43	15	4	281	6	61	11	42	3	36.3	3	0	0	0	18
Hickey (hb)	45	169	3.8	0	0	0	0	1	50	0	0	0	0.0	1	0	0	0	6
Baldacci (qb-fb)	46	152	3.3	14	7	1	71	8	211	0	0	8	27.8	5	1	1	0	31
Shannon (hb)	37	95	2.6	0	0	0	0	1	10	0	0	0	0.0	1	0	0	0	6
D. Hill (hb-fb)	37	92	2.5	2	1	0	7	0	0	0	0	0	0.0	1	0	0	0	6
Branoff (hb)	20	69	3.5	1	0	1	0	3	47	0	0	0	0.0	1	0	0	0	6
Maddock (qb)	22	37	1.7	35	16	5	293	1	21	0	0	9	36.4	1	1	0	0	6
Corey (hb)	9	21	2.3	0	0	0	0	2	50	1	3	0	0.0	0	0	0	0	0
Barr (hb)	13	21	1.6	3	0	0	0	2	18	0	0	0	0.0	0	0	0	0	0
Kramer (e)	4	17	4.3	0	0	0	0	23	303	3	43	19	41.2	3	15	14	0	32
Knickerbocker (hb-qb)	2	5	2.5	0	0	0	0	0	0	0	0	0	0.0	0	0	0	0	0
Gagalis (fb)	1	4	4.0	0	0	0	0	0	0	0	0	0	0.0	0	0	0	0	0
Hendricks (hb)	3	1	0.3	0	0	0	0	1	53	1	68	0	0.0	1	0	0	0	6
McDonald (qb)	9	-48	-5.3	36	15	6	237	0	0	0	0	2	36.0	0	3	2	0	2
Greenwood (qb)	0	0	0.0	1	0	1	0	0	0	0	0	0	0.0	0	0	0	0	0
G. Williams (e)	0	0	0.0	0	0	0	0	2	24	0	0	0	0.0	0	0	0	0	0
Rotunno (e)	0	0	0.0	0	0	0	0	1	17	0	0	0	0.0	0	0	0	0	0
Veselenak (e)	0	0	0.0	0	0	0	0	1	13	0	0	0	0.0	0	0	0	0	0
Maentz (e)	0	0	0.0	0	0	0	0	1	7	0	0	0	0.0	0	0	0	1	2

Alphabetical Listing
1955 MICHIGAN VARSITY

No.	Name	Pos.	Age	Ht.	Wt.	Class
27	*Baldacci, Louis G.	FB	20	6:1	196	Sr.
28	Baldwin, Paul T.	QB	20	6:0	198	Sr.
41	*Barr, Terry A.	LH	20	6:0	182	Jr.
37	Basford, Michael	FB	19	5:11	180	Jr.
58	*Bates, James V.	C	22	6:0	200	Sr.
65	Berger, Thomas E.	G	19	5:11	183	So.
68	Bochnowski, Alex	G	20	5:9	185	So.
52	Bowman, James	C	22	5:11	194	Sr.
17	*Branoff, Tony D.	HB	21	5:11	190	Sr.
89	Brooks, Charles	E	20	6:1	198	Jr.
15	*Corey, George R.	RH	22	5:10	166	Sr.
67	Corona, Clement	G	20	6:2	221	Jr.
73	Davies, James J.	T	20	5:10	214	Jr.
22	Dickey, James A.	QB	20	6:0	188	So.
57	Eldred, Dale L.	T	22	5:11	199	Jr.
86	Faul, Lawrence J.	E	20	6:0	185	Jr.
66	*Fox, James W.	G	21	6:0	191	Sr.
53	Goebel, Jerry P.	C	19	6:3	211	Jr.
82	Gonser, Jerry I.	E	21	6:0	187	Sr.
77	Gray, James	T	20	6:0	209	Fr.
25	Greenwood, John	QB	20	5:10	170	Jr.
42	*Hendricks, Thomas	LH	21	5:11	188	Sr.
79	Heynen, Richard B.	T	20	6:0	195	Jr.
18	*Hickey, Edward L.	RH	22	5:9	175	Sr.
45	Hill, David J.	FB	23	6:0	188	Jr.
69	*Hill, Richard F.	G	20	5:11	194	Jr.
12	Janecke, Jerry	HB	19	5:10	171	So.
35	Johnson, Earl	FB	25	5:11	194	Sr.
74	Kamhout, Carl R.	T	22	6:2	212	Sr.
83	Ketteman, Dick	E	19	6:1	178	So.
44	Klinge, Walter W.	HB	19	5:11	183	So.
19	*Knickerbocker, Stanley	RH	22	5:11	173	Sr.
75	*Kolesar, William	T	21	6:0	214	Sr.
62	Krahnke, Charles	G	21	6:0	210	Sr.
87	Kramer, Ronald J.	E	20	6:3	222	Jr.
33	Krueger, Frederick	E	19	5:11	181	So.
23	Lousma, Jack R.	QB	19	6:0	187	So.
56	MacPhee, William	C	19	6:0	185	So.
26	*Maddock, James	QB	20	5:11	189	Jr.
85	*Maentz, Thomas	E	19	6:2	207	Jr.
60	*Marion, Robert L.	G	21	5:10	194	Sr.
10	Matulis, Charles	LH	20	5:9	171	Jr.
80	McKoan, Joseph H.	E	20	6:0	193	Jr.
76	*Meads, G. Edgar (Capt)	G	21	6:0	198	Sr.
88	Morrow, Gordon H.	E	20	6:3	220	So.
78	*Morrow, John M.	T	22	6:2	228	Sr.
64	Nyren, Marvin R.	G	20	6:0	204	Jr.
72	Orwig, James B.	T	20	6:0	194	Jr.
71	Owen, David G.	T	19	6:0	214	Jr.
43	Pace, James E.	LH	19	5:11	185	So.
63	Paplomatas, James	G	19	5:10	192	So.
59	Peckham, John	C	20	6:2	227	Sr.
54	Rembiesa, Donald	C	19	5:11	185	So.
84	Rentschler, David F.	E	22	6:0	190	Jr.
81	Rotunno, Michael	E	20	6:1	192	Jr.
16	*Shannon, Edward	RH	20	5:8	172	Jr.
14	Shatusky, Mike	HB	25	5:10	172	Jr.
70	Sigman, Lionel A.	T	24	5:10	215	Sr.
46	Sriver, Robert E.	HB	22	5:11	178	Sr.
61	Steinmeyer, Bill	G	19	5:11	198	Jr.
24	VanPelt, James S.	QB	20	5:11	178	So.
38	Zervas, Stephen J.	FB	19	6:0	193	Sr.

*Lettermen

1955 TEAM

Left to right, Front Row: Ed Hickey, Tony Branoff, H. O. Crisler (direc[tor] of athletics), Ed Meads (captain), Bennie Oosterbaan (coach), Tom Mae[ntz] captain-elect), Bill Kolesar.
Second Row: John Peckham, Carl Kamhout, John Morrow, Lou Baldacci, J[im] Bates, Tom Hendricks, Dale Eldred, George Corey.
Third Row: Clement Corona, Dick Hill, Stanley Knickerbocker, Dave Rentschle[r], Jim Fox, Jim Bowman, Bob Marion, Ed Shannon, Jim Maddock.
Fourth Row: Jim Hunt (trainer), Jim Davies, Charles Brooks, Ron Kramer, M[e]... Rotunna, Lawrence Faul, Terry Barr, Casper Grathwol (manager).
Fifth Row: Al Sigman, Jim Pace, Dick Heynen, Jim Van Pelt, Jerry Goebe[l], Marvin Nyren, James Orwig, John Greenwood.

1955

Michigan		Opponent	
Michigan	42;	Missouri	7
Michigan	14;	Michigan State	7
Michigan	26;	Army	2
Michigan	14;	Northwestern	2
Michigan	14;	Minnesota	13
Michigan	33;	Iowa	21
Michigan	6;	Illinois	25
Michigan	30;	Indiana	0
Michigan	0;	Ohio State	17

Season Summary
Games won, 7; Lost, 2; Tied, 0.
Points for Michigan, 179; For Opponents 94

TEAM PLAYERS
MICHIGAN
LE—Kramer, Rentschler
LT—Orwig, Heynen, Kamhout
LG—R. Hill, Fox, Eldred, Marion
C—Goebel, Peckham, Rembiesa
RG—Meads, Nyren, Corona
RT—Sigman, J. Morrow, Davies
RE—Brooks, Rotunno, Maentz, Faul
QB—Maddock, Van Pelt, Greenwood
LH—Barr, Pace, Hendricks
RH—Branoff, Corey, Hickey, Knickerbocker
FB—Shannon, Baldacci, E. Johnson, Basford

ARMY
LE—Johnson, McCaffrey
LT—Chesnauskas, Shea
LG—Slater, Warner, Fadel
C—Szveterz, Kernan
RG—Goodwin, Shannon
RT—Stephenson, Reid
RE—Satterfield, Saunders, Melnik
QB—Holleder, Mericle
LH—Lobel
RH—Zeigler, Lash, Munger, Thiebert
FB—Barta, Byrd

SCORE BY PERIODS

MICHIGAN	6	6	0	14	26
ARMY	0	0	0	2	2

Touchdowns: MICHIGAN—Barr (2), Shannon, Pace.
Conversions: MICHIGAN — Branoff (Run), Van Pelt.
Safety against Michigan (for Army team).

TEAM STATISTICS

	U-M	Army
First Downs	7	11
Rushing	3	11
Passing	3	0
Penalty	1	0
Net yards—Rushing	69	199
Net yards—Passing	95	72
Forward passes—Attempted	13	10
Forward Passes—Completed	7	...
Forward passes intercepted	2	1
Punts—Number	7	...
Average distance	31	36
Kickoffs—Returned by	2	5
Yards kicks returned	136	51
Punts	105	50
Kickoffs	31	10
Fumbles—Number	3	11
Ball lost by	2	5
Penalties—Number	7	6
Yards penalized	61	6...

Wolverines Bottle Up Cadet Bids
97,239 See First Victory Over Foe

ANN ARBOR, Mich., Oct. 8.—Terry Barr, a junior from Grand Rapids, heretofore undistinguishable from other Michigan left halfback, erupted from anonymity with the first touchdown of his varsity career and led the Wolverines into the promised land with a 26-to-2 victory over fumbling Army before a sell-out crowd of 97,239 today.

A ten-year drought ended for Michigan with this crushing triumph over the fumblingest Cadet team Red Blaik ever sent into gridiron battle.

Five times in five meetings since 1945 Army had humbled proud Michigan by an aggregate count of 122-to-40 points

Explosive Thirty Minutes

Varsity Scores Five Touchdowns In Last Half To Defeat Iowa

Reprinted with permission from the **Michigan Alumnus**

MICHIGAN		IOWA
...ostanio (Kramer) (Brooks) (Rentschler)	L E	(Rigney) Gibbons
...erwig (Heynen) (Kamhout)	L T	(Burroughs) Bloomquist
..., Hill (Fox) (Marion)	L G	Deasy
...ates (Goebel) (Bowman)	C	(Van Buren) Suchy
...eads (Nyren) (Corona)	R G	Jones
...ixman (Morrow) (Davies)	R T	(Jehle) (Bowen) Swedberg
...aentz (Brooks) (Faul)	R E	(Hatch) Freeman
...an Pelt (Maddock) (Baldacci) (Greenwood)	Q B	(Ploen) Reichow
...orr (Pace) (Hendricks)	L H B	(Hagler) Dobrino
...ranoff (Hickey) (Shannon) (Corey)	R H B	(Smith) Vincent
(Knickerbocker)		
...aldacci (D. Hill) (Johnson)	F B	Wiegmann

MICHIGAN	0	0	13	20	33
IOWA	7	7	7	0	21

Touchdowns: Vincent, Dobrino 2, Baldacci, Maentz 2, Kramer, Branoff.
Points after touchdown: Freeman 3, Kramer 3.
Officials: Referee, M. J. Delaney; Umpire, Don Elser; Field Judge, Harold Still; Head Lines-man, Charles Leadbetter; Backfield Judge, W. E. Farrell.

Cassady Paces Title Conquest

By Edgar Hayes

Detroit Times Sports Editor

ANN ARBOR, Nov. 19—Michigan's dream of a fourth trip to the Rose Bowl was turned into a nightmare here this afternoon in the wildest game ever seen in Michigan Stadium.

Led by a speedy 168-pound halfback. Howard (Hopalong) Cassady and a tremendous lineman named Jim Parker, Ohio State crushed Michigan 17-0.

The defeat meant Michigan had paved the way for its hated rival Michigan State to go to the Rose Bowl in place of the proud Wolverines. It also meant Ohio State won its second Big Ten title in a row and had defeated Michigan for the first time since 1937 in Michigan Stadium.

Reprinted with permission from the **Detroit Times**

KRAMER

The Illini Do It Again

Varsity's Unbeaten String Snapped By Inspired Illinois Eleven

WHEN Illinois meets Michigan on the gridiron the sensible thing to do is expect the unexpected.

More often than not, it is an Illinois triumph which is unexpected and, more often than not in these past ten years, that is exactly what has occurred.

It was so again last weekend. The unbeaten Wolverines journeyed to Champaign seeking victory number seven of the 1955 campaign. Instead, they were stunned with a smashing 25 to 6 defeat and the longest of long rides back to Ann Arbor.

In recent years Illinois has been far and away Michigan's most troublesome Conference foe. No other team in the land, in fact, has heaped so much adversity on the Wolverines since 1950.

During the past decade — from the fall of 1946 through the frustrating afternoon of November 5, 1955 — Michigan has lost only thirteen Western Conference games. It is a record unapproached by any Big Ten colleague.

Three Conference schools have not defeated Michigan at all in that ten-year span, while three others have managed only one triumph over the Varsity in league play. Two schools. Ohio State and Northwestern, have each won twice. The standout exception is Illinois which now has won six times in the past ten years.

The recent record is even more impressive. Illinois has defeated Michigan five times in the past six years, allowing the Wolverines only 36 points during that span.

MICHIGAN'S 1955 TEAM STATISTICS

	Michigan	Opponents
FIRST DOWNS	107	107
By Rushing	70	88
By Passing	33	17
By Penalty	4	2
NET YARDS RUSHING	1359	1596
Number of Attempts	393	470
Yards per Attempt	3.5	3.4
NET YARDS PASSING	772	402
Forward Passes Attempted	115	86
Forward Passes Completed	44	28
Passes Had Intercepted	12	10
Percent of Passes Completed	38.3	32.6
Yards per Pass Attempt	6.7	4.7
NET YARDS—RUSHING AND PASSING	2131	1998
Number of Plays	508	556
Yards per Play	4.2	3.6
PUNTS	52	59
Yards on Punts	1946	2179
Average Distance per Punt	37.4	36.9
FUMBLES	25	32
Ball Lost by Fumbles	17	19
PENALTIES	54	53
Yards Penalized	499	506
POINTS	179	94
POINTS IN BIG TEN	111	85

CRISLER OVERSHOOTS MARK BY 1,000

3,762 New Seats Raise 'M' Capacity to 101,001

1956 MICHIGAN VARSITY SQUAD

No.	Name	Pos.	Age	Ht.	Wt.	Class	Home Town
41	*Barr, Terry	HB	21	6:0	184	Sr.	Grand Rapids
15	Batsakes, John	HB	21	5:8	174	Jr.	Ann Arbor
65	Berger, Tom	G	20	5:11	185	Jr.	Detroit
68	Bochnowski, Alex	G	20	5:10	190	Jr.	E. Chicago, Ind.
66	Boshoven, Robert	G	19	6:0	205	Jr.	Grand Rapids
84	Bowers, Dave	E	20	6:2	195	Jr.	Traverse City
74	Boyden, Joel	G	19	6:6	249	So.	Muskegon
89	*Brooks, Charles	E	21	6:2	202	Sr.	Marshall
33	Byers, Jim	FB	19	6:0	198	So.	Evansville, Ind.
61	Callahan, Alex	G	19	6:0	190	So.	Wyandotte
67	*Corona, Clem	G	21	6:1	221	Sr.	Berwick, Pa.
73	*Davies, Jim	T	21	5:11	215	Sr.	Muskegon Hts.
32	Dickey, Jim	FB	21	6:1	185	Jr.	Miamisburg, Ohio
63	*Faul, Larry	G	20	6:0	195	Jr.	River Forest, Ill.
77	Gray, Jim	T	21	6:3	215	So.	Battle Creek
25	*Greenwood, John	HB	21	5:9	175	Sr.	Bay City
62	Haller, Dave	G	20	6:1	191	So.	Park Ridge, Ill.
36	Herrnstein, John	FB	18	6:2	212	So.	Chillicothe, Ohio
79	*Heynen, Dick	T	21	6:1	198	Sr.	Grand Rapids
69	*Hill, Dick	G	21	5:11	198	So.	Gary, Ind.
60	Jenks, John	G	19	5:10	202	So.	Chicago, Ill.
82	Johnson, Walter	E	19	6:4	211	So.	Dearborn
83	Ketteman, Richard	E	20	6:1	181	Jr.	Toledo, Ohio
87	*Kramer, Ron	E-HB	21	6:3	216	Sr.	E. Detroit
71	Kreger, John	T	20	6:6	246	Jr.	Flat Rock
80	Krueger, Fred	E	21	5:11	180	Jr.	Allen Park
23	Lousma, Jack	QB	20	6:0	192	So.	Ann Arbor
56	MacPhee, Bill	C	19	6:0	192	Jr.	Grand Haven
26	*Maddock, Jim	QB	21	5:10	187	Sr.	Chicago, Ill.
85	*Maentz, Tom (Capt.)	E	22	6:3	210	Sr.	Holland
78	Marciniak, Jerry	FB	19	6:2	220	So.	Chicago, Ill.
18	McCoy, Ernie	HB	22	5:10	165	Jr.	Ann Arbor
88	Morrow, Gordon	E	21	6:3	208	So.	Ann Arbor
64	*Nyren, Marvin	G	21	6:0	205	Jr.	Des Plaines, Ill.
50	Orvis, Douglas	G	19	5:11	180	So.	Flint
72	*Orwig, Jim	T	21	6:0	196	Sr.	Toledo, Ohio
43	*Pace, Jim	HB	20	5:11	192	Jr.	Little Rock, Ark.
86	Prahst, Gary	E	19	6:4	210	So.	Berea, Ohio
49	Ptacek, Bob	HB	19	6:1	206	So.	Cleveland, Ohio
54	Rembiesa, Don	C	20	5:11	190	Jr.	Dearborn
48	*Rentschler, Dave	HB	23	6:1	195	Jr.	Grosse Pointe
81	*Rotunno, Mike	C	20	6:1	191	Sr.	Canton, Ohio
16	*Shannon, Ed	HB	21	5:8	171	Sr.	River Forest, Ill.
14	Shatusky, Mike	HB	26	5:11	175	Sr.	Menominee
70	*Sigman, Al	T	25	5:11	217	Sr.	Ann Arbor
35	Sisinyak, Eugene	FB	19	6:0	195	So.	Monroe
75	Smith, Willie	T	18	6:2	237	So.	Little Rock, Ark.
58	*Snider, Gene	C	25	6:1	205	Jr.	Hamtramck
22	Spidel, John	QB	19	5:11	174	So.	Greenville, Ohio
76	Stetten, Maynard	T	19	6:2	205	So.	Gibraltar
10	Stovall, Jack	HB	25	5:9	180	Jr.	Howell
28	Sytek, Jim	QB	19	5:11	185	So.	Detroit
24	*VanPelt, Jim	QB	20	5:11	187	Jr.	Evanston, Ill.
55	Wine, Ray	C	22	6:2	200	So.	Port Huron
42	Zachary, John	HB	19	5:10	168	So.	Chicago, Ill.
38	Zervas, Steve	FB	21	5:11	192	Jr.	Hazel Park

*Letterman

1956 Season — Won 7, Lost 2, Tied 0

			Date	Place	Attendance
Michigan 42	U.C.L.A.	13	Sep 29	Ann Arbor	70,159
Michigan 0	Michigan State	9	Oct 6	Ann Arbor	101,001
Michigan 48	Army	14	Oct 13	Ann Arbor	93,402
Michigan 34	Northwestern	20	Oct 20	Ann Arbor	81,718
Michigan 7	Minnesota	20	Oct 27	Ann Arbor	85,566
Michigan 17	Iowa	14	Nov 3	Iowa City	55,896
Michigan 17	Illinois	7	Nov 10	Ann Arbor	75,735
Michigan 49	Indiana	26	Nov 17	Ann Arbor	58,515
Michigan 19	Ohio State	0	Nov 24	Columbus	78,830

'U' Students Apprehended

Six University students were disciplined yesterday by Joint Judiciary Council for participating in a pre-game painting party in East Lansing early yesterday morning.

Meeting in special session at 5 p.m. yesterday, Joint Judic handed out a three point penalty to Duane Kalember, '59, David Partridge, John Lun, Robert Beckman, William Freitag and Theodore Hurchik, '59.

The students will be 1) required to give up their tickets to the next three home football games; 2) confined to student residences during the actual games; 3) required to withdraw from all house and campus activities for the rest of the semester.

Michigan State University Police picked up the students at 2:20 a.m. yesterday. According to a Lansing newspaper, Kalember and Partridge admitted painting a blue "M" on a bench and "U of M" across a sidewalk. Lun and Beckman were observing and Freitag and Hurchik were apprehended later in a car.

Before returning to the University, the students scrubbed off their handiwork and apologized to Dean of Men Thomas King. There were no police charges.

City and campus police here stayed alert last night for possible reprisals from MSU.

Joint Judic Chairman Mike McNerney, '57L, Student Government Council President Bill Adams, '57BAd and Daily Editor Dick Snyder. '57 recently met with MSU representatives to decide ways to prevent and punish paint parties.

State-M Facts

Michigan State	0	0	3	6—9
Michigan	0	0	0	0—0

Michigan State scoring — Touchdown: Mendyk (5, plunge). Field goal: Matsko (29).

	MSU	Mich.
First downs	9	13
Rushing yardage	153	50
Passing yardage	9	79
Passes	0-3	11-21
Passes intercepted by	2	0
Punts	8-46	4-58
Fumbles lost	2	2
Yards penalized	20	15

1956 TEAM

Top Row (left to right): Dave Lundquist (student manager), Jack Lousma, Eugene Sisinyak, John Spidel, Raymond Wine, Walter Johnson, David Bowers, Gerald Marciniak, James Dickey.
Second Row: James Hunt (trainer), Richard Heynen, Eugene Snider, Marvin Nyren, Robert Ptacek, Gary Prahst, John Herrnstein, Thomas Berger, Willie Smith.
Third Row: James Van Pelt, Alex Bochnowski, James Pace, Clement Corona, James Byers, James Davies, Lawrence Faul, Michael Shatusky.
Fourth Row: Al Sigman, Terry Barr, David Rentschler, Ron Kramer, Charles Brooks, Richard Hill, Ed Shannon.
Front Row: John Greenwood, Michael Rotunno, Herbert O. Crisler (athletic director), Tom Maentz, Bennie Oosterbaan (head football coach), James Orwig, James Maddock.

The Illini Finally Fall

Michigan Gains Its Second Win Over Illinois In The Past Seven Years

COACHES Ray Eliot of Illinois and Bennie Oosterbaan of Michigan walked arm-in-arm off the field after the Wolverines had defeated the Illini, 17 to 7, in their tensely-exciting battle of November 10.

Most post-game exchanges between victorious and vanquished coaches last no more than ten seconds, but these two long-time antagonists kept right on talking as they made their way through the crowd and into the Stadium tunnel ramp.

What they said is known only to each other, but the conversation might have started out like this:

Eliot: "Congratulations, Ben, that was a fine victory and your team deserved to win it."

Oosterbaan: "Well, thanks, Ray. It was about time. You've been mighty tough for us to beat."

Nov. 3

IOWA (14)
LE—Gibbons, Langston.
LT—Karras, Burroughs.
LG—Bloomquist, Commings.
C—Suchy, Pierce.
RG—Drake, Bowen, Theer.
RT—Klein, Deasy.
RE—Gilliam, Prescott.
QB—Ploen, Veit, Duncan.
LH—Furlong, Dobrino, Kloewer, Gravel.
RH—Happel, Hagler.
FB—Harris, Nocera.

MICHIGAN (17)
LE—Kramer, Prahst.
LT—Orwig, Heyen, Smith.
LG—Hill Faul.
C—Snider, Rotunno, Wine.
RG—Nyren, Corona, Bochnowski.
RT—Sigman, Davies.
RE—Maentz, Brooks, Ketteman.
QB—Van Pelt, Maddock.
LH—Pace, Ptacek.
RH—Shannon, Shatusky, Barr.
FB—Herrnstein, Byers.

FIRST PERIOD
		TIME
3 0	Kramer (12-yard field goal)	14:31

SECOND PERIOD
3 6	Kloewer (13-yard pass from Duncan)	8:05
3 7	Prescott (placement)	
3 13	Ploen (33-yard run)	12:52
3 14	Prescott (placement)	

THIRD PERIOD
| 9 14 | Shatusky (3-yard run) | 5:09 |
| 10 14 | Kramer (placement) | |

FOURTH PERIOD
| 16 14 | Shatusky (2-yard run) | |
| 17 14 | Kramer (placement) | |

HERBERT O. CRISLER
Michigan's Athletic Director was honored last month by Touchdown Club of New York for outstanding service to football.

Nov. 24

TEAM LINEUPS
MICHIGAN
LEFT ENDS: Kramer, Prahst, Rentschler.
LEFT TACKLES: Orwig, Heynen.
LEFT GUARDS: Hill, Faul, Berger.
CENTERS: Rotunno, Snider, Wine.
RIGHT GUARDS: Nyren, Corona, Bochnowski.
RIGHT TACKLES: Sigman, Davies, Smith.
RIGHT ENDS: Maentz, Brooks.
QUARTERBACKS: Van Pelt, Maddock, Greenwood, Spidel.
LEFT HALFBACKS: Pace, Ptacek.
RIGHT HALFBACKS: Barr, Shannon.
FULLBACKS: Herrnstein, Byers, Sisinyak.

OHIO STATE
LEFT ENDS: Michael, Bowermaster.
LEFT TACKLES: Martin, Schafrath.
LEFT GUARDS: Parker, Baldacci.
CENTERS: Dillman, James.
RIGHT GUARDS: Thomas, Spychalski.
RIGHT TACKLES: Guy, Crawford.
RIGHT ENDS: Brown, Kriss, Katula.
QUARTERBACKS: Ellwood, Kremblas.
LEFT HALFBACKS: Clark, LeBeau.
RIGHT HALFBACKS: Roseboro, Cannavino.
FULLBACKS: Cisco, Vicic.
Michigan Scoring Touchdowns: Barr 2, Maddock.
Conversion: Kramer.

SCORE BY QUARTERS:
| MICHIGAN | 13 | 0 | 0 | 6—19 |
| OHIO STATE | 0 | 0 | 0 | 0— 0 |

Michigan's Ron Kramer sporting a brace on his left hand, reached up to snag a long pass from Terry Barr in a play that covered 60 yards. Three plays later Michigan scored its second TD.

Michigan's football jersey number 87, carried to All-American fame by end Ronald Kramer, will soon join number 47 (Bennie Oosterbaan), number 98 (Tom Harmon) and number 11 (the three Wisterts) in permanent retirement. Kramer was one of the 1956 All-Americans saluted last month on Ed Sullivan's television show.

MICHIGAN'S 1956 TEAM STATISTICS

	Michigan	Opponent
FIRST DOWNS	160	124
By Rushing	109	94
By Passing	46	24
By Penalty	5	6
NET YARDS RUSHING	1943	1629
Number of Attempts	471	433
Yards per Attempt	4.13	3.76
NET YARDS PASSING	1032	579
Forward Passes Attempted	128	100
Forward Passes Completed	66	39
Passes Had Intercepted	8	9
Percent of Passes Completed	51.6	39.0
Yards per Pass Attempt	8.06	5.79
NET YARDS RUSHING AND PASSING	2975	2208
Number of Plays	599	533
Yards per Play	4.97	4.14
PUNTS	32	41
Average Distance per Punt	36.3	35.2
KICKOFFS, RETURNED BY	27	38
FUMBLES	29	34
Ball Lost by Fumbles	15	23
PENALTIES	46	34
Yards Penalized	420	310
POINTS	233	123
POINTS IN BIG TEN	143	96

	RUSHING			PASSING				RECEIVING		PUNT RET.		PUNTING		SCORING				
	Tries	Net Gain	Ave.	Att'd	Comp.	Had Int.	Gain	Cgh't	Gain	No.	Yds.	No.	Avg.	TD	CA	CM	FG	TP
Herrnstein, fb	123	475	3.9	1	0	1	0	0	0	0	0	0	0.0	7	0	0	0	42
Barr, hb	60	366	6.1	6	5	0	187	3	66	6	82	0	0.0	7	0	0	0	42
Ptacek, hb	45	208	4.6	23	15	2	245	7	53	6	36	0	0.0	1	0	0	0	6
Pace, hb	103	498	4.8	12	6	1	97	7	155	4	28	0	0.0	2	0	0	0	12
Shannon, hb	27	90	3.3	3	2	0	25	2	35	7	36	0	0.0	3	1	1	0	19
Kramer, e	5	19	3.8	2	1	0	23	18	353	0	0	2	56.0	2	20	17	2	35
Byers, fb	22	77	3.5	0	0	0	0	2	5	0	0	0	0.0	1	0	0	0	6
Shatusky, hb	24	72	3.0	0	0	0	0	2	21	0	0	2	38.5	3	0	0	0	18
Maddock, qb	25	72	2.9	42	20	3	213	5	79	1	15	7	31.7	3	8	7	0	25
Dickey, fb	7	6	0.8	0	0	0	0	0	0	0	0	0	0.0	1	0	0	0	6
Prahst, e	1	31	31.0	0	0	0	0	4	42	0	0	0	0.0	1	0	0	0	6
Van Pelt, qb	15	3	0.2	33	15	1	221	3	40	0	0	8	32.0	2	2	2	0	14
Sisinyak, fb	5	12	2.4	0	0	0	0	0	0	0	0	0	0.0	0	0	0	0	0
Lousma, hb	2	6	3.0	2	2	0	19	0	0	0	0	0	0.0	0	0	0	0	0
Batsakes, hb	1	0	0.0	0	0	0	0	0	0	0	0	0	0.0	0	0	0	0	0
Greenwood, hb	1	3	3.0	2	0	0	0	0	0	0	0	1	28.0	0	0	0	0	0
Spidel, qb	2	1	0.5	1	0	0	0	1	14	0	0	0	0.0	0	0	0	0	0
Sytek, qb	0	0	0.0	1	0	0	0	0	0	0	0	1	26.0	0	0	0	0	0
Maentz, e	0	0	0.0	0	0	0	0	6	70	0	0	11	40.0	0	2	2	0	2
Brooks, e	0	0	0.0	0	0	0	0	5	62	0	0	0	0.0	0	0	0	0	0
Johnson, e	0	0	0.0	0	0	0	0	1	27	0	0	0	0.0	0	0	0	0	0
Rentschler, e	0	0	0.0	0	0	0	0	1	8	0	0	0	0.0	0	0	0	0	0

Aid To Athletes

The University and its colleagues of the Big Ten Conference last month embarked on the first phase of a far reaching new plan for the control and conduct of intercollegiate athletics.

Final approval was given to legislation which brings into existence a new financial aid program and provides severe penalties for any violation of carefully-defined regulations (see Marcus Plant interview in January 19 issue).

The new program, passed by majority vote of the Big Ten's faculty representatives on February 22, took effect immediately. The vote of the various schools was not announced, although it was known in advance that the proposal was favored by Michigan, Michigan State, Purdue, Illinois, Indiana and Wisconsin.

1957 Season — Won 5, Lost 3, Tied 1

			Date	Place	Attendance
Michigan 16,	U.S.C	6	Sep 28	Los Angeles	43,569
Michigan 26,	Georgia	0	Oct 5	Ann Arbor	84,165
Michigan 6,	Michigan State	35	Oct 12	Ann Arbor	101,001
Michigan 34,	Northwestern	14	Oct 19	Ann Arbor	71,513
Michigan 24,	Minnesota	7	Oct 26	Minneapolis	63,523
Michigan 21,	Iowa	21	Nov 2	Ann Arbor	90,583
Michigan 19,	Illinois	20	Nov 9	Champaign	47,886
Michigan 27,	Indiana	13	Nov 16	Ann Arbor	56,616
Michigan 14,	Ohio State	31	Nov 23	Ann Arbor	101,001

MICHIGAN'S 1957 TEAM STATISTICS

	Michigan	Opponents
FIRST DOWNS	149	132
By Rushing	97	95
By Passing	44	34
By Penalty	8	3
NET YARDS RUSHING	1772	1879
Number of Rushes	482	458
Yards per Attempt	3.7	4.1
NET YARDS PASSING	1009	681
Forward Passes Attempted	146	118
Forward Passes Completed	72	51
Passes Had Intercepted	12	12
Percent of Passes Completed	49.3	43.2
Yards per Pass Attempt	6.9	5.8
NET YARDS RUSHING AND PASSING	2781	2560
Number of Plays	628	576
Yards per Play	4.4	4.4
PUNTS	34	42
Average Distance per Punt	32.6	34.9
KICKOFFS, RETURNED BY	30	38
FUMBLES	29	22
Ball Lost by Fumbles	17	15
PENALTIES	36	44
Yards Penalized	336	432
POINTS	187	147

1957 MICHIGAN VARSITY

No.	Name	Pos.	Age	Ht.	Wt.	Class
15	Batsakes, John	HB	22	5:8	170	Sr.
65	Berger, Thomas	G	21	5:11	185	Sr.
68	Bochnowski, Alex	G	21	5:10	190	Sr.
81	Boshoven, Robert	E	25	6:0	205	Sr.
84	Bowers, David	E	20	6:2	195	Sr.
97	Boyden, Joel	T	20	6:6	260	Jr.
26	Brown, David	QB	19	5:11	185	So.
74	Bushong, Jared	T	20	6:2	210	So.
33	Byers, James	FB	20	6:0	198	Jr.
61	Callahan, Alex	G	20	6:0	185	Jr.
92	Cowan, Keith	T	20	6:0	205	So.
94	Crownley, Ermin	T	20	6:1	226	So.
73	Davies, James	T	22	5:11	220	Sr.
67	DeMassa, Thomas	G	19	5:8	188	So.
57	Dickey, James	C	20	6:0	188	Sr.
52	Dupay, Michael	C	19	6:3	212	So.
63	Faul, Lawrence	G	20	6:0	195	Sr.
69	Fillichio, Mike	G	19	5:10	195	So.
70	Genyk, George	T	19	6:0	190	So.
53	Goebel, Jerry	C	21	6:3	214	Sr.
96	Golvach, Duane	C	21	6:0	210	So.
77	Gray, James	T	22	6:3	221	Jr.
10	Groce, Alvin	HB	19	5:11	175	So.
39	Haller, David	FB	20	6:0	185	Jr.
41	Harper, Darrell	HB	19	6:1	190	So.
36	*Herrnstein, John	FB	19	6:2	212	Jr.
79	Heynen, Richard	T	22	6:1	200	Sr.
51	Hoke, Hugh	G	20	5:9	185	Jr.
89	Johnson, Robert	E	20	6:1	189	Jr.
82	*Johnson, Walter	E	20	6:2	214	Jr.
16	Julian, Fred	HB	19	5:9	178	So.
91	Keller, Dale	E	19	6:1	198	So.
83	Ketteman, Richard	E	21	6:1	187	Sr.
95	Kolcheff, Donald	E	19	6:0	183	So.
71	Kreger, John	T	21	6:6	248	Sr.
80	Krueger, Frederick	E	22	5:11	185	Sr.
45	Leith, Jerry	HB	20	5:9	167	Jr.
48	*Lousma, Jack R.	C	21	6:0	192	Jr.
56	MacPhee, William	C	20	6:0	191	Sr.
78	*Marciniak, Gerald	G	20	6:2	220	Jr.
18	McCoy, Ernest	HB	22	5:10	170	Sr.
40	McPherson, James	QB	19	5:10	185	So.
17	Myers, Bradley	HB	19	6:0	185	So.
88	Morrow, Gordon	E	22	6:3	212	Sr.
27	Noskin, Stanton	QB	19	5:11	180	So.
64	*Nyren, Marvin	G	22	6:0	205	Sr.
62	Olm, Fred	G	18	5:10	210	So.
60	Oppman, Douglas	G	19	5:10	195	Jr.
72	*Orwig, James (Capt.)	T	22	6:0	200	Sr.
43	*Pace, James	HB	21	6:0	195	Sr.
66	Poulos, Paul	G	19	5:11	190	So.
86	*Prahst, Gary	E	20	6:4	210	Jr.
49	*Ptacek, Robert	HB	20	6:1	194	So.
32	Renwick, William	FB	19	6:0	185	Jr.
37	Rio, Anthony	FB	20	6:0	185	Jr.
14	*Shatusky, Michael	HB	26	5:11	175	Sr.
35	*Sisinyak, Eugene	FB	20	6:0	190	Jr.
30	Smith, Gerald	FB	19	5:10	185	So.
75	Smith, Willie	T	19	6:2	240	Jr.
58	*Snider, Gene	C	26	6:1	210	Sr.
22	Spidel, John	QB	20	5:11	178	Jr.
76	Stetten, Maynard	T	20	6:2	205	Jr.
28	Sytek, James	QB	20	5:11	195	Jr.
85	Teuscher, Charles	E	19	6:1	197	So.
24	Van Pelt, James	QB	21	5:11	185	Jr.
59	Vavroch, John	G	20	6:0	205	Jr.
55	*Wine, Raymond	C	23	6:2	196	Jr.
42	Zachary, John	HB	20	5:11	175	Jr.
38	Zervas, Stephen	FB	22	5:11	192	Sr.

*Lettermen

HALFBACKS

JAMES PACE—One of football's fastest backs, Pace will be a senior this fall. Last year he played 289 minutes, averaged 4.8 yards per play as he netted 498 yards on 103 attempts. He scored two touchdowns, completed six of 12 passes for 97 yards. He also caught seven passes and averaged 22 yards with them although he did not score any touchdowns on receptions.

Two years ago he played 98 minutes, racked up 5.4 yards per carry rushing and completed one out of six passes thrown for six yards, having one intercepted. He also caught one aerial for 13 yards and punted once for 41 yards. Although he scored two touchdowns as a sophomore, he had several called back because of rules infractions, offsides, etc., by team-mates.

Pace holds the Big Ten indoor 60-yard sprint title and has won two letters in track as a sprinter. Originally from Grand Rapids, Mich. where he played sandlot football with Terry Barr, former Wolverine ace, when the two were youngsters. Pace played his high school athletics at Dunbar high school in Little Rock, Ark., where he attracted widespread attention both as a halfback and sprinter. He stands five feet, 11 inches tall and weighs 194 pounds. He's 21 and a senior in the College of Education.

The composers of Michigan's two most famous marching songs were assembled during Reunion Weekend and — they say — this is the first time a picture ever has been taken of them together. Left to right are: Dr. John A. Flower, accompanist for the Alumni Sing; Louis Elbel, Composer of "The Victors"; J. Fred Lawton and Dean Earl V. Moore, author and composer of "Varsity"; and Donn M. Chown, Songmaster of the Alumni Sing.

Nov. 2

MICHIGAN (21)
LE—Prahst, Teuscher, Spidel
LT—Orwig, Heynen
LG—Faul, Callahan, Berger
C—Goebel, Snider, Wine
RG—Nyren, Marciniak, Fillichio
RT—Davies, Smith, Bushong
RE—W. Johnson, Boshoven
QB—Van Pelt, Noskin
LH—Pace, Ptacek
RH—Myers, Shatusky
FB—Byers, Herrnstein, Sisinyak

IOWA (21)
LE—Gibbons, Jenkinson, Merz
LT—Karras, Theer
LG—Bloomquist, Grouwinkel
C—Lapham, M. Lewis
RG—Commings, Drake
RT—Klein, Rigney
RE—Norton, Prescott, Livermore
QB—Duncan, Veit
LH—Gravel, Furlong, Jeter, Sessi
RH—Hagler, Jauch, John Brown, Hapoel
FB—Horn, Nocera

IOWA	7	0	7	7—21
MICHIGAN	0	21	0	0—21

Ia.	Mich.		Time
		FIRST QUARTER	
6	0	Nocera (2-yd. run)	
7	0	Prescott (placekick)	7:12
		SECOND QUARTER	
7	6	Pace (65-yd. punt return)	2:00
7	7	Van Pelt (place kick)	
7	13	Prahst (31-yd. pass play from Van Pelt)	5:06
7	14	Van Pelt (place kick)	
7	20	Noskin (71yd. sneak)	10:45
7	21	Van Pelt (place kick)	
		THIRD QUARTER	
13	21	Horn (3-yd run)	6:15
14	21	Prescott (place kick)	
		FOURTH QUARTER	
20	21	Duncan (1-yd. sneak)	8:45
21	21	Prescott (place kick)	

Nov. 9

MICHIGAN		ILLINOIS
Prahst (Teuscher)	LE	Hanson
Orwig (Heynen) (Genyk)	LT	(Nietupski) Adams
Callahan (Berger) (Faul)	LG	(Ash) Burrell
Goebel (Snider) (Wine)	C	(Stapleton) Cherney
Nyren (Marciniak) (Fillichio)	RG	(Patrick) Allen
Davies (Smith)	RT	(Krumrei) (Utz) Johnson
W. Johnson (Boshoven)	RE	(Kreitling) Delaney
Noskin (Van Pelt) (Spidel)	QB	(Schrader) (Hickey) Haller
Pace (Ptacek)	LHB	Mitchell
Shatusky (Myers)	RHB	(Wallace) Bonner
Byers (Herrnstein)	FB	(Delveaux) Nitschke

MICHIGAN	6	0	0	13—19
ILLINOIS	0	13	0	7—20

Touchdowns: Myers, Herrnstein, Teuscher, Delveaux, Bonner 2.
Points after touchdown: Van Pelt, Haller 2.
Officials: Referee, Ross Dean; Umpire, Don Elser; Head Linesman, Charles Leadbetter; Field Judge, Max Mohr; Back Judge, Claude Chrisman.

Jim Pace Selected As All American

TEAM PLAYERS
MICHIGAN
LE—Prahst, Teuscher.
LT—Orwig, Heynen.
LG—Faul, Callahan, Berger.
C—Goebel, Snider.
RG—Nyren, Marciniak, Fillichio.
RT—Davies, Smith, Bushong.
RE—Boshoven, W. Johnson.
QB—Van Pelt, Noskin.
LH—Pace, Ptacek.
RH—Shatusky, Myers.
FB—Rio, Sisinyak, Herrnstein.

OHIO STATE
LE—Houston, Morgan.
LT—Schafrath, A. Crawford.
LG—Jobko, Baldacci, H. Jones, Anders.
C—Fronk, D. James.
RG—Thomas, Spychalski.
RT—Marshall, Martin.
RE—Brown, Bowermaster.
QB—Kremblas, Okulovich.
LH—LeBeau, Connavino, Sutherin.
RH—Trivisonno, Wentz.
FB—White, Cisco.

Nov. 23

SCORE BY PERIODS

MICHIGAN	7	7	0	0—14
OHIO STATE	7	3	14	7—31

Touchdowns: MICHIGAN—Pace, Myers; OHIO STATE—LeBeau (2), Kremblas, Connavino.

Conversions: MICHIGAN—Van Pelt (2); OHIO STATE—Sutherin, Kremblas (3).

Field Goals: OHIO STATE—Sutherin.

TEAM STATISTICS

	MICH.	OSU
FIRST DOWNS	16	19
Rushing	12	17
Passing	3	2
Penalty	1	0
TOTAL NO. OF RUSHES	42	70
NET YARDS—		
Rushing	270	372
Passing	107	49
Total Yards	377	421
FOR'D PASSES ATT'PTED	12	9
Completed	5	3
Intercepted by	0	0
Yds. interceptions ret'ned	0	0
TOTAL PLAYS (Rushes and Passes)	54	79
PUNTS—		
Number	2	4
Average distance	46	30
KICKOFFS, returned by	5	4
YDS. KICKS RETURNED	74	75
Punts	14	4
Kickoffs	60	71
FUMBLES—		
Number	3	0
Ball lost by	2	0
PENALTIES—		
Number	2	4
Yards penalized	6	12

Michigan Inspired "The Victors"

THE VICTORS
(CHORUS)

Hail! to the victors valiant
Hail! to the conquering heroes
Hail! Hail to Michigan, the leaders and best—
   Hail! to the victors valiant
Hail! to the conquering heroes,
   Hail! Hail! to Michigan, the champions of the West.

By Louis Elbel

Composer Louis Elbel leads the band in "The Victors" at the Homecoming of 1939.

Reprinted with permission from the **Michigan Alumnus**

MICHIGAN'S INDIVIDUAL SCORING FOR 1957

	RUSHING			PASSING				RECEIVING		PUNT RET.		PUNTING		SCORING						
	Tries	Net Gain	Ave.	Att'd	Comp.	Had Int.	Gain	Cgh't	Gain	No.	Yds.	No.	Avg.	TD	CA	CM	S	FGA	FG	TP
Herrnstein, fb	31	125	4.0	0	0	0	0	1	−8	0	0	0	0.0	1	0	0	0	0	0	6
Pace, hb	123	664	5.4	3	1	0	−8	11	122	8	98	0	0.0	10	0	0	0	0	0	60
Van Pelt, qb	36	8	0.2	80	42	3	629	0	0	0	0	15	31.1	1	19	17	0	3	1	26
Shatusky, hb	36	149	4.1	1	0	1	0	4	45	2	15	9	33.0	2	0	0	0	0	0	12
Ptacek, hb	60	161	2.7	3	2	0	23	8	88	8	82	0	0.0	0	0	0	0	0	0	0
Myers, hb	69	252	3.7	1	1	0	2	9	159	5	40	8	34.5	4	1	0	0	0	0	24
Noskin, qb	44	70	1.6	52	24	5	344	0	0	0	0	0	0.0	3	6	3	0	0	0	21
Sisinyak, fb	23	77	3.3	0	0	0	0	0	0	0	0	0	0.0	0	0	0	0	0	0	0
Julian, hb	6	1	0.2	0	0	0	0	1	12	0	0	0	0.0	0	0	0	0	0	0	0
Harper, hb	8	37	4.6	0	0	0	0	0	0	1	0	2	35.0	0	1	0	0	0	0	0
Byers, fb	31	161	5.2	0	0	0	0	0	0	0	0	0	0.0	0	0	0	0	0	0	0
Groce, hb	3	2	0.7	0	0	0	0	0	0	0	0	0	0.0	1	0	0	0	0	0	6
Spidel, qb	4	27	6.8	5	2	2	19	0	0	0	0	0	0.0	0	0	0	0	0	0	0
McCoy, hb	2	5	2.5	0	0	0	0	0	0	0	0	0	0.0	0	0	0	0	0	0	0
Rio, fb	6	33	5.5	0	0	0	0	0	0	0	0	0	0.0	0	0	0	0	0	0	0
Sytek, qb	0	0	0.0	1	0	1	0	0	0	0	0	0	0.0	0	0	0	0	0	0	0
Prahst, e	0	0	0.0	0	0	0	0	15	233	0	0	0	0.0	2	0	0	0	0	0	12
Johnson, W., e	0	0	0.0	0	0	0	0	9	122	0	0	0	0.0	0	0	0	0	0	0	0
Bowers, e	0	0	0.0	0	0	0	0	6	111	0	0	0	0.0	2	0	0	0	0	0	12
Boshoven, e	0	0	0.0	0	0	0	0	3	57	0	0	0	0.0	0	0	0	0	0	0	0
Teuscher, e	0	0	0.0	0	0	0	0	5	68	0	0	0	0.0	1	0	0	0	0	0	6
Callahan, g	0	0	0.0	0	0	0	0	0	0	0	0	0	0.0	0	0	0	1	0	0	2

1958 MICHIGAN VARSITY

No.	Name	Pos.	Age	Ht.	Wt.	Class
21	Barger, Phil	QB	19	5:11	188	So.
15	Batsakes, John	HB	23	5:8	172	Sr.
84	Brefeld, Joseph	E	18	6:2	212	So.
26	Brown, Dave	HB	20	5:11	183	Jr.
74	Bushong, Jared	T	20	6:2	209	Jr.
48	Bushong, Reid	HB	18	6:1	179	Jr.
33	Byers, James	C	21	6:0	198	Sr.
61	Callahan, Alex	G	21	6:0	195	Sr.
90	Cowan, Keith	E	21	6:0	205	Jr.
65	Curtis, Guy	G	19	6:1	222	So.
67	DeMassa, Thomas	G	20	5:8	188	Jr.
68	Deskins, Donald	T	27	6:2	241	So.
57	Dickey, James	C	23	6:1	191	Sr.
72	Dupay, Michael	T	19	6:2	207	Jr.
85	Farris, Lovell	E	21	6:3	216	Jr.
69	Fillichio, Mike	G	20	5:10	190	Jr.
32	Fitzgerald, Dennis	FB	22	5:9	184	So.
80	Galarneault, John	E	19	6:2	198	So.
70	Genyk, George	T	20	6:1	200	Jr.
77	Gray, James	T	23	6:3	233	Sr.
97	Grein, Wilfrid	T	20	6:3	226	Jr.
10	Groce, Alvin	HB	20	5:11	166	Jr.
53	Hall, B. Lee	T	20	6:0	206	So.
81	Halstead, John	E	18	6:2	205	So.
20	Hannah, Donald	QB	19	6:0	178	So.
41	Harper, Darrell	HB	20	6:1	195	Jr.
36	Herrnstein, John	FB	20	6:2	215	Sr.
93	Hildebrand, Willard	T	19	6:2	216	So.
64	Jobson, Tom	G	19	6:0	201	So.
89	Johnson, Robert	E	20	6:2	199	Sr.
82	Johnson, Walter	E	22	6:2	214	Sr.
16	Julian, Fred	HB	20	5:9	184	Jr.
88	Kane, Gary	E	19	6:2	215	So.
50	Kerr, Thomas	C	19	6:1	203	So.
83	Kolcheff, Donald	E	20	6:0	192	So.
91	Lanka, Vitauts	E	19	5:11	187	So.
92	Lazik, Arthur	E	20	6:2	210	So.
19	Leith, Jerry	HB	21	5:9	167	Sr.
56	MacPhee, William	C	21	6:0	191	Sr.
96	Maki, Wesley	T	19	5:11	214	So.
78	Marciniak, Jerry	T	21	6:2	236	Sr.
14	McNitt, Gary	HB	19	5:9	196	So.
24	McPherson, James	QB	20	5:10	175	Jr.
58	Morrow, Gordon	C	23	6:3	228	Sr.
17	Myers, Bradley	HB	20	6:0	196	Jr.
46	Newman, Harry, Jr.	HB	20	5:9	185	So.
27	Noskin, Stanton	QB	20	5:11	180	Jr.
62	Olm, Fred	G	19	5:11	223	Jr.
60	Oppman, Douglas	G	22	5:10	192	Jr.
63	Palomaki, David	G	19	6:1	205	So.
66	Poulos, Paul	G	20	5:11	198	Jr.
86	Prahst, Gary	E	21	6:4	220	Sr.
49	Ptacek, Robert	HB	21	6:1	204	Sr.
18	Raeder, Paul	HB	19	5:11	187	So.
37	Rio, Anthony	FB	21	6:0	189	Sr.
35	Sisinyak, Eugene	FB	19	6:0	195	So.
51	Smith, Gerald	C	20	5:11	185	Jr.
75	Smith, Willie	T	20	6:2	243	So.
23	Snow, Daniel	QB	19	6:0	192	So.
22	Spidel, John	QB	21	5:11	180	Sr.
76	Stetten, Maynard	T	21	6:2	206	Sr.
79	Stine, William	T	19	6:1	215	So.
39	Stuart, Henry	FB	19	5:11	191	So.
73	Swanson, Robert	T	19	6:0	212	So.
55	Syring, Richard	C	19	6:0	189	So.
28	Sytek, James	QB	21	5:11	194	Sr.
52	Thorpe, Darrell	C	19	6:0	204	So.
45	Vollmar, James	HB	20	6:0	178	So.
38	Walker, John	FB	20	6:0	195	So.
71	Walls, Grant	T	19	6:0	189	So.
30	Wilson, Willerfred	FB	20	5:10	180	Jr.
42	Zachary, Jack	HB	21	5:9	174	Sr.

Letterman

1958 Season				Won 2, Lost 6, Tie			
				Date	Place	Atten
Michigan	20	U.S.C.	19	Sep 27	Ann Arbor	70
Michigan	12	Michigan State	12	Oct 4	East Lansing	75
Michigan	14	Navy	20	Oct 11	Ann Arbor	80
Michigan	24	Northwestern	55	Oct 18	Evanston	34
Michigan	20	Minnesota	19	Oct 25	Ann Arbor	72
Michigan	14	Iowa	37	Nov 1	Ann Arbor	68
Michigan	8	Illinois	21	Nov 8	Ann Arbor	58
Michigan	6	Indiana	8	Nov 15	Ann Arbor	47
Michigan	14	Ohio State	20	Nov 22	Columbus	79

SEPT. 27

Michigan Edges Trojan

Varsity Opens Campaign Wit

Ten-Point Win In Far We

State Earns A Deadloc

Favored Spartans Surge Fror

Behind To Tie Wolverines

Michigan State has a colorful football custom which never has been publicly followed at Michigan.

After each victory, Spartan Coach Hugh (Duffy) Daugherty presents the game ball to the State player he feels has been the most deserving in the day's play.

There was no victory—as had been expected—in Spartan Stadium on the perfect football afternoon of October 4. But the personable Daugherty made the presentation nonetheless.

Duffy, in a spontaneous action, thrust the ball into the hands of a surprised Bennie Oosterbaan as the two exchanged post-game congratulations out on the turf where, moments before, their teams had battled tensely and furiously to a 12 to 12 deadlock.

This was Duffy's way of paying tribute to a respected antagonist. He has pitted his teams against Bennie's Wolverines for five successive years now. Most observers would agree the Spartans have been blessed with superior manpower during this span, but the two men still stand all even with two victories apiece and one tie.

Moreover, Duffy is still looking upward at Ben's Big Ten coaching record. Oosterbaan, now in his eleventh season, has lost only 18 Conference games and has a winning percentage of .692. Duffy, who never has been forced to face Ohio State, stands at .620.

NOV. 8

The Illini Do It Again

Loss Gives Michigan Its Worst

Defensive Record In History

NOV. 1

Iowa Speeds To Victory

Hawkeyes Win First Michigan

Game In Thirty-Four Years

Middies Upset Michigan

Ben's Last Home Game

Hoosiers Turn Back Michigan's Effort To Win Stadium Finale

FIELDING H. YOST had a ready answer for those opponents who used to complain they had outplayed his Michigan teams but somehow had failed to win.

"The only thing that really counts, y'know, is what shows up there on the scoreboard."

Over the years Michigan has defeated many teams while winding up on the short end of the statistical charts. Occasionally, the reverse has been true, and so it was on the chilled afternoon of October 11 when Navy's Midshipmen paid an infrequent visit to Michigan Stadium.

The Wolverines outran, outpassed, outdowned, and outkicked their resourceful guests from Annapolis. They controlled the ball for 60 per cent of the game, and time after time had the hard-pressed Midshipmen backed up in a resolute defense of the Navy goal.

But the Wolverines also learned the sad truth of Yost's philosophy. "When games are won or lost on the basis of first downs or yardage, then we'll try to do those things. Meanwhile, y'know, we'll just concentrate on the points."

Until the game's final moment, Navy was across midfield and down into Michigan territory only thrice all afternoon. But the opportunistic Midshipmen made each of the three penetrations pay off in a scoreboard dividend.

Michigan had the ball eleven times during the tense afternoon. Nine times the Wolverines drove inside the Navy 35 and six times they were inside the 20. But they scored only twice, and so Navy won the victory, 20 to 14.

Reprinted with permission from the Michigan Alumnus

MICHIGAN'S 1958 TEAM STATISTICS

	Michigan	Opponents
FIRST DOWNS	143	135
Rushing	85	93
Passing	49	35
Penalty	9	7
NET YARDS RUSHING	1253	1835
Number of rushes	431	451
Yards per attempt	2.9	4.1
NET YARDS PASSING	1208	807
Forward passes attempted	176	96
Forward passes completed	93	43
Passes had intercepted	13	7
Per Cent of passes completed	52.8	44.8
Yards per pass attempted	6.9	8.4
NET YARDS—RUSHING & PASSING	2461	2642
Number of plays	607	547
Yards per play	4.1	4.8
PUNTS	47	43
Average distance per punt	37.4	35.4
Punts had blocked	1	1
YARDS KICKS RETURNED	890	941
Punts	188	350
Kickoffs	702	591
FUMBLES	26	28
Ball lost by	11	15
PENALTIES	35	54
Yards penalized	337	416

	RUSHING			PASSING			RECEIVING			PUNT RET.		PUNTING		SCORING							
	Tries	Net Gain	Ave.	Att'd	Comp.	Had Int.	Gain	Cgh't	Gain	No.	Yds.	No.	Ave.	TD	R	P	K	R	C	K	TP
Herrnstein, fb	35	138	3.9	0	0	0	0	2	45	0	0	0	0.0	2	0	0	0	0	0	0	12
Julian, hb	45	180	4.0	1	0	1	0	7	84	0	0	0	0.0	0	0	0	0	0	0	0	0
Myers, hb	81	201	2.5	7	4	0	59	17	169	7	63	27	39.4	3	2	0	3	1	0	1	21
Ptacek, qb	92	124	1.3	115	65	9	763	5	30	8	66	0	0.0	4	2	5	0	1	0	0	26
Groce, hb	4	12	3.0	0	0	0	0	0	0	0	0	0	0.0	0	0	0	0	0	0	0	0
Rio, fb	28	98	3.5	0	0	0	0	0	0	0	0	0	0.0	1	0	0	0	0	0	0	6
Noskin, qb	11	−57	−5.2	29	13	1	204	1	7	0	0	0	0.0	0	0	0	1	0	0	1	1
McNitt, hb	3	10	3.3	0	0	0	0	0	0	0	0	0	0.0	0	1	0	0	1	0	0	2
Harper, hb	55	309	5.6	14	8	0	131	13	137	5	33	19	36.6	3	1	0	3	1	0	2	22
Walker, fb	11	36	3.3	0	0	0	0	0	0	0	0	0	0.0	0	0	0	0	0	0	0	0
Spidel, qb	7	18	2.6	5	2	1	24	0	0	0	0	0	0.0	0	0	0	0	0	0	0	0
R. Bushong, hb	11	19	1.7	3	0	0	0	4	72	0	0	0	0.0	0	1	0	0	0	0	0	2
Newman, hb	10	39	3.9	2	1	1	27	1	14	0	0	0	0.0	2	0	0	0	0	0	0	12
Sisinyak, fb	25	107	4.3	0	0	0	0	0	0	1	2	0	0.0	0	0	0	0	0	1	0	2
Byers, c	9	31	3.4	0	0	0	0	1	2	0	0	0	0.0	0	0	0	0	0	0	0	0
Batsakes, hb	3	3	1.0	0	0	0	0	1	6	0	0	0	0.0	0	0	0	0	0	0	0	0
Halstead, e	0	0	0.0	0	0	0	0	5	82			0	0.0		0	0	0	0	0	0	0
Prahst, e	0	0	0.0	0	0	0	0	22	313			0	0.0	4	0	0	0	0	1	0	26
W. Johnson, e	0	0	0.0	0	0	0	0	4	99			0	0.0		0	0	0	0	0	0	0
Zachary, hb	0	0	0.0	0	0	0	0	1	4			0	0.0		0	0	0	0	0	0	0
R. Johnson, e	0	0	0.0	0	0	0	0	8	119			0	0.0		0	0	0	0	0	0	0
Kane, e	0	0	0.0	0	0	0	0	1	12			0	0.0		0	0	0	0	0	0	0

Bump Elliott To Succeed Oosterbaan

SNUBS GRID-CZAR JOB

Crisler Is Staying In Post at U-M

Oct. 3

BY HAL MIDDLESWORTH
Free Press Staff Writer

The University of Michigan can call off its so-called "search for a new director of athletics." Fritz Crisler isn't leaving, after all, to become czar of the newly formed but still inactive American Football League. Crisler never said he was.

* * *

BUT FOR the past week, stories from "reliable sources" kept popping out, insisting that the most powerful figure in college football was ready to jump to the pros. Some insisted that Crisler already had agreed to a five-year contract at a salary of $50,000 or $60,000 a year.

Crisler ended the talk Sunday night.

Through the university public relations department, he announced at Ann Arbor that he has asked withdrawal of his name from consideration for the commissioner's post in the new league.

Then Crisler hopped a plane for Boston, to attend a four-day gathering of the NCAA executive council.

Oct. 20

1959 Season			Won 4, Lost 5, Tied 0		
			Date	Place	Attendance
Michigan 15,	Missouri	20	Sep 26	Ann Arbor	52,756
Michigan 8,	Michigan State	34	Oct 3	Ann Arbor	103,234
Michigan 18,	Oregon State	7	Oct 10	Ann Arbor	76,020
Michigan 7,	Northwestern	20	Oct 17	Ann Arbor	68,393
Michigan 14,	Minnesota	7	Oct 24	Minneapolis	56,082
Michigan 10,	Wisconsin	19	Oct 31	Ann Arbor	68,756
Michigan 20,	Illinois	15	Nov 7	Champaign	44,768
Michigan 7,	Indiana	26	Nov 14	Bloomington	24,171
Michigan 23,	Ohio State	14	Nov 21	Ann Arbor	88,804

From the Sidelines . . .

The record crowd total of 103 requires a word of explanation s Michigan has added no more seat the Stadium since previous sell were listed at 101,001. Athletic ti manager Don Weir, unable to conv Ohio State—Michigan's perennial r for the nation's seasonal crowd le ership—that only regular ticket-h ers should be included in the offi figures, has now adopted Ohio's me od of counting everyone who is actu in the Stadium. This includes pr and radio people, the players, bar ushers, etc.

This was the twelfth straight y that Michigan and State have playe capacity crowds. It was announce a sellout back in June.

Reprinted with permission from the
Detroit Free Press

Bump's First Defeat

Missouri Edges Wolverines In Final Five Seconds

Chalmers (Bump) Elliott last week achieved a distinction he had striven mightily to avoid.

This personable young man is the twelfth head coach in Michigan's rich 80-year history of collegiate football. He is now the first ever to launch his Wolverine career by absorbing a defeat.

No matter how long he coaches, Elliott will never see a team come closer to victory without gaining it. Michigan's first loss under his direction was a matter of seconds and inches—and both were resolved in favor of the determined Missouri foe.

Fifty-nine minutes and 55 seconds had passed by on the humid, overcast afternoon of September 26 and Michigan was clinging to a 15 to 14 lead. Three seconds later—with only two ticks of the clock left before game's end—Missouri nudged across the lead touchdown by scant inches.

It was the final scrimmage play of an intersectional engagement which moved somewhat uneventfully through the first half, picked up excitement in the third period, and then left all of the 50,553 opening-day Stadium spectators limp at the close.

The final score was Missouri 20, Michigan 15, and it squares the all-time record of the two schools. Four years ago, in another season-opener, Ron Kramer scored 23 points as Michigan swept to a 42 to 7 triumph.

Reprinted with permission from the
Michigan Alumnus

I WANT TO GO BACK TO MICHIGAN

I want to go back to Michigan,
To dear Ann Arbor town,
Back to Joe's and the Orient,
Back to some of the money we sper
I want to go back to Michigan,
To dear Ann Arbor town,
I want to go back; I got to go back
To Michigan. Oh!
Father and Mother pay all the bills
And we have all the fun
In the friendly rivalry of college life
Hooray!
And we have to figure a heckuva lot
To tell what we have done
With the coin we blew at dear old
Michigan!

MICHIGAN'S 1959 TEAM STATISTICS

	Michigan	Opponents
FIRST DOWNS	127	129
Rushing	81	91
Passing	39	37
Penalty	7	1
NET YARDS RUSHING	1278	1634
Number of rushes	441	457
Yards per attempt	2.9	3.6
NET YARDS PASSING	801	886
Forward Passes Attempted	148	122
Forward passes completed	67	57
Passes had intercepted	21	14
NET YARDS — RUSHING & PASSING	2079	2520
Number of plays	589	579
Yards per play	3.5	4.4
PUNTS	44	44
Punts had blocked	0	1
YARDS KICKS RETURNED	816	686
Punts	296	204
Kickoffs	520	482
FUMBLES	28	21
Ball lost by	13	14
PENALTIES	29	31
Yards penalized	254	324

The Jug Stays Home
Harper, Julian And Defense Provide 14 To 6 Triumph

The superlatives were properly applied to a pair of Wolverine halfbacks as the shadows lengthened over Minnesota Stadium on the wind-blown afternoon of October 24.

But in the first flush of upset 14 to 6 victory over Minnesota's massive Gophers, most observers seemed to overlook Michigan's team performance in the less exciting but equally meaningful area of defense.

Darrell Harper and Fred Julian, a pair of Seniors whose Michigan careers more often than not have been rooted in frustration, each deeply deserved every word of spoken and written praise.

Harper returned a punt 83 yards for Michigan's first touchdown and then Julian followed scant minutes later with a 42-yard scoring slash over the momentarily-unbalanced Gophers for another.

Neither had ever before been able to manage so sparkling an achievement during their Wolverine playing days. Together, they were indeed instrumental in Michigan's hard-fought triumph which:

1/ Marked the first Wolverine Big Ten win in exactly 52 weeks.

2/ Enabled the jubilant Blue team to return the fabled Little Brown Jug to its Ann Arbor resting place for at least another year.

3/ Leapfrogged the rebuilding young Michigan team over defending champion Iowa and into a sixth-place tie in the Conference scramble.

4/ And extended Coach Bump Elliott's proud record of never having lost to Minnesota either as player or coach at Michigan.

Nov. 21

MICHIGAN		OHIO STATE
Halstead (Maentz)(Cowan)	LE	(Rowland)(Perdue) Bryant
Jobson (Stine)(Hildebrand)	LT	Michael
Genyk (Hall)(DeMassa)	LG	(Hauer) Ingram
Smith (Grant)(Stieler)	C	(Watkins)(Lindner) Anders
Fillichio (Pavloff)(Poulos)	RG	Hartman
J. Bushong (Curtis)(Deskins)(Schopf)	RT	(Tolford) Tyrer
Johnson (Mans)(Zubkus)	RE	(Fiers) Houston
Noskin (Stamos)(McPherson)	QB	(Matte) Fields
Harper (R. Bushong)(McRae)	LHB	(Hansley)(German)(Kilgore) Ferguson
Julian (Raeder)(Fitzgerald)(Leith)	RHB	(Herbstreit) Houck
Rio (McNitt)(Tureaud)	FB	(Tingley) Detrick

MICHIGAN	7	7	6	3	23
OHIO STATE	6	0	8	0	14

Touchdowns: Rio 2, Noskin, Houston, Detrick.
One-point conversions: Harper 2.
Two-point conversion: Herbstreit (pass from Fields)
Field goal: Harper.
Officials: Referee, Mike Delaney; Umpire, A. N. Smith; Head Linesman, Charles Leadbetter; Field Judge, Wally Marks; Backfield Judge, Robert Baur.

	RUSHING			PASSING			RECEIVING			PUNT RET.		PUNTING		SCORING								
	Tries	Net Gain	Ave.	Att'd	Comp.	Had Int.	Gain	Cgh't	Gain	No.	Yds.	No.	Ave.	TD	P.A.T. Att. R	P	K	P.A.T. R	C	K	F.G.	TP
Julian, hb	72	289	4.0	0	0	0	0	5	42	2	24	1	36.0	2	0	0	0	0	0	0	0	12
Rio, fb	56	222	4.0	0	0	0	0	8	90	0	0	0	00.0	3	0	0	0	0	0	0	0	18
Harper, hb	67	224	3.3	1	0	0	0	4	33	3	101	26	41.0	3	0	0	8	0	0	7	2	31
McRae, hb	76	242	3.2	0	0	0	0	4	102	5	19	0	00.0	2	0	0	0	0	0	0	0	12
Stamos, qb	12	−16	−1.3	9	2	4	35	0	0	0	0	0	00.0	0	0	0	0	0	0	0	0	0
Noskin, qb	44	−29	−0.7	115	61	15	747	0	0	0	0	4	32.0	2	1	4	0	0	0	0	0	12
Tureaud, fb	27	104	3.8	0	0	0	0	6	60	0	0	0	00.0	2	0	0	0	0	0	0	0	12
R. Bushong, hb	14	43	3.1	0	0	0	0	4	27	4	62	6	38.5	0	0	0	0	0	0	0	0	0
Fitzgerald, hb	16	55	3.4	0	0	0	0	1	7	2	36	0	00.0	0	0	0	0	1	0	0	0	2
Raeder, fb	8	25	3.1	0	0	0	0	0	0	4	45	0	00.0	0	0	0	0	0	0	0	0	0
Van Dyne, fb	2	2	1.0	0	0	0	0	0	0	0	0	0	00.0	0	0	0	0	0	0	0	0	0
Newman, hb	6	16	2.7	0	0	0	0	1	9	0	0	0	00.0	0	0	0	0	0	0	0	0	0
Tunnicliff, fb	13	33	2.5	0	0	0	0	1	4	0	0	0	00.0	0	0	0	0	0	0	0	0	0
Hannah, qb	4	11	2.8	13	2	1	10	0	0	0	0	0	00.0	0	0	0	0	0	0	0	0	0
Palmer, qb	3	8	2.7	10	2	1	8	0	0	0	0	0	00.0	0	0	0	0	0	0	0	0	0
McNitt, hb	3	11	2.7	0	0	0	0	1	20	1	5	0	00.0	0	0	0	0	0	0	0	0	0
Myers, hb	17	43	2.5	0	0	0	0	1	25	1	3	1	39.0	0	0	0	0	0	0	0	0	0
G. Mans, e	0	0	0.0	0	0	0	0	1	15	0	0	0	00.0	0	0	0	0	0	0	0	0	0
Johnson, e	0	0	0.0	0	0	0	0	20	264	0	0	0	00.0	0	0	0	0	1	0	0	0	2
Kane, e	0	0	0.0	0	0	0	0	1	3	0	0	0	00.0	0	0	0	0	0	0	0	0	0
Halstead, e	0	0	0.0	0	0	0	0	6	77	0	0	0	00.0	2	0	0	3	0	0	3	2	21
Callahan, g	0	0	0.0	0	0	0	0	1	−6	0	0	0	00.0	0	0	0	0	0	0	0	0	0
Maentz, e	0	0	0.0	0	0	0	0	2	18	0	0	6	41.3	0	0	0	0	0	0	0	0	0

Hall of Fame

Neil Worthington Snow
University of Michigan
All-American End 1901

[certificate text, partially illegible]

Elected
February 1960
New Brunswick, N.J.

The above certificate was awarded to Neil Snow on February 17, 1960. Neil Worthington Snow: University of Michigan End and Fullback 1898-1901. Casper Whitney's All-America 1901. 12 letterman at Michigan, four each in football, baseball and track. Walter Camp said of him "No College ever developed a better all around athlete." An early football official and a very successful businessman, Snow died in 1914 at the age of 34.

Other Michigan players to win this coveted Hall of Fame Award are: Willie Heston, Adolph "Germany" Schulz, Harry Kipke, Benny Friedman, Bennie Oosterbaan and Tommy Harmon, making a total of seven Michigan men. This number is exceeded by only two other institutions, Yale with nine men and Harvard with eight men installed in the Hall of Fame.

In addition, three Michigan coaches have been so honored: Fielding H. Yost, Elton E. Wieman and Michigan's present Athletic Director, H. O. Crisler.

Oct. 1

Game Tale In Figures

MICHIGAN STATE
ENDS—Arbanas, Brandstatter, Oxendine, Sanders, Abrecht, Zorn, Fontes, Harness, Clark, Jones.
TACKLES—Winiecki, Kanicki, Kakela, Bobbitt, Walker, Budde, Szwast.
GUARDS—Azar, Kumiega, Biondo, Hahn, Wendorf, Boylen, Mudd, Ross.
CENTERS—Manders, Behrman.
BACKS—Wilson, Adderley, Hudas, Grimsley, Hrisko, Paterra, Hatcher, Suci Ryan, Roe, Stewart, Ballman, Eaton, Charon, Saimes, Stevenson, Newman.

MICHIGAN
ENDS—Maentz, Johnson, Freehan, Zubkus, Mans, Halstead.
TACKLES—Jobson, Schopf, Stine, Houtman, Curtis.
GUARDS — Poulos, Syring, Hall, O'Donnell.
CENTERS—Smith, Grant.
BACKS—Glinka, McRae, Fitzgerald, Tureaud, Stamos, Chandler, Strobel, Bushong, Raimey, McNitt, Van Dyne, Tunnicliff.

SCORING
MICHIGAN   7 10 0 0—17
STATE   7 7 3 7—24

TOUCHDOWNS: MICHIGAN—Raimey, Fitzgerald; STATE—Wilson, Ballman, Charon.
FIELD GOALS: MICHIGAN—Halstead; STATE—Brandstatter.
EXTRA POINTS: MICHIGAN —Halstead 2 (placement); STATE—Brandstatter 3 (placement).

1960 MICHIGAN VARSITY

No.	Name	Pos.	Ht.	Wt.	Age	Cl
16	Agee, Michael J.	HB	6:0	175	19	S
73	Atchison, John	G	6:0	195	19	S
86	Brown, Robert M.	E	6:5	217	20	S
70	Bryce, Gary L.	T	6:3	215	19	S
48	*Bushong, Reid J.	HB	6:1	185	20	S
20	Chandler, M. Robert	QB	6:3	196	19	S
67	Clappison, Frank D.	G	6:1	192	19	S
72	Conklin, Jon D.	T	6:2	250	19	S
90	*Cowan, Keith E.	E	6:2	207	22	S
77	*Curtis, Guy P.	T	6:0	205	21	S
34	DeStefano, Guy J.	FB	5:11	185	20	Jr.
80	Filar, Robert L.	E	6:4	200	18	S
18	*Fitzgerald, Dennis	HB	5:10	185	24	S
88	Freehan, William A.	E	6:3	195	18	So.
53	Gee, Thomas A.	G	6:0	197	20	Jr.
24	Glinka, David J.	QB	6:1	198	19	S
59	*Grant, Todd P.	C	6:4	225	20	Jr.
23	Griesser, Ralph	QB	5:10	180	19	So.
65	*Hall, B. Lee	G	6:0	208	22	Jr.
81	*Halstead, John C.	E	6:2	208	20	Sr.
22	*Hannah, Don W.	QB	6:0	180	21	Sr.
75	Herrala, Wallace R.	G	5:10	215	20	Jr.
93	*Hildebrand, Willard	T	6:2	210	21	Sr.
12	Hood, E. Edward	HB	5:9	175	19	So.
17	Hornbeck, William H.	HB	6:1	185	20	Jr.
57	Houtman, John L.	C	6:4	230	19	So.
64	*Jobson, E. Thomas	T	6:0	215	21	Sr.
89	*Johnson, Robert	E	6:2	201	22	Sr.
50	Kerr, Thomas	C	6:1	190	21	Sr.
63	Kocan, Ronald R.	G	5:11	205	23	So.
83	*Korowin, James F.	E	6:2	194	20	Jr.
16	Kowalik, John F., Jr.	HB	5:10	180	19	So.
58	Kriska, Nicholas J.	G	6:0	185	19	So.
74	Lehr, John J.	T	6:0	223	19	So.
96	*Maentz, D. Scott	E	6:3	206	20	Jr.
56	Maloney, Frank M.	G	5:11	193	20	Jr.
82	*Mans, George W.	E	6:4	208	20	Jr.
40	McKee, Grant	HB	6:0	187	20	Jr.
14	McNitt, Gary D.	FB	5:10	191	21	Sr.
43	*McRae, Benjamin P.	HB	6:0	170	20	Jr.
62	Minko, John P.	G	6:1	212	18	So.
33	Mongeau, David G.	FB	6:3	211	19	So.
69	O'Donnell, Joseph R.	FB	6:2	208	19	So.
95	Palomaki, Dave	T	6:1	205	21	Sr.
52	Pampu, Virgil R.	C	6:0	190	28	Jr.
60	*Pavloff, Louis	G	6:0	190	20	Jr.
25	Plesha, Robert H.	QB	6:0	174	18	So.
66	*Poulos, Paul K.	G	5:11	205	22	Sr.
35	*Raeder, J. Paul	HB	5:11	192	21	Jr.
19	Raimey, David E.	HB	5:10	190	19	So.
78	Schmidt, Paul R.	T	6:4	235	20	Jr.
76	Schopf, Jon B.	T	6:2	228	20	Jr.
51	*Smith, Gerald (Capt.)	C	5:11	190	22	Sr.
99	Smith, Jeffrey A.	E	6:3	193	20	Jr.
15	Spacht, Ronald L.	HB	5:10	180	20	Jr.
28	*Stamos, John E.	QB	6:1	208	20	Jr.
94	Stawski, Willard S.	T	6:3	209	20	Jr.
79	*Stine, William R.	T	6:2	223	21	Sr.
42	Strobel, Jack A.	HB	5:10	176	19	So.
55	*Syring, Richard E.	G	6:0	192	21	Sr.
36	*Tunnicliff, Wm. H.	FB	6:1	210	20	Jr.
39	*Tureaud, Kenneth E.	HB	6:1	198	20	Jr.
32	*Van Dyne, Rudd D.	FB	6:0	198	22	Sr.
54	*Walker, John C.	C	6:0	200	21	Sr.
61	Walls, Grant W., Jr.	T	6:0	205	21	Sr.
45	Ward, James A.	HB	6:1	195	19	So.
85	*Zubkus, E. James	E	6:1	196	22	Jr.

*Letterman

1960 Season — Won 5, Lost 4, Tied 0

			Date	Place	Attendance
Michigan	21	Oregon	0	Sep 24	Ann Arbor	48,021
Michigan	17	Michigan State	24	Oct 1	East Lansing	76,490
Michigan	31	Duke	6	Oct 8	Ann Arbor	77,183
Michigan	14	Northwestern	7	Oct 15	Ann Arbor	63,027
Michigan	0	Minnesota	10	Oct 22	Ann Arbor	71,752
Michigan	13	Wisconsin	16	Oct 29	Madison	57,629
Michigan	8	Illinois	7	Nov 5	Ann Arbor	63,665
Michigan	29	Indiana	7	Nov 12	Ann Arbor	51,584
Michigan	0	Ohio State	7	Nov 19	Columbus	83,107

Fitzgerald off on 99-yard touchdown dash

Michigan Tops Duke University By 31 To 6 Count

IN five of the last six football seasons, Michigan has scheduled competition with schools never before played by past Wolverine teams.

Each of these encounters has ended in a Michigan victory.

Missouri (1955), U.C.L.A. (1956), Georgia (1957) and Oregon State (1959) all have had losing debuts with Wolverine teams during the last half-dozen years.

Duke University became the latest of the new rivals on October 8 and bowed to the Wolverines, 31 to 6, before a Band Day crowd of 77,183 in Michigan Stadium.

Coach Chalmers (Bump) Elliott's young men achieved victory over their visitors from Durham, North Carolina, despite the absence of two backs who had led the Wolverines in rushing yardage for the first two games of the season. Sitting out the Duke contest were Halfback Ben McRae and Fullback Ken Tureaud, both injured in the Michigan State battle the week before. McRae was favoring an injured ankle while Tureaud nursed a bruised hip.

With these two first-stringers kept out of action, Coach Elliott moved Right Halfback Dennis Fitzgerald to the left half position, elevated speedy Dave Raimey to the starting right half spot and installed Rudd Van Dyne as the first unit's fullback.

The lineup shuffle proved successful as Raimey and Fitzgerald each scored a pair of touchdowns against Duke's Blue Devils.

Gophers Regain The Jug

Minnesota Hands Michigan Its 150th Football Defeat

Michigan recorded its 150th football victory in 1905 and since then Wolverine teams have gone on to win a grand total of 462 games.

Now, for the first time in Michigan's rich and storied gridiron history, rival schools have amassed 150 triumphs.

This bench mark in Wolverine football annals was reached on the afternoon of October 22 as unbeaten Minnesota gained a 10 to 0 Big Ten decision before a Homecoming crowd of 69,352 spectators in Michigan Stadium.

In addition to holding Michigan scoreless for the first time in 40 games, Minnesota also won possession of the Little Brown Jug trophy for the first time since 1956 and maintained its front-running position with Iowa in the race for 1960 Western Conference championship honors.

Bump Edges Pete In First Battle Between Elliotts

IN the long and colorful history of the Western Conference, 9 head football coaches have been former Michigan players.

Only three Big Ten schools — Indiana, Minnesota and Northwestern — never have had an ex-Wolverine as gridmaster.

Five of the men have returned to their alma mater as coaches: Gustave H. Ferbert (1897-99), Elton S. Wieman (1927-28), Harry G. Kipke (1929-37), Ben Oosterbaan (1948-58) and the current mentor, Chalmers W. (Bump) Elliott, who took over in 1959.

Albert Herrnstein coached at Purdue (1905) and Ohio State (1906-09), Kipke at Michigan State (1928) and Ivan B. Williamson at Wisconsin (1949-55). Forest Evashevski has been head coach at Iowa since 1954.

And this year Peter Elliott, Bump's brother, succeeded Ray Eliot as the head grid mentor at Illinois.

Twelve times during the last 55 years, Wolverine alumni have coached Big Ten teams against Michigan. Their combined record is one victory, one tie, and 10 defeats.

When Pete Elliott brought his Illini into Michigan Stadium on November 5 it marked the first time in Big Ten annals that two brothers had been opposing head coaches.

Playing before 62,927 fans, with the season's first snow falling intermittently, Bump's Wolverines edged Pete's Illini with the help of a two-point conversion, 8 to 7.

MICHIGAN			MINNESOTA
Maentz (Halstead) (Freehan)		LE	(Prawdzik) R. Larson
Jobson (Stine) (Houtman)		LT	(Miller) (Frisbee) Bell
Hall (Poulos)		LG	(McNeil) Mulvena
Smith (Walker) (Grant)		C	(Hook) (Annis) G. Larson
Syring (O'Donnell)		RG	(Odegard) Brown
Schopf (Curtis)		RT	(Bergman) Brixius
Johnson (Mans)		RE	(Hall) Deegan
Stamos (Glinka)		QB	(Salem) (Johnson) Stephens
McRae (Bushong) (Strobel) (Hood)		LH	(Mulholland) King
McNitt (Raimey) (Ward) (Fitzgerald)		RH	(Kauth) Munsey
Tureaud (Tunnicliff) (Van Dyne) (Raeder)		FB	(Enga) (Rogers) Hagberg

MICHIGAN	0	0	0	0 — 0	
MINNESOTA	0	7	0	3 — 10	

SCORING: Touchdown—Rogers; Field goal—Rogers; One-point conversion—Rogers.
OFFICIALS: Howard Wirtz, referee; Richard Lowell, umpire; F. G. Skibbie, head linesman; Wally Marks, field judge; Mike Layden, back judge.

Bucks Take The Finale
Ohio State Wins, 7 To 0, On Fourth-Quarter Drive

Before the 1960 season began, football-analysts rated Michigan as a team having strong offensive potential and a weak defense.

As the campaign ran its course, however, the Wolverine defensive unit proved to be more consistent and dependable than the offense.

Going into the final game of the season, Michigan stood second in the Big Ten defensive ratings—and ninth on offense.

This pattern was followed in the 1960 finale on November 19 as Ohio State scored a fourth-quarter touchdown to defeat Michigan, 7 to 0, before 83,107 spectators in Ohio Stadium.

It was a game with no title implications and the result did not change the position of either team in the Big Ten standings—Ohio State remained in third place behind co-champions Iowa and Minnesota, and Michigan stayed in a tie for fifth place. But such special inducements seldom are necessary when these two old rivals meet, and they have played 57 times since the series began in 1897.

Reprinted with permission from the **Michigan Alumnus**

Conference Standings
(Final)

	W	L	T	Pct.	Pts.	Opp. Pts.
Iowa	5	1	0	.833	163	89
Minnesota	5	1	0	.833	105	50
Ohio State	4	2	0	.667	129	83
Michigan State	3	2	0	.600	87	96
MICHIGAN	2	4	0	.333	52	71
Illinois	2	4	0	.333	80	103
Purdue	2	4	0	.333	99	111
Northwestern	2	4	0	.333	60	91
Wisconsin	2	4	0	.333	89	170
*Indiana	0	0	0	.000	0	0

*Games do not count in standings.

MICHIGAN'S 1960 TEAM STATISTICS

	Michigan	Opponents
FIRST DOWNS	145	106
Rushing	97	65
Passing	39	38
Penalty	9	3
NET YARDS RUSHING	1642	1235
Number of rushes	456	873
Yards per attempt	3.6	3
NET YARDS PASSING	878	730
Forward passes attempted	149	151
Forward passes completed	63	63
Passes had intercepted	11	13
NET YARDS RUSHING and PASSING	2520	1968
Number of plays	605	524
Yards per play	4.2	3
PUNTS	48	53
Punts had blocked	0	0
YARDS KICKS RETURNED	764	724
Punts	290	218
Kickoffs	474	506
FUMBLES	29	23
Ball lost by	16	11
PENALTIES	35	34
Yards penalized	348	249

MICHIGAN'S INDIVIDUAL SCORING FOR 1960

	RUSHING Tries	Net Gain	Ave.	PASSING Att'd	Comp.	Had Int.	Gain	RECEIVING Cgh't	Gain	PUNT RET. No.	Yds.	PUNTING No.	Ave.	TD	P.A.T. Att. R	P	K	P.A.T. R	C	K	F.G.	PT
McRae, hb	80	352	4.4	0	0	0	0	7	99	14	113	0	0.0	0	0	1	0	0	1	0	0	2
Raimey, hb	62	292	4.7	0	0	0	0	3	37	4	35	0	0.0	6	0	0	0	0	0	0	0	36
Fitzgerald, hb	66	263	4.0	0	0	0	0	1	5	4	19	0	0.0	3	0	2	0	0	2	0	0	22
Tureaud, fb	60	233	3.9	0	0	0	0	8	90	0	0	0	0.0	1	0	0	0	0	0	0	0	6
Strobel, hb	27	128	4.6	0	0	0	0	1	7	4	10	0	0.0	1	0	0	0	0	0	0	0	6
Tunnicliff, fb	36	107	3.0	0	0	0	0	1	5	0	0	0	0.0	3	0	0	0	0	0	0	0	18
VanDyne, fb	14	59	4.2	0	0	0	0	2	20	0	0	0	0.0	0	0	0	0	0	0	0	0	0
Bushong, hb	19	59	3.1	0	0	0	0	0	0	4	36	39	35.6	0	0	0	0	0	0	0	0	0
Glinka, qb	37	−29	−0.8	124	54	11	755	0	0	0	0	0	0.0	0	0	0	0	0	0	0	0	0
McNitt, hb	12	45	3.8	0	0	0	0	0	0	4	44	0	0.0	0	0	0	0	0	0	0	0	0
Stamos, qb	5	−18	−3.6	12	3	0	55	0	0	0	0	0	0.0	0	0	0	0	0	0	0	0	0
Hornbeck, hb	9	41	4.6	0	0	0	0	0	0	0	0	0	0.0	0	0	0	0	0	0	0	0	0
Ward, hb	12	67	5.6	0	0	0	0	0	0	2	18	0	0.0	0	0	0	0	0	0	0	0	0
Kowalik, hb	3	12	4.0	0	0	0	0	0	0	0	0	0	0.0	1	0	0	0	0	0	0	0	6
Hood, hb	3	12	4.0	0	0	0	0	1	8	0	0	0	0.0	0	0	0	0	0	0	0	0	0
Spacht, hb	3	9	3.0	0	0	0	0	0	0	0	0	2	28.5	0	0	0	0	0	0	0	0	0
Raeder, fb	1	2	2.0	0	0	0	0	0	0	0	0	0	0.0	0	0	0	0	0	0	0	0	0
Hannah, qb	1	5	5.0	9	4	0	52	0	0	0	0	0	0.0	0	0	0	0	0	0	0	0	0
DeStefano, fb	2	2	1.0	0	0	0	0	0	0	0	0	0	0.0	0	0	0	0	0	0	0	0	0
Chandler, qb	3	3	1.0	4	2	0	16	0	0	0	0	1	35.0	0	0	0	0	0	0	0	0	0
Cowan, e	1	2	2.0	0	0	0	0	1	15	0	0	0	0.0	0	0	0	0	0	0	0	0	0
Johnson, e	0	0	0.0	0	0	0	0	15	230	0	0	0	0.0	1	0	0	0	0	0	0	0	6
Maentz, e	0	0	0.0	0	0	0	0	7	128	0	0	6	31.5	2	0	0	0	0	0	0	0	12
Mans, e	0	0	0.0	0	0	0	0	9	136	0	0	0	0.0	1	0	0	0	0	0	0	0	6
Brown, e	0	0	0.0	0	0	0	0	3	59	0	0	0	0.0	0	0	0	0	0	0	0	0	0
Zubkus, e	0	0	0.0	0	0	0	0	1	3	0	0	0	0.0	0	0	1	0	0	1	0	0	2
Halstead, e	0	0	0.0	0	0	0	0	1	9	0	0	0	0.0	0	0	10	0	0	6	1	9
Freehan, e	0	0	0.0	0	0	0	0	1	11	0	0	0	0.0	0	0	2	0	0	2	0	2
Korowin, e	0	0	0.0	0	0	0	0	1	16	0	0	0	0.0	0	0	0	0	0	0	0	0

Tax Money Not Given To Athletes

Fritz Crisler, Michigan Athletic Director, yesterday denied that any state funds intended for scholarships were given to University of Michigan athletes.

"We get nothing from the Legislature and never have," said Crisler.

"Our gate receipts and share of student activities fees pay for everything. Whenever we recruit an athlete from out of state, we must pay the same tuition for him as for any other student," continued Crisler.

The controversy was raised by Senator Garland Lane (D-Flint) who charged last Saturday that Michigan Tech was spending $193,-000 a year to keep Canadian hockey players and other out-of-state students there.

Football Ticket Prices to Rise

By PETE WALDMEIR

The price of Big Ten football is going up.

When the season ticket applications go out from Michigan and Michigan State this spring, both schools plan to tack on an extra 50 cents a game, raising Michigan's price to an even $5 and Michigan State's to $4.50.

The increase already has been approved at State, while Michigan's rise needs only the formal stamp of the athletic board.

And the rest of the conference schools, belabored by rising costs and stagnant revenues, are expected to follow suit, breaking the long-established $4 line, according to Michigan Athletic Director Fritz Crisler.

"In the postwar years costs of operating a football program have risen nearly 500 per cent," Crisler explained, "but ticket prices on the average haven't gone up more than 10 per cent.

"At the Big Ten meetings in December a proposal was made for across the board increases to $5 at all schools, but it was defeated. Instead, it was left up to each institution."

Reprinted with permission from the **Michigan Daily**

1961			
Michigan	29	UCLA	6
Michigan	38	Army	8
Michigan	0	Michigan State	28
Michigan	16	Purdue	14
Michigan	20	Minnesota	23
Michigan	28	Duke	14
Michigan	38	Illinois	6
Michigan	23	Iowa	14
Michigan	20	Ohio State	50

Season Summary
Games won 6; Lost, 3; Tied, 0.
Points for Michigan 212; Opponents, 163.

THEN AND NOW—SIXTY YEARS OF SUCCESS
University of Michigan Athletic Association Financial Report

	September 1900—September 1901		July 1960—June 1961	
	Receipts	Expenses	Receipts	Expenses
Balance	$ 424.73			
Football	10,557.13		$ 725,873.10	
Football		$ 7,786.81		$ 207,867.18
Baseball	2,413.69		291.00	
Baseball		2,169.24		24,618.30
Track	1,598.30		750.84	
Track		2,174.72		56,570.68
Interscholastic Meet	419.11		77.79	
Interscholastic Meet		847.54		
Membership Tickets	2,065.90			
Subscriptions	1,729.50			
All Other Receipts	3,086.71		524,383.47	
All Other Expenses		9,287.27		935,223.28
Total Receipts	$22,295.07		$1,251,376.38	
Total Expenses		$22,265.58		$1,224,279.44
Balance	$ 29.49		$ 27,096.94	
Debts Outstanding		$ 2,320.00		none
Deficit		$ 2,299.51		none

1900-1901:

Item of All Other Receipts includes proceeds from Bills payable.

Item of All Other Expenses includes salaries, stand fund appropriation and a few permanent improvements.

(signed) C. G. Roe
Financial Secretary

September 24, 1901 Balance in my hands: $29.49.

(signed) T. L. Rolinson
Treasurer

1960-1961:

The 1900-1901 report represents a complete financial report. It is difficult to compare the counterpart of every item in the 1901 report. For example, a far more expansive program exists today such as seven additional varsity sports, the golf course and rink, radio, television etc. all figure in the 1961 report.

("This I Remember" Continued on page 21)

MICHIGAN'S 1961 TEAM STATISTICS

	Michigan	Opponents
FIRST DOWNS		
Total No. 1st Downs	135	131
Rushing	94	83
By Passing	34	43
By Penalty	7	5
RUSHING		
Net Yards Rushing	1841	1225
No. Rushes	427	404
Yds. per Attempt	4.3	3.0
PASSING		
Net Yds. Passing	715	1101
Passes Attempted	112	161
Passes Completed	54	80
Passes Had Intercepted	5	7
Touchdown Passes	6	6
Average Gain per Attempt	6.4	6.
Completion percentage	48.2	49.
TOTAL OFFENSE		
Net Yards Gained	2556	2326
No. Offensive Plays	539	565
Average Gain per Play	4.7	4.
PUNTING		
Number	45	51
Total Yards	1587	1859
Average Yards	35.3	36.
Punts Had Blocked	0	1
KICK RETURNS		
Yards Punts Returned	198	239
Yards Kickoffs Returned	667	678
Total Yards Kicks Returned	865	917
FUMBLES		
Total Fumbles	17	22
Ball Lost By	11	11
PENALTIES		
No. of Penalties	41	32
Yards Penalized	401	284

AUG. 8

Top 'M' Grid Player Dies In Crash Here

Philip Garrison Victim; Three Others Injured

University football player Philip Garrison, 19, of Wyandotte, was killed early this morning when the sports car he was driving went out of control and pinned him underneath it on W. Huron River Dr.

County medical examiner Dr. John C. Floyd reported that Garrison, a sophomore tackle. died of asphyxiation from gas, mud and water under the car shortly after the mishap. ,

The accident occurred at about ; a.m. on Huron River Dr. between Maple Rd. and Wagner Rd. in Scio township.

Injured were U-M wrestler Karl Fink, 21, of 2050 Washtenaw Ave., Ypsilanti; Michael D. Morrison, 22, of Kalamazoo, and Carl Quarmistrom, 21, of New Haven.

Fink was a passenger in the car driven by Garrison.

Following In His Car

Morrison was following the Garrison vehicle in another sports car. It went out of control at the same point on the road moments later, skidding upright into a ditch about 60 feet from the overturned Garrison car, Washtenaw sheriff's deputies reported.

Philip Garrison

VS. DUKE

During the three seasons Bump Elliott has been Michigan's head football coach, Wolverine teams have stepped out of the Big Ten seven times to face non Conference opponents.

After a loss to Missouri in Bump's 1959 coaching debut. the Varsity has won six straight games against outside competition. The latest of these triumphs was a 28 to 14 decision over Duke. achieved Nov. 4 before 56,488 fans in Michigan Stadium.

It gave this year's Wolverine team the distinction of having beaten one of the best teams on the West Coast (U.C.L.A.), one of the best in the East (Army), and the 1961 Cotton Bowl champion (Duke).

Michigan scored the second time it had the ball for a series of downs. moving 39 yards in seven plays. Halfback Ben McRae, who tallied the Varsity's first three touchdowns. made this one on a five-yard sprint around right end.

The Wolverines widened the margin to 21 to 0 in the second quarter, with McRae scoring on a 15-yard pass from Quarterback Dave Glinka and a 34-yard runback of a pass interception.

Duke rallied to score a pair of touchdowns in the second half, but Michigan also counted one to keep the game well under control. The final Wolverine TD went to End Bob Brown on a 45-yard pass play from Glinka. Michigan's extra points were scored on a pair of conversion kicks by Doug Bickle and a two-point pass from Glinka to End George Mans.

SEPT. 30

UCLA Ripped, 29 to 6

Wolverines Hit Hard and Fast

	MICHIGAN	UCL
First downs	13	1
Rushing yardage	227	11
Passing yardage	26	58
Passes	2-8	5-1
Passes intercepted	1	0
Punts	5-35	7-37
Fumbles lost	1	2
Yards penalized	70	10

UCLA	0	0	6	
Michigan	13	3	13	0

MICH—Tunnicliff 1 run (Bickle kick).
MICH—Raimey 20 run (kick failed).
MICH—FG Bickle 29.
MICH—McRae 4 run (Bickle kick).
MICH—Tureaud 92 pass interceptio (kick failed).
UCLA—Dimkich 1 run (run failed).

Michigan Victor

MICHIGAN (16)

LE—Maentz, Jeff Smith, Brown.
LT—Bickle, Houtman, Keating, Staw ski.
LG—Minko, Maloney.
C—Walker, Grant.
RG—Hall, Kurtz.
RT—Schopf, Curtis.
RE—Mans, Monzeau.
QB—Stamos, Glinka.
LH—McRae, Strobel.
RH—Raimey, Ward, Hood, McLenna
FB—Tureaud, Tunnicliff, Raeder.

PURDUE (14)

LE—Elwell, Wells.
LT—Brumm, Bowic.
LG—Sczurek, Ohl, Florence.
C—Pennhanna, Paltani.
RG—Krysinski, Stafford.
RT—Russ, Keiser.
RE—Farmer, Greiner, Butcher.
QB—Meyer, Digravio, Hogan.
LH—Miller, Bloom.
RH—Boris, Weil.
FB—Plaskon, Walker, Donaldson.

MICHIGAN	9	0	7	0—1
PURDUE	0	7	7	0—1

FIRST QUARTER

SCORE / TIME

2	0	Safety (Boris tackled in end zone)	5:20
8	0	Raimey (1-yard plunge)	11:10
9	0	Bickle (placement).	

SECOND QUARTER

9	6	Digravio (13-yard run)	6:10
9	7	Ohl (placement).	

THIRD QUARTER

15	7	McRae (72-yard pass from Glinka)	1:1
16	7	Bickle (placement).	
16	13	Elwell (77-yard pass from Digravio)	2:1
16	14	Ohl (placement).	

Oh, Brother! --M Clobbers Illini, 38-6

Bump Hands Pete His 7th Straight '61 Loss

Nov. 11

Nov. 25

Game Story As Reflected Via Figures

Lineups

MICHIGAN

ENDS—Maentz, Maus, Brown, Korowin, Smith, Bickle, Zubkus.
TACKLES — Houtman, Stawski, Keating, Schmidt, Curtis, Schopf.
GUARDS—Minko, Collins, Hall, Szymankls, Kurtz.
CENTERS — Walker, Maloney, Slezak.
BACKS—Stamos, Glinka, Prichard, Chandler, Dougall, Chapman, Hood, Hornbeck, Raimey, McLenna, Watters, Specht, Raeder, Tunnicliff, Tureaud, Ward.

OHIO STATE

ENDS — Bryant, Perdue, Wittmer, Ricketts, Middleton, Tidmore, Van-Raaphorst.
TACKLES—Vogel, Krstolic, Roberts, Laskoski, Sanders, Tolford, Manula, Connor.
GUARDS—Jenkins, Ingram, Moeller, Foster, Stephens, Betz.
CENTER—Armstrong.
BACKS—Hess, Mummey, Sparma, Mrukowski, Warfield, Hartman, Johnson, Klein, Houck, Ferguson, Tingley, Katterhenrich, Francis.

Scoring

MICHIGAN	0 6 6 8—20		
OHIO STATE	7 14 0 29—50		

TOUCHDOWNS: MICHIGAN—Raimey, McLenna, Ward; OHIO STATE—Ferguson 4, Warfield, Klein, Tidmore.

EXTRA POINTS: MICHIGAN—Ward 2 (plunge); OHIO STATE—Van Raaphorst 6 (placements); Tidmore 2 (pass from Sparma).

MICHIGAN'S INDIVIDUAL SCORING FOR 1961

	RUSHING			PASSING				RECEIVING		PUNT RET.		PUNTING		SCORING							
	Tries	Net Gain	Ave.	Att'd	Comp.	Had Int.	Gain	Cgh't	Gain	No.	Yds.	No.	Ave.	TD R	P.A.T. Att. P	P.A.T. Att. K	P.A.T. R	P.A.T. C	P.A.T. K	F.G.	TP
McRae, hb	75	453	6.0	0	0	0	0	10	210	10	39	0	0.0	6	0	0	0	0	0	0	36
Raimey, hb	99	496	5.0	0	0	0	0	3	14	7	92	0	0.0	8	0	0	0	0	0	0	48
Tunnicliff, fb	96	396	4.1	0	0	0	0	0	0	0	0	0	0.0	3	0	0	0	0	0	0	18
Chapman, hb	18	97	5.4	0	0	0	0	1	9	4	24	0	0.0	1	0	0	0	0	0	0	6
Ward, hb	10	43	4.3	0	0	0	0	1	5	0	0	0	0.0	1	0	0	1	0	0	0	8
Tureaud, fb	12	45	3.8	0	0	0	0	2	15	0	0	0	0.0	1	0	0	0	0	0	0	6
Raeder, fb	11	77	7.0	0	0	0	0	1	7	0	0	0	0.0	2	0	0	0	0	0	0	12
McLenna, hb	14	43	3.1	0	0	0	0	0	0	2	12	0	0.0	2	0	0	0	0	0	0	12
Hood, hb	20	56	2.8	0	0	0	0	0	15	3	5	0	0.0	0	0	0	0	0	0	0	0
Prichard, qb	7	53	7.6	2	1	0	10	0	0	0	0	12	30.5	0	0	0	0	0	0	0	0
Strobel, hb	16	42	2.6	0	0	0	0	4	37	5	23	0	0.0	0	0	0	0	0	0	0	0
Dougall, qb	2	6	3.0	1	1	0	17	0	0	0	0	0	0.0	0	0	0	0	0	0	0	0
Kornowa, hb	1	3	3.0	0	0	0	0	0	0	0	0	0	0.0	0	0	0	0	0	0	0	0
Spacht, qb	1	3	3.0	0	0	0	0	0	0	0	0	1	39.0	0	0	0	0	0	0	0	0
Dodd, fb	1	3	3.0	0	0	0	0	0	0	0	0	0	0.0	0	0	0	0	0	0	0	0
Kowalik, hb	1	2	2.0	0	0	0	0	0	0	0	0	0	0.0	0	0	0	0	0	0	0	0
Hornbeck, hb	1	2	2.0	0	0	0	0	1	17	0	0	0	0.0	0	0	0	0	0	0	0	0
Glinka, qb	33	42	1.3	96	46	5	588	0	0	0	0	0	0.0	1	0	0	0	0	0	0	6
Chandler, qb	10	−9	0.9	11	6	0	100	0	0	0	0	0	0.0	0	0	0	0	0	0	0	0
Alix, qb	0	0	0.0	2	0	0	0	0	0	0	0	0	0.0	0	0	0	0	0	0	0	0
Korowin, e	0	0	0.0	0	0	0	0	1	13	0	0	0	0.0	0	0	0	0	0	0	0	0
Brown, e	0	0	0.0	0	0	0	0	6	127	0	0	0	0.0	3	0	0	0	0	0	0	18
Mans, e	0	0	0.0	0	0	0	0	15	149	0	0	0	0.0	1	0	0	0	1	0	0	8
Maentz, e	0	0	0.0	0	0	0	0	5	49	0	0	28	37.3	0	0	0	0	0	0	0	0
Bickle, e	0	0	0.0	0	0	0	0	4	48	0	0	1	22.0	0	0	23	0	0	20	4	32
Tageson, e	0	0	0.0	0	0	0	0	0	0	0	0	1	34.0	0	0	0	0	0	0	0	0
O'Donnell, g	0	0	0.0	0	0	0	0	0	0	0	0	2	41.0	0	0	0	0	0	0	0	0
Hall, g	0	0	0.0	0	0	0	0	0	0	0	0	0	0.0	0	0	0	1	0	0	0	0

Oct. 27

1962

Michigan	13	Nebraska	25
Michigan	17	Army	7
Michigan	0	Michigan State	28
Michigan	0	Purdue	37
Michigan	0	Minnesota	17
Michigan	12	Wisconsin	34
Michigan	14	Illinois	10
Michigan	14	Iowa	28
Michigan	0	Ohio State	28

Season Summary
Games won 2; Lost 7; Tied, 0.
Points for Michigan 70; Opponents, 214.

U-M Shut Out 3rd Time, 17-0

Teams Commit 17 'Mistakes'

BY LYALL SMITH
Free Press Sports Editor

ANN ARBOR—Once upo a time Michigan carried th proud reputation of being "point-a-minute" footba' team.

Memories are made of thi

But for the old grads amon the 65,484 disconsolate fans wh watched the Wolverines of 196 here Saturday, those memorie were long gone, faded and torr

Michigan lost again, 17-0, i a sloppy battle with Minnesot in this Little Brown Jug due to run its streak of scoreles quarters to an astounding 1 as it absorbed its third straigh shutout defeat in as many Big Ten games.

* * *

NOT SINCE 'way back i 1935 has any Michigan squad been blanked on three consecu tive Saturdays.

Since those disastrous days of 27 years ago, other Wolverine teams went through 204 games before they ran into their current scoring drouth.

And if things are going to get better, they'll have to get better at the expense of highly-rated Wisconsin next weekend if this team is to escape the unsavory distinction of becoming the first in U-M history to be blanked four straight times.

* * *

IT WAS STRICTLY no-contest again as they lost to the not-so-golden Gophers in a game which saw the unseemly total of 17 fumbles and pass interceptions on both sides of the line.

Michigan's revised offense was so futile that after 66 plays, the Wolverines gained exactly 50 yards for their afternoon's labors.

1962 MICHIGAN VARSITY SQUAD

No.	Name	Pos.	Ht.	Wt.	Age	Class	Home Town
25	Alix, Denis	QB	6:0	170	20	Jr.	West Bloomfield
57	Anthony, Mel	FB	5:11	195	19	So.	Cincinnati, Ohio
67	Baty, Donald	G	6:2	211	20	Jr.	Hastings
23	Bay, Richard	QB	5:10	168	20	So.	Waukegan, Ill.
59	Blanchard, Don	C	6:3	233	20	Jr.	Sturgis
86	*Brown, Bob (Capt.)	E	6:5	226	22	Sr.	Kalamazoo
77	Butler, Dave	G	6:1	220	19	So.	Detroit
29	Buurma, Roger	QB	6:2	191	19	So.	Holland
20	*Chandler, Bob	QB	6:3	199	21	Jr.	LaGrange, Ill.
46	*Chapman, Harvey, Jr.	HB	5:11	180	20	Jr.	Farmington
68	Collins, Chuck	G	6:1	225	21	Jr.	Grand Rapids
82	Conley, Jim	E	6:3	193	19	So.	Springdale, Pa.
38	Dodd, Bill	FB	5:11	203	20	Jr.	Virden, Ill.
26	Evashevski, Forest	QB	6:0	182	20	Jr.	Iowa City, Iowa
80	Farabee, Ben	E	6:2	201	19	So.	Holland
91	Franzen, Raymond	T	6:0	218	19	So.	Centerline
71	Frontczak, John	T	6:3	230	19	So.	Dowagiac
97	Frontczak, Nick	G	5:10	210	18	So.	Detroit
96	Gallagher, Jim	T	6:4	216	20	Jr.	Chicago, Ill.
90	Ginger, George	E	6:3	208	21	Sr.	Detroit
24	*Glinka, Dave	QB	6:0	194	21	Sr.	Toledo, Ohio
55	Green, Jim	C	6:1	212	19	So.	Trenton
65	Hahn, Dick	G	6:0	195	18	So.	Norton, Ohio
12	*Hood, Ed	HB	5:9	175	21	Sr.	Detroit
57	*Houtman, John	T	6:4	229	21	Sr.	Adrian
41	Jones, Dennis	HB	6:2	191	19	So.	Worthington, Ohio
79	*Keating, Tom	T	6:3	206	20	Jr.	Chicago, Ill.
88	Kocan, Ron	E	5:11	203	25	Sr.	Sharpsville, Pa.
48	Kornowa, Donald	HB	6:1	195	19	Jr.	Toledo, Ohio
50	Kovacevich, Dave	G	5:10	203	20	Jr.	Chicago, Ill.
16	Kowalik, John, Jr.	HB	5:10	181	21	Sr.	Detroit
63	*Kurtz, Dave	G	6:0	204	19	Jr.	Toledo, Ohio
85	Lambert, Fred	E	6:3	215	19	So.	Millburn, N. J.
83	Laskey, Bill	E	6:1	206	19	So.	Milan
76	Lauterbach, Ronald	T	6:3	232	21	Sr.	Dayton, Ohio
94	Mader, Gerald	T	6:3	217	19	So.	Chicago, Ill.
61	Marcum, John	G	6:0	205	20	Jr.	Monroe
93	Mayer, Richard	E	6:2	187	19	So.	Evanston, Ill.
92	McAleer, Pat	E	6:4	222	19	So.	Kenosha, Wis.
95	McLeese, Ronald	T	6:4	250	19	So.	Roseville
15	Miheve, Tom	HB	6:0	168	19	So.	Wakefield
62	*Minko, John	G	6:1	226	20	Sr.	Connellsville, Pa.
84	Morawa, Lawrence	E	6:3	190	20	Jr.	Dearborn
58	Muir, Bill	C	6:0	200	20	Jr.	Cuyahoga Falls, Ohio
66	*Nolan, Deb	G	5:11	210	20	Jr.	Clare
69	*O'Donnell, Joe	T	6:2	219	21	Sr.	Milan
43	Ong, Dave	HB	6:0	185	20	So.	Allen Park
53	Paoletti, Maurice	G	5:10	205	19	So.	Grosse Pointe
54	Pasch, John	C	6:2	202	20	So.	Toledo, Ohio
51	Patchen, Brian	C	5:11	207	19	So.	Steubenville, Ohio
60	*Pavloff, Louis	G	6:0	210	22	Sr.	Hazel Park
78	Piotrowski, Larry	T	6:4	215	19	Jr.	Bay City
21	*Prichard, Tom	HB	5:10	180	20	Jr.	Marion, Ohio
19	*Raimey, David	HB	5:10	195	21	Sr.	Dayton, Ohio
17	Rindfuss, Dick	HB	6:1	188	19	So.	Niles, Ohio
36	Schmitt, Roger	FB	5:11	195	20	Jr.	Buffalo, N. Y.
73	Schram, Dick	T	6:1	220	21	Jr.	Jackson
56	Seamon, David	C	6:3	223	19	So.	Grand Rapids
70	Simkus, Arnold	T	6:4	225	19	So.	Detroit
33	Sparkman, Wayne	FB	5:11	189	20	Jr.	Plymouth
75	Striegel, Dan	T	6:4	220	20	Jr.	Arlington Hts., Ill.
42	*Strobel, Jack	HB	5:9	175	21	Jr.	Maywood, Ill.
64	*Szymanski, Dick	G	5:10	187	21	Jr.	Toledo, Ohio
89	Tageson, Bill	E	6:3	195	19	So.	Bad Axe
28	Timberlake, Bob	QB	6:4	200	19	So.	Franklin, Ohio
44	Vuocolo, Mike	FB	6:0	195	19	Jr.	Lock Haven, Pa.
45	*Ward, Jim	E	6:1	196	21	Jr.	Imlay City
49	Wickstrom, Gregg	G	5:11	206	19	So.	Lapeer
99	Woodward, Paul	T	6:2	221	20	Jr.	Cincinnati, Ohio
81	Yanz, John	E	6:2	201	20	Jr.	Chicago, Ill.

*Letterman

MICHIGAN'S INDIVIDUAL SCORING FOR 1962

	RUSHING			PASSING				RECEIVING		PUNT RET.		PUNTING		SCORING TD			P.A.T.	P.A.T.			F.G.	TP
	Tries	Net Gain	Ave.	Att'd	Comp.	Had Int.	Gain	Cgh't	Gain	No.	Yds.	No.	Ave.	R	P	K	Att.	R	C	X		
Anthony, fb	18	48	2.67	0	0	0	0	0	0	0	0	0	0.0	0	0	0	0	0	0	0	0	0
Chapman, hb	6	9	1.50	0	0	0	0	11	223	4	18	0	0.0	0	1	0	0	1	0	0	0	2
Chandler, qb	28	-63	-2.25	63	29	4	401	0	0	0	0	0	0.0	1	0	0	0	0	0	0	0	6
Dodd, fb	20	101	5.05	0	0	0	0	1	14	0	0	0	0.0	0	0	0	0	0	0	0	0	0
Evashevski, qb	25	10	0.40	35	11	3	83	0	0	0	0	0	0.0	0	0	0	0	0	0	0	0	0
Glinka, qb	8	37	4.63	17	7	1	45	0	0	0	0	0	0.0	1	0	0	0	0	0	0	0	6
Hood, hb	4	8	2.00	0	0	0	0	1	3	1	1	0	0.0	0	0	0	0	0	0	0	0	0
Prichard, hb	16	27	1.69	2	1	0	3	2	8	4	16	5	33.3	0	0	0	0	0	0	0	0	0
Raimey, hb	124	385	3.11	0	0	0	0	11	45	6	3	0	0.0	5	0	0	0	0	0	0	0	30
Rindfuss, hb	20	57	2.85	0	0	0	0	1	9	0	0	3	31.0	1	0	0	0	0	0	0	0	6
Sparkman, fb	35	133	3.80	0	0	0	0	2	22	0	0	0	0.0	0	0	0	0	0	0	0	0	0
Strobel, hb	21	68	3.23	0	0	0	0	3	29	1	7	0	0.0	1	0	0	0	0	0	0	0	6
Timberlake, qb	73	104	1.42	34	16	3	179	11	164	0	0	0	0.0	0	0	0	3	1	0	0	0	14
Brown, e	0	0	0.0	0	0	0	0	2	15	0	0	0	0.0	0	0	0	0	0	0	0	0	0
Conley, e	0	0	0.0	0	0	0	0	5	47	0	0	0	0.0	0	0	0	0	0	0	0	0	0
Farabee, e	0	0	0.0	0	0	0	0	4	33	0	0	0	0.0	0	0	0	0	0	0	0	0	0
Kocan, e	0	0	0.0	0	0	0	0	5	49	0	0	0	0.0	0	0	0	0	0	0	0	0	0
Lambert, e	0	0	0.0	0	0	0	0	1	9	0	0	0	0.0	0	0	0	0	0	0	0	0	0
Laskey, e	0	0	0.0	0	0	0	0	2	13	0	0	0	0.0	0	0	0	0	0	0	0	0	0
Ward, e	0	0	0.0	0	0	0	0	3	30	0	0	0	0.0	0	0	0	0	0	0	0	0	0
O'Donnell, t	0	0	0.0	0	0	0	0	0	0	0	0	54	34.8	0	0	0	0	0	0	0	0	0

Tom Harmon, Michigan All-American, was saluted by the Michigan band as it formed his initials and his football number, which has been retired by the Wolverine team.

MICHIGAN'S 1962 TEAM STATISTICS

	Michigan	Opponents
FIRST DOWNS		
Total No. 1st Downs	98	152
Rushing	61	91
Passing	28	47
By Penalty	9	14
RUSHING		
Net Yards Rushing	891	1839
Number of Rushes	400	440
Yards per Attempt	2.23	4.18
PASSING		
Net Yards Passing	711	909
Passes Attempted	152	159
Passes Completed	64	75
Passes Had Intercepted	11	13
Touchdown Passes	1	10
Average Gain per Completion	11.1	12.1
Completion %	42.1	47.2
TOTAL OFFENSE		
Net Yards Gained	1602	2748
Number Offensive Plays	552	598
Average Gain per Play	2.91	4.60
PUNTING		
Number	62	36
Average Distance	34.4	33.2
Punts Had Blocked	0	0
KICK RETURNS		
Yards Punts Returned	64	429
Yards Kickoffs Returned	639	464
Total Yards Kicks Returned	703	893
FUMBLES		
Total Fumbles	20	31
Ball Lost By	14	16
PENALTIES		
Number of Penalties	53	46
Yards Penalized	477	375

Free Substitution Back In Football

By the Associated Press

The country's college football coaches tossed away their scorecards today, verbally approved the newly adopted free substitution rule as "good for the game" and indicated they now have enough room to manipulate their forces despite a couple of annoying strings.

"I think it will make a better game," said Coach Dan Devine of Missouri. "It's a great rule change," said North Carolina's Jim Hickey. "I'm delighted."

"Very wise — very sound," said Bump Elliott of Michigan.

The new rule, as adopted by the Football Rules Committee of the National Collegiate Athletic Association at its meeting in Coronado, Calif., Saturday, calls for more liberalized substitution. There are certain restrictions, however.

Completely free substitution will be permitted any time the clock stops and on all plays in a series except fourth down and when the ball changes hands. In each of the restrictive cases, only two men can be sent in. The substitution rules have not been that lax since unlimited substitution went out 10 years ago.

1963 FOOTBALL RESULTS

MICHIGAN	27	So. Methodist	16
Michigan	13	NAVY	26
Michigan	7	Michigan State	7
Michigan	12	PURDUE	23
Michigan	0	MINNESOTA	6
MICHIGAN	27	Northwestern	6
MICHIGAN	14	Illinois	8
Michigan	21	Iowa	21
Michigan	10	OHIO STATE	14
Totals	131	Totals	127

The Deadlock With State

Michigan had lost only 16 of the 55 games in the long Michigan State series before this year's engagement, but every Wolverine player and many of the 101,450 who jammed into the Stadium October 12 was keenly aware of recent Spartan domination which has held Michigan without victory since 1955.

The Wolverines broke on top in this 1963 defense-dominated renewal with a first period score, then saw it matched by the resurgent Spartans in the third quarter. Both teams mounted later threats but the scoreboard remained unchanged at 7 to 7.

Neither side was completely happy. "Playing a tie game is like getting a kiss from your sister," said State's Duffy Daugherty.

"I was satisfied with the way our team played," said Wolverine Coach Bump Elliott, "but I wasn't satisfied with the result."

The Jug Whitewash

It was Homecoming up in Minneapolis where the Wolverines ventured October 26 for their first out-of-town journey of the fall and all over town was visible the Gopher theme of the day, "Wish Again, Michigan."

The slogan was not too imaginative, perhaps, but it could hardly have been more prophetic. After a hard-fought game full of Wolverine frustrations, Michigan did indeed wish it could play again any one of three or four key plays.

Both the final score, favoring Minnesota by 6 to 0, and the action on the field were reminiscent of old-time battles for the Little Brown Jug. The hitting was hard, the line play tough, and the game's outcome in doubt until the final minute.

There were 62,107 on hand in windswept Memorial Stadium even though by this mid-point mark in their respective seasonal campaigns neither team had anything to gain other than the Jug and personal pride.

Reprinted with permission from the **Michigan Alumnus**

SEPT. 2

MICHIGAN	0	21	6	0—2	
SOUTH METHODIST	0	0	0	16—1	

SECOND QUARTER

M-SMU				Time
6	0	Rindfuss (18-yard run)		2:0
7	0	Timberlake (placement)		
13	0	O'Donnell (59-yard run)		6:5
14	0	Timberlake (placement)		
20	0	Lasky (4-yard pass from Evashevski)		12:48
21	0	Timberlake (placement)		

THIRD QUARTER

27	0	Anthony (1-yard run)		12:52

FOURTH QUARTER

27	6	Gannon (3-yard run)		8:30
27	8	Thomas (run)		
27	14	Thomas (1-yard run)		
27	16	Tenny (pass from Thomas)		

The Navy Aerial Show

The Midshipmen are openly boosting Junior quarterback Roger Staubach for All-American honors. Before the season ever started Navy coach Wayne Hardin declared flatly that Staubach "is destined to be the greatest quarterback that has ever played for Navy."

An eastern writer said: "The Brigade of Midshipmen believes that Staubach can walk on water and maybe he can."

A total of 55,877 fans showed up in Michigan Stadium the afternoon of October 5 to see for themselves if Staubach could live up to his advance raves. He surpassed them with a superlative performance rated by many a longtime Michigan observer as the best ever by any opposing quarterback, and Navy won the game, 26 to 13.

Before the day was done Staubach personally accounted for more than 300 yards, scored one touchdown himself, passed for two others, and brought the crowd to its feet time after time in roaring admiration of his brilliance.

BRIEF STATISTICS	Navy	Mich
First downs	18	1
Net yards gained	391	22
Passes attempted	16	1
Passes completed	14	1
Yards gained passing	237	14
Passes intercepted by	1	
Fumbles lost	3	
Yards penalized	54	1

Reprinted with permission from the **Michigan Alumnus**

M's First Grid Coach Dies At 93

(Special to The News)

FREEPORT, Me. — Frank Crawford, Michigan's first official football coach, died yesterday at the age of 93.

Reprinted with permission from the **Michigan Alumnus**

Nov. 2

RTHWESTERN	0	0	0	6 — 6
CHIGAN	0	7	14	6 — 27

M		Time

SECOND QUARTER
6 Clancy (33-yard pass from Timberlake) — 12:59
7 Timberlake kick

THIRD QUARTER
13 Henderson (23-yard pass interception) — 3:16
14 Timberlake kick
20 Henderson (24-yard pass from Timberlake) — 12:21
21 Timberlake kick.

FOURTH QUARTER
27 Conley (33-yard pass from Timberlake) — 6:03
Pass failed
27 Proffitt (4-yard pass from Milam) — 14:52
Pass failed

LSON—No. 36
0 SPORTS—MICH.

FACES TELL THE STORY: Downhearted Illinois coach, Pete Elliott (left), is consoled by his brother, Coach Bump Elliott of Micigan, after the Wolverines' 14-8 upset victory. The brothers, just one year apart in age (Bump is 38 and Pete 37), are former All-Americas at Michigan. Pete was a quarterback and Bump a halfback.

Reprinted with permission from the **Michigan Alumnus**

1963 MICHIGAN VARSITY

No.	Name	Pos.	Ht.	Wt.	Age	Class	Home Town
	Alix, Denis	QB	6:0	185	21	Sr.	West Bloomfield
	*Anthony, Melvin	FB	6:0	202	20	Jr.	Cincinnati, Ohio
	Bay, Richard	QB	5:10	170	21	Jr.	Waukegan, Ill.
	Blanchard, Don	T	6:3	226	21	Sr.	Sturgis
	Brigstock, Thomas	HB	6:0	186	20	So.	Battle Creek
	Butler, David	G	6:1	218	20	Jr.	Detroit
	Cecchini, Thomas	C	6:0	195	19	So.	Detroit
	*Chandler, Robert	QB	6:3	208	22	Sr.	LaGrange, Ill.
	Chapman, Harvey	HB	5:11	177	21	Sr.	Farmington
	Clancy, Jack	QB	6:1	196	19	So.	Detroit
	*Conley, James	E	6:3	191	20	Jr.	Springdale, Pa.
	Dehlin, Charles	FB	5:11	198	19	So.	Flushing
	*Dodd, William	HB	6:0	204	21	Sr.	Virden, Ill.
	*Evashevski, Forest	QB	6:0	185	21	Sr.	Iowa City, Iowa
	*Faribee, Ben	E	6:3	206	20	Jr.	Holland
	Flanagan, Dennis	E	6:2	208	19	So.	Niles, Ohio
	Frontczak, Stanley	G	5:11	208	19	Jr.	Detroit
	Green, James	C	6:1	210	20	Jr.	Trenton
	*Hahn, Richard	G	6:0	206	20	Jr.	Norton, Ohio
	Haverstock, Thomas	T	6:3	219	19	So.	Harrisburg, Pa.
	Henderson, John	E	6:3	185	20	Jr.	Dayton, Ohio
	Houtman, John	G	6:4	244	22	Sr.	Adrian
	Hoyne, Jeffrey	E	6:1	197	19	So.	Chicago, Ill.
	Kabealo, Geoffrey	FB	6:0	205	19	So.	Columbus, Ohio
	*Jones, Dennis	HB	6:2	185	20	Jr.	Worthington, Ohio
	Keating, Thomas	T	6:3	240	21	Sr.	Chicago, Ill.
	Keating, William	G	6:1	221	18	So.	Chicago, Ill.
	Kines, Charles	T	6:1	228	19	So.	Niles, Ohio
	Kirby, Craig	E	6:1	179	19	So.	Royal Oak
	Kovachevich, David	G	5:10	215	21	So.	Chicago, Ill.
	*Kurtz, David	G	6:0	214	20	Sr.	Toledo, Ohio
	*Laskey, William	E	6:1	211	20	Jr.	Milan
	Legacki, Norman	E	6:0	172	19	So.	Philadelphia, Pa.
	Mack, Thomas	E	6:3	216	19	So.	Bucyrus, Ohio
	*Mader, Gerald	T	6:3	220	20	Jr.	Chicago, Ill.
	*Marcum, John	G	6:0	208	21	Jr.	Monroe
	McDonald, Kenneth	E	6:1	198	19	So.	Detroit
	Miheve, Thomas	HB	6:0	166	20	Jr.	Wakefield
	*Muir, William	C	6:0	210	21	Sr.	Cuyahoga Falls, Ohio
	*O'Donnell, Joseph (Capt.)	G	6:2	239	22	Sr.	Milan
	Pasch, John	G	6:2	212	21	Sr.	Toledo, Ohio
	Patchen, Brian	C	5:11	212	20	Jr.	Steubenville, Ohio
	*Prichard, Thomas	QB	5:10	180	21	Sr.	Marion, Ohio
	Quist, Robert	HB	5:11	191	20	So.	Grand Rapids
	Reid, Dorie	HB	5:7	165	19	So.	Ferndale
	Ries, Richard	G	6:2	225	18	So.	Royal Oak
	*Rindfuss, Richard	HB	6:0	191	20	Jr.	Niles, Ohio
	Rowser, John	HB	6:0	176	19	So.	Detroit
	Ruzicka, Charles	T	6:1	239	19	So.	Skokie, Ill.
	Sarnecke, Phil	E	6:1	193	20	Jr.	Detroit
	Scharl, James	HB	6:0	202	19	So.	Detroit
	Schick, Gary	FB	6:2	205	19	So.	Grosse Pointe
	Schmidt, Robert	T	5:10	230	19	So.	Cincinnati, Ohio
	*Simkus, Arnold	T	6:4	237	20	Jr.	Detroit
	Smith, Stephen	E	6:5	228	19	So.	Park Ridge, Ill.
	*Sparkman, Wayne	FB	5:11	186	21	Sr.	Plymouth
	*Szymanski, Richard	C	5:10	185	22	Sr.	Toledo, Ohio
	*Timberlake, Robert	QB	6:4	211	20	Jr.	Franklin, Ohio
	Wells, Richard	HB	5:9	172	19	So.	Grand Rapids
	*Woodward, Paul	G	6:2	216	20	Jr.	Cincinnati, Ohio
	Wright, Kenneth	C	6:1	207	19	So.	Bay City
	*Yanz, John	T	6:3	215	21	Sr.	Chicago, Ill.
	Yearby, William	T	6:3	223	19	So.	Detroit

*Letterman

The Tie With Iowa

A total of 46,582 fans assembled in Michigan Stadium to watch the November 16 engagement with Iowa. It turned out to be a free-wheeling affair, with yardage totals almost even and the final score exactly so at 21 to 21.

Iowa dominated first-half action, with all but 67 of its 366 net yards coming in the opening two periods, but still achieved only a 14 to 7 scoreboard margin. The second half was almost a complete reversal.

Fullback Anthony scored all three of Michigan's touchdowns. The first came on a 13-yard slant to culminate a 94-yard upfield drive in the first quarter. Iowa counted twice in the second period, with quarterback Gary Snook rolling 13 for one and tossing 12 yards to end Cloyd Webb for the other.

Michigan rolled all the way after the second half kickoff with Anthony diving over left tackle for the score. The Wolverines were right back again the following play sequence, with Anthony this time hitting 3 yards into the end zone.

Iowa bounced back once more early in the final period on the wings of an aerial attack, with Paul Krause catching a Snook pass and completing a 25-yard scoring play. The conversion knotted the count at 21 and there it remained, though each team threatened again mildly with field goal attempts which fell short.

BRIEF STATISTICS

	Iowa	Mich.
First downs	19	20
Net yards gained	366	369
Passes attempted	19	13
Passes completed	9	5
Yards gained passing	158	93
Passes intercepted by	0	0
Fumbles lost	1	3
Yards penalized	40	34

Reprinted with permission from the **Michigan Alumnus**

Ohio State Air Attack Surprises U-M

By JERRY GREEN
Detroit News Sports Writer

ANN ARBOR, Nov. 30.—Ohio State, out of character with daring and imaginative football, overcame a 10-point deficit and defeated the much-too-cautious University of Michigan, 14-10, today.

The Buckeyes used the forward pass, a bomb banned during most of Woody Hayes' 13-year career in Columbus, as their most devastating weapon. It probed at Michigan's weakest spot, a defense that had been leaky against passes most of the season.

The Wolverines, bidding for their highest Big Ten finish in seven years, piled into a 10-0 lead in the first 21 minutes of play. But then Michigan was content to sit back cozy, trying to protect what it had built up with ease and Ohio State took away the momentum.

Michigan thus ended its season clogged in a fifth-place tie with Wisconsin and Northwestern with a 2-3-2 won-lost-tied record in the Big Ten. The Wolverines were 3-4-2 overall, their third losing season in Bump Elliott's five-year coaching regime.

MICHIGAN'S 1963 TEAM STATISTICS

	Michigan	Oppon
FIRST DOWNS		
Total No. 1st Downs	130	149
Rushing	80	79
Passing	47	62
By Penalty	3	8
RUSHING		
Net Yards Rushing	1180	1251
Number of Rushes	392	408
Yards per Attempt	3.02	3.
PASSING		
Net Yards Passing	963	1391
Passes Attempted	154	176
Passes Completed	75	98
Passes Had Intercepted	9	9
Touchdown Passes	7	8
Average Gain per Completion	12.82	14.
Completion %	.488	
TOTAL OFFENSE		
Net Yards Gained	2143	2642
Number Offensive Plays	546	584
Average Gain per Play	3.925	4.
PUNTING		
Number	55	51
Average Distance	36.0	37.7
Punts Had Blocked	0	0
KICK RETURNS		
Yards Punts Returned	254	99
Yards Kickoff Returned	383	391
Total Yards Kicks Returned	637	490
FUMBLES		
Total Fumbles	24	20
Ball Lost By	11	16
PENALTIES		
Number of Penalties	39	37
Yards Penalized	324	372

MICHIGAN'S INDIVIDUAL SCORING FOR 1963

	RUSHING			PASSING				RECEIVING		PUNT RET.		PUNTING			SCORING							
	Tries	Net Gain	Ave.	Att'd	Comp.	Had Int.	Gain	Cgh't	Gain	No.	Yds.	No.	Ave.	TD	P.A.T. Att. R	P	K	P.A.T. R	C	K	F.G.	TP
Anthony, fb	103	394	3.82	0	0	0	0	1	4	0	0	0	0.0	5	0	0	0	0	0	0	0	30
Chandler, qb	13	-61	-4.69	33	16	2	216	0	0	0	0	0	0.0	0	0	0	0	0	0	0	0	0
Chapman, hb	6	19	3.16	0	0	0	0	1	34	0	0	0	0.0	0	0	0	0	0	0	0	0	0
Clancy, hb	34	109	3.21	0	0	0	0	4	78	10	105	0	0.0	1	0	0	0	0	0	0	0	6
Dodd, hb	2	9	4.50	0	0	0	0	0	0	2	14	0	0.0	0	0	0	0	0	0	0	0	0
Dehlin, fb	21	76	3.62	0	0	0	0	0	0	0	0	0	0.0	0	0	0	0	0	0	0	0	0
Evashevski, qb	22	49	2.22	23	12	3	154	0	0	0	0	0	0.0	0	0	0	0	0	0	0	0	0
Henderson, e	1	-8	-8.00	0	0	0	0	27	330	0	0	0	0.0	5	0	1	0	0	1	0	0	32
O'Donnell, g	1	50	50.0	0	0	0	0	0	0	0	0	48	36.4	1	0	0	0	0	0	0	0	6
Quist, hb	2	-1	-0.50	0	0	0	0	0	0	0	0	0	0.0	0	0	0	0	0	0	0	0	0
Reid, hb	1	10	10.00	0	0	0	0	0	0	0	0	0	0.0	0	0	0	0	0	0	0	0	0
Rindfuss, hb	58	211	3.64	0	0	0	0	10	100	11	96	4	36.8	3	0	0	0	0	0	0	0	18
Rowser, hb	11	40	3.63	0	0	0	0	4	24	1	14	0	0.0	0	0	0	0	0	0	0	0	0
Schick, fb	5	17	3.40	0	0	0	0	0	0	0	0	0	0.0	0	0	0	0	0	0	0	0	0
Sparkman, fb	9	25	2.78	0	0	0	0	1	10	0	0	0	0.0	0	0	0	0	0	0	0	0	0
Wells, hb	5	25	5.00	0	0	0	0	0	0	4	25	0	0.0	0	0	0	0	0	0	0	0	0
Timberlake, qb	98	231	2.36	98	47	4	593	0	0	0	0	0	0.0	2	0	0	0	0	12	1	27
Conley, e	0	0	0.00	0	0	0	0	6	114	0	0	0	0.0	1	0	0	0	0	0	0	0	6
Laskey, e	0	0	0.00	0	0	0	0	7	105	0	0	0	0.0	1	0	0	0	0	0	0	0	6
Hoyne, e	0	0	0.0	0	0	0	0	1	19	0	0	0	0.0	0	0	0	0	0	0	0	0	0
Kirby, e	0	0	0.0	0	0	0	0	13	166	0	0	0	0.0	0	0	0	0	0	0	0	0	0
Prichard, qb	0	0	0.0	0	0	0	0	0	0	0	0	2	35.0	0	0	0	0	0	0	0	0	0
Stagg, g	0	0	0.0	0	0	0	0	0	0	0	0	1	15.0	0	0	0	0	0	0	0	0	0

HENRY HATCH
Keeper of the Little Brown Jug

The story of the Little Brown Jug in reality is not about pottery, but about people. The people who purchased and misplaced the Jug to begin it all, the players of two Big Ten universities whose efforts in one game each football season determine the ownership of the Jug for twelve more months, and—to anyone who has witnessed the "Jug Game"—it must be obvious that the history of the Jug cannot be written without the name of one man, Henry Hatch. As Equipment Manager, Henry served Michigan and Michigan athletics—they were one and the same to him—for forty-four of his sixty-four years. During that time, when the Jug was in Michigan's possession, it was in his possession. He guarded it carefully year after year as Michigan won the Jug, and he relinquished it with reluctance the years Minnesota was the victor. No scoreboard was ever needed to determine the outcome of the game when Michigan played Minnesota. One look at Hank told the story. An ear-to-ear grin meant a Michigan victory, a low walk back to the dressing room meant Minnesota had the Jug. And a Michigan victory that reclaimed the Jug from Minnesota was always a special one for Hank. He was the first man across to the Gopher sideline to gather in the Jug for the Maize and Blue as the game ended. His quick dash across midfield was slowed not one bit as he congratulated his wonderful Wolverines as he went. Hank will not be on the field to claim 'his' Jug when next Michigan wins it back. His sudden and untimely death occurred in April of 1964. This great personal contribution to the tradition of Michigan athletics which began in 1919 has ended. But as the thread of his life is woven in the history of the Little Brown Jug, so his devotion to Michigan and Michigan men all over the world will continue, a force for good in the lives of all who knew Henry Hatch. To this man, we dedicate this program.

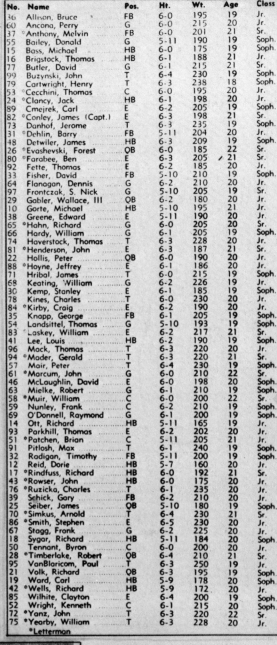

No.	Name	Pos.	Ht.	Wt.	Age	Class
36	Allison, Bruce	FB	6-0	195	19	Jr.
60	Ancona, Perry	G	6-2	215	20	Jr.
37	Anthony, Melvin	FB	6-0	201	21	Sr.
55	Bailey, Donald	G	5-11	190	19	Soph.
15	Bass, Michael	HB	6-0	175	19	Soph.
16	Brigstock, Thomas	HB	6-1	188	21	Jr.
77	Butler, David	G	6-1	215	21	Sr.
99	Buzynski, John	T	6-4	230	19	Soph.
79	Cartwright, Henry	T	6-3	238	18	Soph.
53	Cecchini, Thomas	C	6-0	195	20	Jr.
24	*Clancy, Jack	HB	6-1	198	20	Jr.
89	Cmejrek, Carl	E	6-2	205	19	Soph.
82	Conley, James (Capt.)	E	6-3	198	21	Sr.
73	Danhof, Jerome	T	6-3	235	19	Soph.
31	*Dehlin, Barry	FB	5-11	204	20	Jr.
48	Detwiler, James	HB	6-3	209	19	Soph.
26	*Evashevski, Forest	QB	6-0	185	22	Sr.
80	*Farabee, Ben	E	6-3	205	21	Sr.
92	Fette, Thomas	E	6-2	185	20	Jr.
33	Fisher, David	FB	5-10	210	20	Soph.
64	Flanagan, Dennis	G	6-2	210	20	Jr.
97	Frontczak, S. Nick	G	5-10	205	19	Sr.
29	Gabler, Wallace, III	QB	6-2	180	20	Jr.
10	Gorte, Michael	HB	5-10	195	21	Jr.
38	Greene, Edward	E	5-11	190	20	Jr.
65	*Hahn, Richard	G	6-0	205	20	Sr.
66	Hardy, William	G	6-1	205	19	Soph.
74	Haverstock, Thomas	T	6-3	228	20	Jr.
81	*Henderson, John	E	6-3	187	21	Sr.
22	Hollis, Peter	QB	6-0	190	19	Jr.
88	*Hoyne, Jeffrey	E	6-1	186	20	Jr.
71	Hribal, James	T	6-0	215	19	Soph.
68	Keating, William	G	6-2	226	19	Jr.
30	Kemp, Stanley	E	6-1	185	19	Soph.
78	Kines, Charles	T	6-0	230	20	Jr.
84	*Kirby, Craig	E	6-2	190	20	Jr.
35	Knapp, George	FB	6-1	205	20	Soph.
54	Landsittel, Thomas	G	5-10	193	19	Soph.
83	*Laskey, William	E	6-2	217	21	Sr.
41	Lee, Louis	HB	6-2	190	19	Soph.
96	Mack, Thomas	T	6-3	220	20	Jr.
94	*Mader, Gerald	T	6-3	220	21	Sr.
57	Mair, Peter	T	6-4	230	19	Soph.
61	*Marcum, John	G	6-0	210	22	Sr.
46	McLaughlin, David	E	6-0	198	20	Soph.
63	Mielke, Robert	G	6-1	210	19	Soph.
58	*Muir, William	C	6-0	200	22	Sr.
59	Nunley, Frank	C	6-2	210	19	Soph.
69	O'Donnell, Raymond	G	6-1	200	19	Soph.
14	Ott, Richard	HB	5-11	165	19	Jr.
93	Parkhill, Thomas	E	6-2	202	20	Jr.
51	*Patchen, Brian	C	5-11	205	21	Sr.
91	Pitlosh, Max	T	6-1	240	19	Soph.
32	Radigan, Timothy	FB	5-11	200	19	Jr.
12	Reid, Dorie	HB	5-7	160	20	Jr.
17	*Rindfuss, Richard	HB	6-0	192	21	Sr.
43	Rowser, John	HB	6-0	175	20	Jr.
76	*Ruzicka, Charles	T	6-1	235	20	Jr.
39	Schick, Gary	FB	6-2	210	20	Jr.
25	Seiber, James	QB	5-10	180	19	Soph.
70	*Simkus, Arnold	T	6-4	230	21	Sr.
86	*Smith, Stephen	E	6-5	230	20	Jr.
67	Stagg, Frank	G	6-2	225	20	Jr.
18	Sygar, Richard	HB	5-11	184	20	Soph.
50	Tennant, Byron	C	6-0	200	20	Jr.
28	*Timberlake, Robert	QB	6-4	210	21	Sr.
95	VanBlaricom, Paul	T	6-3	250	19	Jr.
21	Volk, Richard	QB	6-3	195	19	Soph.
19	Ward, Carl	HB	5-9	178	20	Jr.
42	*Wells, Richard	HB	5-9	172	20	Jr.
85	Wilhite, Clayton	E	6-4	200	19	Soph.
52	Wright, Kenneth	C	6-1	215	20	Soph.
72	*Yanz, John	T	6-3	220	22	Sr.
75	Yearby, William	T	6-3	228	20	Jr.

*Letterman

ROBERT W. TIMBERLAKE, 6-4, 215, 21, a senior in the LSA College. Bob has been a standout back for two seasons. As a sophomore two years ago he played more than any other back, 325 minutes, as left half and quarterback . . . drafted to left half to fill gap, he did outstanding job. In 1962 he rushed 104 yards net on 74 tries, completed 16 of 34 passes for 179 yards and scored 14 points on a touchdown, a field goal, five conversion points and by rushing for two extra points after touchdown.

Last year, although handicapped by an arm injury which limited his services to only a few minutes the first four games, he wound up with 168 minutes of playing time, averaging 2.36 yards on rushing attempts and passing 98 times for 47 completions to total 593 yards and three touchdowns. He also scored 27 points himself on a pair of TD's, a field goal and 12 extra points in 13 attempts . . . earned All-American and all-state honors at Franklin, Ohio, high school as quarterback, playing for Coach Alan Parr . . . also captained football, basketball and golf teams. A "B" student in the classroom, he also handles assignments smartly on the playing field. A powerful runner with fair speed, and a fine passer, he should give the Wolverines a real lift again this fall . . . born October 18, 1943, in Middletown, Ohio.

WILLIAM YEARBY, 6-3, 222, 20, a junior in Education . . . from Detroit Eastern high school where he played under Harry Collins. Transferred from end where his strong, aggressive play attracted attention of coaches . . . captained high school team, also lettered in track, basketball . . . could be one of Big Ten's top tackles if he continues to improve . . . played 258 minutes last season as soph . . . born July 24, 1944, Birmingham, Ala.

TIMBERLAKE

YEARBY

AP Poll (1964)
1. Alabama
2. Arkansas
3. Notre Dame
4. MICHIGAN
5. Texas
6. Nebraska
7. L.S.U.
8. Oregon State
9. Ohio State
10. Southern Cal.

UPI Poll (1964)
1. Alabama
2. Arkansas
3. Notre Dame
4. MICHIGAN
5. Texas
6. Nebraska
7. L.S.U.
8. Oregon State
9. Ohio State
10. Southern Cal.

	1964		
Michigan	24	Air Force	7
Michigan	21	Navy	0
Michigan	17	Michigan State	10
Michigan	20	Purdue	21
Michigan	19	Minnesota	12
Michigan	35	Northwestern	0
Michigan	21	Illinois	6
Michigan	34	Iowa	20
Michigan	10	Ohio State	0

Season Summary
Games won, 8; Lost, 1; Tied, 0.
Points for Michigan, 201; For Opponents 76
1965 ROSE BOWL GAME

WOLVERINES TOP STAUBACH, NAVY, 21 TO 0

Abandon Ship

NAVY [0]		MICHIGAN [21]
Neil Henderson	L. E.	Steve Smith
Pat Philbin	L. T.	Charles Kines
John Connolly	L. G.	Dave Butler
Bruce Kenton	C.	Brian Patchen
Fred Marlin	R. G.	John Marcum
Jim Freeman	R. T.	Tom Mack
Doug McCarty	R. E.	John Henderson
Roger Staubach	Q. b.	Bob Timberlake
Tom Leiser	L. H.	Jim Detwiler
Ed Orr	R. H.	Carl Ward
Pat Donnelly	F. B.	Mel Anthony

Navy .... 0 0 0 0— 0
Michigan .... 0 6 8 7—21

Scoring—
Michigan: Ward, 2-yard run.
[Center fumbled.] 7 0
Michigan: Ward, 4-yard run.
[Farabee, pass from Timberlake.] ..14-0
Michigan: Fisher, 4-yard run.
[Timberlake, kick.] 21-0

Substitutions—Michigan: Ends, Kirby, Conley, Hoyne, Farabee, Laskey, Parkhill, Wilhite, Kemp, McLaughlin; tackles, Simkus, Yearby, Hribal, Ruzicka, Mader, Cartwright, Haverstock; guards, Keating, Hahn, Mielke, Flanagan, Yanz, Landstittle, O'Donnell; centers, Cecchini, Nunley, Muir, Wright; backs, Dehlin, Volk, Rindfuss, Sygard, Gabler, Evashevski, Gabler, Bass, Lee, Wells, Fisher, Gorte, Reid, Ott, Hollis, Kemp, Radigan, Brigstock.
Navy: Ends, Broomall, Norton, Hill, Mickelson, Studt, Williams, Ryan; tackles, Wittenberg, Buschbom, Moosally, Taylor; guards, Kocisko, Riley, Gillespie, Hardman; centers, Dittman, Downing; backs, Bickel, Paskewich, Schrawder, Goebel, Roodhouse, McQueen, Havasy, Ingraham, Orr, Wong, Szabo.

The Win At Iowa

Michigan took to the road for its final pair of games, with the first one out at Iowa City on a balmy November 14 before 56,791 fans. They saw a spectacular contest marked both by brilliant play and by some action remindful of the sandlots.

For the most part, Michigan looked like a considerably stronger team and yet it was not until close to the end before the outcome was assured. The final score was 34 to 20 and it was a real quarterback-fullback day for Michigan. Timberlake ran and passed for 216 yards, directed all five touchdowns, scored one himself and passed for another, and kicked four extra points. Fullback Anthony ran for 121 yards, scoring three touchdowns, while his alternate Sophomore Dave Fisher added another 33 yards.

The Purdue Defeat

The ultimate consequences of the loss to Purdue in a thrilling 21 to 20 affair before 60,424 Stadium spectators were uncertain at mid-season. But if it turns out to have cost Michigan the major seasonal objectives, there's a certainty the Wolverines who played the game will replay it mentally for a long time to come.

This was one of those battles where one team out-ran, out passed and out-kicked the opponent but was edged where it counts most, on the scoreboard. Michigan piled up a massive yardage total of 435 almost two lengths of the gridiron more than Purdue.

But Michigan was also beset with such misadventures as three lost fumbles, a pair of pass interceptions, and the unusual total of 89 penalty yards. Once a perfectly-thrown Bob Timberlake pass was dropped by a racing halfback as he neared the Purdue goal unchallenged by defenders. Two of the fumbles were particularly disheartening offensively. One came at the Purdue 3, with the ball bouncing over the goal. A Michigan lineman tried desperately to cover it for the touchdown, but a Boilermaker was adjudged to have possession after the huge pileup was untangled. The final fumble halted a surging Wolverine drive in the game's final moments.

Along with the defeat, Michigan sustained loss for the balance of the season of two of its regular members of the defensive unit, Senior Rick Hahn and Junior Barry Dehlin, both of whom required knee surgery within hours after the game.

BRIEF STATISTICS

	Pur.	Mich.
First downs	15	22
Net yards gained	268	435
Passes attempted	25	23
Passes completed	10	10
Yards gained passing	149	192
Passes intercepted by	2	1
Fumbles lost	1	3
Yards penalized	38	89

MACK

Oct. 24

TIMBER WOLVE

Minnesota	0 0 6	6
Michigan	7 3 9	0

SCORE-BY-SCORE

Minn.	Mich.	First Quarter	
0	6	Anthony (1-yd. plunge)	
0	7	Timberlake (place kick)	7
		Second Quarter	
0	10	Timberlake (29-yd. field goal)	10
		Third Quarter	
0	12	Ball out of end zone on attempted punt for automatic safety	
0	18	Timberlake (1-yd. plunge)	10
0	19	Timberlake (place kick)	
		Fourth Quarter	
6	19	Kramer (11-yd. pass from Hankinson)	
6	19	Hankinson (pass incomplete)	
12	19	Lofquist (91-yd. run with intercepted pass)	5
12	19	Hankinson (pass incomplete)	

STATISTICS

	Minn.	Mi
First downs	16	1
Yards rushing	84	31
Yards passing	163	
Passes attempted	27	
Completed	17	
Intercepted by	1	
Punts	5	
Average	40	32
Fumbles lost	0	0
Yards penalized	30	5

Helms Group Picks Wistert

LOS ANGELES (AP) Albert Wistert, star tackle of the University of Michigan 1940-41-42 football teams, was elected to the Helms College Football Hall of Fame Monday. Wistert was among a dozen to be honored, including Angelo Bertelli, Notre Dame quarterback of the 1940s, and Johnny Lattner, Notre Dame halfback of the 1950s.

Judge Has His Day In Court

It may not have been particularly sedate, but it was sweet music to the ears of Ben J. Goldman, common pleas judge of Clark county, Ohio, and a 1927 graduate of The University of Michigan Law School.

We refer to his playing of a recording of "The Victors" in his courtroom on the Monday following Michigan's 10-0 triumph over Ohio State. Most of the attorneys appearing in Judge Goldman's court are Ohio State graduates. Since 1959 they have taken great pleasure in ribbing the judge about each successive Buckeye win over the Wolverines.

Not only did Judge Goldman play the Michigan fight song. He ordered everyone to stand and told them they would be in contempt of court if they refused.

'M' EARNS ROSE BOWL BID

Gridders Blank OSU, 10-0; Clinch Big Ten Championship

FINAL 1964 CONFERENCE STANDINGS
Team Standings

Team	W	L	T	Pct.	Pts.	Opp. Pts.	Off. Rank*	Def. Rank*
MICHIGAN	6	1	0	.857	156	69	1	3
Ohio State	5	1	0	.833	102	41	6	1
Purdue	5	2	0	.714	136	112	3	6
Illinois	4	3	0	.571	96	79	8	2
Minnesota	4	3	0	.571	89	85	9	4
Michigan State	3	3	0	.500	97	79	5	5
Northwestern	2	5	0	.286	61	133	10	7-t
Wisconsin	2	5	0	.286	74	152	7	10
Indiana	1	5	0	.167	91	121	4	7-t
Iowa	1	5	0	.167	108	139	2	9

*Based on comparative grading of points, first downs and yards per play.

Bowl Comments

Here is what some others thought after viewing or participating in the 1965 Rose Bowl game:

"I said before the game that Michigan was the best team I had seen this year in person, on film, or on TV, and I'm more impressed than ever after playing them" Oregon State Coach Tommy Prothro.

Big 10 Has Too Much for 'Easy 8'

By JOE HENDRICKSON

Michigan unleashed two break-away runners and a break-away pig in crushing Oregon State 34-7 before 100,423 Rose Bowl spectators Friday.

Mel Anthony sprinted a record 84 yards and Carl Ward spurted 43 yards to score touchdowns that broke the game open in the second quarter after Paul Brothers' accurate pitching arm had given underdog Oregon State a 7-0 lead.

Wolverine fans became so elated they unleashed a maize smoke bomb, then a speedy pig named Cleopatra. At least Cleopatra it should be as a gent named Anthony was the leading man this sunny, crisp afternoon. The Michigan fullback scored three touchdowns, fell on a blocked punt and gained 123 yards from scrimmage. His 84-yard touchdown run was the longest in Rose Bowl history, three yards longer than a sprint by Iowa's Bob Jeter in 1959.

Cleopatra ran the wrong way on her scoring dash. The fleet pig executed the most notable Corrigan effort in the Arroyo saucer's colorful history since Roy Riegels' famed mistake. After "scoring," Cleo tried to amend by coming back the right way. A fan made a diving tackle to halt the little critter. If the fan was from Oregon State, he made the best Oregon State tackle of the day.

It was inability to stop the Michigan ground game that ruined the West. The Beaver defense was far below expectations and yielded 332 yards on the ground.

OSU Defense Fails

If Tommy Prothro is the next UCLA football coach, he was introduced to Los Angeles area fans in a manner more cruel than he deserved. Prothro's team played 23 opening minutes of hopeful football, especially on attack. But Prothro's defense, highly regarded before the game, couldn't.

This decay in tackling and deciphering Michigan pitch-outs and rollouts plus off-guard counters undid a six-straight pass completion streak by Brothers which netted the Easy Eight representatives a go-ahead touchdown early in the second quarter.

The Anthony and Ward dashes put Michigan ahead 12-7, and then Bob Timberlake directed a complete demolition job in the second half.

Timberlake, a strong-running quarterback, wound up with quite an afternoon of attainment—57 yards running and 7 pass completions in 10 tries. He scored a touchdown and a two-point conversion.

1965 ROSE BOWL STATISTICS

	MICH.	ORE. STATE
NET YDS. RUSHING	332	64
Passes Attempted	11	33
Passes Completed	8	19
Passes Had Intercepted	0	0
NET YDS. PASSING	83	179
YDS. RUSHING & PASSING	415	243
First Downs Rushing	11	4
First Downs Passing	6	10
First Downs Penalties	1	0
TOTAL FIRST DOWNS	18	14
Yds. Kickoff Returned	48	89
Number of Punts	5	9
Average Length Punts	33.6	43.5
Yds. Punts Returned	85	0
Penalties	6	5
Yds. Lost on Penalties	55	57
Ball Lost on Downs	0	2
Number of Fumbles	2	1
Ball Lost on Fumbles	1	1

SCORING

	TD	CK	CPR	FG	TP
Anthony	3	0	0	0	18
Timberlake	1	2	1	0	10
Ward	1	0	0	0	6

RUSHING

	Tries	Gains	Loss	Net	Ave.
Anthony	13	123	0	123	9.4
Detwiler	5	16	0	16	3.2
Timberlake	12	71	14	57	4.7
Ward	10	88	0	88	8.8
Sygar	1	8	0	8	8.0
Fisher	5	30	0	30	6.0
Volk	1	1	0	1	1.0
Lee	1	5	0	5	5.0
Wells	1	3	0	3	3.0
Dehlin	1	0	0	0	0.0
Gabler	1	1	0	1	1.0

PASSING

	Att.	Comp.	Int.	Yds.	TD
Timberlake	10	7	0	77	0
Evashevski	1	1	0	6	0

RECEIVING

	Number	Yards	TD
Anthony	1	5	0
Henderson	4	34	0
Farabee	1	8	0
Detwiler	1	30	0
Kirby	1	6	0

PUNTING

	Number	Yards	Ave.
Kemp	5	168	33.60

Anthony's (37) Record 84-Yard Rose Bowl Run With Tom Mack Escorting

	RUSHING			PASSING				RECEIVING		PUNT. RET.		PUNTING		SCORING				
	Tries	Net Gain	Ave.	Att'd	Comp.	Had Int.	Gain	Cgh't	Gain	No.	Yds.	No.	Ave.	TD	CK	CPR	FG	TP
Timberlake, qb	144	574	3.9	127	63	5	807	0	0	0	0	0	00.0	8	20	0	4	80
Detwiler, hb	70	282	4.0	0	0	0	0	10	184	0	0	0	00.0	3	0	0	0	18
Ward, hb	91	427	4.7	0	0	0	0	1	5	0	0	0	00.0	3	0	0	0	18
Anthony, fb	132	579	4.3	0	0	0	0	0	0	0	0	0	00.0	6	0	0	0	36
Fisher, fb	43	175	4.0	0	0	0	0	0	0	0	0	0	00.0	2	0	0	0	12
Sygar, hb	4	11	2.8	2	1	0	31	3	24	12	68	0	00.0	1	1	0	0	7
Evashevski, qb	8	23	2.8	7	1	1	12	0	0	0	0	0	00.0	0	0	0	0	0
Bass, hb	7	13	1.9	0	0	0	0	0	0	1	8	0	00.0	0	0	0	0	0
Reid, hb	2	8	4.0	0	0	0	0	0	0	0	0	0	00.0	0	0	0	0	0
Lee, hb	3	7	2.3	0	0	0	0	1	9	1	10	0	00.0	0	0	0	0	0
Gabler, qb	3	-7	-2.3	2	0	0	0	0	0	0	0	0	00.0	0	0	0	0	0
Volk, qb	5	23	4.6	1	1	0	33	0	0	1	27	0	00.0	0	0	0	0	0
Allison, fb	3	25	8.3	0	0	0	0	0	0	0	0	0	00.0	0	0	0	0	0
Radigan, fb	1	1	1.0	0	0	0	0	0	0	0	0	0	00.0	0	0	0	0	0
Hollis, qb	0	0	0.0	2	0	0	0	0	0	0	0	0	00.0	0	0	0	0	0
Rindfuss, hb	0	0	0.0	2	1	0	47	3	31	7	40	0	00.0	0	0	0	0	0
Wells, hb	0	0	0.0	0	0	0	0	0	0	2	15	0	00.0	0	0	0	0	0
Kirby, e	0	0	0.0	0	0	0	0	6	38	0	0	0	00.0	0	0	0	0	0
Farabee, e	0	0	0.0	0	0	0	0	8	88	0	0	0	00.0	0	0	0	1	2
Henderson, e	0	0	0.0	0	0	0	0	27	393	0	0	0	00.0	3	0	0	0	18
Smith, e	0	0	0.0	0	0	0	0	8	131	0	0	0	00.0	1	0	1	0	8
Kemp, e	0	0	0.0	0	0	0	0	0	0	0	0	42	36.2	0	0	0	0	0
Greene, e	0	0	0.0	0	0	0	0	0	0	0	0	1	34.0	0	0	0	0	0

TIMBERLAKE GETS TRIBUNE AWARD TODAY

Silver Football to Michigan Star

Ann Arbor, Mich., Feb. 19—Bob Timberlake, All-American quarterback, who directed Michigan's football team to a Western conference championship and victory in the Rose Bowl, will receive THE CHICAGO TRIBUNE's Silver Football tomorrow afternoon. The presentation will be made by Wilfrid Smith, sports editor of THE TRIBUNE, at half time of the Michigan-Ohio State basketball game.

Timberlake is the 41st Western conference football player to receive the trophy, a sterling silver replica of a football mounted on an ebony base. The first was presented to Harold [Red] Grange of Illinois in 1924 by the late Harvey Woodruff.

The Carolina Victory

This was Michigan's first football game against North Carolina and the participating Wolverines are apt to remember the circumstances far longer than the final score which turned out to be a free-wheeling 31 to 24 affair.

Picturesque Kenan Stadium, nestled in the wooded Chapel Hill campus, was the September 18 site and 41,000 fans were on hand. The temperature out at nearby Raleigh-Durham airport was up around the 86-degree mark, but the guess is that at stadium turf level it was a terrifically humid 100.

BRIEF STATISTICS	NC	Mich.
First downs	16	19
Net yards gained	290	329
Passes attempted	41	12
Passes completed	24	6
Yards gained passing	199	74
Passes intercepted by	1	1
Fumbles lost	1	5
Yards penalized	71	30

1965 MICHIGAN VARSITY SQUAD
(Alphabetical)

No.	Name	Pos.	Ht.	Wt.	Age	Class	Home Town, High School & Coach
60	Ancona, Perry	G	6-0	215	21	Sr.	Madeira, O., Madeira, John Rape
55	*Bailey, Donald	G	5-11	198	20	Jr.	Greensburg, Pa., Greensburg, Bob Williams
15	*Bass, Michael	HB	6-0	182	20	Jr.	Ypsilanti, Ypsilanti, Bob Moffett
97	Berline, James	E	6-0	195	19	Soph.	Niles, O., McKinley, Tony Mason
16	Brigstock, Thomas	HB	6-1	197	22	Soph.	Battle Creek, Lakeview, Dick Colburn
61	Broadnax, Stanley	G	6-0	217	19	Soph.	Cincinnati, O., Taft, Will Hundemer
99	Buzynski, John	T	6-4	215	20	Jr.	Detroit, Notre Dame, Walt Bazylewisch
77	Byers, David	T	6-2	221	19	Soph.	Warren, Warren, Steve Nowak
79	Cartwright, Henry	T	6-3	235	19	Jr.	Detroit, Central, Corky Foster
53	*Cecchini, Thomas (Capt.)	C	6-0	194	21	Sr.	Detroit, Pershing, Mike Haddad
24	*Clancy, Jack	E	6-1	195	21	Jr.	Detroit, Redford St. Mary, Nick Galante
73	Danhof, Jerome	T	6-3	228	20	Sr.	Detroit, Denby, Ed Rutherford
56	Day, Floyd	G	6-2	202	20	Jr.	Canton, O., McKinley, Pete Ankeny
58	Dayton, Joseph	G	6-2	218	19	Soph.	Detroit, Cooley, Roger Parmentier
31	*Dehlin, Barry	G	5-11	215	21	Sr.	Flushing, Flushing, Al Gratsch
51	D'Eramo, Paul	C	5-10	212	19	Soph.	Youngstown, O., Austintown Fitch, Bob Winterburn
48	*Detwiler, James	HB	6-3	215	20	Jr.	Toledo, O., DeVilbiss, Dave Hardy
30	Doty, Alfred	FB	5-10	205	19	Soph.	Mount Morris, Mount Morris, Pete Fusi
33	*Fisher, David	FB	5-10	215	20	Jr.	Kettering, O., Fairmont, James Hoover
64	Flanagan, Dennis	G	6-2	215	21	Sr.	Niles, O., McKinley, Tony Mason
29	Gabler, Wallace	QB	6-2	195	21	Sr.	Royal Oak, Kimball, Pin Ryan
65	Goss, Thomas	T	6-2	217	19	Soph.	Knoxville, Tenn., Austin, George Lennon
38	Greene, Edward	E	5-11	200	21	Sr.	Flat Rock, Flat Rock, Marv Mittelstatt
90	Hanna, Henry	E	6-0	220	20	Jr.	Youngstown, O., Cardinal Mooney, Dennis Barrett
66	Hardy, William	T	6-1	225	20	Jr.	Detroit, Pershing, Mike Haddad
82	Heffelfinger, Jon	E	6-2	201	19	Soph.	Battle Creek, Central, Jack Finn
22	Hollis, Peter	QB	6-0	190	21	Sr.	Detroit, Redford, Ed Larimore
88	*Hoyne, Jeffrey	E	6-1	190	21	Jr.	Chicago, Ill., Weber, Joe Sassano
71	Hribal, James	T	6-0	225	20	Jr.	Dearborn, H. H. Lowrey, Ralph Bach
26	Humphries, Derrick	E	6-2	192	19	Soph.	Detroit, Chadsey, Irving Petross
10	Irwin, John	HB	5-11	175	19	Soph.	Allegan, Allegan, Charles Armatage
62	Johnson, Paul	T	6-0	226	18	Soph.	Bay City, Central, Elmer Engel
68	*Keating, William	G	6-2	226	20	Sr.	Chicago, Ill., St. Patrick, Fred Dempsey
80	*Kemp, Stanley	E	6-1	185	20	Sr.	Greenville, Greenville, Jack McAvoy
78	*Kines, Charles	T	6-1	238	21	Sr.	Niles, O., McKinley, Tony Mason
84	*Kirby, Craig	E	6-2	185	21	Sr.	Royal Oak, Kimball, Pin Ryan
35	Knapp, George	G	6-1	225	20	Jr.	Bay City, Handy, Al Sigman
50	Lancaster, George	C	6-1	190	19	Soph.	Struthers, O., Struthers, Bob Cummings
41	*Lee, Louis	HB	6-2	192	20	Jr.	Willow Grove, Pa., Abington, Charles Weber
40	Legacki, Norman	HB	6-1	188	21	Sr.	Philadelphia, Pa., Father Judge
23	Leslie, Kent	FB	6-0	198	19	Soph.	Ann Arbor, Ann Arbor, Jay Stielstra
96	*Mack, Thomas	T	6-3	235	21	Sr.	Bucyrus, O., Cleveland Hts., Jim Roberts
57	Mair, Peter	T	6-4	228	20	Jr.	Allentown, Pa., Wm. Allen, Perry Scott
92	McLaughlin, Donald	E	6-0	205	21	Jr.	Chelsea, Chelsea, Alan Conklin
63	*Mielke, Robert	G	6-1	218	20	Jr.	Chicago, Ill., Carl Schurz, Fred O'Keefe
34	Morgan, Dennis	FB	5-11	222	19	Soph.	Phoenixville, Pa., Bishop Kenrick, Dan Hoey
44	Nelson, Douglas	HB	6-0	180	18	Soph.	Adrian, Adrian, Gary McNitt
59	*Nunley, Frank	C	6-2	222	20	Jr.	Belleville, Belleville, Harry Hidenfelter
69	O'Donnell, Raymond	E	6-1	208	20	Jr.	Milan, Milan, Cliff Hall
93	Parkhill, Thomas	E	6-2	205	21	Sr.	Ada, O., Ada, Richard Watson
72	Phillips, Raymond	T	6-3	222	19	Soph.	Evanston, Ill., Evanston Twnshp., Murney Lazier
91	Pitlosh, Max	G	6-1	250	20	Jr.	Detroit, St. Thomas, Paul Mandzira
70	Porter, David	G	6-3	221	19	Soph.	Lansing, Sexton, Russ Maples
81	Pullen, Thomas	E	6-4	190	20	Soph.	Ottawa, Can., Glebe C. I., Ralph Thornton
32	Radigan, Timothy	FB	5-11	206	19	Jr.	Lansing, St. Mary, Paul Pozega
83	Rosema, Roger	E	6-3	208	19	Soph.	Grand Rapids, Central, Russ Posthumus
43	*Rowser, John	HB	6-0	182	21	Jr.	Detroit, Eastern, Harry Collins
76	*Ruzicka, Charles	T	6-1	238	21	Jr.	Skokie, Ill., St. George, Max Burnell
89	Salmi, Terry	E	6-1	205	19	Soph.	Wakefield, Wakefield, Duane Lane
39	Schick, Gary	FB	6-2	215	21	Sr.	Grosse Pointe, St. Paul, Ed Lauer
25	Seiber, James	QB	5-10	180	20	Jr.	Niles, O., McKinley, Tony Mason
17	Sharpe, Ernest	HB	5-11	190	19	Soph.	Palos Hts., Ill., Carl Sandburg, Joe Devine
86	*Smith, Stephen	E	6-5	229	21	Sr.	Park Ridge, Ill., Maine East, Bud Gates
45	Spencer, Royce	E	6-1	205	19	Soph.	Chicago, Ill., Morgan Park, Joe Stepanek
18	*Sygar, Richard	HB	5-11	180	21	Sr.	Niles, O., McKinley, Tony Mason
54	Tennant, Byron	C	6-0	212	21	Sr.	Worthington, O., Worthington, Ralph Sabach
95	VanBlaricom, Paul	T	6-3	241	22	Sr.	Kalamazoo, University, Ray Walters
27	Vidmer, Richard	QB	6-0	184	20	Soph.	Greensburg, Pa., Hempfield, Bill Abrahams
49	*Volk, Richard	HB	6-3	190	20	Jr.	Wauseon, O., Wauseon, Larry Fruth
19	*Ward, Carl	HB	5-9	177	21	Jr.	Cincinnati, O., Taft, Joe Corcoran
42	*Wells, Richard	HB	5-9	178	21	Jr.	Grand Rapids, Ottawa Hills, Rip Collins
85	Wilhite, Clayton	E	6-4	204	20	Jr.	Bay City, Handy, Al Sigman
52	Wright, Kenneth	G	6-1	215	21	Jr.	Bay City, Central, Elmer Engel
67	Yanz, Richard	G	6-2	204	19	Soph.	Chicago, Ill., Brother Rice, Nick Adduci
75	*Yearby, William	T	6-3	230	21	Sr.	Detroit, Eastern, Harry Collins
14	Yedinak, Martin	HB	5-8	175	19	Soph.	Alpena, Alpena, Michael Yedinak

*Letterman

WARD

NUNLEY

Reprinted with permission from the **Michigan Alumnus**

1965 FOOTBALL RESULTS

MICHIGAN	31	North Carolina	24
MICHIGAN	10	California	7
Michigan	7	GEORGIA	15
Michigan	7	MICHIGAN STATE	24
Michigan	15	PURDUE	17
Michigan	13	MINNESOTA	14
MICHIGAN	50	Wisconsin	14
MICHIGAN	23	Illinois	3
Michigan	22	NORTHWESTERN	34
Michigan	7	OHIO STATE	9
	185	Total	161

Season Record: Won 4, Lost 6 — Big Ten: Won 2, Lost 5

The California Triumph

There was considerably less scoring but even more apprehension near game's end the following week when Michigan's home opener unfolded September 25 before 81,417 Band Day fans.

As in the opener, Michigan broke on top, added to the early margin, and seemed to have matters well in hand. The score was 10-0, in fact, before the Bears from Berkeley even managed their initial first down.

BRIEF STATISTICS	Cal.	Mich.
First downs	14	17
Net yards gained	228	326
Passes attempted	12	16
Passes completed	4	8
Yards gained passing	45	103
Passes intercepted by	2	1
Fumbles lost	1	3
Yards penalized	57	45

State 24, Michigan 7

A capacity throng announced at 103,219 jammed Michigan Stadium October 9 for the Michigan State game, a free-wheeling affair far closer than the final 24-7 score indicates.

The outcome was in doubt, in fact, until just the last couple of minutes when State added a clinching 9 points to put the game beyond Michigan's reach.

The Spartans capitalized an early opportunity to open the scoring. It was set up by a Michigan aerial which hit the intended receiver right in the helmet before he turned around. The ball bounced up and was grabbed by State's George Webster on a diving catch at the Michigan 18. Three plays later Steve Juday sneaked for a 1-yard touchdown and State broke on top by 6-0. The conversion attempt was wide to the left.

Early in the second period the Wolverines culminated a 57-yard drive, mostly by air with Wally Gabler at the controls, and scored on Gabler's 1-yard sneak over guard. Sygar converted the one-pointer to put Michigan ahead by 7-6.

But, almost immediately, the Wolverines were in deep trouble again when Gabler fumbled and State recovered at the Michigan 26. The Spartans turned this into 3 points when Dick Kenney lofted a 20-yard field goal, and State took a 9-7 lead into the half-time intermission.

Midway through the third period the Spartans struck quickly on a 38-yard completion from Juday to Gene Washington and then a 10-yard scoring slash by Clinton Jones to widen the margin to 15-7.

The Wolverines twice launched scoring bids deep into Spartan territory, once dropping a pass on the 3 yard line, but State's outstanding defense held firm enough through the final quarter. Kenney kicked another field goal for 35 yards and then, on the game's final scrimmage play, Bob Apisa broke over a relaxed Michigan defense for a startling 39-yard touchdown run.

BRIEF STATISTICS	State	Mich.
First downs	13	16
Net yards gained	318	249
Passes attempted	17	40
Passes completed	8	17
Yards gained passing	117	287
Passes intercepted by	2	0
Fumbles lost	0	3
Yards penalized	78	21

Lineups

MICHIGAN
ENDS—Hoyne, Kemp, Pullen, Smith, Wilhite, Clancy.
TACKLES — Kines, Mack, Johnson, Yearby, Hardy.
GUARDS — Flanagan, Bailey, Wright, Mielke, Hanna.
CENTERS—Dayton, Cecchini, Nunley.
BACKS — Vidmer, Detwiler, Ward, Schick, Fisher, Bass, Volk, Gabler, Wells, Sygar, Radigan, Morgan, Sharpe.

GEORGIA
ENDS—Richter, Hodgson, Adams, Varnado, Creech, Kohn, Tootle.
TACKLES — Patton, Chandler, Arkwright, Smaha, Pillsbury, Evans, Harber, Hayes.
GUARDS — Whidden, Denney, Kasey, Steele, Brantley, Dennard, Phillips.
CENTERS—K. Davis, J. Davis.
BACKS—Ridlehuber, Taylor, Hurst, McWhorter, Wheeler, Sellers, Hughes, Swinford, Cooper, Lawhorne, Dickens, Jenkins, Etter, Neuhaus, Moore, Crawford, McFalls, Mosher.

Officials

N. M. Cavette, referee; Don Elser, umpire; Harry Sharp, head linesman; Joe Schneider, field judge; Leonard Heinz, back judge.

Scoring

MICHIGAN	0	7	0	0
GEORGIA	3	3	0	9

TOUCHDOWNS: MICHIGAN Rad (one-yard plunge); GEORGIA Hog (10-yard pass from Ridlehuber).
EXTRA-POINT: MICHIGAN — S (placement).
FIELD GOALS: GEORGIA Ette (34 yards, 44 yards and 31 yards).

Team Statistics

	M
First downs	13
Rushing	8
Passing	5
Penalty	0
Total number of rushes	45
Net yards—Rushing	129
Passing	107
Forward passes attempted	13
Completed	7
Intercepted by	2
Yards interceptions returned	4
Total plays (rushes and passes)	58
Punts, number	5
Average distance	29
Kickoffs, returned by	4
Yards kicks returned	85
Punts	59
Kickoffs	26
Fumbles, number	3
Ball lost by	1
Penalties, number	4
Yards penalized	51

Purdue 17, Michigan 15

For the fourth time in five weeks the Wolverines were faced with an undefeated opponent as Purdue came to the Stadium October 16. It was Homecoming and a throng of 85,905 was on hand.

The Boilermakers were favored to win this one, but they were trailing by a point, at 15-14, until the final 55 seconds when a Bob Griese field goal from 35 yards out shattered the Wolverines.

For the first time all season Michigan managed to eliminate fumbles and interceptions from the attack. Twice in the first period the Wolverines marched within field goal distance but each time Sygar's attempts were unsuccessful.

Griese was brilliant in the final Purdue aerial surge which started from the Boilermaker 11 and carried just close enough in the final minute of play to permit Griese's 35-yard field goal to win the game.

BRIEF STATISTICS	Purd.	Mich.
First downs	19	22
Net yards gained	300	308
Passes attempted	38	29
Passes completed	22	9
Yards gained passing	273	137
Passes intercepted by	0	1
Fumbles lost	1	0
Yards penalized	56	45

Michigan 23, Illinois 3

Against much stronger opposition the Wolverines turned in another superb effort a week later down in Champaign on November 6. Illinois had won four straight games, including a smashing 21-0 shutout over Purdue seven days earlier, and was poised to give Coach Pete Elliott his first triumph over brother Bump.

But the Wolverines chose this day before 50,136 Illini fans to unfurl what probably was their best all around performance of the year. After spotting the Illini an opening 3 lead, Michigan pounded back for 2 points to give Bump his seventh straight coaching success against this old-time foe.

The Illinois score came on its first offensive thrust. Michigan stiffened inside the Wolverine 10, so quarterback Fred Custardo settled for a 3 point field goal. Never again the balance of the day could the Illini advance beyond the Michigan 38 despite the dangerous thrusts of All American fullback Jim Grabowski who closed out his Illini career without scoring a single touchdown against Michigan.

Michigan, meanwhile, pounded the Illini defenses for a net of 423 yards with the elusive Ward carrying for 139 yards in 19 tries.

BRIEF STATISTICS	Ill.	Mich.
First downs	17	21
Net yards gained	254	423
Passes attempted	22	13
Passes completed	10	8
Yards gained passing	124	117
Passes intercepted by	1	1
Fumbles lost	0	1
Yards penalized	30	70

Minnesota 14, Michigan 13

Seven days later, up in Minneapolis on October 23, another heartbreaker for Michigan unfolded before the 519 fans who watched the annual battle for the Little Brown Jug.

The Wolverines fought furiously to give the Jug round trip transportation back to Ann Arbor, but wound up leaving it there as a last-minute victory bid fell short.

Halfback Rick Volk intercepted a Gopher pass and returned it 19 yards to the Minnesota 35 midway through the first period to set up the initial Wolverine score. Five ground slashes moved the ball down to the 14 and then Ward resourcefully passed to fullback Fisher for the touchdown on broken play intended to be an end sweep. Sygar's conversion made 7-0.

Each team had passes intercepted at the 2-yard line as the half concluded with no additional scoring.

The Gophers tied it up in the third period, following an unsuccessful Michigan field goal try, with a 51-yard drive climaxed by Joe Holmberg's 8-yard run. The conversion attempt was good and the game was knotted at 7-7.

Then, in the fourth period, Minnesota gained both ball possession and field position when a short Gopher punt hit a Michigan blocker and was recovered by Minnesota near midfield. Quarterback John Hankinson drove his team skillfully to the end zone, carrying himself on the last three plays, and the conversion kick put Minnesota out front by 14-7.

With the clock ticking away Michigan unfurled a successful 52-yard surge. Gabler completed four successive passes during the drive and scored the touchdown himself on a 4-yard keeper play, narrowing the margin to 14-13.

Only 82 seconds now remained and Michigan disdained the probable tie from a kick conversion, choosing instead to go for two points and victory. Gabler sent a man in motion to the right, then swung out to the left on an optional run or pass effort for the 3 yards. The Gophers alertly shut off the run, put heavy pressure on Gabler as he faded back to look for a receiver, and the ball arched harmlessly into the end zone.

"I thought we were the hard-luck team," said Minnesota coach Murray Warmath later, "but it looks like Michigan wins the prize."

BRIEF STATISTICS	Minn.	Mich.
First downs	14	20
Net yards gained	271	303
Passes attempted	12	24
Passes completed	3	14
Yards gained passing	67	138
Passes intercepted by	1	2
Fumbles lost	0	1
Yards penalized	94	66

Ohio State 9, Michigan 7

The Wolverines had the most opportunities but the Buckeyes managed the payoff points in the November 20 seasonal finale before 77,733 Stadium fans.

The finish was almost a carbon copy of Michigan's earlier last minute loss to Purdue, with the Bucks driving downfield against the clock and barely managing a successful field goal to win the game, 9 to 7.

Oddly, it was the third Big Ten game Ohio State had won by a combined total of five points, the exact opposite of Michigan's trio of losses by the same margin and the outcome gave the Buckeyes a second-place Conference finish behind unbeaten Michigan State.

Michigan, substantially outgaining Ohio for the day, mounted seven scoring threats but capitalized only on one. The Buckeyes managed to cross midfield only three times but placed points on the scoreboard twice. The ultimate difference was supplied by kicking accuracy.

The first of Ohio's drives came early, with most of the yardage supplied on the wings of a passing game most unusual for a Woody Hayes team. It began at the Ohio 24 and moved into the end zone on a 5 yard aerial from Don Unverferth to Bill Anders. Kicking specialist Bob Funk sliced his one point conversion try wide to the right to hold the lead at 6 to 0, but he was destined to walk off the field a hero at the end.

Michigan dominated the action most of the rest of the way. A 71-yard drive in the second quarter reached the Buckeye 6 before it ground out on downs. But the field position thus gained helped set up the equalizing touchdown as defensive halfback Mike Bass intercepted an Ohio pass at the 25 and moved down to the Buckeye 15. From this point the Wolverines crunched over the goal line in four successive plunges by fullback Fisher. Sygar's conversion put Michigan on top by 7-6.

Moments later Michigan moved to the Ohio 10 but a holding penalty helped scramble this drive and the Wolverines lost the ball on downs at the 16.

Early in the third period the Wolverines unfurled a 70-yard drive to the Ohio 6 but, on fourth down, Sygar's field goal attempt went wide to the left. He tried another from the Ohio 25 in the last quarter but this one, too, was unsuccessful.

For more than 30 minutes Ohio had not been able to move out of its own half of the field. But when it counted most, in the final few minutes of play, the Buckeyes did sustain a drive from their own 9 deep into Michigan territory. Finally the Wolverines stiffened, but Funk was now within range and lofted a 28-yard field goal over the crossbar for the 9-7 victory.

In the final 75 seconds of the unhappy 1965 season Michigan managed to move 40 yards and try still another field goal. But, characteristic of the overall Wolverine season, it fell far short of the objective.

BRIEF STATISTICS	OSU	Mich.
First downs	19	18
Net yards gained	261	335
Passes attempted	29	16
Passes completed	15	7
Yards gained passing	123	86
Passes intercepted by	0	2
Fumbles lost	1	0
Yards penalized	10	35

Northwestern 34, Michigan 22

Michigan's new-found prosperity was short-lived.

The back-to-back triumphs over Wisconsin and Illinois—and the manner in which they were achieved—gave the Wolverines hope for a garrison finish of four straight victories and a winning season.

But Northwestern's supercharged Wildcats out-hit the Wolverines 34 to 22 in a November 13 battle at Evanston before 40,007 chilled spectators. Both in yardage yielded and in scoreboard points, it was Michigan's weakest defensive performance in three years.

There wasn't much wrong with Michigan's own offense; the defense simply couldn't hold the Wildcats.

BRIEF STATISTICS	NU	Mich.
First downs	20	21
Net yards gained	328	332
Passes attempted	11	20
Passes completed	8	10
Yards gained passing	117	116
Passes intercepted by	0	0
Fumbles lost	1	1
Yards penalized	71	53

FINAL 1965 CONFERENCE STANDINGS

	W	L	T	Pct.
Mich. State	7	0	0	1.000
Ohio State	6	1	0	.857
Minnesota	5	2	0	.714
Purdue	5	2	0	.714
Illinois	4	3	0	.571
Northwestern	3	4	0	.429
Michigan	2	5	0	.286
Wisconsin	2	5	0	.286
Indiana	1	6	0	.143
Iowa	0	7	0	.000

Bill Yearby Cleaning Up Grid Honors

(From News Wire Services)

Although the past Michigan football season was far from being exceptional, coaches and sportswriters recognized several Wolverines for turning in top performances.

Defensive tackle Bill Yearby leads the parade of honors by being selected for the 1965 American Football Coaches Association All America squad.

The 6-2, 222 pound senior from Detroit also repeated on the Associated Press and United Press International Big Ten squads.

YEARBY

Safetyman Rich Volk, a 6-3, 195-pound junior from Wauseon, O., joined Yearby on the Associated Press Big Ten defensive team. He also made the first string UPI team.

Two Wolverines made the AP and UPI Big Ten first team offensive squads. They are tackle Tom Mack, a 6-3, 228 pound senior from Bucyrus, O., and halfback Carl Ward, a 5-9, 178 pound junior from Cincinnati.

MICHIGAN'S 1965 TEAM STATISTIC[S]

	Michigan	Oppone[nts]
FIRST DOWNS	196	161
Rushing	117	93
Passing	68	61
Penalty	12	7
NO. OF RUSHES	531	440
Net Yds.—Rush.	2023	1436
Net Yds.—Pass.	1337	1324
FORWARD PASSES ATT'D	200	226
Completed	94	118
Intercepted by	14	10
Yds. Int'cpt Ret'd	123	154
TOTAL PLAYS	731	666
PUNTS, NUMBER	49	61
Ave. Dist.	36.2	28.8
KICKOFFS, returned by	35	37
YARDS KICKS RETURNED	779	833
Punts	294	89
Kickoffs	485	744
FUMBLES	35	22
Ball lost by	15	8
PENALTIES, Number	52	54
Yards Penalized	446	562

MICHIGAN'S INDIVIDUAL SCORING FOR 1965

	RUSHING			PASSING				RECEIVING		PUNT RET.		PUNTING		SCORING				
	Tries	Net Gain	Ave.	Att'd	Comp.	Had Int.	Gain	Cgh't	Gain	No.	Yds.	No.	Ave.	TD	CK	CPR	FG	TP
Ward, hb	112	639	5.7	3	2	0	7	3	37	0	0	0	0.0	3	0	0	0	18
Fisher, fb	139	575	4.1	0	0	0	0	1	14	0	0	0	0.0	4	0	0	0	24
Gabler, qb	85	265	3.1	125	58	2	825	0	0	0	0	0	0.0	7	0	0–3	0	42
Sygar, hb	61	253	4.1	2	1	1	26	4	51	10	121	0	0.0	1	18–19	0–2	5–11	39
Sharpe, hb	18	73	4.1	0	0	0	0	4	62	0	0	0	0.0	1	0	0	0	6
Schick, fb	12	62	5.2	0	0	0	0	0	0	0	0	0	0.0	0	0	0	0	0
Detwiler, hb	17	61	3.6	0	0	0	0	1	18	0	0	0	0.0	2	0	0	0	12
Radigan, fb	18	60	3.3	0	0	0	0	0	0	0	0	0	0.0	1	0	0	0	6
Rowser, hb	13	42	3.2	0	0	0	0	0	0	0	0	0	0.0	0	0	0	0	0
Morgan, fb	6	11	1.8	0	0	0	0	1	1	0	0	0	0.0	0	0	0	0	0
Brigstock, hb	4	10	2.5	0	0	0	0	0	0	0	0	0	0.0	0	0	0	0	0
Hollis, qb	2	−7	−3.5	0	0	0	0	0	0	0	0	0	0.0	0	0	0	0	0
Vidmer, qb	43	−10	−0.2	68	32	7	472	0	0	0	0	0	0.0	1	0	0	0	6
Kemp, e	1	−11	−11.0	0	0	0	0	0	0	0	0	49	36.2	0	0	0	0	0
Clancy, e	0	0	0.0	0	0	0	0	52	762	0	0	0	0.0	5	0	0	0	30
Smith, e	0	0	0.0	0	0	0	0	21	314	0	0	0	0.0	0	0	0	0	0
Kirby, e	0	0	0.0	0	0	0	0	3	51	0	0	0	0.0	0	0	0	0	0
Wilhite, e	0	0	0.0	0	0	0	0	3	32	0	0	0	0.0	0	0	0	0	0
D'Eramo, c	0	0	0.0	0	0	0	0	0	0	0	0	0	0.0	0	0–1	0	0–2	0
Volk, qb	0	0	0.0	0	0	0	0	0	0	10	73	0	0.0	0	0	0	0	0
Wells, hb	0	0	0.0	0	0	0	0	7	89	0	0	0	0.0	0	0	0	0	0

1966 MICHIGAN

Name	Pos.	Ht.	Wt.	Age	Class
				Alphabetical	
*Bailey, Donald	OG	6-0	225	21	Sr.
Banks, Terry	HB	5-8	188	18	Soph.
*Bass, Mike	DHB	6-0	180	19	Sr.
Banar, James	OT	6-0	218	19	Soph.
Baumgartner, Robert	OG	6-0	215	19	Soph.
Beemer, Dennis	QB	5-10	155	19	Soph.
Beier, Michael	DHB	5-11	191	19	Soph.
Berline, James	OE	6-0	188	20	Jr.
Broadnax, Stanley	OT	6-0	230	20	Jr.
Brown, Dennis	QB	5-10	178	19	Soph.
Buzynski, John	C	6-4	230	21	Sr.
Byers, David	DT	6-3	235	20	Jr.
*Clancy, John (Capt.)	OE	6-1	192	22	Sr.
Danhof, Jerry	C	6-3	228	21	Jr.
*Dayton, Joseph	C	6-2	229	21	Jr.
*Dehlin, Barry	LB	5-11	205	22	Sr.
*D'Eramo, Paul	LB	5-10	208	20	Jr.
*Detwiler, James	HB	6-3	215	21	Sr.
Doane, Thomas	HB	5-10	207	19	Soph.
Doty, Alfred	DHB	5-10	195	20	Jr.
Duffy, James	OG	6-1	215	19	Soph
Farabee, David	OHB	6-0	185	19	Soph.
*Fisher, David	FB	5-10	210	20	Sr.
Frysinger, Terry	C	6-2	210	19	Soph.
Goss, Thomas	MG	6-2	225	20	Jr.
*Hanna, Henry	OG	6-0	220	21	Sr.
*Hardy, William	OT	6-1	229	21	Sr.
Hartman, Gerald	DHB	6-1	168	19	Soph.
Heffelfinger, Jon	OE	6-2	203	20	Jr.
Hoey, George	OHB	5-10	170	19	Soph.
Hribal, James	OT	6-0	220	21	Sr.
Humphries, Derrick	OE	6-2	190	19	Jr.
Jobe, Theodore	OHB	6-0	178	19	Soph.
Johnson, Paul	DT	6-0	231	19	Jr.
Johnson, Ronald	OHB	6-1	192	19	Soph.
*Kemp, Stanley	OE	6-1	185	20	Sr.
Kieta, Robert	QB	6-0	181	19	Soph.
Knapp, George	OG	6-1	218	21	Sr.
Kramer, Jon	DE	6-3	213	19	Soph.
Kunsa, Joseph	OG	6-0	207	19	Soph.
Landsittel, Thomas	OG	5-10	198	21	Sr.
Lee, Louis	DHB	6-2	195	21	Jr.
Leslie, Kent	LB	6-0	217	20	Jr.
Lynch, John	DHB	5-10	175	19	Soph.
Mair, Peter	OT	6-4	233	21	Sr.
*Mielke, Robert	DT	6-1	223	21	Sr.
Miklos, Gerald	DT	6-3	225	19	Soph.
Monthei, Dennis	MG	6-2	198	20	Jr.
*Morgan, Dennis	LB	5-11	230	20	Jr.
Nelson, Douglas	DHB	6-0	186	19	Soph.
*Nunley, Frank	LB	6-2	218	21	Sr.
Penksa, Robert	OT	6-1	228	19	Soph.
*Phillips, Raymond	OT	6-3	228	20	Jr.
*Porter, David	MG	6-3	237	20	Jr.
*Pullen, Thomas	OE	6-3	195	20	Jr.
*Radigan, Timothy	FB	5-11	206	21	Sr.
Reynolds, John	FB	5-10	218	19	Soph.
*Rosema, Roger	DE	6-2	214	20	Jr.
*Rowser, John	DHB	6-0	183	22	Sr.
Salmi, Terry	DE	6-1	208	20	Jr.
Schwartz, Thomas	OHB	6-1	195	19	Soph.
*Sharpe, Ernest	OHB	5-11	191	20	Jr.
Sipp, Warren	OE	6-1	216	19	Soph.
Sirosky, Dennis	LB	6-0	197	19	Soph.
Spencer, Royce	OE	6-1	208	20	Jr.
Stincic, Thomas	DE	6-3	217	19	Soph.
*Sygar, Richard	DHB	5-11	185	21	Sr.
Tackett, Richard	OT	6-3	227	19	Soph
Thomas, John	QB	6-1	192	20	Jr.
Thompson, Ronald	OE	6-1	195	19	Soph.
*Vidmer, Richard	QB	6-1	185	21	Jr.
*Volk, Richard	DHB	6-3	192	21	Sr.
*Ward, Carl	OHB	5-9	178	22	Sr.
Washington, Martin	OG	5-10	194	19	Soph.
Wedge, Robert	DHB	6-2	193	19	Soph.
*Wilhite, Clayton	OE	6-4	210	21	Sr.
Wilhite, James	OHB	6-3	204	19	Soph.
Williamson, Richard	DT	6-4	225	20	Jr.
*Wright, Kenneth	DT	6-1	230	22	Sr.
Yanz, Richard	OG	6-1	212	19	Soph.

*Letterman

JACK D. CLANCY is captain of the 1966 Wolverines and a strong candidate for All America honors this season. Shifted to right end last year from his previous halfback post, Clancy scored five touchdowns for 30 points and set a new Michigan pass-receiving record of 52 passes for 762 yards. His speed and shiftiness, plus the experience gained at end last year, should bring him his best season. Originally a quarterback, Clancy was shifted to halfback three years ago. He averaged 3.21 yards per play in his first season in that spot. Early in 1964 he was injured and granted an additional year of eligibility by the Big Ten. A graduate of Redford St. Mary's where he played for Nick Galante, he earned All-American honorable mention, all-state and all-Catholic honors. The 6-1, 192-pound Wolverine leader was born in Fort Dodge, Ia., June 18, 1944, which makes him 22. He is a senior in the College of Literature, Science, and the Arts.

JAMES M. MANDICH, 6-3, 215, from Solon, O., is a sophomore standout and a top candidate for the tight-end post vacated by Warren Sipp, who has been shifted to fullback. A rugged power player with great competitive instincts. He was coached by Arch Tunnel at Solon High where he won 12 letters, three each in football, basketball, baseball and track. He was an All-State gridder and also placed on the All-American squad. He is 19 and was born in Solon, July 30, 1948.

Michigan 41, Oregon State 0

There were 56,097 fans in Michigan Stadium for the September 17 opener and all but the visiting Beaver partisans were pulled out of their seats early by some explosive offensive action.

The Wolverines first gained ball possession back on their 30-yard line. In four plays they moved the 70 yards to the goal, with the long gainers a 49-yard Vidmer to Clancy pass and a 16-yard left end sweep by Carl Ward for the touchdown. Rick Sygar converted the first of his five extra point kicks and the Wolverines had a 7 to 0 lead before the season was five minutes old.

The count doubled on Michigan's next opportunity. This drive spanned 53 yards in eight plays, with Ward diving over left guard the final few feet.

Two tries, two touchdowns, and Oregon State still did not have a first down. Beaver Coach Dee Andros sorrowfully observed later that "Michigan was more ready to play than any team I've ever seen."

Reprinted with permission from the **Michigan Alumnus**

Mandich

Clancy

NORTH CAROLINA

ENDS—Carr, Warren, Hume, Davis, Rogers, Buskey, Wood, Duncan.

TACKLES—Ingle, Blank, Rowe, Ringwalt, Sadler, Renedo, Spain, Smith, Cowan, Barnes.

GUARDS—Alexander, Pukal, Richey, Powell, Horvat, Shea, Masino, Connally.

CENTER—Battistello.

BACKS—Talbott, Riggs, Lampman, Mazza, Milgram, Dodson, Davenport, Bomar, Karrs, Beaver, Darnall, Link, Wesolowski, Fortune.

MICHIGAN

ENDS—Sipp, Clancy, Kramer, Stincic, Kemp.

TACKLES—Phillips, Hribal, Hardy, Mair, Williamson, Porter, Goss.

GUARDS—Bailey, Hanna, Mielke, Nunley, Dehlin.

CENTER—Dayton.

BACKS—Vidmer, Sharpe, Ward, Fisher, Volk, Detwiler, Rowser, Sygar, Bass, Morgan, Reynolds, Johnson, Lee.

Scoring

NORTH CAROLINA	0	7	7	7	21
MICHIGAN	7	0	0	0	7

TOUCHDOWNS: NORTH CAROLINA Lampman (12-yard pass from Talbott), Wesolowski (five-yard run), Talbott (one-yard run). MICHIGAN—Fisher (one-yard run).

EXTRA POINTS: NORTH CAROLINA Talbott 3 (placement). MICHIGAN Sygar (placement).

1966 FOOTBALL RESULTS

MICHIGAN	41	Oregon State	0
MICHIGAN	17	California	7
Michigan	7	NORTH CAROLINA	21
Michigan	7	MICHIGAN STATE	20
Michigan	21	PURDUE	22
MICHIGAN	49	Minnesota	0
MICHIGAN	28	Wisconsin	17
Michigan	21	ILLINOIS	28
MICHIGAN	28	Northwestern	20
MICHIGAN	17	Ohio State	3
Total	236	Total	138

Big Ten: Won 4, Lost 3   Season: Won 6, Lost 4

RICHARD VOLK, 6-3, 192, a senior, has been one of the best defensive backs in the Big Ten for two seasons. As a sophomore he was shifted from quarter to defensive half and quickly became a standout on the Big Ten and Rose Bowl championship outfit. The Wauseon, O., athlete was groomed again this past spring as a quarterback while recovering from minor knee surgery. His great defensive ability probably will be used again but he could be available in case of emergency. Rick is the nephew of Bob Chappuis, All-American halfback on Michigan's 1947 Conference and Rose Bowl champs. Coached by Larry Fruth at Wauseon, he was a scholastic All-American. Born in Toledo, O., March 15, 1945.

Volk

The Statistical Story

Oct. 8

Lineups

MICHIGAN
ENDS—Slipp, Clancy, Spencer, Kramer, Kemp, Stincic.
TACKLES—Phillips, Hribal, Williamson, Porter.
GUARDS — Hanna, Bailey, Mielke, Hardy, Nunley, Dehlin, Morgan, D'Eramo.
CENTER—Dayton.
BACKS—Vidmer, Sharpe, Ward, Fisher, Volk, Johnson, Detwiler, Rowser, Brown, Bass, Sygar, Reynolds, Hartman, Lee.

MICHIGAN STATE
ENDS—Brenner, Washington, Thornhill, C. Smith, Chatlos, Pruiett.
TACKLES—Przybycki, West, Hoag, McLoud, Ruminski, Bailey.
GUARDS—Conti, Techlin, Bradley, Gallinagh, Zindell, Brawley, Jordan.
CENTERS—L. Smith, Richardson, Redd, Ranieri.
BACKS—Raye, Lee, C. Jones, Apisa, Cavender, Berlinski, Waters, Wedemeyer, Webster, Summers, J. Jones, Phillips, Garrett, Armstrong, Mullen, Lawson, Super, Kenney, Feraco.

Officials

Eugene Calhoun, referee; Donald Elsass, umpire; Harold Still, back judge; William Filson, head linesman; Steve Slattery, field judge.

Scoring

MSU	7 0 0 13—20
MICHIGAN	0 0 0 7— 7

TOUCHDOWNS: MICHIGAN — Detwiler (15-yard pass from Vidmer); MSU—Raye (five-yard run), Apisa (six-yard run), Washington (24-yard pass from Raye). EXTRA POINTS: MICHIGAN — Sygar (placement); MSU—Kenney 2 -(placements).

PASSING
MICHIGAN

	Att.	Comp.	Yds.	Int.
Vidmer	47	18	168	0
Brown	1	0	0	0

MSU

	Att.	Comp.	Yds.	Int.
Raye	9	3	45	0
Wedemeyer	2	0	0	0

PASS RECEIVING
MICHIGAN

	No.	Yds.
Clancy	9	98
Spencer	2	7
Sipp	3	31
Detwiler	2	33
Sharpe	2	9
Totals	18	168

MSU

	No.	Yds.
Brenner	1	8
Jones	1	13
Washington	1	24

PUNTING
MICHIGAN

	No.	Yds.	Ave.
Kemp	11	440	40

MSU

	No.	Yds.	Ave.
Kenney	6	240	40

Detwiler

MINNESOTA
ENDS—Last, Anderson, Sanders, Williams, Litten, Jessen.
TACKLES—Klick, Boston, Kamzelski, Duren, Jones, Hermann, Bedney.
GUARDS — Laskso, Enderlo, Walter, Reierson, Brown.
CENTERS—Killan, Parr.
BACKS—Wilson, Bryant, Whitlow, Connell, Newsom, Sakal, Wintermute, Carlson, Stephens, Wheeler, Hale, Jenkins, Baldridge, Hatfield, Lee, Seitz, Forte.

MICHIGAN
ENDS—Kramer, Stincic, Clancy, Rosema, Stipp, Salmi, Berline, Kemp, Humphries.
TACKLES—Hardy, Porter, Hribal, Phillips, Williamson, Miklos, Wright, Ma Penksa.
GUARDS — Mielke, Nunley, Bailey, Hanna, Dehlin, Goss, Lanstittel, Yanz, Morgan.
CENTERS—Dayton, D'Eramo, Danhof.
BACKS—Vidmer, Bass, Sygar, Volk, Fisher, Rowser, Detwiler, Brown, Wedge, Ward, Radigan, Hartman, Lee, Nelson, Sharpe, Reynolds, Doty, Jobe, Johnson.

Scoring

MICHIGAN	14 21 7 7—49
MINNESOTA	0 0 0 0— 0

TOUCHDOWNS: MICHIGAN—Detwiler 2 (one-yard run, one-yard run), Sygar (57-yard punt return), Clancy 2 (24-yard pass from Vidmer, 56-yard pass from Vidmer), Ward (five-yard pass from Vidmer), Sharpe (four-yard run). EXTRA POINTS: Sygar 7 (placements).

THOMAS D. STINCIC, 6-3, 217, and a sophomore, comes from Cleveland John Marshall high school where he was coached by Bill Quayle. A standout frosh defensive end, he won the John Maulbetsch Award given annually to the freshman male student demonstrating capacity for leadership and success. The 19-year-old newcomer led his high school team and earned all-conference and northeast Ohio honors. He was born November 24, 1946 in Clevland.

Stincic

MICHIGAN 17, OHIO STATE 3

Oftimes in the past — including as recently as 1964 — a championship has been riding on the outcome of this traditional finale. Pride was the chief prize at stake this fall for the November 19 renewal at Columbus before 83,403 onlookers.

They were rewarded with the customary hard-hitting contest and the Michigan partisans among them were additionally treated to one of the top Wolverine defensive efforts of the season. This, coupled with sharp offensive play, provided a decisive 17 to 3 triumph, vaulted the Wolverines into third place in the Big Ten race, and forced Woody Hayes to accept his second losing campaign in a most productive 16-year span at Ohio.

The Wolverines, with the offensive line blocking crisply, had the better of the early going but three challenging first period drives produced only a 3 to 0 margin on Sygar's 24-yard field goal. Ohio State matched this in the second quarter with a 26-yard field goal by Gary Cairns.

Just before the close of the half, however, the Wolverines sustained a big 66-yard scoring effort. Vidmer to Clancy aerials clicked for 15 and 34 yard gains, and finally Detwiler — who rushed 20 times for 140 yards — swept to the right for the final seven yards.

The score reached its final margin midway through the third quarter when the Wolverines climaxed a 56-yard drive on a Vidmer to Wilhite 28-yard scoring play. There was plenty of action after that but Michigan managed to turn back each Buckeye threat. With the gun marking the season's close, the jubilant Wolverines lofted Coach Bump Elliott to their shoulders. "I'm so pleased for this entire team," said Bump later. "The Seniors, especially, have done a tremendous job . . . I just wish a couple of plays during the season could have gone differently."

ILLINOIS 28, MICHIGAN 21

The Wolverines still had a slim chance for a Rose Bowl journey but long-suffering Illinois — loser of seven straight games to Michigan — wiped it out with a spectacular fourth-quarter comeback before 59,322 unbelieving fans at the Stadium on November 5.

The Illini tallied first with Bob Naponic sneaking the final yard of a 61-yard drive. Michigan retaliated immediately on a march of identical length with Detwiler moving the final six yards into the end zone. In the third quarter the teams again traded touchdowns, Illinois slashing 90 yards in three plays with Naponic racing the final 20, and then Michigan moving 58 and scoring on a Vidmer to Clancy pass for the climactic 16 yards.

This carbon copy format continued when Sygar returned an Illini punt 64 yards for a go-ahead touchdown, only to have Mick Smith race 60 yards to the end zone with a Michigan punt. The Illini failed to tie the count, however, when the conversion attempt by Jim Stotz soared to the right and left Illinois trailing, 21 to 20.

This set the stage for a frustrating finish which rivaled that of the Purdue game. The Wolverines pounded back in an effort to widen the margin, once moving to the Illini six-yard line before losing the ball on downs and moments later marching half the field again to the Illinois six. There, on a third down play, Vidmer tried to hit Clancy in the end zone. But Clancy had fallen, the ball was tipped in the air by one defender to the eager hands of another, Bruce Sullivan, who raced 98 yards for the touchdown and Illinois victory.

...HIGAN'S 1966 TEAM STATISTICS

	Mich.	Opp.
...DOWNS	186	165
...ushing	97	94
...assing	79	50
...enalty	10	21
... NUMBER RUSHES	467	489
...et Yards, Rushing	1845	1596
...et Yards, Passing	1682	953
...ARD PASSES ATTEMPTED	232	196
...ompleted	121	82
...ntercepted by	9	7
...ards Interceptions Returned	67	159
...L PLAYS	698	685
...S, NUMBER	51	55
...verage Distance	39.1	38.6
...Had Blocked	1	0
...OFFS, Returned By	28	47
...S KICKS RETURNED	719	1194
...Punts	385	266
...Kickoffs	334	928
...LES	24	27
...Ball Lost by	13	12
...LTIES, Number	52	36
...Yards Penalized	603	437

All America

Clancy, Volk Receive Recognition

(From News Wire Services)

Michigan Captain Jack Clancy has been placed on two teams in recognition of his outstanding ability as a pass receiver.

Clancy was named to the first team of the All America squad picked by the American Football Coaches Association.

The 6-1, 192-pounder from Detroit was also selected for All Big Ten first string honors at end by the Associated Press.

Also being named to the All America team as an honorable mention selection was defensive back Rick Volk. The 6-3, 192-pound senior was accorded first team honors on the All Big Ten outfit.

	RUSHING			PASSING				RECEIVING		PUNT RET.		PUNTING		SCORING				
	Tries	Net Gain	Ave.	Att'd	Comp.	Had Int.	Gain	Cgh't	Gain	No.	Yds.	No.	Ave.	TD	CK	CPR	FG	TP
...er fb	131	673	5.1	0	0	0	0	0	0	0	0	0	0.0	5	0	0	0	30
...rd, hb	128	499	3.9	0	0	0	0	10	146	1	2	0	0.0	7	0	0	0	42
...wiler, hb	86	413	4.8	1	0	0	0	9	165	0	0	0	0.0	10	0	0	0	60
...rpe, hb	32	105	3.3	1	1	0	28	7	63	0	0	0	0.0	2	0	0	0	12
...wn, qb	11	44	4.0	4	3	0	43	0	0	0	0	0	0.0	0	0	0	0	0
...nson, R., hb	12	44	3.7	0	0	0	0	0	0	0	0	0	0.0	0	0	0	0	0
...ynolds, fb	7	35	5.0	0	0	0	0	0	0	0	0	0	0.0	0	0	0	0	0
...mer, qb	67	30	0.4	226	117	7	1611	0	0	0	0	0	0.0	1	0	0	0	6
...lk, s	1	8	8.0	0	0	0	0	0	0	14	149	0	0.0	0	0	0	0	0
...be, hb	1	4	4.0	0	0	0	0	0	0	0	0	0	0.0	0	0	0	0	0
...digan, fb	1	4	4.0	0	0	0	0	0	0	0	0	0	0.0	0	0	0	0	0
...mp, e	1	−14	−14.0	0	0	0	0	0	0	0	0	50	40.0	0	0	0	0	0
...ancy, e	0	0	0.0	0	0	0	0	76	1079	0	0	0	0.0	4	0	0	0	24
...Wilhite, e	0	0	0.0	0	0	0	0	8	136	0	0	0	0.0	1	0	0	0	6
...erline, e	0	0	0.0	0	0	0	0	2	33	0	0	0	0.0	1	0	0	0	6
...pp, e	0	0	0.0	0	0	0	0	5	43	0	0	0	0.0	0	0	0	0	0
...pencer, e	0	0	0.0	0	0	0	0	2	7	0	0	0	0.0	0	0	0	0	0
...umphries, e	0	0	0.0	0	0	0	0	2	10	0	0	0	0.0	0	0	0	0	0
...ygar, s	0	0	0.0	0	0	0	0	0	0	9	180	0	0.0	2	32-32	0-1	2	50

Whitey Wistert Voted To 'Hall'

(Special to The News)

NEW YORK — Francis (Whitey) Wistert, All-America tackle at Michigan in 1933, will be one of nine former players inducted into the National Football League Hall of Fame for 1967.

Wistert, who helped the Wolverines to an unbeaten 7-0-1 record his senior year, was the first of three brothers to become All-America tackles at Michigan.

Brother Albert won the honor in 1942 and brother Alvin was tapped in both 1948 and 1949.

Chester J. LaRoche, president of the National Football Foundation, announced Wistert's nomination Thursday.

Wistert and the other players were honored along with former college and professional coach Greasy Neale. All will be inducted at the 10th annual Awards Banquet Dec. 5.

The players honored include six linemen and three backs. They are: Slade Cutter, Navy tackle; Nathan Dougherty, Tennessee guard; Joel Hunt, Texas A&M back; Wear Schoonover, Arkansas end; Paul Schwegler, Washington tackle; Herb Stein, Pittsburgh center; Cecil Isbell, Purdue back, and Abe Mickal, Louisiana State back in addition to Wistert.

Reprinted with permission from the Ann Arbor News

1967 MICHIGAN VARSITY SQUAD
Alphabetical

No.	Name	Pos.	Ht.	Wt.	Age	Class	Hometown
95	Bonar, James	OT	6-0	218	20	Jr.	Chicago,
60	Baumgartner, Bob	OG	6-0	219	20	Jr.	Chicago,
97	Berline, Jim	OE	6-0	185	21	Sr.	Niles,
61	Broadnax, Stan	OT	6-0	226	21	Sr.	Cincinnati
22	Brown, Dennis	QB	5-10	175	20	Jr.	Lincoln
66	Brown, Richard	OT	6-1	215	19	So.	Au
56	Caldarazzo, Dick	OG	5-10	210	19	So.	Melrose Park
25	Craw, Garvie	OB	6-2	211	19	So.	Montclair,
25	Curtis, Tom	DHB	6-2	184	19	So.	Aurora
58	*Dayton, Joe (Capt.)	C	6-2	225	22	Sr.	De
52	Denzin, David	C	6-2	220	20	Jr.	Xenia
51	*D'Eramo, Paul	C	5-10	214	21	Sr.	Mt.
30	Doty, Alfred	SB	5-10	187	21	Sr.	Youngstown,
50	Drehmann, Peter	OT	6-1	206	19	So.	Mt. Cleme
70	Duffy, James	OG	6-1	215	21	Sr.	Abington,
93	Falkenhagen, Curt	DE	6-2	198	19	So.	Winchester,
23	Farabee, David	OHB	6-0	185	20	Jr.	Bridges
37	Federico, Eric	FB	5-11	197	19	So.	Holl
64	Francis, Alan	MG	5-10	190	19	So.	Tren
54	Frysinger, Terry	DT	6-2	212	20	Jr.	Euclid,
18	Gabler, John	OHB	6-2	208	19	So.	Royal
8	*Goss, Tom	DT	6-2	225	20	Sr.	Knoxville,
77	Hall, Werner	DT	6-0	226	19	So.	Sandusky,
57	Hankwitz, Mike	LB	6-1	194	19	So.	Scotty
80	Harris, William	OE	6-1	184	19	So.	Mt. Clem
26	*Hartman, Gerald	SB	6-1	170	21	Jr.	Ann Ar
13	Healy, Brian	DHB	6-1	170	19	So.	Sandusky,
82	Heffelfinger, Jon	DE	6-2	205	21	Sr.	Battle C
12	Hoey, George	DHB	5-10	169	20	Jr.	Fl
86	Humphries, Derrick	OE	6-2	192	20	Sr.	Detr
62	Johnson, Paul	OT	6-0	231	20	Sr.	Bay C
42	*Johnson, Ronald	OHB	6-1	196	20	Jr.	Detr
21	Kieta, Robert	SB	6-0	181	20	Jr.	Chicago,
84	*Kramer, Jon	MG	6-3	215	20	Jr.	Toledo,
68	Kunsa, Joseph	OG	6-0	207	20	Jr.	W. Braddock,
28	Lynch, John	DHB	5-10	175	20	Jr.	Chicago, I
73	Mair, Peter	OE	6-3	225	19	So.	Allentown, P
72	Mandich, James	OE	6-3	215	19	So.	Solon,
94	Miklos, Gerald	DT	6-3	227	20	Jr.	Chicago, Ill
74	Monthei, Dennis	MG	6-2	201	21	Sr.	Detr
34	Morgan, Dennis	LB	5-11	215	21	Sr.	Phoenixville, P
71	Mouch, William	OT	6-5	260	19	So.	Cincinnati, O
44	Nelson, Douglas	SB	6-0	181	21	Jr.	Adria
76	Penksa, Robert	OT	6-1	225	20	Jr.	Niles,
72	*Phillips, Ray	OG	6-3	229	19	So.	Evanston, I
70	Pierson, Barry	DHB	6-0	173	19	So.	St. Ignace
70	*Porter, Dave	DT	6-3	231	21	Sr.	Lansing
55	Pryor, Cecil	LB	6-4	218	19	So.	Corpus Christi, Tex
81	*Pullen, Tom	OE	6-3	198	22	Sr.	Ottawa, Can.
69	Ritley, Robert	OT	6-0	228	19	So.	Garfield Hgts., O.
83	Rosema, Roger	DE	6-2	225	21	Sr.	Grand Rapids
46	Jansom, Elijah	DHB	6-1	191	20	Jr.	Detroit
59	Sarantos, Peter	C	6-0	207	19	So.	Elkhart, Ind.
91	Seymour, Philip	DE	6-4	195	19	So.	Berkley
17	*Sharpe, Ernest	OHB	5-11	191	21	Sr.	Palos Hts., Ill.
33	Sipp, Warren	FB	6-1	209	20	Jr.	Akron, O.
19	Sirosky, Dennis	LB	6-0	221	20	Jr.	Ecorse
19	Sorenson, Eric	OE	6-0	188	19	So.	Royal Oak
45	Spencer, Royce	OE	6-1	208	21	Sr.	Ecorse
90	*Stincic, Tom	DE	6-3	217	20	Jr.	Chicago, Ill.
20	Thomas, John	QB	6-1	188	19	So.	Cleveland, O.
31	Titas, Frank	FB	6-2	205	19	So.	Walled Lake
27	*Vidmer, Richard	QB	6-1	181	22	Sr.	Cleveland, O.
32	Wadhams, Timothy	DHB	6-1	178	19	So.	Greensburg, Pa.
36	Washington, Martin	OG	5-10	194	20	Jr.	Ann Arbor
10	Wall, Kenneth	DHB	6-2	180	19	So.	Ecorse
53	*Wedge, Robert	LB	6-2	201	20	Jr.	LaGrange, Ill.
85	Weinmann, Tom	OE	6-2	214	19	So.	Port Huron
49	Werner, Mark	DHB	6-2	188	19	So.	Ann Arbor
43	White, Robert	OHB	6-2	190	19	So.	Cincinnati, O.
92	Wilhite, James	MG	6-3	204	20	Jr.	Middleville
75	*Williamson, Dick	DT	6-4	227	21	Jr.	Bay City
96	Woolley, Edwin	DE	6-3	218	19	So.	East Detroit
67	Yanz, Richard	OG	6-1	217	19	So.	Pitman, N.J.
							Chicago, Ill.

OE Off. End
DE Def. End
OT Off. Tackle
DT Def. Tackle
OG Off. Guard
MG Middle Guard
C Center
QB Quarterback
OHB Off. Halfback
FB Fullback
LB Linebacker
DHB Def. Halfback
SB Safety Back

*Denotes lettermen

1967 FOOTBALL RESULTS

10	MICHIGAN	Duke 7
9	Michigan	CALIFORNIA 10
21	Michigan	NAVY 26
0	Michigan	MICHIGAN STATE 34
20	Michigan	INDIANA 27
15	Michigan	MINNESOTA 20
7	MICHIGAN	Northwestern 3
21	MICHIGAN	Illinois 14
27	MICHIGAN	Wisconsin 14
14	Michigan	OHIO STATE 24
144	TOTAL	TOTAL 179

BIG TEN: Won 3, Lost 4   SEASON: Won 4, Lost 6

FINAL 1967 CONFERENCE STANDINGS
Team Standings

	W	L	T	Pct.	Ave.	Opp. Ave.	Off.* Rank	Def.* Rank
Indiana	6	1	....	.857	17.4	16.1	3	6
Minnesota	6	1	....	.857	18.1	12.0	5	3
Purdue	6	1	....	.857	32.1	13.0	1	1
Ohio State	5	2	....	.714	15.4	15.1	7	4
Michigan	3	4	....	.429	14.9	19.4	8	7
Illinois	3	4	....	.429	14.6	20.9	10	8
Michigan State	3	4	....	.429	19.6	15.9	4	5
Northwestern	2	5	....	.286	17.9	20.4	6	2
Iowa	0	6	1	.071	16.1	24.9	2	10
Wisconsin	0	6	1	.071	13.3	21.7	9	9

Based on comparative grading of points, first downs and yards per play.

DENNIS M. BROWN, 5-10, 175, is a junior signal caller from Lincoln Park who saw about 13 minutes of varsity action last fall. He showed quickness, good speed and fair passing ability, and should see more action this fall. In high school he was a quarterback and safety man, gaining all-state honors. He was co-captain of both his football and basketball teams. His grid coach at Lincoln Park was Ron Pascuzzi. Dennis was born in Detroit, August 16, 1947.

Captain

Dayton

D. Brown

Sept. 25

The Lineups
DUKE
ENDS—Hayes, Carter, DeBolt, Hepler, Courtillet, Joseph, Dearth.
TACKLES—Bombard, Parker, Rasberry, Bodkin, Zirkle, Renneker, Lasky.
GUARDS—Goins, Edwards, Biddle, Foyle, Newman, Padgett, Compitello, Grace.
SENTERS—Murphy, Morris.
BACKS—Woodall, Ryan, Hicklin, Calabrese, Baglien, Brannon, Riesenfeld, Dempsey, Beath, Schafer, Wuerstle, Davis, Vann.

MICHIGAN
ENDS—Stincic, Rosema, Berline, Mandich, Seymour, Weinmann.
TACKLES—Porter, Goss, Mair, Penksa, Hankwitz, Miklos, Drehmann, Williamson.
GUARDS—Monthei, Yanz, Kramer, Phillips.
CENTERS—Wedge, Dayton, Morgan.
BACKS—Vidmer, Healy, Titas, Sipp, Johnson, Sharpe, Brown, Hartman, Curtis, Craw, Hoey, Gabler.

Scoring

DUKE	7 0 0 0—	7
MICHIGAN	0 0 7 3—	10

TOUCHDOWNS: DUKE—Ryan (four yards). MICHIGAN—Sharpe (seven yards).
EXTRA POINTS: DUKE—Riesenfeld (placement). MICHIGAN—Titas (placement).
FIELD GOAL: MICHIGAN—Titas (27 yards).

Lineup

Individual Figures

RUSHING
INDIANA

	T	G	L	N
	18	101	0	101
	14	63	0	63
Cole	9	32	0	32
Gonso	10	38	21	17
Grove	1	5	0	5

MICHIGAN

Johnson	16	35	7	28
Brown	30	131	4	127
Craw	9	32	3	29
Gabler	1			

ENDS — Gill, McCaa, Norman, Gage, Lunas, Stolberg, Snowden, Price, TACK. Isenbarger, S., Crusan, Geers, Dunn, Schmidt, Krivoshia, Bergman, Christ, Grecco, GUARDS — Calfe, Snodeck, Cassells, Russell, arks, DeSalle, CENTERS — Kaezm..., .rk, Mauro, Applegate, Pankratz, .CKS — Gee, Kaenda, Cunningham, .uquman, Dorty, Butcher, Isenbarger, .eal, Warner, Cole, Krivoshia, Mathias, .rove, Nichols,

MICHIGAN

ENDS — Mandich, Berline, Kramer, effelfinger, Stincic, Seymour; TACKLES — ..., Weinmann, Mair, Porter, Penksa, .oss, Drehmann, P. Johnson, William- .on, GUARDS — Phillips, Baumgartner, .roadnax, Morgan, Miklos, Rosema, .edge, Hankwitz, Wilhite; CENTERS — .ayton, Monthei; BACKS — Brown, Gab- .er, Johnson, Titas, Craw, Curtis, Nelson, .ieta, Hoey, Hartman, Pierson, Doty, .Healy, Sipp.

Scoring

INDIANA	14	6	0	7	—27
MICHIGAN	0	7	7	6	—20

TOUCHDOWNS. INDIANA — Isenbarg- er 2 (28-yard run and one-yard run), Stolberg (seven-yard pass from Gonso), Butcher (41-yard pass from Isenbarger). MICHIGAN — Brown 2 (two-yard run and one-yard run), Johnson (one-yard run).

EXTRA POINTS: INDIANA — Warner 3 (placements); MICHIGAN — Hank- witz 2 (placements).

PASSING
INDIANA

Att.	Comp.	Int.	Yds.
11	5	0	78
3	2	1	79

MICHIGAN

Gonso	31	18	1	211
Isenbarger				

PASS RECEIVING
INDIANA

	No.	Yds.
Butcher	3	82
Stolberg	1	7
Gage	2	40
Krmradt	1	18

MICHIGAN

	No.	Yds.
Berline	7	93
Gabler	10	101
Mandich	1	17

PUNTING
INDIANA

	No.	Ave.
Isenbarger	4	36.7

MICHIGAN

Drehmann	2	55

Officials

Howard Wirtz, referee; Robert Hepler, umpire; William Filson, head linesman; Victor Wukovits, field judge; Jerry Markbreit, back judge.

By running or passing on 61 plays, Brown eclipsed a 14-year-old record held by Minnesota's Paul Giel who had 53 plays against Michigan on Oct. 24, 1953, at Minneapolis.

By totaling 338 yards (211 on 18 completions in 31 passes and 127 rushing), Brown topped the record 317 set by Purdue's Bob Griese last season against Illinois.

Michigan halfback Ron Johnson (40) swings outside a flying Navy tackler and sets out for the goal line 62 yards away. The play, the Wolverines' second of the game, featured near-perfect block- ing to spring Johnson loose for the first score of the game. Johnson produced a Michigan record 270 yards rushing and two long-run touchdowns in 26 carries against Navy.

R. Johnson

'M' Struggles to 500th Win

Michigan 7, Northwestern 3: It wasn't easy, as the score testifies, but this November 4 game in the Stadium turned out to be the long-awaited 500th football victory. The 62,063 fans witnessed a tough, tight game in which all the scoring was confined to the second period. A 28-yard field goal put the Wild- cats out in front but Michigan came right back with a 70-yard drive climaxed by Brown's one-yard sneak across the goal line. Hankwitz converted to provide the game's final point. Johnson reached the Big Ten record books by carrying 42 times, netting 167 of Michigan's 184 rushing yards.

The Lineups

NORTHWESTERN

ENDS — Buckner, Anderson, Paquette, Clawson, Hubbard, Proskine; TACKLES— Brandt, Hahn, Denny, Ekl, Blue, Ziol- kowski; GUARDS — Loukas, Gunstra, Angelo, Mied; CENTERS — Rudnay, Spenko; BACKS — Melzer, Olson, Kur- zawski, Anstey, Garretson, Field, White, Boothe, Dennis, Piccuta, Emmerich, Dan- iels, Coyne, Cornell, Hudson, Smeeton, Glass, Dean, Ross, Laissoo, Forsthoffer.

MICHIGAN

ENDS — Weinmann, Berline, Kramer, Mandich, Seymour; TACKLES — Penksa, Mair, Drehmann, Miklos, Porter, Hankwitz; GUARDS — Phillips, Baumgartner, Broadnax, Stincic, Wedge, Rosema; CENTERS — Dayton, Morgan, Heffelfinger; BACKS — Brown, Gabler, Johnson, Craw, Healy, Curtis, Hoey, Hartman, Doty, Pierson, Titas, Nelson.

Scoring

NORTHWESTERN	0	3	0	0—3
MICHIGAN	0	7	0	0—7

TOUCHDOWN: MICHIGAN — Brown (one-yard run).
EXTRA POINT: MICHIGAN — Hank- witz (placement).
FIELD GOAL: NORTHWESTERN — Emmerick (28 yards).

MICHIGAN

Johnson	42	168	1	167
Brown	15	33	16	17

PASSING

NORTHWESTERN

	Att.	Comp.	Int.	Yds.
Melzer	23	8	1	98
Kurzawski	1	0	1	0

MICHIGAN

Brown	22	10	0	77

RECEIVING

NORTHWESTERN

	No.	Yds.
Olson	3	17
Anderson	3	41
Hubbard	3	36
Kurzawski	1	4

MICHIGAN

	No.	Yds.
Gabler	4	19
Berline	4	43
Mandich	2	15

PUNTING

NORTHWESTERN

	No.	Aev.
Kurzawski	5	25

MICHIGAN

Drehmann	6	40.5

Minnesota 20, Michigan 15: The Wolverines, playing their best first half of the year before 50,006 at Memorial Stadium in Minneapolis, moved to a 15-0 lead over the favored Gophers. Johnson scored an early touchdown on a 59-yard pitchout play, then reached the end zone moments later after a Curtis interception had given Michigan possession at the Minnesota 5. The Wolverines missed both kick conversions, but later widened the lead to 15 points on a 21-yard field goal by Mike Hankwitz. The Gophers, however, came back strong, scoring one touchdown just before the half and two more in the fourth quarter. Michigan twice threatened in the closing moments but could not again reach the scoreboard and Minnesota regained the coveted Little Brown Jug.

Michigan 21, Illinois 14: The Illini moved off to a 14-0 lead before 44,236 fans at Champaign and it looked like a long afternoon for the Wolverines. Instead, this game turned into one of the three greatest comebacks in Michigan's 88 years of football history. A third-quarter touchdown pass from Brown to Berline put the Wolverines on the scoreboard, then they quickly reached it again on Hoey's spectacular 60-yard punt return. Tom Weinmann caught a Brown pass for a two-point conversion, making it 14-14. The tie-breaking score came in the final quarter, with Johnson slashing the final three yards of a 44-yard drive.

Michigan 27, Wisconsin 14: The Badgers, playing before 44,721 in their Camp Randall Stadium, scored first and last but the Wolverines had their season best offensive day with a four-touchdown surge. Brown was a standout with 274 running and passing yards. He ran 44 yards for the first Michigan score, set up the second with a 37-yard pass to Johnson, hit Berline on a 60-yard play for the third, and then combined again with Johnson on a 31-yard pass play for the final touchdown.

Ohio State 24, Michigan 14: Both teams brought three-game win streaks into this traditional finale before 64,144 Stadium fans and a regional TV audience. At the outset, Ohio was all-powerful while Michigan was inexplicably flat. The Bucks moved seemingly at will through the Wolverine defenses and also stalled each Michigan offensive move. Midway through the second quarter Ohio had a 21-0 lead and appeared to be a runaway victor. The margin was cut just before the close of the half when the Wolverines unfurled an 80-yard drive climaxed by Brown's 6-yard touchdown toss to Berline. Fumbles and penalties hampered Michigan's third quarter efforts, but in the final period the Wolverines moved 47 yards to the second touchdown with Brown firing a 13-yard pass to Sophomore John Gabler. Ohio came back strong, however, and a 37-yard field goal put the battle out of Michigan reach in the final two minutes.

Reprinted with permission from the **Michigan Alumnus**

Williamson

Morgan

Overall, the 1967 squad finished with four victories in the ten-game slate. It was outscored by the opponents, 176 to 144. The Big Ten record was 3-4. Indiana, Minnesota and Purdue deadlocked for the championship with 6-1 marks. Ohio State wound up 5-2. Illinois and Michigan State joined the Wolverines at 3-4. Northwestern was eighth with 2-5, and Wisconsin and Iowa shared the cellar at 0-6-1.

At season's end, underclassmen were carrying the major burden for the Wolverines. The entire offensive backfield and the entire defensive secondary returns intact next year. Included are some individual standouts who excelled statistically even in the losing campaign. Junior Ron Johnson, who earlier established Michigan's one-game rushing record, wound up the year as the first Wolverine ever to top the 1,000-yard mark in rushing with a net of 1,005. Junior Dennis Brown, who did not make his first start until the season's fifth game, finished as the Big Ten's runnerup in both the passing and total offense categories.

Sophomore Tom Curtis tied a Big Ten record with seven pass interceptions for the year, while his defensive backfield mate, Junior George Hoey, far surpassed all other Conference performers in punt return effectiveness. There was honor, as well, for one of Michigan's eight departing Senior starters — split end Jim Berline — who placed second in the Big Ten in pass receptions with 41.

Berline

Curtis

Porter

P. Johnson

Goss

Mair

MICHIGAN'S 1967 TEAM STATISTICS

	Mich.	Opp.
FIRST DOWN	168	167
Rushing	97	109
Passing	66	49
Penalty	5	9
TOTAL NUMBER RUSHES	488	516
Net Yards, Rushing	1635	1808
Net Yards, Passing	1302	1153
FORWARD PASSES ATTEMPTED	244	174
Completed	120	74
Intercepted By	14	13
Yards Interceptions Returned	178	80
TOTAL PLAYS	732	690
PUNTS, NUMBER	55	61
Average Distance	37.6	35.1
KICK-OFFS, Returned By	32	31
YARDS KICKS RETURNED	999	849
Punts	384	317
Kickoffs	615	532
FUMBLES	22	28
Ball Lost By	16	15
PENALTIES, Number	40	43
Yards Penalized	443	388

MICHIGAN'S INDIVIDUAL STATISTICS FOR 1967

	RUSHING			PASSING				RECEIVING		PUNT RET.		PUNTING		SCORING				
	Tries	Net Gain	Ave.	Att'd	Comp.	Had Int.	Gain	Cgh't	Gain	No.	Yds.	No.	Ave.	TD	CK	CR	FG	TP
Johnson, R. hb	220	1005	4.6	0	0	0	0	13	179	0	0	0	0.0	8	0	0	0	48
Brown, qb	137	358	2.6	156	82	7	913	0	0	0	0	0	0.0	4	0	0	0	24
Sipp, fb	24	104	4.3	0	0	0	0	0	0	0	0	0	0.0	1	0	0	0	6
Craw, fb	29	101	3.4	0	0	0	0	1	5	0	0	3	24.3	0	0	0	0	0
Sharpe, hb	33	98	2.9	0	0	0	0	5	58	0	0	0	0.0	1	0	0	0	6
Gabler, hb	16	25	1.6	0	0	0	0	20	173	0	0	0	0.0	2	0	0	0	12
Titas, fb	2	9	4.5	0	0	0	0	0	0	0	0	0	0.0	0	7-11	0	1-2	10
Federico, fb	2	3	1.5	0	0	0	0	0	0	0	0	0	0.0	0	0	0	0	0
Vidmer, qb	25	—68	—2.7	88	38	6	376	0	0	0	0	0	0.0	0	0	0	0	0
Berline, e	0	0	0.0	0	0	0	0	54	624	0	0	0	0.0	3	0	0	0	18
Mandich, e	0	0	0.0	0	0	0	0	26	256	0	0	0	0.0	0	0	0	0	0
Drehman, lb	0	0	0.0	0	0	0	0	0	0	0	0	52	38.4	0	0	0	0	0
Hankwitz, lb	0	0	0.0	0	0	0	0	0	0	1	—1	0	0.0	0	6-7	0	2-6	11
Hoey, hb	0	0	0.0	0	0	0	0	0	0	12	299	0	0.0	1	0	0	0	6
Weinmann, fb	0	0	0.0	0	0	0	0	0	0	0	0	0	0.0	0	1-1	0	0	2
Hartman, hb	0	0	0.0	0	0	0	0	0	0	8	64	0	0.0	0	0	0	0	0
Curtis, hb	0	0	0.0	0	0	0	0	0	0	5	22	0	0.0	0	0	0	0	0

Don Canham Named Athletic Director

Donald Canham

Michigan's track coach for the past 19 years and a successful businessman in his own right, Donald B. Canham, has been named director of athletics and physical education at the University by the Regents upon recommendation of President Robben W. Fleming.

The 49-year-old Canham will succeed H. O. (Fritz) Crisler, who retires June 30.

In announcing the appointment, President Fleming indicated that Canham has agreed to divest himself of his business interests. Canham heads an Ann Arbor corporation which manufactures and sells gymnasium, playground, and athletic equipment as well as scientific and teaching aid products.

Under a reorganized structure for physical education and athletics, announced earlier, positions were created for an associate director of intercollegiate athletics and an associate director of physical education and athletics. Appointments to these positions will come at the recommendation of the new athletic director.

During his 19-year tenure as track coach, Canham's Michigan teams have won 12 Big Ten championships, all of them in the past dozen years, and his squads have occupied the runner-up position no less than 14 times. For 14 of 19 seasons, Michigan under Canham has finished among the top three teams in Conference title meets. His squads have established more than 80 records both indoors and outdoors, including world, American and Big Ten marks, his relay teams, in particular, being remarkably successful.

Counting dual, triangular and quadrangular competition, Canham's teams have a record of over .800 per cent in 115 meets, and Michigan has never had a losing season under his direction while competing against the country's foremost teams.

A native of Oak Park, Illinois, Canham was born there April 27, 1918, and after attending public schools there, graduated from Oak Park High School in 1937. Entering the University of Michigan that same year, he became NCAA high jump champion and also took four Big Ten titles. He received his B. S. degree from the University in physical education, history and science. He received a master's degree in 1948.

Canham taught history and coached basketball and football at Kankakee, Illinois, High School until 1942, when he enlisted as a private in the U. S. Army Air Force during World War II. He was discharged as a captain in 1946. He became assistant track coach at his alma mater that same year and two years later was elevated to the head coaching post.

In 1954 he started a small instructional sports film company to manufacture various types of playground and athletic equipment as well as scientific and teaching aid products. In recent years, however, he has gradually withdrawn from management of the concern.

The energetic Wolverine director has conducted coaching clinics in Finland, Africa, Germany, Trinidad, Canada, and other countries. He has made six foreign coaching trips in the interest of track and field and is permanent executive director of the United States Track Coaches Association with headquarters in Ann Arbor. During the past five years, he has been one of the leading organizers of the U. S. Track and Field Federation. He has served the U. S. State Department as a representative abroad and as consultant for the U. S. Army in Germany.

Canham also founded and directed the first NCAA Indoor Track and Field history, with gross revenue exceeding $80,000 per year. All profits were returned to the competing schools. In 1968 he served as promotional director of the Madison Square Garden Invitational Track Meet in New York.

Canham was married in 1941 to the former Marilyn Norris, '42, at Grand Rapids, Michigan. They are the parents of two children, Clare Ann Canham, 14, St. Thomas High School, and Donald Norris Canham, 19, University of Michigan sophomore.

Athletic Directors Honor Fritz Crisler

(Special to The News)

MINNEAPOLIS — Fritz Crisler, retiring athletic director at Michigan, has been named winner of the second James J. Corbett Memorial Award.

The award is for outstanding achievements throughout the years in intercollegiate athletics and is presented by the National Association of Collegiate Directors of Athletics (NACDA). The announcement was made by Mike Cleary, executive director of NACDA.

The award is named after James J. Corbett, the late director of athletics at Louisiana State, who was the first president of NACDA.

The presentation of the award to Crisler will be made by Bill Orwig, athletic director at Indiana, at NACDA's third national convention in Cleveland June 25.

Crisler has been Michigan's director of athletics since 1941. He retires on June 30. Crisler was named in 1954 to the Football Foundation's Hall of Fame. He had coached at Minnesota (1930-31), Princeton (1932-37) and Michigan (1938-1947), winning more than 72 per cent of his games.

Crisler also is a life member-at-large of the NCAA Football Rules committee.

Will Perry, assistant sports editor of the Grand Rapids Press, today was named sports information director at Michigan by the Board in Control of Intercollegiate Athletics.

The board also approved appointment of Larry Zimmer, sports director of radio station WAAM, Ann Arbor, as co-ordinator of radio and television for the athletic department. He will continue to broadcast football and basketball on a contractual basis. Zimmer will assume duties of the newly-created post, July 1. The two appointees will be the first named to serve under Don Canham, newly-appointed director of athletics, who succeeds Fritz Crisler, who will retire on June 30.

The 34-year-old Perry succeeds Les Etter, who also retires June 30, after 24 years of service at Michigan.

A Michigan graduate in 1955, Perry served two years as information specialist in the Army, and later worked as sports editor and political writer on the Belvidere (Ill.) Daily Republican and the Morris (Ill.) Herald, before joining the Grand Rapids Press in 1960.

Perry was a pitcher for the Michigan baseball team for two years although he did not earn a letter.

He is married to the former Patricia Pezet of Grand Rapids. They have three children, Stephan, 11; Karen, 9; and Susan, 6.

1968 MICHIGAN

Alphabetical

No.	Name	Pos.	Wgt.	Hgt.	Age	Class
3	ABRAHAMS, Morris	DT	225	6-2	25	Junior
5	BANAR, James	DT	218	6-0	20	Junior
0	BAUMGARTNER, Robert	OG	215	6-0	21	Senior
8	BERUTTI, William	QB	178	6-2	19	Sophomore
3	BETTS, Jim	OHB	180	6-4	19	Sophomore
1	BROADNAX, Stanley	OG	226	6-0	22	Senior
2	BROWN, Dennis	QB	175	5-10	21	Senior
4	BROWN, Richard	LB	215	6-1	20	Junior
6	CALDARAZZO, Richard	OG	210	5-10	20	Junior
7	CATALLO, Giulio	DT	260	6-4	19	Sophomore
8	CRAW, Garvie	FB	211	6-2	20	Junior
5	CURTIS, Thomas	DHB	184	6-1	20	Junior
2	DENZIN, David	C	220	6-2	21	Senior
2	DIERDORF, Daniel	OT	255	6-3	19	Sophomore
6	DOANE, Tom	LB	207	5-10	21	Junior
0	DREHMANN, Peter	OT	206	6-1	20	Junior
9	DUFFY, James	MG	230	6-0	21	Junior
5	DUTCHER, Gerald	OE	175	6-2	19	Sophomore
2	FARABEE, David	OHB	185	6-1	21	Senior
7	FEDERICO, Eric	FB	197	5-11	20	Junior
3	FLANAGAN, Stephen	DE	193	6-2	19	Sophomore
1	FRANCIS, Alan	DG	190	5-10	20	Junior
4	FRYSINGER, Terry	DT	210	6-2	22	Senior
8	GABLER, John	OHB	208	6-2	20	Junior
5	GOSS, Thomas	DT	225	6-2	22	Senior
5	HALL, Werner	OT	225	6-0	20	Junior
1	HANKWITZ, Michael	OE	190	6-2	20	Junior
1	HARPRING, Jack	OT	215	6-4	19	Sophomore
0	HARRIS, William	OE	195	6-1	20	Junior
7	HARRISON, Gregory	OHB	183	5-11	19	Sophomore
6	HARTMAN, Gerald	DHB	170	6-1	22	Senior
4	HEALY, Brian	DHB	170	6-1	20	Junior
9	HILL, Henry	DG	200	5-10	19	Sophomore
2	HOEY, George	DHB	169	5-10	21	Senior
0	HUFF, Ralph	LB	220	6-2	19	Sophomore
6	IMSLAND, Jerry	OE	210	6-2	19	Junior
0	JOHNSON, Ronald	OHB	196	6-1	21	Senior
3	JONES, Joseph	OG	195	6-0	20	Junior
1	KIETA, Robert	OHB	181	6-0	21	Senior
5	KILLIAN, Timothy	LB	220	6-4	19	Sophomore
4	KRAMER, Jon	DE	215	6-3	21	Senior
8	KUNSA, Joseph	OG	207	6-0	21	Senior
7	LUKZ, Joseph	OT	210	6-1	20	Junior
8	MANDICH, James	OE	215	6-3	20	Junior
3	MANDLER, Jay	LB	210	5-10	21	Junior
9	McCAFFREY, Thomas	OE	185	6-2	19	Sophomore
8	McCOY, Richard	DT	230	6-4	19	Sophomore
4	MIKLOS, Gerald	DG	227	6-3	21	Senior
7	MOORE, Edward	LB	200	6-1	19	Sophomore
7	MOORHEAD, Donald	QB	197	6-3	19	Sophomore
2	NEWELL, Peter	DE	218	6-4	19	Sophomore
3	NIEMAN, Thomas	OE	200	6-1	19	Sophomore
4	PARKS, Daniel	DT	235	6-5	19	Sophomore
6	PENKSA, Robert	OT	225	6-1	21	Senior
9	PIERSON, Barry	DHB	173	6-0	20	Junior
9	PRUSIECKI, John	DT	245	6-2	19	Junior
5	PRYOR, Cecil	LB	218	6-4	20	Junior
9	RITLEY, Robert	OT	228	6-0	20	Junior
1	SAMPLE, Fred	C	225	6-0	19	Sophomore
4	SAMS, Kirby	OHB	195	6-0	19	Sophomore
6	SANSOM, Elijah	DHB	188	6-1	21	Senior
9	SARANTOS, Peter	C	200	6-0	20	Junior
5	SCHEFFLER, Lance	OHB	190	6-0	19	Sophomore
1	SEYMOUR, Philip	DE	193	6-4	20	Junior
3	SIPP, Warren	FB	209	6-1	21	Senior
2	SIROSKY, Dennis	LB	197	6-0	22	Senior
9	SORENSON, Eric	OHB	185	6-0	20	Junior
0	STAROBA, Paul	OE	195	6-3	19	Sophomore
0	STINCIC, Thomas	DE	217	6-3	21	Senior
0	THOMAS, John	QB	198	6-1	22	Senior
4	TITAS, Frank	OG	205	6-2	20	Junior
1	WADHAMS, Timothy	OHB	178	6-1	20	Junior
0	WALL, Kenneth	DHB	180	6-2	19	Sophomore
6	WASHINGTON, Martin	OG	194	5-10	20	Junior
8	WEDGE, Robert	DHB	193	6-2	21	Senior
9	WERNER, Mark	DHB	185	6-2	21	Junior
3	WHITE, Robert	OHB	190	6-2	20	Junior
2	WILHITE, James	DG	204	6-3	20	Junior
6	WOLFF, John	OG	220	6-1	19	Sophomore
6	WOOLEY, Edwin	DE	218	6-1	20	Junior
8	ZUGANELIS, George	C	212	6-0	20	Junior

1968			
Michigan	7;	California	21
Michigan	31;	Duke	10
Michigan	32;	Navy	9
Michigan	28;	Mich. State	14
Michigan	27;	Indiana	22
Michigan	33;	Minnesota	20
Michigan	35;	Northwestern	0
Michigan	36;	Illinois	0
Michigan	34;	Wisconsin	9
Michigan	14;	Ohio State	50

Season Summary

Games won 8; Lost 2; Tied 0
Points for Michigan 277; For Opponents 155

This 'Retirement' Spotlights Football Tribute

You can't tell the players without a scorecard, or in the case of a football game, without a program. That adage is largely true, except in the case of a 98 or a 77 or a 47.

These numbers and several more became so nationally known because of the exploits of the players that wore them that the universities involved — Michigan and Illinois — retired them permanently.

Retirement of a jersey number is a rare honor. Five schools in the Big Ten (Indiana, Minnesota, Purdue, Ohio State and Northwestern), never have retired a number.

Michigan has retired four numbers as tribute to seven players. Number 98 still is associated with Tom Harmon, twice an All-American halfback (1939-40) for the Wolverines. Bennie Oosterbaan's 47 was put in storage after he became the school's only three-time All-American (1925-26-27).

FRANCIS WISTERT

And Ron Kramer, like Oosterbaan, an end, had his 87 retired after three brilliant seasons (1954 - 55 - 56) under Coach Oosterbaan.

One of the rarest college football accomplishments was turned in by the Wistert brothers — Francis (1933), Albert (1942), and Alvin (1948). All were Michigan All-Americans and all wore number 11. It was fitting that,

ALBERT WISTERT

ALVIN WISTERT

after Alvin completed his career and there were no more future Wolverines in the Wistert family, Michigan retired this jersey number.

California 21—Michigan 7

September 21 Ann Arbor Attendance—71,386

The Wolverines' season opened on a sour note against the fired-up Golden Bears. California jumped off to a quick 14-0 lead in the first quarter as tailback Gary Fowler scored twice. Meanwhile, Michigan's pass receivers had trouble hanging on to the football. Tight end Jim Mandich was the only consistent receiver hauling in 6 for 73 yards, including a second period touchdown pass which left the Wolverines trailing at halftime 14-7. Fowler again scored in the fourth period to put the game on ice for Cal.

Michigan 31—Duke 10

September 28 Durham, N. C. Attendance—25,000

It was a different Michigan team on this sunny day in the South. All-American Ron Johnson, who had rushed for only 48 yds. against California, gained 205 yards and scored two touchdowns, while quarterback Dennis Brown connected on 13 of 23 passes for 180 yards. Brown's pass to Jerry Imsland got Michigan on the scoreboard in the first quarter, but a long pass from Blue Devil quarterback Leo Hart to Marcel Courtillet tied it up early in the second quarter. Johnson put the Wolverine back on top to stay with a 53-yard TD run minutes later. Michigan added a field goal in the third period and two touchdowns in the final stanza as Johnson scored from in close and sophomore linebacker Marty Huff intercepted a pass and rambled in from 44 yards out.

Michigan 32—Navy 9

October 5 Ann Arbor Attendance—56,501

After Navy jumped off to a first quarter lead with a field goal, George Hoey leveled the Middies with a broadside of punt returns. The Wolverine speedster grabbed a second period Navy punt on the Michigan 31 and raced it back to the Midshipman 6-yard line. In two plays Ron Johnson scored. Minutes later Dennis Brown completed passes to Mandich and Imsland, then carried the ball over the goal line himself for the second Wolverine score. With little more than a minute remaining in the half Hoey broke loose with another Navy punt and sailed to the 19. On the next play Brown hit Mandich for another score. Johnson raced 39 yards for a third touchdown, and reserve quarterback Bill Berutti passed for the final tally in the fourth stanza.

Michigan 28—Michigan State 14

October 12 Ann Arbor Attendance—102,785

A sky-high Michigan team ended four years of frustration against its up-state rival in a stirring victory before the nation's largest crowd of the season. On the fifth play of the game, Ron Johnson exploded for a 38-yd. touchdown run. Michigan State retaliated quickly as flanker Charley Wedemeyer dashed 37 yards on a reverse. The Spartans missed the extra point and the Wolverines still led. Michigan increased the lead when Dennis Brown hit John Gabler with a 33-yard scoring strike. The score remained 13-6 until the opening play of the fourth period when Earl Anderson climaxed a long Spartan drive with a touchdown. MSU faked a kick which would have tied the score, and instead Wedemeyer passed to Frank Foreman for two points to give the Spartans a 14-13 lead. Midway in the final quarter, a scrambling Brown whipped a pass down the sidelines to Jim Mandich who ran to the end zone in a play that covered 53 yards. Brown threw for two points to put more pressure on the Spartans and Garvie Craw applied the clincher by breaking loose for a 25-yard scoring run.

Michigan 27—Indiana 22

October 19 Bloomington, Ind. Attendance—51,951

Before a sellout Indiana homecoming crowd had settled in its seats, Michigan moved 93 yards for its first score in a drive highlighted by a 37-yard scamper by Ron Johnson, and climaxed by his 18-yard dash to the end zone. A pair of long runs tied it for Indiana in the second quarter. A Hoosier field goal gave IU a 10-7 lead in the third quarter, but then Michigan struck quickly. Jerry Hartman picked off a Harry Gonso pass and ran 62 yards for a touchdown. On the following kickoff, Ed Moore recovered a Hoosier fumble and seconds later Dennis Brown passed to John Gabler for another score to make it 20-10. The never-say-die Indiana club kept coming back, but Brown's touchdown pass to Bill Harris in the final quarter clinched the victory for the Wolverines.

Craw

Mandich

RUSHING Michigan				
	Att.	Gaines	Losses	Net
Brown	8	15	1	14
Johnson	31	210	5	205
Craw	13	78	7	71
Scheiffler	3	10	0	10
Baglien	5	20	0	20
Duke				
Hart	11	19	40	-21
Chesson	7	13	1	12
Baglien	5	20	0	20
Trice	5	24	0	24
Cappellano	6	10	0	10
Asack	2	6	0	6
Carter	3	17	0	17

Hoey

Gabler   Hartman

Brief Statistics	MSU	Mich.
First downs	25	16
Net yards gained	356	420
Passes attempted	13	16
Passes completed	6	9
Yards gained by passing	61	177
Passes intercepted by	2	2
Fumbles lost	2	0
Yards penalized	35	20

THE YELLOW AND BLUE

Sing to the colors that float in the light;
Hurrah for the Yellow and Blue!
Yellow the stars as they ride through the night,
And reel in a rollicking crew;
Yellow the fields where ripens the grain,
And yellow the moon on the harvest wane;
Hail! Hail to the colors that float in the light;
Hurrah for the Yellow and Blue!

Michigan 34, Wisconsin 9

At the outset, there were 51,117 fans in the Stadium for what turned out to be Ron Johnson's classic November 16 performance. At the close, only a few thousand could truthfully say they had watched every minute of it in person.

A light rain at the beginning of a cold, gust-torn afternoon turned into a downpour which drove the bulk of the fans home at halftime. When they left the score was 9-7, with Wisconsin on top, and none could guess what was yet to come. But most departed with the knowledge they could watch the rest on TV — and what they subsequently saw will be remembered for years.

Johnson's great day began spectacularly. He carried Michigan's first scrimmage play from the Wolverine 39 to the 50. A 15-yard penalty advanced the ball to the Badger 35. From there, on first down, Johnson broke off left tackle and pounded all the way to the goal line. A Killian conversion kick gave Michigan a quick 7-0 lead.

Wisconsin fought back with a first period touchdown of its own, scoring on a deflected pass play from the Michigan 12 after recovering a Wolverine fumble. Then, just before the half, the Badgers went ahead, 9-7, on a 34-yard field goal.

Seemingly in deep trouble at the intermission, Johnson and his Wolverine colleagues scored touchdowns four of the next five times they had the ball — on runs of 67, 1, 60 and 50 yards. The final touchdown burst came just 20 seconds into the fourth quarter, raised the score to 34-9, and sent Johnson to the sidelines for the final 14 minutes.

Altogether, the Wolverine Captain carried 31 times for a net of 347 yards, an average of 11.2 per try. His five scoring runs averaged out at 42.6 yards, a total of 213. His other 26 carries netted 134 yards, or 5.15 per try. By quarters, Johnson's performance went like this: 1st, 10 carries for 73 yards and 1 touchdown; 2nd, 9 for 45; 3rd, 11 for 179 yards and 3 touchdowns; and 4th, 1 carry for 50 yards and 1 touchdown.

Grange had his Britton and Harmon had Evashevski as principal blocking mates. All season long, fullback Garvie Craw has been a key blocker for Johnson. He was magnificent in this game and so, too, were the men up front like Jim Mandich, Stan Broadnax, Bob Penksa, Dave Denzin, Dick Caldarazzo and Dan Dierdorf.

Brief Statistics	Wis.	Mich.
First downs	12	19
Net yards gained	189	481
Passes attempted	24	15
Passes completed	5	6
Yards gained by passing	53	117
Passes intercepted by	1	1
Fumbles lost	0	1
Yards penalized	15	60

Reprinted with permission from the **Michigan Alumnus**

Michigan 33—Minnesota 20

October 26　　　Ann Arbor　　　Attendance—69,384

"I've never seen a better game from a quarterback." Those are the words of Minnesota coach Murray Warmath after Michigan quarterback Dennis Brown engineered a complete rout of the Gophers to bring the Little Brown Jug back to Ann Arbor. Brown was sensational as Michigan opened up a 33-0 lead early in the third quarter before leaving the mopping-up job to the reserves.

The game was just underway when Brown passed to Paul Staroba for the first touchdown. Then George Hoey returned a punt 40 yards to set up a score by Ron Johnson. Tom Curtis intercepted a pass, and again Johnson scored a touchdown. Brian Healy had a turn at pilfering a pass and that led to a touchdown pass from Brown to Bill Harris. Before the first half had ended Tim Killian booted two field goals to give Michigan a 30-0 lead.

Killian tied a modern Big Ten record and set a new Michigan record by kicking his third field goal of the game in the third period. In all, Michigan intercepted five Gopher passes, recovered two fumbles, and blocked a punt, and not even a 20 point Minnesota spurt in the fourth quarter could take away from the Wolverine domination in the game.

Michigan 35—Northwestern 0

November 2　　　Evanston, Ill.　　　Attendance—40,101

Michigan was at its explosive best on a grey afternoon in Dyche Stadium. Outmanned Northwestern battled the Wolverines on even terms for a quarter, but the Wolverines erupted for 28 points in the second period with three touchdowns in 73 seconds.

Ron Johnson broke the deadlock with a 3-yard plunge, then with time running out in the half, Michigan put on a devastating display which started with a fourth down touchdown pass from Dennis Brown to Bill Harris. Two plays later, Tom Curtis intercepted a pass leading to a Johnson touchdown from the Wildcat five yard line. On the first play after the next kickoff, defensive tackle Dan Parks pulled down a deflected pass and lumbered 50 yards for another six-pointer. Lance Scheffler added final touchdown in the fourth period.

Michigan 36—Illinois 0

November 9　　　Ann Arbor　　　Attendance—56,775

Michigan rolled to its seventh straight victory with Dennis Brown and Ron Johnson again leading the way. Johnson scored twice early in the game on short plunges and Brown gave the Wolverines a 20-0 halftime cushion by connecting with Bill Harris on a 69-yard pass play. In the second half Brown passed for a touchdown to Paul Staroba, Tim Killian kicked a field goal and Don Moorhead threw a scoring pass to Mike Hankwitz as the Wolverines wrapped up their second shutout in a row. It was a red-letter day for Tom Curtis who intercepted his eighth pass of the Big Ten season to set a new conference record for pass interceptions.

Ohio State 50—Michigan 14

November 23　　　Columbus, O.　　　Attendance—85,371

Everything was on the line in this game. Both the Wolverines and Buckeyes were unbeaten in conference play and the title and Rose Bowl bid went to the winner. Michigan stunned the overflow crowd in the first period as Ron Johnson broke away for 39 yards, Dennis Brown hit Jim Mandich with a pass covering 21 yards and then Johnson crashed into the Buckeye end zone from the one. Ohio State was not to be denied. They roared back for two straight scores by Jim Otis and Rex Kern. Then it was Michigan's turn again, as Johnson again his paydirt to tie the contest at 14-14. The turning point came late in the second quarter as Ohio put together an 86-yard sustained march that ate up most of the period and ended in the Wolverine end zone to give the Buckeyes a 21-14 lead at intermission. The third quarter started the same way with another long Buckeye drive that resulted in a 27-14 OSU lead. Michigan hopes ended as a Wolverine drive died on the Ohio State 14 yard line. The Buckeyes turned it into a rout with 23 points in the fourth period as Michigan gambled to get back into the game. Ohio State's convincing victory earned them the national championship.

Michigan No. 12 In Final Grid Poll

1. Ohio State (44)		10-0	968
2. Penn State (2)		11-0	782
3. Texas (2)		9-1-1	762
4. Southern California		9-1-1	693
5. Notre Dame		7-2-1	482
6. Arkansas (1)		10-1	478
7. Kansas		9-2	465
8. Georgia		8-1-2	349
9. Missouri		8-3	297
10. Purdue		8-2	263
11. Oklahoma		7-4	257
12. MICHIGAN		8-2	197
13. Tennessee		8-2-1	165
14. Southern Methodist		8-3	143
15. Oregon State		7-3	105
16. Auburn		7-4	36
17. Alabama		8-3	32
18. Houston		6-2-2	31
19. Louisiana State		8-3	23
20. Ohio U.		10-1	22

Other teams receiving votes, listed alphabetically: Arizona State, Florida, Florida State, Harvard, Minnesota, North Texas State, Richmond, Wyoming, Yale.

Big Ten Honors M Tailback

Tailback Ron Johnson, elected by his teammates as Michigan's most valuable football player for the 1968 season, also has been named the most valuable player in the Big Ten.

Number 40 — More Than Records

Ron Johnson moved the football 3,467 yards during three seasons at Michigan and woven in that career are proud moments, ponderous records and heartbreak.

He did everything ever expected of a football player. He stood at the college football summit after rushing for an outstanding 347 yds. against Wisconsin. He was an All-American that day in victory. A week later he broke right for 39 yards, then came back left to smash for one touchdown; and later to score again. He blocked and he tackled and remained an All-American in Ohio State's great moment of victory.

He was accorded every honor his teammates could direct toward No. 40. His coach, Bump Elliott, was moved to praise him as "the best

JOHNSON THE WARRIOR

football player and best captain I had during my coaching career."

Here is the Ron Johnson story of 1966-67-68.

Year	RUSHING Atts.	Yards	RECEIVING No.	Yards	SCORING TD	CPR	TP	KO Ret'ns No.	Yds.	Yd
1966	12	44	0	0	0	0	0	5	37	8
1967	220	1005	13	179	8	0	48	27	498	168
1968	255	1391	14	166	19	1	116	9	147	170
Total	487	2440	27	345	27	1	164	40	681	346

NCAA RECORDS

Yards Rushing single game—347 (Wisconsin 11-16-68)

BIG TEN RECORDS

Yard Rushing Season—1017 (1968)
Yards Rushing Game—347
Total Offense—347
Rushes Single Game—42
Touchdowns Game—5
Points Single Game—30
Points Season—92 (1968)

RECORDS TIED (BIG TEN)

Most kickoffs returned season—18 (1967)
Most Touchdowns Season—15 (1968)

MICHIGAN RECORDS

Rushing attempts career (487), rushing attempts season (255), net yards rushing career (2440), net yards rushing season (1391), touchdowns season (19), kickoff returns season (27), net yards rushing game (347), touchdowns single game (5), points single game (30), total offense single game (347), rushing attempts single game (42).

HONORS—1967

First Team—All-Big Ten
Most Valuable Player—Michigan

HONORS—1968

All-American (Football Writers, Football News)
First Team All-Big Ten
Most Valuable Player—Michigan
Most Valuable Player—Big Ten
Back of the Week against Duke (UPI); Michigan State (Sports Illustrated); Wisconsin (Sports Illustrated, UPI).
Michigan Captain
Big Ten Conference Medal of Honor
Senior Athlete Award—Michigan
Doc Losh Award—Michigan
First Round Draft Pick—Cleveland

RUSHING

	Atts.	Yds.Gain	Yds. Lost	Net Yds.	Avg.
Johnson	255	1474	83	1391	5.5
Craw	81	324	17	307	3.8
Brown	115	432	217	215	1.9
Scheffler	55	196	5	191	3.5
Moorhead	16	106	8	98	6.1
Sipp	10	24	0	24	2.4
Harrison	2	17	0	17	8.5
Federico	1	6	0	6	6.0
Thomas	2	3	2	1	0.5
Berutti	1	0	0	0	0.0
Werner	1	19	0	19	19.0

PASSING

	Atts.	Comp.	Int.	Yds.	TD
Brown	209	109	10	1562	12
Moorhead	25	10	2	122	1
Johnson	1	0	1	0	0

RECEIVING

	No.	Yds.	TD
Mandich	43	576	3
Imsland	19	269	1
Harris	16	369	4
Johnson	14	166	0
Staroba	11	158	2
Gabler	8	110	2
Betts	4	29	0
Others	4	7	1

PUNTING

	No.	Yds.	Avg.
Werner	66	2438	36.9

PUNT RETURNS

	No.	Yds.	LP
Hoey	19	228	63
Curtis	8	49	21
Healy	2	4	4
Seymour	1	8	8

SCORING

	TD	CK	CPR	FG	TP
Johnson	19	0	1	0	116
Killian	0	22	0	0	37
Mandich	3	0	0	0	18
Gabler	2	0	0	0	12
Harris	4	0	0	0	24
Others	11	0	2	0	70
Michigan Totals	39	22	3	5	217
Opponents Totals	21	10	2	5	155

INTERCEPTIONS

	No.	Yds.	LP	TD
Curtis	10	182	43	0
Hoey	2	32	31	0
Healy	3	20	20	0
Wedge	2	11	0	0
Huff	1	44	44	1
Hartman	1	62	62	1
Parks	1	50	50	1
Kieta	1	24	24	0
Newell	1	19	19	0
Werner	1	0	0	0
McCoy	1	3	3	0
Killian	1	3	3	0

KICKOFF RETURNS

	No.	Yds.	LP
Hoey	12	221	39
Johnson	9	147	24
Scheffler	3	69	48
Craw	3	11	11
Mandich	1	4	4
Harrison	1	20	20

FUMBLES RECOVERED

Hill, Moore, Pryor	2
Curtis, Wedge, Johnson, Hoey, Dierdorf, White, Huff, Seymour, Harris	1

1968 Team Statistics

	Mich.	Opp.		Mich.	Opp.
FIRST DOWNS	214	201	TOTAL NUMBER RUSHES	539	546
Rushing	124	130	Net Yards		
Passing	76	60	Rushing	2270	1993
Penalty	14	11	Passing	1683	1270
FORWARD PASSES			TOTAL PLAYS	794	795
ATTEMPTED	255	249	Net Total Yardage	3953	3252
Completed	119	96			
Intercepted By	25	13			
Yds. Int'cpt Ret'd	447	227	NUMBER of PUNTS	67	59
			Average Distance	36.5	36.
KICKOFF, RETURNED BY	30	51			
			YARDS, KICKS RETURNED	773	1343
FUMBLES/FUMBLES LOST	16/5	26/14	Punts	299	178
			Kickoffs	474	1165
NUMBER PENALTIES/ YARDS	59/562	35/383			

TACKLES

	S	A	TL
Seymour	81	21	3
Stincic	55	47	4
Goss	54	31	9
Hill	50	22	16
Moore	30	15	4
Curtis	30	11	1
Hoey	28	11	1

Michigan's Coaching Staff

Kneeling, left to right: Jerry Hanlon, Chuck Stobart, Frank Maloney and head coach Bo Schembechler. Standing, left to right: Gary Moeller, Larry Smith, Louie Lee, Jim Young, Dick Hunter, George Mans.

It's Bouncing Boy For U-M's Bo

Bo Schembechler won't have to be making any emergency trips during Saturday's Michigan-Washington football game.

The baby he and his wife Millie were expecting Saturday caught an early stork and arrived at noon Wednesday, leaving ol' dad to concentrate on the football game.

The seven-pound, 14-ounce boy hadn't been named when Schembechler had to leave for football practice Wednesday afternoon. "But he looks like an offensive guard," Bo grinned. Both the lad and his mother are in good condition.

AP Poll (1969)
1. Texas
2. Penn State
3. Southern Cal.
4. Ohio State
5. Notre Dame
6. Missouri
7. Arkansas
8. Mississippi
9. MICHIGAN
10. L.S.U.

UPI Poll (1969)
1. Texas
2. Penn State
3. Arkansas
4. Southern Cal.
5. Ohio State
6. Missouri
7. L.S.U.
8. MICHIGAN
9. Notre Dame
10. U.C.L.A.

TOM CURTIS

1969		
Michigan	42; Vanderbilt	14
Michigan	45; Washington	7
Michigan	17; Missouri	40
Michigan	31; Purdue	20
Michigan	12; Michigan State	23
Michigan	35; Minnesota	9
Michigan	35; Wisconsin	7
Michigan	57; Illinois	0
Michigan	51; Iowa	6
Michigan	24; Ohio State	12

Season Summary

Games won 8; Lost 2; Tied 0

1970 Rose Bowl

Michigan	3; Southern Cal.	10

Points for Michigan 352; For Opponents 148

Schembechler Leads Young Football Staff

Glenn Edward (Bo) Schembechler opens his first season as head football coach at the University of Michigan, the 13th person to hold this position since the sport was organized here in 1879. He was appointed in December, 1968.

Schembechler (pronounced SHEM-beck-lur), 39, comes to Michigan with outstanding football credentials. In the last six seasons as head football coach at Miami his teams posted a 40-17-3 record overall, and a 27-8-1 record in the Mid-American Conference. His teams won two MAC co-championships (1965 and 1966), and finished second twice and tied for third once. Last season Miami was 7-3 overall and 5-1 in the conference for a second place finish. He never coached a losing team.

Schembechler was the fourth straight head coach at Miami to take over a Big Ten team. Woody Hayes (Ohio State), Ara Parseghian (Northwestern), and John Pont (Indiana) had coached Miami teams since 1949. He replaced Bump Elliot as head coach at Michigan and becomes only the fourth coach of the Wolverines since Fritz Crisler was appointed head coach in 1938.

Voted MAC Coach of the Year in 1965 and Ohio Coach of the Year in 1966, Schembechler engineered upsets of Northwestern in 1964 (28-27) and Indiana in 1966 (20-10).

Schembechler, who graduated from Miami University in 1951 and received a master's degree in education from Ohio State in 1952, has an extensive coaching background. He started as a graduate assistant coach under Hayes at Ohio State in 1951. He served two years in the Army, coaching both the football and baseball teams at Camp Rucker, Alabama. He was a line coach at Presbyterian College in 1954, a line coach at Bowling Green in 1955, and joined Parseghian's staff at Northwestern as a line coach in 1956. Schembechler rejoined Hayes at Ohio State in 1958 and served five seasons as line coach there before taking over the head job at Miami in 1963.

The former Barberton, Ohio, prep all-stater was an offensive tackle at Miami for three years, playing under George Blackburn and Hayes.

JIM MANDICH . . . 6-3, 220, senior, from Solon, Ohio . . . Another in a long list of outstanding ends at Michigan . . . Could be the 12th end to gain All-American honors . . . An exceptionally fine blocker at tight end with unusual strength and quickness . . . Going into third season, he ranks as third all time Michigan pass receiver . . . Caught 43 for 576 yards as junior, including a 53-yard that defeated Michigan State . . . 13.4 yards average on receptions . . . All-Big Ten selection. Earned 12 prep letters . . . High school All American in football . . . Born July 30, 1948 in Solon, O.

JIM MANDICH

(Yr.)	(No.)	(Yds.)	(TD)	Avg.)
1967	26	256	0	9.9
1968	43	576	3	13.4

Michigan 42, Vanderbilt 14

September 20   Ann Arbor   Attendance 70,18

Michigan coach Bo Schembechler's Wolverine coaching debut w successful, as his Wolverines scored 28 points in the final quarter break open what had been a tight game with Vanderbilt, and win goin away. 42-14

Before 70,183 fans on high school Band Day, senior fullback Garvi Craw opened up the scoring for Michigan in the first period with one-yard plunge for a touchdown. In the second quarter, Glenn Dought indicated he might be the replacement for departed All-American Ro Johnson, as he high-stepped 80 yards for a score.

Vanderbilt roared back on the opening series of the second hal to close the gap to 14-7. The capable field generalship of Wolverin signal caller Don Moorhead, who gained 103 yards in 11 carries, alon with an alert defense that created two scoring opportunities, allowe Michigan to pull away in a fourth quarter scoring display.

Michigan	7	7	0	28—42
Vanderbilt	0	0	7	7—14

SCORING

Mich—Craw (run, 1 yd), Titas kick.
  Doughty (run, 80 yds), Titas kick.
  Moorhead (run, 2 yds), Titas kick.
  Huff (punt return, 31 yds), Titas kick.
  Moorhead (run, 4 yds), Titas kick.
  Federico (run, 1 yd), Titas kick.
Vand—Mathews (run, 1 yd), Wilins kick.
  Valput (run, 2 yds), Wilins kick.

STATISTICS

	MICH	VAN
First Downs	17	1
Net Yards Rushing	367	5
Net Yards Passing	56	12
Passes Attempted	11	2
Passes Completed	5	1
Intercepted by	1	
Punting	6-30.5	8-4
Return Yardage	105	12
Fumbles	2	

Here's the run-down on Michigan's touchdowns:

1—7:13 elapsed in the first period. Moorhead passed nine yards to Mandich who caught the ball while on the ground in the end zone. Forty-two yard drive. Conversion attempt no good following bad pass from center.

2—4:28 elapsed in the second period. Moorhead rolled around end for five yards. Sixty-three-yard drive. Two-point play fails.

3—4:27 elapsed in the third period. Moorhead scores from the one-yard line. Seventy-four-yard drive. Two-point play fails.

4—9:43 elapsed in the third period. Moorhead rolled around end for nine yards. Seventy-six-yard drive. Two-point play fails.

5—1:23 elapsed in the fourth ter. Jim Betts passed 59 yards through Washington. Sixty-seven-yard drive. Frank Titas converted.

6—7:36 elapsed in the fourth period. Craw at center for one yard. Eighty-yard drive. Ttias converted.

7—9:37 elapsed in fourth quarter. Jim passes 59 yards to Bill to Bill Harris following Washington punt out of bounds. Titas converted.

Behind the blocking of Michigan Capt. Jim Mandich (88), Wolverine halfback Glenn Doughty breaks into the clear on an 80-yard touchdov gallop midway in the second period. The play followed a Vanderbilt punt that rolled through the end zone. In the center is Michigar Paul Staroba (30). Note the special cleats used on Michigan's new artificial turf.

Michigan 45, Washington 7

The Huskies from Washington were huge in stature but lacking a bit in quickness and fleetness. Michigan went over, around and through them to such an extent that two modern-era team offensive records were set: a total of 34 first downs and a net yardage output of 581, which bettered by 50 the former Michigan mark set against Ohio State 26 years ago.

Quarterback Don Moorhead had a rush-pass total of 288 yards and scored three of Michigan's seven touchdowns. Sophomore Glenn Doughty netted 191 yards running and scored once. The other touchdowns went to Captain Jim Mandich, fullback Garvie Craw and end Bill Harris. Meantime, Tom Curtis and Barry Pierson each had two interceptions as the Wolverine defense also mastered the Huskies.

TOM DARDEN, 6-1½, 186, sophomore from Sandusky, O. . . . Michigan's first Wolfman . . . plays linebacker and in defensive secondary . . . broke up five passes in single game (Purdue) . . . strong tackler with fine speed . . . could play any position in secondary.

No.	Name	Pos.	Wgt.	Hgt.	Age	Class
3	ABRAHAMS, Morris	OT	230	6-3	25	Senior
4	ALEXANDER, Joe	DB	200	5-8	19	Sophomore
2	BALDWIN, Ed	OG	207	6-0	20	Junior
0	**BAUMGARTNER, Bob	OG	215	6-0	22	Senior
9	BECKMAN, Tom	DT	230	6-7	19	Sophomore
8	BERUTTI, William	QB	194	6-2	20	Junior
3	*BETTS, Jim	QB	185	6-3½	20	Junior
6	BRANDSTATTER, Jim	OT	235	6-3	19	Sophomore
4	BROWN, Richard	MG	212	6-2	21	Senior
6	CALDARAZZO, Dick	OG	215	5-11	21	Senior
4	CARPENTER, Al	DE	210	6-2	19	Sophomore
6	COIN, Dana	DE	213	6-2	19	Sophomore
0	CONNELL, Dennis	QB	178	6-2	19	Sophomore
8	**CRAW, Garvie	FB	218	6-2	21	Senior
5	**CURTIS, Tom	DB	188	6-1	21	Senior
5	DARDEN, Tom	DB	186	6-1½	19	Sophomore
2	*DIERDORF, Dan	OT	243	6-4	20	Junior
2	DOUGHTY, Glenn	TB	195	6-2	18	Sophomore
6	DUTCHER, Gerald	DB	180	6-2	20	Junior
1	ELLIOTT, Bruce	DB	172	6-0	18	Sophomore
7	*FEDERICO, Eric	FB	200	5-11	21	Senior
1	*FRANCIS, Al	MG	195	5-10	21	Senior
8	**GABLER, John	WB	203	6-2	21	Senior
2	GRAMBAU, Fred	DT	227	6-4	19	Sophomore
4	GUSICH, Frank	DB	187	6-0	19	Sophomore
5	*HALL, Werner	OT	219	6-0	21	Senior
1	**HANKWITZ, Mike	TE	203	6-1	21	Senior
1	*HARPRING, Jack	OT	218	6-4	20	Junior
0	*HARRIS, William	SE	189	6-1	21	Junior
7	HARRISON, Gregory	FB	188	5-11	20	Junior
4	**HEALY, Brian	DB	167	6-1	21	Senior
4	HENRY, Preston	TB	185	6-0	18	Sophomore
9	*HILL, Henry	MG	224	5-11	20	Junior
0	*HUFF, Marty	LB	228	6-2	20	Junior
9	HUISKENS, Tom	TE	200	6-2	19	Sophomore
2	HULKE, Scott	C	207	6-5	18	Sophomore
6	*IMSLAND, Jerry	SE	203	6-2	21	Senior
3	JONES, Joseph	LB	191	6-0	20	Junior
0	KELLER, Mike	DE	205	6-3	19	Sophomore
7	*KILLIAN, Tim	C	215	6-4	20	Junior
8	LINDENFELD, Dick	DB	185	6-1	19	Sophomore
7	LUKZ, Joseph	OG	202	6-2	21	Senior
8	**MANDICH, Jim	TE	217	6-3	21	Senior
7	*MOORE, Ed	LB	210	6-1	20	Junior
7	*MOORHEAD, Don	QB	193	6-3	20	Junior
3	MURDOCK, Guy	C	210	6-2	19	Sophomore
8	*McCOY, Dick	DT	240	6-4	20	Junior
5	McKENZIE, Reggie	OG	236	6-3	19	Sophomore
2	*NEWELL, Pete	DT	226	6-4	20	Junior
3	NIEMAN, Tom	TE	205	6-1	20	Junior
4	OLDHAM, Mike	SE	195	6-3	19	Sophomore
4	*PARKS, Dan	DT	234	6-5	20	Junior
9	**PIERSON, Barry	DB	175	6-0	21	Senior
5	*PRYOR, Cecil	DE	240	6-5	21	Senior
9	RITLEY, Robert	OT	218	6-0	21	Senior
5	ROSEMA, Bob	DE	197	6-4	19	Sophomore
6	ROSS, William	QB	203	6-3	19	Sophomore
9	SARANTOS, Pete	C	205	6-0	20	Senior
5	*SCHEFFLER, Lance	TB	193	6-0	20	Junior
2	SCHMITZ, Jim	WB	167	6-0	19	Sophomore
2	SEYFERTH, John	FB	198	6-3	19	Sophomore
5	SEYMOUR, Paul	SE	235	6-5	19	Sophomore
1	**SEYMOUR, Phil	DE	200	6-4	21	Senior
1	SHAW, Donald	OG	200	6-1	19	Sophomore
0	SMITH, Mike	C	218	6-4	19	Sophomore
0	*STAROBA, Paul	WB	201	6-3	20	Junior
3	TAKACH, Thomas	DE	215	6-1	21	Senior
2	TAYLOR, Bill	TB	195	5-10	19	Sophomore
3	TAYLOR, Mike	LB	210	6-1½	20	Sophomore
4	**TITAS, Frank	OG	215	6-2	21	Senior
1	WADHAMS, Tim	DB	185	6-1	20	Senior
9	*WERNER, Mark	DB	191	6-2	22	Senior
3	WHITE, Robert	DB	189	6-2	21	Senior
6	WOLFF, John	OG	220	6-1	20	Junior
6	ZUCCARELLI, David	DB	183	6-0	19	Sophomore
8	ZUGANELIS, George	LB	200	6-0	21	Senior

* Letters Won

Missouri 40, Michigan 17

Missouri possessed in abundance some of the attributes lacked by Washington. And the highly-ranked Tigers also exploited to maximum advantage a seemingly endless assortment of Wolverine misadventures: 11 penalties, four lost fumbles, a blocked punt, an interception and other hampering errors.

By halftime, Michigan was at a 24-3 deficit. The Wolverines fought back with two Craw touchdowns to make it 24-17 at the start of the fourth quarter. But then the blocked punt opened the door and Missouri poured across 16 more points. Michigan wound up with more first downs but the proud Tigers had a runaway victory which enabled Missouri to join Cornell and Wesleyan as the only schools to hold a series edge over the Wolverines.

Michigan 31, Purdue 20

Through most of this decade, Purdue has been Michigan's most troublesome foe. The Boilermakers had five straight wins, the last three by a net total of four points.

For a while, in this fall's October 11 renewal of the series, the 80,411 Stadium fans thought the pattern might be repeated. Michigan opened with two long scoring drives, capped by Doughty and Craw touchdowns, for a 14-0 lead. But Purdue knotted the count just before halftime with a pair of equalizing touchdowns.

The third period belonged to Michigan. A 28-yard field goal by Tim Killian followed by a Moorhead touchdown sneak made it 24-14. Then the Wolverines unfurled a 90-yard drive in the fourth quarter to put it away. Captain Mandich scored this one on a pass from Moorhead — his 10th reception of the afternoon for 156 yards. Altogether, Moorhead completed 15 of 25 for 247 yards. Purdue's heralded Mike Phipps threw for 250 — including a consolation touchdown in the game's final minute — but lost four of his 44 tosses to Michigan defenders, three to linebacker Marty Huff and one to Curtis.

Michigan State 23, Michigan 12

A year ago in this intra-state classic, State won the statistics but lost the ball game, 28-14. This time, Michigan had more first downs, ran more plays and had a bulging edge in aerial yardage. But the hard-hitting Spartans, in firm control most of the way, ripped the Wolverines on the ground and excelled in the basics of blocking and tackling.

Michigan scored first, on a 29-yard Killian field goal, and last, on a fourth-quarter Doughty touchdown followed by a gift safety. But the surging Spartans dominated everything in between, built up a 23-3 lead, and forced Michigan to a catch-up style of play — and, in the end, to a catch-up situation for the last half of the season.

Michigan 35, Wisconsin 7

The Badgers were 2-1 in the Conference race when they journeyed to Ann Arbor for this November 1 Homecoming test, so the loser was destined to drop out of serious contention.

The suspense lasted only a few brief minutes. First, Taylor broke a 37-yard touchdown run on a well-blocked counter play, then soon after he raced 51 yards on a spectacular tackle-breaking effort. Before the half was concluded the hard-driving Wolverines added three more touchdowns. Fullback Craw crashed over on a one-yard plunge, Barry Pierson rambled 51 yards on a punt return, and Moorhead hit Captain Jim Mandich on a 12-yard pass play.

Placekicker Frank Titas ran his record to 22 conversions in 23 attempts by kicking the five extra points so Michigan took a 35-0 lead into the dressing room. The second half scoring all belonged to Wisconsin, but the Wolverines had long since insured the key triumph.

Taylor was used only sparingly in the second half and wound up with 142 yards in 15 carries.

Michigan 35, Minnesota 9

A road game at Minneapolis is an unlikely place to launch a comeback bid — particularly when you've left your two starting halfbacks at home because of injuries.

Michigan usually beats the Gophers in Ann Arbor but until this October 25 game had not won at Minnesota in a full decade. And it was done this time without the services of regular wingback John Gabler and Sophomore Glenn Doughty, the exceptional runner who had netted 531 yards in his first five Michigan games despite some hampering injuries.

Doughty's absence opened a spot in the starting lineup for another Sophomore, Bill Taylor, and he hasn't left it yet. Injured himself earlier in the fall, Taylor had carried the ball only 15 times prior to the Minnesota challenge. But in this game he was called upon for 31 rushes and responded with 151 yards and three touchdowns.

The Wolverines scored a lone touchdown in the first half — an 8-yard touchdown toss from Don Moorhead to Taylor — but trailed, 9-7, at the intermission as Minnesota booted a third long field goal with one second left before halftime.

The second half, as Coach Schembechler was to reflect later, might have been the turning point of Michigan's entire season. The Wolverines unfurled two long touchdown drives in the third period to move ahead, 21-9, with Taylor furnishing the climactic yardage each time. Then, in the final quarter, Moorhead and Lance Scheffler added the fourth and fifth touchdowns to wrap it up, 35-9.

Meanwhile, Michigan's defense never let the Gophers penetrate beyond the 18-yard line and held the foe to 75 net yards on the ground — 210 less than the Wolverine total. The achievement looked better and better in retrospect, for it turned out this was Minnesota's last loss of the year. The Gophers went on to win all of their November games to finish fourth in the Big Ten standings.

Reprinted with permission from the **Michigan Alumnus**

Michigan	0	7	14	14—35
Minnesota	3	6	0	0— 9

SCORING

Mich—Moorhead-Taylor (pass 8 yds), Titas kick.
Taylor (run, 3 yds), Titas kick.
Taylor (run, 1 yd), Titas kick.
Moorhead (run, 6 yds), Titas kick.
Scheffler (run, 10 yds), Titas kick.
Minn—Nygren (field goal, 35 yds).
Anderson (field goal, 42 yds)
Anderson (field goal, 37 yds).

STATISTICS

MICH		MINN
23	First Downs	16
285	Net Yards Rushing	75
103	Net Yards Passing	182
13	Passes Attempted	37
9	Passes Completed	21
2	Intercepted by	0
5-30	Punting	5-42.6
54	Return Yardage	112
3	Fumbles	2
0	Ball Lost By	1

Wolverine Honors in '69

Coach of the Year

Glenn E. Bo Schembechler (Writers, Coaches, Walter Camp)

All-Americans

End — Jim Mandich (AP, UPI, Writers, Central Press)
Safety — Tom Curtis (AP, UPI, Writers, Central Press)

All-American Second Team

Tackle — DAN DIERDORF (Central Press)

Records Fall As Wolverines Run Over Iowa

By Wayne DeNeff

IOWA CITY, Iowa — The Roses have bloomed again for Michigan — not in the snow as they did in 1950 but in the bright sun at Iowa Stadium.

The Wolverines, a precision machine on a cold but sunny day on the midwest plains, hammered out a 51-6 victory over the Hawkeyes who were no less stunned than the 45,981 fans who sat in solemn silence through the unbelievable slaughter.

It's hard to see how the Wolverines can be anything except the Rose Bowl choice of the faculty representatives after they

Won their fourth straight game by an overwhelming margin.

Set a Big Ten total offense record of 673 yards.

Set a Big Ten rushing record of 524 yards and set a Big Ten record of 34 first downs.

On the basis of their tremendous victory here, the Wolverines are assured of no worse than a tie for second and they could share the championship with a victory over Ohio State in the season's finale at Ann Arbor next Saturday.

And don't discount Michigan's chances although the Buckeyes truly are one of the great teams of all time.

MICHIGAN

ENDS: Mandich, Keller, Pryor, Carpenter, Harris, Hankwitz, Moore, Coin, Imsland.
TACKLES: Harpring, Grambau, Parks, Hall, Beckman, Dierdorf, Newell, Brandstatter, McCoy.
GUARDS: Baumgartner, Titas, Caldarazzo, Hill, Francis.
CENTERS: Murdock, M. Taylor, Sarantos, Killian.
BACKS: Moorhead, Curtis, Werner, Betts, B. Taylor, Seyferth, Staroba, Elliott, Craw, Pierson, Doughty, Healy, Scheffler, Gabler, Henry, Darden, Gusich.

ILLINOIS

ENDS: Kaiser, Smith, Pickering, Jeske, Krieger, Dieken, Bucklin, Mauzey.
TACKLES: Scott, Pnazek, Samojedny, Levanti, Cole, Clements, Rotzoll, Fletcher, Zochert.
GUARDS: Redmann, Coleman, Sliva, Mortscheiser, Sautini, Vyborny, Brennan, Kristak.
CENTERS: McMillin, Kelly, Baskin, Ornatek.
BACKS: Livas, McKissic, Wintermute, Lange, Jackson, Ryan, Jones, Spiller, Beck, Bargo, Dufflmeier, Wright, McSwine, Darlington, Kmiec, Bess, Robinson, McCarthy, Masar, Singleton.

SCORING

MICHIGAN	0	23	7	27—57
ILLINOIS	0	0	0	0— 0

TOUCHDOWNS: MICHIGAN—Craw 4, B. Taylor, Betts, Gabler, Elliott.
CONVERSIONS: MICHIGAN—Titas 4 (by kicks), Harris 1 (pass).
FIELD GOALS: MICHIGAN—Killian.
OFFICIALS: Ross Dean, referee; Lowell Wrigley, umpire; William Filson, head linesman; Norman Kraga, field judge; Donald Hakes, back judge.

Reprinted with permission from the **Ann Arbor News**

Michigan 24, Ohio State 12

November 22	Ann Arbor	Attendance 103,588

Before the largest crowd ever to see a college football game, Michigan defeated the number-one ranked Ohio State Buckeyes, breaking their 22-game winning skein, and earning a share of the Big Ten championship.

Ohio scored early and the Buckeyes scored first, as they had been doing all year. Undaunted, the Wolverines came right back, moving 55 yards in 10 plays from the three-yard line for the score. Behind for the first time in 1969, by a score of 7-6, OSU took the ball downfield for another score, missing a two-point conversion attempt.

That was the last time the Buckeyes led. Billy Taylor set up the second Michigan touchdown with a 28-yard ramble that carried to the Ohio State five-yard line. Craw busted over the goal line again. Frank Titas converted, making the score 14-12, Michigan in front.

When Ohio State failed to move the ball, it punted from its own 27-yard line. Barry Pierson hauled it in, and danced 60-yards to the Ohio State three-yard line, Don Moorhead crashing over for the score two plays later. Tim Killian added a 25-yard field goal to complete the game's scoring.

Michigan	7	17	0	0—24
Ohio State	6	6	0	0—12

SCORING

Mich—Craw (run, 3 yds).
Craw (run, 1 yd).
Moorhead (run, 2 yds).
Killian (field goal, 25 yds).
Titas, 3 conversions.
Ohio State—Otis (run, 1 yd).
Kern-. White (pass, 22 yds).

STATISTICS

MICH		OSU
21	First Downs	20
266	Net Yards Rushing	222
108	Net Yards Passing	155
20	Passes Attempted	28
10	Passes Completed	10
6	Intercepted by	1
3-41.6	Punting	3-27.0
229	Return Yardage	229
0	Fumbles	
0	Ball Lost By	1

Michigan's Schembechler Is Named Coach-of-Year

Big Ten Standings

	W	L	Pts.	Opp.
MICHIGAN	6	1	245	77
Ohio State	6	1	280	79
Purdue	5	2	248	180
Minnesota	4	3	135	135
Indiana	3	4	173	165
Iowa	3	4	149	179
Northwestern	3	4	121	187
Wisconsin	3	4	145	224
Michigan State	2	5	124	163
Illinois	0	7	62	293

ALL-TIME TEAM

Bennie Oosterbaan, Michigan's three-time All American end, has been voted the U-M's greatest all-time football player in a poll of Michigan alumni and friends.

The poll, taken to commemorate college football's 100th anniversary, also selected the U-M's all-time team.

Here are the results:

Ends: Bennie Oosterbaan, 1925, '26, '27; and Ron Kramer; 1954, '55, '56.

Linemen: Adolph Schulz, 1904, '05, '07, '08; Julius Franks, 1941, '42; Francis Wistert; 1931, '32, '33; Alvin Wistert, 1947, '48, '49; and a tie between Mervin Pregulman, 1941, '42, '43, and Bill Yearby, 1963, '64, '65.

Backs: Tom Harmon, 1938, '39, '40; Willie Heston, 1901, '02, '03, '04; Ron Johnson, 1966, '67, '68; and Benny Friedman, 1924, '25, '26.

1969 Team Statistics

	Mich.	Opp.		Mich.	Opp.
First Downs	*242	185	Total Plays	*918	763
Rushing	*154	95	Total Offense	*4492	*3351
Pass	*82	*76	No. of Punts	56	60
Penalty	6	14	Average	37.8	37.0
No. of Rushes	*673	489	Kickoffs Ret'n by	31	50
Net Yds. Rushing	*2938	*1851	Yds. Kicks Ret'n by	884	580
Net Yds. Passing	1554	*1500	Punts	359	261
Passes Attempted	245	*274	Kickoffs	525	319
Completed	119	*130	Fumbles	22	*35
Intercepted	24	7	Ball Lost by	7	18
			Penalties, Number	68	43
			Yds. Penalty	636	374

Score by Quarters

Opponents	12	66	35	35 — 148
Michigan	51	118	71	112 — 352

*New Michigan School Season Record

SCORING

	TD	CK	CRP	FG	TP
Garvie Craw	13	0	0	0	78
*Don Moorhead	9	0	0	0	54
*Billy Taylor	8	0	0	0	48
Frank Titas	0	35-39	0	0	35
*Glenn Doughty	4	0	0	0	24
Jim Mandich	4	0	0	0	24
*Tim Killian	0	4-4	0	7-16	25
*Jim Betts	3	0	0	0	18
*Bill Harris	1	0	1	0	8
Barry Pierson	1	0	0	0	6
John Gabler	1	0	0	0	6
*Bruce Elliott	1	0	0	0	6
*Marty Huff	1	0	0	0	6
Eric Federico	1	0	0	0	6
*Lance Scheffler	1	0	0	0	6

Michigan's 1969 Individual Statistics

(11-Game Totals)

RUSHING

	Att	Gain	Loss	Net	Ave
*Billy Taylor	141	878	14	864	6.1
*Glenn Doughty	150	762	30	732	4.9
*Don Moorhead	170	808	183	625	3.7
Garvie Craw	117	344	0	344	2.1
*Jim Betts	32	157	27	130	4.0
John Gabler	25	100	6	94	3.8
*Lance Scheffler	19	89	0	89	4.7
Eric Federico	3	20	0	20	6.7
*Preston Henry	10	22	5	17	1.7
*Bill Berutti	1	15	0	15	15.0
*Greg Harrison	1	6	0	6	6.0
*Fritz Seyferth	4	3	1	2	.5

PASSING

	Att	Comp	Int	Yds	TD
*Don Moorhead	210	103	7	1261	5
*Jim Betts	33	16	0	293	3
*Bill Berutti	2	0	0	0	0

RECEIVING

	No.	Yds	TD
Jim Mandich	50	662	4
*Bill Harris	15	302	1
Mike Hankwitz	13	155	0
*Paul Staroba	12	141	0
John Gabler	6	67	1
Garvie Craw	7	59	1
Jerry Ismland	5	60	0
*Glenn Doughty	3	17	0
*Preston Henry	2	31	0
*Mike Oldham	4	33	0
*Billy Taylor	2	14	1

*Player Returning

PUNT RETURNS

	No.	Yds	Ave	TD
Barry Pierson	21	293	14.6	1
*Marty Huff	1	31	31.0	1
Tom Curtis	11	21	1.9	0
Brian Healy	1	0	0.0	0
*Bruce Elliott	1	14	14.0	0

PUNTING

	No.	Yds	Ave
Mark Werner	54	2115	37.8
Team	2	0	0.0

BO SUFFERS HEART ATTACK

Michigan's Greatest Loss Came Hours Before Kickoff---Coach III

Michigan		0	3	0	0—	3
USC		3	0	7	0—	10

SCORING	STATISTICS		
		MICH	USC
Mich—Killian (20 yd field goal).	20	First Downs	16
USC—Ayala (25 yard field goal).	162	Net Yards Rushing	195
Chandler (33 yds, pass Jones),	127	Net Yards Passing	195
Ayala kick.	32	Passes Attempted	17
	14	Passes Completed	10
	0	Intercepted by	1
	6-36.2	Punting	5-40.6
	56	Return Yardage	75
	1	Fumbles	2

Michigan's football forces sustained two major setbacks on New Year's Day of 1970.

One was clear cut. The 10-3 loss to Southern California will stand in the record books forever as Michigan's first Rose Bowl defeat after a glittering series of triumphs in the Pasadena classic.

The full impact of the other is yet to be determined. Head Coach Glenn (Bo) Schembechler was forced to leave his team scant hours before the game on January 1 and was rushed to the hospital instead.

There, while a record throng of 103,878 jammed into the picturesque stadium in Arroyo Seco and millions more watched on TV, Schembechler was secluded in St. Luke's intensive coronary care unit, unable even to listen to the game action.

In late December the 40-year-old Schembechler had been acclaimed by the nation's grid writers as the collegiate coach of the year. "All I've ever wanted to do," he told a press group at the time, "was coach football."

But fate prevented him from coaching the biggest game of his brilliant career and now no one knows what lies ahead for him. The early reports were promising — "no massive heart damage" — and it was thought that after a fortnight or so in the Pasadena hospital he might be able to return to Ann Arbor.

Beyond that, only the developments of the future can resolve the uncertainties which inevitably stem from the initial "mild heart attack" diagnosis announced to the Wolverine team that crucial morning.

The Michigan players were stunned when they heard the news from Bo's assistants about three hours before game time, shortly after he was hastened to the hospital. At the moment, none could know how serious it might turn out to be and suddenly their concern for the USC battle was replaced by personal prayers that their coach's life be spared.

Later, after all the field action was concluded, some tried to express their feelings.

"I'm not trying to make any kind of excuse," said Captain Jim Mandich. "USC played a fantastic game. But it was a great shock to the team and our mental capacities were diverted from the game itself. We were upset both from the fact that Bo was ill and that he wasn't here with us."

"We couldn't help being broken up about it," said quarterback Don Moorhead. "Bo brought us here and worked so hard. It was a terrible blow. Did you know he left the hotel only one night all the time we've been out here? He has studied movies, talked with players and set the same kind of example he has all year. Without his example we wouldn't be here. He is always my inspiration on the sidelines and there's no question his leadership on the field was missed."

Defensive end Cecil Pryor declared: "I know my play was affected, at least early in the game until I convinced myself we had to carry on. And I think Bo's loss affected the younger guys even more. They draw on him a lot. He has a very dominant personality."

Jim Young, Michigan's 34-year-old defensive coordinator who assumed the position of head coach for the day, said: "Bo's absence was a tremendous blow to all of us."

All season long Schembechler has called all of Michigan's offensive plays. In this emergency, Young continued to call the defensive signals as in the past and responsibility for the offensive calls was shared by three other coaches. "They did all they could," said another Wolverine player, "but it just wasn't the same without Bo."

With or without Bo, of course, Southern Cal is a great defensive team with a huge and mobile forward wall which USC Coach John McKay thinks is perhaps the finest in college football history. And, without reservations, McKay termed this "my best defensive team ever — better even than my national champions."

Statistically, it was a near even battle. Michigan made 20 first downs and USC had 16. USC gained 195 yards on the ground and Michigan had 162. USC made 128 yards passing and Michigan had 127.

The overall net yardage advantage for the Trojans was 34 — a figure which included a 33-yard aerial game breaker for the lone touchdown which Michigan could not match.

Thus ended the 1969 season — extended to the first day of 1970 by virtue of the Big Ten co-championship. Overall, Michigan was 8-3 and ranked No. 9 in the nation by the final post-game Associated Press poll. Of the country's Top Twenty teams, the Wolverines defeated two, No. 4 Ohio State and No. 18 Purdue, and lost to two, No. 3 Southern Cal and No. 6 Missouri.

Coach Schembechler was not the Rose Bowl effort's only Wolverine casualty. Just before Christmas Day, Sophomore running standout Glenn Doughty incurred a severe knee injury which required surgery and left him sidelined. Then, in the game's final moments, Junior Bill Harris, trying desperately to grab a pass in the end zone, crumpled to the turf and underwent a similar knee operation.

Hopefully, all three will be back in perfect form for the 1970 season. Thirty-three of the 50 Rose Bowl squad members have eligibility remaining, including six starting Sophomores and seven starting Juniors. Nine starting Seniors will graduate — Captain Mandich, guards Bob Baumgartner and Dick Caldarazzo, fullback Craw, wing back John Gabler, defensive end Pryor, and defensive backs Pierson, Healy and All-American Tom Curtis. Other departing Seniors include Mike Hankwitz, Pete Sarantos, Frank Titas, Werner Hall, Jerry Imsland, Eric Federico, Al Francis, and Mark Werner.

J-M coach to rest

Bo is home again —tired but happy

A Farewell To Bump

A BRIDGE over troubled waters is what Bump Elliott will have to be in his new job as athletic director at the University of Iowa.

We wish Bump well and much success at Iowa City. He inherits a troubled athletic situation and quite likely some morale and dissension problems, but Bump, we suspect, knows what he's walking into. And is confident, as we are, that he can handle the job.

We will miss him in Ann Arbor. As player, coach and administrator, he is a Michigan tradition. The Elliott name is a proud one in Michigan sports history. Bump coached some fine Wolverine teams, including the 1964 squad which went on to a Rose Bowl win.

To all who know Bump as a gentleman friend of young people, sportsman and family man, his leavetaking is one we accept with reluctance.

ALL-TIME GRIDDERS:
Big Ten best tabbed

The Big Ten Skywriters, a group of veteran Big Ten football observers, today named their All-Time Big Ten Football Team featuring 22 of the conference's greatest players.

The list included the legendary Tom Harmon at halfback and former Michigan ends Ron Kramer and Bennie Oosterbaan on the first team while honorable mention awards were given to tackle Whitey Wistert and quarterback Benny Friedman, both former Michigan All-Americans.

Bo Receives Unique Honor

Michigan football Coach Bo Schembechler had some distinguished company yesterday as he received a distinguished honor.

Schembechler, who guided the Wolverines to a share of the Big Ten championship in his first season as coach, was made a member of the varsity M Club.

And he received the honor in the presence of seven members of Michigan's 1920 team who were holding their 50th reunion.

It was the first time any Michigan coach has been inducted into the club after only one year at the university. Schembechler, a 1951 graduate of Miami of Ohio, also was given a plaque for winning the football championship at the M Club annual spring meeting.

AP Poll (1970)	UPI Poll (1970)
1. Nebraska	1. Texas
2. Notre Dame	2. Ohio State
3. Texas	3. Nebraska
4. Tennessee	4. Tennessee
5. Ohio State	5. Notre Dame
6. Arizona State	6. L.S.U.
7. L.S.U.	7. MICHIGAN
8. Stanford	8. Arizona State
9. MICHIGAN	9. Auburn
10. Auburn	10. Stanford

Michigan's 1970 Season

(Won 9, Lost 1)

Date	Opponent (site)	Mich.	Opp.	Attendance
Sept. 19	Arizona (Ann Arbor)	20	9	80,386
Sept. 26	Washington (Seattle)	17	3	57,500
Oct. 3	Texas A&M (Ann Arbor)	14	10	71,732
Oct. 10	Purdue (Lafayette)	29	0	69,022
Oct. 17	Michigan State (Ann Arbor)	34	20	103,580
Oct. 24	Minnesota (Ann Arbor)	39	13	83,496
Oct. 31	Wisconsin (Madison)	29	15	72,389
Nov. 7	Illinois (Ann Arbor)	42	0	70,781
Nov. 14	Iowa (Ann Arbor)	55	0	66,189
Nov. 21	Ohio State (Columbus)	9	20	87,331
	Ave.	28.8	9	76,240
	Total	288	90	762,406

Dan Dierdorf

72 DAN DIERDORF, 6-4, 250, senior, Canton, Ohio . . . Definite All-American prospect . . . All-Big Ten last year, was second team selection as a sophomore . . . key man in clearing holes for Taylor and Doughty as power tackle . . . very strong and quick for size . . . married and has one son . . . majoring in economics and history . . . born 6-29-49.

1970 Football Roster

No.	Name	Pos.	Wt.	Ht.	Class
99	*BECKMAN, Thomas C.	DT	245	6-5½	Jr.
28	*BERUTTI, William J.	WB	189	6-0½	Sr.
23	**BETTS, N. James	S	185	6-4	Sr.
76	*BRANDSTATTER, James P.	OT	244	6-4	Jr.
94	*CARPENTER, Alden J. (Butch)	DE	206	6-2	Jr.
24	CIPA, Lawrence A.	QB	204	6-3	Soph.
40	COAKLEY, Gary R.	SE	200	6-2	Soph.
36	*COIN, Dana S.	K-LB	210	6-1	Jr.
73	COODE, James E.	OT	239	6-3½	Soph.
60	COYLE, Thomas J.	OG	228	6-0	Soph.
19	DANIELS, John W.	DB	192	6-4	Soph.
35	*DARDEN, Thomas V.	DB	190	6-2	Jr.
72	**DIERDORF, Daniel L.	OT	250	6-4	Sr.
22	*DOUGHTY, Glenn M.	TB	195	6-2	Jr.
59	DUFFY, Mark F.	C	210	5-11	Sr.
46	DUTCHER, Gerald E.	DB	185	6-1	Sr.
86	EATON, Donald R.	DB	185	6-4	Soph.
21	*ELLIOTT, Bruce N.	DB	176	6-0	Jr.
68	ELLIS, Gregory A.	MG	215	6-2	Soph.
77	FERCHAU, Thomas D.	OT	220	6-0	Soph.
92	*GRAMBAU, Fredrick E.	DT	242	6-2½	Jr.
14	*GUSICH, Frank J.	Wolf	187	6-0	Jr.
75	**HALL, Werner W.	OG	219	6-0	Sr.
71	**HARPRING, John J.	OT	224	6-4	Sr.
80	**HARRIS, William J.	SE	189	6-1	Sr.
17	HARRISON, Gregory W.	DB	197	5-10	Sr.
56	HART, William J.	C	215	6-4	Soph.
43	HASLETT, William D.	SE	169	5-10	Soph.
44	*HENRY, Preston	WB	185	6-0	Jr.
39	**HILL, Henry W.	MG	220	5-11	Sr.
70	**HUFF, R. Martin (Marty)	LB	231	6-2	Sr.
89	HUISKENS, Thomas A.	TE	207	6-2½	Jr.
52	HULKE, Scott E.	C	215	6-5	Jr.
37	KEE, Thomas G.	Wolf	204	5-11½	Soph.
90	*KELLER, Michael F.	DE	210	6-3	Jr.
57	**KILLIAN, Timothy J.	K-OG	225	6-3	Sr.
41	LOGAN, Randolph	WB	200	6-2	Soph.
25	McBRIDE, John R.	QB	189	6-2½	Soph.
78	**McCOY, C. Richard, Jr.	DT	240	6-4	Sr.
65	*McKENZIE, Reginald	OG	221	6-4	Jr.
97	**MOORE, Edward M.	LB	210	6-1	Sr.
27	**MOORHEAD, Donald W.	QB	199	6-2	Sr.
64	MORAN, William F.	LB	183	6-0½	Soph.
53	*MURDOCK, Guy B.	C	215	6-2	Jr.
82	**NEWELL, Peter J.	DT	226	6-4	Sr.
83	NIEMAN, Thomas S.	TE	205	6-1	Sr.
84	*OLDHAM, Michael	SE	200	6-3	Jr.
29	PIGHEE, John A.	DB	190	6-3	Soph.
79	POPLAWSKI, Thomas	OT	230	6-4	Soph.
15	RATHER, David E. (Bo)	DB	175	6-1	Soph.
95	ROSEMA, Robert J.	DE	200	6-3	Jr.
26	ROSS, William A.	QB-DE	212	6-3	Jr.
45	**SCHEFFLER, Lance G.	TB	199	5-10	Sr.
81	SCHUMACHER, Gerald F.	TE	215	6-2	Soph.
32	*SEYFERTH, John F. (Fritz)	FB	202	6-3	Jr.
85	SEYMOUR, Paul C.	TE	235	6-5	Jr.
91	**SEYMOUR, Philip H.	DE	215	6-4	Sr.
50	SMITH, Michael C.	C	220	6-2	Jr.
74	SMITH, Tony L.	DT	225	6-5	Soph.
96	SPEARMAN, Clinton	DE	213	6-3	Soph.
30	**STAROBA, Paul L.	SE	209	6-3	Sr.
55	SWAN, Robert P.	LB	218	6-3½	Soph.
33	*TAYLOR, Michael	LB	217	6-1½	Jr.
42	*TAYLOR, William L.	FB	200	5-10	Jr.
49	WALKER, Alan G.	TB	192	6-1½	Soph.
66	WOLFF, John L.	OG	220	5-11	Sr.
16	ZUCCARELLI, David C.	DB	188	5-11½	Jr.

* Letters Won

Henry Hill

39 HENRY HILL, 5-11, 220, senior, Detroit . . . non-scholarship player who became a star . . . second team All-Big Ten for two seasons . . . very quick and has thrown runners for losses 23 times in two seasons . . . is on academic scholarship . . . business law major . . . born 10-31-48.

Reprinted with permission from the **University of Michigan Football Program**

'Whiskey'—World Smallest Halftime Show in Football

By Robin Wright

Among the many football traditions originated at Michigan, there's a new one that's likely to stay exclusive to the school—a 'letterman' dog.

Her name is Whiskey and she's unofficially a mascot in residence.

The three-year-old white, wired-haired fox terrier has gained considerable recognition for her half-time performances at Michigan football games.

She recently began her third season of half-time shows which feature a run from goal post to goal post pushing a maize and blue ball while weaving through U-M band members' legs and eluding perplexed officials. After three seasons, Whiskey's skill is matched only by her popularity and acceptance.

It all started during half-time of the 1968 Michigan-Michigan State game. Attendants saw a little terrier in a maize and blue jacket push a green and white ball across the field.

Fans cheered as the tiny pooch knocked the ball across the goal line, then pushed it the entire length of the field in the opposite direction to dodge officials, who were not as pleased with her performance.

Whiskey, in theatrical terms, was an immediate hit.

In fact, demand for a return performance became so great that the athletic department asked the student paper to request information on the dog.

Although the ad was not immediately answered, the dog mysteriously turned up at the next game and entertained the crowds with another half-time performance.

No official word ever came from Whiskey's owners, who continued to secretly sneak the dog and her famed ball in and out of the stadium. But Michigan fans were content that she was at least coming back.

By the climactic moment of the 1968 season—the Ohio State game—Michigan had a new tradition. It seemed quite appropriate that Michigan's only female football performer should accompany the team to the championship game—just for good luck, of course.

Michigan Marching Band — Volga Boatman Formation

Revelli Plans Final Season

Dr. Revelli, left; Prof. Cavender

The 1970 football season will mark Dr. William D. Revelli's 36th and final year as Conductor of Bands at the University of Michigan and as Director of the famed Michigan Marching Band.

His guiding genius has been the force which has brought Michigan Bands to a position of foremost excellence among the bands of the world. On the gridiron, his imagination, his search for the new and different, his refusal to compromise musically and his total dedication to perfection has brought the Michigan Marching Band to new pinnacles of greatness.

September 19th, when Michigan opens the season against Arizona, will be the 22nd Annual Band Day in the Michigan Stadium with 125 bands from all parts of the state gathered together for one of the fall football half-time extravaganzas at Michigan.

The Minnesota game on October 24th will be the occasion of the Band Alumni Reunion, so appropriately called "The Blast From The Past." Plans call for a special show honoring Dr. Revelli's retirement after 36 years as Director of the Marching Band, and all band alumni are urged to return on this date to make this the greatest reunion ever.

The Michigan Marching Band with approximately 200 members, is traditionally an all male organization and counts men from almost every school and college on campus in its membership. One of the most active student organizations on campus, membership in the marching band is a prized accomplishment.

The Marching Band is one of seven University of Michigan Bands with a combined membership of approximately 500. Other bands are the Symphony Band, Wind Ensemble, Concert Band, Varsity Band, Wolverine Band and Jazz Band.

George Cavender, Assistant Conductor of Bands, will be serving his 19th season with the Marching Band.

Michigan 20, Arizona 9

September 19 — Ann Arbor — Attendance 80,386

The Wolverines opened the 1970 season hosting the Wildcats from Arizona, marking the first meeting between Michigan and a Western Athletic Conference school.

Before a Band Day crowd junior placekicker Dana Coin split the uprights with a 42-yard field goal, the longest in Wolverine history, to put Michigan in front, 3-0, midway through the first quarter. The Wolverines promptly moved 63 yards in eight plays to score the season's first touchdown, Billy Taylor getting the six points on a 29-yard screen pass from Don Moorhead.

Michigan's offense bogged down and early in the fourth quarter Arizona's Steve Hurley kicked his third field goal, cutting the Wolverine lead to one at 10-9. At that point the tenacious Michigan defense provided the spark to set up Coin's second field goal and linebacker Marty Huff picked off another aerial to set up Lance Scheffler's clinching touchdown.

Michigan	10	0	0	10	20
Arizona	3	3	0	3	9

SCORING

Mich—Coin (42-yard field goal)
Taylor (29-yard pass from Moorhead)
Coin (20-yard field goal)
Scheffler (6-yard run)
Killian (2 PAT's)
Ariz—Hurley (29-yard field goal)
Hurley (44-yard field goal)
Hudley (33-yard field goal)

STATISTICS

	MICH	ARIZ
First Downs	18	10
Net Yards Rushing	186	84
Net Yards Passing	168	143
Passes Attempted	24	32
Passes Completed	11	15
Intercepted By	4	0
Punting	10-40.1	9-41.8
Return Yardage	82	140
Fumbles/Lost	3/1	5/0

Michigan 14, Texas A & M 10

The Aggies of Texas A & M were a first-time foe for Michigan although the Wolverines have faced and defeated Southern Methodist from the same Southwest Conference.

For most of this hard-fought October 3 battle before 71,732 fans in Michigan Stadium, the Aggies held the dominant edge both in the field action and in the scoreboard count. But finally, with only 180 seconds left, the Wolverines pushed over a go-ahead touchdown and then hung on for a 14-10 triumph.

"The defense just wouldn't crack," said a relieved Schembechler in the locker room. "That was the story. The defense just kept getting the ball back for us until we finally got our offense going."

Michigan 29, Purdue 0

October 10 — Lafayette — Attendance 69,022

Michigan's offense finally exploded as had been expected during the pre-season, but not until the fourth quarter. Entering the final 15 minutes the Wolverines held a slim 6-0 lead, then ripped off 23 points to bury Purdue, 29-0.

The Michigan defense was once again brilliant, a style of play that was becoming ordinary for them. The defenders racked up their first shutout of the year and broke Purdue's 13 game home field winning streak. The Wolverines picked off three passes, setting up two touchdowns, and limited the Boilermakers to just 36 yards rushing.

Quarterback Don Moorhead fired two touchdown passes for the offense and tailback Billy Taylor, running to his 1969 form, rushed for 89 yards and crossed the goal line once. Preston Henry also scored on the ground as the Wolverines untracked the running game to gain 221 yards. The passing game also improved as Glenn Doughty moved from tailback to wingback and proved to be a dangerous receiver.

The opening game of the Big Ten season had been a key one and Michigan put its game together just in time, as the big grudge game with Michigan State was next on the agenda.

Michigan	0	6	0	23	29
Purdue	0	0	0	0	0

SCORING

Mich—Taylor (1-yard run)
Coin (32-yard field goal)
Scheffler (7-yard pass from Moorhead)
Seymour (10-yard pass from Moorhead)
Killian (2 PAT's)

STATISTICS

	MICH.	P
First Downs	18	11
Net Yards Rushing	221	36
Net Yards Passing	92	176
Passes Attempted	17	27
Passes Completed	9	16
Intercepted By	3	1
Punting	5-40.1	9-39.4
Return Yardage	116	27
Fumbles/No. Lost	3/1	2/1

Michigan 34, Michigan State 20

October 17 — Ann Arbor — Attendance 103,580

Before the second largest crowd ever to see a regular season college football game Michigan avenged its 1969 defeat to Michigan State by dropping the Spartans, 34-20.

It wasn't easy, though, as Michigan State came out roaring and immediately drove 74 yards for a touchdown. But Michigan wasn't to be denied as Billy Taylor ran 26 yards for a tying score and then scored again at the end of the half to send the teams off deadlocked, 13-13.

Michigan then locked the game away in the third quarter as Taylor scored for the third time, the first Wolverine to do so against State since Bob Chappuis in 1947, and Don Moorhead fired an eight-yard touchdown pass to Fritz Seyferth. Glenn Doughty slammed into the end zone on the first play of the fourth quarter for an insurance touchdown and Michigan had its fifth straight win of the season.

Michigan	7	6	14	7	34
Michigan State	10	3	0	7	20

SCORING

Mich—Taylor (26-yard run)
Taylor (2-yard run)
Taylor (4-yard run)
Seyferth 8-yard pass from Moorhead)
Doughty (5-yard run)
MSU— Allen (42-yard run)
Tripplett (3-yard run)
Shlapak (25-yard field goal)
Shlapak (46-yard field goal)
Shlapak (2 PAT's)

STATISTICS

	MICH	MSU
First Downs	23	20
Net Yards Rushing	304	194
Net Yards Passing	156	200
Passes Attempted	19	30
Passes Completed	12	15
Intercepted By	1	1
Punting	2-35.0	3-30.3
Return Yardage	85	106
Fumbles/No. Lost	1/1	0/0

Michigan 39, Minnesota 13

Many Wolverine partisans were apprehensive about a letdown following the previous week's victory over Michigan State, but Michigan tripled the score on Minnesota, 39-13, and placed a new name in the record books.

Few among the 83,496 fans for this October 24 Homecoming battle could have readily identified Fritz Seyferth before kickoff. But the Junior fullback, starting only his second game in Michigan Stadium, scored twice as many touchdowns as the Gophers and helped mightily in keeping the Little Brown Jug in Ann Arbor at least a year longer.

Seyferth crossed the goal line four times, a feat surpassed in Michigan grid annals only by Ron Johnson who scored five against Wisconsin two years ago. The achievement paired him with Tom Harmon and Garvie Craw as the only other Wolverines in modern times to score four TDs in one game.

Tailback Billy Taylor punched in Michigan's first touchdown with a 17-yard slash, then went on to net 151 rushing yards for the afternoon. Seyferth's initial score, a short plunge, made it 12-0, but the Gophers hit two long passes late in the second quarter for gains totaling 61 yards and a touchdown.

That was the last time it was close, however, for Seyferth tallied once more before intermission, then twice in the second half before Minnesota gained its final score. Lance Scheffler provided Michigan's last touchdown.

Brief Statistics	Minn.	Mich.
First downs	13	28
Net yards gained	283	518
Rushing net yardage	69	414
Passes attempted	38	18
Passes completed	16	7
Yards gained by passing	214	104
Passes intercepted by	0	3
Fumbles lost	1	1
Yards penalized	58	66

Michigan 55, Iowa 0

There was more of the same November 14 when 66,189 braved intermittent snow for the home finale against Iowa. Like Illinois, the Hawkeyes had come off a pair of impressive performances with 56 points against Minnesota and Indiana the previous two weekends.

But Iowa never was able to cross midfield until the game's final 25 seconds and Michigan piled up 561 offensive yards.

Tailback Taylor, who gained 189 in a shortened appearance because of elbow injury, was the lone player scoring more than one touchdown in the eight-touchdown barrage. He made two, while Doughty, Moorhead, Seyferth, Scheffler, Tom Darden and Dave Zuccarelli had one apiece. Meanwhile, Dana Coin converted all but the last extra-point kick.

Brief Statistics	Iowa	Mich.
Total first downs	6	33
Net yards gained	122	561
Rushing net yardage	88	468
Passes attempted	8	17
Passes completed	3	7
Yards gained by passing	34	93
Passes intercepted by	0	0
Fumbles lost	5	1
Yards penalized	23	74

Reprinted with permission from the Michigan Alumnus

Michigan 29, Wisconsin 15

| October 31 | Madison | Attendance 72,38 |

Michigan's All-Big Ten passing combination of Don Moorhead an Paul Staroba combined to shoot down Wisconsin, 29-15, as Moorhea fired 11 completions in 22 attempts for 223 yards with Staroba catchin six for 178 yards and a touchdown.

Moorhead started the Wolverine rolling early in the first quarter afte Jim Betts recovered a Badger fumble, hitting Fritz Seyferth with an eight yard scoring pass. Moorhead kept throwing in the second quarter as th Wolverines struck quickly. He combined with Staroba on a sensationa 70-yard pass play that carried to the Wisconsin three and set up Sey ferth's second touchdown. The Wolverines came right back on a 76-yar drive with Preston Henry scoring and Staroba catching a two-point con version pass.

But the tide began to turn at the end of the first half when the Badger got on the board with seconds remaining to make the score 21-6. Whe Danny Crooks took off on an 87-yard punt return in the second half an the Badgers added a field goal, the score was cut to 21-15 and Wisconsin appeared to have the momentum for an upset.

Moorhead and Staroba were prepared for the emergency, though, com bining on a 24-yard touchdown play that safely put the game away.

Michigan	7	14	0	8—29
Wisconsin	0	6	9	0—15

SCORING

Mich—Seyferth (8-yard pass from Moorhead)
Seyferth (3-yard run)
Henry (4-yard run)
Staroba (24-yard pass from Moorhead)
Killian (1 PAT)
Staroba (1 PAT—pass from Moorhead)
Taylor (1 PAT—run)
Wisc—Thompson (17-yard pass from Graff)
Crooks (87-yard punt return)
Jaeger (32-yard field goal)

STATISTICS

	MICH		WISC
First Downs	24		17
Net Yards Rushing	227		79
Net Yards Passing	223		168
Passes Attempted	22		23
Passes Completed	11		11
Intercepted By	1		0
Punting	4-42.8		6-41.2
Return Yardage	66		234
Fumbles/No. Lost	4/3		1/1

Michigan 42, Illinois 0

| November 7 | Ann Arbor | Attendance 70,781 |

The Wolverines had their most balanced offense of the season as they overpowered a young Illinois team, 42-0. Michigan rushers charged for 259 yards while Don Moorhead and his backup, Jack McBride, passed for another 166.

Wingback Glenn Doughty put on the finest individual performance as he ran for 40 yards, caught five passes for 81 yards and scored the first two Michigan touchdowns. Almost all of the Wolverine runners got in on the show as Lance Scheffler led the team with only 75 yards. Scheffler, starting in place of the slightly injured Taylor, also scored once. Taylor returned to action himself late in the first half and got 66 yards and two touchdowns while seeing limited duty.

The defense displayed its usual form as the season's second shutout was put on the board. The Illini could manage only eight first downs as the Wolverines shut them out for the 14th straight quarter, dating back to 1968.

Michigan	7	14	14	7—42
Illinois	0	0	0	0—0

SCORING

Mich—Doughty (3-yard run)
Doughty (4-yard run)
Taylor (2-yard run)
Schumacher (4-yard pass from Moorhead)
Taylor (7-yard run)
Scheffler (1-yard run)
Coin (6 PAT's)

STATISTICS

	MICH		ILL
First Downs	24		8
Net Yards Rushing	259		71
Net Yards Passing	166		101
Passes Attempted	16		18
Passes Completed	11		7
Intercepted By			1
Punting	3-50.0		5-40.1
Return Yardage	64		133
Fumbles/No. Lost	0/0		3/1

Big Ten 1970 Statistics

	CONFERENCE GAMES						ALL GAMES		
	W	L	T	Pct.	Pts. Ave.	Opp. Pts.	Off. Rank	Def. Rank	W-L-T
Ohio State	7	0	0	1.000	26.1	10.0	2	3	9-0-0
MICHIGAN	6	1	0	.857	33.9	9.7	1	2	9-1-0
Northwestern	6	1	0	.857	27.4	13.3	3	1	6-4-0
Iowa	3	3	1	.500	15.0	24.7	8	7	3-6-1
Michigan State	3	4	0	.429	20.9	18.6	4	5	4-6-0
Wisconsin	3	4	0	.429	21.1	20.6	5	6	4-5-1
Minnesota	2	4	1	.357	15.6	23.0	6	8	3-6-1
Purdue	2	5	0	.286	17.1	18.1	7	4	4-6-0
Illinois	1	6	0	.143	15.6	34.3	9	10	3-7-0
Indiana	1	6	0	.143	9.9	30.3	10	9	1-9-0

Ohio State 20, Michigan 9

"Is this our best team ever?" Woody Hayes echoed his questioner. "Well, today it was. Today, this was the best we've ever been."

No one on the Michigan side would quarrel with that assessment. "You have to give them credit," said Schembechler. "They are a real championship team."

The largest home crowd in Ohio history, 87,331, jammed into the big horseshoe stadium and millions of televiewers across the nation also watched the November 21 action. Most would probably agree with Schembechler's appraisal: "We made mistakes, but I just can't fault our effort."

Later, he amplified a bit: "If we couldn't run against them we weren't going to win. And we couldn't run." In the end, Michigan netted only 37 yards on 30 rushing efforts, barely more than 1 yard per try.

"That was the story," said Schembechler. "We played with great effort and enthusiasm. But we didn't move the football on the ground and we gave up almost all their points on our mistakes — fumbles, dropped passes, penalties and an interception."

A lost fumble on the opening kickoff placed the Wolverines in a deep hole right at the outset, and Fred Schram's 28-yard field goal provided an early 3-0 margin. Michigan, playing catchup football all afternoon, evened the count following a Jim Betts pass interception and Dana Coin's 31-yard field goal.

Ohio moved ahead again late in the second period. A 73-yard Staroba punt was nullified by a face mask penalty call, so Staroba booted again and the Bucks had the ball at Michigan's 47. They pushed it on down to the 25. The Wolverine defenders twice stopped Ohio and it was third-and-11 at the 26 when Rex Kern fired a perfect pass to Bruce Jankowski for the touchdown. Schram converted what proved to be a very important extra point and the Bucks went on top again, 10-3.

The entire third period was dominated by Michigan. A 50-yard scoring drive — mostly by air — was capped by a Moorhead to Staroba pass in the left corner of the end zone for the final 13 yards. But Buckeye Tim Anderson blocked Coin's extra-point try and the Wolverines still trailed, 10-9.

It stayed that way until the fourth quarter when Ohio's longest offensive surge of the day provided field position for Schram's second field goal, a 27-yarder which upped the count to 13-9 and made it necessary for Michigan now to score a touchdown in order to take the lead.

But the battle's final touchdown went to the surging Buckeyes. A Moorhead pass — his first interception since way back in the Michigan State game — was grabbed off by Stan White at the Wolverine 23 and returned all the way to the 9. Three plays later Leo Hayden rounded right end for the decisive touchdown and Ohio had perhaps its most satisfying victory in Buckeye football annals.

Michigan was still not through but a dropped fourth down pass at the Ohio 13 killed the last real chance to pull closer and retain opportunity to win.

Two of Michigan's standout players on this unhappy final day wound up their careers by moving into the Wolverine record books — Staroba for his season-long punting average of 41.5 yards and Moorhead for a whole cluster of school career records which include: 3,641 yards running and passing; 200 pass completions; and 2,540 yards passing.

	1	2	3	4	
Michigan	0	3	6	0	— 9
Ohio State	3	7	0	10	—20

SCORING

Mich—Coin (31-yard field goal)
  Staroba (13-yard pass from Moorhead)
OSU— Schram (28-yard field goal)
  Jankowski (26-yard pass from Kern)
  Schram (27-yard field goal)
  Hayden (4-yard run)
  Schram (2 PAT's)

STATISTICS

	MICH		OSU
First Downs	10		18
Net Yards Rushing	37		242
Net Yards Passing	118		87
Passes Attempted	26		12
Passes Completed	12		8
Intercepted By	1		1
Punting	7-41.4		6-28.1
Return Yardage	67		86
Fumbles/No. Lost	3/2		3/1

Dana Coin

Paul Staroba

Don Moorhead

INDIVIDUAL

RUSHING

	Att	Gain	Loss	Net	Ave.	LP
Bill Taylor	197	928	18	911	4.6	41
Don Moorhead	97	431	63	368	3.8	39
Fritz Seyferth	86	337	4	333	3.9	19
Preston Henry	70	325	11	314	4.5	30
Glenn Doughty	67	277	19	258	3.8	53
Lance Scheffler	48	215	0	215	4.5	12
Bill Berutti	10	37	1	36	3.6	11
Randy Logan	6	27	0	27	4.5	11
Dave Zuccarelli	4	21	0	21	5.2	7
Greg Harrison	6	21	0	21	3.5	5
Jack McBride	6	13	9	4	0.7	10

(Players returning in bold face type)

PASSING

	Att	Comp	Int	Yards	TD	LP
Don Moorhead	190	87	6	1167	8	70
Jack McBride	8	3	0	55	0	41

SCORING

	TDr	TDp	K	PR	FG	Pts.
			PAT			
Bill Taylor	10	1	0	1/1	0	68
Fritz Seyferth	6	2	0	0	0	48
Dana Coin	0	0	15/17	0	5/13	30
Lance Scheffler	4	1	0	0	0	30
Glenn Doughty	4	0	0	0	0	24
Preston Henry	4	0	0	0	0	24
Tim Killian	0	0	14/19	0	0	14
Paul Staroba	0	2	0	1/1	0	14
Don Moorhead	2	0	0	0/2	0	12
Tom Darden	*1	0	0	0	0	6
Jerry Schumacher	0	1	0	0	0	6
Paul Seymour	0	1	0	0	0	6
Dave Zuccarelli	1	0	0	0	0	6

* Scored on Fumble Recovery

RECEIVING	No.	Yards	TD	LP
Staroba	35	519	2	70
Doughty	22	298	0	41
Seymour, Paul	13	194	1	41
Taylor, B.	6	82	1	29
Scheffler	4	39	1	20
Schumacher	3	33	1	16
Seyferth	3	16	2	8
Henry	2	14	0	9
Berutti	1	17	0	17
Harris	1	10	0	10

FUMBLES RECOVERED

2 Betts
2 Darden
2 Gusich
1 Beckman
1 Coin
1 Henry
1 Kee
1 Newell
1 McKenzie
1 Seymour, Paul
1 Spearman

PASSES BROKEN UP

10 Darden
9 Betts
5 Taylor, M
4 Huff
4 Gusich
4 Newell
3 Beckman
3 Moore
2 Rather
1 Elliott
1 Hill
1 Keller
1 McCoy

BLOCKED PUNTS

Rather — 1 punt partially blocked

BLOCKED PAT

Opponents blocked 1 placement attempt

KICKOFF RETURNS

	No.	Yards	Ave.	LP
Taylor, B.	2	45	22.5	23
Seyferth	2	44	22.0	24
Rather	3	62	20.7	38
Henry	6	104	17.3	20
Doughty	7	116	16.0	20
Scheffler	3	26	8.7	12
Harpring	1	0	0.0	0

PUNTING

	No.	Yards	Ave	LP
Staroba	54	2240	*41.5	64

* new Wolverine season record

PUNT RETURNS

	No.	Yards	Ave	LP
Rather	1	44	44.0	44
Darden	18	153	8.5	21
Elliott	12	57	4.8	10

INTERCEPTIONS

	No.	Yards	TD	LP
Huff	5	85	0	51
Darden	5	46	0	19
Betts	3	78	0	45
Elliott	2	21	0	12
Moore	1	9	0	9
Kee	1	7	0	7
Gusich	1	0	0	0
Rather	1	0	0	0
Taylor, M.	1	0	0	0

TEAM

	Mich.	Opp.
First Downs	203	130
Rushing	131	57
Passing	60	66
Penalties	12	7
Total Offensive Plays	795	663
Total Offensive Yards	3730	2478
Rushing Attempts	597	416
Rushing Yardage	2508	1051
Passing Attempts	198	247

	Mich.	Opp.
Pass Completions	90	121
Passing Yardage	1222	1427
Passes Intercepted by	20	6
Punt Returns	31	32
Punt Ret. Yardage	254	311
Fumbles/Lost	26/15	29/14
Penalties/Yds.	45/484	48/441
No. of Punts	54	73
Avg. Distance	41.5	39.0

Wolverine Honors in '70

All-Americans

Tackle — Dan Dierdorf (AP, UPI, NEA, Coaches, Football News, Writers)
Linebacker — Marty Huff (Coaches)
Middle Guard — Henry Hill (Central Press)

All-American Second Team

Tackle — Dan Dierdorf (Central Press)
Linebacker — Marty Huff (UPI, AP)
Middle Guard — Henry Hill (NEA, AP)

Honorable Mention All-American

Middle Guard, Henry Hill (UPI); Defensive Back, TOM DARDEN (UPI); Defensive Back, Jim Betts (UPI); Tailback, BILLY TAYLOR (UPI).

Sophomore All-American

Guard — TOM COYLE (Football News Sophomore All-American)

Cavender Takes Over 'M' Band

Prof. George Cavender
'M' Band Director

The 1971 football season will bring with it many new changes for the famed University of Michigan Marching Band. Foremost among these will be a change in conductors after a period of 36 years with the retirement of William D. Revelli.

Professor George Cavender, former assistant conductor of bands for 19 years, has been appointed "Coordinator of Bands" for 1971-72 at Michigan and will assume complete charge of the Michigan Marching Band this fall season.

Professor Cavender's work, as assistant conductor, did much to raise the Michigan Marching Band to a position of foremost eminence among the bands of the nation. Active as a marching band clinician across the United States, he has, along with marching band arranger Jerry Bilik, co-authored several texts and numerous shows for marching bands which have received national acceptance. Unique is his ability to work very successfully in both the concert and marching band fields.

September 18th, when Michigan meets Virginia, marks the date of Michigan's 23rd Annual Band Day with bands gathered together from all parts of Michigan for one of the nations great half-time extravaganzas.

The Indiana game on October 30th will be the occasion of the Band Alumni reunion, so appropriately called "The Blast From The Past", and all former Michigan Bandsmen are urged to make their plans to attend.

The Michigan Marching Band with approximately 200 members, is traditionally an all male organization and counts men from almost every school and college on campus in its membership. One of the most active student organizations on campus, membership in the marching band is a prized accomplishment.

MICHIGAN'S FOOTBALL STAFF (Left to right) Head Coach Bo Schembechler, Larry Smith (interior offensive line), Dick Hunter (defensive backs), Gary Moeller (defensive ends), Frank Maloney (defensive line) Jerry Hanlon (offensive line), Chuck Stobart (offensive backs), Jim Young (defensive coordinator), Tirrel Burton (freshman coach), George Mans (receivers).

Michigan's 1971 Season

(Won 11, Lost 1)

Date	Opponent (site)	Mich.	Opp.	Attendance
Sept. 11	Northwestern (Evanston)	21	6	42,472
Sept. 18	Virginia (Ann Arbor)	56	0	81,391
Sept. 25	UCLA (Ann Arbor)	38	0	89,177
Oct. 2	Navy (Ann Arbor)	46	0	68,168
Oct. 9	Michigan State (E. Lansing)	24	13	80,093
Oct. 16	Illinois (Ann Arbor)	35	6	73,406
Oct. 23	Minnesota (Minneapolis)	35	7	44,176
Oct. 30	Indiana (Ann Arbor)	61	7	75,751
Nov. 6	Iowa (Ann Arbor)	63	7	72,467
Nov. 13	Purdue (Lafayette)	20	17	65,254
Nov. 20	Ohio State (Ann Arbor)	10	7	104,016
Jan. 1	Stanford (Rose Bowl)	12	13	103,154
	Average	35.1	6.9	74,917
	Total	421	83	899,525
	Home Average			80,639
	Road Average			67,038

AP Poll (1971)
1. Nebraska
2. Oklahoma
3. Colorado
4. Alabama
5. Penn State
6. MICHIGAN
7. Georgia
8. Arizona State
9. Tennessee
10. Stanford

UPI Poll (1971)
1. Nebraska
2. Alabama
3. Oklahoma
4. MICHIGAN
5. Auburn
6. Arizona State
7. Colorado
8. Georgia
9. Tennessee
10. L.S.U.

Big Ten 1971 Statistics

	CONFERENCE GAMES								All Games	
	W	L	T	Pct.	Pts. Ave.	Opp. Pts.	Off. Rank	Def. Rank	W - L - T	
MICHIGAN	8	0	0	1.000	33.6	8.8	1	1	11 - 1 - 0	
Northwestern	6	3	0	.667	21.3	14.1	7	4	7 - 4 - 0	
Illinois	5	3	0	.625	18.7	16.3	8	6	5 - 6 - 0	
Michigan State	5	3	0	.625	24.0	16.3	5	2	6 - 5 - 0	
Ohio State	5	3	0	.625	21.8	12.1	6	3	6 - 4 - 0	
Minnesota	3	5	0	.375	18.3	24.0	4	7	4 - 7 - 0	
Purdue	3	5	0	.375	21.0	22.7	3	8	3 - 7 - 0	
Wisconsin	3	5	0	.375	20.1	25.0	2	9	4 - 6 - 1	
Indiana	2	6	0	.250	15.7	29.3	9	5	3 - 8 - 0	
Iowa	1	8	0	.111	9.7	33.5	10	10	1 - 10 - 0	

Sons of former Wolverine All-American: Pete Elliot

Bruce Elliott

Dave Elliott

No.	Name	Pos.	Ht.	Wt.	Class
20	BANKS, Harry	TB	5-10	177	Soph.
99	**BECKMAN, Thomas C.	DT	6-5	246	Sr.
24	BRANDON, David A.	Wolf	6-3	202	Soph.
76	**BRANDSTATTER, James P.	OT	6-4	245	Sr.
80	CALIN, Peter J.	SE	6-3	177	Soph.
94	**CARPENTER, Alden J. (Butch)	DE	6-2	215	Sr.
12	CASEY, Kevin	QB	6-2	175	Soph.
19	CEDERBERG, Jon C.	TB	5-10	177	Soph.
70	CHERRY, John A.	OT	6-5	230	Soph.
13	CIPA, Lawrence A.	QB	6-3	203	Jr.
40	COAKLEY, Gary R.	SE	6-2	197	Jr.
36	**COIN, Dana S.	K-LB	6-1	229	Sr.
39	COLEMAN, Don	FB	6-2	210	Soph.
73	COODE, James E.	Ot	6-3½	235	Jr.
60	COYLE, Thomas J.	OG	6-0	233	Jr.
35	**DARDEN, Thomas W.	DB	6-2	195	Sr.
57	DAY, Michael J.	LB	6-1	201	Soph.
25	DOTZAUER, Barry S.	DB	6-1	162	Soph.
22	**DOUGHTY, Glenn M.	WB	6-2	204	Sr.
28	DRAKE, Thomas E.	DB	5-11	175	Soph.
59	DUFFY, Mark F.	C	5-11	224	Sr.
86	*EATON, Donald R.	DE	6-4	194	Jr.
21	*ELLIOTT, Bruce N.	DB	6-0	175	Sr.
45	ELLIOTT, David L.	DB	6-2	170	Soph.
68	*ELLIS, Gregory A.	MG	6-2	223	Jr.
89	FEDIUK, Arthur W.	TE	6-2	212	Soph.
71	GALLAGHER, David D.	DT	6-4	225	Soph.
92	*GRAMBAU, Fredrick E.	DT	6-2½	234	Jr.
14	**GUSICH, Frank J.	Wolf	6-0	188	Sr.
48	GUSTAFSON, Lawrence J.	WB	5-11	176	Soph.
69	HAINRIHAR, Gary	OG	6-2	220	Soph.
56	HART, William J.	C	6-4	227	Jr.
43	HASLERIG, Clinton E.	WB	6-1	182	Soph.
61	HOBAN, Michael A.	OG	6-2	232	Soph.
52	HULKE, Scott E.	OT	6-5	224	Sr.
82	JOHNSON, Larry L.	DE	6-1	203	Soph.
27	JOHNSTON, James D.	Wolf	5-11	175	Soph.
37	*KEE, Thomas G.	LB	5-11	210	Jr.
90	**KELLER, Michael F.	DE	6-3	215	Sr.
10	KOSS, Gregory	QB	6-5	180	Soph.
41	LOGAN, Randolph	DB	6-2	192	Jr.
72	LYALL, James M.	DT	6-5	224	Soph.
18	*McBRIDE, John R.	QB	6-2½	191	Jr.
65	**McKENZIE, Reginald	OG	6-4	232	Sr.
62	MASTERSON, Kevin J.	OG	6-0	227	Soph.
93	MIDDLEBROOK, John P.	LB	6-0	210	Sr.
53	**MURDOCK, Guy B.	C	6-2	210	Sr.
34	MUTCH, Craig A.	LB	6-1	203	Soph.
84	*OLDHAM, Michael	SE	6-3	198	Sr.
79	POPLAWSKI, Thomas	OT	6-4	225	Jr.
15	*RATHER, David E. (Bo)	SE	6-1	180	Jr.
95	ROSEMA, Robert J.	DE	6-3	193	Sr.
63	*SCHUMACHER, Gerald F.	OG	6-2	224	Jr.
83	SEAL, Paul N.	TE	6-6	213	Soph.
55	SEXTON, Walter E.	MG	5-11	200	Soph.
32	**SEYFERTH, John F. (Fritz)	FB	6-3	218	Sr.
85	*SEYMOUR, Paul C.	TE	6-5	231	Jr.
31	SHUTTLESWORTH, Eugene Ed.	FB	6-2	235	Soph.
17	SLADE, Thomas A.	QB	6-1	198	Soph.
74	*SMITH, Tony L.	DT	6-5	230	Jr.
96	*SPEARMAN, Clinton	DE	6-3	223	Jr.
64	STAVEREN, Howard M.	DT	6-7	278	Soph.
38	STEGER, Geoffrey C.	Wolf	6-0	188	Soph.
23	SZYDLOWSKI, Ron E.	WB	5-9	160	Soph.
44	TAYLOR, Lonnie	DB	5-10	180	Soph.
33	*TAYLOR, Michael	LB	6-1½	224	Sr.
42	**TAYLOR, William L.	TB	5-11	195	Sr.
66	THOMAS, John E.	C	6-3	215	Soph.
30	THORNBLADH, Robert N. M.	FB	6-2	224	Soph.
75	TROSZAK, Douglas	DT	6-3	241	Soph.
78	TUCKER, Curtis J.	OT	6-1	243	Soph.
46	VERCEL, Jovan	MG	6-0	214	Soph.
49	WALKER, Alan (Cowboy)	TB	6-1½	202	Jr.
54	WARNER, Donald R.	MG	5-11	197	Soph.
67	WEST, Alfred L.	DT	6-3	223	Jr.
91	WILLIAMSON, Walter L.	DE	6-4	224	Soph.
16	ZUCCARELLI, David C.	WB	6-0	196	Jr.

* Letters Won

Michigan 21, Northwestern 6

September 11   Evanston   Attendance 42,47_

As the Big Ten moved to an 11-game schedule Michigan was face_ with a conference opponent for the opener for the first time in 25 year_ Northwestern was the foe and, having finished tied for second in 197_ considered to be a prime contender for the Big Ten title.

Michigan responded to the challenge, pounding out a 21-6 victo_ as split end Bo Rather made an auspicious debut on offense. Rathe_ ran 18 yards with an end-around to score one touchdown and recovere_ a blocked field goal in the end zone for another. Michigan's final sco_ was racked up by Billy Taylor, who gained 105 yards.

The Michigan defense showed its strength by continually shutting o_ the Wildcats and not allowing a score until a penalty-marred fourt_ quarter march by Northwestern.

Michigan		0	7	14	0 —	21
Northwestern		0	0	0	6 —	6

SCORING   STATISTICS

Mich—Rather (18-yard run)
    Rather (fumble recovery)
    Taylor (5 yard run)
    Coin (3 PAT'S)
NW —Cooks (2-yard pass from
    Daigneau)

	MICH		N'
15	First Downs		1
213	Net Yards Rushing		7
34	Net Yards Passing		19
11	Passes Attempted		3
4	Passes Completed		1
3	Intercepted By		
4-37	Punting		2-3
70	Return Yardage		3
1/0	Fumbles/No. Lost		1/

Bo Rather   **Tom Beckman**   **Fritz Seyferth**

Michigan 56, Virginia 0

September 18   Ann Arbor   Attendance 81,391

In their home debut, the Wolverines gave Michigan fans plenty to cheer about as they rolled up 56 points on Virginia. The Cavaliers were never in the game as Michigan scored 35 points in the first half, including two touchdowns by Billy Taylor and a kickoff recovery in the end zone by soph Dave Elliott.

For the first time, Michigan displayed its powerful bench with reserves Ed Shuttlesworth, Bob Thornbladh and Harry Banks all scoring. The defense was just as awesome, holding the Cavaliers to just seven first downs and a record -1 yard passing. For the day Virginia could complete only one pass and gain 78 yards rushing while the Wolverines piled up 491 yards on the ground.

Michigan		14	21	14	7 —	56
Virginia		0	0	0	0 —	0

SCORING   STATISTICS

Mich—Taylor (10-yard run)
    Taylor (8-yard run)
    Seyferth (1-yard run)
    Shuttlesworth (4-yard run)
    D. Elliott (kickoff recovery)
    Banks (4-yard run)
    Banks 5-yard run)
    Thornbladh (5-yard run)
    Coin (8 PAT'S)

	MICH		VIR
33	First Downs		7
491	Net Yards Rushing		78
71	Net Yards Passing		-1
10	Passes Attempted		13
3	Passes Completed		1
3	Intercepted By		0
1-43	Punting		8-34.4
37	Return Yardage		169
3/2	Fumbles/No. Lost		2/1

Mike Keller   **Paul Seymour**   **Guy Murdock**

Michigan 38, UCLA 0

"In all my years as a coach," said UCLA's Pepper Rodgers, "I have never had a team so completely dominated."

Such was the post-game appraisal on September 25 after his Bruins had been blanked, 38-0. Many of the Michigan partisans among the home crowd of 89,177 would agree that the Wolverines were indeed over-powering, particularly during a first half in which every UCLAN effort was blunted while 24 points were posted against them.

In all, five Wolverines tallied touchdowns: Fritz Seyferth, Ed Shuttlesworth, Bo Rather, Tom Darden and Harry Banks. But kicker Dana Coin wound up as the day's leading scorer with five extra points and a 31-yard field goal.

One of the most spectacular efforts in Michigan Stadium history was unfurled by Wolverine safety Darden who picked off a pass attempt and weaved his way 92 yards to the opposite end zone. It was three yards short of the Michigan record for a pass interception return, held by Tom Harmon who happened this day to be up in a radio booth broadcasting the game back to his West Coast listeners.

Reprinted with permission from the **Michigan Alumnus**

Michigan 35, Illinois 6

October 16   Ann Arbor   Attendance 73,406

Illinois became the first team to score on Michigan in the first quarter and also the first club to take a lead on the Wolverines. The mistake-prone Wolverines appeared ripe for an upset, but the defense held strong, the offense began to mesh and Michigan was headed for its sixth straight victory.

Tom Slade got Michigan rolling by running 25 yards for one score and then Glenn Doughty took over, catching a Slade pass for one touchdown and running for two others. Billy Taylor added Michigan's other marker on a 10-yard run.

Despite their early touchdown, the Illini never could get untracked, gaining only 83 yards for the afternoon.

Michigan		7	14	0	14 — 35
Illinois		6	0	0	0 — 6

SCORING		STATISTICS	MICH		ILL
Mich—Slade (25-yard run)			22	First Downs	8
Doughty (19-yard pass from Slade)			268	Net Yards Rushing	52
Taylor (10-yard run)			87	Net Yards Passing	31
Doughty (1-yard run)			10	Passes Attempted	17
Doughty (32-yard run)			6	Passes Completed	5
Coin (5 PAT'S)			0	Intercepted By	2
Ill—Wilson (10-yard run)			4-41	Punting	11-40.9
			136	Return Yardage	103
			3/2	Fumbles/No. Lost	2/1

Michigan 61, Indiana 7

"I didn't want to win like that," said Schembechler after the Wolverine squad devasted Indiana, 61-7, in Michigan Stadium. He and John Pont, the Indiana coach, were teammates together in their playing days at Miami of Ohio. "He's one of my best friends and a good coach. You better believe it," said Bo.

But nothing could stop the Maize and Blue on this October 30th. It was the first time that Michigan had put more than 60 points on the board since Fritz Crisler's "Mad Magicians" buried Pittsburgh, 69-0 in 1947.

Michigan netted 452 yards on the ground. "That running game is just tremendous," said Indiana Coach Pont. "We had people in the right spots, but they just couldn't fight off those blocks."

Michigan 46, Navy 0

October 2   Ann Arbor   Attendance 68,168

Michigan started slowly, then blasted away at the Middies for 21 points in the fourth quarter and a 46-0 victory.

The Wolverines only had 15 points at halftime but their superior manpower began to show against the spirited sailors in the second half and the bench made the game a runaway. Backup tailback Alan Walker scored twice and reserve Harry Banks once. Mike Oldham completed the scoring on a 49-yard aerial strike from Larry Cipa.

The defense recorded its third straight shutout, allowing Navy only 71 yards in total offense.

Michigan		7	8	10	21 — 46
Navy		0	0	0	0 — 0

SCORING		STATISTICS		
			MICH	NAVY
Mich—Seyferth (1-yard run)		First Downs	25	3
Walker (1-yard run)		Net Yards Rushing	275	34
Shuttlesworth (2 pt. conversion)		Net Yards Passing	153	37
Walker (17-yard run)		Passes Attempted	16	15
Coin (38-yard field goal)		Passes Completed	9	6
Taylor (1-yard run)		Intercepted By	0	0
Banks (1-yard run)		Punting	5-50.2	11-44.1
Oldham (49-yard pass from Cipa)		Return Yardage	111	54
Coin (6 PAT'S)		Fumbles/No. Lost	2/2	3/3

Michigan 24, Michigan State 13

"It was an emotional game, as they always are, and our players gave it everything." So said Coach Schembechler at the close of this nationally televised October 9 battle in Spartan Stadium.

And it took just about everything to turn back the surging Spartans who were down, 10-0, at one point, then seriously threatened to take over the lead in third-period action before the Wolverines managed to turn things around again.

Two plays, each with just one second remaining on the scoreboard clock, had a lot to do with the final margin of 24-13. The first came at the end of the first half. State quarterback Frank Kolch rolled out to his left and dove a final yard into the end zone to reduce the Michigan lead to 10-7. The second came on the game's final play with the Wolverines on State's 1-yard line this time. The Spartans stopped the thrust short of goal, preventing the Michigan total from rising still higher. Thus, two seconds and two plays; had the results been reversed, the score would have been 31-6.

Michigan's yardage advantage on the ground was 322 to 59 and Billy Taylor had 117 of them despite an ailing shoulder which kept him out of action much of the time. Taylor scored a 38-yard touchdown the first time the Wolverines had the ball, then came back in the fourth period to tally another. Quarterback Tom Slade ran a 9-yard keeper for the last one, while Coin had three extra points and a 27-yard field goal.

Reprinted with permission from the **Michigan Alumnus**

Michigan 35, Minnesota 7

The famed "Little Brown Jug" remained safely in Ann Arbor's keeping as the Wolverines set a Big Ten record for rushing plays (85), rammed in three long touchdown drives and buried the Minnesota Gophers, 35-7, on October 23 at Minneapolis.

Senior Billy Taylor, always a problem for Minnesota, turned in his best performance yet against the Gophers, rambling for 166 yards as the Wolverines amassed a net rushing yardage of 391.

Michigan 63, Iowa 7

November 6	Ann Arbor	Attendance 72,467

The Wolverines put on their most awesome display of the season, smashing through Iowa for 63 points and 493 yards rushing while holding the Hawkeyes to eight yards on the ground. Place kicker Dana Coin set an NCAA record, running his extra point string to 51.

Sophomore fullback Ed Shuttlesworth took advantage of a chance to start and scored three touchdowns and gained 112 yards. Alan Walker came off the bench to score twice while Tom Slade showed the Wolverine aerial arm, hitting Bo Rather with a 24-yard scoring strike.

The Michigan defense was just as strong, intercepting three Iowa passes, recovering a fumble and holding the Hawks to only 97 yards in total offense.

Michigan	14	7	28	14 — 63
Iowa	0	7	0	0 — 7

SCORING / STATISTICS

Mich—Shuttlesworth (5-yard run)
Shuttlesworth (3-yard run)
Shuttlesworth (3-yard run)
Taylor (5-yard run)
Doughty (2-yard run)
Rather (24-yard pass from Slade)
Walker (28-yard run)
Thornbladh (3-yard run)
Walker (9-yard run)
Coin (9 PAT'S)
Iowa—Triplett (11-yard pass from Sunderman)
Kokolus (1 PAT)

	MICH		IOWA
First Downs	30		8
Net Yards Rushing	493		8
Net Yards Passing	66		89
Passes Attempted	6		26
Passes Completed	3		1
Intercepted By	3		1
Punting	4-38.7		9-38.2
Return Yardage	82		203
Fumbles/No. Lost	4/2		3/1

Michigan 10, Ohio State 7

The marbles had been won by the time Saturday, November 20, arrived. The Big Ten championship was locked up. So was the Rose Bowl. But there are always plenty of incentives lying around unused when Michigan goes against Ohio State.

The largest crowd in modern collegiate football history (104,016) gathered on this ominous Saturday afternoon and the Michigan Stadium playing surface was white with sleet as the kick-off neared.

Michigan put together three solid offensive drives in the first half but came up with only a 3-0 lead at half-time. One drive was stopped when the tenacious Buckeyes halted Ed Shuttlesworth on fourth and inches at the Ohio 23, and another went for zero when Billy Taylor fumbled deep in Buckeye-land.

Ohio's fine defensive back Tom Campana sent the Scarlet and Gray followers into a delighted frenzy when he shot 85 yards for a touchdown late in the third quarter on a punt return. That made it 7-3 Ohio, and it stayed that way as the Michigan tension mounted. Just over seven minutes of playing time remained when the Wolverines took over on their own 28-yard line.

Michigan, with its backs to the upset wall, powered down the field with second string quarterback Larry Cipa in command. Three times Michigan came up with a third and long yardage situation. Twice they made the precious territory on the third try. On the last one, with third and five at the Ohio 28, the Buckeyes stopped Taylor inches short, but Fullback Fritz Seyferth leaped head-first through the line for the first down.

On the next play, a quarterback option, Cipa timed his pitch to Taylor perfectly. Taylor burst around the corner. Seyferth delivered a memorable block on Campana and Billy Taylor romped into the end zone.

Michigan 20, Purdue 17

There weren't many leaves raked in Ann Arbor yards on the afternoon of November 13. Thousands of Wolverine fans fully intended to clean up their premises that afternoon as Michigan went against an aroused Purdue football team in Lafayette, Ind. But the cliff-hanger the two teams put on kept the Michigan fans who hadn't made the trip on the edge of their radios.

It wasn't until only 43 seconds showed on the Ross-Ade Stadium clock that Dana Coin kicked a field goal to give Michigan a 20-17 win, a Big Ten championship and the coveted trip to the Rose Bowl.

Michigan took a 10-7 lead into the dressing room at halftime, but Purdue erased that when, on the fourth play from scrimmage in the second half, the Boilermakers' Gary Danielson whipped a touchdown pass to flanker Daryl Stingley.

Michigan went back on top, 17-14, with an 83-yard drive with Glenn Doughty scoring. Purdue came back with a field goal and Michigan drove 59 yards in the final 4½ minutes to set up Coin's winning boot. The Blue had a 307-to-125 superiority in net yards rushing.

Ohio State Coach Woody Hayes disputed the call on a Michigan interception of a dying-moments Ohio State pass. Here, he argues with the referee, which brought him a 15-yard penalty. Seconds later he tore up the down markers on the sideline.

Wolverine Honors in '71

All-Americans

...ety	Tom Darden (Coaches, Football News)
...ebacker	Mike Taylor (Coaches, AP, UPI, Football News, Writers)
...ard	Reggie McKenzie (AP, UPI, Football News, Writers)
...ilback	Billy Taylor (Football News)

All-American Second Team

...fety	Tom Darden (UPI, AP)
...ilback	Billy Taylor (UPI, Captains)

All-American Third Team

...ilback	Billy Taylor (AP)
...efensive End	Mike Keller (UPI, AP)

Sophomore All-American

...llback	Ed Shuttlesworth (Football News)
...efensive Tackle	David Gallagher (Football News)

Reggie McKenzie

Tom Darden

Mike Taylor

Bill Taylor

Michigan's 1971 Statistics

(12-Game Totals)
INDIVIDUAL

RUSHING

	Att.	Gain	Loss	Net	Ave.	LP
...aylor	249	1358	61	1297	5.2	66
...uttlesworth	182	877	2	875	4.8	28
Doughty	98	490	16	474	4.9	32
Walker	65	407	4	403	6.2	42
Slade	77	365	99	266	3.5	25
Seyferth	56	195	1	194	3.5	14
Thornbladh	30	125	1	124	4.1	11
Banks	21	115	6	109	5.2	31
...ather	6	68	0	68	11.3	20
Cipa	21	80	14	66	3.1	15
Gustafson	5	30	3	27	5.4	17
Haslerig	4	25	0	25	6.2	11
Casey	17	69	54	15	0.9	29
Coleman	3	19	4	15	5.0	12
McBride	4	15	6	9	2.2	11
Zuccarelli	3	7	0	7	2.3	3
Szydlowski	1	4	0	4	4.0	4

(Players returning in bold face type)

PASSING

	Att	Comp	Int	Yards	TDs	LP
Slade	63	27	4	364	2	28
Casey	34	14	1	165	1	32
Cipa	25	27	2	146	2	49
McBride	3	2	0	34	0	22

SCORING

	TDr	TDp	TDo	PAT K	PAT P/R	FG	TP
Coin	0	0	0	55/55	0	8/14	79
...Taylor	13	0	0	0	0	0	78
...huttlesworth	6	0	0	0	1/1	0	38
Doughty	5	1	0	0	0	0	36
Seyferth	5	0	0	0	0	0	30
Walker	5	0	0	0	0	0	30
Banks	4	0	0	0	0	0	24
...Rather	1	2	1	0	0	0	24
Slade	4	0	0	0	0	0	24
Thornbladh	4	0	0	0	0	0	24
Darden	0	0	2	0	0	0	12
Elliott	0	0	1	0	0	0	6
Gustafson	0	1	0	0	0	0	6
Oldham	0	1	0	0	0	0	6
two safeties	.	.	.	.	.	.	4

TDr — run   TDp — pass   TDo — other

RECEIVING

	No.	Yards	TDs	LP
Doughty	16	203	1	22
Rather	11	181	2	32
Oldham	7	136	1	49
Seymour	6	63	0	13
Gustafson	4	57	1	28
Haslerig	3	49	0	22
Seal	1	13	0	13
Seyferth	1	5	0	5
B. Taylor	1	2	0	2

BLOCKED KICKS

M. Taylor —— 1 field goal blocked.

PUNTING

	No.	Yards	Ave	LP
Dotzauer	60	2416	40.3	56

PUNT RETURNS

	No.	Yards	Ave	LP
Darden	24	237	9.9	47
B. Elliott	26	202	7.8	36
Drake	2	23	11.5	25
D. Elliott	1	10	10.0	10

FUMBLES RECOVERED

4	Keller
2	Carpenter
2	**Dotzauer**
2	Gusich
2	**Ellis**
1	Beckman
1	Coin
1	**Coleman**
1	**Coyle**
1	Drake
1	B. Elliott
1	**Grambau**
1	Kee
1	**Rather**
1	Spearman
1	M. Taylor
1	**Warner**

PASSES BROKEN UP

9	B. Elliott
7	M. Taylor
3	Darden
3	Kee
3	Logan
3	Steger
2	Carpenter
1	Coin
1	Beckman
1	Drake
1	Eaton
1	Ellis
1	Gallagher
1	Grambau
1	Gusich
1	Sexton
1	Williamson

KICKOFF RETURNS

	No.	Yards	Ave	LP
Rather	12	240	20.0	30
Banks	5	120	24.0	45
Doughty	3	50	16.7	21
B. Taylor	2	36	18.0	22
Gustafson	1	21	21.0	21
Oldham	1	8	8.0	8
Schumacher	1	0	0.0	0
Seymour	1	0	0.0	0

INTERCEPTIONS

	No.	Yards	TDs	LP		No.	Yards	TD	LP
Darden	4	163	2	92	Kee	2	0	0	0
M. Taylor	2	9	0	9	**Gallagher**	1	3	0	3
Gusich	2	2	0	2	Keller	1	0	0	0
B. Elliott	2	0	0	0	Rosema	1	0	0	0

TEAM

	Mich.	Opp.		Mich.	Opp.
First Downs	271	146	Pass Completions	50	128
Rushing	229	53	Passing Yardage	709	1571
Passing	34	77	Passes Inter-		
Penalties	8	16	cepted by	15	7
Total Offensive			Punt Returns	53	31
Plays	967	699	Punt Ret. Yardage	472	284
Total Offensive			Fumbles/Lost	27/13	36/25
Yards	4687	2360	Penalties/Yds.	54/613	43/365
Rushing Attempts	842	441	No. of Punts	60	84
Rushing Yardage	3978	789	Avg. Distance	40.3	40.0
Passing Attempts	125	258			

SCORING					
STANFORD	0	0	3	10	— 13
MICHIGAN	0	3	0	9	— 12

TOUCHDOWNS: MICHIGAN — Fritz Seyferth
STANFORD — Jackie Brown
CONVERSIONS: MICHIGAN — Dana Coin (by kick)
STANFORD — Rod Garcia (by kick)
FIELD GOALS: MICHIGAN — Dana Coin 1 (30 yards)
STANFORD — Rod Garcia 2 (42 and 31 yards)
SAFETY: MICHIGAN — Ed Shuttlesworth, by tackle

	Stanford	Michig..
First downs	22	1..
By rushing	4	1..
By passing	18	C
By penalty	0	C
Number attempts		
rushing	23	74
Yards rushing	118	290
Yards lost rushing	25	26
Net yards rushing	93	264
Net yards passing	290	26
Passes attempted	44	11
Passes completed	24	3
Had intercepted	0	1
Total offensive plays . . .	67	85
Total net yards	383	290

The 1971 Michigan football team set three major goals for itself before the season ever started — winning the Big Ten championship outright (they did), winning all eleven of the regular season games (they did), and winning the Rose Bowl game. They came within 12 seconds of accomplishing that, too, but a superb Stanford team took it away with some last-minute heroics culminating in a 31-yard field goal that gave the Indians the victory, 13-12.

To say that it was a bitterly disappointing finish to a fine season is putting it blandly. "The whole story of the game is that we didn't get the first downs," Head Coach Bo Schembechler said as darkness closed in on the picturesque stadium in Arroyo Seco and the crowd of 103,154 moved to their cars and buses. "We didn't play well offensively. Stanford deserved to win."

The one-point loss was keenly disappointing to the thousands of Michigan rooters attending the 50th Rose Bowl game, among them the 900-plus alumni who took part in the Alumni Association's Rose Bowl tour from Detroit and Chicago. But it was just about the only off-night in a splendid week of alumni activity on the West Coast for the tour participants, nearly half of whom opted for a two-night extension in either San Francisco or Las Vegas.

After more than a week of rain, the Southern California weather cleared for the Wolverine rooters the day after the charter planes landed in Los Angeles. It stayed beautiful all week long as the tour participants took in the many Los Angeles attractions, heard the Michigan Marching Band in concert on the lawn of the Ambassador Hotel, attended the Big Ten Dinner of Champions and a special New Year's Eve party.

The sun rose brightly on the morning of January 1 as the Michigan group reached the site of the Rose Bowl parade in Pasadena. Excitement mounted as kick-off time neared and many on the Michigan side of the field thought back to two years ago when Schembechler suffered the heart attack just hours before the Wolverines, stunned by that announcement, lost to Southern California.

This year's contest started out as a defensive struggle. All Stanford could muster in the way of a scoring

threat in the first half was two long field goal a[t]tempts, neither one of which came close. Michiga[n] punched out the best drive in the first half, movin[g] 59 yards in 17 plays and scoring on Dana Coin[']s eighth field goal of the season, a 30-yarder, for a 3[-0] half-time lead.

In the third quarter, the Wolverines pounded o[ut] yardage on the ground down to a first down on Stan[ford's nine. Ordinarily very effective at that rang[e,] Michigan was stopped on the one by a great Stanfor[d] forward wall. It gave the Indians new strength an[d] they moved down the soggy turf for a tying field goa[l.]

Michigan then ripped off a 71-yard drive with ful[l-]back Fritz Seyferth plunging into the end zone t[o] put the Wolverines ahead, 10-3, after Coin cashe[d] in his 55th straight extra-point attempt of the yea[r.]

Stanford's quarterback, Don Bunce (voted the mo[st] valuable player of the game) brought the Indian[s] back, however. They roared 67 yards for a score, th[e] tally coming on a sprint through the line when Mich[-]igan was obviously protecting against the pass, makin[g] it 10-10.

Shortly after, Michigan tried a long field goal an[d] Stanford's Jim Ferguson grabbed Coin's kick in th[e] end zone and started out. Seeing a wall of Wolver[-]ines closing in, he started to retreat and was downe[d] in the end zone by Michigan's Ed Shuttlesworth fo[r] a two-point safety, giving the Blue a 12-10 lead.

Michigan couldn't move after receiving the kick-of[f] and it proved fatal. Bunce moved the Indians dow[n] the field with pin-point passing until — with 12 sec[-]onds showing — he had his team in beautiful field goal position. Rod Garcia, who had missed five field goal attempts in Stanford's embarrassing 13-12 loss to San Jose State earlier in the season, atoned for his previous errors by booting the fall through the up[-]rights for the victory.

"It's a hell of a thing to lose the Rose Bowl when we had it won," said Schembechler. Nobody was inclined to disagree with him.

the ROSE BOWL

Michigan's Oosterbaan

As an athlete, a coach, a person, Benjamin Gaylord osterbaan for 48 years has offered his special commit- ent to excellence in athletics at Michigan.

He was three times a football All-American as well an All-Time All-American, the Big Ten's leading hit- r in baseball, a basketball All-American, football cap- in, and coach who produced championships his first ree seasons and won 66 per cent of all his games.

His accomplishments as a man were immense and gure heavily in what is known as Michigan Tradition.

This 1972 Gridiron Guide is dedicated to Bennie osterbaan.

AP Poll (1972)
1. Southern Cal.
2. Oklahoma
3. Texas
4. Nebraska
5. Auburn
6. MICHIGAN
7. Alabama
8. Tennessee
9. Ohio State
10. Penn State

UPI Poll (1972)
1. Southern Cal.
2. Oklahoma
3. Ohio State
4. Alabama
5. Texas
6. MICHIGAN
7. Auburn
8. Penn State
9. Nebraska
10. L.S.U.

BO

77 PAUL SEYMOUR, 6-5, 250, sr., Berkley . . . two year starter at tight end who has been switched to tackle . . . will handle the key strong tackle position . . . considered to be one of finest blocking tight ends in country last year . . . extremely powerful . . . had good spring making adjustment . . . caught 19 passes, one for TD, in two seasons . . . brother of Chicago Bears end Jim Seymour . . . will be key man for Michigan . . . physical education major . . . born 2-6-50.

	Receptions	Yards	Average	TDs
1970	13	194	14.9	1
1971	6	63	10.5	0

Paul Seymour

Dave Brown

Tom Coyle

Randy Logan

41 RANDY LOGAN, 6-2, 192, sr., Detroit . . . did excellent job at short side halfback . . . moved from offense . . . proved to be great hitter . . . made 68 tackles, four for losses . . . was tough against sweeps . . . broke up three passes . . . has excellent speed and size . . . may move to safety to take advantage of natural skills . . . brother is a minister in Detroit . . . business major . . . born 5-1-51.

1972 Football Roster

No.	Name	Pos.	Ht.	Wt.	Class	Hometown
58	ARMOUR, Jim	OG	6-4	220	Jr.	Detroit
20	*BANKS, Harry	TB	5-10	177	Jr.	Cleveland
32	BANKS, Larry	MG	6-2	210	Jr.	Cleveland
85	BRANDON, Dave	DE	6-3	202	Jr.	Plymouth
6	BROWN, Dave	S	6-1	185	Soph.	Akron, O.
8	BURKS, Roy	DB	6-2	185	Soph.	Midland
46	CARPENTER, John	TB	5-11	175	Soph.	Detroit
12	*CASEY, Kevin	QB	6-2	175	Jr.	Grand Rapids
19	*CEDERBERG, Jon	TB	5-10	177	Jr.	Plymouth
24	CHAPMAN, Gil	WB	5-9	185	Soph.	Elizabeth, N. J.
70	CHERRY, John	OT	6-5	230	Jr.	Willard, O.
13	*CIPA, Larry	QB	6-3	203	Jr.	Cincinnati, O.
40	*COAKLEY, Gary	SE	6-2	197	Sr.	Detroit
39	COLEMAN, Don	DE	6-2	210	Jr.	Toledo, O.
73	COODE, Jim	OT	6-4	235	Jr.	Mayfield, O.
60	*COYLE, Tom	OG	6-0	233	Sr.	Chicago, Ill.
80	*DANIELS, John	SE	6-4	199	Sr.	Newark, O.
57	DAY, Mike	LB	6-1	201	Jr.	Livonia
84	DenBOER, GREG	TE	6-6	233	Soph.	Kentwood
25	*DOTZAUER, Barry	DB	6-1	162	Jr.	Cincinnati, O.
28	*DRAKE, Tom	DB	6-1	175	Jr.	Midland
86	**EATON, Don	DE	6-4	194	Sr.	Lancaster, O.
45	*ELLIOTT, Dave	DB	6-2	170	Jr.	Coral Gables, Fla.
68	**ELLIS, Greg	MG	6-2	223	Sr.	Connersville, Ind.
89	FEDIUK, Art	TE	6-2	212	Jr.	Livonia
9	FRANKLIN, Dennis	QB	6-1	185	Soph.	Massillon, O.
42	FRANKLIN, Glenn	WB	5-10	185	Soph.	Warren, O.
50	FRANKS, Dennis	C	6-1	218	Soph.	Bethel Park, Pa.
71	*GALLAGHER, Dave	DT	6-4	225	Jr.	Piqua, O.
92	**GRAMBAU, Fred	DT	6-2	234	Sr.	Ossineke
48	*GUSTAFSON, Larry	WB	5-11	176	Jr.	Mays Landing, N. J.
69	HAINRIHAR, Gary	C	6-2	220	Jr.	Cicero, Ill.
22	HARDEN, Linwood	DB	6-1	185	Soph.	Detroit
56	**HART, Bill	C	6-4	227	Sr.	Rockford
43	*HASLERIG, Clint	WB	6-1	182	Jr.	Cincinnati, O.
44	HEATER, Chuck	TB	6-0	205	Soph.	Tiffin, O.
61	*HOBAN, Mike	OG	6-2	232	Jr.	Chicago, Ill.
93	HOBAN, Bill	DE	6-3	210	Soph.	Chicago, Ill.
7	JACOBY, Mark	DE	6-1	190	Soph.	Toledo, O.
35	JEKEL, Rick	FB	5-9	195	Soph.	Clio
82	JOHNSON, Larry	DE	6-1	203	Jr.	Munster, Ind.
27	JOHNSTON, Jim	Wolf	5-11	175	Jr.	Dallas, Tex.
21	KAMPE, Kurt	DB	5-10	165	Soph.	Defiance, O.
37	**KEE, Tom	LB	5-11	210	Sr.	Wheaton, Ill.
67	KING, Steve	OT	6-5	225	Soph.	Tiffin, O.
10	KOSS, Greg	S	6-5	180	Jr.	Cuyahoga Falls, O.
88	KUPEC, C. J.	TE	6-8	235	Soph.	Oak Lawn, Ill.
36	LANTRY, Mike	PK	6-2	220	Soph.	Oxford
41	*LOGAN, Randy	Wolf	6-2	192	Sr.	Detroit
95	LONG, Norm	MG	6-3	230	Soph.	Trenton
72	LYALL, Jim	DT	6-5	224	Jr.	N. Olmstead, O.
26	MACKENZIE, Doug	S	6-3	175	Soph.	Warren
76	McCLAIN, Mark	OT	6-3	225	Soph.	Thornridge, Ill.
62	MASTERSON, Kevin	MG	6-0	227	Jr.	Cleveland, O.
65	METZ, Dave	OG	6-2	225	Soph.	Harrison, O.
34	MUTCH, Craig	LB	6-1	203	Jr.	Detroit
97	PERLINGER, Jeff	DT	6-3	225	Soph.	Crystal, Minn.
29	PIGHEE, John	S	6-3	194	Sr.	Cleveland, O.
90	POLLISTER, Ed	DE	6-3	195	Soph.	Elk Rapids
79	*POPLAWSKI, Tom	OT	6-4	225-	Jr.	Warren
15	**RATHER, Bo	SE	6-1	180	Sr.	Sandusky, O.
33	RUSS, Carl	LB	6-2	215	Soph.	Muskegon Heights
63	**SCHUMACHER, Jerry	OG	6-2	224	Sr.	Chicago, Ill.
83	*SEAL, Paul	TE	6-6	213	Jr.	Detroit
55	*SEXTON, Walt	MG	5-11	200	Jr.	Massapequa, N. Y.
77	**SEYMOUR, Paul	OT	6-5	250	Sr.	Berkley
31	*SHUTTLESWORTH, Ed	FB	6-2	227	Jr.	Cincinnati, O.
17	*SLADE, Tom	QB	6-1	198	Jr.	Saginaw
74	**SMITH, Tony	DT	6-5	230	Sr.	Detroit
14	SPAHN, Jeff	QB	5-11	170	Soph.	Steubenville, O.
96	**SPEARMAN, Clint	DE	6-3	223	Sr.	Hamilton, O.
59	STRINKO, Steve	LB	6-3	235	Soph.	Middletown, O.
23	SZYDLOWSKI, Ron	WB	5-9	160	Jr.	Wyandotte
66	THOMAS, John	C	6-3	215	Jr.	Detroit
30	*THORNBLADH, Bob	FB	6-2	224	Jr.	Plymouth
75	*TROSZAK, Doug	DT	6-3	241	Jr.	Warren
78	*TUCKER, Curtis	OG	6-1	239	Jr.	Cleveland, O.
64	TUMPANE, Pat	OT	6-4	240	Soph.	Midlothian, Ill.
94	VanTONGEREN, Rick	DE	6-1	196	Soph.	Holland
52	VERCEL, Jovan	LB	6-0	214	Jr.	Highland, Ind.
54	WARNER, Don	MG	5-11	197	Jr.	Dearborn
91	WILLIAMSON, Walt	DE	6-4	224	Jr.	Detroit
53	WOJTYS, Ed	LB	5-2	210	Soph.	Detroit
16	*ZUCCARELLI, Dave	Wolf	6-0	196	Sr.	Chicago, Ill.

*Denotes letters won

1972

Michigan	7;	Northwestern
Michigan	26;	UCLA
Michigan	41;	Tulane
Michigan	35;	Navy
Michigan	10;	Michigan State
Michigan	31;	Illinois
Michigan	42;	Minnesota
Michigan	21;	Indiana
Michigan	31;	Iowa
Michigan	9;	Purdue
Michigan	11;	Ohio State

Season Summary
Games won 10; Lost, 1; Tied, 0.
Points for Michigan 264; For Opponents

Big Ten 1972 Statistics

	CONFERENCE GAMES				Pts. Ave.	Opp. Pts. Ave.	Off. Rank	Def. Rank	ALL GAMES		
	W	L	T	Pct.					W	L	T
MICHIGAN	7	1	0	.875	20.3	4.3	4	1	10	1	0
Ohio State	7	1	0	.875	24.9	12.1	2	5	9	2	0
Purdue	6	2	0	.750	24.5	7.6	1	2	6	5	0
Michigan State	5	2	1	.688	17.0	8.5	6	3	5	5	1
Minnesota	4	4	0	.500	18.9	22.9		7	4	7	0
Illinois	3	5	0	.375	18.6	19.5		4	3	8	0
Indiana	3	5	0	.375	16.4	25.6	8		5	6	0
Iowa	2	6	0	.278	8.9	20.3	10	6	3	7	1
Wisconsin	2	6	0	.250	10.4						

Ed Shuttlesworth

Dave Gallagher

Michigan 7, Northwestern 0

September 16　　　**Ann Arbor**　　　**Attendance 71,757**

Michigan unveiled its young Wolverines of 1972, but one facet of their operations hadn't changed — the defense. Using interceptions by Tom Kee and Craig Mutch, Michigan held NU to 49 yards passing in rolling up its first shutout of the season. The offense had problems, but soph QB Dennis Franklin did fire a 21-yard TD pass to Bo Rather. Fullback Ed Shuttlesworth gained 75 yards after entering the game in the second period.

Michigan	0	7	0	0 — 0
Northwestern	0	0	0	0 — 0

SCORING	STATISTICS		
	MICH		**NU**
Mich—Rather, 21-yard pass from Franklin	17	First Downs	10
Lantry (1 PAT)	199	Net Yards Rushing	129
	60	Net Yards Passing	49
	9	Passes Attempted	11
	4	Passes Completed	6
	2	Intercepted By	0
	7-40.4	Punting	8-40.8
	31	Return Yardage	22
	3/1	Fumbles/No. Lost	0/0

Michigan 26, UCLA 9

September 23　　　**Los Angeles**　　　**Attendance 57,129**

Michigan had its first big challenge of the season, traveling to Los Angeles to meet UCLA, conquerors of Nebraska. A bone-crushing ground attack by Michigan highlighted an excellent game that saw neither team commit a turnover. 'M' put together scoring drives of 74, 60, 80 and 53 while rolling up 381 yards on the ground and controlling the clock. Ed Shuttlesworth gained 115 yards and scored twice. On defense, the Wolverines put the clamps on Kermit Johnson and James McAlister, holding them to 38 and 36 yards, respectively, and throttling the wishbone.

Michigan	7	6	7	6 — 26
UCLA	0	3	6	0 — 9

SCORING	STATISTICS		
	MICH		**UCLA**
Mich — Haslerig, 4-yard run	28	First Downs	11
Banks, 2-yard run	381	Net Yards Rushing	189
Shuttlesworth, 1 yard run	41	Net Yards Passing	60
Shuttlesworth, 1 yard run	6	Passes Attempted	10
Lantry (2 Pat's)	4	Passes Completed	4
UCLA—Herrera, 39-yard field goal	0	Intercepted By	0
McAlister, 1-yard run	3-34.6	Punting	4-49.5
	53	Return Yardage	58
	0/0	Fumbles/No. Lost	0/0

Michigan 35, Navy 7

October 7　　　**Ann Arbor**　　　**Attendance 81,131**

For the second straight season the Wolverine attack sputtered in the first half against Navy but a 28-point third-quarter explosion locked away a 35-7 victory.

The Wolverine attack was ignited by Chuck Heater, who gained 94 yards rushing, almost all of it in the second half, and soph safety Dave Brown who roared 83 yards with a punt to tie a Michigan record.

QB Dennis Franklin fired 2 touchdown passes and scored once himself.

The Michigan defense was once again tough, holding Navy scoreless until a last-quarter touchdown pass.

Michigan	0	7	28	0 — 35
Navy	0	0	0	7 — 7

SCORING	STATISTICS		
	MICH		
Mich—Franklin (6-yard run)	18	First Downs	14
Rather (9-yard pass from Franklin)	299	Net Yards Rushing	64
Brown (83-yard punt return)	35	Net Yards Passing	145
Heater (13-yard run)	12	Passes Attempted	37
Seal (10-yard pass from Franklin)	3	Passes Completed	16
Lantry (5 PAT'S)	2	Intercepted By	4
Navy—Ameen (3-yard pass from Glenny)	8-37.5	Punting	9-35.5
Lanning (1 PAT)	97	Return Yardage	83
	4/1	Fumbles/No. Lost	2/2

Brief statistics	Mich.	Tulane
First downs	19	12
Net yards gained	350	205
Rushing net yardage	298	56
Passes attempted	12	28
Passes completed	5	10
Yards gained by passing	52	149
Passes intercepted by	2	0
Fumbles lost	0	0
Yards penalized	69	45

Michigan 41, Tulane 7

The Wolverines, amassing almost 300 yards on the ground, ran over an outmanned Tulane team, using early Green Wave mistakes to open a quick 21-0 lead and settle the issue.

Junior Fullback Ed Shuttlesworth ran for 151 yards and scored three touchdowns to pace the Blue. Said Head Coach Bo Schembechler afterward: "We are getting better and we will continue to improve. We still have a long way to go, but we will be a decent team."

Michigan 10, Michigan State 0

October 14　　　**Ann Arbor**　　　**Attendance 103,735**

In a crushing defensive battle, Michigan used the flying feet of Gil Chapman to post its second straight Big Ten win and shutout.

Chapman got loose on a fourth quarter end-around to outrun the Spartan defense for 58 yards and the game-clinching touchdown. Until that time, the Michigan defense had protected a slender 3-0 lead provided by Mike Lantry's 22-yard second quarter field goal.

Both defenses dominated and mistakes were prevalent. The Wolverines lost 2 fumbles and State one while the 'M' defense also picked off 3 Spartan passes. MSU was unable to complete a single aerial.

The key play, though, came on the Michigan 41 when State elected to gamble on fourth down. Clint Spearman stopped the thrust and one play later Chapman broke loose.

Michigan	0	3	0	7 — 10
Michigan State	0	0	0	0 — 0

SCORING	STATISTICS		
	MICH		**MSU**
Mich—Lantry (22-yard field goal)	19	First Downs	8
Chapman (58-yard run)	323	Net Yards Rushing	176
Lantry (1 PAT)	32	Net Yards Passing	0
	8	Passes Attempted	10
	3	Passes Completed	0
	3	Intercepted By	0
	6-35	Punting	7-47.7
	55	Return Yardage	29
	2/2	Fumbles/No. Lost	3/1

Clint Spearman

Fred Grambau

Dennis Franklin

Gary Coakley

Dave Zuccarelli

Michigan 31, Illinois 7

October 21	Champaign	Attendance 64,290

The Wolverines put on an awesome first-half display while vaulting to a 24-0 lead as they ruined the Illini Homecoming.

Chuck Heater gave a punishing performance, gaining 96 yards (155 for the game) and scoring twice in the first half.

Michigan rolled up 312 on the ground.

Dennis Franklin added 103 yards through the air and Gil Chapman ran a kickoff 73 yards for a touchdown.

The Michigan defense was just as tough, allowing only one score and stopping the Illini once inside the 10-yard line.

Michigan	7	17	7	0 —	31
Illinois	0	0	7	0 —	7

SCORING

Mich—Heater (2-yard run)
Shuttlesworth (1-yard run)
Heater (1-yard run)
Lantry (31-yard field goal)
Chapman (73-yard kickoff return)
Lantry (4 PAT'S)
Ill —Uremovich (18-yard run)
Wells (1 PAT)

STATISTICS

	MICH		ILL
24	First Downs		19
312	Net Yards Rushing		151
103	Net Yards Passing		105
12	Passes Attempted		20
7	Passes Completed		9
0	Intercepted By		2
2-38.0	Punting		6-35.3
121	Return Yardage		144
3/2	Fumbles/No. Lost		5/3

Michigan 42, Minnesota 0

October 28	Ann Arbor	Attendance 84,190

Michigan continued to improve as the Wolverines demolished Minnesota, 42-0. As against Illinois, Michigan did the damage in the first half, scoring 4 times with Ed Shuttlesworth gaining the final yards in every drive.

Shuttlesworth finished his short afternoon's work with 86 yards in addition to his 4 touchdowns.

The pass defense continued to show why it ranked among the country's best as the Gophers were held to 39 yards in the air while the Wolverines pulled in 4 interceptions, including one by Dave Brown for 68 yards and a touchdown.

The shutout was Michigan's third of the year.

Michigan	14	14	14	0 —	42
Minnesota	0	0	0	0 —	0

SCORING

Mich—Shuttlesworth (1-yard run)
Shuttlesworth (4-yard run)
Shuttlesworth (4-yard run)
Shuttlesworth (1-yard run)
Brown (68-yard interception return)
Franklin (1-yard run)
Lantry (6 PAT'S)

STATISTICS

	MICH		MINN
17	First Downs		14
245	Net Yards Rushing		161
111	Net Yards Passing		39
12	Passes Attempted		13
6	Passes Completed		5
4	Intercepted By		
5-44.8	Punting		6-36.6
52	Return Yardage		103
0/0	Fumbles/No. Lost		3/1

Michigan 31, Iowa 0

November 11	Iowa City	Attendance 43,176

Michigan rebounded from its mistake-filled Indiana game to put on another strong first-half performance in beating Iowa, 31-0. For the Wolverine defense, it was the fourth shutout of the season and kept it on top of the national stats.

With FB Ed Shuttlesworth out with a sprained ankle, junior Bob Thornbladh powered his way for 98 yards and Michigan's first touchdown. But the rest of the day on offense belonged to soph QB Dennis Franklin, who threw for 107 yards and 2 touchdowns, including a 37-yard bomb to the speedy Gil Chapman. He also rushed for 37 yards and another touchdown.

Michigan's other score came on Mike Lantry's 30-yard field goal.

Michigan	10	7	14	0 —	31
Iowa	0	0	0	0 —	0

SCORING

Mich—Thornbladh (5-yard run)
Lantry (30-yard field goal)
Seal (15-yard pass from Franklin)
Franklin (1-yard run)
Chapman (37-yard pass from Franklin)
Lantry (4 PAT'S)

STATISTICS

	MICH		IOWA
21	First Downs		13
251	Net Yards Rushing		117
107	Net Yards Passing		93
12	Passes Attempted		23
6	Passes Completed		9
1	Intercepted By		
4-32.5	Punting		5-32.0
67	Return Yards		151
1/1	Fumbles/No. Lost		1/0

David Fish
Senior Manager

Linwood Harden

SCORING

MICHIGAN	0	7	0	14—2	
INDIANA	0	0	0	7—	

TOUCHDOWNS: MICHIGAN — Dennis Franklin 2, Chuck Heater; INDIAN — Dennis Cremeens.
CONVERSIONS: MICHIGAN — Mik Lantry 3 (by kicks).

Michigan 9, Purdue 6

November 18	Ann Arbor	Attendance 88,42

Michigan claimed a share of the Big Ten title as the defense rose to its greatest heights and Mike Lantry kicked a pressure-packed field goal with just one minute remaining in the contest.

The two teams settled into a defensive struggle almost immediately. The Wolverines stopped Purdue's awesome attack on the Michigan 8 and forced the Boilermakers to take a field goal.

The 3-0 lead held up, though, as neither team was able to score for the remainder of the first half.

Michigan struck back instantly in the second half behind Dennis Franklin's passing arm. He hit Bo Rather for 20 yards and Clint Haslerig for 52, setting up an 11-yard scoring strike to Paul Seal. Lantry missed the extra point, though, and Frank Conner's field goal tied the score as the third quarter ended.

The Wolverines had not allowed a touchdown all day and they were not to allow even a field goal in the crucial last minutes. Randy Logan intercepted a pass with three minutes left to open the drive which ended when Lantry was called in to kick a 30-yard field goal, giving the Wolverines their third conference title in four years.

Michigan	0	0	6	3—9	
Purdue	3	0	3	0—6	

SCORING

Mich—Seal (11-yard pass from Franklin)
Lantry (30-yard field goal)
Pur —Conner (25-yard field goal)
Conner 20-yard field goal

STATISTICS

	MICH		PUR
16	First Downs		
100	Net Yards Rushing		126
143	Net Yards Passing		141
15	Passes Attempted		18
10	Passes Completed		9
1	Intercepted By		
5-37.2	Punting		4-42.7
62	Return Yardage		69
3/1	Fumbles/No. Lost		1/0

Ohio State 14, Michigan 11

November 25	Columbus	Attendance 87,040

Michigan's bid for a second straight Rose Bowl appearance was denied by fate and two goal line stands by Ohio State, giving the Buckeyes the trip to Pasadena and a share of the Big Ten title with the Wolverines.

Michigan started off dominating the game but a penalty killed the first Wolverine drive. The Wolverines finally got on the board early in the second quarter when Mike Lantry booted a 35-yard field goal.

But the Bucks retaliated with a touchdown drive and went ahead, 7-3.

Michigan then moved right back down field only to stall at the Ohio one as the half ended. Chuck Heater slipped twice on the wet field with the end zone in sight and on fourth down Franklin lost the snap from center, denying Michigan a last shot at scoring.

The Buckeyes came out in the second half and scored immediately, Archie Griffin racing the final 30 yards.

Michigan then tightened the contest up again by marching in for a touchdown as Ed Shulttlesworth powered in from the one. Franklin passed to Clint Haslerig for two points and Michigan was ready for its final drive.

But victory was denied in the fourth quarter as first Harry Banks, then Franklin, were stopped from the one-yard line. M had an edge in first downs 21-10 and passing and rushing.

Michigan	0	3	8	0 —	11
Ohio State	0	7	7	0 —	14

SCORING

Mich—Lantry (35-yard field goal)
    Shuttlesworth (1-yard run)
    Haslerig (2-point pass from Franklin)
OSU—Henson (1-yard run)
    Griffin (30-yard run)
    Conway (2 PAT's)

STATISTICS

	MICH		OSU
21	First Downs		10
184	Net Yards Rushing		175
160	Net Yards Passing		17
23	Passes Attempted		3
13	Passes Completed		1
1	Intercepted By		0
2-37.0	Punting		5-38.4
74	Return Yardage		45
1/0	Fumbles/No. Lost		0/0

Bill Hart

Greg Ellis

Jim Coode

Receiving

	No.	Yards	TDs	LP
Paul Seal	18	243	3	35
Bo Rather	15	197	2	14
Gil Chapman	9	125	1	37
Clint Haslerig	9	175	0	52
Bob Thornbladh	4	33	0	11
Chuck Heater	3	31	0	16
Larry Gustafson	2	18	0	9
Ed Shuttlesworth	1	14	0	14
John Daniels	1	16	0	16
Greg DenBoer	1	17	0	17

Interceptions

	No.	Yards	TD	LP
Logan	4	37	1	32
Brown	3	91	1	68
Mutch	2	18	0	18
Burks	2	24	0	18
Dotzauer	2	0	0	0
Kee	1	7	0	7
Koss	1	0	0	0
Ellis	1	0	0	0
Zuccarelli	1	14	0	14

Punt Returns

	No.	Yds.	Ave.	TD	LP
Brown	13	200	15.4	1	83
Chapman	20	180	9.0	1	49
Kee	1	6	6.0	0	6

Kickoff Returns

	No.	Yds.	Ave.	TD	LP
Chapman	8	276	34.5	1	73
Banks	2	37	18.5	0	29
Thornbladh	2	16	8.0	0	16
Haslerig	2	40	20.0	0	24
Heater	2	62	31.0	0	40

Punting

	No.	Yards	Ave.	LP
Dotzauer	53	2027	38.2	63

Michigan's 1972 Statistics

11-Game Totals

INDIVIDUAL

Rushing

	Att.	Gain	Loss	Net	Ave.	LP
Ed Shuttlesworth	157	726	3	723	4.6	33
Chuck Heater	139	670	15	655	4.7	22
Dennis Franklin	143	668	157	511	3.6	29
Bob Thornbladh	81	348	1	347	4.3	19
Harry Banks	70	278	5	273	3.9	15
Clint Haslerig	40	177	9	168	4.2	20
Gil Chapman	26	150	1	149	5.7	58
Larry Cipa	6	18	11	7	1.2	11
Larry Gustafson	3	7	3	4	1.3	4
Tom Slade	2	5	1	4	2.0	5
Bo Rather	1	4	0	4	4.0	4

(Players returning in bold face type)

Passing

	Att	Comp	Int	Yards	TDs	LP
Dennis Franklin	123	59	2	818	6	52
Larry Cipa	11	4	2	51	0	17
Tom Slade	1	0	0	0	0	0

Scoring

	TDr	TDp	TDo	PAT K	P/R	FG	TP
Ed Shuttlesworth	11	0	0	0	0	0	66
Mike Lantry	0	0	0	31/35	0	5/14	46
Dennis Franklin	5	0	0	0	0	0	30
Chuck Heater	4	0	0	0	0	0	24
Gil Chapman	1	1	2	0	0	0	24
Paul Seal	0	3	0	0	0	0	18
Bo Rather	0	2	0	0	0	0	12
Dave Brown	0	0	2	0	0	0	12
Bob Thornbladh	2	0	0	0	0	0	12
Clint Haslerig	1	0	0	0	0	1	8
Harry Banks	1	0	0	0	0	0	6
Randy Logan	0	0	1	0	0	0	6

TDr — run   TDp — pass   TDo — other

TEAM

	Mich.	Opp.		Mich.	Opp.
First Downs	219	142	Pass Completions	63	82
Rushing	162	88	Passing Yardage	869	932
Passing	47	44	Passes Intercepted		
Penalty	10	10	By	17	4
Total Offensive			Punt Returns	34	27
Plays	803	680	Punt Ret. Yardage	386	193
Total Offensive			Fumbles/Lost	22/11	25/13
Yards	3714	2372	Penalties/Yards	51/513	49/427
Rushing Attempts	668	480	No. of Punts	53	71
Rushing Yards	2845	1440	Avg. Distance	38.2	39.7
Passing Attempts	135	200			

Wolverine Honors in '72

All-Americans

Wolf	Randy Logan (UPI, Football News, Coaches)
Tackle	Paul Seymour (Football Writers, Coaches)

Sophomore All-American

Safety	Dave Brown (Football News)

All-Big Ten

FIRST TEAM

Offense

Tackle — Paul Seymour (API, UPI, Chicago Tribune)
Guard — Tom Coyle (AP, UPI, Chicago Tribune)
Quarterback — Dennis Franklin (Chicago Tribune)
Fullback — Ed Shuttlesworth (UPI)

Defense

End — Clint Spearman (UPI)
Tackle — Fred Grambau (AP, UPI, Chicago Tribune)
Defensive Back — Randy Logan (AP, UPI, Chicago Tribune)
Defensive Back — Dave Brown (UPI, Chicago Tribune)

Don Weir of Michigan

Don Weir has retired as Michigan's ticket manager, a job he performed with distinction for 26 years. During that period he directed the sale of 15 million tickets to Michigan athletic events and generally was regarded as the best at his job in all of athletics. He also became the friend of thousands of Michigan fans, a respected colleague of other managers around the country, and an important member of Michigan's administrative team. His duties were varied over the years: business manager, traveling secretary, accountant, and security director were among his tasks. This 1973 Gridiron Guide is dedicated to a grand gentleman, Donald A. Weir.

Bo's Record Third Best in Nation

Glenn E. (Bo) Schembechler, Michigan's 13th head football coach, is in his fifth season in charge of the Wolverines and during that time his teams have won 86 per cent of their games.

Going into the 1973 season Bo ranks third among all active coaches in winning percentage with a mark of .764·built over 10 years as head football coach at Miami of Ohio and Michigan.

During his tenure at Michigan Bo's teams have:

- Won 38 games and lost 6,
- Won or shared 3 Big Ten titles,
- Won 22 straight home games,
- Ranked in the Top Ten every season.

Meanwhile, Bo has been voted national Coach of the Year (1969) and the Big Ten's Coach of the Year (1972) as he compiled the best winning percentage of any Michigan football coach since 1900 (.864).

UPI Poll (1973)	AP Poll (1973)
1. Alabama	1. Notre Dame
2. Oklahoma	2. Ohio State
3. Ohio State	3. Oklahoma
4. Notre Dame	4. Alabama
5. Penn State	5. Penn State
6. MICHIGAN	6. MICHIGAN
7. Southern Cal.	7. Nebraska
8. Texas	8. Southern Cal.
9. U.C.L.A.	9. Arizona State
10. Arizona State	9. Houston
	10. Houston

Meet Don Canham

Don Canham became Michigan's fifth director of intercollegiate athletics in 1968 and since that time has maintained that the future of college athletics would be determined by the people who operate them. His belief in modern athletic facilities, inspired coaching and broad promotional ventures to inform the sporting public of the excitement of college athletics is being shared more and more by directors across the nation.

A track coach at Michigan for 20 years with a record of 12 Big Ten titles, Canham brought unique credentials to his job. He had been an NCAA champion high jumper, a team captain, coach and businessman. He once sold out Madison Square Garden for a track meet and has directed the highly successful NCAA Indoor Track Championships in Detroit since it was originated in 1965.

He is chairman of the NCAA Promotions Committee and a member of the important NCAA TV committee. His direct mail philosophy which puts ticket coupons in 4 million homes has made an impact with universities, large and small, throughout the country.

Some of the projects undertaken at Michigan since Canham's appointment five years ago include:

- 1968—installed twin electric scoreboards
- 1969—carpeted stadium with Tartan Turf
- 1971—constructed sports service building and lighted practice field.
- 1972—installed tartan outdoor running track
- 1973—reconverted Yost Fieldhouse to 8,000-seat hockey arena.
- 1973—constructed $1.1 million facility for indoor track, baseball, tennis courts.
- 1973—Proposed two new intramual buildings for campus areas and a conversion of old hockey arena into IM facility.

Michigan's 1973 Varsity Football Roster

Name	Pos.	Ht.	Wt.	Class
ARMOUR, Jim	OG	6-3	230	Sr.
BANKS, Larry	DE	6-2	200	Sr.
BELL, Gordon	TB	5-9	175	Soph.
BRANDON, Dave	DE	6-3	210	Sr.
*BROWN, Dave	S	6-1	188	Jr.
*BURKS, Roy	DB	6-2	190	Jr.
CAPUTO, Matt	DE	6-3	210	Soph.
*CASEY, Kevin	QB	6-2	180	Sr.
CEDERBERG, Jon	TB	5-10	185	Sr.
*CHAPMAN, Gil	TB	5-9	180	Jr.
CHERRY, John	OT	6-6	235	Sr.
**CIPA, Larry	QB	6-4	210	Sr.
*COLEMAN, Don	DE	6-2½	217	Sr.
COLLINS, Jerry	SE	6-2	185	Soph.
**COODE, Jim	OT	6-4	245	Sr.
COYNE, Mike	DT	6-3	250	Soph.
CZIRR, Jim	C	6-3	220	Soph.
DAVIS, Tim	MG	5-10	200	Soph.
DAY, Mike	LB	6-1	210	Sr.
*DENBOER, Greg	TE	6-6	233	Jr.
DEVICH, Dave	LB	6-2	210	Soph.
**DOTZAUER, Barry	DB	6-1	162	Sr.
*DRAKE, Tom	DB	5-11	175	Jr.
DUFEK, Don	Wolf	6-0	195	Soph.
*EATON, Don	DE	6-4	194	Sr.
*ELLIOTT, Dave	DB	6-1	170	Jr.
ELZINGA, Mark	QB	6-3	195	Soph.
FAIRBANKS, Jack	DB	6-0	185	Soph.
FEDIUK, Art	TE	6-2	212	Sr.
*FRANKLIN, Dennis	QB	6-1	180	Jr.
FRANKLIN, Glenn	WB	5-10	185	Jr.
FRANKS, Dennis	C	6-1	223	Jr.
**GALLAGHER, Dave	DT	6-4	245	Sr.
GONZALEZ, Eduardo	TB	5-11	190	Soph.
**GUSTAFSON, Larry	WB	5-11	180	Sr.
*HAINRIHAR, Gary	OG	6-2	223	Sr.
**HASLERIG, Clint	WB	6-1	194	Sr.
*HEATER, Chuck	TB	6-0	200	Jr.
*HOBAN, Bill	DT	6-3	223	Jr.
**HOBAN, Mike	OG	6-2	235	Sr.
HOLMES, Mike	Wolf	6-3	195	Soph.
JACOBY, Mark	Wolf	6-1	195	Jr.
JENSEN, Tom	C	6-3	220	Jr.
JILEK, Dan	DE	6-3	205	Soph.
JOHNSON, Keith	SE	6-0	170	Soph.
JOHNSON, Larry	DE	6-1	200	Sr.
KAMPE, Kurt	DB	5-11	182	Jr.
KING, Steve	OT	6-5	245	Jr.
KOSCHALK, Rich	MG	6-2	205	Soph.
*KOSS, Greg	S	6-5	190	Sr.
*LANTRY, Mike	PK	6-2	210	Jr.
LEWIS, Kirk	OT	6-3	220	Soph.
LYALL, Jim	DT	6-6	224	Sr.
MACKENZIE, Doug	SE	6-2	185	Jr.
METZ, Dave	OG	6-2	235	Jr.
MILES, Les	OG	6-1	220	Soph.
MOORE, Frank	OG	5-11	220	Soph.
MORTON, Greg	DT	6-3	230	Soph.
*MUTCH, Craig	LB	6-1	210	Sr.
O'NEAL, Calvin	LB	6-2	222	Soph.
PERLINGER, Jeff	DT	6-3	235	Jr.
PRZYGODSKI, George	TE	6-3	215	Soph.
RANDOLPH, Chuck	DT	6-3	230	Soph.
RUSS, Carl	LB	6-2	215	Jr.
**SEAL, Paul	TE	6-6	215	Sr.
**SHUTTLESWORTH, Ed	FB	6-2	225	Sr.
**SLADE, Tom	QB	6-0	195	Sr.
SPAHN, Jeff	QB	5-11	175	Jr.
*STEGER, Geoff	Wolf	6-0	195	Jr.
STRABLEY, Mike	LB	6-1	218	Soph.
STRINKO, Greg	DE	6-3	213	Soph.
*STRINKO, Steve	LB	6-3	230	Jr.
SZYDLOWSKI, Ron	WB	5-9	175	Sr.
THOMAS, John	C	6-2	220	Sr.
**THORNBLADH, Bob	FB	6-2	220	Sr.
**TROSZAK, Doug	DT	6-4	240	Sr.
**TUCKER, Curtis	OT	6-2	230	Sr.
TUMPANE, Pat	OT	6-4	235	Jr.
VERCEL, Jovan	LB	6-0	214	Sr.
WARNER, Don	MG	5-11	195	Sr.
WHEELER, Alan	OT	6-5	235	Soph.
*WILLIAMSON, Walt	DE	6-4	224	Sr.

*Denotes letters won

Michigan's 1973 Season

(Won 10, Lost 0, Tied 1)

Date		Opponent (Site)	Mich.	Opp.	Attendance
Sept.	15	IOWA (Iowa City)	31	7	52,105
Sept.	22	STANFORD (Ann Arbor)	47	10	80,177
Sept.	29	NAVY (Ann Arbor)	14	0	88,042
Oct.	6	OREGON (Ann Arbor)	24	0	81,113
Oct.	13	MICHIGAN STATE (E. Lansing)	31	0	78,263
Oct.	20	WISCONSIN (Ann Arbor)	35	6	87,723
Oct.	27	MINNESOTA (Minneapolis)	34	7	44,435
Nov.	3	INDIANA (Ann Arbor)	49	13	76,432
Nov.	10	ILLINOIS (Ann Arbor)	21	6	76,461
Nov.	17	PURDUE (Lafayette)	34	9	56,485
Nov.	24	OHIO STATE (Ann Arbor)	10	10	105,223
		Average	30.0	6.1	75,131
		Total	330	68	826,450
		Home Average			85,025
		Road Average			57,822

Big Ten 1973 Statistics

Standings

	CONFERENCE GAMES						ALL GAMES					
	W	L	T	Pct.	Pts. Avg.	Opp. Pts.	W	L	T	Pct.	Pts.	Opp. Pts.
MICHIGAN	7	0	1	.938	30.6	7.3	10	0	1	.954	33.0	6.1
Ohio State	7	0	1	.938	38.4	4.6	9	0	1	.950	37.1	4.3
Minnesota	6	2	0	.750	24.1	24.9	7	4	0	.636	23.6	26.7
Illinois	4	4	0	.500	15.9	13.6	5	6	0	.454	14.9	14.3
Michigan State	4	4	0	.500	8.6	13.5	5	6	0	.454	10.4	14.9
Northwestern	4	4	0	.500	20.3	27.5	5	6	0	.454	17.1	27.2
Purdue	4	4	0	.500	18.4	20.3	5	6	0	.454	18.2	19.4
Wisconsin	3	5	0	.375	17.3	20.1	3	8	0	.273	19.6	21.5
Indiana	0	8	0	.000	12.0	28.5	2	9	0	.182	12.8	24.6
Iowa	0	8	0	.000	11.8	37.0	0	11	0	.000	12.7	36.0

Don Coleman

Mike Hoban

Doug Troszak

Carl Russ

Mike Lantry

Michigan 31, Iowa 7

Playing away from home against a Big Ten foe in the season opener always stirs up little gnawing worries, but the Wolverines, after sputtering a bit at first, banged Iowa, 31-7, at Iowa City.

Michigan looked a bit different in uniform (wearing white pants instead of maize), but not much different in their execution of a year ago when they defeated the Hawkeyes, 31-0.

"We felt Iowa would be vulnerable outside," said Head Coach Bo Schembechler, "We probed a little inside and then went to the pitch outside and it worked real well for us." It certainly did. Michigan rushed for 440 yards, completely dominating Iowa, especially in the second half.

Brief Statistics	Iowa	Mich.
First downs	14	28
Net yards gained	233	475
Rushing net yardage	118	440
Passes attempted	19	9
Passes completed	10	3
Yards gained by passing	115	35
Passes intercepted by	2	1
Fumbles lost	4	1
Yards penalized	0	70

Reprinted with permission from the **Michigan Alumnus**

Michigan 47, Stanford 10

September 22   Ann Arbor   Attendance 80,

Michigan's home opener came against a powerful Stanford team a the Wolverines shocked the nation by blasting the Cardinals, 47-

The Wolverines came out roaring, using a brutal ground attack tough defense that forced two Stanford turnovers. Within 12 minu Michigan had a 21-0 lead. The rout continued in the second quarte Dennis Franklin passed to Larry Gustafson for one score and M Lantry pounded field goals of 50 and 51 yards.

The Michigan pace slowed in the second half but the Wolverines s scored two more times and continued to frustrate Stanford. For day, the Michigan defense held the Cardinals to minus five yards ru ing while the Wolverine offense was racing for 335 total yards.

Michigan	21	13	7	6 —	47
Stanford	0	0	7	7 —	10

SCORING		STATISTICS	
Mich—Heater, 7-yard run	**MICH**		S
Shuttlesworth, 3-yard run	19	First Downs	
Chapman, 1-yard run	240	Net Yards Rushing	
Gustafson, 4-yard pass	95	Net Yards Passing	
from Franklin	15	Passes Attempted	
Shuttlesworth, 1-yard run	8	Passes Completed	
Chapman, 6-yard run	2	Intercepted By	
Lantry, 50-yard field goal	3-49.0	Punting	5-3
Lantry, 51-yard field goal	72	Return Yardage	
Lantry (5 PAT's)	2/1	Fumbles/No. Lost	
Stan— Garcia, 37-yard field goal			
Ishman, 19-yard pass from Boryla			
Garcia, (1 PAT)			

Michigan 14, Navy 0

September 28   Ann Arbor   Attendance 88,042

Michigan had a letdown after the great Stanford game and found itself struggling to defeat Navy, 14-0.

The Middies battled the Wolverines for every inch and the solid Wolverine defense was called upon to attain what was almost a necessary shutout. Although Navy got 20 first downs, the Mids could never penetrate the goal line and Michigan was able to capitalize on a fumble for one score and put together one drive for the other.

While Michigan's pride may have been hurt a little, the greatest blow was discovered after the game when it was learned that Dennis Franklin had a broken finger on his left hand and would be a doubtful starter in upcoming weeks.

Michigan	7	0	7	0 —	14
Navy	0	0	0	0 —	0

SCORING		STATISTICS	
	MICH		**NAVY**
Mich—Heater, 8-yard run	15	First Downs	20
Shuttlesworth, 1-yard run	268	Net Yards Rushing	83
Lantry (2 PAT's)	134	Net Yard Passing	173
	3	Passes Attempted	30
	1	Passes Completed	17
	3	Intercepted by	0
	8-38.7	Punting	6-37.1
	42	Return Yardage	43
	1/1	Fumbles/No. Lost	6/1

Larry Cipa

Chapman's 83 yard jaunt disheartens Ducks, 24-0

	Oregon	U-M
First Downs	14	12
Rushes—Yards	37-106	50-185
Passing Yards	161	93
Return Yards	3	110
Passes	17-38-3	7-16-1
Punts	9-39	9-39
Fumbles—Lost	3-1	5-2
Penalties	5-47	4-50

Oregon	0	0	0	0 — 0
Michigan	0	14	0	10 — 24

MICH—Thornblad 1 run (Lantry kick))
MICH—Seal 4 pass from Cipa (Lantry kick)
MICH—Chapman 83 punt return (Lantry kick)
MICH—FG Lantry 39.
A—81,113.

Gil Chapman

Michigan 35, Wisconsin 6

October 20   Ann Arbor   Attendance 87,72

In contrast to the MSU game, the track was dry in Michigan Stadiur and the Wolverines rolled up 523 yards in offense en route to stoppin Wisconsin, 35-6.

The Wolverines opened the scoring quickly as Dennis Frankli connected with Paul Seal on a 46-yard bomb. In the second quarter th ground attack, paced by Gil Chapman, began to roll. Chapman had 9 yards in the first half and one score as Michigan vaulted to 21-0 lead

The assault continued in the second half as Chuck Heater an Gordon Bell each scored on the Wolverines' patented option play. Th only break in the Michigan charge came when a pass was deflected t Wisconsin's Bill Marek, who raced in untouched for the Badgers onl score.

Michigan	7	14	7	7 —	35
Wisconsin	0	0	0	6 —	6

SCORING		STATISTICS	
	MICH		**WISC**
Mich—Seal, 46-yard pass from	29	First Downs	1
Franklin	415	Net Yards Rushing	10
Chapman, 3-yard run	108	Net Yards Passing	12
Franklin, 1-yard run	11	Passes Attempted	1
Heater, 4-yard run	5	Passes Completed	
Bell, 7-yard run	0	Intercepted By	
Lantry (5 PAT's)	3-36.3	Punting	8-42.
Wisc—Marek, 65-yard pass from Bohlig	48	Return Yardage	6
	2/1	Fumbles/No. Lost	

Michigan 31
Michigan State 0

Playing in a steady rainstorm, the Wolverines picked up their fifth and sweetest victory of the 1973 season on Oct. 13, by defeating Michigan State in Spartan Stadium, 31-0.

Before the kickoff, Michigan backers were apprehensive because the Blue had turned in two rather lacklustre performances in a row on the preceding Saturdays, and because State had lost by only four points to apparently powerful Notre Dame a week earlier.

But it was strictly no contest on this rain-soaked day as the Spartans dropped the ball nine times (losing it to Michigan six of those times), mounted no appreciable offense and in general looked as if their minds were on something else.

Michigan's Dave Brown ran a punt back 53 yards for the first TD and Gil Chapman zipped through the State line for an identical-length touchdown run to highlight the scoring output. Coach Schembechler said before the game: "If this rain keeps up, I just have a feeling this is a Chapman game because he's built near the ground and keeps his footing." It was. The speedy tailback collected 117 yards in all.

Meanwhile, the defense cut the Spartans off at the pass — and the run, registering its third consecutive shutout.

Clint Haslerig

Tom Slade

Reprinted with permission from the **Michigan Alumnus**

Kirk Lewis

Walt Williamson

Michigan 34, Purdue 9

The Boilermakers gave Michigan fans a bad case of nerves for half on November 17. The Blue was ahead by only 6 to 3 at the intermission down at West Lafayette, but they came out and took charge in the second half, running up 28 points in the final rehearsal for the big one in Ann Arbor against the Buckeyes.

Michigan's first-string tailback, Gil Chapman, stayed home with a groin injury, but his replacement, Chuck Heater, led the ground assault with 86 yards, and his replacement, Gordon Bell, picked up an additional 64.

And so the stage was set, once again, for the showdown against Ohio State in Michigan Stadium. On the line are the championship of the Big Ten, the Rose Bowl invitation, and, very possibly, the number one ranking in collegiate football.

Michigan 34, Minnesota 7

| October 27 | Minneapolis | Attendance 44,435 |

In a game reminiscent of past battles, Michigan beat Minnesota, 34-7, in a ground war to retain possession of the Little Brown Jug.

A total of only 11 passes were thrown in the game as line play became the key to victory and Michigan won on both sides. The Wolverine offense moved the Gophers for 275 yards while the Michigan defense was holding Minnesota to 106 yards and just five first downs for the day.

Ironically, Minnesota's only score came on a pass as Rick Upchurch and Vince Fuller connected on the halfback option late in the third quarter.

But Michigan had compiled a 27-0 lead by that time as the Wolverines cashed in on two fumbles in the first quarter and added a long drive for 17 points. On each of the touchdowns, Ed Shuttlesworth bulled his way into the end zone.

| Michigan | 17 | 7 | 3 | 7 — 34 |
| Minnesota | 0 | 0 | 7 | 0 — 7 |

SCORING

		MICH	STATISTICS	MINN
Mich—Lantry, 27-yard field goal		16	First Downs	5
Shuttlesworth, 6-yard run		275	Net Yards Rushing	106
Shuttlesworth, 1-yard run		50	Net Yards Passing	36
Bell, 2-yard run		9	Passes Attempted	2
Lantry, 28-yard field goal		5	Passes Completed	1
Bell, 1-yard run		0	Intercepted By	.
Lantry, (4 PAT's)		4-36.0	Punting	7-34.1
Minn—Fuller, 36-yard pass from Upchurch		103	Return Yardage	141
Goldberg (1 PAT)		4/1	Fumbles/No. Lost	6/4

Michigan 49, Indiana 13

| November 3 | Ann Arbor | Attendance 76,432 |

One of the greatest first half explosions in Michigan history highlighted the Wolverines 49-13 triumph over Indiana. In just 19 minutes of the first and second quarters, Michigan put 42 points on the board and basically ended the game.

The Blue wave began rolling when Chuck Heater raced nine yards for a score and moments later, Ed Shuttlesworth powered in for another score.

Then the big plays began to break. Heater broke through the middle, cut to the outside and raced 71 yards for his second touchdown. Gordon Bell soon scored from 29 yards out, and Dennis Franklin on the option ran 49 yards to score.

Steve Strinko returned an interception to the Indiana 10 and on the next play Bob Thornbladh scored to complete the point barrage.

| Michigan | 14 | 28 | 7 | 0 — 49 |
| Indiana | 0 | 7 | 0 | 6 — 13 |

SCORING

		MICH	STATISTICS	IND
Mich—Heater, 9-yard run		22	First Downs	14
Shuttlesworth, 1-yard run		385	Net Yards Rushing	81
Heater, 71-yard run		96	Net Yards Passing	176
Bell, 29-yard run		13	Passes Attempted	29
Franklin, 49-yard run		6	Passes Completed	18
Thornbladh, 10-yard run			Intercepted By	1
Shuttlesworth, 2-yard run		5-39.6	Punting	11-35.3
Lantry (7 PAT's)		140	Return Yardage	58
Ind — Smock, 5-yard pass from Jones		3/2	Fumbles/No. Lost	3/0
Cremeens, 8-yard run				
Stavroff (1 PAT)				

Michigan 21, Illinois 6

| November 10 | Ann Arbor | Attendance 76,461 |

Illinois came to Michigan Stadium with an attack based upon counter plays to offset the Wolverines' flowing defense and the results proved to be effective. But the Michigan defense was able to adjust and the Wolverines came out with a 21-6 victory.

In the first half, though, Illinois seriously threatened and Michigan found itself down, 6-0, through the efforts of Dan Beaver's field goal kicking. When Illinois fumbled late in the half Michigan took but four plays to score, Ed Shuttlesworth getting the last yard.

Gil Chapman's 33-yard dash gave 'M' an insurance TD.

The final score came in the fourth quarter on one of the rarest plays in football. Chuck Kogut of the Illini broke up an attempted pitch out and the ball bounced wildly. Paul Seal raced in for Michigan, picked up the loose ball, reversed his field and scored the clinching touchdown.

| Michigan | 0 | 7 | 0 | 7 — 21 |
| Illinois | 0 | 6 | 0 | 0 — 6 |

SCORING

		MICH	STATISTICS	ILL
Mich—Shuttlesworth, 1-yard run		18	First Downs	10
Chapman, 33-yard run		295	Net Yards Rushing	135
Seal, 20-yard run		36	Net Yards Passing	84
Lantry (3 PAT's)		4	Passes Attempted	20
Ill — Beaver 41-yard field goal		3	Passes Completed	8
Beaver 29-yard field goal		1	Intercepted By	0
		4-31.2	Punting	6-36.3
		113	Return Yardage	85
		6/4	Fumbles/No. Lost	3/1

'M' ties Ohio State; Rose Bowl decision awaits Big 10 vote

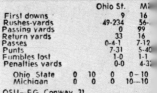

	Ohio St.	Mi
First downs	9	16
Rushes-yards	49-234	56-
Passing yards	0	99
Return yards	33	16
Passes	0-4-1	7-12
Punts	7-31	5-40
Fumbles lost	1-0	1-1
Penalties yards	0-0	4-3?

Ohio State	0	10	0	0-10	
Michigan	0	0	0	10-10	

OSU—FG Conway 31
OSU—Johnson 5 run (Conway kick)
MICH—FG Lantry 30
MICH—Franklin 10 run (Lantry kick
A—105,223

INDIVIDUAL LEADERS

RUSHING—Ohio State, Griffin 30-1
Greene 8-32, P. Johnson 5-22, Elia 4-
Lippert 2-4; Michigan, Shuttlesworth
116, Chapman 19-58, Franklin 4-17, Hea
5-12.

RECEIVING—Ohio State, none; Mi
igan, Haslerig 5-64, Seal 1-27, Sh
tlesworth 1-8.

PASSING—Ohio State, Hare 0-4-1,
yards; Michigan, Franklin 7-11-1,
yards.

Michigan 10, Ohio State 10

November 24	Ann Arbor	Attendance 105,223

Curtis Tucker

Craig Mutch

Michigan and Ohio State, which had won or tied for the last five Big Ten titles, finally played what must have seemed inevitable—a 10-10 tie before a record crowd of 105,223 and millions of viewers on national television.

Following a scoreless first period, the Buckeyes' Archie Griffin slashed his way to the Michigan 14 before the Wolverines stiffened and Ohio State settled for a field goal.

A clipping penalty on the ensuing kickoff cost Michigan field position and the Bucks scored again, freshman Pete Johnson blasting the final five yards.

The Wolverines began to move in the second half. They slashed up field, only to be stopped by an interception, but early in the fourth quarter, Mike Lantry kicked a 30-yard field goal.

The Buckeyes were immediately stopped and in only six plays Dennis Franklin had scored, daringly sliding into the end zone from 10 yards out on a fourth down play.

Then the dramatics became heavy. Michigan started a long drive but during it Franklin broke his collarbone. Lantry barely missed a 58-yard field goal attempt but Tom Drake intercepted to give Michigan one more chance. With time running out, Lantry's 44-yard attempt was wide and the two superpowers left the field deadlocked.

For the Wolverines, it closed an undefeated season as Ohio State won the Rose Bowl vote. It gave Michigan and coach Bo Schembechler their third consecutive Big Ten title and fourth in the last five seasons.

Bob Thornbladh

Buckeyes win Big Ten Rose Bowl vote

An Editorial

Why Is Big 10 Giving In to Woody Hayes?

THE PEOPLE OF WISCONSIN have a right to know how Athletic Director Elroy Hirsch voted on whether Michigan or Ohio State should represent the Big Ten in the Rose Bowl.

The excuse that the Big Ten Commissioner pledged the athletic directors to secrecy is not satisfactory. Neither Hirsch nor any other athletic director from a publicly-supported institution has the right to agree to such an illegal stipulation.

Hirsch evidently has "hinted" to some sports writers that he voted to send Ohio State. There is no reason to be so coy about the matter. He should announce publicly how he voted and give his reasons.

The secrecy on this matter is symptomatic of the whole disturbing trend toward professionalism in the Big Ten since Wayne Duke became commissioner.

BY THE STANDARDS of amateurism, fair play and good sportsmanship — which should be the hallmarks of inter-collegiate competition — Michigan clearly deserved to go to the Rose Bowl. Although the game ended in a tie, Michigan, on that day, was clearly the superior team.

By the rules which had prevailed until just a few years ago — no successive trips by one team — there would have been no question about Michigan going, since Ohio State had gone — and lost — last year.

But the Big Ten is no longer moved by considerations of equity and sportsmanship. Only winning counts. The whole prestige of the conference was riding on Ohio State winning the Michigan game and retaining its "Number One" rating.

Michigan is hardly an example of amateurism itself, but in this case it is being punished for having had the temerity to knock Woody Hayes' Ohio State out of the No. 1 spot, opening the way for the likes of Alabama or Notre Dame.

So the Big Ten, using the outrageous and cowardly excuse that a couple of Michigan players are hurt, has decided to give Ohio State another chance to retain its No. 1 spot.

For that to happen, Ohio State would hav on New Year's Day, Alabama and Notre Da to tie, Penn State would have to lose — but on? The whole thing is ridiculous beyond w

It is time for the faculties of the Big Ten to stop arguing about their parking space for and take a whole new, searching look at wh ing done in the names of their institutions athletic directors.

For a start, they should rescind the r rule, abolish the Rose Bowl pact, and ins round robin schedule among the member s Then perhaps college football can become a again and not a professional spectacle.

Don Eaton

Paul Seal

Kevin Casey

Barry Dotzauer

Larry Gustafson

Wolverine Honors in '73

Dave Gallagher

All-Americans

ckle.........Dave Gallagher (AP, UPI, Coaches, Chicago Tribune, Football Writers, NEA, Sporting News, Time Magazine)
afety..............Dave Brown (Coaches, Football Writers, UPI, Chicago Tribune)
cker...............................Mike Lantry (Football News)

All-Big Ten
FIRST TEAM

Offense	Defense
uard.....Mike Hoban (AP, UPI)	Tackle...Dave Gallagher (AP, UPI, Chicago Tribune)
uarterback.....Dennis Franklin (Chicago Tribune, AP, UPI)	Safety.....Dave Brown (AP, UPI, Chicago Tribune)
ullback......Ed Shuttlesworth (Chicago Tribune, AP, UPI)	Linebacker.......Steve Strinko, (Chicago Tribune)
ingback....Clint Haslerig (UPI)	

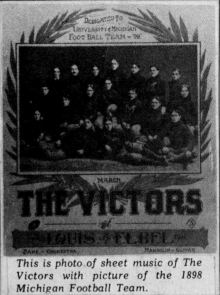

This is photo of sheet music of The Victors with picture of the 1898 Michigan Football Team.

INDIVIDUAL

Rushing

	Att.	Gain	Loss	Net	Avg.	LP
d Shuttlesworth	193	746	1	745	3.8	15
huck Heater	114	690	24	666	5.8	71
il Chapman	111	568	26	542	4.8	53
ennis Franklin	101	530	105	425	4.2	49
ordon Bell	88	475	11	464	5.2	24
ob Thornbladh	52	206	0	206	3.9	31
arry Cipa	24	91	31	60	2.5	15
lint Haslerig	7	63	0	63	9.0	34
ob Lytle	3	6	0	6	2.0	3
aul Seal	1	20	0	20	20.0	20
arry Gustafson	1	11	0	11	11.0	11

(Players returning in bold face type)

Passing

	Att.	Comp.	Int.	Yds.	TDs	LP
Dennis Franklin	67	36	5	534	4	46
Larry Cipa	35	13	2	163	1	10
Kevin Casey	3	1	1	10	0	10

Scoring

	TDr	TDp	TDo	PAT K	PAT P/R	FG	TP
Mike Lantry	0	0	0	42/43	0	8/13	66
Ed Shuttlesworth	9	0	0	0	0	0	54
Gil Chapman	6	0	1	0	0	0	42
Chuck Heater	6	0	0	0	0	0	36
Dennis Franklin	6	0	0	0	0	0	36
Bob Thornbladh	5	0	0	0	0	0	30
Gordon Bell	4	0	0	0	0	0	24
Paul Seal	1	3	0	0	0	0	24
Larry Gustafson	0	1	0	0	0	0	6
Dave Brown	0	0	1	0	0	0	6
Clint Haslerig	0	1	0	0	0	0	6

TDr — run   TDp — pass   TDo — other

Receiving

	No.	Yds.	TDs	LP
Paul Seal	14	254	3	46
Clint Haslerig	13	210	1	41
Keith Johnson	9	108	0	19
Bob Thornbladh	3	22	0	12
Jim Smith	2	28	0	18
Larry Gustafson	2	22	1	10
Gil Chapman	2	14	0	10
Gordon Bell	2	8	0	6
Chuck Heater	1	21	0	21
Greg DenBoer	1	12	0	12
Ed Shuttlesworth	1	8	0	8

Punt Returns

	No	Yds	Avg	TD	LP
Dave Brown	14	125	8.9	1	53
Gil Chapman	13	179	13.8	1	83
Tom Drake	9	139	15.4	0	54

Kickoff Returns

	No.	Yds	Avg	TD	LP
Gil Chapman	6	135	22.5	0	28
Clint Haslerig	6	127	22.4	0	31
Chuck Heater	4	84	21.0	0	28
Bob Thornbladh	3	36	12.0	0	18
Gordon Bell	2	47	23.5	0	23
Tom Drake	1	15	15.0	0	15

Punting

	No	Yds	Avg	LP
Barry Dotzauer	53	2111	39.0	63

Interceptions

	No	Yds	Avg	TDs	LP
Barry Dotzauer	3	13	4.3	0	12
Dave Brown	2	38	19.0	0	24
Tom Drake	2	12	6.0	0	7
Don Coleman	2	6	3.0	0	17
Steve Strinko	1	17	17.0	0	17
Greg Koss	1	3	3.0	0	3
Roy Burks	1	1	1.0	0	1
Don Dufek	1	0	.0	0	0
Carl Russ	1	0	.0	0	0

Fumbles Recovered

5	Dufek	1	L. Johnson
4	Drake	1	Steger
3	Brown	1	Eaton
3	Burks	1	Jilek
2	Russ	1	Troszak
2	Coleman	1	Warner
2	Mutch	1	Elliott
1	Williamson	1	Strinko

TEAM

	Mich	Opp		Mich	Opp
Total First Downs	211	134	Total Number of		
Rushing	165	65	Punts	55	71
Passing	35	62	Total Yards	2128	2542
Penalty	11	7	Average Per Punt	38.6	35.9
Total Offensive			Total Kick Returns		
Plays	800	661	Yards	57/871	59/949
Rushing Attempts	695	444	Punt Returns	36/444	22/182
Rushing Yards	3208	1075	Kickoff Returns		
Passing Yards	707	1321	Yards	21/427	37/767
Passing Attempts	105	217	Interceptions/		
Pass Completions	50	111	Yards	14/90	9/109
Total Offensive			Fumbles/Lost	30/15	44/21
Yards	3915	2396	Penalties/Yards	58/560	34/295

Michigan's 1974 Varsity Football Roster

No.	Name	Pos.	Ht.	Wt.	Class
66	ANDERSON, Steve	LB	6-2	220	Soph.
31	ANDREWS, Phil	FB	6-2½	225	Soph.
58	ARMOUR, James	OG	6-3	230	Sr.
20	**BANKS, Harry	DB	5-10	185	Sr.
32	BANKS, Larry	DE	6-2	210	Sr.
5	*BELL, Gordon	TB	5-9	175	Jr.
22	BOLDEN, Jim	DB	5-10	180	Soph.
6	**BROWN, Dave	S	6-1	188	Sr.
30	BROWN, Phil	DB	6-0	170	Soph.
4	BRUMBAUGH, Phil	DB	5-9	160	Jr.
48	CANADY, Al	DB	6-0	180	Soph.
13	CEDDIA, John	QB	6-1	190	Soph.
24	**CHAPMAN, Gil	WB	5-9	180	Sr.
29	COLLINS, Jerry	SE	6-2	185	Jr.
75	COYNE, Mike	DT	6-3	250	Jr.
52	*CZIRR, Jim	C	6-3	220	Jr.
56	*DAVIS, Tim	MG	5-10	220	Jr.
84	**DENBOER, Greg	TE	6-6	233	Sr.
55	DEVICH, Dave	LB	6-2	210	Jr.
28	*DRAKE, Tom	DB	5-11	175	Sr.
35	*DUFEK, Don	Wolf	6-0	195	Jr.
45	**ELLIOTT, Dave	DB	6-1	170	Sr.
16	ELZINGA, Mark	QB	6-3	195	Jr.
41	FAIRBANKS, Jack	DB	6-0	185	Jr.
9	**FRANKLIN, Dennis	QB	6-1	180	Sr.
42	FRANKLIN, Glenn	WB	5-10	185	Jr.
50	**FRANKS, Dennis	C	6-1	223	Sr.
54	GRAVES, Steve	MG	6-2	220	Soph.
53	HACKETT, Jim	LB	6-2	220	Soph.
70	HALL, Jim	OT	6-4	235	Soph.
44	**HEATER, Chuck	FB	6-0	205	Sr.
95	HEFFERNAN, Jack	DT	6-2	250	Soph.
46	HENEVELD, Bill	DB	5-10	180	Soph.
71	HENNESSY, John	DT	6-4	235	Soph.
93	**HOBAN, Bill	DT	6-3	223	Sr.
40	HOLMES, Mike	DE	6-3	200	Jr.
7	JACOBY, Mark	Wolf	6-1	195	Sr.
51	*JENSEN, Tom	C	6-3	220	Jr.
81	*JILEK, Dan	DE	6-3	210	Jr.
34	JOHNSON, Alex	TB	5-9	170	Soph.
27	*JOHNSON, Keith	SE	6-3	170	Jr.
82	*JOHNSON, Larry	DE	6-1	200	Sr.
21	KAMPE, Kurt	DB	5-11	182	Sr.
67	*KING, Steve	OT	6-5	245	Sr.
92	KOSCHALK, Rick	MG	6-2	205	Jr.
62	LANG, Bob	DT	6-2	240	Soph.
36	**LANTRY, Mike	PK	6-2	210	Sr.
74	*LEWIS, Kirk	OG	6-3	220	Jr.
25	LYTLE, Rob	TB	6-1	190	Soph.
65	*METZ, Dave	OG	6-2	235	Sr.
63	MILES, Les	OG	6-1	220	Jr.
93	MILLER, Aubrey	DT	6-0	210	Soph.
68	MOORE, Frank	OG	5-11	220	Jr.
77	MORTON, Greg	DT	6-3	230	Jr.
96	O'NEAL, Calvin	LB	6-2	222	Jr.
97	*PERLINGER, Jeff	DT	6-3	235	Jr.
90	PHELPS, Eric	DE	6-1	200	Soph.
80	*PRZYGODSKI, George	TE	6-3	215	Jr.
76	RANDOLPH, Chuck	DT	6-3	230	Jr.
33	**RUSS, Carl	LB	6-2	215	Sr.
37	*SMITH, Jim	SE	6-3	200	Soph.
14	SPAHN, Jeff	QB	5-11	175	Sr.
57	STEFAN, Terry	LB	6-1	210	Jr.
38	**STEGER, Geoff	Wolf	6-0	195	Sr.
85	STEPHENSON, Curt	SE	5-11	170	Soph.
49	STRABLEY, Mike	LB	6-1	218	Jr.
94	STRINKO, Greg	DE	6-3	213	Jr.
59	**STRINKO, Steve	LB	6-3	235	Sr.
57	SZAFRANSKI, Roger	MG	5-11	225	Soph.
69	SZARA, Gerry	OG	6-3	240	Soph.
89	TRABER, Pete	TE	6-3	220	Soph.
19	TRUITT, Darrell	Wolf	6-1	190	Soph.
64	*TUMPANE, Pat	OT	6-4	235	Sr.
39	VOGELE, Jerry	FB	6-3	235	Soph.
1	WHITEFORD, Dave	DB	6-1	185	Jr.
3	WOOD, Bob	PK	5-9	170	Jr.
8	ZUVER, Jerry	S	6-3	187	Soph.

*Denotes letters won

Michigan's 1974 Season

(Won 10, Lost 1)

Date	Opponent (Site)	Score	Attendance
Sept. 14	Iowa (Ann Arbor)	24- 7	76,80
Sept. 21	Colorado (Ann Arbor)	31- 0	91,20
Sept. 28	Navy (Ann Arbor)	52- 0	104,23
Oct. 5	Stanford (Palo Alto)	27-16	52,50
Oct. 12	Michigan State (Ann Arbor)	21- 7	104,68
Oct. 19	Wisconsin (Madison)	24-20	78,91
Oct. 26	Minnesota (Ann Arbor)	49- 0	96,28
Nov. 2	Indiana (Bloomington)	21- 7	32,87
Nov. 9	Illinois (Champaign)	14- 6	60,67
Nov. 16	Purdue (Ann Arbor)	51- 0	88,90
Nov. 23	Ohio State (Columbus)	10-12	88,24
	Average (for 11 Games)	30- 6.1	79,57
	Total (for 11 Games)	324-75	875,302

Home Attendance....562,105   Average at Home....93,684
Road Attendance....313,197   Average on Road....62,640

Big Ten 1974 Statistics

Standings

	CONFERENCE GAMES						ALL GAMES					
	W	L	T	Pct.	Pts.	Opp. Pts.	W	L	T	Pct.	Pts.	Opp. Pts.
MICHIGAN	7	1	0	.875	214	59	10	1	0	.909	324	65
Ohio State	7	1	0	.875	299	85	10	1	0	.909	420	111
Michigan State	6	1	1	.813	223	121	7	3	1	.682	270	196
Wisconsin	5	3	0	.625	240	179	7	4	0	.636	341	243
Illinois	4	3	1	.563	134	149	6	4	1	.590	210	206
Purdue	3	5	0	.375	171	218	4	6	1	.410	223	261
Minnesota	2	6	0	.250	110	241	4	7	0	.364	161	332
Iowa	2	6	0	.250	133	230	3	8	0	.273	157	308
Northwestern	2	6	0	.250	116	277	3	8	0	.273	140	385
Indiana	1	7	0	.125	124	205	1	10	0	.091	166	292

AP Poll (1974)	UPI Poll (1974)
1. Oklahoma	1. Southern Cal.
2. Southern Cal.	2. Alabama
3. MICHIGAN	3. Ohio State
4. Ohio State	4. Notre Dame
5. Alabama	5. MICHIGAN
6. Notre Dame	6. Auburn
7. Penn State	7. Penn State
8. Auburn	8. Nebraska
9. Nebraska	9. N.C. State
10. Miami (Ohio)	10. Miami (Ohio)

Bo Schembechler — Head Coach

Michigan 24, Iowa 7

An opener is always an uncertain thing — especially when, just before kickoff, you learn that your starting quarterback won't even dress for the game.

That happened in Ann Arbor on Sept. 14 as the Iowa Hawkeyes came to town with the intention of proving they were much better than their 1973 winless season indicated.

Just before game time, it was announced that Dennis Franklin, Michigan's premier senior quarterback, would not play. A virus had laid him low and recovery was slow in coming. Happily, second stringer Mark Elzinga proved a most capable replacement. Although his passing (two completions out of 11 attempts) left something to be desired, he directed the attack solidly.

As always, the Wolverines' defense was rugged. By the end of the first quarter, Michigan led, 14-0. Iowa got on the board late in the game with their only sustained drive of the day.

Reprinted with permission from the **Michigan Alumnus**

Steve Strinko

Dennis Franklin

Chuck Heater

Michigan 31, Colorado 0

September 21   **Ann Arbor**   **Attendance 91,203**

Dennis Franklin, back from the sick list, hit on 11 of 16 passes for 115 yards, rushed for 69 more, recovered a fumble in the end zone for a TD and David Brown returned a punt a school record 88 yards to score as Michigan won for the first time in four games over a Big 8 foe.

Soph split end Jim Smith caught five passes, a couple of them spectacular, for 50 yards, and tight end Greg DenBoer caught a 5-yard TD pass from Franklin. DenBoer's TD was set up by Gordon Bell's 25-yard run.

Senior defensive end Larry Johnson injured his knee and was lost for the season. Chuck Heater, playing his second game at fullback after two seasons at tailback, rushed for 74 yards, Lytle had 66.

Michigan	7	7	7	10 — 31
Colorado	0	0	0	0 — 0

SCORING		STATISTICS	
	MICH		COL
Mich—Brown, 88-yard punt return	21	First Downs	10
Franklin, fumble recovery in end zone	273	Net Yards Rushing	64
Heater, 6-yard run	115	Net Yards Passing	117
Lantry, 19-yard field goal	17	Passes Attempted	27
DenBoer, 5-yard pass from Franklin	11	Passes Completed	13
Lantry (4 PAT's)	1	Intercepted By	0
	4-40.2	Punting	9-37.5
	120	Return Yardage	143
	1-0	Fumbles/No. Lost	1-1

Michigan 52, Navy 0

September 28   **Ann Arbor**   **Attendance 104,232**

Navy, upset winner over Penn St. the previous week 7-6, ran into a buzz-saw as Michigan ran its total in three games to 221 plays without a turnover. Third straight win jumped Wolverines to 4th in AP Poll as second largest crowd in Michigan history saw the Band Day game.

Michigan's speed was evident as Gordon Bell scored 3 times, tackle Jeff Perlinger set up a TD with a pass interception in the Navy backfield, Franklin completed 5 of 6 passes for 85 yards, and Rob Lytle, used mostly in the second half, gained 101 yards in 15 carries.

"We got inundated," said Navy coach George Welsh.

Michigan	7	24	14	7 — 52
Navy	0	0	0	0 — 0

SCORING		STATISTICS	
	MICH		NAVY
Mich—Heater, 1-yard run	26	First Downs	10
Heater, 3-yard run	340	Net Yards Rushing	142
Bell, 3-yard run	119	Net Yards Passing	50
Bell, 25-yard run	11	Passes Attempted	16
Lantry, 31-yard field goal	7	Passes Completed	5
Bell, 2-yard run	3	Intercepted By	0
Smith, 29-yard pass from Franklin	5-38.6	Punting	8-38.9
Lytle, 6-yard run	38	Return Yardage	60
Lantry (7 PAT's)	3-0	Fumbles/No. Lost	4-3

Still No Turnovers

BY WAYNE DENEFF
News Sports Editor

Would you believe 221 offensive plays without turning over the football?

That's the most incredible fact about the Michigan football team. The Wolverines have defeated Iowa (24-7), Colorado (31-0) and Navy (52-0) and they have yet to give up the football by fumble or interception.

The Wolverines challenged fate a few times Saturday. Quarterback Dennis Franklin let the ball get away twice and reserve quarterback John Ceddia lost it once, but each time they made their own recoveries. There also were a couple of deflected passes when the ball was up for grabs.

Reprinted with permission from the **Ann Arbor News**

Michigan 27, Stanford 16

October 5   **Palo Alto**   **Attendance 52,500**

Dennis Franklin ran for 2 TDs and guided a 78-yard final scoring drive as Michigan rallied from a 9-6 halftime deficit for its fourth straight win. Franklin hit on 6 of 13 passes for 85 yards and rushed for 72 yards, while Rob Lytle added 96 in 17 trips.

Franklin directed a 94-yard drive in the third period to put the UPI's third-rated team ahead for the first time and later hit on three key passes, two of them 28-yarders to Jim Smith, for Michigan's clinching score. In between, Larry Banks set up a score as Michigan had 21 second-half points.

Michigan	0	6	14	7 — 27
Stanford	6	3	0	7 — 16

SCORING		STATISTICS	
	MICH		STAN
Mich—Bell, 1-yard run	21	First Downs	14
Franklin, 12-yard run	317	Net Yards Rushing	62
Franklin, 4-yard run	85	Net Yards Passing	229
Corbin, 2-yard run	13	Passes Attempted	40
Lantry (3 PAT's)	6	Passes Completed	21
Stan—Langford, 52-yard field goal	1	Intercepted By	1
Langford, 42-yard field goal	7-41.3	Punting	7-37.3
Langford, 42-yard field goal	82	Return Yardage	115
Laidlaw, 7-yard pass from Waldvogel	0	Fumbles/No. Lost	3-1
Langford (PAT)			

Michigan 21, Michigan State 7

"We did a poor job of coaching in the second half," said Bo Schembechler in the locker room after his Wolverines had beaten arch-rival Michigan State on Oct. 12.

"In the second half, we were sloppy. We should have run right at them. We should have stuck to gut football," the coach said. But, he added, "in a game like this, we are happy to win."

On a dark, drizzly day in Ann Arbor, the Wolverines picked up their 21 points in the first half, the third touchdown coming dramatically with five seconds left on the clock. Dennis Franklin arched a beautiful pass to Sophomore Jim Smith, who had somehow gotten completely clear of all Spartan defenders, for the tally.

The State score came in the fourth quarter after a pass interference call against Michigan had given the Spartans fine field position. State Quarterback Charlie Baggett rifled a pass to Mike Cobb deep in the end zone.　M

Dennis Franks

Michigan 51, Purdue 0

As though in dress rehearsal for the Big One down in Columbus, the Michigan football team smashed Purdue with an awesome thoroughness in Ann Arbor on Nov. 16.

The defense, nut-tough all year, turned in its fourth shutout of the season, limiting the Boilermakers to just 68 yards on the ground and 117 in the air.

Meanwhile, the offense, which has known less than brilliant moments on occasion, rushed for nearly 400 yards, plus another 185 passing. Senior Placekicker Mike Lantry used the occasion to set a Michigan career record for extra points (109) and booted three field goals.

"This," said a pleased Coach Schembechler, "is exactly what we needed to propel us into the big game next Saturday. The team is really looking forward to the Ohio State game. Don't underestimate us. We'll be ready."

Michigan 24, Wisconsin 20

With an upset uppermost in their minds, the Badgers of Wisconsin played a strong game Oct. 19 in Madison before succumbing to the Wolverines, 24-20.

"We knew Wisconsin would come back after last week (when Ohio State drubbed them). We're just happy to get out of here with a win," said Bo Schembechler.

The Badgers dominated the first half but could put only seven on the board. Michigan matched that before the intermission and then developed two long, time-eating drives in the second half to boost its lead to 21-7. Wisconsin wasn't through, however. The Badgers scored another TD, thanks in part to a Michigan pass interference call in the Blue end zone. Then the Wolverines drove downfield, settling for a Mike Lantry field goal, only to see matters tightened to 24-20 when Wisconsin scored again and then failed to convert on a two-point play.

Michigan 14, Illinois 6

Somehow the Wolverines manage to make things tough for themselves when they play away from home this year. It happened again Nov. 9 when Michigan absolutely dominated the first half at Champaign, Ill., but stopped itself time and again with fumbles and costly penalties.

As a result, Bo's boys left the field at halftime with only a 14-0 lead. Illinois came back with inspired football in the second stanza, scored once on a pretty punt return gallop and scared Michigan with an aerial bombardment as the game closed.

"We should have put the game out of reach in the first half, but when you're playing on the road and you let the home team off the hook, this is what can happen," said Schembechler.

And so now it comes down to the final two — Purdue at home and Ohio State in Columbus, an Ohio State that was upset on national TV by Michigan State.

Michigan 49, Minnesota 0

"The Little Brown Jug" stays in Ann Arbor for the seventh straight year as a result of Michigan's most powerful showing of the season, a 49-0 blanking of old-rival Minnesota on Oct. 26.

A Homecoming crowd of 96,000 watched in awe as the Wolverines pounded for a total of 620 yards on the ground and in the air. The Michigan defense didn't allow the Gophers even a smell of the goal line.

Brief Statistics	Minn.	Mich.
First downs	7	33
Rushing net yardage	100	521
Passes attempted	12	8
Passes completed	4	6
Yards gained by passing	49	99
Passes intercepted by	0	2
Fumbles lost	1	2
Yards penalized	38	10

Jeff Perlinger

Don Dufek

Michigan 21, Indiana 7

Michigan added win Number Eight down at Bloomington, Ind., on Nov. 2, but it was anything but easy. Fired-up Indiana, urged on by a small but vociferous crowd of 32,000, nearly pulled off the year's biggest upset. Michigan didn't get its third — and decisive — touchdown until there were only 36 seconds left on the clock.

"Indiana played a heckuva game," said a relieved Bo Schembechler. "They didn't give the ball away and we coughed it up three times (two fumbles and an interception). That was the story of the game."

So Near . . . So Close . . . So Frustrating!

Michigan 10, Ohio State 12

In the showdown, Michigan came up short.

Two points short.

Ohio State defeated the Wolverines, 12 to 10, as all the western world must know, on the strength of four field goals. And, the following day, the Big Ten athletic directors met in Chicago and voted to send the Buckeyes back to the Rose Bowl for the third straight year. They'll face Southern California on Jan. 1.

The statistical story was slightly in Michigan's favor — and how close the valiant Wolverines came in the last 18 seconds! Mike Lantry booted a 33-yard field goal just a few inches left of the upright to end Michigan's final, desperate rally. "Don't blame Lantry," Head Coach Bo Schembechler said after the game. "I'm not holding Mike responsible. We should have put the game out of reach by then.

"I feel real frustrated," he went on, "but I'm real proud of this team. They were a highly motivated bunch of kids who did a helluva job of rebuilding this year. We lost 30 seniors from last year. Ohio State had just about everybody back."

And so another football year is in the books. Michigan and Ohio State are once again co-champions of the conference with identical 7-1-0 records.

Brief Statistics	OSU	Mich.
First downs	14	18
Rushing net yardage	195	195
Passes attempted	6	14
Passes completed	3	5
Yards gained by passing	58	96
Passes intercepted by	2	0
Fumbles lost	2	1
Yards penalized	25	16

Reprinted with permission from the **Michigan Alumnus**

Jim Smith (37) Grabs Michigan TD Pass

2 U-M Players Very Bitter

BY CHARLIE VINCENT
Free Press Sports Writer

A couple of University of Michigan seniors, members of the Wolverine squads that compiled a 30-2-1 record in three seasons but didn't get a single Rose Bowl trip for their efforts, reacted bitterly to Sunday's decision to send Ohio State back to Pasadena.

"Maybe it doesn't sound like we've got too much class," said offensive guard Dave Metz, "but we want to express our feelings. We feel we've been done dirt the last few years and we're very bitter."

Metz and center Denny Franks called the Free Press Sunday after hearing the unfounded television report stating the vote had ended in a tie that would automatically send Michigan to the Rose Bowl, only to find an hour later that was untrue and Ohio State would again represent the Big

Ten on New Year's Day.

"From what we hear on TV it was a tie vote," Franks said, "and we would appreciate knowing who made the vote. We feel like we've been one of the top teams in the country the last three years and we've got nothing to show for it."

THE PLAYERS were going against an order from coach Bo Schembechler by commenting on the balloting.

"We're not supposed to be talking to anybody," Franks admitted, "but I've got to say something."

Reprinted with permission from the **Detroit Free Press**

NEW ROSE BOWL FORMULA

The new procedure has a four-point formula:

● The conference champion, determined by the highest winning percentage of conference games, will get the Rose Bowl nod.

● If there is a tie, the winner of the game between the two top contenders will represnt the conference.

● If there still is a tie and the two teams did not meet during the regular season, the representative will be determined by the highest wining percentage of all games played, including non-conference.

● If there still is a tie, the most recent team to represent the conference in the Rose Bowl will be eliminated from consideration.

In the event that more than two teams tie for the Big Ten title, the selection procedure may boil down to a vote by the athletic directors.

Michigan's 1974 Statistics

11-Game Totals

INDIVIDUAL

Rushing

	Att.	Gain	Loss	Yds.	Avg.	LP
Bell	174	1072	24	1048	6.0	39
Lytle	140	807	5	802	5.7	38
Heater	153	662	2	660	4.3	22
Franklin	108	425	135	290	2.7	20
Chapman	41	237	9	228	5.6	38
Corbin	29	160	0	160	5.5	16
Elzinga	20	115	18	97	4.9	49
Richardson	14	88	0	88	6.2	20
King	3	18	0	18	6.0	13
Holland	1	1	0	1	1.0	1
Moore	1	0	0	0	0.0	0
Ceddia	2	0	20	-20	-10.0	

(Players returning in bold face type)

Passing

	Att.	Comp.	Int.	Yds.	TDS	LP
Franklin	104	58	5	933	8	52
Elzinga	21	5	0	104	2	36
Spahn	1	0	0	0	0	

Scoring

	TDr	TDp	TDo	P/R	ExP	FG	TP
Bell	11	0	0	0	0	0	66
Lantry	0	0	0	0	40-42	8/20	64
Heater	7	0	0	0	0	0	42
Chapman	3	3	0	0	0	0	36
Franklin	3	0	1	0	2	0	26
Smith	0	4	0	0	0	0	24
Lytle	2	1	0	0	0	0	18
DenBoer	0	2	0	0	0	0	12
Elzinga	2	0	0	0	0	0	12
Corbin	2	0	0	0	0	0	12
Brown	0	0	0	1	0	0	6
Jilek	0	0	1	0	0	0	6

TDr = run   TDp = pass   TDo = other

Receiving

	No.	Yds.	Avg.	TDs	LP
Chapman	23	378	16.4	3	48
Smith	21	392	18.7	4	52
DenBoer	8	103	12.8	2	26
Lytle	4	65	16.2	1	36
K. Johnson	3	44	14.6	0	18
Przygodski	2	30	15.0	0	16
Heater	1	14	14.0	0	14
Bell	1	11	11.0	0	11

Punt Returns

	No.	Yds.	Avg.	TD	LP
Brown	21	206	9.8	1	88
Chapman	13	103	7.9	0	16
Hicks	2	20	10.0	0	10
Drake	2	13	6.5	0	9
L. Banks	1	25	25.0	0	25

Kickoff Returns

	No.	Yds.	Avg.	TD	LP
Chapman	12	231	19.3	0	30
Bell	1	40	40.0	0	40
Lytle	2	30	15.0	0	19
Smith	1	-11	-11.0	0	-11

Punting

	No.	Yds	Avg.	LP
Anderson	41	1577	38.5	55

Interceptions

	No.	Yds.	TD
Brown	4	73	-
Drake	4	30	-
L. Johnson	1	20	-
Perlinger	1	10	-
Devich	1	2	-
D. Dufek	1	0	-
Steger	1	0	-
H. Banks	1	0	-

Fumbles Recovered

2 S. Strinko	1 Davis
1 L. Banks	1 Jilek
1 Brown	1 Lantry
1 Devich	1 Morton
1 D. Dufek	1 Randolph
1 Elliott	

Passes Broken Up

4 Dave Brown	1 Dave Devich
4 Tom Drake	1 Greg Morton
4 Calvin O'Neal	1 Jerry Zuver
3 Steve Strinko	1 Dwight Hicks
2 Dan Jilek	1 John Hennessy
2 Dave Elliott	1 Mike Holmes
2 Harry Banks	1 Mike Strabley

TEAM

	Mich	Opp		Mich	Opp
Total First Downs	245	144	Total No. of Punts	41	7?
Rushing	186	73	Total Yards	1577	286?
Passing	54	61	Average Per Punt	38.5	38.?
Penalty	5	10			
Total Offenseive	812	659	Total Kick Returns	55/657	67/92?
Rushing Attempts	686	438	Punt/Ret/Yds	39/367	22/17?
Rushing Yards	3372	1163	Kickoff/Ret/Yds	6/290	45/74?
Passing Yards	1037	1190			
Passing Attempts	126	221	Inter/Yds	14/135	5/54?
Pass Completions	63	106	Fumbles/Lost	23/9	23/12?
Total Offensive	4409	2353	Penalties/Yards	38/384	43/365?

Wolverine Honors in 1974

All-American

DAVE BROWN, DB (AP, UPI, Coaches, Walter Camp, NEA, Writers, Time, FN)
CHUCK HEATER, RB (Churchmen's All-American)
KIRK LEWIS, OT, (Academic All-American)
STEVE STRINKO, LB (UPI, FN — Second Team)
DENNIS FRANKS, C (FN — Third Team)

Honorable Mention

DENNIS FRANKLIN, QB (UPI, FN)   GORDON BELL, RB (FN)
DON DUFEK, DB (UPI)   DAN JILEK, DE (FN)
TIM DAVIS, MG (UPI)   JEFF PERLINGER, DT (FN)

6 **DAVE BROWN, S, 6-1, 188, sr., Akron, O.** . .All-American safety. . .All-Big Ten for two seasons. . .premier defensive back in league, if not in country. . .has five interceptions, five fumble recoveries in two years. . .returned on intercept for a score. . .has two TD's as a punt returner. . .combines exceptional speed, quickness, hands and hitting ability. . .provides solid backline for Michigan defense. . .should reap honors again this year. . .speech (radio-TV) major. . .born 1-16-53.

	Punt Ret.	Yds.	Avg.	Tds
1972	13	200	15.4	1
1973	14	125	8.9	1
Totals	27	325	12.0	2

Rob Lytle

Larry Johnson

Gordon Bell

Dave Brown

Tom Drake

Steve King

...wman named to Hall of Fame

...ormer Michigan All-American ...arterback Harry Newman has ...en named to the National Foot-...l Foundation Hall of Fame. ...wman, who led the Wolverines ...a national championship in 1932, ...ow retired and lives in Pompano ...ach, Florida. He came to Mi...h-...n from Detroit Northern High ...hool and later went on to star in ...e National Football League with ...e New York Giants.

Band Facts

Conductor—George Cavender
Organized—1859 with 15 members
Present Size—235 members
Band Day—Originated High School Band Day in 1949 by Dr. William Revelli. First event featured 29 bands.
1975 Band Day—Baylor game Sept. 27 with 160 high school bands and 13,500 musicians.
Movies—First Big Ten band to be featured in a 'movie short' by major studio (RKO-Pathe).

Canham's Marketing Policy Pays Off at the Gate

Don Canham was appointed ...ichigan's fifth athletic director ... 1968 and since then the ...olverines have experienced the ...ost dramatic six-year growth in ...ootball attendance in the ...chool's history.

During Canham's first season ...e Wolverines averaged 67,991 ...ans for six home games, but in ...974 that figure had skyrocketed ...o an impressive 93,684. Here's a ...reakdown of Michigan's atten-...ance figures for both six and ...even-home game schedules:

Year	Attendance	Average
	Six Games	
1968	407,948	67,991
1969	428,780	71,360
1970	476,165	79,360
1972	513,398	85,566
1974	563,105	93,684
	Seven Games	
1971	564,376	80,622
1973	595,162	85,023

Of course, Bo Schembechler's record of 58-5-1 and two Rose Bowl appearances have played a large role in this steady atten-dance growth. But Michigan has had Big Ten and National Cham-pionship teams in the past, in years before television and when the entertainment dollar was not the object of such intense com-petition from professional leagues. "Even the best product on the shelf has to be promoted," insists Canham, who has brought a new marketing approach to intercollegiate football.

Canham's philosophy has been to "make it easy for a fan to buy a ticket." The cornerstone of this approach has been a steady increase in ticket information sent direct to the homes of potential customers. From a basic list of 'M' Alumni in 1968, direct mail ticket coupons are now sent to more than a million families in Michigan, Indiana and Ohio. Canham has directed a vast news-paper advertising campaign and put the Michigan football mes-sage between the covers of such magazines as Time, Fortune, Sports Illustrated, Business News — all on a regional basis.

But marketing has been only part of Canham's fast-moving administration. He has spent more than $3 million on new build-ings and facilities, and this entire amount has been financed through athletic department reve-nues. The budget has grown from around $2 million to more than $4 million in six years.

Some of the capital expendi-tures include two artificial grass football fields ($600,000), conver-sion of Yost Field House into a 8,000-seat hockey arena ($500,000), indoor track-tennis building ($1,000,000), outdoor track ($200,000), football service building ($380,000) and improve-ments in Michigan Stadium ($500,000).

Additionally, the old hockey rink was converted into an intra-mural building at a cost of $140,000 and given to The Univer-sity for student use.

And through promotions and retirements, Canham had to appoint new head coaches in football, basketball, hockey, ten-nis, wrestling, golf and track. Michigan's coaching staff has led the Wolverines to 22 Big Ten team championships in the last seven years.

Tim Davis

Don Dufek

Dan Jilek

Bob Wood

Michigan's 1975 Varsity Football Roster

No.	Name	Pos.	Ht.	Wt.	Class
86	*ANDERSON, John	DE	6-3	215	So.
66	ANDERSON, Steve	DT	6-2	230	So.
31	ANDREWS, Phil	FB	6-1	217	So.
61	BARTNICK, Greg	OG	6-3	225	So.
5	**BELL, Gordon	TB	5-9	178	Sr.
12	BETTIS, Roger	QB	6-3	185	So.
22	*BOLDEN, Jim	DB	6-1	177	Jr.
45	BROWN, Woody	S	5-11	175	So.
4	BRUMBAUGH, Phil	DB	5-9	160	Sr.
15	BUSH, Ken	Wolf	5-11	200	So.
14	CARIAN, Rob	QB	6-1	195	Jr.
29	COLLINS, Jerry	SE	6-2	185	Sr.
34	*CORBIN, Scott	FB	6-1	220	So.
52	**CZIRR, Jim	C	6-3½	225	So.
56	**DAVIS, Tim	MG	5-10	201	Sr.
55	*DEVICH, Dave	LB	6-1	210	Sr.
60	DONAHUE, Mark	OG	6-3½	237	So.
72	DOWNING, Walt	OG	6-4	232	So.
73	*DUFEK, Bill	OT	6-4	255	So.
35	*DUFEK, Don	Wolf	6-0	195	Sr.
16	*ELZINGA, Mark	QB	6-2½	190	Jr.
54	GRAVES, Steve	MG	6-1	217	So.
53	HACKETT, Jim	C	6-1	220	Jr.
70	HALL, Jim	OT	6-4	235	Jr.
83	HARDING, Dave	TE	6-4	223	So.
71	*HENNESSY, John	DT	6-4	235	Jr.
17	*HICKS, Dwight	S	6-2	180	So.
93	*HOBAN, Bill	DT	6-4	238	Sr.
40	*HOLMES, Mike	DE	6-3	210	Sr.
10	*HOWARD, Derek	DB	6-2	187	So.
7	JACKSON, Andy	DB	6-0	170	So.
51	**JENSEN, Tom	OG	6-3	225	Sr.
81	**JILEK, Dan	DE	6-2	212	Sr.
27	**JOHNSON, Keith	SE	6-0	175	Sr.
20	JOHNSON, Ray	S	6-0	177	So.
21	*KAMPE, Kurt	DB	5-11	182	Sr.
78	KENN, Mike	OT	6-6½	243	So.
36	KING, Kevin	FB	6-2	215	So.
67	**KING, Steve	OT	6-5	245	Sr.
99	KNICKERBOCKER, Steve	PK	6-1	180	So.
92	*KOSCHALK, Rick	MG	6-2	193	Sr.
62	*LANG, Bob	DT	6-1	230	Jr.
74	**LEWIS, Kirk	OG	6-3½	240	Sr.
41	*LYTLE, Rob	FB	6-1	190	Jr.
49	MACKALL, Rex	LB	6-4	215	So.
49	MANDICH, John	DB	6-1	184	So.
63	MILES, Les	OG	6-1	225	Sr.
77	*MORTON, Greg	DT	6-2	225	Jr.
50	NAUTA, Steve	C	6-2	227	So.
96	*O'NEAL, Calvin	LB	6-2	230	Jr.
97	**PERLINGER, Jeff	DT	6-4	242	Sr.
90	PHELPS, Eric	DE	6-1	208	So.
18	PICKENS, Jim	S	6-2	188	So.
80	**PRZYGODSKI, George	TE	6-3	215	Sr.
76	RANDOLPH, Chuck	DT	6-3	227	Sr.
26	RICHARDSON, Dennis	TB	5-11	182	So.
43	*RICHARDSON, Max	WB	6-1	187	So.
37	**SMITH, Jim	WB	6-3½	198	Jr.
44	SMITH, Mike	TB	5-8	175	So.
58	STEFAN, Terry	C	6-0	210	Jr.
85	STEPHENSON, Curt	SE	6-1	170	Sr.
42	STRABLEY, Mike	LB	6-0	218	Sr.
94	STRINKO, Greg	DE	6-3	213	Sr.
57	SZAFRANSKI, Roger	MG	5-11	193	Jr.
69	SZARA, Gerry	OG	6-2	250	So.
99	TEDESCO, Dominic	DE	6-4	210	So.
19	TRUITT, Darrell	WB	6-0	190	So.
39	*VOGELE, Jerry	LB	6-3	235	Jr.
84	WHITE, Rick	SE	6-5	195	Jr.
1	WHITEFORD, Dave	S	6-1	185	Sr.
3	WOOD, Bob	PK	5-8	170	Jr.
8	*ZUVER, Jerry	Wolf	6-2	195	Jr.

*Denotes letters won

Michigan's 1975 Season

(Won 8, Lost 2, Tied 2)
(Big Ten 7-1-0)

Date	Opponent (Site)	Score	Attendance
Sept. 13	Wisconsin (Madison)	23- 6	79,022
Sept. 20	Stanford (Ann Arbor)	19-19	92,304
Sept. 27	Baylor (Ann Arbor)	14-14	104,248
Oct. 4	Missouri (Ann Arbor)	31- 7	104,578
Oct. 11	Michigan State (East Lansing)	16- 6	79,776
Oct. 18	Northwestern (Ann Arbor)	69- 0	86,201
Oct. 25	Indiana (Ann Arbor)	55- 7	93,857
Nov. 1	Minnesota (Minneapolis)	28-21	33,191
Nov. 8	Purdue (Ann Arbor)	28- 0	102,415
Nov. 15	Illinois (Champaign)	21-15	45,077
Nov. 22	Ohio State (Ann Arbor)	14-21	105,543*
Jan. 1	Oklahoma (Orange Bowl-Miami, Fla.)	6-14	80,307
	Average (12 Games)	27-10.8	83,877
	Total (12 Games)	324-130	1,006,519

Home Attendance...689,146*   Average at Home.....98,449*
Road Attendance....317,373   Average on Road.....63,475
* NCAA Record

1975 Big Ten Standings

	CONFERENCE GAMES						ALL GAMES					
	W	L	T	Pct	Pts	Opp Pts	W	L	T	Pct	Pts	Opp Pts
Ohio State	8	0	0	1.000	284	43	11	1	0	.917	384	102
Michigan	7	1	0	.875	254	76	8	2	2	.800	324	130
Michigan State	4	4	0	.500	161	136	7	4	0	.636	222	167
Illinois	4	4	0	.500	169	166	5	6	0	.455	229	260
Purdue	4	4	0	.500	119	170	4	7	0	.363	128	220
Wisconsin	3	4	1	.438	98	194	4	6	1	.409	174	269
Minnesota	3	5	0	.375	167	185	6	5	0	.545	236	192
Iowa	3	5	0	.375	149	212	3	8	0	.273	182	279
Northwestern	2	6	0	.250	126	243	3	8	0	.273	149	318
Indiana	1	6	1	.188	73	175	2	8	1	.227	104	254

AP Poll (1975)	UPI Poll (1975)
1. Oklahoma	1. Oklahoma
2. Arizona State	2. Arizona State
3. Alabama	3. Alabama
4. Ohio State	4. Ohio State
5. U.C.L.A.	5. U.C.L.A.
6. Texas	6. Arkansas
7. Arkansas	7. Texas
8. MICHIGAN	8. MICHIGAN
9. Nebraska	9. Nebraska
10. Penn State	10. Penn State

Michigan 14, Baylor 14

For the second straight week in a row, the Wolverines settled for a tie when the Baylor Bears made their first-ever-in-history appearance in Michigan Stadium Sept. 27.

Unlike the preceding week's standoff against Stanford, this time the Wolverines were happy to get out of the affair without a loss. The Baylor team, champions of the Southwest Conference a year ago, came to play football. They outgained the Blue, 338 yards to 219, and, had a last minute field goal not gone awry, could well have gone back to Texas a winner.

The game was viewed by 104,248 people, the third largest crowd in Michigan history. Included in the total were 13,000 high school bandsmen from all over the state.

Reprinted with permission from the Michigan Alumnus

George Przygodski

Scott Corbin

Dave Devich

Tom Jensen

Steve King

Mike Holmes

Michigan 23, Wisconsin 6

The folks in Madison, Wis., h over the past year, largely c vinced themselves that this was be their year to waylay the W verines. After all, they had los Michigan by only four points 1974 and they figured to be bet — and they had premier runni back Billy Marek, and, well, Badgers were ready.

The Wolverines were even re ier. Bo's boys rushed for 394 yar and completely dominated the position, winning, 23 to 6, on crisp early fall afternoon in Can Randall Stadium in Madison.

And, oh, the defense! As Sche bechler said after the game, was the best defensive game have ever played!'' The high rated Billy Marek went virtual no place as the Wolverines he the Badgers to 98 on the groun and 38 by air.

For the first time in Michig football history, the Maize ar Blue started a *freshman* at quarte back. Rick Leach, a Flint, Mich product, played the entire gam running the option play to ne perfection. Unhappily, he thre three pass interceptions. Thos together with an early-in-the game fumble on the Blue 33 yard-line, and a long punt retur by Wisconsin, kept the Badge somewhat in the game. But eac time, the defense held magni icently — and Wisconsin had t settle for a pair of field goals.

Speaking of running backs Michigan's senior tailback, Gor don Bell rambled for a net of 21 yards and Rob Lytle tossed i another 91 from the fullback spot.

It was a tremendous start — o the road — for Michigan as it pre pared for three non-conference en counters before meeting you know-who at East Lansing on Oc tober 11.

Michigan 19, Stanford 19

September 20   Ann Arbor   Attendance 92,304

Stanford kicked a field goal with 9 seconds left in the game to earn a tie. Mike Cordova exploited the young Wolverine secondary by completing 24 of 44 passes for 290 yards, including two for touchdowns. Michigan's Rick Leach completed 6 of 17 for 145 yards, including a touchdown pass of 48 yards to Jim Smith. Rob Lytle gained 113 yards as Michigan rushed for 322 yards. Bob Wood set a single game record for Michigan with four field goals, the last one a 42-yard effort with 1:36 left in the game. Smith caught 5 passes for 143 yards, while Stanford's Tony Hill caught 8 for 126 yards.

Michigan	0	7	6	6 — 19
Stanford	6	0	0	13 — 19

SCORING		STATISTICS	MICH	STAN
Mich—Smith, 48-yard pass from Leach		First Downs	17	21
Wood, 27-yard field goal		Net Yards Rushing	322	46
Wood, 29-yard field goal		Net Yards Passing	145	285
Wood, 32-yard field goal		Passes Attempted	17	44
Wood, 42-yard field goal		Passes Completed	6	24
Wood (PAT)		Intercepted By	2	1
Stan—Hill, 25-yard pass from Cordova		Punting	5-35.8	8-33.4
T. Anderson, 4-yard deflected pass from Cordova		Return Yardage	29	110
Langford, 40-yard field goal		Fumbles No./Lost	3-2	1-1
Langford, 33-yard field goal				
Langford (PAT)				

Michigan 31, Missouri 7

October 4   Ann Arbor   Attendance 104,578

Michigan's defense turned in one of its strongest games of the season while the offense rolled for 400 yards in an impressive win over the nation's fifth-rated team from the Big Eight. Gordon Bell ran for 119 yards and Rick Leach had 97 on the ground as Michigan broke open a tight game with two, third-period touchdowns. Bob Wood's 40-yard field goal was his eighth of the season and tied a Michigan record as the Wolverines played before their second straight home crowd of 100,000 plus.

Michigan	7	3	14	7 — 31
Missouri	0	0	0	7 — 7

SCORING		STATISTICS	
	MICH		MO
Mich—Lytle, 1-yard run	24	First Downs	14
Wood, 40-yard field goal	372	Net Yards Rushing	132
Lytle, 19-yard run	28	Net Yards Passing	121
Leach, 12-yard run	11	Passes Attempted	23
Huckleby, 11-yard run	3	Passes Completed	11
Wood (4 PAT's)	0	Intercepted By	1
Missouri—Douglass, 5-yard pass	4-42.0	Punting	7-42.1
from Woods	36	Return Yardage	140
Gibbons (PAT)	1-1	Fumbles No./Lost	4-3

Michigan 16, Michigan State 6

October 11   East Lansing   Attendance 79,776

Michigan returned to Big Ten competition and again it was defense that keyed the Wolverines. Michigan State was held to 279 yards in total offense, while Gordon Bell with 105 yards and Rob Lytle with 111 paced the Wolverine ground attack. The teams matched field goals in the first half as Bob Wood kicked two more for a school record, then Michigan scored 10 points in the fourth period to win it. Bell scored on a 19-yard run and Wood added his third field goal to account for the 10 points. The game was on national TV (ABC) and Bell (offense) and Don Dufek (defense) were selected as recipients of the Chevrolet Outstanding Player Scholarship awards.

Michigan	0	6	0	10 — 16
Michigan State	3	0	3	0 — 6

SCORING		STATISTICS	
	MICH		MSU
Mich—Wood, 33-yard field goal	14	First Downs	17
Wood, 46-yard field goal	268	Net Yards Rushing	117
Bell, 19-yard run	38	Net Yards Passing	162
Wood, 25-yard field goal	6	Passes Attempted	16
Wood (PAT)	2	Passes Completed	10
MSU—Nielsen, 46-yard field goal	0	Intercepted By	1
Nielsen, 43-yard field goal	5-38.6	Punting	7-37.3
	48	Return Yardage	79
	3-3	Fumbles No./Lost	5-3

Michigan 55, Indiana 7

October 25   Ann Arbor   Attendance 93,857

Rob Lytle with 147 yards and Gordon Bell will 117 paced another heavy ground assault that netted 490 in Michigan's Homecoming win. Lytle scored four touchdowns and freshman fullback Russell Davis scored twice as Michigan opened a 34-0 first-half lead. Indiana broke a Michigan defensive streak of not allowing a touchdown on the ground for 35 straight quarters when the Hoosiers punched over a touchdown in the fourth period. Wingback Jim Smith, on his only rushing attempt of the game, ran 77 yards to record the sixth longest touchdown run in Michigan history.

Michigan	14	20	14	7 — 55
Indiana	0	0	0	7 — 7

SCORING		STATISTICS	
	MICH		IND
Mich—Smith, 77-yard run	30	First Downs	13
Bell, 53-yard run	490	Net Yards Rushing	120
Lytle, 1-yard run	86	Net Yards Passing	76
Lytle, 7-yard run	9	Passes Attempted	18
Lytle, 1-yard run	5	Passes Completed	6
R. Davis, 2-yard run	1	Intercepted By	0
R. Davis, 3-yard run	3-38.0	Punting	8-37.8
Lytle, 12-yard run	110	Return Yardage	164
Wood (6 PAT's)	0-0	Fumbles No./Lost	1-1
Willner (PAT)			
Ind— Jones, 1-yard run			
Stavroff (PAT)			

Jim Czirr

Keith Johnson

Kurt Kampe

Reprinted with permission from the **Michigan Alumnus**

Michigan 69, Northwestern 0

The night before the Northwestern game, Coach Schembechler looked again at some Northwestern films and "I got worried. I went down to some of the players' rooms in the hotel and tried to get everybody up for the game."

Michigan was up, all right. Sixty-nine points up in the worst thrashing a Wolverine team has administered since the Blue pulverized Pittsburgh in 1947.

The Wolverines ripped hapless Northwestern for 10 touchdowns and 573 yards on the ground while the defense refused to let the Wildcats even get within field goal distance.

After Michigan rolled up its fourth touchdown — the fourth time it had the ball, midway in the second quarter — the first unit was removed. Among other things, this allowed Freshman Tailback Harlan Huckleby to become Michigan's leading ground gainer with 157 yards on 18 carries.

Brief Statistics	N'western	Mich.
First downs	6	31
Rushing net yardage	91	573
Passes attempted	13	5
Passes completed	2	2
Yards gained by passing	24	32
Passes intercepted by	1	1
Fumbles lost	5	2
Yards penalized	36	30

Chuck Randolph

Phil Brumbaugh

Michigan 28, Minnesota 21

November 1   Minneapolis   Attendance 33,191

Gordon Bell ran 23 yards to score with 6:56 left in the game to lift Michigan over an inspired Minnesota team which had tied the game in the third period. Bell gained 172 yards rushing for Michigan, while Minnesota's Tony Dungy completed 17 or 31 passes for 198 yards. Michigan rushed for 345 yards, while the Wolverine defenders held the Gopher ground attack to 64 yards and checked Dungy with 5 completions in the second half after the talented junior had completed 12 of 16 in the first half.

Michigan	7	14	0	7 — 28
Minnesota	7	7	7	0 — 21

SCORING		STATISTICS	
	MICH		MINN
Mich—Lytle, 4-yard run	21	First Downs	16
Bell, 5-yard run	345	Net Yards Rushing	64
Leach, 3-yard run	17	Net Yards Passing	198
Bell, 23-yard run	6	Passes Attempted	31
Wood (4 PAT's)	1	Passes Completed	17
Minn—Sims, 1-yard pass from Dungy	0	Intercepted By	0
Kullas, 14-yard pass from Dungy	7-31.4	Punting	7-37.0
Holmes, 16-yard run	94	Return Yardage	105
Kocourek (3 PAT's)	2-1	Fumbles No./Lost	1-1

GORDON BELL

Michigan 28, Purdue 0

November 8   Ann Arbor   Attendance 102,415

Michigan quarterback Rick Leach turned in his finest passing afternoon of the season to spark a shutout victory over a strong Purdue team. Leach connected on six of nine passes for 218 yards, including an 83-yard touchdown pass to Jim Smith. Smith came within 14 yards of breaking Michigan's reception record as the junior wingback caught 5 for 184. Michigan's rushing attack, led by Gordon Bell's 94 yards, netted 283 for a total offense of 501. Bell caught a pass for 34 yards and returned a kickoff for 22 in another exceptional performance.

| Michigan | 14 | 0 | 0 | 14 — 28 |
| Purdue | 0 | 0 | 0 | 0 — 0 |

SCORING		STATISTICS	
	MICH		PUR
Mich—Bell, 20-yard run	23	First Downs	15
Smith, 83-yard pass from Leach	283	Net Yards Rushing	173
Bell, 3-yard run	218	Net Yards Passing	115
Leach, 2-yard run	9	Passes Attempted	15
Wood (4 PAT's)	6	Passes Completed	7
	0	Intercepted By	0
	1-48.0	Punting	5-38.8
	39	Return Yardage	13
	2-2	Fumbles No./Lost	2-0

Michigan 21, Illinois 15

November 15   Champaign   Attendance 45,07

Illinois again proved a tough opponent for Michigan in Champaign, scoring 15 points in the fourth period in an upset bid. Michigan led 21- at halftime as Gordon Bell scored twice and Rick Leach once. Si fumbles, three of them lost, thwarted Michigan's offensive attack. Kur Steger, after one completion in nine attempts, hit 10 of 14 in the secon half to spark the Illini comeback. Bell again paced Michigan's running with 141 yards. The victory was Michigan's seventh straight in the Big Ten and set up a championship finale with Ohio State.

| Michigan | 14 | 0 | 7 | 0 — 21 |
| Illinois | 0 | 0 | 0 | 15 — 15 |

SCORING		STATISTICS	
	MICH		ILL
Mich—Bell, 2-yard run	16	First Downs	16
Bell, 1-yard run	218	Net Yards Rushing	137
Leach, 1-yard run	27	Net Yards Passing	103
Wood (PAT)	1	Passes Attempted	24
Lytle (PAT run)	1	Passes Completed	11
Ill— Johnson, 5-yard pass	3	Intercepted By	0
from Steger	4-40.8	Punting	6-41.3
Phillips, 2-yard run	12	Return Yardage	44
Beaver (PAT)	6-4	Fumbles No./Lost	3-1
Johnson (PAT pass from Steger)			

Bill Hoban

Rob Lytle

Rick Koschalk

Calvin O'Neal

Mark Donahue

OSU 'Rosy'

Ohio State 21, Michigan 14

November 22   Ann Arbor   Attendance 105,543

Michigan and Ohio State met for the 15th time to decide the Big Ten title and the Buckeyes prevailed with two touchdowns in the last 3 minutes, 18 seconds of the game. Ohio, shut off without a first down after its opening touchdown drive in the first period until midway in the fourth quarter, went to the air and completed three straight passes in driving 80 yards to the tying score. A pass interception seconds later set up OSU's winning touchdown as Michigan, playing for a victory, was operating from its 11-yard line. Michigan, controlling most of the game, received an 11-yard tailback pass from Gordon Bell to Jim Smith for one score and Rick Leach dove in for the second. Bell gained 124 yards and Rob Lytle 104, while OSU's Archie Griffin was checked with 46. A record NCAA regular season crowd of 105,543 pushed Michigan's average home attendance to 98,449, an all-time college record.

| Michigan | 0 | 7 | 0 | 7 — 14 |
| Ohio State | 7 | 0 | 0 | 14 — 21 |

SCORING		STATISTICS	
	MICH		OSU
Mich—Smith, 11-yard pass from Bell	19	First Downs	12
Leach, 1-yard run	248	Net Yards Rushing	124
Wood, (2 PAT's)	113	Net Yards Passing	84
OSU— Johnson, 7-yard pass	21	Passes Attempted	16
from Greene	8	Passes Completed	7
Johnson, 1-yard run	2	Intercepted By	3
Johnson, 3-yard run	6-29.5	Punting	8-44.6
Klaban (3 PAT's)	37	Return Yardage	11
	2-2	Fumbles No./Lost	1-1

Michigan Sets New Record For Attendance

SHAWNEE MISSION, Kan. (AP) — The University of Michigan drew the six largest crowds of the 1975 college football season and set all-time attendance marks by drawing 689,146 to its home games and averaging 98,449 per contest.

The biggest 1975 turnout was 105,543 for the Michigan-Ohio State game at Ann Arbor, Mich., a national regular-season record for the 28 years of official National Collegiate Athletic Association attendance figures.

Michigan ended Ohio State's streak of 14 consecutive national attendance championships in 1972. The Buckeyes regained the crown in 1973 but Michigan won it back in 1974.

LINEUPS

Michigan

ENDS K Johnson, Stephenson, Schmerge, G Johnson, Przygodski, Jilek, Seabron, Holmes, J Anderson
TACKLES S King, Lang, B Dufek, Hall, Perlinger Morton
GUARDS Donahue, Miles, Downing, T Davis, Koschalk
CENTERS Czirr
LINEBACKERS O'Neal, Mackall, Devich
BACKS G Bell, Lytle, R Davis, Corbin, Leach, Elzinga, J Smith, Richardson, D Dufek, Zuver, Howard, Bolden, Pickens, Hicks
PUNTER J Anderson
PLACE KICKER Wood

Oklahoma

ENDS Hicks, T Owens, Brooks, Hover, Phillips, Baccus, Elrod, Brown
TACKLES Baldischwiler, Vaughan, Kulbeth, L Selmon, Murray, Bryant, Tabor
GUARDS Evans, Dodds, Webb, D Selmon, Cozeaux
CENTERS Buchanan, Bodin
LINEBACKERS Thomas, Moore, Sellzyer, Dalke, Hunt
BACKS Davis, Washington, Sims, Peacock, Rogers, Littrell, Culbreath, Anderson, Van Camp, R Owens, Brown, Peters, McReynolds, Hill, Birke, Henderson, Reese

TEAM FIGURES

	M	O
FIRST DOWNS	12	16
RUSHES-YARDS	52-169	65-282
PASSES	2-20-3	3-5-0
PASSING YARDS	33	63
PUNTS-AVERAGE	10-38.6	9-34.9
PENALTIES-YARDS	5-24	9-90
FUMBLES-LOST	1-0	5-2
RETURN YARDAGE	52	16

SCORING

MICHIGAN	0	0	0	6—	6
OKLAHOMA	0	7	0	7—	14

O—Brooks 39-yard run (DiRienzo kick)
O—Davis 9-yard run (DiRienzo kick)
M—Bell 2-yard run (Leach run failed)
ATTENDANCE 80,307

Sooner Defense 'Stonewalls' M

BY WAYNE DENEFF
News Sports Editor

MIAMI, Fla. — Michigan prides itself on great defense, but it also knows now how it feels to crash your head into a stone wall.

Oklahoma, very likely to be named national collegiate football champion when the polls are released Saturday morning, blunted everything Michigan tried to do for a 14-6 Orange Bowl victory before a sell-out crowd of 80,307.

Oklahoma, 11-1, is ranked No. 2 by United Press International and Michigan, 8-2-2, is ranked No. 4, but the Sooners figure to make that one big step ahead of the top-ranked Ohio State Buckeyes who were upended by UCLA, 23-10, in the Rose Bowl. Both Oklahoma and Michigan were a notch lower in the Associated Press poll, but that poll was taken a few weeks ago and does not reflect two consecutive losses by second ranked Texas A & M.

Michigan had heard a lot about the Selmon brothers, Leroy and Dewey, and big Jimbo Elrod. They proved just as tough in the flesh, playing rock-'em sock-'em football that left the Wolverines with their lowest offensive output in many, many games, 202 yards.

The Sooners stopped Michigan's 1,000-yards-a-season rushers, Gordon Bell and Rob Lytle, with 53 and 32 yards, respectively, and that tells a lot about what happened in Michigan's first appearance ever in the Orange Bowl.

When the Selmons and the Elrods weren't knocking over Bell and Lytle, they were putting a big rush on quarterback Rick Leach and the Michigan freshman had a bad night throwing the ball.

Leach, who was knocked groggy just before the half and didn't play at all in the third quarter, threw 15 passes, completed two and had two intercepted.

His running was just about his best ever, and he was Michigan's top ground gainer with 62 yards.

Going against a bigger, stronger opponent, Michigan figured it had to do some gambling and started right off throwing the ball.

But the air attack fizzled, and there really wasn't much hope the Wolverines could overpower their opponents on land.

Michigan's defense played well, in fact, very well considering how often and how long it was on the field, but it couldn't hold off the Sooners all night.

With about five minutes to play in the half, Oklahoma erupted for 79 yards in just two plays for a 7-0 lead and then pounded out 68 yards in 12 plays to go ahead, 14-0, on the first play of the fourth quarter.

True through the final game of the season, the Sooners were their own worst enemies.

They scored that second touchdown despite the fact on successive plays they fumbled the ball out of bounds, completed a one-hop lateral and were penalized 15 yards for clipping.

End Billy Brooks scored the first touchdown on an end-around, bursting for 39 yards, and the second TD was the result of a nine-yard run by quarterback Steve Davis who did a neat job of faking out the Wolverines.

Michigan's lone touchdown was a gift.

Linebacker Calvin O'Neal pounced on a fumble on the handoff between Davis and fullback Jim Culbreath and the Wolverines had first-and-goal at the two-yard line.

Bell scored on the next play and it was 14-6 with 7:06 left in the game.

Michigan's try for two extra points was thwarted when Leach was stacked up just inches short.

An onside kick backfired and the Wolverines were kept on their own side of the field after that.

Don Dufek (35) Keys Michigan's Defense

Wolverine Honors in 1975

All-American

DON DUFEK, WOLF — Coaches Kodak, Walter Camp Foundation, Football Writers Association, Football News. Second team AP, UPI.
TIM DAVIS, MG — Second team AP, UPI.
GORDON BELL, TB — Third team AP, FN
JIM SMITH, WB — Third team, FN
DAN JILEK, DE — Academic All-American First team.
BOB WOOD, K — Churchman's All-American First team.

Honorable Mention

Calvin O'Neal, LB   Dan Jilek, DE
Greg Morton, DT   Rob Lytle, FB

Michigan's 1975 Statistics

12-GAME STATISTICS

Individual

Rushing

	Att	Gain	Loss	Yds	Avg	LP
G. Bell	273	1441	53	1388	5.1	53
Lytle	193	1055	15	1040	5.4	47
Leach	113	663	83	552	4.9	44
J. Smith	31	253	16	237	7.6	77
Huckleby	31	228	0	228	7.4	27
R. Davis	40	183	4	179	4.5	17
Elzinga	28	126	26	100	3.6	22
Corbin	17	90	0	90	5.3	18
M. Richardson	5	18	0	18	3.6	8
F. Bell	2	8	0	8	4.0	4
Carian	1	5	0	5	5.0	5
K. King	3	3	0	3	1.0	2

Passing

	Att	Comp	Int	Yds	TD	LP
Leach	100	32	12	680	3	83
Elzinga	23	8	2	133	1	28
G. Bell	2	1	1	11	1	11

Scoring

	TDr	TDp	TDo	P/R	ExP	FG	TP
G. Bell	13	1	0	0	0	0	84
Wood	0	0	0	0	32/35	11/16	65
Lytle	10	0	0	0	2	0	62
Leach	5	0	0	0	0	0	30
J. Smith	1	4	0	0	0	0	30
Huckleby	3	0	0	0	0	0	18
R. Davis	2	0	0	0	0	0	12
Elzinga	1	0	0	0	0	0	6
Devich	0	0	1	0	0	0	6
Seabron	0	0	1	0	0	0	6
Willner	0	0	0	0	5/5	0/2	5

TDr = rush   TDp = pass   TDo = other

Receiving

	No	Yds	Avg	TD	LP
J. Smith	24	553	23.0	4	83
G. Bell	7	84	12.0	1	34
K. Johnson	6	130	21.7	0	29
M. Richardson	1	28	28.0	0	28
Schmerge	1	13	13.0	0	13
Lytle	1	12	12.0	0	12
G. Johnson	1	4	4.0	0	4

Punting

	No	Yds	Avg	LP
J. Anderson	53	2018	38.1	67

Punt Returns

	No	Yds	Avg	TD	LP
J. Smith	26	210	8.1	0	50
Hicks	9	63	7.0	0	21
G. Bell	4	18	4.5	0	7
Bolden	1	0	0.0	0	0

Kickoff Returns

	No	Yds	Avg	TD	LP
G. Bell	9	227	25.2	0	64
Lytle	5	84	16.8	0	21
Huckleby	2	30	15.0	0	16
J. Smith	1	16	16.0	0	16
Corbin	1	12	12.0	0	12

Interceptions

	No	Yds	TD	LP
Seabron	*	40	1	40
D. Dufek	2	28	0	27
Devich	2	23	1	23
Hicks	2	20	0	20
Jilek	1	11	0	11
Pickens	1	7	0	7
Kampe	1	0	0	0
Bolden	1	0	0	0
Mackall	1	0	0	0

* Fumble interception return

Fumble Recoveries

3 - D. Dufek	1 - Vogele
2 - Pickens	1 - Hicks
2 - Koschalk	1 - T. Davis
2 - Morton	1 - J. Anderson
2 - Holmes	1 - Devich
2 - Jilek	1 - O'Neal

Passes Broken Up

8 - Bolden	2 - Devich
6 - Hicks	2 - Pickens
5 - O'Neal	1 - Morton
4 - Zuver	1 - Howard
4 - D. Dufek	1 - Hennessy
3 - Jilek	1 - J. Anderson
	1 - Vogele

Team Statistics

	Mich	Opp		Mich	Opp
Total First Downs	242	175	Total No. of Punts	53	84
Rushing	199	93	Total yards	2018	3285
Passing	34	72	Average per punt	38.1	39.1
Penalty	9	10			
Total Offensive	863	783	Total Kick Ret	58/660	64/956
Rushing Attempts	738	549	Punt Ret/Yds	40/291	15/145
Rushing Yards	3848	1605	Kickoff Ret	18/369	49/811
Passing Yards	824	1391	Intercep./Yds	11/132	15/174
Passing Att.	125	234	Fumbles/Lost	27/19	36/20
Pass Com.	41	113	Penalties/Yards	31/319	42/410
Total Off. Yds.	4672	2996			

Bo out of hospital

From Wire Service Reports

ANN ARBOR — University of Michigan football Coach Bo Schembechler was released from St. Joseph Mercy Hospital yesterday just two weeks after undergoing open heart surgery.

Doctors said the 49-year-old Schembechler, who suffered a heart attack on the eve of the Rose Bowl game in 1971, must still spend about another four to six weeks recovering from the bypass operation at home.

Schembechler was described as "doing a little better than normal for this type of surgery," by a U-M spokesman.

They said they were very pleased at his progress.

Schembechler has said he plans to resume his coaching duties as soon as he is able.

Doctors bypassed four arteries in the six-hour-long operation May 20 to correct a circulatory problem that will improve the flow of blood to previously deprived parts of Schembechler's heart.

Reprinted with permission from the **Michigan Daily**

AP Poll (1976)
1. Pittsburgh
2. Southern Cal.
3. MICHIGAN
4. Houston
5. Oklahoma
6. Ohio State
7. Texas A & M
8. Maryland
9. Nebraska
10. Georgia

UPI Poll (1976)
1. Pittsburgh
2. Southern Cal.
3. MICHIGAN
4. Houston
5. Ohio State
6. Oklahoma
7. Nebraska
8. Texas A & M
9. Alabama
10. Georgia

Michigan's 1976 Season

(Won 10, Lost 2)
(Big Ten 7-1)

Date	Opponent (Site)	Score	Attendance
Sept. 11	Wisconsin (Ann Arbor)	40-27	101,347
Sept. 18	Stanford (Ann Arbor)	51- 0	103,741
Sept. 25	Navy (Ann Arbor)	70-14	101,040
Oct. 2	Wake Forest (Ann Arbor)	31- 0	103,241
Oct. 9	Michigan State (Ann Arbor)	42-10	104,211
Oct. 16	Northwestern (Evanston)	38- 7	31,045
Oct. 23	Indiana (Bloomington)	35- 0	39,385
Oct. 30	Minnesota (Ann Arbor)	45- 0	104,426
Nov. 6	Purdue (Lafayette)	14-16	57,205
Nov. 13	Illinois (Ann Arbor)	38- 7	104,107
Nov. 20	Ohio State (Columbus)	22- 0	88,250
Jan. 1	Southern Cal (Rose Bowl-Pasadena)	6-14	106,182
	Average (12 Games)	36-7.9	87,015
	Total (12 Games)	432-95	1,044,180*

Home Attendance......722,113* Average at Home......103,159*
Road Attendance......322,067 Average on Road.......64,413
*NCAA Record

Final 1976 Big Ten Football Standings

	CONFERENCE GAMES					ALL GAMES				
	W	L	T	Pct	Pts	Opp Pts	W L T	Pct	Pts	Opp Pts
Michigan	7	1	0	.875	274	67	10 2 0	.833	432	95
Ohio State	7	1	0	.875	235	100	9 2 1	.792	305	149
Minnesota	4	4	0	.500	145	149	6 5 0	.445	201	211
Purdue	4	4	0	.500	133	159	5 6 0	.455	188	233
Illinois	4	4	0	.500	178	194	5 6 0	.455	235	248
Indiana	4	4	0	.500	76	172	5 6 0	.455	130	254
Iowa	3	5	0	.375	113	170	5 6 0	.455	161	234
Wisconsin	3	5	0	.375	194	197	5 6 0	.455	298	266
Michigan State	3	5	0	.375	178	213	4 6 1	.409	236	278
Northwestern	1	7	0	.125	119	224	1 10 0	.091	134	311

1976 Varsity Football

No.	Name	Pos.	Ht.	Wt.	Class
86	**ANDERSON, John	DE	6-3	208	Jr.
66	ANDERSON, Steve	MG	6-2	225	Jr.
31	ANDREWS, Phil	FB	6-1	217	Jr.
64	ARBEZNIK, John	OG	6-4	230	Soph.
61	BARTNICK, Greg	OG	6-3	235	Jr.
12	BETTIS, Roger	QB	6-3	185	Jr.
22	**BOLDEN, Jim	DB	6-1	177	Sr.
28	BRAMAN, Mark	DB	6-2	190	Soph.
45	BROWN, Woody	S	5-11	175	Jr.
13	CEDDIA, John	QB	6-0	185	Jr.
33	*DAVIS, Russell	FB	6-2	215	Soph.
92	DeSANTIS, Mark	DE	6-4	212	Soph.
60	*DONAHUE, Mark	OG	6-3½	245	Jr.
72	*DOWNING, Walt	C	6-4	250	Jr.
73	**DUFEK, Bill	OT	6-4	250	Jr.
68	GIESLER, Jon	DT	6-4	265	Soph.
54	GRAVES, Steve	MG	6-1	217	Soph.
95	GREER, Curtis	DT	6-4	220	Soph.
2	GRIEVES, Chris	PK	6-0	155	Soph.
53	HACKETT, Jim	C	6-1	220	Sr.
83	HARDING, Dave	TE	6-4	223	Jr.
71	**HENNESSY, John	DT	6-4	235	Sr.
17	*HICKS, Dwight	S	6-2	180	Jr.
94	HOLLWAY, Bob	DE	6-3	200	Soph.
10	**HOWARD, Derek	Wolf	6-2	187	Jr.
25	*HUCKLEBY, Harlan	TB	6-11½	195	Soph.
93	JACKSON, William	DT	6-4	230	Soph.
88	*JOHNSON, Gene	TE	6-4	220	Soph.
20	JOHNSON, Ray	S	6-0	177	Jr.
9	JOHNSON, Stacy	QB	6-2	185	Soph.
51	KADELA, Dave	OT	6-2	235	Soph.
55	KEITZ, Dale	MG	6-2	230	Soph.
78	*KENN, Mike	OT	6-6½	245	Jr.
36	KING, Kevin	FB	6-2	215	Jr.
19	LABUN, Nick	PK	5-11	172	Jr.
62	**LANG, Bob	MG	6-1	230	Sr.
7	*LEACH, Rick	QB	6-1	180	Soph.
74	**LEWIS, Kirk	OG	6-3½	235	Sr.
63	LINDSAY, Rock	OG	6-1	230	Soph.
41	**LYTLE, Rob	TB	6-1	195	Sr.
49	*MACKALL, Rex	LB	6-4	215	Jr.
45	MALINAK, Tim	LB	6-1	215	Soph.
38	MELITA, Tom	MG	6-11½	211	Soph.
46	METER, Jerry	LB	6-3	205	Soph.
77	**MORTON, Greg	DT	6-2	225	Sr.
50	*NAUTA, Steve	C	6-2	227	Jr.
96	**O'NEAL, Calvin	LB	6-2	230	Sr.
24	PATEK, Bob	Wolf	6-2	190	Soph.
89	PEDERSON, Chip	TE	6-5½	222	Soph.
90	*PHELPS, Eric	DE	6-1	208	Jr.
18	*PICKENS, Jim	DB	6-2	188	Jr.
43	**RICHARDSON, Max	WB	6-1	187	Jr.
82	SCHMERGE, Mark	TE	6-3	235	Soph.
91	*SEABRON, Tom	DE	6-3½	212	Soph.
37	***SMITH, Jim	WB	6-3	195	Sr.
99	SMITH, Lewis	DT	6-4	235	Soph.
44	SMITH, Mike	DB	5-8	175	Jr.
85	*STEPHENSON, Curt	SE	6-1	175	Jr.
57	SZAFRANSKI, Roger	MG	5-11	210	Sr.
69	SZARA, Gerry	OG	6-2	240	Jr.
99	TEDESCO, Dom	DE	6-4	210	Jr.
79	TORZY, Mark	OT	6-4	240	Soph.
39	**VOGELE, Jerry	LB	6-3	235	Sr.
84	WHITE, Rick	SE	6-5	205	Jr.
65	WILLIAMS, Kyron	MG	6-1	205	Soph.
1	WILLNER, Gregg	PK	5-10	145	Soph.
3	*WOOD, Bob	PK	5-8	170	Sr.
21	WOODFORD, Tony	DB	5-9	170	Soph.
8	**ZUVER, Jerry	Wolf	6-2	195	Sr.

*Denotes letters won

Michigan 40, Wisconsin 27

September 11   Ann Arbor   101,347

Michigan jumped off to a 23-point first quarter lead, then had to withstand a record Wisconsin aerial assault that produced the most points any team would score on the Wolverine defense all season. The Badgers completed more passes against Michigan than any team in history as Mike Carroll completed 25 of 44 for 268 yards and two touchdowns.

Wisconsin's total offense of 426 caused Coach Bo Schembechler some concern, but Michigan's offensive performance was equal to the task. The Wolverines had 62 plays that netted 455 yards for a 7.3 per play average. Sophomore Harlan Huckleby, who scored Michigan's first touchdown on a 56-yard option play, gained 131 yards, while quarterback Rick Leach, who completed six of eight passes for 105 yards and two touchdowns, averaged 9.3 yards on nine running plays. Huckleby scored three touchdowns and split receiver Jim Smith hauled down scoring passes of 12 and 25 yards. Co-captain Calvin O'Neal led the defense with 18 tackles.

Wisconsin	0	13	7	7 — 27
Michigan	23	10	0	7 — 40

SCORING
First Quarter
M — Team, Safety
M — Huckleby, 56-yd run (Wood)
M — Huckleby, 4-yd run (Wood)
M — Smith, 12-yd pass from Leach (Wood)
Second Quarter
Wis.—Egloff, 26-yd pass from Carroll (Lamia)
M—Smith, 25-yd pass from Leach (Wood)
Wis.—Lamia, 42-yd FG
M—Wood, 36-yd FG
Wis.—Lamia, 42-yd FG
Third Quarter
WIS.—Canada, 6-yd run (Lamia)
Fourth Quarter
M—Huckleby, 1-yd run (Wood)
Wis.—Charles, 7-yd pass from Carroll (Lamia)

STATISTICS		
MICH		WIS
22	First Downs	24
350	Net Yards Rushing	158
105	Net Yards Passing	268
8	Passes Attempted	44
6	Passes Completed	25
0	Intercepted	1
2/38.0	Punts/Average	3/48.3
101	Return Yardage	84
4/4	Fumbles/Lost	4/2

Top Individuals
Rushing — Huckleby (M) 19-131; Leach (M) 9-84; Lytle (M) 16-76
Passing — Leach (M) 6-8-105; Carroll (W) 25-44-268
Receiving — J. Smith (M) 4-70; Bailey (W) 7-63; Lytle (M) 2-35

Michigan 70, Navy 14

September 25   Ann Arbor   101,040

An inspired Navy team battled Michigan on even terms for two periods, but the Wolverines scored 28 points in a five-minute span in the third quarter to win easily.

Rick Leach fired a 31-yard touchdown pass to Jim Smith with just 27 seconds left in the first half to snap a 14-14 tie. Leach passed for 197 on just eight completions, while Gene Johnson caught his first touchdown pass. Bob Wood tied a Michigan record with nine extra points and his 51-yard field goal also tied a school record. The 70-point total was the highest for a Michigan team since an 85-0 rout of Chicago in 1939. Coach Bo Schembechler was not elated at being rated No. 1 in both polls (advancing there after last week's win.) "We are not great. Today we were outplayed in the first half. We could have been beaten. That's the kind of thing that can happen when you're No. 1."

Navy	7	7	0	0 — 14
Michigan	7	14	28	21 — 70

SCORING
First Quarter
Navy—Kurowski, 20-yd run (Tata)
M—Lylte, 3-yd run (Wood)
Second Quarter
M—Team, Safety
M—Wood, 51-yd FG
Navy—Klawinski, 1-yd run (Tata)
M—Team, Safety
M—Smith, 31-yd pass from Leach (Wood)
Third Quarter
M—Leach, 6-yd run (Wood)
M—O'Neal, 29-yd pass interception (Wood)
M—Leach, 7-yd run (Wood)
M—Johnson,G.,5-yd pass from Leach(Wood)
Fourth Quarter
M—Johnson, S., 4-yd run (Wood)
M—King, 13-yd run (Wood)
M—Reid, 2-yd run (Wood)

STATISTICS		
MICH		NAVY
29	First Downs	9
342	Net Yards Rushing	75
209	Net Yards Passing	42
14	Passes Attempted	10
10	Passes Completed	5
0	Intercepted	1
2/36.5	Punts/Average	8/37.0
65	Return Yardage	62
1/1	Fumbles/Lost	2/0

Top Individuals
Rushing — Reid (M) 7-79; Huckleby (M)11-79
Passing — Leach (M) 8-12-179; S. Johnson (M) 2-2-30
Receiving — J. Smith (M) 4-147; G. Johnson (M) 2-20; Harding (M)1-16

Calvin O'Neal

Rick Leach

Jim Smith

Harlan Huckleby

Gene Johnson

Rob Lytle

Russell Davis

Kirk Lewis

Greg Morton

Michigan 51, Stanford 0

All week long, Michigan's defense had lived with the chagrin of those 27 points piled up by Wisconsin. But on the sunny afternoon of Sept. 18, the defense, in the words of one of its members, "played hellish, aggressive football for four quarters."

As a result, the heralded Stanford passing attack never put a point on the board. The Wolverine forwards swarmed in on the Cardinal throwers and runners, and the defensive backfield roamed with a previously unseen quickness to thwart the West Coast visitors.

Meanwhile, the Maize and Blue offense blazed away with all of its guns, running up 531 yards from scrimmage. Three Michigan backs — Harlan Huckleby, Rob Lytle and Russell Davis — each topped 100 yards for the day.

Davis, a fullback who thinks he is a halfback when he gets beyond the line of scrimmage, dashed for 85 yards in one burst. That run tied him for second place as the second longest touchdown run from scrimmage in Michigan history. He now shares the record with Bill Culligan, who ran the same number of yards against Wisconsin in 1944. The record — 86 yards — is held by Tom Harmon, who turned in the feat in 1940 against California.

But it was the defense on this day that won the adulation of the crowd of 103,741. They intercepted three Stanford passes and recovered two fumbles. Three of those five turnovers were turned into Wolverine scores.

And now it's Navy and Wake Forest before getting into the Big Ten season by hosting Michigan State.

Michigan 31, Wake Forest 0

ANN ARBOR, Mich., Oct. 2 (AP)— Rob Lytle, a fullback, scored two touchdowns today and passed Tom Harmon on the Michigan career rushing list as the Wolverines trounced Wake Forest, 31-0.

Lytle scored on a 9-yard run in the second quarter and on a 25-yard burst in the final period as Michigan won its fourth game without a loss before a crowd of 103,281.

Lytle rushed for 110 yards in 14 carries for a total of 2,187 for his career. He moved into fifth place ahead of Harmon's 2,134.

The other Michigan touchdowns were scored by Rick Leach on a 2-yard run in the first quarter, a 13-yarder by tailback Harlan Huckleby in the third and a 23-yard field goal by Bob Wood in the second period.

Michigan, favored by as many as 40 points, led only 17-0 at halftime and it's high-powered offense never really got untracked. The Deacons intercepted three passes.

Michigan Romps Over Mich. State

ANN ARBOR, Mich., Oct. 9 (AP)—Harlan Huckleby scored three touchdowns today and Rob Lytle rushed for 180 yards as Michigan crushed Michigan State, 42-10, in a Big Ten football game.

The point total for Michigan was its largest against the Spartans since a 55-0 triumph in 1947.

Lytle, a fullback, scored on a 75-yard run on Michigan's fourth play from scrimmage after Michigan State had taken a 3-0 lead. The Spartans had surprised the Wolverines by recovered a fumble and score in the first two minutes on a 24-yard field goal by Hans Nielsen.

Huckleby scored his first touchdown on a 38-yard run in the first period. He added touchdowns on plunges of - yard in the second quarter and 2 yards in the third.

The other touchdowns for Michigan, now 5-0 overall and 2-0 in the Big Ten, came on a 3-yard run by Rick Leach, a quarterback, in the second quarter and a 59-yard interception return by Jerry Zuver in the final period.

Michigan 38, Northwestern 7

"I'd love to get into a slugfest where a yard means a yard," said Schembechler after his Wolverines demolished Northwestern at Evanston, Ill., before 31,045 chilly fans.

"We've had too many games like this. We play good football at times and then we don't. We haven't had to sustain it yet, and I think that hurts us. There are several teams still on our schedule who can beat us if we don't play well."

After a slow first quarter, Michigan exploded for four touchdowns in nine minutes, putting matters out of reach of the Wildcats.

Rob Lytle had another great day running. He rushed for 172 yards, thus surpassing Ron Johnson and becoming the third on the list of all-time Michigan rushers. Only Gordon Bell and Billy Taylor are ahead of him.

Brief Statistics	N'western	Mich
First downs	7	38
Rushing net yardage	162	366
Passes attempted	16	7
Passes completed	11	3
Yards gained by passing	111	101
Passes intercepted by	2	2
Fumbles lost	0	0
Yards penalized	50	55

Reprinted with permission from the Michigan Alumnus

Michigan 45, Minnesota 0

A crowd of 104,426 jammed Michigan Stadium for the start of the Little Brown Jug battle, but, as the Michigan score went up and the raindrops came down, three-quarters of the group left the scene before the final gun.

The scenario was pretty much the same as it has been all season: the Wolverines proved unstoppable on offense and unbeatable on defense. It wasn't until the last minute of play that the Gophers got the ball across the 50-yard-line.

Senior Rob Lytle had still another fine game, rushing for 129 yards in 20 tries and scoring a pair of touchdowns. Just like the week before, Sophomore Quarterback Rick Leach threw four times and completed all four, two of them for touchdowns.

The Jug stays in Ann Arbor for another year.

Purdue shocks 'No. 1'

Purdue 16, Michigan 14

Michigan missed tackles, couldn't keep its offense going and generally played a poor game. Purdue lived up to its "Spoilermaker" reputation and downed the Wolverines before 57,205 fans — most of them hysterical — on a sunny Nov. 6 afternoon.

Purdue, coming off a sound thrashing by Michigan State, played superbly against what was the number one team in the nation. Michigan had plenty of chances to chalk up its ninth straight win — but it failed to score with first down on the Purdue four-yard-line, usually reliable Jim Smith dropped a certain touchdown pass, and, in the closing seconds, Bob Wood barely missed a field goal.

It was a superlative upset for the Boilermakers and they deserved the roars of appreciation that shook West Lafayette as it has seldom been shaken.

Dwight Hicks

Jerry Zuver

Michigan 35, Indiana 0

Ocotber 23   Bloomington   39,416

Michigan, playing on the road for the second straight week, received another remarkable performance from Rob Lytle in defeating a capable Indiana team. Lytle gained 175 yards, while Rick Leach was almost flawless at quarterback, directing Michigan to touchdowns the first three times it had possession. Michigan, leading the nation in rushing offense, picked up 383 yards on the ground and showed a total offense of 493 yards. Dwight Hicks returned to action at his free safety position for the first time since Stanford and Russell Davis saw extensive action at fullback with Lytle moving to tailback.

Michigan	7	14	14	0 — 35
Indiana	0	0	0	0 — 0

SCORING
First Quarter
M—Davis, 1-yd run (Wood)
Second Quarter
M—Lytle, 16-yd run (Wood)
M—Johnson, G., 9-yd pass from Leach (Wood)
Third Quarter
M—Davis, 15-yd pass from Leach (Wood)
M—Huckleby, 1-yd run (Wood)

STATISTICS	MICH	IND
First Downs	28	11
Net Yards Rushing	383	123
Net Yards Passing	110	63
Passes Attempted	6	14
Passes Completed	5	5
Intercepted	0	2
Punts/Average	1/45.0	7/36.0
Return Yardage	30	59
Fumbles/Lost	5/2	4/1

Top Individuals
Rushing — Lytle (M) 25-175; R. Davis (M) 15-69; Harkrader (I) 15-65
Passing — Leach (M) 4-4-102; Arnett (I) 5-14-63
Receiving — J. Smith (M) 2-78; Edgar (I) 2-24; Fishel (I) 1-18

Walt Downing

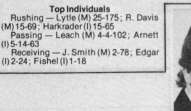
Mark Donahue

Michigan 38, Illinois 7

November 13   Ann Arbor   104,107

There were questions about Michigan's ability to bounce back and they were answered against Illinois. The Wolverines broke a 7-7 tie with two second-period touchdowns to set up a championship game the next week with Ohio State. Jim Smith caught six passes for 127 yards and Greg Morton had 15 tackles for Michigan. Punter John Anderson missed the game with a knee injury. It was Michigan's ninth straight home game before more than 100,000 fans. "This is a good win for us. It pleases me very much," said Bo Schembechler. "This team had all its hopes destroyed last week and it came back strong. We're already looking toward the game in Columbus."

Illinois	7	0	0	0 — 7
Michigan	7	14	14	3 — 38

SCORING

First Quarter
M—Leach, 11-yd run (Wood)
Ill. — Phillips, 2-yd run (Beaver)
Second Quarter
M—Lytle, 5-yd pass from Leach (Wood)
M—Schmerge, 7-yd pass from Leach (Wood)
Third Quarter
M—Lytle, 13-yd run (Wood)
M—Lytle, 2-yd run (Wood)
Fourth Quarter
M—Wood, 37-yd FG

STATISTICS

MICH		ILL
21	First Downs	12
240	Net Yards Rushing	101
156	Net Yards Passing	79
16	Passes Attempted	17
10	Passes Completed	7
1	Intercepted	3
2/33.5	Punts/Average	6/43.8
52	Return Yardage	70
2/1	Fumbles/Lost	1/1

Top Individuals

Rushing — Lytle (M) 21-89; Phillips (I) 21-78; R. Davis (M) 11-65
Passing — Leach (M) 9-15-151; Steger (I) 7-13-79
Receiving — J. Smith (M) 6-127; Friel (I) 3-51

Dominic Tedesco

John Anderson

Jim Bolden

Jim Pickens

Mike Kenn

Jerry Vogele

Michigan Beats Ohio State, 22-0, And Gains a Rose Bowl Berth

After five years of pure frustration, the Michigan Wolverines are once again on their way to Pasadena to meet the Trojans of Southern California in the greatest collegiate football game of them all — the Rose Bowl!

As everyone in the country with a smidgen of interest in college football must know, the Wolverines defeated the Buckeyes of Ohio State, 22-0, in Ohio Stadium before a record crowd of 87,250. Of that number, 4,000 were deliriously happy. The rest were struck numb by a second-half display of power and speed that figured to carry Michigan nearly back to the Number One national ranking it had held before the episode at Purdue.

As this is written, hundreds of excited Michigan alumni are signing up to take the Alumni Association's Official Rose Bowl Tour to Los Angeles to see the January 1 confrontation with Southern California.

Ann Arbor went literally berserk as the gun sounded, giving Michigan the football co-championship with the Buckeyes. Students and townspeople poured out of taverns and homes and filled the street with jubilation.

The victory was probably even more sweet because the Ohio State forces were shut out. The last time any team blanked the Buckeyes was in 1964. Michigan did it that time too.

The Wolverines, on this sunny, crisp Nov. 20 in Columbus, had heroes aplenty. Bo Schembechler says the overriding factor was the superb defense thrown up by his Wolverines. Ohio threatened only once and that was late in the first half. A Buckeye drive put them on Michigan's 10-yard-line, but an ill-conceived and poorly executed pass into the end zone was picked off by Jim Pickens and the Wolverines were out of trouble.

Michigan's execution improved in the second half and the Wolverines broke for two touchdowns, plus a two-point conversion (on a bit of trickery not recently seen in these parts), and the game was in hand.

Here are some of the dressing room quotes from Michigan players:

Greg (Mo) Morton, who made 14 tackles: "This is the biggest thing in my collegiate career. It's the climax of everything."

Rob Lytle, whose 165 yards rushing was a major factor in the win: "We've worked so hard as a team. It's one of the greatest feelings you can have."

Calvin O'Neal, the middle linebacker: "I've been here before. In 1974 we didn't give up a touchdown to them, either (Ohio won, 12-10, on four field goals). This makes my career at Michigan."

And from Ohio State Coach Woody Hayes: "Any team that can beat us that badly has to be Number One."

Reprinted with permission from the **Michigan Alumnus**

Bill Dufek

Bob Wood

Curt Stephenson

Bob Lang

Rose Bowl
Southern Cal 14, Michigan 6

| Jan. 1, 1977 | Pasadena | 106,182 |

Southern California extended its record of Rose Bowl victories to 16 with a strong defense and a superb passing performance by Vince Evans, defeating Michigan 14-6. Evans completed 14 of 20 passes for 181 yards, but all the scoring was done on the ground. Rob Lytle gave Michigan a 6-0 lead on a yard run in the second period, but USC went ahead 7-6 on Evans' rollout run from the one and Glen Walker's conversion kick. A fourth-period TD by freshman tailback Charles White, who rushed for 114 yards, sealed it for USC, but Michigan, behind two pass completions by Rick Leach, moved to the Trojan 17 before running out of downs. USC's Rickey Bell and M's Jerry Zuver both were injured early and missed the rest of the game.

Michigan	0	6	0	0 —	6
Southern Cal	0	7	0	7 —	14

SCORING

Second Quarter
M—Lytle, 1-yd run (KB)
USC—Evans, 1-yd run (Walker)
Fourth Quarter
SC—White, 7-yd run (Walker)

Top Individuals
Rushing — White (SC) 32-114; Lytle (M) 18-67; Tatupu (SC) 7-60; Davis (M) 10-39
Passing — Evans (SC) 14-20-181; Leach (M) 4-12-76

Receiving — Diggs (SC) 8-98; Robinson (SC) 4-42; Smith (M) 2-52

STATISTICS

MICH		USC
12	First Downs	19
155	Net Yards Rushing	200
76	Net Yards Passing	181
12	Passes Attempted	20
4	Passes Completed	14
0	Intercepted	1
5/45.0	Punts/Average	3/29.7
64	Return Yardage	2/17
4/2	Fumbles/Lost	2/1

Wolverine Honors in 1976

JOHN ANDERSON, DE — All-America (Academic, Churchmen's), All-Big Ten (UPI First Team, AP Second Team, Academic).

JIM BOLDEN, DB — All-Big Ten (AP Honorable Mention).

MARK DONAHUE, OG — Consensus All-America (UPI, Football News, NEA, Walter Camp, College Football Writers, AP Honorable Mention) All-Big Ten (AP, UPI, Chicago Tribune).

WALT DOWNING, C — All-America (AP Honorable Mention), All-Big Ten (AP, UPI, Chicago Tribune).

BILL DUFEK, OT — All-America (Tom Harmon, AP Honorable Mention), All-Big Ten (AP, UPI, Chicago Tribune).

DWIGHT HICKS, S — All-Big Ten (AP Second Team).

GENE JOHNSON, TE — All-Big Ten (UPI Second Team).

MIKE KENN, OT — All-Big Ten (UPI Second Team, AP Honorable Mention)

BOB LANG, MG — All-Big Ten (Academic).

RICK LEACH, QB — All-America (AP Honorable Mention), 14th in balloting for Heisman Trophy, All-Big Ten (AP, UPI, Chicago Tribune).

KIRK LEWIS, OG — All-America (UPI Honorable Mention, Churchmen's), All-Big Ten (AP Second Team, Academic Honorable Mention), Arthur D. Robinson Award (for team scholarship).

ROB LYTLE, TB — Consensus All-America (AP, UPI, Kodak Coaches, Walter Camp, Football News, Churchmen's), Wiseman Trophy Winner, third in balloting for Heisman Trophy, Big Ten Silver Football (as conference MVP), Louis B. Hyde Memorial Award (as team MVP), All-Big Ten (AP, UPI, Chicago Tribune).

GREG MORTON, DT — All-America (AP Honorable Mention, Churchmen's), Defensive Lineman of the Year (ABC-TV), All-Big Ten (AP, UPI, Chicago Tribune).

CALVIN O'NEAL, LB — Consensus All-America (UPI, Sporting News, Tom Harmon, Churchmen's, AP Second Team, Football News Third Team), All-Big Ten (AP, UPI, Chicago Tribune).

JIM PICKENS, DB — All-Big Ten (UPI Second Team, AP Honorable Mention, Academic).

JIM SMITH, WB — Consensus All-America (AP, Football News, Sporting News, Walter Camp, College Football Writers, UPI Second Team), All-Big Ten (AP, UPI, Chicago Tribune).

CURT STEPHENSON, SE — All-Big Ten (Academic).

DOMINIC TEDESCO, DE — All-Big Ten (Academic).

BOB WOOD, PK — All-America (Churchmen's Second Team), All-Big Ten (UPI Second Team).

JERRY ZUVER, WOLF — All-America (Churchmen's Second Team), All-Big Ten (UPI Second Team, AP Honorable Mention).

Michigan's 1976 Statistics

12-GAME STATISTICS

Individual

Rushing

	Att	Gain	Loss	Yds	Ave	LP
Lytle	221	1474	5	1469	6.6	75
Huckleby	155	938	26	912	5.9	56
Leach	114	735	97	638	6.0	48
R. Davis	105	596	0	596	5.7	85
J. Smith	25	158	1	157	6.3	51
Reid	16	107	0	107	6.7	18
K. King	20	85	1	84	4.2	13
S. Johnson	21	92	9	83	3.9	27
Clayton	9	52	0	52	5.7	6
Richardson	4	35	0	35	8.8	13
Andrews	4	28	0	28	7.0	15
M. Davis	3	11	0	11	3.7	6
R. Smith	3	11	2	9	3.0	6
Ceddia	2	3	0	3	1.5	3
Willner	1	0	16	-16		
Wangler	3	0	24	-24		

Passing

	Att	Comp	Pct.	Int	Yds	TD	LP
Leach	105	50	.476	8	973	13	64
S. Johnson	3	2	.667	0	30	0	16
Wangler	2	1	.500	0	8	0	8
Ceddia	1	1	1.000	0	5	0	5

Scoring

	TDr	TDp	TDo	ExP	FG	TP
Lytle	14	2	0	0	0	96
Wood	0	0	0	55-57*	7/10	76
Huckleby	11	0	0	0	0	66
Leach	10	0	0	0	0	60
J. Smith	0	6	0	0	0	36
R. Davis	5	1	0	0	0	36
G. Johnson	0	3	0	0	0	18
Zuver	0	0	1	1+	0	8
O'Neal	0	0	1	0	0	6
Reid	1	0	0	0	0	6
S. Johnson	1	0	0	0	0	6
King	1	0	0	0	0	6
Schmerge	0	1	0	0	0	6
Team safeties	0	0	0	0	0	6

*Blocked + Ran for 2 pt. conversion

Receiving

	No.	Yds	Avg	TD	LP
J. Smith	26	714	27.5	6	64
Lytle	9	81	9.0	2	20
G. Johnson	9	78	8.7	3	15
White	3	38	12.7	0	14
R. Davis	2	27	13.5	1	15
Clayton	2	13	6.5	0	8
Stephenson	1	42	42.0	0	42
Harding	1	16	16.0	0	16
Schmerge	1	7	7.0	1	7

Punting

	No.	Yds	Avg	LP
J. Anderson	30	1244	41.5	55
Willner	3	108	36.0	41

Punt Returns

	No.	Yds	Avg	TD	LP
J. Smith	25	313	12.5	0	41
Pickens	4	18	4.5	0	13
Harden	2	40	20.0	0	40
Hicks	2	12	6.0	0	8
Jolly	1	1	1.0	0	1

1976 Statistics (Cont'd.)

Kickoff Returns

	No.	Yds	Avg	TD	LP
J. Smith	15	288	19.2	0	36
Lytle	1	26	26.0	0	26
Clayton	1	17	17.0	0	17
Reid	1	19	19.0	0	19
Richardson	1	5	5.0	0	5

Interceptions

	No.	Yds	TD	LP
Zuver	6	110	1	60
O'Neal	3	60	1	29
J. Anderson	3	27	0	25
Pickens	3	16	0	16
Hicks	2	52	0	51
Harden	1	27	0	27
Tedesco	1	18	0	18
Simpkins	1	5	0	5
Meter	1	2	0	2
Bolden	1	0	0	0
Howard	1	0	0	0

Fumble Recoveries

3 - J. Anderson		1 - Hicks
3 - Tedesco		1 - O'Neal
1 - Howard		1 - Vogele
1 - Zuver		1 - Graves

Passes Broken Up

8 - Zuver		3 - Bolden
7 - Hicks		1 - Morton
7 - O'Neal		1 - Simpkins
4 - J. Anderson		1 - Harden
4 - Howard		1 - Jackson
3 - Pickens		

Touchdown Saves

4 - Bolden
3 - Hicks
1 - Patek

Team Statistics

	Mich	Opp		Mich	Opp
Total First Downs	264	177	Total No. of Punts	33	75
Rushing	211	83	Total yards	1352	2811
Passing	40	87	Average per punt	41.0	37.5
Penalty	13	7			
Total Offensive Plays	817	796	Total Kick Ret	53/739	53/671
Rushing Attempts	706	512	Punt Ret/Yds	34/384	11/38
Rushing Yards	4144	1454	Kickoff Ret	19/355	42/633
Passing Yards	1016	1593	Intercep./Yds	23/317	8/43
Passing Att.	111	284			
Pass Com.	54	155	Fumbles/Lost	30/19	28/12
Total Off. Yds.	5160	3047	Penalties/Yards	30/307	44/357

Canham Keys Broad Success In 'M' Athletics

Michigan Athletic Director Don Canham often is invited by universities to discuss the administration of intercollegiate athletics. His first suggestion is to "surround yourself with capable people."

Building administrative and coaching staffs has been a priority since Canham was appointed athletic director, just the fifth in 'M' history, in 1968. Two of Canham's former assistants, Bump Elliott and Dave Strack, became athletic directors, while five assistant football coaches went on to head coaching positions. Promotions and retirements have forced complete turnovers in all but two sports.

Despite these changes, the Wolverines have won 31 of their 199 Big Ten titles over this nine-year period. Last season the football team won the Big Ten title and went to the Rose Bowl, the cross-country team won its third straight title, the basketball team won the conference title and made a record fourth straight trip to the NCAA tournament, the hockey team battled to the finals of the NCAA Championships, the tennis team won its 10th straight title and a berth in the NCAAs, while the baseball team, after two straight titles, finished second, but still competed in the NCAA.

In addition to this across-the-board excellence in competition, Michigan offers one of the finest athletic plants in the nation as Canham has earmarked more than $4 million in expansion and improvement of facilities. This was totally funded by athletic department revenues.

He also spearheaded the $7.2 million construction of two recreational sports buildings (financed by the University), transferred the IM Building to the University, financed a $140,000 renovation of the old ice arena, turning it into a general sports building. Michigan now has 333,000 square feet of indoor recreational sports space, more than any university in the nation.

Nationally, Canham serves on various Big Ten and NCAA committees, including the important NCAA television and promotions committees. The former Michigan track coach has directed a football promotional campaign that has helped Michigan break all NCAA attendance records.

Canham operated a highly successful sports equipment business that was placed in trust upon his appointment. He was a national high jump champion, captain of the Wolverines track team and as Michigan's track coach won 12 Big Ten titles.

MICHIGAN'S STAFF—The 1977 Wolverine staff includes (left to right): Kneeling—
Darrel Burton, Jerry Hanlon, Bo Schembechler, Paul Schudel, Don Nehlen. Rear—
Larry Pierson and Bob Thornbladh (special assistants), Tom Reed, Bill McCartney,
Jack Harbaugh, Dennis Brown, and Jerry Zuver and Tim Davis (parttime young
assistants).

Michigan 37, Illinois 9

There was a fair amount of apprehension in the Wolverine camp just before the season opener with the Illini. For one thing, it was at Champaign-Urbana. For another, Gary Moeller, a Michigan assistant just a year ago, is the new head coach at Illinois and no one knew exactly what he had installed for an offense. For a third, Michigan had experienced some upsetting injuries in the line and had to leave some valuable people at home.

But, with the exceptions of two fumbles and two pass interceptions, the Wolverines made it known to the college football world that they are likely to be one of the best in the nation again in 1977. Indeed, two days after the game, the UPI coaches' poll said the Big Blue was Number One.

"I don't think we played as well as we are capable of playing," said Bo Schembechler, "but, all in all, I have to be satisfied with it for a first game. You have to remember that Illinois is a team that knows everything about us. We both made a lot of mistakes. We gave them nine points and they gave us some."

SCORE BY QUARTERS					
ILLINOIS	3	0	0	6	— 9
MICHIGAN	13	7	10	7	— 37

SUMMARY OF SCORING

ILL — Finzer, 42 FG — 11:55 1Q
MICH — Clayton, 30 pass from Leach (Willner kick) — 3:16 1Q
MICH — Huckleby, 15 run (kick wide) — 42 1Q
MICH — Huckleby, 3 run (Willner kick) — 2:50 2Q
MICH — G. Johnson, 11 pass from Leach (Willner kick) — 1:20 3Q
MICH — Davis, 4 run (Willner kick) — 7:31 4Q
ILL — Baker, 1 run (kick wide) — 2:25 4Q

Michigan Stadium, the largest college-owned football stadium in the nation, has a seating capacity of 101,701.

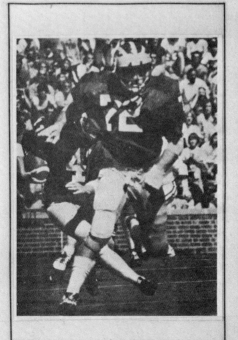

WALT DOWNING

Michigan 21, Duke 9
Sept. 17/at Ann Arbor

Michigan looked anything but the No. 1 ranked team in the nation in defeating Duke. An intercepted pass and a fumble recovery led to two Michigan touchdowns in the first half as Rick Leach scored from seven yards out and Russell Davis from four. The Blue Devils held the Wolverines scoreless in the third period and Mike Dunn, passing effectively, led a 77-yard march, and scored the TD himself from the three. Early in the fourth period Duke narrowed it to 14-9 on a field goal. Michigan immediately responded with an 80-yard drive as Leach scored from the one. The Wolverine defense then intercepted a pass and recovered a fumble to stop Duke twice and preserve the victory. John Anderson was Defensive Champion, but the staff decided not to name an Offensive Champion. Rick Leach, however, was UPI Big Ten Player of the Week, running for 98 yards and passing for 76.

Michigan 14, Navy 7
Sept. 24/at Ann Arbor

Michigan again struggled through a scoreless first period, then Harlan Huckleby scored twice in the second quarter to give the Wolverines a halftime lead of narrow proportions. Navy, as is its custom, battled all the way, scoring a touchdown in the third period, while Michigan's offense struggled without a first down during the entire 15 minutes of action. The fourth quarter was scoreless. Navy actually had more first down (17-16) and moved 194 yards through the air on the passing of Bob Leszczynski. Ron Simpkins had 19 tackles for the Wolverines, while Curtis Greer, voted Defensive Champion, had 10 with two sacks. Tackle Mike Kenn was the Offensive Champion. Michigan slipped from No. 1 to third in the polls as a result of this game.

Michigan
ENDS: Gene Johnson, Schmerge, White, Stephenson.
TACKLES: Powers, Kenn, Keitz, Godfrey, Greer.
GUARDS: Szara, Donahue, Arbenzik, Graves, Melita.
CENTERS: Downing, Lilja.
LINEBACKERS: Tedesco, Seabron, John Anderson, Simpkins, Meter, Owens.
BACKS: Clayton, Richardson, Russell Davis, Huckleby, Leach, Hicks, Patek, Jolly, Howard, Braman, Harden, Pickens, Willner, Labun.

Navy
ENDS: McConkey, Jones, Hendershot, Cellon, Nixon, Stephens.
TACKLES: Lippard, Ryan, Merrill, Trass, Redvict.
GUARDS: Kremer, Bott, Schafer, Thompson.
CENTER: Fritsch.
LINEBACKERS: Paulk, Zingler, DeStafney, Mygas, Thorton.
BACKS: Leszynski, Gattuso, Callahan, Miller, Klawinski, Walker, Kurowski, Milo, Klein, McCormick, Flanagan, Sturges, Ross, Wilson, Galpin, Chanian, Gilbert, Tata.

TEAM FIGURES

	Michigan	Navy
First Downs	14	7
Rushes-Yards	55-241	41-107
Passes	4-5-0	16-28-1
Passing Yards	36	194
Total Plays-Offense	60-277	69-301
Return Yards	64	34
Punts-Average	6-45.0	6-37.5
Penalties	4-40	5-43
Fumbles-Lost	1-1	0-0

SCORING

NAVY	0 0 7 0 — 7
MICHIGAN	0 14 0 0 — 14

M — Harlan Huckleby 13-yard run (Greg Willner kick)
M — Harlan Huckleby 22-yard run (Greg Willner kick)
N — Sandy Jones 34-yard pass from Bob Leszynski (Bob Tate kick)

MIKE KENN

Kevin King

Rex Mackall

Ron Simpkins

Russell Davis

Michigan 56, Wisconsin 0
Oct. 15/at Ann Arbor

Michigan met an undefeated team for the second straight week with Wisconsin posing a definite threat for the Big Ten title. 'M' took charge immediately, scoring with the opening kickoff with Rick Leach capping an 81-yard drive by passing 10 yards to Doug Marsh. Leach and Roosevelt Smith had short TD runs in the second period and two more scores put it out of reach in the third period. Smith, subbing for the injured Harlan Huckleby, gained 157 yards and scored twice. Leach, with 127 yards passing and 2 TD strikes, was Michigan's Offensive Champion, while Derek Howard was the Defensive Champion. The victory moved Michigan into No. 1 position in both wire polls.

SCORING

WISCONSIN	0 0 0 0 — 0
MICHIGAN	7 14 14 21 — 56

M — Doug Marsh 7-yard pass from Rick Leach (Gregg Willner kick)
M — Rick Leach 2-yard run (Gregg Willner kick)
M — Roosevelt Smith 2 yard run (Gregg Willner kick)
M — Gene Johnson 22-yard pass from Rick Leach (Gregg Willner kick)
M — Russell Davis 37-yard run (Nick Labun kick)
M — Roosevelt Smith 2-yard run (Nick Labun kick)
M — Stan Edwards 3-yard run (Nick Labun kick)
M — Brian Dickey 3-yard run (Nick Labun kick)

Nick Labun

John Anderson

ANN ARBOR, Mich., Oct. 1 (AP) — After losing two fumbles, Russell Davis ran for two touchdowns that put Michigan on its way to an overwhelming 41-3 rout of mistake-prone Texas A. & M. today.

The Aggies got a 24-yard field goal from Tony Franklin in the first quarter, five plays after Mike Williams recovered a Davis fumble at the Michigan 27. But it was the Wolverines' game the rest of the way before a crowd of 104,802.

Davis wound up with 110 yards rushing in 19 carries, his touchdowns coming on a 4-yard run in the second quarter and a 1-yard plunge in the third as the Wolverines took a 13-0 lead.

Michigan's other touchdowns were a 35-yard pass from Rick Leach to Curt Stephenson, an 8-yard run by Harlan Huckleby, a recovered punt in the end zone by Jim Pickens and a 50-yard interception return by Mike Jolly.

TEAM FIGURES

	Michigan	Texas A&M
First Downs	12	12
Rushes-Yards	44-197	70-208
Passes	7-19-0	1-10-2
Passing Yards	103	3
Total Plays-Total Offense	63-300	80-211
Return Yards	111	140
Penalties-Yards	11-102	4-40
Fumbles Lost	2-2	4-3

SCORING

TEXAS A&M	3 0 0 0 — 3
MICHIGAN	0 7 13 21 — 41

A&M — Tony Franklin 24-yard field goal
M — Russell Davis 4-yard run (Gregg Willner kick)
M — Russell Davis 1-yard run (run failed)
M — Curt Stephenson 35-ayrd pass from Rick Leach (Gregg Willner kick)
M — Harlan Huckleby 8-yard run (Gregg Willner kick)
M — Jim Pickens blocked punt (Gregg Willner kick)
M — Mike Jolly 50-yard interception return (Gregg Willner kick)

Michigan 24, Michigan State 14

It was anything but easy! The Spartans, much improved over a year ago and playing on their home field, battled from gun to gun before falling to the Wolverines.

With something like 10 minutes left, it was anybody's ball game. Many in the Michigan section were casting uneasy glances at each other as State, behind by only 10, moved the ball from its own 20 to the Wolverine 36. But a fumble recovery by the Big Blue ended the threat and Michigan was on the Spartans' 1-yard line when time ran out.

The game, played before 78,183, see-sawed back and forth and the weather did the same. A violent thundershower hit the stadium in the second half and a stiff wind prevailed throughout the contest.

Brief Statistics	MSU	Mich.
First downs	13	19
Rushing net yardage	107	302
Passes attempted	23	10
Passes completed	14	4
Yards gained by passing	147	111
Passes intercepted by	1	1
Fumbles lost	4	2
Yards penalized	38	42

Minnesota 16, Michigan 0

Were these the same players who represented Michigan seven days earlier in the 56-0 rout of Wisconsin? Their names and numbers were the same, but after that, the similarity is short-lived.

In what Bo Schembechler called "the poorest offensive game we've ever played," the Wolverines could muster only 80 yards on the ground. As a result, they threw 29 times, many of the passes coming in desperation in the final few minutes.

One of Michigan's troubles was that the offense never got cranked up. It ran three plays and — if it didn't fumble or get intercepted — punted. "We can't leave our defense on the field like that. Three plays and punt, that's ridiculous." It was the first time in 113 games that Michigan failed to score.

And so, the Little Brown Jug takes up residence in Minnesota, at least temporarily, and the Wolverines find that they must win all the rest in order to get to Pasadena.

Brief Statistics	Minn.	Mich.
First downs	13	12
Rushing net yardage	190	80
Passes attempted	10	29
Passes completed	6	13
Yards gained by passing	60	122
Passes intercepted by	2	0
Fumbles lost	0	3
Yards penalized	40	12

```
              SCORING
MICHIGAN                  0  0  0  0— 0
MINNESOTA                10  3  0  3—16
MN — Rogindn 41 field goal
MN — Barber 3-run (Rogind kick)
MN — Rogind 37 field goal
MN — Rogind 32 field goal
```

Michigan 40, Purdue 7
Nov. 12/at West Lafayette

Michigan avenged a 1976 loss to Purdue, settled any question about winning on grass, and, most importantly, set up another title showdown with Ohio State. Again, however, 'M' found itself behind as Purdue scored on a Mark Herrmann pass in the first period. Gregg Willner's field goal made it 7-3. Playing on prescription grass, Michigan began to move, rolling up 317 yards rushing. Rick Leach tossed two more touchdown passes, giving him 29 in 34 games. Russell Davis, voted Offensive Champion of the Game, gained 167 yards, while tailbacks Stanley Edwards had 66 and Roosevelt Smith 53 as Harlan Huckleby again was idled by injury. Gene Johnson also missed the game, but the tight end position appeared solid as Mark Schmerge caught two TD passes. Michigan's defense intercepted three passes of frosh sensation Herrmann, including a 30-yard TD steal

Michigan 23, Iowa 6
Oct. 29/at Ann Arbor

Michigan faced a must-win situation for three straight weeks, starting with Iowa, and quarterback Rick Leach took charge of the first challenge. The junior southpaw fired three touchdown passes, passed for a season high 202 yards, and rushed for 59 yards to spark the victory. His first TD toss came on a broken play and went 63 yards to Russell Davis. Iowa scored early in the fourth period, but the 'M' defense, led by Dom Tedesco's sack of quarterback Tom McLaughlin in the end zone for a safety, was overpowering. Center Walt Downing, on his way to All-American honors, and tackle Dale Keitz were named the week's champions.

```
            Michigan 26, Iowa 3
Iowa ... ... ... ... ...   0  0  0  6— 6
Michigan ... ... ... ...   7  7  7  2—23
 Mich—R. Davis 63 pass from Leach
    (Willner kick)
 Mich—G. Johnson 6 pass from Leach
    (Willner kick)
 Mich—White 32 pass from Leach (Will-
    ner kick)
 Iowa—McLaughlin 1 run (run failed)
 Mich—Safety, McLaughlin tackled in
    end zone
    A—104,617

                         Iowa  Michigan
First downs                12      19
Rushes-yards            36-50   57-208
Passing yards             174     202
Return yards                0       0
Passes                  16-22-0  9-12-0
Punts                    7-37    3-43
Fumbles-lost              2-1     2-2
Penalties-yards          5-70    5-35
```

Dominic Tedesco

Max Richardson

by linebacker Dom Tedesco. Ron Simpkins had 10 tackles and deflected two passes to earn Champion of the Game.

```
              SCORING
PURDUE  ... ... ... ...    7  0  0  0— 7
MICHIGAN ... ... ... ...   3 14 21  2—40
P — Mark Hermann 6-yard pass to Dave
  Young (Scott Sovereen kick good)
M — Gregg Willner 28-yard field goal
M — Rick Leach 28-yard pass to Mark
  Schmerge (Willner kick good)
M— Roosevelt Smith 2-yard run (Willner kick
  good)
M — Russell Davis 24-yard run (Willner kick
  good)
M — Dominic Tedesco 30-yard interception re-
  turn (Willner kick good)
M — Rick Leach 6-yard pass to Mark
  Schmerge (Willner kick good)
M — Tom Seabron tackles Mark Herrmann for
  safety
```

Michigan 63, Northwestern 20

A crowd of 103,211 — the 15th straight crowd in excess of 100,000 in Michigan Stadium — watched the Wolverines sputter through the first half and then rip the out-manned Wildcats unmercifully in the second half to win, 63-20.

Something like 77 Michigan players got into the game, leading Schembechler to comment, "We needed a game like this. It's especially great for our demonstration team players. It's a great morale booster. These kids bust their necks all week long and seldom get to play."

The Wolverines, largely thwarted in the first half of the contest, glued it all together in the second stanza, scoring 49 of their 63 points. Quarterback Rick Leach had another good throwing day, completing eight of 11 passes for 155 yards.

On the ground, Michigan ran for 323 yards, lead by Fullback Russell Davis.

```
              SCORING
NORTHWESTERN — 7  0  0 13—20
MICHIGAN — 0 14 28 21 — 63
N — Scott Stranski 1-yard run (Sam Poulos
  kick)
M — Harlan Huckleby 4-yard run (Gregg
  Willner kick)
M — Gene Johnson fumble recovery (Gregg
  Willner kick)
  Rick Leach 21-yard run (Gregg Willner kick)
M — Rich Leach 4-yard run (Gregg Willner
  kick)
M — Stanley Edwards 26-yard pass from
  Rick Leach (Gregg Willner kick)
M — Ralph Clayton 41-yard pass from Rick
  Leach (Gregg Willner kick)
M — Lawrence Reid 19-yard run (Gregg
  Willner kick)
N — Todd Sheets 28-yard pass from Scott
  Stranski (Sam Poulos kick)
M — Mike Smith 15-yard run (Gregg Willner
  kick)
M — Alan Mitchell 33-yard pass from John
  Wangler (Gregg Willner kick)
N — Mark Bailey 8-yard pass from Scott
  Stranski (pass failed)
```

MARK DONAHUE

Michigan 14, Ohio State 6

It is not at all clear that the better team won in Michigan Stadium on Saturday, Nov. 19. But the team with the most points did.

And so the Wolverine football squad — co-champions of the Big Ten — is headed west once more to represent the Western Conference in the Rose Bowl game. Whether Bo's boys will play Washington or U.C.L.A. had not been determined at this writing.

Ohio State won the statistics in the big game, but Michigan got the points and the 14-6 victory evens up matters between Schembechler and Woody Hayes in their nine meetings. Each has four victories and there was one tie.

As everyone who is even remotely interested must know by this time, it was Michigan's tenacious defense that stopped the Buckeyes time and again when it looked as though Ohio would rip into Michigan's end zone.

"Our defense was terrific," grinned Schembechler. "They came up with the big plays when we had to have them. This is a great Ohio State offense and we have now held them out of the end zone for three of the last four games."

The Buckeyes moved the ball for 203 yards on the ground and 144 through the air — enough to win most ball games. But Michigan pounced on two Ohio fumbles and stopped the Buckeyes when they had to.

"It was a great victory," beamed Bo. "This team has overcome more adversity than any team I've had in 25 years of coaching. Our injuries were devastating, but they kept coming back. I feel great for these kids. They never give up."

Millions on television and 106,024 — the largest assemblage ever for a regular-season football game — can attest to that.

Brief Statistics	Ohio	Mich.
First downs	23	10
Rushing net yardage	203	141
Passes attempted	16	9
Passes completed	13	3
Yards gained by passing	144	55
Passes intercepted by	0	0
Fumbles lost	2	1
Yards penalized	5	5

U-M Marching Band Director George Cavender (right) achknowledges the ovation of an enthusiastic Homecoming crowd in Michigan Stadium as he is presented with a plaque denoting his 25 years of service to the University. Dr. Daniel Kutt, president of the Michigan Band Alumni (left), made the presentation.

Reprinted with permission from the **Michigan Alumnus**

Steve Graves

Jim Pickens

Roger Bettis

Rick White

Reprinted with permission from the Michigan Alumnus

U-M Attendance Sets NCAA Mark

MISSION, Kan. — (AP) — The Michigan Wolverines drew record-breaking crowds to their seven home games this season and won the national college football attendance battle for the fourth straight year, the NCAA Statistics Service reported Thursday.

An average of 104,203 fans attended at Michigan, which topped last year's record of 103,159 Michigan fans. Michigan also held the 1975 record with 98,499 at Ann Arbor.

Ohio State had dominated the national attendance figures between 1949 and 1974 with 14 straight titles before Michigan ended the streak in 1972. Ohio State won again in 1973 and then Michigan took the title.

The Buckeyes held the second spot this year with an average of 87,589 fans. The battle between the two teams drew a regular season game record of 106,024 fans.

TEAM
RECORD: 10-1 (Big Ten 7-1)

Date	M		Opp	Attend
9/10	37	at Illinois	9	60,477
9/17	21	Duke	9	104,072
9/24	14	Navy	7	101,800
10/1	41	Texas A&M	3	104,802
10/8	24	at Mich. State	14	78,183
10/15	56	Wisconsin	0	104,892
10/22	0	at Minnesota	16	44,165
10/29	23	Iowa	6	104,617
11/5	63	Northwestern	20	103,211
11/12	40	at Purdue	7	68,003
11/19	14	Ohio State	6	106,024

SCORES BY QUARTERS

	1	2	3	4	Total
MICHIGAN	30	108	114	81	333
Opponents	33	10	16	38	97

Curt Stephenson

Derek Howard

UNIVERSITY OF MICHIGAN ROSTER

No.	Name	Pos	Hgt	Wgt	Class	Hometown
86	***Anderson, John	OLB	6-3	219	Sr	Waukesha, WI
64	Arbeznik, John	OG	6-3	237	Jr	University Hts., OH
61	*Bartnick, Greg	OG	6-2	233	Jr	Detroit
65	Becker, Kurt	OT	6-6	230	Fr	Aurora, IL
48	Bednarek, Jeff	ILB	6-4	237	So	Trenton
42	Bell, Gene	S	6-2	196	So	East Liverpool, OH
12	Bettis, Roger	QB	6-2	190	Sr	Minerva, OH
28	Braman, Mark	DHB	6-1	192	Jr	Midland
8	Breaugh, Jim	QB	6-2	188	Fr	West Bloomfield
45	Brown, Woody	S	5-10	175	Sr	East Detroit
41	Cannavino, Andy	OLB	6-1	203	Fr	Cleveland, OH
34	Christian, Chuck	OLB	6-3½	203	Fr	Detroit
22	Clayton, Ralph	TB	6-3	211	So	Detroit
33	**Davis, Russell	FB	6-1	220	Jr	Woodbridge, VA
92	*DeSantis, Mark	OLB	6-3	215	Jr	Harper Woods
6	Dickey, Brian	QB	6-0	185	Fr	Ottawa, OH
29	Diggs, Gerald	TB	6-0	186	So	Chicago, IL
60	**Donahue, Mark	OG	6-3	245	Sr	Oak Lawn, IL
72	**Downing, Walt	C	6-4	254	Sr	Coatesville, PA
32	Edwards, Stanley	RB	6-2	205	Fr	Detroit
13	Feaster, Rodney	WR	6-2	180	Fr	Flint
68	*Giesler, Jon	OT	6-4	253	Jr	Woodville, OH
51	Gilmore, Keith	ILB	6-1	204	So	Highland Park
74	Ginley, Neal	OT	6-7	250	Fr	Parma, OH
90	Godfrey, Chris	DT	6-4	239	So	Miami Lakes, FL
54	*Graves, Steve	MG	6-1	218	Sr	Cleveland, OH
95	*Greer, Curtis	DT	6-4	237	Jr	Detroit
4	Harden, Michael	DHB	6-1	179	So	Detroit
83	Harding, Dave	ILB	6-3	226	Sr	Northville
31	Harris, Stuart	DB	6-2	190	Fr	Chagrin Falls, OH
17	***Hicks, Dwight	S	6-1	180	Sr	Pennsauken, NJ
10	***Howard, Derek	Wolf	6-1	193	Sr	Hamilton, OH
25	**Huckleby, Harlan	TB	6-1½	199	Jr	Detroit
58	Humphries, Jim	MG	5-11	209	So	Detroit
97	Jackson, Jeff	DE	6-7½	228	Fr	Toledo, OH
93	*Jackson, William	DT	6-3	226	Jr	Richmond, VA
88	**Johnson, Gene	TE	6-3	227	Jr	Flint
15	Johnson, Irvin	OLB	6-2	200	So	Warren, OH
81	Johnson, Oliver	OLB	6-3½	220	Fr	Detroit
16	*Jolly, Michael	DHB	6-3	178	So	Melvindale
44	Jones, Rick	ILB	6-3	215	Fr	Detroit
51	Kadela, Dave	OT	6-2	236	Jr	Dearborn
81	Kasparek, Ed	WR	6-1	180	Jr	Dearborn
55	Keitz, Dale	DT	6-1	240	Jr	Columbus, OH
94	Keller, Tom	OLB	6-2	203	So	Grand Rapids
78	**Kenn, Mike	OT	6-6½	244	Sr	Evanston, IL
57	Keough, Kelly	DT	6-3	230	Fr	Merrillville, IN
36	*King, Kevin	FB	6-2	212	Sr	Oak Lawn, IL
39	Kligis, Mike	Wolf	6-3	195	Fr	Lombard, IL
6	Kozlowski, Jim	DHB	5-11	180	So	Detroit
70	Kwiatkowski, Dan	OT	6-4½	235	Fr	Detroit
3	Labun, Nick	PK	5-11	172	Sr	Rockford, IL
7	**Leach, Rick	QB	6-1	192	Jr	Flint
76	Leoni, Mike	OT	6-3	255	So	Flint
34	Leoni, Tony	Wolf	5-10	194	So	Flint
59	Lilja, George	C	6-4	239	So	Palos Park, IL
63	Lindsay, Rock	OT	6-2	235	Jr	Lapeer
49	**Mackall, Rex	ILB	6-4	220	Sr	Berea, OH
45	Malinak, Tim	ILB	6-1	222	Jr	Flemington, PA
80	Marsh, Doug	TE	6-3	229	So	Akron, OH
38	Melita, Tom	MG	6-1	224	Jr	Penns Grove, NJ
46	*Meter, Jerry	ILB	6-3	206	Jr	Birmingham
30	Mitchell, Alan	WR	6-2	190	Fr	Detroit
52	Motley, Fred	DT	6-2½	215	Fr	Dayton, OH
27	Murray, Dan	Wolf	6-0	194	So	Ann Arbor
83	Needham, Ben	Wolf	6-5	215	Fr	Groveport, OH
96	Nicolau, Dave	DT	6-5	235	Fr	Arlington Hts., IL
56	Novak, Richard	OT	6-5	244	So	Calumet City, IL
79	Osbun, Tony	DT	6-5	240	Fr	Kenton, OH
53	Owens, Mel	OLB	6-2	222	So	DeKalb, IL
93	Payne, Dave	OLB	6-1	196	So	Detroit
18	**Pickens, Jim	DHB	6-0	182	Sr	Sylvania, OH
67	Powers, John	OG	6-3	261	So	Oak Park, IL
71	Prepolec, John	OT	6-4	240	Fr	Bloomfield Hills
70	Quinn, Gary	OT	6-3	242	So	Quincy, MA
23	Reid, Lawrence	FB	6-1	206	So	Philadelphia, PA
43	***Richardson, Max	WB	6-0	187	Sr	Fort Wayne, IN
82	**Schmerge, Mark	TE	6-3	229	Jr	Cincinnati, OH
91	**Seabron, Tom	OLB	6-3	208	Jr	Detroit
40	*Simpkins, Ron	ILB	6-1	221	So	Detroit
44	Smith, Mike	TB	5-10	170	Sr	Kalamazoo
26	Smith, Roosevelt	TB	5-10	198	So	Detroit
85	**Stephenson, Curt	WR	6-1	177	Sr	La Jolla, CA
69	**Szara, Gerry	OG	6-1	240	Sr	Oak Lawn, IL
99	*Tedesco, Dominic	OLB	6-4	212	Sr	Riverside, IL
79	Torzy, Mark	OT	6-4	241	Jr	Warren
77	Trgovac, Mike	MG	6-2	220	Fr	Austintown, OH
66	Wandersleben, Tom	OG	6-3½	250	Fr	Euclid, OH
5	Wangler, John	QB	6-2	189	So	Royal Oak
62	Weber, Gary	DT	6-2	241	So	Matawan, NJ
84	*White, Rick	WR	6-4	200	Sr	Cincinnati, OH
19	Williams, Virgil	WB	5-10	185	So	Lorain, OH
1	Willner, Gregg	PK	5-10	156	Jr	Miami Beach, FL
56	Wunderli, Greg	DT	6-6	230	Fr	St. Louis, MO
37	Yearian, Kirk	DHB	6-0	185	Fr	Downers Grove, IL

* Letters won

Mike Smith

BO SCHEMBECHLER'S COACHING RECORD

at Miami

1963	5-3-2	.625
1964	6-3-1	.667
1965	7-3	.700
1966	9-1	.900
1967	6-4	.600
1968	7-3	.700
Total	40-17-3	.702

at Michigan

1969	8-3	.727
1970	9-1	.900
1971	11-1	.917
1972	10-1	.909
1973	10-0-1	1.000
1974	10-1	.909
1975	8-2-2	.800
1976	10-2	.833
1977	10-1	.909
Totals	86-12-3	.878
15-year Totals	126-29-6	.813

Woody Brown

Dwight Hicks

Gerry Szara

Dave Harding

MICHIGAN FINAL STATS

11 GAMES

Rushing	TCB	YG	YL	NET	Avg	TD	LP
R. Davis	207	1015	2	1013	4.9	7	44
Huckleby	160	769	26	743	4.6	6	31
Leach	106	488	118	370	3.5	7	21
R. Smith	57	313	5	308	5.4	4	25
Edwards	33	161	9	152	4.6	1	12
King	20	77	0	77	3.9	0	14
Dickey	7	79	21	58	8.3	1	74
Reid	8	57	0	57	7.1	1	19
M. Smith	6	32	0	32	5.3	1	15
Clayton	7	24	8	16	2.3	0	20
Wangler	2	10	0	10	5.0	0	8
Richardson	3	4	3	1	0.3	0	2
UM	616	3029	192	2837	4.6	29	74
OPP	488	—	—	1287	2.6	6	—

Passing	PC	PA	HI	Yds	Pct	TD	LP
Leach	76	147	7	1109	.517	13	63
Wangler	1	2	1	33	.500	1	33
Dickey	1	3	0	−3	.333	0	−3
UM	78	152	8	1139	.513	14	63
OPP	121	221	13	1327	.548	5	—

Receiving	No.	Yds	Avg	TD	LP
Clayton	19	393	20.7	2	41
G. Johnson	13	187	14.4	3	31
Huckleby	12	104	8.7	0	15
R. Davis	12	148	12.3	1	63
Marsh	5	52	10.4	1	22
R. Smith	5	46	9.2	0	22
Edwards	4	55	13.8	1	26
White	3	59	19.7	2	32
Stephenson	2	48	24.0	1	35
Schmerge	2	14	7.0	2	8
Mitchell	1	33	33.0	1	33
UM	78	1139	14.6	14	63
OPP	121	1327	11.0	5	—

Scoring	TD	PAT	FG	Saf	TP
Willner	—	40-41	3-12		49
R. Davis	8	—	—		48
Leach	7	—	—		42
Huckleby	6	—	—		36
R. Smith	4	—	—		24
G. Johnson	4	—	—		24
Edwards	2	—	—		12
White	2	—	—		12
Clayton	2	—	—		12
Schmerge	2	—	—		12
Dickey	1	—	—		6
Reid	1	—	—		6
M. Smith	1	—	—		6
Stephenson	1	—	—		6
Marsh	1	—	—		6
Mitchell	1	—	—		6
Jolly	1	—	—		6
Pickens	1	—	—		6
Tedesco	1	—	—		6
Labun	—	4-4	—		4
Team	—	0-1		4	8
UM	29	44-46	3-12	4	333

Punting	No	Yds	Avg	LP
Anderson	52	2099	40.4	56
OPP	74	2721	36.7	—

Punt Rets.	No.	Yds	Avg	TD	LP
Hicks	16	161	10.1	0	49
Harden	14	86	6.1	0	19
Jolly	3	28	9.3	0	11
UM	34	279	8.2	0	49
OPP	23	149	6.5	0	—

Kickoff Rets.	No.	Yds	Avg	TD	LP
Clayton	7	137	19.6	0	24
Huckleby	4	90	22.5	0	38
R. Smith	4	80	20.0	0	26
Harden	3	49	16.3	0	20
Edwards	2	86	43.0	0	62
Hicks	1	14	14.0	0	14
UM	21	456	21.7	0	62
OPP	52	861	16.6	0	—

Interceptions	No.	Yds	Avg	TD	LP
Hicks	3	32	10.1	0	22
Jolly	2	54	27.0	1	50
Howard	2	14	7.0	0	14
Pickens	2	0	0.0	0	0
Tedesco	1	30	30.0	1	30
Harris	1	21	21.0	0	21
Murray	1	13	13.0	0	13
Anderson	1	0	0.0	0	0
UM	13	164	12.6	2	50
OPP	8	88	11.0	0	—

FUMBLE RECOVERIES
5 - Simpkins, 4 - Tedesco, 2 - Meter, 2
Stephenson, 1 - Jolly, 1 - G. Johnson,
Keitz, 1 - Nicolau, 1 - O. Johnson, 1
Anderson, 1 - Howard
PASSES BROKEN UP
4 - Simpkins, 3 - Howard, 3 - Meter, 3
Hicks, 2 - Tedesco, 2 - Pickens, 1
Anderson, 1 - Jolly, 1 - Seabron
TOUCHDOWN SAVES
1 - Howard, 1 - Pickens, 1 - Owens
BLOCKED PUNT   SAFET
Simpkins   1 - Tedesco, 1 - Seabro

TACKLES	Solo	Asst	Total	TL	Y
Simpkins	113	45	158	8	
Meter	62	34	96	3	
Greer	54	34	88	11	
Anderson	51	36	87	6	
Hicks	45	27	72	2	
Pickens	43	22	65	-	
Tedesco	36	27	63	10	7
Howard	33	24	57	-	
Keitz	24	30	54	1	
Graves	35	16	51	3	
Owens	30	15	45	2	
Jolly	29	14	43	3	
Harden	30	5	35	-	
Seabron	23	9	32	6	4
Godfrey	19	7	26	2	2
Melita	14	11	25	2	1

TEAM STATISTICS	MICH	OPP
Total Points	333	97
Avg pts/Game	30.3	8.8
Touchdowns	46	11
by Rush	29	6
by Pass	14	5
Other	3	0
First Downs	204	153
by Rush	150	87
by Pass	50	60
by Penalty	4	5
Rushing Attempts	616	488
Yards Gained	3029	—
Yards Lost	192	—
Net Yards Rushing	2837	1287
Avg/Carry	4.6	2.6
Avg/Game	257.9	117.0
Passes Completed/Att.	78/152	121/221
Passes Had Inter.	8	13
Percentage	.513	.548
Net Yards Passing	1139	1327
Avg/Comp.	14.6	11.0
Avg/Game	103.5	120.6
Total Plays	768	708
Total Net Yards	3976	2614
Yds/Play	5.2	3.7
Yds/Game	361.2	237.6
Punts/Net Yds	52/2099	74/2721
Average	40.4	36.7
Punt Returns/Yds	34/279	23/149
Avg/Return	8.2	6.5
Kickoff Returns/Yds	21/456	52/861
Avg/Return	21.7	16.6
Interceptions/Yds	13/164	8/88
Avg/Inter.	12.6	11.0
Penalties/Yds	47/432	30/294
Fumbles/Lost	26/19	31/19

Rick Leach Sets
Record for Yards

Valiant Comeback Falls Short

By Wayne DeNeff
NEWS SPORTS EDITOR

PASADENA, Calif. — Michigan batted back valiantly from just about total disaster in the 64th Rose Bowl game but couldn't save itself from its 7th straight bowl defeat, 27-20, at the hands of Washington.

The Big Ten co-champs were on the verge of being blown out.

It was 24-0 midway through the third period.

But quarterback Rick Leach, often the target of critics who say he can't pass, unleashed a spectacular aerial blitz.

He passed for two touchdowns and set up a third with passes.

It almost rescued Michigan, but not quite.

Washington saved victory in its first Rose Bowl appearance since 1964 on a pair of classy interceptions, one by All-Pac-8 linebacker Mike Jackson at the two-yard line and another by cornerback Nesby Glasgow at the 10.

The crowd of 105,312 and about 71,000,000 television viewers were no doubt stirred by Michigan's determination and outstanding success so late in the game but 15 or 20 minutes of football do not make a full game make.

Reprinted with permission from the **Ann Arbor News**

The complete 1977 FOOTBALL NEWS All-American team follows:
FIRST TEAM

OFFENSE		DEFENSE	
E	Ken MacAfee, N.D.	DL	Art Still, Kentucky
E	Ozzie Newsome, Ala.	DL	Ross Browner, N.D.
T	Chris Ward, Ohio St.	DL	Brad Shearer, Texas
T	Dan Irons, Tex. Tech	DL	Randy Holloway, Pitt.
G	Mark Donahue, Mich.	DL	Dee Hardison, N.C.
G	Greg Roberts, Okla.	LB	Daryl Hunt, Okla.
C	Walt Downing, Mich.	LB	Jerry Robinson, UCLA
QB	Guy Benjamin, S'ford	LB	Gary Spani, Kans. St.
RB	Terry Miller, Okla. St.	DB	Zac Henderson, Okla.
RB	Earl Campbell, Texas	DB	Luther Bradley, N.D.
RB	Wes Chandler, Fla.	DB	Dennis Thurman, USC

Leach Cool In Defeat

Rick Leach came of age in the Rose Bowl game.

Open season on the ability of the Michigan junior as a quarterback should come to an end after the way he performed in Monday's 27-20 football loss to the University of Washington.

Never in Coach Bo Schembechler's nine years at Michigan have the Wolverines trailed by 24-0, or even 17-0 as they did against the Huskies — except for the 40-17 loss to Missouri in 1969 in a game that was close until the closing minutes.

But Leach, unaccustomed to such a deficit, was as cool as he ever has been. He had the poise of a pro, nearly pulling out a victory in the waning minutes with his leadership and passing accuracy.

"I've never doubted my ability as a quarterback," he said the next day. "All I have to please is myself and Bo. I'm not worried about what other people say. I give 100 per cent every time I am on the field.

THE LINEUPS
Michigan
ENDS: White, Stephenson, Clayton, Schmerge, Gene Johnson, Marsh.
TACKLES: Kenn, Giesler, Keitz, Motley, Godfrey, Greer.
GUARDS: Donahue, Szara, Graves, Trogvac, Melita.
CENTERS: Downing, Lilja.
LINEBACKERS: Tedesco, Seabron, Anderson, DeSantis, Simpkins, Gilmore, Meter, Owens.
OFFENSIVE BACKS: Leach, Davis, Reid, Edwards, Smith, Clayton, Richardson, Mitchell.
KICKER: Willner.
DEFENSIVE BACKS: Howard, Jolly, Harris, Hicks, Bell, Needham, Pickens, Harden.

Washington
ENDS: Gaines, Bean, Greenwood, Moraga, Rumberger.
TACKLES: Westlund, Marsh, Toews, Sanford, VanDivier, Martin, Browning, Grant.
GUARDS: Foreman, Chavira, Sherwood, Bauer, Cromer, Betja, Cupic.
CENTERS: Bush, Turnure.
LINEBACKERS: Kerley, Gagliardi, Richardson, Pence, Jackson, Tormey, McClain, Harrell, Caloia.
OFFENSIVE BACKS: Moon, Gipson, Smith, Tyler, Steele, Rowland, Stevens, Briggs, Richardson.
DEFENSIVE BACKS: Glasgow, Theodele, Lee, Grimes, Edwards, Leeland, Gardner, Heinrich, Roche.
KICKERS: Robbins, Wilson.

Officials
REFEREE — Otho Kurtz, UMPIRE — Henry Sadorus, HEAD LINESMAN — Ed Scheck, LINE JUDGE — Gaylord Bryan, FIELD JUDGE — John Everett, BACK JUDGE — Steve Higgins.

TEAM FIGURES
	Michigan	Washington
First Downs	22	17
Rushes-Yards	48-149	48-164
Passes	14-27-2	13-24-2
Passing Yards	239	234
Total Plays-Offense	75-388	72-398
Fumbles-Lost	2-1	0-0
Penalties-Yards	3-11	6-47
Punts-Average	442.5	5-39.0
Return Yards	172	92
Third-Down Efficiency	8-16	8-19
Time Of Possession	29:18	30:42

SCORING
WASHINGTON	7	10	10	0—27
MICHIGAN	0	0	7	13—20

W—Moon two-yard run (Robbins kick)
W—Robbins 30-yard field goal
W—Moon one-yard run (Robbins kick)
W—Gaines 28-yard pass from Moon (Robbins kick)
M—Stephenson 76-yard pass from Leach (Willner kick)
W—Robbins 28-yard field goal
M—Davis two-yard run (Willner kick)
M—Edwards 32-yard from Leach (kick failed)

All-America
OFFENSE

Pos.	Player and College	Cl.	Age	Ht.	Wt.	Hometown
WR	Wes Chandler, Florida	Sr.	21	6:01	188	N. Smyrna Bch, Fla.
WR	Ozzie Newsome, Alabama	Sr.	21	6:03	210	Leighton, Ala.
TE	Ken MacAfee, Notre Dame	Sr.	21	6:04	250	Brockton, Mass.
T	Chris Ward, Ohio St.	Sr.	21	6:04	272	Dayton, O.
T	Gordon King, Stanford	Sr.	21	6:06	265	Fair Oaks, Cal.
G	George Collins, Georgia	Sr.	22	6:04	225	Robins, Ga.
G	Mark Donahue, Michigan	Sr.	21	6:03	245	Oak Lawn, Ill.
C	Walt Downing, Michigan	Sr.	21	6:04	254	Coatesville, Pa.
QB	Doug Williams, Grambling	Sr.	22	6:04	214	Baton Rouge, La.
RB	Earl Campbell, Texas	Sr.	22	6:01	220	Tyler, Tex.
RB	Terry Miller, Okla. St.	Sr.	21	6:00	196	Colo. Spgs, Colo.

Regents Field 1893-1905

Ferry Field 1906-1926

Michigan Stadium 1927-1977

Michigan Football Awards

Each year, three special awards are given to players on the Michiga football team. The awards are the John F. Maulbetsch Award, the Meye Morton Award, and the Frederick C. Matthaei Scholarship Award

Maulbetsch Award

The John F. Maulbetsch Award is given to the freshman football ca didate after spring practice on the basis of desire, character, capaci for leadership and future success both on and off the gridiron. It wa established by Frederick C. Matthaei in 1954 in honor of the late John F Maulbetsch, All-American halfback on the 1914 team.

Meyer Morton Award

The Meyer Morton Award is given to the football player who show greatest development and most promise as a result of the annual sprin practice. The award is given in honor of the late Meyer Morton, note Big Ten official.

Matthaei Award

The Frederick C. Matthaei Award is given to the junior-to-be gridde who has displayed leadership, drive, and achievement on the athleti field and in the classroom. The award was established by Frederick C Matthaei in 1968.

Michigan Award Winners

Years	MOST VALUABLE	MEYER MORTON	JOHN F. MAULBETSCH	FREDERICK MATTHAEI
1977		John Anderson	Ron Simpkins	Jerry Meter
1976	Rob Lytle	Greg Morton	Rick Leach	John Anders
1975	Gordon Bell	Dan Jilek	Dwight Hicks	Jim Smith
1974	Steve Strinko	Dennis Franklin	Rob Lytle	Kirk Lewis
1973	Paul Seal	Paul Seal	Don Dufek	Dave Brown
1972	Randy Logan	Randy Logan	Dennis Franklin	Tom Drake
1971	Billy Taylor	Guy Murdock	Dave Gallagher	Tom Kee
1970	Don Moorhead & Henry Hill	Jim Betts	Tom Coyle	Bruce Elliott
1969	Jim Mandich	Don Moorhead	Glenn Doughty	Jack Harpring
1968	Ron Johnson	Bob Baumgartner	Marty Huff	Tom Curtis
1967	Ron Johnson	Dick Yanz	Jim Mandich	
1966	Jack Clancy	Don Bailey	Tom Stincic	
1965	Bill Yearby	Bill Keating	Rocky Rosema	
1964	Bob Timberlake	Tom Mack	Clayton Wilhite	
1963	Tom Keating	Tom Keating	Rick Sygar	
1962	Dave Raimey	John Minko	Bob Timberlake	
1961	John Walker	Dave Raimey	Harvey Chapman	
1960	Dennis Fitzgerald	Bill Freehan	Jack Strobel	
1959	Tony Rio	Willard Hildebrand	Bob Brown	
1958	Bob Ptacek	Dick Syring	John Walker	
1957	Jim Pace	Charles Teusher	George Genyk	
1956	Dick Hill	John Herrnstein & Bob Ptacek	John Herrnstein	
1955	Terry Barr	Jim VanPelt		
1954	Fred Baer	Ron Kramer		
1953	Tony Branoff	Don Dugger & Tony Branoff		
1952	Ted Topor	Gene Knutson		
1951	Don Peterson	Merritt Green		
1950	Don Dufek	Roger Zatkoff		
1949	Dick Kempthorn	Don Dufek		
1948	Dominic Tomasi	Leo Koceski		
1947	Bump Elliott	Alvin Wistert		
1946	Bob Chappuis	Bob Ballou		
1945	Harold Watts			
1944	Don Lund			
1943	Bob Wiese	Clem Bauman		
1942	Al Wistert	Bob Wiese		
1941	Reuben Kelto	Mervin Pregulman		
1940	Tom Harmon	George Ceithaml		
1939	Tom Harmon	Ralph Fritz		
1938	Ralph Heikkinen	Archie Kodros		
1937	Ralph Heikkinen	Fred Trosko		
1936	Matt Patanelli	John Jordan		
1935	Bill Renner	Bob Cooper		
1934	Gerald Ford	Matt Patanelli		
1933	Herman Everhardus	Mike Savage		
1932	Harry Newman	Gerald Ford		
1931	Bill Hewitt	Herman Everhardus		
1930	Jack Wheeler	Estil Tessmer		
1929	James Simrall	Roy Hudson		
1928	Otto Pommerening	Danny Holmes		
1927	Bennie Oosterbaan	LeVerne Taylor		
1926	Benny Friedman	George Rich		
1925		Ray Baer		

Jerry Meter
Matthaei Award

Ron Simpkins
Maulbetsch Award

John Anderson
Morton Award

Michigan's Future Football Schedules

1978
September 16	Illinois	Ann Arbor
September 23	Notre Dame	South Bend
September 30	Duke	Ann Arbor
October 7	Arizona	Ann Arbor
October 14	Michigan State	Ann Arbor
October 21	Wisconsin	Madison
October 28	Minnesota	Ann Arbor
November 4	Iowa	Iowa City
November 11	Northwestern	Evanston
November 18	Purdue	Ann Arbor
November 25	Ohio State	Columbus

1979
September 8	Northwestern	Evanston
September 15	Notre Dame	Ann Arbor
September 22	Kansas	Ann Arbor
September 29	California	Berkeley
October 6	Michigan State	East Lansing
October 13	Minnesota	Ann Arbor
October 20	Illinois	Champaign
October 27	Indiana	Ann Arbor
November 3	Wisconsin	Ann Arbor
November 10	Purdue	West Lafayette
November 17	Ohio State	Ann Arbor

1980
September 13	Northwestern	Ann Arbor
September 20	Notre Dame	South Bend
September 27	South Carolina	Ann Arbor
October 4	California	Ann Arbor
October 11	Michigan State	Ann Arbor
October 18	Minnesota	Minneapolis
October 25	Illinois	Ann Arbor
November 1	Indiana	Bloomington
November 8	Wisconsin	Madison
November 15	Purdue	Ann Arbor
November 22	Ohio State	Columbus

1981
September 12	Wisconsin	Madison
September 19	Notre Dame	Ann Arbor
September 26	Navy	Ann Arbor
October 3	Indiana	Bloomington
October 10	Michigan State	East Lansing
October 17	Iowa	Ann Arbor
October 24	Northwestern	Ann Arbor
October 31	Minnesota	Minneapolis
November 7	Illinois	Ann Arbor
November 14	Purdue	West Lafayette
November 21	Ohio State	Ann Arbor